ENCHANTED DRAWINGS

ENCHANTED DRAWINGS

The History of Animation

Charles Solomon

WINGS BOOKS
New York • Avenel, New Jersey

Copyright © 1989, 1994 by Charles Solomon

All rights reserved under International and Pan-American Copyright Conventions.

This 1994 edition is published by Wings Books, distributed by Random House Value Publishing, Inc., 40 Engelhard Avenue, Avenel, New Jersey 07001, by arrangement with Alfred A. Knopf, Inc.

Grateful acknowledgment is made to the following for permission to reprint previously published material:

MCA Music Publishing: Excerpt from "Boogie Woogie Bugle Boy," words and music by Don Raye and Hughie Prince. Copyright 1940, 1941 by MCA Music Publishing, a Division of MCA Inc., New York, NY 10019. Copyright renewed. Used by permission. All rights reserved.

Warner/Chappell Music, Inc.: Excerpt from "I Haven't Got a Hat" by Buddy Burnier and Robert D. Emmerich. Copyright 1934 by Warner Bros. Inc. (renewed). All rights reserved. Used by permission.

Random House
New York • Toronto • London • Sydney • Auckland

Printed and bound in China

Library of Congress Cataloging-in-Publication Data

Solomon, Charles.
    The history of animation: enchanted drawings / Charles Solomon.
      p.   cm.
    Rev. ed. of: Enchanted drawings. 1st ed. 1989.
    Includes bibliographical references and index.
    ISBN 0-517-11859-9
    1. Animated films—United States—History. 2. Animated films—History. I. Solomon, Charles. Enchanted drawings. II. Title.
NC1766.U5S68 1994
741.5′8′09—dc20   94-17283
                                            CIP

8 7 6 5 4 3 2 1

For H.B., who was always there

Although it describes a variety of filmmaking techniques, *animation* has been synonymous with drawn cartoons throughout most of its history. Two characteristics distinguish animation from live action: the image is recorded on film frame by frame; and the illusion of motion is created, rather than recorded.

In live action, film is exposed in "takes," which may last from a few seconds to several minutes. The result is usually projected at the same speed at which it was recorded; twenty-four frames per second is standard for sound film. In animation, each frame is exposed individually. Between exposures, the artist must change cels, alter the positions of puppets, and so on.

In animation, the motions exist only on film: Bugs Bunny didn't ask, "What's up, Doc," the California Raisins didn't dance and King Kong didn't scale the Empire State Building until the film was projected.

The distinctions between live action and animation have tended to blur since the 1970s, as filmmaking and video techniques have grown increasingly sophisticated. The debate over definitions and other issues reflects the growing acceptance of animation as an art form that has developed since the late 1960s, an acceptance that vindicates a statement Walt Disney made in 1941:

"I have had a stubborn, blind confidence in the cartoon medium, a determination to show the skeptics that the animated cartoon was deserving of a better place; that it was more than a mere 'filler' on the program; that it was more than a novelty; that it could be one of the greatest mediums of fantasy and entertainment yet developed."

ACKNOWLEDGMENTS

It would literally have been impossible to write this book without the cooperation of the artists who shared their time in interviews and their talent in the illustrative materials.

Special thanks are due to many individuals for their contributions to this work. In addition to providing hospitality, John Canemaker generously shared both his published and unpublished research with me, including his interviews with J. R. Bray and Dave Hilberman. Harvey Deneroff and Joe Adamson were equally gracious about sharing research; Joe's oral histories with Friz Freleng, Dave Fleischer and Dick Huemer proved particularly valuable. Steve Schneider shared both his library and his boundless enthusiasm for animation with me. Mark Kausler, animation's encyclopedist, made a variety of research materials available to me, as did John Lange, Tim Walker and Donald Crafton. Nick and Tee Bosustow provided access to the papers of their late father, Stephen.

Special thanks are also owed the following people: At The Walt Disney Company: Dave Smith and Paula Sigman of the Disney Archives; the indefatigable Howard Green (still the best publicist I've ever met); Richard Jordan, his able assistant; Steve Rogers; Joanne Warren; Wayne Morris. At the Disney animation department: Tony Anselmo, Hendel Butoy, Andreas Deja, Mark Henn, Glen Keane and Tom Sito; four of Disney's "Nine Old Men"—Frank Thomas, Ollie Johnston, Marc Davis and Ward Kimball.

At Warner Brothers: Kathy Helppie, Steven Green and Patricia Brown. Faith Hubley of the Hubley Studio; Sarah Baisley at Taft Entertainment; Lou Scheimer, John Gruse and Leda Gloddell at Filmation; Robert Rosen, Dan McLaughlin and Phil Denslow at UCLA; James Blinn and Sylvie Rueff at the Jet Propulsion Laboratory; Elfriede Fischinger; Al Dinoble at Metrolight; Billie Ward at the Jay Ward Studio; Michael Whit- ney at Whitney-Demos; John Whitney, Sr.; Linda Jones at Chuck Jones Enterprises; Bill Kroyer of Kroyer Films; Sody Clampett; Lee Mishkin; Eric Goldberg of Pizzazz Pictures, London; Kemp Niver and his secretary, Bebe Bergson; Richard Balzer; Peter Bylsma and Faith Frenz-Heckman at Universal; Tyrus Wong; Ralph Guggenheim at Pixar; Nancy St. John at Pacific Data Images; Joshua Arfer of Christie's East; J. D. Halver; Tom Wilhite; Jerry Rees; Jerry Beck; Arnold Leibovit.

Mike and Jeanne Glad graciously opened their home to me—as well as their extraordinary collection of animation art. They provided an inordinate number of illustrations, including many from films I thought it would be impossible to represent visually.

Much of the research for this book was initially done for articles that appeared in the Los Angeles *Times,* and I would like to thank the editors and writers who encouraged me to cover animation when most major journals ignored the art form: Sheila Benson, Charles Champlin, David Crook, David Fox, Connie Koenenn, Irv Letofsky, Aileene MacMinn, Lee Margulies, Jack Miles, Barbara Saltzman, Art Seidenbaum and William Wilson.

For several years I had considered writing a book along the lines of this one, but it was Ronald Haver of the Los Angeles County Museum of Art film department who convinced me to pursue the idea seriously. My thanks to him for his goading, his friendship and several excellent dinners. Ron also introduced me to my agent, Bob Cornfield, who answered myriad questions with more patience than I would have shown.

The estimable Martha Kaplan proved that a good editor is the best friend a writer can have. She answered countless questions and showed exceptional sensitivity, intelligence and forbearance while trimming my original manuscript down to a book a reader can lift without fear of rupture. Like a sculptor working a recalcitrant lump of clay, designer Peter Andersen took hundreds of pages of manuscript and literally thousands of transparencies, drawings and prints and transformed them into an attractive and coherent entity.

Dennis M. Johnson proofread the manuscript three times, correcting an embarrassing number of typos and making many helpful suggestions. Lewis Segal offered valuable editorial advice on the television chapter when the prospect of writing it seemed insurmountably dreary. Greg Clarke shot much of the artwork for the illustrations, often improvising to compensate for inadequate equipment and/or less than ideal conditions.

My thanks also to several friends who made contributions to all phases of the work, not the least of which was putting up with all the "writing this thing is driving me crazy" phone calls: Stuart Sumida, Kevin Caffey, Anne Pautler and Jim Brunet, Paul Basta, Detrik Hohenegger, Adrienne Parks, Hank Cato, Lee Nordling, Bill Cohn, Bruce Bardfield and Joe Cocozza. My family—Rose Solomon, Ann Solomon, Marsha and Marvin Francis and S. W. Bunce—always encouraged my fascination with animation, instead of pressuring me to find a more respected and lucrative profession.

PREFACE TO THE NEW EDITION

The five years that have passed since the completion of *Enchanted Drawings* have been a time of change for the art of animation. The animated feature has enjoyed both unprecedented success and failure, like a glacier that advances and retreats simultaneously. Nothing in the history of the medium can match The Walt Disney Studio's recent string of smash hits. But their phenomenal popularity must be balanced against the box office failure of a record number of features. While it seems premature to declare the 1990s a new "Golden Age," it's clear that a renaissance has occurred in theatrical features, albeit a somewhat erratic and one-sided one.

Computer animation has continued to develop at an extraordinary pace, and has largely supplanted stop-motion techniques in special effects; at the same time, a new generation of animators has been extending the boundaries of stop-motion animation, especially the use of clay characters.

The advent of the cable networks and the rising popularity of the weekday afternoon and Sunday morning markets have spurred record production of animated television programs. At the same time, the allegedly violent content of television cartoons has become the focus of increasingly acrimonious debate. Some of the calls for governmentally enforced guidelines and/or censorship recall Dr. Frederic Wertham's notorious campaign to clean up comic books during the early 1950s. Amid this brouhaha, no one seems to have noticed that many of the most creative members of the baby-boom generation cheerfully acknowledge being influenced by the theatrical shorts and early television cartoons that occupied so much of their childhoods. The ongoing debate will probably ensure a place for animation stories in the popular media.

The enormous sums animated features have earned at the box office and through video cassette sales should continue to spur an accelerating rate of production. During the late 1980s, some producers expressed concern that the market might become glutted with animated product; those fears have proved groundless. The recent Disney features have shown that the audience for high quality animation is virtually limitless. However, whether another studio can match Disney's blend of well-structured stories, state-of-the-art animation, imaginative songs and skillful promotion remains to be seen.

Preparing this edition enabled me to correct misspellings (notably, the name of the Van Beuren Studio) and rectify misidentifications in some captions. Many new people generously gave their time in interviews, their talent in films and their assistance in corralling the supplemental material needed. At The Walt Disney Studio: Jeffrey Katzenberg, Roy E. Disney, Steve Rogers, Peter Schneider, Tom Schumacher and Terry Press. Also at Disney, the tireless Howard Green and his cheerful assistant Fumi Kitahara went beyond the call of duty to provide aid, comfort and illustrations. At Disney animation, Andreas Deja, Will Finn, Eric Goldberg, Don Hahn, T. Dan Hofstedt, Glen Keane, Duncan Marjoribanks, John Musker, John Pomeroy, David Pruiksma and Nik Ranieri provided drawings, suggestions, information and company.

Special thanks are also due to Jeff Segal, Jonathan Rosenthall and Lorna Bold at the Universal Cartoon Studio; David Kirschner and his assistant, Susan Roberts; Antonia Coffman, Matt Groening and David Silverman at Fox Television; Carl Rosendahl, Al DiNoble and Monica Corbin at Pacific Data Images; John Hughes, Suzanne Datz and Ellen Bauman at Rhythm & Hues; Mike Patterson and Candace Reckinger; Bill Kroyer; Denny Cline; Richard Lewis at DIC Entertainment; Jean MacCurdy, Maura Sullivan, Gino D'Bois and Cathy

Helpie at Warner Bros.; Marvin Levy; Tom Wilhite and Kurt Albrecht at Hyperion Pictures; Gary Goldman at Don Bluth Ireland, Ltd.; Carol Block at Will Vinton Entertainment; Bob Kurtz of Kurtz and Friends; Stephen Johnson; Sarah Baisley at FilmRoman; Miles Perkins at Industrial Light & Magic; Pam Hamilton at Colossal Pictures; Mike Kunkes at Klasky-Csupo; Alexis Hunter at Nickelodeon; Jim Ballantine and Steve Guy of "Ren & Stimpy."

My agent, Robert Cornfield, did his usual exemplary job of shepherding the project through to completion.

Once again, my friends listened—more or less patiently—to my complaints about the horrors of writing and deadlines. In addition, Scott Johnston offered valuable suggestions on the sections involving computer animation; Dennis M. Johnson proofread much of the manuscript and Martha Kaplan offered her customary insights. My interest in animation was again supported by my family, which now includes Socrates, the recalcitrant arnab.

Charles Solomon
April 1994

CONTENTS

ENCHANTED DRAWINGS

81

Gertie bridles at the entrance of Jumbo, the woolly mammoth, in "Gertie the Dinosaur" (1914). In this landmark film, Winsor McCay began to explore the principles of character animation, the art of making a drawn figure move in ways that express the character's personality.

PRECURSORS
AND EXPERIMENTS

Sir Francis Bacon described minds under the influence of powerful ideas as "dancing in little rings like persons bewitched." Animation (and all filmmaking) emerged from a fascination with light and motion—a series of interlocking dancers' rings that began with the "new science" of the seventeenth century.

By the middle of the century, ideas were circulating more freely in Europe than ever before. Refinements in techniques for grinding lenses and prisms and improved mathematics (especially calculus) made it possible to study light and motion with new accuracy. Science was not yet the restricted domain of specialists. All educated people—major thinkers like Sir Isaac Newton and countless interested amateurs—debated and discussed the new knowledge.

It was in this heady atmosphere that the Jesuit scholar/inventor Athanasius Kircher published his *Ars Magna Lucis et Umbrae* (*The Great Art of Light and Shadow*) in Rome in 1645. In the last chapter, he described a new invention—the magic lantern, a simple device that consisted of a box containing a light source (either a candle or a lamp) and a curved mirror.

When Kircher demonstrated his new device, there were mutterings about witchcraft, and more than one churchman advised the disgruntled inventor to go back to studying mathematics. Despite this initial skepticism, magic lanterns became the object of immediate and widespread interest. All over Europe, scientists began experiments which included explo-

rations of their potential for entertainment. In 1666, Samuel Pepys noted in his diary a visit from the optician Richard Reeves, who "did also bring a lanthorn with pictures in glasse, to make strange things to appear on a wall, very pretty." Three days later, Pepys bought two telescopes from Reeves and "the lanthorn that shows tricks."

But Kircher was interested in education, not projecting pretty pictures. In the revised edition of the *Ars Magna* (1671), he explained how a revolving glass disc with a series of painted images could be used to present a story to an audience. Kircher had wanted to become a missionary, and chose scenes from the life of Christ. The pictures on the disc were intended to be seen separately. This was not animation—yet.

Scientists continued to experiment with magic lanterns. In 1685, in the Netherlands, Johannes Zahn published instructions for making a lantern into a projecting clock. Fifty years later, another Dutchman, Pieter van Musschenbroek, demonstrated that a revolving disc, similar to Kircher's but with sequential images, could produce an illusion of motion. In 1736, he astonished the visiting Abbé Nollet with visions of a windmill with revolving arms, a man raising his hat and a woman bowing. Later, Musschenbroek used multiple lanterns, synchronized slide changes and long slides (which he slowly passed before the projecting beam) to present more elaborate illusions, such as a storm at sea: the first animated entertainments.

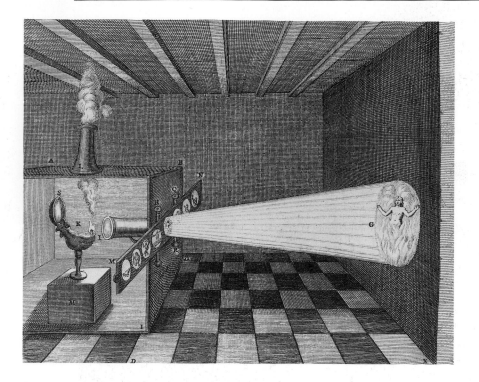

The magic lantern from Kircher's *The Great Art of Light and Shadow* (1645). Reflected light emerges from a small hole in the housing, then passes through an image painted on a glass slide and a lens. In a darkened room, the magnified image can be seen projected on a wall.

Kircher's diagram of a glass disc with scenes from the life of Christ. The images were to be shown separately, to illustrate lectures or sermons.

Musschenbroek's discoveries were quickly popularized in Abbé Guyot's *Nouvelles Récréations Physiques et Mathématiques*, translated as *Rational Recreations in Which the Principles of Numbers and Natural Philosophy Are Clearly and Copiously Elucidated, by a Series of Easy, Entertaining, Interesting Experiments*. The text was somewhat less long-winded than the title, and included instructions for a "magical theater" presentation of the siege of Troy.

By the middle of the eighteenth century, the traveling show had become a popular form of entertainment, and the itinerant showman with a lantern strapped to his back was a familiar sight.

The greatest of all the lantern showmen was Etienne Gaspard Robert of Liège, who billed himself as "Robertson." In 1794 he opened his eerie "Fantasmagorie" in Paris; it proved so successful that in 1797 he moved to the crumbling remains of an abandoned Capuchin monastery—a site in keeping with the contemporary taste for ruins.

The audience sat in a darkened room, still decorated with the skulls and bones the monks had kept as reminders of mortality. Robertson showed lantern slide portraits of recently dead heroes of the French Revolution. By masking the edges of the pictures with black paint, he eliminated the circle of white light that usually surrounded lantern projections, and made them appear to be free-floating. He heightened the effects by projecting the slides onto mirrors, glass, smoke and sheets of gauze soaked with translucent wax. As a finale, the Grim Reaper appeared: "the fate that awaits us all."

Like modern horror movies, the "Fantasmagorie" shows enjoyed an immense popularity. The magician Paul de Philipstahl brought a similar show, "Phantasmagoria," to London in 1801. Within a year *The Lady's Magazine* was publishing complaints from parents whose children stole money and stayed out late to see these entertainments. Another "Phantasmagoria" opened in New York in 1803; later, shows were held in other American cities.

The weakness of these shows was the difficulty of rendering an image that would look convincing when projected—a problem that still bedevils animators. In 1832, Sir David Brewster, the inventor of the kaleidoscope, wrote: "Even Michael Angelo [*sic*] would have failed in executing a figure an inch long with transparent varnishes, when all its imperfections were magnified. In order, therefore, to perfect the art of representing phantasms, the objects must be living ones, and in place of chalky ill drawn figures mimicking humanity by the most absurd gesticulations, we shall have the phantasms of the most perfect delineation, clothed in real drapery, and displaying all the movements of life."

In 1863, John Henry Pepper and Henry Dircks received patents for "projecting images of living persons in the air." These projections were used in a new series of ghost shows at the Royal Polytechnic Institute in London (which had opened

The magic lantern as a parlor amusement. A middle-class English family observes "royalty" in 1823.
The pseudo-oriental setting of the image reflects the continuing interest in *chinoiserie*.

in 1836 with elaborate lantern entertainments like "The Adventures of Sinbad" and "The Siege of Dehli"). The techniques for producing "Pepper's Ghosts"—lanterns, lights and one- and two-way mirrors—remained standards in the magician's repertoire well into this century.

Magic lantern slides of less grisly subjects served as popular parlor entertainments during the nineteenth century. In *Remembrance of Things Past*, Proust compared the lantern shows of his childhood to moving stained-glass windows.

Midway between the discoveries of Musschenbroek and the debut of Robertson's ghastly shows, another important precursor of animation appeared in the West: shadow puppets. A popular entertainment in China since the Tang dynasty (618–907), shadow theaters were introduced in Europe around 1760, as part of a craze for *chinoiserie*. The puppets were known as *ombres chinoises,* or Chinese shadows.

Dominique Séraphin, the most famous of the shadow theater proprietors, began presenting shows at Versailles in 1772. Séraphin moved to Paris in 1784, where his theater was maintained until 1870. The only thing Chinese about these *ombres*

Another important ancestor of animation: shadow puppets. The intricate figures are cut from water buffalo hide and manipulated behind a screen.

PHANTASMAGORIA,

THIS and every EVENING till further Notice,
AT THE
LYCEUM, STRAND.

As the Advertisement of various Exhibitions under the above Title, may possibly mislead the unsuspecting Part of the Public (and particularly Strangers from the Country) in their Opinion of the ORIGINAL PHANTASMAGORIA, M. DE PHILIPSTHAL, the Inventor, begs Leave to state that they have no Connexion whatever with his Performances. The utmost Efforts of Imitators have not been able to produce the Effect intended; and he is too grateful for the liberal Encouragement he has received in the Metropolis, not to caution the Public against those Spurious Copies, which, failing of the Perfection they assume, can only disgust and disappoint the Spectators.

M. DE PHILIPSTHAL
Will have the Honour to EXHIBIT (as usual) his

Optical Illusions and Mechanical Pieces of Art.

At the LYCEUM, and at no other Place of Exhibition in London.

SELECT PARTIES may be accommodated with a MORNING REPRESENTATION at any appointed Hour, on sending timely Notice.

☞ To prevent Mistakes, the Public are requested to Notice, that the PHANTASMAGORIA is on the Left-hand, on the Ground Floor, and the EGYPTIANA on the Right-hand, up Stairs.

The OPTICAL PART of the EXHIBITION

Will Introduce the PHANTOMS or APPARITIONS of the DEAD or ABSENT, in a way more to the Eye in a public Theatre, as the Objects freely originate in the Air, and unfold themselves as the Imagination alone has hitherto painted them, occasionally assuming the Figure and most perfect Resemblance of the Characters of past and present Times.

This SPECTROLOGY, which professes to expose the Practices of artful Impostors and pretended Exorcists, who still foster an absurd Belief in GHOSTS or DISEMBODIED SPIRITS, will, it is presumed, afford also a pleasing Entertainment; and in order to render these Apparitions more interesting, they will be preceded by a Thunder Storm, accompanied with vivid Lightning, Hail, Wind, &c.

The MECHANICAL PIECES of Art

Include the following principal Objects, a more detailed Account of which will be given in the Bills.

Two elegant ROPE DANCERS, the one, representing a Spaniard nearly Six Feet high, will mark the Time of the Music with a small Whistle, smoke his Pipe, &c.—The other, called the Little Farmer, will surpass the former in Skill and Agility.

The INGENIOUS SELF-DEFENDING CHEST—The superior Excellence and Utility of this Piece has always a Safe-guard against Depredators; for the concealed Battery of Four Pieces of Artillery fire on the Stranger tries to force open the Chest.—This has been acknowledged by several Professional Men, who think its equal Advantage be applied to the Protection of Property in Counting-houses, Post Chaises, &c.

The MECHANICAL PEACOCK, which so exactly imitates the Actions of that stately Bird, that it eats, drinks, &c. at command, unfold its Tail in a brilliant Circle, and in every respect seems to understand the Thoughts of the Company.

The BEAUTIFUL COSSACK, enclosed in a small Box, opens it when ordered, and presents a Nosegay, which, as soon as desired, she changes with astonishing Quickness into a most Elegant Garland, and dances after the Manner of the Cossacks, she will also resolve different Questions. &c. &c.

The SELF-IMPELLED WINDMILL, which is put in Motion, or stands still by the most astonishing Manner which apparently does away the Idea of all Mechanical Agency.

The whole to conclude with a superb OPTICAL and MECHANICAL FIRE-WORK Changes.

↓ Doors to be opened at SEVEN o'Clock, the Concert to begin at EIGHT.

BOXES, 4s.—PIT, 2s.

Left: A poster from the English version of Robertson's eerie "Fantasmagorie" (1803). Below: Three nineteenth-century engravings. Clockwise, one published in Robertson's *Memoires* in 1831; one that appeared in *Le Magasin Pittoresque* in 1849; and an undated illustration of the final image in the show—"the fate that awaits us all."

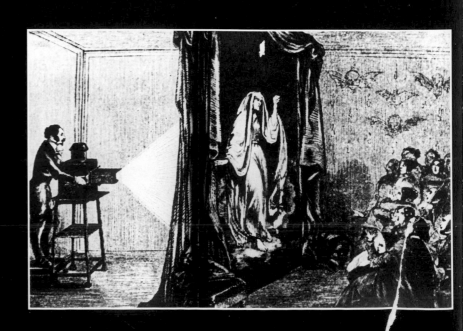

The thaumatrope, a nineteenth-century animation toy. When the disc is spun on its string, the bird seems to appear inside the cage.

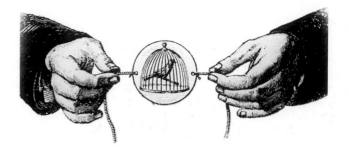

THAUMATROPE,
1825

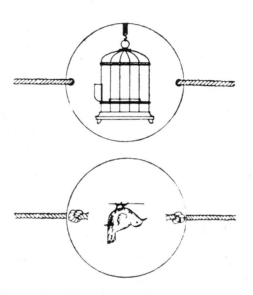

chinoises was their name. The puppets and scenery were all made in Western styles, and the subjects ranged from the Temptation of St. Anthony to adaptations of Molière's plays to popular farces such as "The Broken Bridge."

Shadow theaters enjoyed an even greater vogue at the turn of this century. In 1887, the first shows were presented at Le Chat Noir (The Black Cat), a cabaret in Montmartre run by Rodolphe Salis. The Chat Noir was an informal place, frequented by writers and artists, who sometimes staged satirical puppet plays. One evening, the painter Henri Rivier cut a caricature of a policeman out of cardboard and manipulated it to the tune of a popular song.

The cabaret soon became the site of increasingly elaborate shadow shows, with Salis providing spontaneous commentaries. Rivier, Caran d'Ache and Steinlen were among the popular artists and cartoonists who made the figures out of cardboard and thin sheets of zinc. While many of these plays were simple satires, some were complicated dramas involving subtle effects borrowed from lantern shows. Clouds, atmospheric effects and moving water were painted on long glass slides and moved behind the puppets. Caran d'Ache's *"L'Epopée,"* an epic about Napoleon I, had two acts and fifty scenes; Rivier presented a mystery play of the life of Christ, *"La Marche à l'Etoile"* ("The Journey to the Star") in 1890.

Like lantern shows, shadow plays were also presented in simpler forms. From the late 1830s, the traveling "gallanty shows" (from the street cries of *"galante,"* meaning "fine" in Italian) were a common sight in Europe, especially England. Many entertainers presented Punch and Judy shows by day and shadow plays by night. For home entertainment, children bought sheets of human and animal silhouettes, which they pasted onto cardboard and cut out. Included with the silhouettes were instructions on constructing a shadow theater and, often, scripts for simple plays. Similar instructions and scripts appeared in children's magazines.

The nineteenth century was also the great era of "philosophical" or animation toys, beginning with the invention of the *thaumatrope* in 1826, probably by John Ayrton Paris. (It has also been attributed to Sir John Herschel, Charles Babbage, Dr. William Fitton and Dr. William Wollaston.) The thaumatrope is a very simple device to be the object of so much controversy. It consists of a disc with an image painted on each side and threaded with a string. When the disc is spun, the images seem to combine: the wig appears on the bald

man's head; the jockey astride the horse. Advertised as "rounds of amusement," thaumatropes proved quite popular.

Around the same time, considerable interest was focused on "the wheel phenomenon": why the spokes of a rapidly spinning wheel seem to turn backward or forward or seem to stand still at different times. Among the scientists investigating the effect was Peter Mark Roget (of *Thesaurus* fame), who published *Persistence of Vision with Regard to Moving Objects* in 1824. While not all of Roget's conclusions were correct, he did describe the important fact that the human eye will blend a series of sequential images into a single motion if the images are presented rapidly, with sufficient illumination, and interrupted regularly.

Research into the question of the wheel led the Belgian scientist Joseph Plateau to invent the *phenakistoscope* or *fantoscope*, a more complex animation device that depended on the persistence of vision, between 1828 and 1832. The phenakistoscope was made up of two discs; one with sequential images painted around its edge, the other with slits. When the discs were spun at the correct rates, the viewer saw a moving image. The slits acted as a shutter; the spaces between them provided the interruptions the eye requires to meld the images into motions. (At about the same time, Simon von Stampfer, an Austrian geologist, came up with a similar device that he called the *stroboscope*.) The phenakistoscope remained popular for the rest of the century. Virtually any action that could be presented as a cycle of movement was printed on discs—wheels turning, horses trotting, clowns juggling, bicyclists pedaling, acrobats turning flips.

In 1834, William Horner of Bristol created a device he called the *Daedalum*, or Wheel of the Devil. Nothing much was done with the invention until the 1860s, when it was renamed and marketed as the *zoetrope*, or Wheel of Life. Like the phenakistoscope, the zoetrope depended on the persistence of vision. A strip of paper with sequential images was placed inside a hollow drum with slits in its sides. When the drum was spun, the images, seen through the slits, appeared to move. The zoetrope also proved to be a popular amusement, and hundreds of strips were printed depicting every sort of action from a seal balancing a ball on its nose to a black boy biting into a slice of watermelon.

Invented in 1868, the *kineograph*, or flipbook, proved to be one of the simplest and least expensive but most popular and durable animation toys. A flipbook consists of a few dozen sequential drawings or photographs, bound in order, that the viewer flips through with his thumb: the rapidly changing images appear to move. Flipbooks were sometimes given away as advertisements or as bonuses with merchandise. In 1905, one cigarette manufacturer offered a series of flipbooks of photographs entitled "Turkish Trophies," which showed a woman in tights doing what looked like a hootchy-kootchy dance but was supposed to be a set of deep-breathing exercises.

Thomas Edison took the principle further with the *mutoscope*, a sort of mechanical flipbook he devised in 1895. Sequential photographs were set in a ring attached to a crank. When a viewer turned the crank, it flipped the pictures. The mutoscope was one of several devices Edison created while exploring ways to record visual images to accompany his sound recordings. It remained little more than an amusement park novelty, although some of the original mutoscopes were still in use in the early 1960s and the independent animator Oskar Fischinger did animation for a mutoscope as late as 1946.

The most advanced and sophisticated of all the animation devices was the *praxinoscope*, invented by Emile Reynaud in 1877. Like the zoetrope, the praxinoscope involved a rotating drum and a strip of painted images. Instead of staring through slits in the drum, the viewer saw the motions reflected in a series of mirrors. Around 1882, Reynaud combined his invention with a projector and began drawing animated stories, first on long strips of paper, then on celluloid. (No other artist would draw directly onto film until the mid-1930s, when Len Lye and Norman McLaren began experimenting with cameraless animation in England.)

In 1892, he opened his Théâtre Optique at the Musée Grevin, a wax museum in Paris, to present the films, which he called *Pantomimes Lumineuses*. Essentially short plays, "Pauvre Pierrot" ("Poor Pierrot," 15 minutes), "Un Bon Bock" ("A Good Glass of Beer," 15 minutes) and "Clown et Ses Chiens" ("A Clown and His Dogs," 10 minutes) had musical accompaniments and electrically triggered sound effects. The Théâtre Optique was a huge success: Reynaud gave almost 13,000 performances between 1892 and 1900, to an estimated audience of 500,000—an extraordinary figure for that time.

Performances of the Théâtre Optique continued to draw customers five years after the first cinematic projections by the Lumières (1895). But Reynaud, a single artist who worked alone, could not compete with the burgeoning film industry. His work was supplanted by the creations of Emile Cohl, Georges Méliès and others who could adapt their talents to the new medium. Financially ruined and depressed, he threw most of his films and equipment in the Seine one evening in

1910. He died eight years later in a sanatorium, wretched and forgotten.

Reynaud's place in the history of animation remains the subject of considerable debate. He presented colored, animated films with story lines and synchronized sound tracks long before anyone else. His films have been rediscovered in recent years and presented at various festivals and exhibits, and they retain a distinct, ingenuous charm. But he was not a great draftsman or animator, and there is no evidence that any of the early animators attended his performances or knew his work.

Around the time Reynaud was perfecting the praxinoscope, Eadweard Muybridge began his research into the use of sequential photography in the analysis of human and animal motion. (Photography, another manifestation of the nineteenth-century interest in light, had been invented in the late 1820s by Nicéphore Niepce and Louis Daguerre.)

In 1872–73, Leland Stanford hired Muybridge to investigate the question of "unsupported transit": whether or not a trotting horse ever has all four feet off the ground. The familiar story that the former governor of California had a $25,000 bet on the outcome may or may not be true, but he was eager to improve the performance of his horses and the controversy over unsupported transit was hotly debated in sporting circles. For his initial studies, Muybridge took up to twenty-five sequential photographs per second. The results were somewhat dim and shadowy, but they proved that a trotting horse does have all four feet off the ground at certain moments.

Muybridge returned to Stanford's Palo Alto horse farm in 1877–79 to make more thorough photographic analyses of the gaits of the horse, with clearer results. These experiments attracted considerable attention in the scientific and artistic communities. The French physiologist Etienne Jules Marey and the editors of *Scientific American* suggested that the Palo

Above: Emile Reynaud demonstrating the projecting praxinoscope from his Théâtre Optique in 1892.

Opposite and left, other animation toys. Opposite left: A hand-held phenakistoscope (British, 1833). The images on the disc were seen reflected in a mirror. Opposite right: The Ludoscope, a free-standing phenakistoscope (American, 1904). The images were viewed directly, rather than in a mirror. Left: An English biscuit tin in the shape of a zoetrope, with two strips of images (c. 1920).

Alto photographs should be issued as strips for the zoetrope. By late January 1879, zoetrope strips of horses in silhouette were on sale in France. The painter Thomas Eakins adapted the photographs to create zoetrope strips that gave "a perfect representation of the motion."

Spurred by these experiments with his work, Muybridge constructed the *zoopraxinoscope* in 1879–80. The zoopraxinoscope was a projecting magic lantern with a rotating disc that held up to two dozen slides; a counterrotating, slotted disc acted as a shutter. Images from sequential photographs were traced onto the glass slides. Muybridge used the instrument to illustrate his lectures.

Some film historians have described these illustrated lectures as the first motion picture projections. The question becomes one of definition. Franz von Uchatius, an Austrian officer, had devised a similar system in 1853; and several attempts had been made to simulate motion by projecting posed photographs. Muybridge described the zoopraxinoscope as the prototype machine for "synthetically demonstrating movements analytically photographed from life."

Largely through the efforts of Eakins, Muybridge moved to the University of Pennsylvania in Philadelphia, where he continued his photographic analyses of the movements of humans and animals. His efforts culminated in the two volumes *Animals in Motion* (1899) and *The Human Figure in Motion* (1901), which have remained basic references for animators.

The zoetrope as parlor amusement: an advertisement from an optician.

This free kit from the Boston *Sunday Herald* (1896) provided everything needed to make a toy Wheel of Life, including strips of images.

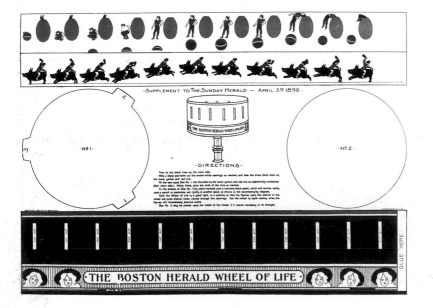

Magic lantern shows, magician's tricks, shadow theaters, animation devices and sequential photography are only some of the manifestations of the continuing interest in light and motion. Film animation could have evolved from any of them if the technology had been available. The first motion pictures, which were far less sophisticated than the better magic lantern shows or the shadow plays of the Chat Noir, met with delight and amazement. It was only a question of time before someone used the inventions of Edison and the Lumière brothers to create movement.

The career of James Stuart Blackton links many of the ancestors of animation. Relatively little is known about his life, and much of the information that does exist is unreliable, as Blackton often lied about his age and background. He was born in Sheffield, England, on January 4, probably in 1875, and came to America as an infant, after the death of his father. He displayed an early talent for painting and published a book of marine sketches while still in his teens.

In 1894, Ronald Reader introduced Blackton to Albert E. Smith, another British immigrant. The three young men decided to quit their jobs and go into show business as "Reader, Smith and Blackton," or "The International Novelty Company." Reader performed sleight-of-hand magic; Smith was an "illusionist"—his tricks involved technical devices (including some derived from the magic lantern shows and "Pepper's Ghosts"); Blackton, "The Komikal Kartoonist," did quick sketching and chalk talk routines.

The act was not a great success: their first performance was given to an audience of two—one of whom was the janitor, waiting to clean the theater. Nor were subsequent audiences amused at the "Lightning Landscape Paintings" of "Mlle. Stuart": the muscular Blackton incongruously disguised in spangled tights and a wig.

By July 1895, Smith and Blackton realized their act needed something to bolster it; perhaps a rendition of "Rip Van Winkle" illustrated with lantern slides. They were discussing the prospect when they saw an Edison Kinetograph, a kind of motion picture peep show. Viewers watched the flickering images through a small square of glass. According to Smith's memoirs, the two men immediately realized that if larger images could be projected onto a screen, more people could see them—and would pay to see them. Smith set to work on his own version of the motion picture projector.

In January of 1896 or 1897, the magicians founded the Vitagraph Company, which would become one of the most impor-

tant film studios of the silent era. Meanwhile, Blackton began working as an illustrator/cartoonist for the New York *Evening World*. In April, the paper sent him to interview and sketch Thomas Edison, who had just unveiled his motion picture projector. Edison then made a short film of the artist at work. Film historian Anthony Slide quotes a talk Blackton gave at the University of Southern California in 1929:

Then he asked me if I could draw that picture of him on a big paper on a board. I told him that I could and he said, "You come on out to the Black Maria," and we did and he had them get boards and wide white paper and some charcoal, and right then and there he had the camera recording your humble servant drawing a picture of Thomas A. Edison. He said, "Put your name on that board," and, "This will be a good ad for you. It will go all over the country in the show houses." I did, and that was my entry into the motion picture industry. I finished that picture with the name of Blackton, Cartoonist of the New York *Evening World*, written all over the top of that board.

Artists doing caricatures and "Lightning Sketchers," music-hall cartoonists who turned one drawing into a succession of

Muybridge's sequential photographs of the horse "Sallie Gardner" proved that a trotting horse does raise all four feet off the ground at certain moments.

THE HORSE IN MOTION.
Illustrated by
MUYBRIDGE.
"SALLIE GARDNER," owned by LELAND STANFORD; running at a 1.40 gait over the Palo Alto track, 19th June, 1878.

different images by adding a few lines, were often used as subjects for films at this time.

In 1899, Smith and Blackton went to Cuba to shoot news footage of the Spanish-American War, but missed the naval engagement at Santiago Bay. When the partners returned to New York and discovered that audiences and theater owners were clamoring for newsreels of the battle, Blackton suggested they create one.

He made cutouts of the American and Spanish ships from large photographs street vendors were selling, and painted a miniature set that held about an inch of water. Smith and Blackton used fine black threads to maneuver the ships, while Mrs. Blackton and an office boy puffed on cigarettes and cigars to provide the smoke of battle. Pinches of gunpowder were ignited to simulate explosions. The primitive lenses, film and projection equipment helped disguise any technical errors. "The Battle of Santiago Bay," one of the first examples of creating special effects with animated miniatures, was a smashing success. Audiences accepted the two-minute film as an authentic record of the destruction of the Spanish fleet. Unfortunately, the prints all seem to have been destroyed in a fire in 1910.

A painted tin magic lantern made by Augustin Lapierre in France c. 1880.

An eighteenth-century French engraving of a traveling lantern showman. The weak light source required the performer to stand close to the screen.

Smith claimed he and Blackton also made the first purely stop-motion film, "The Humpty Dumpty Circus," using "my little daughter's set of toy wooden circus performers and animals, whose movable joints enabled us to place them in balanced positions. It was a tedious process inasmuch as movement could be achieved only by photographing separately each change of position. I suggested we obtain a patent on the process; Blackton felt it wasn't important enough."

The story is hard to accept. Blackton's casual attitude is at odds with the pride he later expressed in his animation for "The Haunted Hotel" (1907). The Vitagraph partners quickly patented other innovations, and were involved in lawsuits with Edison over the patents on the motion picture process. Also, the joints in most toys are too unresponsive for even crude stop-motion animation. No print survives of "The Humpty Dumpty Circus."

In 1900, Blackton returned to Edison's laboratory for another animation project, "The Enchanted Drawing." The premise is a simple one: Blackton stands by an easel with a tablet and draws various objects—a hat, a cigar, a bottle of wine—which magically appear in his hand. A face drawn on the tablet scowls as Blackton takes away the objects, but smiles when given a drink from the bottle. Blackton plays the scene with the hammy expressions and exaggerated gestures of the vaudeville stage. The effects in "The Enchanted Drawing" were achieved by stopping the camera between frames and making substitutions, rather than by conventional anima-

Cinema and animation pioneer J. Stuart Blackton. Left: A poster from his vaudeville act with Ronald Reader and Albert Smith. Above: A frame from "The Enchanted Drawing" (1900) shows Blackton holding the bottle that "magically" appeared from the drawing on the easel.

tion. The same technique was used in a number of early motion pictures known as trick-films.

Blackton was apparently interested in the possibilities of frame-by-frame filmmaking, but his duties as producer, director and, sometimes, actor at the rapidly expanding Vitagraph Studio occupied his time and attention. He continued his experiments in 1906 with "The Humorous Phases of Funny Faces," generally considered to be the animated film.

"Humorous Phases" is composed of several unrelated vignettes, some of them obviously adapted from Blackton's vaudeville chalk talks. The artist's hand is seen drawing the faces of a man and a woman, which change expressions after the hand is withdrawn. The man blows a cloud of cigar smoke and obliterates the woman; Blackton erases the board. In the second sequence, the profile of a man in a bowler hat seems to draw itself. The man tips his hat, an effect achieved by using a cutout arm, hand and hat. The combination of techniques is quite subtle, and it's difficult to tell when the image changes from a drawing to a cutout. Next, the profiles of a man and a woman disappear, line by line, until the screen is blank. A cutout clown doing a comic balancing act with a poodle follows. Blackton concludes the film by turning the words "Coon" and "Cohen" into caricatures of a black and a Jew. "Humorous Phases" is not a great film, but it was a beginning.

Blackton continued his experiments. He used stop-motion techniques to create eerie effects such as a loaf of bread slicing itself in "The Haunted Hotel" (1907), which enjoyed a tremendous success in the United States and Europe. Slide quotes Blackton as recalling: "What pride I took in carrying out all the weird happenings in 'The Haunted Hotel.' By means of a stop mechanism on the shutter, I endowed every piece of furniture with airy animation. The knife sawed through the loaf of bread unassisted, 'in a manner calculated to baffle the spectators,' as our catalogue might have said."

The premise of a hapless traveler caught in a room full of invisible ghosts had already been explored on the stage and in other films in America, England and France. But Blackton's technical aplomb (no wires or other evidence of trickery could be seen), combined with Vitagraph's advertising campaign and a craze for things American, made the film a hit. Nor was Blackton ignorant of the work of his European counterparts. "The Magic Fountain Pen" (1909) and "Princess Nicotine, or The Smoke Fairy" (1909) clearly show the influence of Emile Cohl and Georges Méliès.

Whether Blackton lost interest in animation or, as seems more probable, his duties at Vitagraph kept him too busy to pursue his interest (by 1910, he was supervising all the company's productions), he stopped working in the medium. He resigned from the studio in 1919 to form an independent production company, but made only live-action films. The sale

This color poster announced the theatrical release of Winsor McCay's "Gertie the Dinosaur," November 1914. McCay completed the film and began using it in his vaudeville act in February of that year.

of Vitagraph to Warner Brothers in 1926 made Blackton a wealthy man, but he soon lost the money in various business ventures. By 1931, he was bankrupt. Penniless and forgotten, Blackton died in 1941 after being hit by a bus.

J. Stuart Blackton may have invented animated filmmaking, but it was Winsor McCay who demonstrated the artistic potential of the new medium and inspired generations of animators. An extraordinary draftsman, McCay was not only the greatest of the pioneer animators but one of the undisputed masters of the newspaper comic strip and a respected editorial cartoonist.

McCay was born on September 26, in Spring Lake, Michigan, probably in 1867. He studied drawing and painting, and his cartoons and animation are distinguished by their solid three-dimensionality and extraordinary sense of perspective.

McCay wanted to become a humorous artist like A. B. Frost,

the celebrated illustrator of *Uncle Remus*. In a frequently quoted letter to cartoonist Clare Briggs, McCay declared: "The principal factor in my success has been an absolute desire to draw constantly. I never decided to be an artist. Simply, I could not stop myself from drawing. I drew for my own pleasure. I never wanted to know whether or not someone liked my drawings. I drew on walls, the school blackboard, old bits of paper, the walls of barns. Today I'm still as fond of drawing as when I was a kid—and that's a long time ago." He

Two strips of film from "Little Nemo" (1911). McCay had each frame of the original 35mm print tinted to match the colors in his newspaper comic strip.

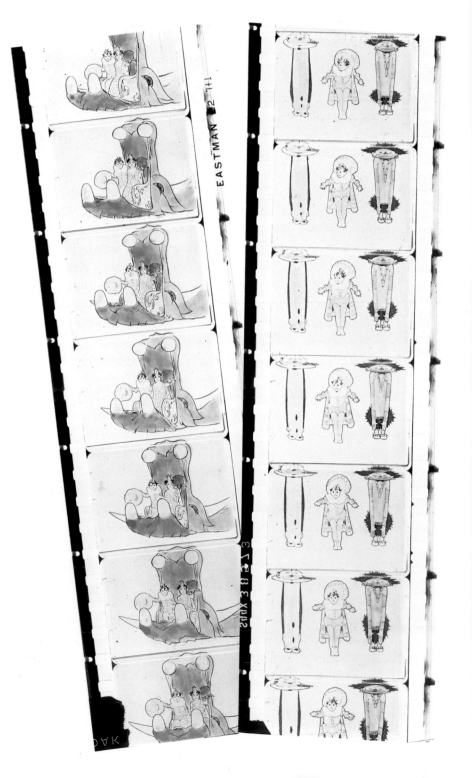

soon found a job at a company that made posters for traveling carnivals, circuses and melodrama companies.

Around 1889, McCay came to Cincinnati, Ohio. Two years later, he married Maud Dufour; their two children, Robert Winsor and Marion, later served as the models for Little Nemo and the Princess of Slumberland. McCay worked at the Vine Street Dime Museum, drawing posters and scenery for the exotic animal acts and freak shows.

He became a reporter/illustrator for the *Commercial Tribune* and, later, the Cincinnati *Enquirer*—a position similar to the one Blackton held at the New York *Evening World*. At the *Enquirer*, McCay drew his first comic strip, "Tales of the Jungle Imps by Felix Fiddle": parodies in verse of Kipling's *Just So Stories* written by George Chester.

The "Imps" ran in the Sunday supplement of the *Enquirer* for only forty-three weeks in 1903, but it caught the attention of James Gordon Bennett, Jr., the flamboyant publisher of the New York *Herald* and *Evening Telegram*. Bennett brought McCay to New York to work as an illustrator, but he was soon doing comic strips for the Bennett papers. The most interesting of his early efforts appeared in the *Herald*: "Little Sammy Sneeze" (1904), about a child whose catastrophic sneezes destroyed everything around him, and "Hungry Henrietta" (1905), the misadventures of a ravenous moppet.

That same year, McCay scored his first big success with "Dreams of the Rarebit Fiend" in the *Telegram*. Like most of his earlier strips, the "Rarebit Fiend" has a single story line: someone who has eaten a Welsh rarebit before going to bed suffers a terrible nightmare, and awakens vowing never to touch fried cheese again. The dream sequences gave McCay ample opportunity to display his imagination and graphic skills: a furnace becomes a demon-headed monster; a jockey tries to ride a dinosaur skeleton in a horse race; a crocodile bag turns into a hungry reptile and attacks its owner. Dreamers shrink, grow and metamorphose in sequences that recall the fun-house mirrors of McCay's circus posters. The "Rarebit Fiend" also reveals the artist's wry sense of humor; a missionary is captured by cannibals who complain that he's too tough and stringy ("He'll do for one of those cheap boarding houses"); a married couple must face the horror of moving to Brooklyn.

In 1905, McCay also began his masterpiece in the *Herald*: "Little Nemo in Slumberland," one of the most extraordinary illustrated narratives ever created. Again, the story line is simple. In his dreams, Nemo visits the sometimes beautiful, sometimes frightening wonders of Slumberland. He shares adventures with the other major characters: the lovely Princess of Slumberland and her father, King Morpheus; Flip, the rambunctious nephew of the Guardian of the Dawn; Dr. Pill and Impy, a mischievous cannibal child. In the last panel, Nemo awakens—sometimes reluctantly, sometimes in fright. Many experts rank "Little Nemo" second only to George

Winsor McCay, c. 1925. A consummate draftsman, McCay was an undisputed master of both animated and print cartoons.

Herriman's "Krazy Kat" in the annals of newspaper comic strips.

"Little Nemo" was an immediate success, appearing in other newspapers, both in the United States and abroad. Its popularity enabled McCay to create a vaudeville act for himself in 1906. He drew panels of the "Rarebit Fiend" and "Little Nemo" at a chalkboard with lightning speed, and sketched members of the audience. McCay's most famous routine was "The Seven Ages of Man": he would draw the faces of a baby boy and girl on the board, and take the characters through childhood, maturity and old age by adding and erasing lines. The act was also a success. McCay earned up to $500 a week, and appeared on bills with W. C. Fields, Will Rogers and Harry Houdini.

In 1908, McCay drew design suggestions for the scenery of an elaborate three-act operetta based on "Little Nemo" with music by Victor Herbert. Although it received good reviews—"as refined and wholesome as it was beautiful and merry," wrote one critic—and spawned a line of "Nemo" merchandise that included sandals and pocket watches, the show ran for only 111 performances in New York and has never been revived.

McCay claimed that he invented the animated cartoon in 1909, inspired by his son's "flippers." The Sunday supplement of the New York *American* included a page of sequential cartoons, printed on heavy paper, for children to cut out and bind with rubber bands. These flipbooks were actually advertisements, designed to generate interest in the movies.

His assistant, John Fitzsimmons, told animation scholar John Canemaker that McCay's first film resulted from a saloon bet with George McManus, the creator of "Bringing Up Father," in 1910:

> I think McManus kidded McCay because he was such a fast worker. . . . Jokingly, McManus suggested that McCay make several thousand drawings, photograph them onto film and show the results in theatres. . . . McCay claimed he would produce enough line drawings to sustain a four- or five-minute animated cartoon showing his Little Nemo characters and would use the film as a special feature of his already popular vaudeville act.

Even a cursory glance at McCay's comic strips suggests that he had been thinking of animation for several years. While most cartoonists used successive panels to present isolated incidents in a narrative, McCay often showed a slight change in an action or a metamorphosis or the point of view. In a six-panel page of "Sammy Sneeze" from September 24, 1905, the first four drawings show the title character preparing to sneeze. His face contorts as he struggles against the unbearable tickling in his nose. The sneeze shatters the fifth panel, and Sammy sits in the last drawing, festooned with the fragments. The animals in motion in "Little Nemo" are so accurately rendered that a biologist can identify their gaits.

McCay made four thousand drawings for the film "Little Nemo," working in India ink on translucent rice paper. A wooden holder and cross hairs in the corners of the paper kept the drawings in register. He timed movements to the split second with a stopwatch and flipped the drawings on a homemade mutoscope to check their smoothness. No records indicate how or when McCay met Blackton, or how well they knew each other; but the drawings were photographed at the Vitagraph Studio in Brooklyn, and Blackton directed the live-action prologue. The film was completed in early January 1911, and McCay hand-tinted each frame to match the colors of the comic strip. It premiered on April 12 at the Colonial Theatre in New York as part of McCay's vaudeville act.

"Little Nemo" is a series of plotless episodes involving the main characters from the strip. From the opening shot of Flip's profile, when the words "Watch me move" appear, there is constant motion on the screen. Flip and Impy run and tumble like circus clowns. McCay did not use backgrounds, but suggested movement in perspective by enlarging or shrinking characters. Fragments of lines coalesce to form Nemo—an effect that anticipates the look of computer graphics. The figures of Impy, Flip and Nemo stretch and distort like reflections in a fun-house mirror. Nemo sketches the Princess of Slumberland and she comes to life. Bosco, a green dragon with a chair in his móuth, lumbers in and bears Nemo and the Princess away. Flip and Impy drive through in a ramshackle jalopy that explodes: they fly through the air and land on Dr. Pill as the film ends.

No one knew what to make of "Little Nemo." No one had seen anything like it. The films of Blackton and Cohl showed simple line or stick figures performing elementary motions. McCay's sophisticated animation depicted fully rendered characters who moved smoothly and realistically. To the artist's chagrin, audiences assumed he had made the film using some sort of trick photography of live actors.

Posterity has judged this beautiful film more enthusiastically. Nearly seventy years later, it inspired Bob Kurtz when he began the Chevron Oil commercials that featured a clutch of blue dinosaurs: "The work McCay did so very early is so wonderful; it looks seventy or eighty years ahead of its time—as if he had really been born in 2025, acquired a complete knowledge of animation, then took a time capsule back to 1911 and faked it."

McCay's second film, "How a Mosquito Operates" (1912), also known as "The Story of a Mosquito," met with similar reactions. Audiences enjoyed the antics of Steve, the dapper mosquito who sucks too much blood from a fat man and explodes, but assumed McCay had rigged a dummy mosquito on wires. To avoid competing with himself, McCay would not allow the film to be shown in the United States while he was using it in his act; Universal released it in 1916 with a live-action prologue as "Winsor McCay and His Jersey Skeeters."

Around the time McCay completed "Mosquito," he began to declare that animation—which had been regarded as an amusing curiosity—was a new art form that would supplant the traditional pictorial arts.

> Take, for instance, that wonderful painting which everyone is familiar with, entitled *The Angelus*. There will be a time when people will gaze at it and ask why the objects remain rigid and stiff. They will demand action. And to meet this demand the artists of that time will look to motion picture people for help and the artists, working hand in hand with science, will evolve a new school of art that will revolutionize the entire field.

Two original drawings from "Gertie the Dinosaur" (1914). Below: Gertie reaches for the apple McCay pretended to give her as a treat. Bottom: She prepares to take a nap.

For his next film, McCay chose a subject that couldn't be faked: a prehistoric animal. The result was "Gertie the Dinosaur" (1914), arguably his greatest achievement—and a landmark in the history of animation. McCay made more than five thousand drawings for "Gertie," again working in India ink on rice paper. He hired John Fitzsimmons, then a young man in his teens, to retrace the background in each drawing. Meanwhile, McCay strove to improve his animation, checking his own breathing with a stopwatch to time Gertie's.

He integrated this film into his vaudeville act, rather than showing it as an interlude or a novelty. McCay would give a command and Gertie would respond—in her own good time. When McCay coaxed, she coyly emerged from her cave to bow to the audience and raise first one, then the other of her mighty front feet. But Gertie was not the most tractable performer. She paused to devour a nearby tree, got distracted by a passing sea serpent and quarreled with Jumbo, the woolly mammoth. When McCay scolded her, she cried until he tossed her an apple as a treat. (He pretended to throw her a cardboard apple, and Gertie appeared to catch a drawn one.) As a finale, McCay walked behind the screen as Gertie placed a drawing of him on her back and strolled off, her tail lashing.

In this film, McCay laid the foundations of *character animation*, the art of delineating a character's personality through a unique style of movement. The endearing, somewhat childish personality of the dinosaur is communicated through her motions—the angle at which she cocks her head while listening to a command; the impudence with which she flicks her tail while disobeying it.

Audiences finally realized they were seeing something new: a film composed of drawings. It was later released with a live-action prologue in which George McManus bets McCay an expensive dinner that he can't bring a dinosaur to life through his drawings. ("Gertie" proved so popular that J. R. Bray produced a crude counterfeit version, which still surfaces occasionally.) Within McCay's audiences were a number of young men who were so impressed by what they saw that they decided to become animators, including Walter Lantz, Dave Fleischer and Dick Huemer. The routine made such a strong impression on Huemer that he was able to re-create McCay's role from memory for a "Disneyland" program in 1955.

It's easy to understand their enthusiasm, even today. For a character who represents both the prehistory of life and the prehistory of animation, Gertie wears her years very lightly. More than twenty-five years would elapse before anyone did more polished animation. Many artists feel that McCay's work has been surpassed only by the very best animators—the top artists at Disney, Warners or MGM—at the height of their powers.

On May 7, 1915, without warning, a German submarine torpedoed the Cunard liner *Lusitania* off the coast of Ireland;

An autographed cel from "The Sinking of the *Lusitania*" (1918), McCay's brooding editorial cartoon-in-motion.

1,198 people were killed, including 124 Americans. Incensed at this brutal act, McCay decided to make an animated film that would serve as both a depiction and a protest. Even with Fitzsimmons and another friend, Apthorp Adams, as assistants, it took McCay twenty-two months to complete 25,000 drawings for "The Sinking of the *Lusitania*." For the first time, he worked on cels: clear sheets of celluloid that could be laid over the background, eliminating the need to retrace it in every drawing. Inspired by a ring-bound ledger book, Fitzsimmons devised a system of pegs that held the punched cels in register.

Released in July 1918, "The Sinking of the *Lusitania*" attracted widespread attention. The opening scenes are so precisely timed and drawn in such perfect perspective that they resemble live-action footage.

Between 1918 and 1921, McCay worked on several animation projects. "The Centaurs," "Flip's Circus" and "Gertie on Tour" survive only in fragments. Three short films based on "Dreams of the Rarebit Fiend" were released in 1921. (Edwin S. Porter filmed a seven-minute live-action version of one strip for the Edison Company in 1906.) The most famous of the three is "The Pet," in which a bizarre, puppylike beast grows until it is several stories tall. The gigantic creature wanders

through a city and is attacked by airplanes in scenes that seem to anticipate "King Kong." Like Steve the Mosquito, the monster finally explodes.

In "Bug Vaudeville," a sleeping hobo dreams of a weird theater in which grasshoppers, roaches, beetles and daddy longlegs perform. The titles for "The Flying House" read: "Drawn by Robert Winsor McCay using the Winsor McCay process of animated drawing," but the film probably resulted from a father-son collaboration. In an effort to evade their creditors, a husband and wife transform their house into an airplane, but they miscalculate and end up flying beyond the moon.

No one knows why McCay gave up animation after the "Rarebit" films. He would have been in his early fifties, and he may have lost the incredible energy that had enabled him to give two performances a day while drawing three weekly comic strips and designing the posters and programs for the "Little Nemo" operetta. McCay had moved to the Hearst papers in 1911, and Hearst made him curtail his vaudeville tours in 1917.

But the main reason for abandoning the medium was probably his distaste for the studio cartoons of the silent era, which he correctly regarded as inferior to his own work. In the magazine *Cartoonist Profiles*, I. Klein, whose animation career began at Hearst's International Film Service in 1918, described a testimonial dinner honoring McCay, given by the artists of the fledgling animation industry in 1927. After a fulsome introduction, McCay gave a short speech. "He wound up with a statement that has remained in my mind . . . 'Animation should be an art, that is how I conceived it . . . but as I see what you fellows have done with it is making it into a trade . . . not an art, but a trade . . . *bad luck.*' He sat down. There was some scattered applause."

During the 1920s and '30s, McCay did more drawing for the editorial page than the comics section. (He died in 1934.) His animated films were largely forgotten, supplanted first by Felix the Cat, then by Mickey Mouse. The editorial cartoons he drew seem stiff and unmoving by modern standards, but the level of draftsmanship remained high.

McCay's films survived only by accident. Robert McCay gave them to Irving Mendelsohn, a friend of his father's; the cans of perishable nitrate film sat and rusted in the Mendelsohn garage for years. In 1947, Jack Mendelsohn (Irving's son and later one of the writers of "Yellow Submarine") invited his friend Robert Brotherton, a film editor, to examine the material in his father's garage.

Realizing the value of the material—and the potential danger of the deteriorating nitrate stock—the three men set about sorting and housing McCay's work and, eventually, transferring it to safety stock. (The surviving originals are now in the Library of Congress.) This difficult and expensive task was completed in time for the films to be shown at the Animation Symposium at Expo '67 in Montreal. In 1966, the Metropolitan Museum of Art in New York presented "Two Fantastic Draftsmen," an exhibit of the work of McCay and Herbert Crowley, another cartoonist. Canemaker organized programs of McCay's films for the New York Animation Festival in 1975 and the Whitney Museum of American Art in 1976. These programs, coupled with other screenings and exhibits in the United States and Europe, helped to restore McCay to his proper place in the history of American film and graphic arts.

Although he might have disdained the title, McCay was truly the father of the American animated film. His talent and achievements continue to inspire artists half a century after his death. Commercial animator Bob Kurtz summarized the profound respect most animators reserve for McCay and his work: "He produced the most extraordinary body of animation ever created by one person: There was no Winsor McCay Studio—although you might suspect he kept twenty duplicates of himself in the back room to do all that drawing. On the intimate level at which he worked, no one can even approach him."

A Sunday page from "In the Land of Wonderful Dreams," the later version of "Little Nemo in Slumberland" (1912). Although McCay switched to conventional, rectangular panels, his draftsmanship lost none of its vivid originality.

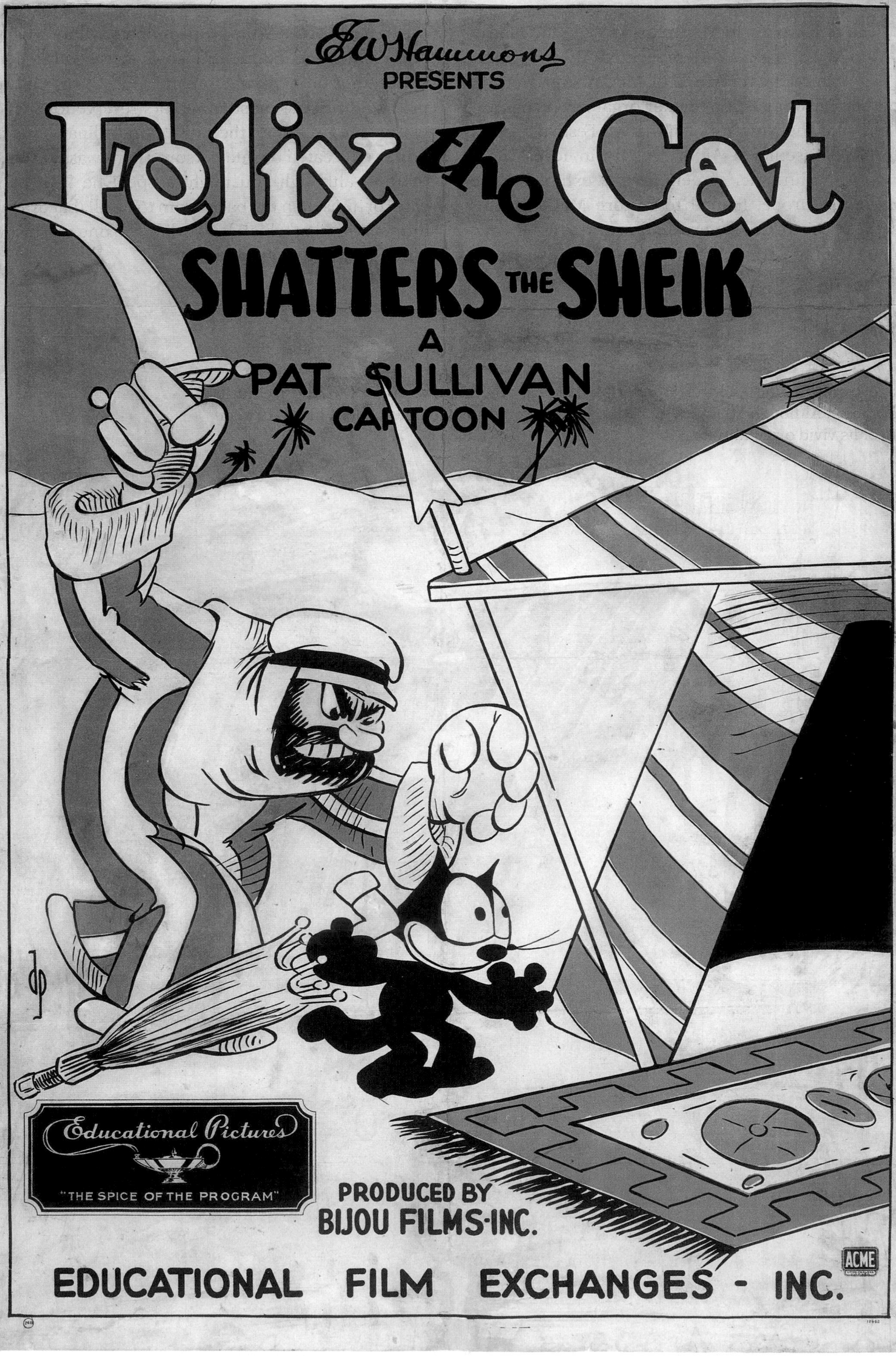
E.W. Hammons
PRESENTS
Felix the Cat
SHATTERS THE SHEIK
A
PAT SULLIVAN
CARTOON
Educational Pictures
"THE SPICE OF THE PROGRAM"
PRODUCED BY
BIJOU FILMS-INC.
ACME
EDUCATIONAL FILM EXCHANGES - INC.

THE SILENT ERA, 1914–1928

By 1927–28, audiences would groan when a cartoon came on. Animation had worn out its welcome. The novelty was gone. If sound hadn't come in, the cartoon would have vanished.

—SHAMUS CULHANE

Almost as soon as there was animation, there were studios to produce it. The medium that Winsor McCay had envisioned as an extension of the pictorial arts and a means of personal expression quickly became a popular entertainment and an assembly-line product.

Film historians estimate that between one-half and two-thirds of the films made before 1950 have been lost. For animation from the silent era, the toll is even higher. Perhaps two hundred silent animated shorts remain in distribution: a tiny fraction of the thousands of cartoons that were released between 1913 and 1928. More do exist, in archives and private collections, but they are rarely screened.

The record of the development of animation and filmmaking has largely vanished. Most of the written records that could supplement the surviving films were destroyed decades ago, when the studios closed or merged. Animation did not receive much serious attention in the popular press and trade journals during the teens and twenties—nor does it today.

A chart of the silent studios would be as complicated and

A poster for a Felix the Cat short (1926). Created in 1919 by Otto Messmer, Felix was the most popular, best animated and most imaginative cartoon character of the 1920s.

involuted as the plot of a television soap opera. Studios were repeatedly opened, closed, merged and split off; the same artists constantly joined and left the various studios, depending on who had work, who offered better salaries and/or conditions and who got along with whom.

For example: around 1910, Raoul Barré, an artist whose comic drawings had been published in France, Canada and the United States, began working with William C. Nolan, doing experimental animation and, later, advertising films. In 1913, he opened the Raoul Barré studio in New York—the first professional animation studio. Three years later, he entered into a partnership with Charles Bowers (who had begun producing cartoons based on the comic strip "Hans and Fritz" in 1916 and had founded a studio, Mutt & Jeff, Inc.) to form the Barré-Bowers studio. Bowers left in the early 1920s to form the Charles Bowers studio, which split into the Ch. Bowers and Queen Plaza studios in 1924–25. The old Barré-Bowers studio became the Bud Fisher studio (named for the artist/producer who drew the "Mutt and Jeff" strip), which was dissolved in 1927.

Often, more than one studio animated the same characters —at least four made films with Mutt and Jeff—and screen credits were given casually, when they were given at all. Many producers put their own names on the films and let it go at that. Veteran animator Grim Natwick recalled that well into the 1930s at the Fleischer studio, when a cartoon was about to

Raoul Barré, the founder of the first animation studio.

be released, someone would go around asking, "Who hasn't had his name on a film in a while?"

The silent cartoons were more than a training ground for animators and directors; they created an audience that could appreciate and accept the movements and expressions of characters composed of ink lines. Without Dinky Doodle, Colonel Heeza Liar, Bobby Bumps, Oswald Rabbit, Felix the Cat and Ko-Ko the Clown, there could never have been Mickey Mouse, Bugs Bunny, Donald Duck, Tom and Jerry, Betty Boop or Wile E. Coyote.

The animation industry, like the burgeoning live-action film industry, was centered in New York. Silent cartoons were popular—despite the disclaimers of some of the artists who made them. By 1918, only four years after the premiere of "Gertie the Dinosaur," there were at least a dozen studios operating in the city, some of them producing films as fast as one per week. The Raoul Barré studio (1913), the John Randolph Bray studio (1914) and William Randolph Hearst's International Film Service (1915) dominated production between 1913 and 1919.

The early producers had to find ways to produce animation quickly and cheaply. Winsor McCay could take months to make a film if he chose, doing all the drawings himself and not worrying about the cost. But studio producers, with deadlines and budgets to meet, needed to streamline this new, highly labor-intensive medium.

One problem was keeping the drawings in register—ensuring that each one was in exactly the same place on the paper. If the image was off by even a fraction of an inch, the results would shimmer and vibrate on the screen. McCay devised a wooden holder that fit against the carefully cut bottom edge of the paper. He also put cross hairs—similar to the ones used by technical draftsmen—in the corners of each sheet.

Barré is credited with devising the peg system of registration. Identical pegs were set into each animator's drawing table, and the paper was punched to match the pegs. The pegs held the paper in place, not only while the animator was drawing but also when the drawings were inked and photographed. This system remains in use today.

The earliest studio cartoons were drawn on paper, and any background elements had to be redrawn every time, which was inefficient and bored the artists. Barré's solution was the "slash system." The animation was drawn on one sheet; the background would be drawn on a second page that was laid over or under the first. If the background was on the top sheet, a hole would be cut in it to show the animated character; if the background was on the lower sheet, most of the page surrounding the character would be cut away to reveal it.

If Ko-Ko the Clown is walking through a room to pick up a ball, only his figure and the ball will be on the top page. Everything but the area immediately around him will be cut away from that sheet of paper. The bottom page will have the walls of the room and the furniture. (If the clown is supposed to pass in front of a table or a chair, that piece of furniture would have to be drawn on the upper level.) The slash system was also sometimes used on characters. If Ko-Ko was to raise his arm, his body would be drawn on the bottom sheet and a series of arms in successive positions would appear on separate pieces of paper—most of which would be cut away.

The slash system is very rarely used today, because the edge of the paper can be seen as a line on the screen. But the cruder lenses, film stocks and processing of the teens were not sensitive enough to capture the difference between the two layers of white paper. Although the cels quickly became the industry standard after they were introduced in 1915, the slash system did not disappear entirely. Dick Huemer remembered using it at the Fleischer studio for Ko-Ko shorts during the early 1920s.

Bill Nolan discovered that if a background drawn on a long piece of paper was passed under the drawings of a character walking, an illusion of horizontal motion was produced. This discovery was the basis for all pan movements in animated films.

With these innovations and a staff that included Nolan, Frank Moser, Gregory LaCava and Pat Sullivan, Barré began making films. In May 1915, he launched one of the first series, the Animated Grouch Chasers, for Edison; it featured cartoon inserts in live-action comedies. He also worked with LaCava and Frank Moser of Hearst's International Film Service on a series of "Phables," based on a comic strip by Tom Powers. A group of little gnomes who represented "Joys" and "Glooms" appeared at the bottom of the frame in the Phables films.

In 1916, Barré accepted an offer from Charles Bowers

(sometimes referred to as Thomas Bowers) to form a partnership. Bowers had been making cartoons based on "Hans and Fritz," "Happy Hooligan" and other comic strips. In 1916, he adapted Harry "Bud" Fisher's enormously popular "Mutt and Jeff" strip for the screen.

The combined Bowers-Barré staff included a number of artists who later made significant contributions to animation, including George Stallings, Ted Sears, Mannie Davis, Burt Gillett, Ben Sharpsteen, Dick Huemer and Vladimir "Bill" Tytla. Despite this array of talent, conditions at the studio were humble, at best. Huemer recalled:

> The Barré studio was in an enormous bare loft, about a hundred feet by about seventy-five feet . . . without any breaks . . . at one end there was a wall for an office. The studio part had these long benches, with room for three or four light boards on each side, facing each other. . . . No curtains or carpets. We had bare flooring. . . . That loft was very bleak and it was very cold in the winter. The heating was totally inadequate. We often had to go home because our fingers got stiff from the cold.

The films were released under Fisher's name, and in interviews he pontificated about how hard he worked on scenarios for the films. In fact, he seems to have contributed nothing to them. According to veterans of the studio, Fisher appeared rarely, and only to survey his domain—usually for the benefit of a female companion.

Fisher and Bowers gradually edged Barré out of the business. In 1919, the weary and disgusted Barré retired from animation and plunged into a deep depression. He spent the next seven years painting and working in illustration and advertising. Barré returned to animation in 1927–28, when he worked on the Felix the Cat series at the Pat Sullivan studio. Fisher fired Bowers later in 1919 because of financial irregularities in the way he ran the studio, but rehired him the next year. The cartoons continued for several more years, although Fisher later fired Bowers a second time for padding the studio payroll and other shady dealings.

Barré's foremost rival was the most redoubtable producer of the silent era: John Randolph Bray, sometimes called the Henry Ford of animation. Barré was quiet, modest and unassuming, and everyone who remembers him speaks of him fondly; Bray was aloof and remote. Shamus Culhane, who began his long animation career as an office boy in the Bray studio, found the boss such an intimidating figure that he could never summon up the nerve to say "good morning" to him.

Born in 1879, in Addison, Michigan, Bray decided to be an artist, and by 1903 he had a staff position on the Brooklyn *Daily Eagle*, one of the largest papers in the New York area. A year and a half later, he married the energetic and strong-willed Margaret Till. Bray apparently wearied of his staff duties and wanted to become a free-lance artist.

In 1906, Bray began selling cartoons to major magazines like *Judge, Life* and *Harper's*. The next year, his most popular print work debuted in *Judge:* "Little Johnny and the Teddy Bears," drawn in the style of nineteenth-century children's book illustrations.

Although Bray maintained that he began the experiments that led to his first film, "The Artist's Dream," in 1908 or 1909, that seems unlikely. As Donald Crafton observed, " 'The Artist's Dream' is usually dated 1910 or 1911, but it was uncharacteristic for Bray or his distributor Pathé to withhold a potentially lucrative item. It was not released until June 12, 1913, and there is no reason to believe that it was completed much in advance of that date."

The plot of "The Artist's Dream" is reminiscent of McCay's "How a Mosquito Operates" (1912). An artist (Bray) draws pictures of sausages, which an animated dachshund devours as soon as the man's back is turned. The greedy pooch grows larger and larger, and finally explodes. "The Artist's Dream" was a crowd pleaser, and Bray signed a contract with Pathé to produce one cartoon each month. He hired six artists and set up a studio in his apartment in New York City.

John Randolph Bray at his desk in 1917. In his efforts to organize the production of animated films, he transformed the medium into an assembly-line product.

More than any other early producer, Bray saw that the process of animation would have to be streamlined and organized. He was also the first to realize that any innovations he devised could be protected by patents. His first was for a system of printing the backgrounds on sheets of paper "by ordinary zinc etching." The animation could be sketched on

Below: "Colonel Heeza Liar's African Hunt" (1914). The star of one of the first cartoon series, the Colonel began as a caricature of Teddy Roosevelt. Bottom: Walter Lantz poses with another version of Colonel Heeza Liar, in what is probably a publicity photo for one of the live-action/animation combination films of the later 1920s.

plain paper, then traced onto the sheets printed with backgrounds. Conflicting lines were inked over or erased.

Bray soon moved his studio to a farm up the Hudson River, where nothing could distract the men from their work. When the artists were released and paid on Friday night, many of them got so drunk they were too hung over to work on Monday morning—if they showed up at all. Margaret Bray is credited with the idea of switching payday to Monday, a tradition still observed in some studios.

In January 1914, Pathé released Bray's "Colonel Heeza Liar's African Hunt," often referred to as "Colonel Heeza Liar in Africa." The title character was essentially a Baron Munchausen figure who used animated gimmicks to escape the predicaments in his fantastic adventures. But the Colonel's tales also spoofed a familiar American figure. The opening verse describes him as roaming the desert "to snuff out T.R.'s candle," an obvious allusion to Teddy Roosevelt's recent shooting expeditions in Africa.

For years, "Colonel Heeza Liar's African Hunt" was considered the first installment in the oldest extant cartoon *series,* but in 1988, one of the thirteen films George McManus and Emile Cohl produced in 1913 based on McManus's strip "The Newlyweds" was discovered in a midwestern archive. Bray continued to make films featuring the potbellied, balding Colonel well into the 1920s. The animation in these early films is at best adequate, far removed from McCay's elegant work. Instead of cutting to title cards, as live-action films did, the action halts while the captions appear inside balloons.

The films were successful enough for Bray to open a new studio at Madison Avenue and Twenty-sixth Street in New York, organized according to the division of labor. His policy of giving foremen freedom to make the series as they saw fit resulted in many of them leaving the studio to become competitors.

Meanwhile, Bray was attempting to devise a system of patents that would give him control over the animation process. McCay never attempted to patent his techniques; the notion was incompatible with his concept of animation as an art form. Smith and Blackton don't seem to have attached enough importance to their discoveries to bother registering them.

In December 1914, Earl Hurd obtained a patent on the use of clear sheets of celluloid (abbreviated to "cels" almost immediately) in animation. Despite the importance of his contributions, Hurd remains one of the shadowiest figures in the history of animation: almost nothing is known about him.

The transparent cels made Bray's printed backgrounds unnecessary. The characters could be drawn on cels and laid over a single background, or vice versa. If only part of the character was moving, that part could be drawn on one cel level and laid over one drawing of the rest of the character. If Ko-Ko was raising his arm, his head and body would be on one

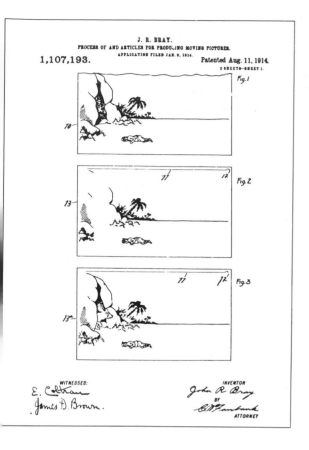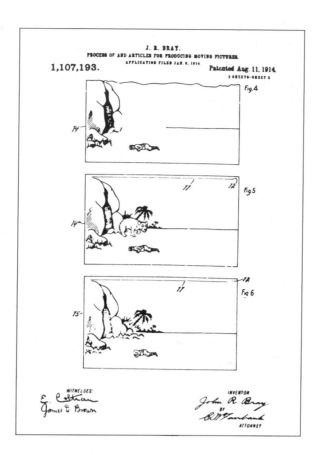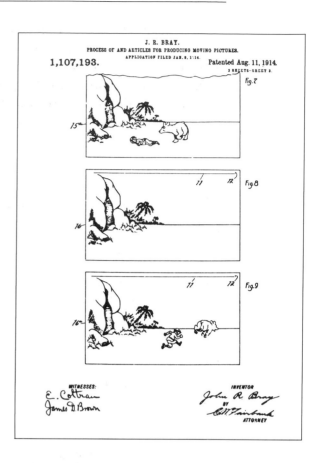

Illustrations from J. R. Bray's patent application (1914), showing how the preprinted backgrounds and other elements could be added to a scene.

cel; a series of cels with the arm in successive positions would be placed on top, one at a time. As the cels were not perfectly transparent, no more than three levels could be used without making the background seem too dark. The cel system quickly became the industry standard, and remains so today.

Bray and Hurd met—no one knows how or where—and agreed to pool their resources to form the Bray–Hurd Processing Company in 1914. With an additional patent obtained by Bray in 1916, the company held a virtual monopoly on the animation process. Assisted by his wife and legal staff, Bray set out to enforce his claim, compelling other animators to buy licenses and pay royalties. In a magazine interview in 1915, he defended his actions, insisting he was not trying to establish a monopoly but rather to ensure a fair salary for animators and maintain a standard of quality in animation:

> From the first, I have tried to uphold the dignity of the animated cartoon, and in doing this have naturally opposed the circulation of poor work that would give the public and exhibitors a wrong impression. . . . Some of the film released was so entirely without merit that it harmed the business prospects of all artists engaged in making cartoon drawings.

This rather ingenuous stance failed to win the sympathy of other producers and animators. Bitterly fought legal battles over Bray's patents and licensing went on through the early 1920s. (Bray even tried to take McCay to court but had to settle—in McCay's favor. McCay received a small percentage of the royalties each quarter.) The patents expired in 1932 because Bray failed to make any improvements on them, and the animation process entered the public domain.

While the courts upheld Bray's suits, it is obvious now that much of what he claimed to have invented had actually been devised by McCay, Barré and others. John Fitzsimmons remembered McCay giving a detailed explanation of his animation process to an unknown young man posing as a journalist: Fitzsimmons believed the "journalist" was actually Bray.

Curiously, Earl Hurd—whose patent ultimately proved far more important than Bray's—worked as an employee in the studio. In 1915, he began the Bobby Bumps series, which featured a stocky little boy and his dog, Fido—the first of many cartoon boy-and-dog teams. (R. F. Outcault created the prototype in 1902 with his popular "Buster Brown" strip.) The first installments were fairly routine, but the series grew wilder as it progressed. Bobby began to interact with the unseen animator, prefiguring later conflicts between Ko-Ko and Max Fleischer.

Above: A poster for a late Colonel Heeza Liar short, drawn by Clyde Geronimi. The devil's features and pince-nez suggest a partial caricature of J. R. Bray. Below: Farmer Al Falfa confronts a horde of rodents in "Rats in His Garret" (1927). The artists at all the silent studios drew virtually identical rats. (Note their similarity to the ones in "Alice Rattled by Rats," on page 40.)

In "Bobby Bumps Puts a Beanery on the Bum" (1918), the title character is seen riding on a cutout of Hurd's hand, which writes "Get off my hand" on a sheet of paper. When a cat calls Fido a cur, the dog announces: "I'm going to make him eat those words." He grabs the dialogue balloon, wads it up and shoves it down the cat's gullet. While the animation relies rather heavily on poses and expressions, these later, surreal Bobby Bumps shorts are far more entertaining to modern audiences than the Colonel Heeza Liar films or most of the other Bray products.

In 1915, Bray signed a contract with Paramount to produce comedies at the extraordinary rate of one thousand feet per week, beginning in 1916. Soon after that contract began, he discovered another lucrative market: instructional films for the military.

After an experimental series of six films made in 1916 for cadets at West Point proved successful, Bray began to produce large numbers of training films. These films became so important to the Army that when Max Fleischer was drafted in 1919, Bray succeeded in having him shipped to Fort Sill, Oklahoma, where he oversaw the production of more films.

In 1919, Bray broke with Paramount and entered into an agreement with Samuel Goldwyn to produce three entertainment shorts a week. The next year, Goldwyn bought controlling interest in the Bray studio, reorganized it and began turning out two cartoons each week. Among them was the first color cartoon, "The Debut of Thomas Cat" (1920), made with an experimental process called Brewster Color, which was deemed too expensive to continue. There seems to have been surprisingly little public reaction to this major first—certainly nothing to compare with the sensation that "Flowers and Trees," the first Technicolor cartoon, caused in 1932.

Although Bray released cartoons through 1928, his interest had shifted to training films by the end of World War I. He continued to make educational, health, safety and travel films for schools, industry and the military until his retirement in the late 1960s. Raoul Barré established the first animation studio, but John Randolph Bray organized the first animation factory, setting the pattern for the great Hollywood studios and the Saturday-morning television houses.

The last of the major early silent studios was the short-lived animation division of the International Film Service (IFS), established in 1915 by William Randolph Hearst as an outgrowth of his International News Service (INS), a wire service intended to compete with the Associated Press. He set up a studio on Seventh Avenue in New York and took out a cel license from Bray; by February 1916, IFS was releasing cartoons. Hearst intended to use comic strip characters from his papers in these films. (It has been suggested that IFS was established as a sort of promotional unit for those comics.) Some of the most popular cartoonists of the time, including

A publicity drawing of Walt Disney's Oswald the Lucky Rabbit, c. 1927.

Fred Opper ("Happy Hooligan"), Harry Hershfield ("Abie the Agent"), George Herriman ("Krazy Kat"), Thomas "Tad" Dorgan ("Silk Hat Harry"), Cliff Sterrett ("Polly and Her Pals"), George McManus ("Bringing Up Father") and Winsor McCay, were listed as future contributors.

The animated adaptations relied on what quickly became formula gags, rather than the original artists' styles of humor. (Not that the IFS films are appreciably worse than contemporary products from Bray or Barré; there is little discernible difference among the earliest studio releases.)

Hearst hired animators away from other studios the same way he had hired writers and editors away from rival newspapers. To head the studio, he chose Gregory LaCava, formerly of Barré–Bowers. The staff included Frank Moser, Bill Nolan and George Stallings. Among the young animators who got their start at IFS were Isadore "Izzy" Klein, Walter Lantz and Grim Natwick. Despite these impressive talents, IFS was constantly beset by problems. A series based on "The Katzenjammer Kids"—a potentially very successful property—proved especially troublesome.

Hearst's increasingly unpopular pro-German/anti-British sympathies led to the banning of his publications (including cartoons) in Britain, France and Canada in 1916. The reputation of IFS was blackened by association after a 1917 scandal that involved the theft of news stories from the Associated Press by INS. The animation branch closed on July 6, 1918. The animators moved on to other studios; LaCava switched to live action, and he became an accomplished comedy director.

While many of the early animators were talented draftsmen, they had no training in making their drawings move convincingly. There was no place to learn animation except the studios, where the men learned from each other and by trial and error. The speed of production precluded the hours of drawing and redrawing required to perfect a movement. The early studio cartoons resemble modern kidvid programs: something to be finished, shown and forgotten in a short time on a small budget. (The entire budget for a cartoon short during the late teens or early twenties might run as low as $1,000–$1,500.)

The crucial weakness of the early shorts is that they are uninteresting as *films*. The artists did not know how to structure a film (or even an individual gag), giving it the necessary beginning, middle and end. Dick Huemer recalled: "We used to look at our own work and laugh like hell. We did, we thought it was great. But in the theater, they didn't. Our mistake was that we weren't establishing anything first. We were giving the payoff without the buildup. We never seemed to bother much with that, or perhaps it never occurred to us to do it. Disney always very carefully planned things, so that everything was understandable, and one thing happened after another, logically."

"Farmer Al Falfa's Wayward Pup" (1917)—the debut film of Paul Terry's genial hayseed, who became one of the few silent cartoon characters to survive the transition to sound.

Animators during the teens produced cartoons with the innocent casualness of Judy Garland and Mickey Rooney deciding to put on a show. There were no scripts or storyboards. Story meetings consisted of the animators sitting around tossing out ideas for a theme or individual gags.

"The stories were pretty simple," says Natwick. "We could throw in any gags we thought were funny—it was expected of us. We could exaggerate and make a neck *this* long if we wanted to. The gags were largely put into the pictures by the animators as we were animating."

"You were given part of the picture, and you did what you wanted," said Huemer. "If it was a picture about ice skating, you took a scene of somebody on ice skates and you used your own gags, and made it all up. We'd spend an evening talking about [a story idea]. Generally it was picking up a theme. We'd say, 'Let's do a Hawaiian picture.' 'Fine. I'll do the surf stuff, you do the cannibals,' or whatever else. Five animators would do it, and we'd do it all in a week."

This lack of organization helps explain why the film adaptations of the early comic strips so often lack the humor that the print originals retain. Five or six animators contributing gags without reference to each other or any finished scenario could hardly be expected to maintain the personality of a character or the style of humor that a single artist had refined over a period of years.

In these early films, the artists are obviously imitating the poses used in the newspaper strips and trying to make them move. An aesthetic revolution began around 1917 at the Bray studio when Bill Nolan started experimenting with what came to be called "rubber hose" animation in "The Spider and the Fly," a Happy Hooligan short. He began to turn the characters' limbs into lengths of flexible tubing: instead of bending stiffly at the elbow, an arm could move with enormous freedom.

"The early animators tried to make straight, angular characters move," explains Natwick, "and the results would strobe between each step: you'd see a flicker of light on the white background. By rounding the shapes and kind of swinging them into the motions, Nolan avoided that flicker: a curve in one drawing will flow into the curve in the next one."

Rubber hose animation quickly became the dominant style and remained so—with some modifications—until the Disney artists began giving their characters weight and realistic movements.

By the end of World War I, new animators and new studios were coming to the fore. Like many of the other early animators, Paul Terry began his career as a cartoonist/illustrator for various newspapers and magazines. By 1911, he was working for the New York *Press* and drawing a short-lived comic strip, "Alonzo," for Hearst's King Features Syndicate. After seeing McCay's "Gertie the Dinosaur," he set to work on his first film, a live-action/animation spoof of Hermann, a well-known magician, entitled "Little Herman."

According to an often-repeated anecdote, Terry screened the film for distributor Lewis Selznick, who offered him a dollar a foot for it. When Terry protested that the film alone had cost more than that, Selznick replied that the film had been worth more before Terry drew on it. (Terry later sold "Little Herman" to the Thanhouser Company for $405, or $1.35 per foot.)

Undaunted by this unenthusiastic reception, Terry tried to interest Bud Fisher in a series of Mutt and Jeff films. Terry lost the job to Charles Bowers, and Terry went to work at the Bray studio, where he soon became a foreman. One of his first creations was "Farmer Al Falfa's Cat-Astrophe" (1916), in which he introduced the familiar round-nosed, white-bearded bumpkin. Although never particularly interesting or well animated, Farmer Al Falfa proved to be one of the most durable characters of the silent era: he continued to appear in cartoons for almost fifty years.

After the war, Terry made Farmer Al Falfa cartoons for Paramount. In 1920, he joined with writer Howard Estabrook to make a series of cartoons based loosely on *Aesop's Fables*. The studio underwent the customary changes of name but is usually known as Fables Pictures.

The first Fable, "The Cat and the Mice," was released in 1921. Although billed as "sugar coated pills of wisdom" (each one ends with some sort of moral, usually in the form of a joke or

The staff of Paul Terry's studio in 1926. From left to right and back to front: Norman Ferguson, Bill Tytla, George Williams, Jerry Sheilds, Frank Chambers, Harry Bailey, Mannie Davis, Eddie Link, Bill Hicks, Eddie Donnelly, Oscar Van Brunt, George MacAvoy, Frank Moser, Paul Terry, Hicks Lokey, Frank Sherman, John McManus, Horvath, John Foster, Jim Tyer, Ted Waldyer and Vet Anderson.

zinger), the majority of the stories have little to do with Aesop. Most of the characters were animals, although Terry shrewdly incorporated Farmer Al Falfa into some. The films were highly praised in the press, and Terry turned out more than four hundred over the next eight years. To modern viewers, the Fables seem terribly repetitious and formulaic, populated with enough identically drawn mice to discourage even the Pied Piper.

Terry's real contribution to animation was technical. He is credited with developing and exploiting the time- and labor-saving possibilities of the cel system. Terry's studio must rank among the earliest animation assembly lines. He managed to turn out all those Fables with a relatively small staff and fought Bray over the licensing issue until 1926.

Max and Dave Fleischer created some of the brightest and most imaginative cartoons of the silent era. Audiences still watch their films as entertainments, rather than as curiosities.

Max Fleischer was born in Vienna in 1883. The family emigrated to America soon after, and David was born in New York in 1894. There were five Fleischer brothers—Charles, Max, Joe, Lou and Dave. All of them had some measure of both artistic and mechanical ability, and all of them worked together at various times. After studying art and mechanics, Max got a job at the Brooklyn *Eagle*, and by 1914 he had become art editor of *Popular Science Monthly*, writing and illustrating articles on new inventions. Dave had gone to work the year before as an editor at Pathé.

Around 1915, the two brothers began their first experiments with the *rotoscope*, a device that enabled an animator to trace live-action footage frame by frame. A modified projector showed one frame of film on a glass plate, fitted with a holder for the paper. The artist drew whatever he needed from that frame with the projection lamp serving as an underlight, then advanced the film to the next frame. It is not clear who originated the idea; the brothers later had a major falling-out and each claimed credit. Max applied for the patent in late 1915; it was granted in 1917.

The first tests for the rotoscope were shot on the roof of Max's apartment building. Dave wore a black clown suit that stood out against a white sheet tacked to a wall. It took the brothers nearly a year to complete 100 feet of animation based on this footage, but Max soon figured out ways to produce the film faster, and persuaded Pathé to hire them to make a film using their invention. Rather than develop the clown character, Max insisted on doing a satire of Teddy Roosevelt hunting a bird. The film was judged unsatisfactory and the brothers were fired.

Max then took the clown film to an old associate from the *Eagle*, J. R. Bray, who hired him to produce one cartoon a month for his Bray Pictograph series in 1916. The outbreak of World War I interrupted this arrangement, and Max spent the war making training films. The rotoscope enabled his film crews to reproduce the complicated motions involved in assembling equipment and similar tasks. Dave worked as a film editor for the War Department.

After the Armistice, Bray put Max in charge of developing a series based on the rotoscoped clown. The first Out of the Inkwell film premiered in 1919 to considerable enthusiasm. An article in the *New York Times* on February 22, 1920, reported: "This little inkwell clown has attracted favorable attention because of a number of distinguishing characteristics. His motions, for one thing, are smooth and graceful. He walks, dances and leaps as a human being, as a particularly easy-limbed human being might."

The story goes on to assure the reader that "no dummy substitutes for the clown when he takes his hazardous jour-

An illustration from Max Fleischer's patent application for the rotoscope, dated 1917. The rotoscope enabled animators to reproduce realistic movements by tracing live-action footage frame by frame.

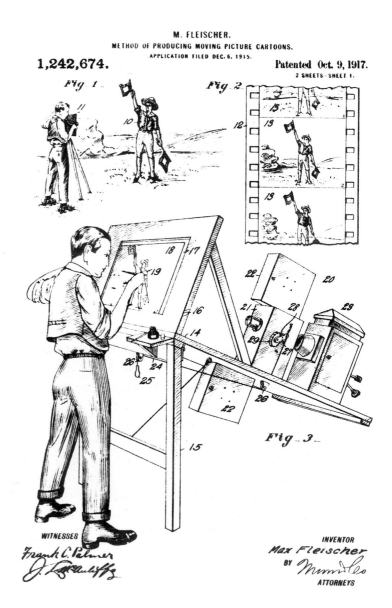

neys around the room." While Max declined to describe the rotoscope process, the article does say that "a real man dressed as a clown poses for him in the principal positions to be assumed by the animated figure." Despite his popularity, the clown (named Ko-Ko in 1923) appeared on the screen only sporadically.

In 1919, the Fleischers struck out on their own and founded Out of the Inkwell, Inc.; Dave was listed as the director of all the cartoons, Max as the producer. Margaret Winkler, the first woman to distribute and produce animated films, handled their output.

After a series of attempts to reorganize and changes in distributors, the studio became Fleischers (or the Fleischer studio) with Paramount handling the releases in 1927, an arrangement that continued until 1942. Max retained the copyrights on the characters, but signed over all the other rights to the films to Paramount—a decision he would later regret.

The Fleischers were not the first to use the image of the artist creating a character, or to combine live-action and animated figures, but they did both with exceptional imagination and wit. The opening of each cartoon was a variation of Ko-Ko emerging from the inkwell. In "Perpetual Motion" (c. 1920), Max blows on a blob of ink that comes to life and assumes the form of the clown. Ko-Ko reverses the process in "Ko-Ko Gets Egg-cited" (1926), and draws in the live-action background—including Max. Max always appeared in the films as the cartoonist, and served as a foil for Ko-Ko.

The Fleischers achieved some of their striking combinations of live action and animation by using black-and-white photographs of objects and landscapes as backgrounds and placing cels over them. In "Bedtime" (1923), Ko-Ko grows taller than a skyscraper and walks through Manhattan, searching for Max. At one point, he reaches into a multistory building and rummages inside, his fingertips emerging through the windows. Similarly, photographs of the desks and chairs in the studio enabled the animators to turn their character loose within its confines.

Max also devised the *rotograph*, a variation on the earlier rotoscope. The projector showed one frame of film on a glass plate, the cels with the characters were laid over the glass and the combined image was rephotographed with an animation camera. Although great care had to be taken to ensure correct registration of the images, the rotograph gave the animators the ability to insert Ko-Ko into motion sequences. Clever cutting between live-action and animated scenes heightened the illusion.

In "Perpetual Motion" (1920), Max sends Ko-Ko around the office to hide in the perpetual-motion machine an inventor has built at a nearby desk. The clown spins the wheel of the device, convincing the inventor that his creation works. When Ko-Ko annoys a sculptor in "Modeling" (1921), the irritated

Out of the Inkwell: Fitz metamorphoses into a window to escape detection by Ko-Ko in "Ko-Ko the Cop" (1927).

artist throws a blob of real clay that pins the frantically struggling clown to the drawing board. At the end of "Ko-Ko the Cop" (1927), Ko-Ko and his dog, Fitz, try to run away. The camera pulls back to reveal they're on a long strip of paper Max is turning like a treadmill. He cuts the paper between the characters, to their astonishment. Ko-Ko even feels the rough edge.

The animation in these cartoons is loose and free. If an artist wanted to stretch a limb or distort a character to get a laugh or highlight a gag, he did. When Ko-Ko scolds Fitz for trying to pull the lever that will end the world in "Ko-Ko's Earth Control" (1928), his wagging index finger stretches until it's several feet long: rubber hose animation had grown rubberier. The characters were drawn on both cels and paper, using a modified slash system.

Not all of the Out of the Inkwell cartoons are wonderful, but a surprisingly large number retain their humor and freshness. Which brother's vision was reflected in the films is the subject of some debate. But by the early 1920s, Max seems to have devoted his time to business and administrative matters exclusively. Huemer, who came to the studio in 1923, remembered Dave circulating among the animators, making suggestions and devising gags.

The Fleischers' output was not limited to the Out of the Inkwell series. In 1923, Max produced "Einstein's Theory of Relativity," a long film (about an hour) that combined live action, still photographs, charts and some simple animation. The film received enthusiastic reviews, including a favorable notice from Einstein himself. Max followed with a similar work, "Darwin's Theory of Evolution," which drew objections from fundamentalists. (The film was released during the Scopes trial.) Ko-Ko appeared in a film sponsored by AT&T in 1927, "That Little Big Fellow's Voice," and in a similar work about film sound tracks for Western Electric in 1929, "Finding His Voice."

Far more popular with general audiences than these experiments were the Song Car-Tunes, a series that began in 1924 with "Oh, Mabel." It was common practice for theaters to show slides of song lyrics and encourage the audience to sing along with the orchestra or organ. The well-known songwriter Charles K. Harris ("After the Ball") came to the Fleischers and asked if they could devise a way to get an audience to sing with a cartoon.

Both brothers subsequently claimed to have invented the famous Bouncing Ball, which wasn't animated at all. The song lyrics, printed in white on black, were mounted on the drum of an old washing machine that was turned to reveal one line at a time to the camera. A man wearing a black sleeve and glove (often Lou Fleischer, the musician of the family) moved a black baton with a white ball or disc on the end from word to word at a carefully calculated pace. Animation was added for the choruses of some songs to provide variety.

The Car-Tunes were a big hit with audiences. Huemer, who saw "Oh, Mabel" at the Circle Theatre in New York, said: "It brought down the house, it stopped the show. They applauded and stamped and whistled into the following picture, which they finally stopped and took off, and put back the 'Oh, Mabel' cartoon again. They ran it again to the delight of the audience. I always say that was an indication of what sound would someday do for the animated cartoon."

The popularity of the Inkwell cartoons led other studios to produce similar films. Walter Lantz, a veteran of IFS who succeeded Max at the Bray studio, began a live-action/animation series in 1924. The title character was an animated little boy named Dinky Doodle who shared his adventures with his dog, Weakheart; Lantz appeared as their cartoonist and friend. Lantz also appeared in the Hot Dog cartoons, featuring Pete the Pup, that succeeded the Dinky Doodle series in 1926.

The live-action/animation combinations in these films were created by shooting the live-action footage and making a large print of each frame. These pictures were used as backgrounds for the animation, which was drawn on cels. A sequence in "The Lunch Hound" (1927), in which Lantz tries to grab the nimble Pete, stands out as an example of how effective the technique could be. These Lantz-Bray films retain a certain freshness and enthusiasm, but they lack the more original appeal of the Inkwell shorts.

Not all the animation done in America during the teens and twenties was drawn. C. Allan Gilbert made a short-lived series of Silhouette Fantasies for Bray. Howard Moss used puppet animation in a series he called Motoy Films, beginning in 1917. Tony Sarg, an illustrator who had also worked as a puppeteer, made several cut-paper silhouette films between 1919 and 1923; only one, "Adam Raises Cain," survives.

In 1976, three previously unknown American live-action comedies by Charles Bowers, the former partner of Raoul Barré, were discovered in the Toulouse Cinémathèque. Further research in France and at the Cinémathèque Québecoise in Canada led to the restoration of several more comedies, which reveal that Bowers was a master of stop-motion techniques.

In "Egged On" (1926), Bowers portrays an eccentric inventor who hides a basket of eggs in the engine compartment of a Model T Ford. When the eggs hatch, tiny Model T's emerge from the shells and scuttle around the barn. They seek shelter under the full-sized car, which settles over them like a brooding hen, protectively lowering its running boards.

The inventor character reappears in "A Wild Rumor" (1926) and creates a household robot with articulated hands. The hands fashion a doll that comes to life after a tiny heart is sewn into its chest. When the doll awakens, it discovers—to its great embarrassment—that it is naked. The hands gently dress the doll, which then curtsies to the audience. The entire sequence is handled with extraordinary delicacy.

Most amazing of all is "Now You Tell One" (1926), in which a house is overrun by particularly nasty mice: the little rodents shoot tiny guns at cats and people. When Bowers sprinkles growth elixir on a spray of pussy willow, one of the fuzzy buds swells and grows into a live cat. But Bowers forgets to keep an eye on the plant, which continues to sprout cats at a furious rate until the place is flooded with felines.

Unfortunately, these comedies are not very entertaining films. They lack the timing, pacing, acting and comedic vision of Chaplin or Keaton, Bowers's obvious models, and are interesting only for their animated sequences.

Walter Lantz at work on the Universal lot, c. 1928. The image of Oswald in the upper right corner shows how the character had been redesigned.

The most popular, best-animated and financially most successful cartoon character of the silent era was the Pat Sullivan studio's irrepressible Felix the Cat. Although it has been estimated that three-quarters of the world's population had seen or could recognize Felix at the height of his fame, the true story of his creation remained unknown to all but a few animators. It was not until the mid-1970s that animation historian John Canemaker followed up the veteran artists' stories and discovered Felix's real creator.

Born in Sydney, Australia, in 1887, Pat Sullivan had been a newspaper cartoonist, a music-hall performer, a sailor, a motion picture exhibitor and a lightweight boxer before he found a job at the New York *World* assisting William Marriner on his "Sammy Johnsin" comic strip. In 1914, Marriner died and Sullivan went to work for Raoul Barré. Having learned animation techniques from Barré, Sullivan opened his own studio in 1915 to produce War Bond pictures. The next year, he hired Otto Messmer to work on a series based on the "Sammy Johnsin" strip and on the films of Charlie Chaplin.

After studying art and fashion illustration, Otto Messmer had begun selling cartoons to *Life* and other periodicals around 1910. A performance of Winsor McCay's vaudeville act with "Gertie the Dinosaur" in 1914 aroused Messmer's interest in animation. He signed a contract with Universal and made a one-minute test film, "Motor Matt and His Fliv."

The Universal executives were so pleased with the results that they put Messmer in contact with the internationally famous cartoonist Hy Mayer. The two men collaborated on Travels of Teddy, an animated series featuring yet another caricature of Teddy Roosevelt. After the series ended in 1916, Messmer went to work for Sullivan.

No one knows how Sullivan persuaded Charlie Chaplin to let him do an animated version of the already famous comic. But Messmer studied Chaplin's silent shorts, frame by frame, learning the nuances of his pantomime gestures and expressions—knowledge that would prove valuable when he animated Felix.

World War I interrupted Messmer's animation career, but in 1919 he returned to the Sullivan studio, where he worked with Earl Hurd, Frank Moser and other artists on four-minute cartoons for Paramount's Screen Magazine. On a free-lance basis, Messmer created "Feline Follies," in which the as yet unnamed Felix made his debut.

It was successful enough for Paramount to request another of the same: "Musical Mews" (1919). After the success of this film, producer John King gave Felix his name, which played off the Latin words for cat (*felis*) and good luck (*felix*). Messmer made the character solid black because he wanted to avoid drawing a lot of outlines; he also found that solid masses moved better on the screen.

The original Felix was rather angular and doglike, with a blocky head, sharp-cornered limbs and rectangular feet. Bill Nolan helped Messmer redesign Felix in 1922, giving the cat his familiar rounded and appealing shape. What set the Felix cartoons apart from their more prosaic counterparts was their use of animation.

"I had him sparkling all the time," Messmer told Canemaker in 1976. "Most of the cartoons [by other studios] were like a dummy, just jumping—so I used an extreme amount of eye motion, wriggling the eyes and turning his whiskers, and this seemed to be what hit the public—expressions!"

Something subtler than facial expressions contributed to Felix's appeal: a unique style of movement that expressed his personality. Using principles explored by McCay and Chaplin, Messmer gave Felix a way of moving as recognizable as any silent comic's. The Felix shorts contain the most sophisticated character animation done before Disney's breakthrough film, "Three Little Pigs" (1933).

By 1925, Felix was the most popular cartoon character in the world, due to a combination of the excellence of his films and Sullivan's astute promotion. Sullivan took all the credit and spoke of the work he invested in Felix, of the burden of his fame, of how the character had been inspired by Kipling's "The Cat That Walked by Himself" and by his wife's predilection for bringing home stray cats. A successful line of toys, dolls and merchandise was instituted in 1926. That same year, a popular song took its title from one of the cartoons, "Felix Kept Walking."

Nor was Felix's appeal limited to the mass audience and the popular press. In his essay "Where Are the Movies Moving?" Aldous Huxley praised the Felix shorts as the outstanding illustration of his dictum: "What the cinema can do better than literature or the spoken drama is to be fantastic." He also suggested that Felix offered a lesson to the European Expressionist filmmakers in how to avoid the pretentiousness and humorlessness that marred their work. Paul Hindemith composed a score—now lost—for "Felix at the Circus" in 1926–27. In 1928, Marcel Brion of the Académie Française wrote:

He has escaped the reality of the cat; he is made up of an extraordinary personality. When he is walking like a man preoccupied, with his head buried in his shoulders, his paws behind his back, he becomes the impossible in cats, the unreal in man. . . . Nothing is more familiar to him than the extraordinary, and when he is not surrounded by the fantastic, he creates it . . . and it is this creative faculty which quite rightly holds us in Felix. It arises from two mental attitudes: astonishment and curiosity, the virtues of poets and scholars. . . . Felix constructs a universe, using only two properties, both originating in him, material signs of the state of his own soul: the exclamation point and the question mark. Nothing more is needed for building a world.

While Sullivan, who rarely even visited the studio after 1925, was posing as Felix's creator and earning an enormous income from the character (toys alone brought him an estimated $100,000 per year), Messmer labored for a modest salary with self-effacing dedication. He managed the studio, wrote and directed all the films and, beginning in 1923, drew Felix's adventures for a Sunday comic page (which earned Sullivan an additional $80,000 or so annually) —anonymously.

Messmer devised the scenarios for all the films, which he produced at the rate of one every two weeks for more than a decade. Al Eugster, who came to the studio as an inker in 1922, remembered with amazement that Messmer could animate a scene from one film while working out the story line for another.

The animation was done on paper, and the inkers traced over the animators' drawing on the same page. The backgrounds—which were kept relatively simple—were inked onto cels and laid over the drawings. The studio camera lacked the gears and sliding peg bars needed to film trucking and panning moves, so Messmer and his staff animated the characters in perspective, including the many times Felix ran toward the camera, the black of his open mouth providing a "wipe" to the next scene. Special effects, like the animated playing cards in "Felix Hits the Deck" (1927), were done by Messmer under the camera.

Given these working conditions, it is a tribute to Messmer's genius (a word he would have modestly eschewed) that the Felix films were so unflaggingly imaginative. The plucky cat retained a child's sense of wonderment that made his cartoon world seem perennially new and fresh. Inevitably, certain

An original drawing of Felix by Otto Messmer.

Otto Messmer

motifs recurred, like the famous "Felix walk" that so impressed Brion. But the Felix shorts lack the formula sameness of so many contemporary studio cartoons.

Felix calmly defied perspective, gravity and logic to manipulate the world around him. Anything could—and did—happen. Felix's tail was interchangeable with question marks and exclamation points, depending on what was needed. It might also serve as an ice-cream scoop. If he sang, the musical notes he produced could be turned into skates, a motor scooter or anything else.

In "Oceanantics" (1930), a hungry Felix tries to find a way into a grocery store. He reaches out with his tail to the small doorway of a distant house and pulls it over. The door stays small, despite its move in perspective. Felix places it against the wall of the store, walks through it and gets his lunch.

When the artist forgets to blacken him in "Comicalamities"

(1928), Felix gets some shoe polish and does it himself. In the same film, Felix redraws the face of the lady cat he's wooing to make her prettier. She asks for a pearl necklace, which Felix sets out to find. The quest appears to be a washout, and the film starts to iris out. Felix stretches the circle back open and announces: "This picture isn't over by a long shot!" When she rejects him after all his efforts, Felix grabs the paper she's drawn on and tears her up.

The graphic sophistication of many of these films remains impressive. Messmer alternates positive and negative frames in "Felix Trifles with Time" (1925), a technique that was heralded as bold and innovative when experimental filmmakers began employing it in the late 1960s and early 1970s. Nothing in contemporary animation approached the dramatic use of shadows and silhouetted images in the eerie "Sure-Locked Homes" (1927).

The Pat Sullivan studio in 1926. The image of Sullivan in the foreground appears to have been cut from another photograph. At the drawing tables, from left: Otto Messmer, Raoul Barré, Dana Parker, Harold Walker, Al Eugster, Jack Nogle, George Canata, Tom Byrne—and Felix.

If imitation is truly the sincerest form of flattery, Felix was one of the most flattered characters in the history of animation. In 1923, Paul Terry introduced his own black cat named Felix. The character was quickly renamed Henry, and his design altered, presumably at the urging of Sullivan or his lawyers. The most important animal character in Walt Disney's live-action/animation Alice in Cartoonland shorts (1924–27) was Julius the Cat. Disney's Oswald the Lucky Rabbit (1927) bore more than a passing resemblance to Felix, as did the early versions of Mickey Mouse. Bosko, created by Hugh Harman and Rudolf Ising in 1930, was also cut from the same cloth.

Felix was still near the zenith of his popularity when he met his unhappy end. On March 26, 1932, Sullivan's wife fell seven stories to her death when she leaned too far out a window. Sullivan, who had suffered from a drinking problem for years, lapsed into acute alcoholism and died of pneumonia in February 1933.

"He left everything in a mess, no books, no nothing," Messmer recalled. "So when he died the place had to close down, at the height of popularity, when everybody, RKO and all of them, for years they tried to get hold of Felix. . . . I didn't have that permission [to continue the character] 'cause I didn't have legal ownership of it."

It's uncertain how much longer the character would have survived, as Sullivan refused to adapt Felix to sound and color. Sullivan's brother made a few color-and-sound Felix shorts with the Van Buren studio (and without Messmer) in 1935. They were notably unsuccessful. Joe Oriolo made more than two hundred Felix cartoons for television in 1959—without Messmer or the imagination of the originals.

Messmer continued to draw the Felix strip and comic books until 1951. He then worked on various animation projects, including animated electric signs, and retired in 1972. Although his achievements were finally recognized during the last years of his life, Messmer shrugged off the acclaim. At tributes held at the Museum of Modern Art and the Whitney in 1976, he declined to make any speeches, saying that, like his character, he was silent. He died in 1982 at the age of ninety-one. Although Felix earned millions, Messmer never received a dime in royalties from the character he created.

To an observer in 1928, Walt Disney would have seemed an unlikely choice as the man who would revolutionize both the art and the industry of animation. His films were good, but by no means extraordinary; Ko-Ko and Felix were far more popular than Disney's Oswald Rabbit.

Walter Elias Disney was born on December 5, 1901, in Chicago. His father, Elias Disney, never achieved much success in the various businesses he tried, and the family moved throughout the Midwest during Walt's childhood. Many efforts—perhaps too many—have been made to tie the fond memories of the farm in Marceline, Missouri, the Disneys tended between 1905 and 1910 to the later use of barnyard settings and farm animals in Disney cartoons. (No one has bothered to subject Paul Terry's childhood and his Farmer Al Falfa films to similar analyses.)

By all accounts, Elias Disney was a hard man and a stern father. Some biographers have suggested that Walt sought refuge in drawing from the harsh conditions of his childhood; certainly he showed an early talent for art. He worked as a cartoonist and photographer for his high school magazine, while studying at the Art Institute of Chicago. Disney left high school in 1918 to serve as a driver in the American Ambulance Corps in France. He returned the next year, determined to pursue a career in art, despite his father's objections.

Disney's first job in his chosen field was an apprenticeship at the Pesmen-Rubin Commercial Art Studio in Kansas City, doing rough drawings and cartoons for print advertisements. There he met a talented young artist of Dutch descent, Ubbe Iwwerks. (He later shortened his unusual name to Ub Iwerks.) The two eighteen-year-olds became fast friends, and launched their own studio, Iwerks-Disney Commercial Artists, in late 1919. The company lasted about a month.

In January 1920, Disney got a job as a cartoonist at the Kansas City Slide Company, which soon became the Kansas City Film Ad Company. He persuaded his employers to hire Iwerks two months later. The Film Ad Company produced one-minute theatrical commercials that featured  simple animation of jointed cutout figures. Disney learned the techniques involved, but apparently wanted to emulate the more sophisticated drawn animation of studio cartoons like the Out of the Inkwell series.

According to Bob Thomas's biography, Disney and Iwerks essentially taught themselves animation by studying Carl Lutz's book on basic techniques and Muybridge's photographs of human and animal motions. In addition to their jobs at the studio, the two men began making animated films at night, using a borrowed camera. Disney persuaded Frank Newman, who ran a chain of theaters in Kansas City, to buy a series of one-minute topical cartoons, which he called the Newman Laugh-O-Grams.

In 1922, Disney set out to expand his animation work. With a crew that consisted primarily of student artists who worked in exchange for cartooning lessons, he made a longer film, "Little Red Riding Hood." Pleased by the results, Disney quit the Film Ad Company and managed to persuade local investors to put up $15,000 to organize Laugh-O-Gram Films. The staff included Iwerks, Hugh Harman and Rudolf Ising.

The studio produced six cartoons based on fairy tales,

124   Animated Cartoons

Then in the performances of the jugglers and in the pranks of the knock-about comedians, the animator finds much to spur him on to creative imagery. The pictorial artist for graphic or easel work, in any of these cases, intending to make an illustration, is content with some representative position that he can grasp visually, or, which is more likely to be the case, the one that is easiest for him to draw. But the animator must have sharp and quickly observing eyes and be able

WALKING MOVEMENTS, SOMEWHAT MECHANICAL.
Suitable for a droll theme.

On Movement in the Human Figure   125

PHASES OF MOVEMENT FOR A LIVELY WALK.
Lower diagram shows how the drawings, on separate sheets of paper, are placed with respect to each other to continue the figure across the scene.

to comprehend and remember the whole series of phases of a movement.

A fancy dancer, especially, is a rich study. To follow the dancer with his supple joints bending

Above: Pages from Lutz's book *Animated Cartoons* (1920), explaining walks and runs. Walt Disney and Ub Iwerks studied this early manual while teaching themselves animation. Below: A publicity photo for the Alice comedies shows Disney with the child actress Margie Gay; the cartoon animals were drawn by Hugh Harman. (Note how the two cats in the foreground bear a marked resemblance to Felix.)

beginning with "The Four Musicians of Bremen." The surviving Laugh-O-Grams contain some amusing moments, but they seem crude compared to the work being done at the Fleischer and Sullivan studios. No major distributor was interested in them. Disney bankrupted the company producing his first live-action/animation combination, "Alice's Wonderland," in 1923. He soon left Kansas City to join his brother Roy, who was convalescing from tuberculosis in Los Angeles.

There Disney managed to interest distributor Margaret Winkler in a series based on his "Alice" film. In the fall of 1923, he signed a contract to make six films at $1,500 apiece, followed by six more at $1,800. Roy helped him raise the money needed to make the first one ("Alice's Day at Sea"), and the Disney Bros. Studio was set up in a one-room office.

Films that featured animated characters in live-action settings had become standard fare by this time. Disney reversed the situation and put a live-action little girl in a cartoon setting. He animated the first six films himself, assisted by Rollin "Ham" Hamilton. In May 1924, Disney persuaded Iwerks to come to California; soon he was doing most of the animation. Harman and Ising followed at the end of the year. Although the Alice shorts are uneven, Iwerks's animation holds up surprisingly well in some sequences such as the mouse's dance in "Alice Rattled by Rats" (1925).

Disney was already trying to improve the quality of his films, which meant he needed higher budgets. But Margaret Winkler's distribution business had been taken over by her more aggressive husband, Charles L. Mintz, who balked at increasing the price. The Alice shorts did well, earning favorable reviews, and Disney was able to move to a new studio on Hyperion Avenue.

By late 1926, the Alice series had run its course. The format of a live actress in a cartoon world seemed more of a gimmick and offered fewer opportunities than the reverse situation favored by the Fleischers. The appearance of Alice sometimes served as little more than a framing device for what was essentially an animated film. Goaded by Mintz (and, probably, Carl Laemmle of Universal, who bought the films), Disney and his staff set to work developing a new animated character, Oswald the Lucky Rabbit.

Although Thomas cites documents from the negotiations over Oswald in which Disney offered to redo "my" sketches, the character was almost certainly designed by Iwerks. By 1926, Disney had given up drawing for production and organizational duties. This switch in focus later gave rise to the rumor that Disney couldn't draw—a rumor fueled by the fact that he never learned to draw Mickey Mouse well. Disney was a capable artist, but he was not in the same league as Iwerks, who ranks as one of the outstanding animators of the silent era.

Iwerks's animation was rubbery, loose-limbed and weightless, punctuated with exaggerated gestures and expressions. He infused his characters with a rambunctious vitality that remains evident today. Equally important in a studio setting, Iwerks was extraordinarily fast. While working on "Plane Crazy" in 1928, he did seven hundred drawings in a single day. He had heard Bill Nolan had once done five or six hundred for a Felix short and decided to break that record.

A rather dumpy version of Oswald made an unimpressive debut in June 1927 in "Poor Papa." Disney and Iwerks refined and redesigned the character, and soon the Oswald films were garnering good reviews. Disney's real talents as an organizer and story man began to emerge during the making of the Oswald series.

Perhaps no one in the history of film has had as thorough an understanding of story structure and pacing as Walt Disney. While he did not use scripts or storyboards yet, he kept a watchful eye on each film and the results were readily apparent. Careful structuring, combined with Iwerks's visual touches—such as having Oswald shatter into a dozen tiny images of himself in "Bright Lights" (1928)—strengthened the appeal of the Disney cartoons. In 1928, *Moving Picture World* praised their "astounding feat of jumping into first-run favor overnight."

But Disney was not satisfied. He disliked the way so many cartoons were being ground out quickly and cheaply, and saw "rigor mortis" setting into the medium. But he remained confident: ". . . with more money and time, I felt that we could make better pictures and shake ourselves out of the rut."

With these thoughts in mind, Disney went to New York in February to ask Mintz to raise the price per film from $2,250 to $2,500. The distributor insisted that he take a cut—to $1,800—or lose the character and his studio. Mintz had covertly signed up the entire staff of animators. Everyone except Iwerks had agreed to leave Disney and go to work for his erstwhile distributor.

This underhanded deal changed the course of animation and American popular culture. Mintz produced Oswald cartoons for a year, then Universal gave Oswald to Walter Lantz. Disney went on to create Mickey Mouse, the most successful of all animated characters.

According to the often-quoted story, Disney devised Mickey on the train ride back from New York. (In some versions, the whistle is supposed to have sounded like "a m-m-mowaouse" to him.) The character's jaunty personality and his original name, Mortimer, were taken from a mouse Disney had adopted as a pet while working on the Laugh-O-Grams in Kansas City. His wife rejected the name Mortimer as too pretentious and/or sissy; she (or Disney himself in some accounts) suggested Mickey instead. Diane Disney Miller wrote that her father insisted this account was true, and it may be, although no one knew the value of a good story better than Disney.

While Disney supplied the character's personality and, for many years, his voice, Iwerks designed his physical appearance. Although Mickey was the first mouse to be the central character in a series, Sullivan, Terry and IFS had all used similar mice in various films. The rats in "Alice Rattled by Rats" are clearly Mickey's graphic ancestors. Herriman's Ignatz seems to have been the prototype.

Walt Disney poses with his Moon, c. 1928. He later sold the car to help pay for the sound track for "Steamboat Willie."

Ub Iwerks at the drawing board, c. 1929. One of the greatest animators of the silent era, Iwerks designed the physical appearance of Oswald Rabbit and Mickey Mouse.

For Mickey's first film, Disney came up with a story that played off the popularity of Charles Lindbergh. (He said the first scenario came to mind at the same time he created the character.) Iwerks started drawing and animated all of "Plane Crazy" by himself in two weeks. "Gallopin' Gaucho" followed soon after. But distributors weren't interested in the first two Mickey cartoons. They were very similar to the Oswald shorts and Disney was asking for $3,000 per film.

What saved Mickey and Disney was sound. Warner Brothers' "The Jazz Singer" had premiered in October 1927; after some initial resistance, all the studios were rushing to switch over to sound film. Disney saw the possibilities the new technology offered. Working with the young animator Wilfred Jackson, he and Iwerks created "Steamboat Willie," which was to be synchronized to two songs, "Steamboat Bill" and "Turkey in the Straw." Using their wives as a test audience, the animators showed "Willie" while performing the music on harmonica, washboard and slide whistle. The reactions confirmed their belief in the film's potential.

On the way to New York to find a distributor, Disney stopped in Kansas City to see an old friend and supporter, theater organist Carl Stalling. Working from the marks Iwerks had put on the film to act as a metronome, Stalling composed the sound track for the cartoon. In New York, Disney had the music recorded for the film, using Pat Powers's Cinephone system.

The initial reaction to the cartoon among distributors was cool, but Disney managed to book it into the Colony Theatre in New York for two weeks. "Steamboat Willie" premiered on November 18, 1928, and the rest is animation history. The cartoon was a smash hit. Audiences were delighted with the bold little mouse who did a jaunty clog step and played "Turkey in the Straw" on a cow's teeth.

Offers for distribution poured in, which Disney turned down. He insisted on retaining his independent status with control over his characters. He was determined not to repeat the error he had made with Oswald. Stalling went to Los Angeles to compose scores for "Plane Crazy," "Gallopin' Gaucho" and the newly completed "The Barn Dance." Disney signed a distribution deal with Powers.

"Steamboat Willie" is often described as the first sound cartoon, which isn't true. The Fleischers had been releasing their Song Car-Tunes since 1924, and some European avant-garde animators had been experimenting with sound. Paul Terry's Fable "Dinner Time" had premiered with a sound track several weeks earlier. (Disney previewed "Dinner Time" and pronounced it "terrible.") But these previous efforts do not diminish the magnitude of Disney's achievement. In his

The rat dancing the Charleston in "Alice Rattled by Rats" (1925) was obviously one of Mickey Mouse's graphic forebears.

unflagging search for excellence in his cartoons, he pioneered the use of sound technology without any backers. And he used the potential that sound offered more effectively than any of his predecessors.

It is difficult to look at "Steamboat Willie" today and imagine how boldly innovative it must have appeared in 1928. The modern viewer can't help being aware of its significance as Mickey's debut film, the film that launched the Disney empire. Yet "Willie" remains an enchanting and well-executed film that continues to delight audiences. After seeing it, silent shorts must have seemed flat and passé. When Mickey Mouse whistled "Steamboat Bill" in the opening scene, he unwittingly sounded the death knell of the silent era in American animation.

Mickey Mouse performs "Turkey in the Straw" in "Steamboat Willie" (1928), the film that ushered in the sound era in animation. The impact lines near the barrel/bass drum are a convention retained from print cartoons.

THE DISNEY ERA, 1928–1941

Sometimes I think Walt's greatest achievement was getting us all to work together without killing each other. —MARC DAVIS

The years 1928–41 are often referred to as the "Golden Age of Animation"; during this time, the medium underwent a growth and transformation unparalleled in the history of the visual arts. Only twelve years separate the premieres of "Steamboat Willie" (November 18, 1928) and "Fantasia" (November 13, 1940), but the aesthetic gap between these films is staggering. It was as if painting had gone from the flat, conventionalized style of Byzantine icons to the rich three-dimensionality of a Rembrandt portrait in a few decades.

This transformation was largely achieved through the dedication, talent and vision of Walt Disney and the artists he employed. Virtually every tool and technique in the animator's repertoire was discovered, invented or perfected at the Disney studio during this era.

The studio was never a monolithic entity; personal styles and counteropinions flourished beneath the surface. But it was Disney's vision that prevailed. The breadth of that vision —and his willingness to sacrifice immediate profits to the long-range benefits of increased excellence—made him the dominant figure in animation during the 1930s, not only in America but throughout the world. Animated films are still judged by the standards the Disney artists set half a century ago.

His distribution contract with Pat Powers enabled Disney to begin the Mickey Mouse series in 1928–29, with an animation staff that included Ub Iwerks, Wilfred Jackson, Les Clark and Johnny Cannon. "Gallopin' Gaucho" and "Plane Crazy" were released with sound tracks, followed by "The Barn Dance," "The Opry House" and "When the Cat's Away," all to very favorable audience response. Mickey was already beginning to rival Felix the Cat in popularity.

Instead of remaining content with Mickey's success, Disney struck out in an entirely new direction with a series of music-oriented fantasies he called Silly Symphonies. Organist/composer Carl Stalling initiated the idea when he suggested setting a graveyard romp to Edward Grieg's "March of the Dwarfs." Disney agreed, and the result was "The Skeleton Dance."

"The Skeleton Dance" represented a radical departure from the standard cartoon format. The film has no real characters or gags or story line: it is essentially a mood piece, and an eerie one at that. Four skeletons emerge from the grave to dance a jaunty rigadoon and play each other's ribs like xylophones. When a cock crows at dawn, they return to their tomb in an untidy rush that scrambles all their bones.

Opposite: Snow White sings to the animals in Disney's "Snow White and the Seven Dwarfs" (1937), one of the most beloved and influential films in the history of American animation.

"The Skeleton Dance"—an eerie mood piece that represented a break with the traditional structure and tone of American cartoons.

Iwerks animated almost the entire film. Disney, who felt his chief animator's time was too valuable to squander making every single drawing, objected to his working without assistants, but Iwerks refused. This seems to have been the first evidence of friction between the two men.

Powers rejected "The Skeleton Dance," and told Disney succinctly: "More mice!" Disney persuaded Fred Miller to show the film at his prestigious Carthay Circle Theater in Los Angeles, where it pleased both audiences and critics. A successful engagement at the Roxy in New York followed, and the Silly Symphonies took off.

By the end of 1929, it was obvious that the arrangement with Powers was not working out. Instead of paying the Disneys their share of the films' earnings, Powers just sent a check for a few thousand dollars whenever funds at the studio ran short. According to Bob Thomas, by January 1930 Disney had delivered the first twelve Mickeys and the first six Silly Symphonies, at a cost of $116,500, or $6,500 per film; they had grossed more than $300,000, or almost $17,000 apiece.

No one had expected Mickey Mouse to become so popular. Powers had apparently intended to use Disney's films to publicize his Cinephone sound system for one year. Now he desperately wanted to hang on to this lucrative property. He offered to take over the studio and pay Disney the enormous salary of $2,500 per week to run it. Undoubtedly remembering Oswald and Universal, Disney refused. When he asked to examine the books, Powers refused to show them to him until he agreed to a deal.

Powers then announced that he had signed Ub Iwerks to create a new cartoon series (for a considerably more modest

$300 per week). Disney was stunned by what he regarded as a betrayal by an old friend. Not only had he and Ub worked together for a decade, but Iwerks also owned a 20 percent share in the studio (which he sold back to Disney for $2,920—an infinitesimal fraction of its ultimate worth). Iwerks cited "artistic differences" as his reason for leaving.

Powers probably assumed that signing Iwerks would force Disney to come to terms. Instead, Walt broke with Powers and signed a two-year deal with Columbia Pictures that included a $7,000 advance for each cartoon.

The fifty Mickey cartoons and Silly Symphonies Disney produced under the arrangement with Columbia (1929–32) are generally ignored in animation histories and retrospectives. They were not bad films for their time. "The Ugly Duckling" (1931) represented one of the first attempts to generate real sympathy for a cartoon character. But the Disney shorts that would soon follow are so entertaining and beautifully animated that they have eclipsed their predecessors.

Despite the larger advances from Columbia, the Disney studio was slipping into debt as Walt hired more artists and strove to make his films better. By 1931, the cartoons had noticeably tighter story lines and better animation. But the harder Disney worked to improve his pictures, the more expensive they became. The strain finally proved too great, and in late 1931 Disney had a nervous breakdown. Rest, travel and exercise (he took up horseback riding and, later, polo) proved therapeutic, and Walt was soon back at the helm.

When it came time to renew the contract with Columbia in 1932, Disney asked for a raise in the advance from $7,000 to $15,000 per film, as his cost per cartoon was now averaging $13,500. Harry Cohn balked at the price and Disney signed with United Artists. The terms of the contract were generous, and the studio, founded by Mary Pickford, Douglas Fairbanks, Charlie Chaplin and D. W. Griffith, was regarded as the most prestigious in Hollywood.

Disney made twenty shorts per year for United Artists, and his production costs kept rising: by 1935 costs were up to an average of $28,000 a film. "Three Little Pigs" (1933) cost $16,000; "Who Killed Cock Robin?" (1935), $27,000; the more ambitious "The Goddess of Spring" (1934), $37,000. During the middle 1930s, prints, advertising, shipping, etc., nearly doubled those costs, bringing the total budget of each seven-minute short to about $50,000. ("King Kong," which was released in 1933, cost only $600,000.) Richard Schickel estimates that Disney earned $48,000 from each cartoon during its first year of distribution, $22,000 the second: many cartoons didn't earn a profit until the year after they were released.

What saved the studio was the phenomenal popularity of Mickey Mouse. Mickey had supplanted Felix the Cat as the most popular cartoon character in the world. By 1931, more than a million children were members of the Mickey Mouse

Club. Franklin Roosevelt, Benito Mussolini, Mary Pickford, George V of England, Queen Mary and the Nizam of Hydera-bad were among his more prominent adult fans. Theater marquees announced "A Mickey Mouse Cartoon" along with the feature titles, and "What, no Mickey Mouse?" became synonymous with disappointment.

Articles about Mickey and Walt appeared regularly in publi-cations ranging from *Harper's* and *Scribner's* to *Scientific American.* By 1933, Disney could spoof his character's celeb-rity in "Mickey's Gala Premiere" in which caricatures of Char-lie Chaplin, Eddie Cantor, the Marx Brothers, Lionel Bàrrymore and Greta Garbo congratulate Mickey at the open-ing of his latest cartoon.

This popularity led to a spate of Mickey Mouse products that outdid Sullivan's merchandising of Felix. The marketing cam-paign started very modestly. In 1929, Disney was offered $300 for permission to put Mickey Mouse on writing tablets. As he needed the money, he accepted. But this was only the beginning.

In January 1930—only fourteen months after the pre-miere of "Steamboat Willie"—the Mickey Mouse comic strip appeared, distributed by Hearst's King Features. Iwerks and his assistant, Win Smith, did the strip for the first few months; then Floyd Gottfredson took over and drew it for the next forty-five years. In February, Roy and Walt authorized the George Borgfeldt Company to license Mickey and Minnie Mouse products. The Dis-ney characters were reproduced on hand-kerchiefs, drums, "cricket" noisemakers, rubber balls and other toys.

Borgfeldt was replaced by the more energetic Herman "Kay" Kaymen in 1932, and the flood of Disney products began in earnest. Mickey's likeness soon appeared on everything from soap to ice-cream cones to Cartier diamond bracelets ($1,250). The sale of 253,000 Mickey Mouse handcars—a tin toy that sold for $1.00—saved the Lionel Com-pany from bankruptcy in 1934. The Inger-soll Wa-

terbury Company sold 2.5 million Mickey Mouse watches in two years. According to *Fortune* magazine, Disney's annual profits on films and merchandise topped $600,000 by 1934.

Early Disney products are highly prized by collectors today, and Mickey remains the most popular license character in the world. He currently appears on more than 7,500 items, not counting publications.

"Sometimes I've tried to figure out why Mickey appealed to the whole world," Disney later wrote. "Everybody's tried to figure it out. So far as I know, nobody has. He's a pretty nice fellow who never does anybody any harm, who gets into scrapes through no fault of his own, but always manages to come up grinning. Why, Mickey's even been faithful to one girl, Minnie, all his life. Mickey is so simple and uncompli-cated, so easy to understand that you can't help liking him."

Mickey's fame also had its negative side: as he became more popular, he grew more limited as a character. The early Mickey could be quite rowdy. In "Plane Crazy," he tried repeatedly to kiss Minnie until she got fed up and jumped out of the plane. In "Steamboat Willie," he played a chorus of "Turkey in the Straw" by yanking the tails of a nursing sow's piglets to make them squeal. Once he became famous, this sort of behavior was forbidden. Whenever Mickey did anything that could be construed as unkind or naughty, the studio would be deluged with letters from concerned and/or indignant parents.

Mickey's original personality was rather amorphous: Walt described him as "simply a little personality assigned to the pur-pose of laughter." (Except for the ever-resourceful Felix, few—if any—silent cartoon characters had identifiable

Walt Disney surrounded by Mickey Mouse dolls, c.1930. Future Warners director Bob Clam-pett designed the original Mickey doll for his aunt, Charlotte Clark.

personalities; they simply reacted to whatever situation the animators devised for them.) As many observers noted, there was a good bit of Chaplin's Little Tramp in Mickey; he was usually the irrepressible underdog (undermouse?) who came from behind to win. He also had many of Disney's characteristics, and much has been written about him acting as a sort of alter ego for Walt.

During the 1930s, Mickey was gradually relegated to the role of Mr. Niceguy, often playing straight man to three increasingly popular new characters: Pluto, Goofy and Donald Duck. Pluto first appeared as an anonymous bloodhound in "The Chain Gang" (1930). Disney was pleased with animator Norm Ferguson's handling of the dog's expressions, especially the way he sniffed, and they continued to develop the character. Ferguson's use of expressions, anticipation, action and body language in the classic "flypaper sequence" in "Playful Pluto" three years later demonstrates just how flexible the character had become.

"That sequence was regarded as a milestone at the time," comments veteran Disney animator Ward Kimball. "Pluto actually seemed to be thinking. That was one of the first scenes in which the characters weren't just bouncing around to music or acting out a gag. The humor was built out of the situation of Pluto trying to extricate himself from his predicament, rather than a simple gag tableau."

Although the good and bad sides of Pluto's nature were occasionally personified—as in "Lend a Paw" (1941)—words were rarely used to convey his thoughts and feelings. Unlike many Disney characters, Pluto always remained a dog, rather than a human in animal guise.

Originally known as Dippy Dawg, Goofy made his debut as a hayseed in the crowd in "Mickey's Revue" (1932). His blithe stupidity made him an effective foil for the straightforward Mickey and the hot-tempered Donald in such excellent shorts as "Clock Cleaners" (1937), "Moving Day" (1936) and "Lonesome Ghosts" (1937). In his "Analysis of the Goof" (as the animators invariably called the character), Art Babbitt explained:

> Think of the Goof as a composite of an everlasting optimist, a gullible Good Samaritan, a half-wit, a shiftless, good-natured hick. . . . Yet the Goof is not the type of half-wit that is to be pitied. He doesn't dribble, drool or shriek. He has music in his heart even though it may be the same tune forever and I see him humming to himself while working or thinking. He talks to himself because it is easier for him to know what he is thinking if he hears it first.

Although there was a reference to Donald Duck as one of Mickey's friends in the 1931 book *The Adventures of Mickey Mouse*, the character didn't appear on the screen until "The Wise Little Hen," three years later. In that Silly Symphony, a rather dumpy bird with a long beak and a sailor suit used an imaginary bellyache as an excuse not to help the Hen plant or harvest her corn.

"The Duck began as a very crude character," comments Jack Hannah, who directed nearly a third of the 170 Donald cartoons. "Clarence Nash came along at just the right time with just the right voice, and that helped establish the character."

Nash was a boy when he created the barely comprehensible accent he provided Donald. It was an imitation of the baby goat he kept as a pet. He later used the voice for a little girl trying to recite "Mary Had a Little Lamb." Disney heard him—either on the radio or in person (the accounts vary)—and exclaimed, "That's our duck!"

Donald's personality really began to emerge in his second film, "The Orphan's Benefit" (1934, remade in color in 1941). When the crowd of nasty little mice jeered his attempts to recite "Mary Had a Little Lamb" and "Little Boy Blue," the Duck threw the first of his famous temper tantrums.

The best of the early Donald films was "The Band Concert" (1935), the first color Mickey Mouse short and one of the true classics of the Hollywood cartoon. Resplendent in an outsized scarlet uniform whose sleeves constantly flop over his hands, Mickey attempts to lead the local band in the *William Tell* Overture. Donald, a raucous peanut vendor, distracts the musicians by playing "Turkey in the Straw" on a fife. Anima-

Animator Ward Kimball at the Hyperion studio, c. 1935. He recalls that the desks were painted white and the shelves edged with red Spanish tile.

An original cel and background of Mickey and his musicians taking a bow at the opening of "The Band Concert" (1935), the first color Mickey Mouse short.

tion, color, music and direction are skillfully combined to present the conflict between Mickey, who is so intent on his conducting that he fails to notice when a tornado sweeps the entire band into the clouds, and Donald, who fusses at the conductor, an annoying bee and the storm itself.

"Even in 'The Band Concert,' the Duck was still pretty crude-looking," continues Hannah, "but his personality was beginning to develop. We started using rounder shapes when we drew him because they were cuter and more appealing. They also animated better and allowed us to get more vivid expressions."

All the Disney characters were being similarly redesigned, for a variety of reasons. Rounded shapes did animate better. As Bill Nolan had discovered in 1917, curved shapes seem to flow into each other more smoothly on the screen. Also, using circles and ovals as the basis of a character's design makes it easier to ensure uniform drawings. If the animators know that a character's head is basically a circle with the bottom of the eyes touching its equator, they can keep the proportions of the head correct more easily than if they have to try to approximate the shape freehand. (Some animators used to trace around a quarter for Mickey's head and a nickel for his ears.)

Left: The first Technicolor cartoon, "Flowers and Trees" won the first Academy Award given to an animated film. Below: The more pleasing appearance of Mickey Mouse in "Mickey's Garden" (1935) reveals the increasing sophistication of Disney animation during the mid-1930s.

Another factor is the process some psychologists refer to as "shaping": the more often an artist draws a particular shape, the more rounded it becomes as the muscles of the forearm move through an increasingly familiar pattern.

Finally, humans react favorably to creatures with soft, rounded forms. The Disney artists discovered that characters with the proportions of a human baby would be perceived as cute: a large head with big, low-set eyes and a small nose and mouth; a little, rounded body; chubby limbs with tiny hands and feet. (The concept has been carried to absurd extremes in contemporary characters like Strawberry Shortcake.) The rounder, jovial Mickey in "Brave Little Tailor" (1938), whose proportions Fred Moore had redesigned along these principles, has an immediate appeal and charm that the more angular Mickey of "Steamboat Willie" lacked.

Moore and his fellow animators were able to develop and expand the characters because Disney plowed almost every cent he earned back into the studio. The money from the films and the attendant merchandise of the popular characters enabled Walt to embark on a program of training and experimentation that would take the medium of animation in entirely new directions. One of his first innovations was the introduction of color.

By 1932, Technicolor had a version of the three-strip color process that could be used for animation. Disney signed an agreement that guaranteed him exclusive use of the technique for two years. He decided to make "Flowers and Trees," a short that was already in production, the first color release. Roy was horrified. Half the film had already been shot, and he knew that color would add considerably to expenses without bringing any increase in advances. Walt went ahead, insisting that the added appeal of color would produce longer play dates for the films, which would result in higher revenues—eventually.

Considerably more was involved than just reshooting the film on the new color film stock. For the black-and-white shorts, the cels were painted with black, white and gray inks. These cels were then washed and reused two or three times, until they became scratched. Colored paints that would adhere to the slick surface of the cels had to be formulated. These paints stained the cels so they could no longer be reused, which added to expenses. Backgrounds had to be repainted in color, and some changes had to be made in the character designs and animation to make use of the possibilities color offered.

"Flowers and Trees," a pastoral fantasy about a young tree defeating a malign old stump to win the love of a graceful willow, caused the sensation Disney must have hoped for. It won the first Academy Award for an animated short film. All future Silly Symphonies were made in color, although the Mickey Mouse films remained in black and white until 1935.

A photograph of Bill Tytla taken by his friend Art Babbitt during the late 1930s captures the artist's brooding intensity.

Cartoons from other studios, shot in various two-strip processes, looked garish when compared with the more subtle and realistic palette Technicolor provided. The Silly Symphonies, which had taken a back seat to the Mickey Mouse cartoons, became the testing ground for the Disney experiments in animation.

Throughout the early 1930s, Disney had continued to hire the best artists and animators he could find. There were still relatively few trained animators, and whenever Disney saw a piece of animation that impressed him, he would try to hire the artist. He lured prominent New York animators like Grim Natwick, Bill Tytla and Shamus Culhane to Hollywood with offers of generous salaries. Only Otto Messmer remained impervious to Disney's overtures; he refused to leave the East Coast.

But Disney's films were often his most effective recruiting device. Art Babbitt abandoned a successful career in commercial art to become an animator after seeing "The Skeleton Dance." "Who Killed Cock Robin?" convinced Marc Davis he might have something to offer the studio and the medium.

Jobs were scarce during the Depression, and jobs for artists were especially scarce. Many of the men who answered the ads that read "Walt Disney is looking for artists" did so out of economic necessity, rather than an interest in animation. A beginning animator at Disney received a starting salary of

about $17 a week, which was a living wage at the time. An artist with substantial training and/or demonstrated ability earned a little more.

The top animators, such as Moore and Ferguson, earned what were considered staggering salaries. Babbitt remembers averaging about $300 a week by the later 1930s—enough to pay for a large house, two servants and three cars. Most studios required animators to produce about 30 feet (or 20 seconds of screen time) per week. At Disney, the footage requirements were much lower, and Walt paid bonuses for exceptional animation. Natwick recalls getting a $600 bonus for his work on "Alpine Climbers" (1936); Babbitt received $1,500 for his animation of the title character in "The Country Cousin" (1936).

By 1934, Disney had assembled the extraordinary team of key animators who would both draw many of the classic films and train the next wave of artists: Fred Moore, Hamilton Luske, Norm Ferguson, Art Babbitt and Bill Tytla.

In 1930, nineteen-year-old Fred Moore came to Disney with a portfolio of sketches hastily done on old shirt cardboards; he was immediately hired. Although he had little artistic training, Moore quickly became one of the most influential artists at the studio. He was at his best working with any cute or childlike character, such as the Three Little Pigs or Mickey. Kimball recalled that Moore was the first to stop using a hard circle for Mickey's head, giving him flexible cheeks that moved when he chewed or talked.

"He broke away from the rubber hose and round circle school of drawing and put more squash and stretch in his drawings than others did," wrote animator Ollie Johnston.

"But his biggest contribution was the tremendous appeal and charm that he gave his characters. Under his influence the style of Disney drawing changed markedly for the better."

"I credit Fred as the one that really created the Disney style," agrees Marc Davis, another key Disney animator. "The drawing people think of when they think of Disney was inspired by Fred Moore."

Although Hamilton "Ham" Luske also had virtually no art training when he came to the studio in 1931, he made important contributions to many films, including his animation of the jet-propelled braggart, Max Hare, in the Oscar-winning short "The Tortoise and the Hare" (1934). Leo Salkin, who was working on Oswald Rabbit shorts for Walter Lantz at the time, recalled: "The whole studio was talking about how they got that speed effect. It doesn't look all that fast now, but at the time that exciting visualization of speed was one of the most revolutionary bits of animation anyone had ever encountered."

Davis praises Luske's handling of Jenny Wren—the slinky Mae West caricature in "Who Killed Cock Robin?"—as "a masterpiece of animation." But most animators speak of Luske's exceptional ability to observe and analyze. Nothing escaped his notice, from the way a friend's tie blew in the wind to his partner's golf swing. At the end of 1935, he prepared a step-by-step "General Outline of Animation Theory and Practice" for Disney that remains a masterpiece of brevity and thoroughness.

Kimball offered this evaluation of the work of Norman "Fergy" Ferguson: "When I came to the studio in 1934, Norm was regarded as the best animator in the place. He wasn't

Opposite left: A drawing by Ward Kimball of some of his fellow young artists at the Disney studio, c. 1937, including Marc Davis (far left) and Leo Salkin (second from right). Opposite right: Animator/designer Mel Shaw's sketch of Don Graham lecturing to a class, c. 1937. Left: Some of the freewheeling spirit of the Hyperion studio can be seen in this caricature by Walt Kelly (the future creator of "Pogo"). Left to right, Kelly, Ward Kimball, Larry Clemmons and Fred Moore, c. 1939.

necessarily a great artist, but he had a wonderful sense of timing and acting. His drawings were just a few quick lines, like some of Picasso's sketches, but they described the actions: everything was there. The polish and draftsmanship were added by his cleanup men. If they did their job correctly, the result was a wonderful sequence."

"Walt was just crazy about Fergy's animation and with darn good reason," added Dick Huemer. "Fergy's characters lived and breathed and seemed to have actual thought processes."

Ferguson came to Disney from New York in 1929. In addition to his work with Pluto, Ferguson animated the Wolf in "Three Little Pigs." Although he made significant contributions to many shorts and the first features, his limits as a draftsman caused him to move into the area of story.

Art Babbitt spent three years animating characters like Farmer Al Falfa for Paul Terry before coming to Disney in 1932. His caricatures of Hollywood stars featured prominently in films like "Mickey's Gala Premiere." He worked on "Three Little Pigs" and animated the drunken Abiner in the Oscar-winning Silly Symphony "The Country Cousin." In *The Art of Walt Disney* (1942), Robert Field described that film as "a tour de force. For mastery of animation, apart from technical ingenuity, a point was reached that has never been surpassed."

"Art really developed the Goof out of the Dippy Dawg era with his work in shorts like 'Moving Day,'" said Kimball. "When the Goof walked, Art had him throw out his foot and rotate it 360 degrees at the ankle—which you can only see when you look at it slowed down. He explained to me that you can do a lot of things that defy the laws of gravity and anatomy

to give an extra kick to your animation if you don't let them show."

Babbitt feels he made his greatest contribution by persuading Bill Tytla to come there in 1934: "I think that was the greatest contribution *anyone* ever made to the Disney studio." Vladimir William "Bill" Tytla began his animation career in 1921 in New York, working first for John, then Paul Terry. Later, in Paris, he studied sculpture under Charles Despiau, as well as painting. By the time he came to Disney, he had a reputation as one of the finest animators on the East Coast.

He animated on a number of shorts, working with the jaunty Cookie Boy in "The Cookie Carnival" (1935) and the rooster in "Cock of the Walk" (1935). Although he handled the ponderous Willie the Giant in "Brave Little Tailor" (1938) with exceptional skill, Tytla's best work was done for "Snow White," "Pinocchio," "Fantasia" and "Dumbo."

Meanwhile, eight of the artists who would become the "Nine Old Men," the key group who would create most of the later Disney features, began their careers at the studio, working as in-betweeners: Frank Thomas, Ollie Johnston, Marc Davis, Ward Kimball, Wolfgang "Woolie" Reitherman, Eric Larson, Milt Kahl and John Lounsbery. (The ninth member of the group, Les Clark, had been hired in 1927.) In the same talent pool were artists who would do important work at various studios: Bill Melendez, Stephen Bosustow, Michael Lah, David Hilberman, Emery Hawkins, Leo Salkin, Cal Howard, Clyde Geronimi, Bill Peet and Ken Anderson.

Everyone who worked at Disney agrees that it was a fascinating and unique place. The studio on Hyperion Avenue grew into a crowded rabbit warren of small rooms and additional bungalows as the number of artists increased. Organization seems to have been informal and minimal; cross-pollination flourished.

"There was an atmosphere of discovery, of learning," said Babbitt. "Guys would stay after work to sneak a look at somebody else's stuff, to try to learn from it. Nobody was stingy with his information, they were always happy to tell you how to do something. I really learned how to animate dialogue from Freddy Moore and Ham Luske."

"Something new was happening there every day, something that hadn't been done before," Davis agreed. "It hadn't gotten down to the stage of 'this is the way you do that.' Somebody would do something, and it would have a bit of magic about it. It was primarily a place of wonder."

It soon became obvious that a higher standard of draftsmanship would be required to do better animation. Some of the artists had extensive art training, but many of the new recruits were, in one animator's words, "half-assed newspaper cartoonists." Early in the fall of 1932, Art Babbitt began holding informal life-drawing sessions at his home in the Hollywood Hills. When Walt heard that many of his artists were attending these sessions, he moved them to the studio and paid for the models and supplies.

Babbitt ran the sessions "as a monitor" for a month or so, then writer/animator Hardie Gramatky suggested he contact Don Graham, an instructor at the Chouinard Art Institute. Within two years, Graham was teaching at the studio four days and five nights each week, assisted by Phil Dike. He helped to bring other talented artist-instructors to Disney, including Eugene Fleury, Palmer Schoppe, Jean Charlot and Rico Lebrun. Instruction was expanded to include action analysis, animal anatomy and the principles of acting.

The popularity of the films and the press coverage Disney received made people eager to visit the studio. Alexander Woollcott, H. G. Wells, Frank Lloyd Wright and Charlie Chaplin were among the distinguished guests who came to lecture —or just look around. The ambitious training program, coupled with the influx of ideas, yielded results. The drawing in the Disney films steadily grew in refinement, accuracy and flexibility throughout the 1930s.

But for all the work and study being done there, the Disney studio was a boisterous place. All but a few of the men were in their early twenties to mid-thirties. Bringing so many young, creative minds together inevitably produced an atmosphere in which gags and practical jokes were rife.

"It was dangerous to leave your room; it was dangerous to come back into your room after you left," recalls Davis. "There might be a Dixie cup of water balanced on top of the partly open door—or worse. You could be booby-trapped on anything, and the lower you were on the ladder, the worse things would happen to you, like a dead fish under your light board. We were all young and under tension, and I think we broke the tension with gags. We were in the business of producing comedy, and something funny was going on all the time."

All these diverse elements—the personalities of the animators, the improvements in drawing, the esprit de corps and even the practical jokes—are reflected in the films. With remarkably few exceptions, the Silly Symphonies from the mid to the late 1930s remain as fresh and entertaining today as they were when first released. These cartoons shimmer with the energy and enthusiasm of their youthful creators, who were testing their newly discovered powers and exploring a limitless medium.

No other studio used so many fully animated characters. The trial scene in "Who Killed Cock Robin?" features a full complement of jurors and a crowd of spectators. In the finale of "Mother Goose Goes Hollywood" (1938), the scenery opens like a pop-up book while dozens of celebrity caricatures cavort in and around it. "The Cookie Carnival" includes a beauty pageant with cheering spectators along the parade route.

Changing light and other special effects give the films a heightened sense of atmosphere. The drunken Abiner is puzzled by his wobbly reflection in a cube of gelatin in "The Country Cousin." When the victorious devils dance around a fire in "The Goddess of Spring" (1934), the flames change color and the moving shadows go from orange to blue-violet. The background art ranges from the stylized musical motifs that make up the Land of Symphony and the Isle of Jazz in "Music Land" (1935) to the pastel, patchwork world of "Lullaby Land" (1933) to the realistic interiors in "The Old Mill" (1937).

The most significant of the Silly Symphonies was "Three Little Pigs," one of the landmark films in the history of animation. For the first time, characters who looked alike revealed their individual personalities by the way they moved. Except for their costumes, the three pigs were identical. Only his style of movement distinguished the sensible, hardworking Practical Pig from his frivolous brothers.

"I'm not sure I saw 'Three Little Pigs' right away," comments Warners cartoon director Chuck Jones. "But when I did see it, I realized something was happening there that hadn't happened before. During the twenties, all you needed in animation was action, and a good character just had to look pretty. 'Three Pigs' changed that by proving it wasn't how a character looked but how he moved that determined his personality. All we animators were dealing with after 'Three Pigs' was acting."

" 'Three Little Pigs' was released in 1933. It caused no excitement at its Radio City premiere," Disney wrote in 1941. "In fact, many critics preferred 'Noah's Ark,' which was released at about the same time. I was told that some exhibitors and even United Artists considered 'The Pigs' a 'cheater' because it had only four characters in it. The picture bounced back to fame from the neighborhood theatres. Possibly more people have seen 'The Pigs' than any other picture, long or short, ever made.''

One important reason for its popularity was the song "Who's Afraid of the Big Bad Wolf?" Written by composer/ musician Frank Churchill and story man Ted Sears with some help from Pinto Colvig (better known as the voice of Goofy), the tune became the unofficial anthem of the Depression. Under pressure from United Artists and Roy, Disney made three more films with the same characters: "The Big Bad Wolf" (1934), "Three Little Wolves" (1936) and "The Practical Pig" (1939). None of them duplicated the success of the origi-

nal, which led to Walt's often-repeated remark: "You can't top pigs with pigs."

According to Diane Disney Miller, "Three Little Pigs" was also the first cartoon to have a complete storyboard. Originally devised by Win Smith, Iwerks's former assistant, the storyboard consisted of a series of small drawings and captions pinned to a corkboard wall that showed the action of the film. Preliminary sketches and comic book-like plans had been used on many earlier films. Pinning the drawings to a wall enabled the artists to add, remove or change sketches and to see easily how various sequences within the film related to each other.

A milestone in the art of character animation: "Three Little Pigs" (1933). For the first time, each character's personality was defined by the way he moved, rather than the way he looked.

The storyboard represented Disney's solution to the problem of bringing order and structure to the animated short. Cartoons no longer consisted of haphazardly joined scenes that had been drawn by artists working in virtual isolation. The director could edit the cartoon in advance by plotting the pacing, visual rhythm and exposition before the animation was begun. The storyboard quickly became a standard tool in the animation industry. Today, all commercials and many live-action features are storyboarded before photography begins.

Pinning the drawings to a wall also introduced a new sport among the animators: pushpin throwing. The pin has to be hurled with just the right force or it won't stick in the cork. In addition to contests with a drawn bull's-eye, the artists experimented with trick tosses (behind the back, over the shoulder) and multiple pin throws.

Virtually every Silly Symphony contained some new technique or effect. Two important areas of experimentation were *gravity* and *squash and stretch*. The animators discovered that all movements are performed against the resistance of gravity. This knowledge (and their increasingly polished draftsmanship) enabled them to give their characters convincing weight and mass.

When Mickey picked up the sow and her piglets in "Steamboat Willie," Iwerks merely extended his arms—no strength was required to lift that weightless burden—but Willie the Giant plants each foot so firmly in "Brave Little Tailor" that the audience can see his ponderous bulk settling. When Goofy steps on the precariously balanced boards high above the city in "Clock Cleaners," the weight suggested in each step makes the situation seem so perilous: he's obviously heavy enough to upset the equilibrium and plummet to his doom.

Squash and stretch derives from principles of physics: an object elongates along its axis of acceleration and contracts when it meets with resistance. More simply: a dropped rubber ball will lengthen as it falls, flatten when it hits the floor and lengthen again as it bounces back up. But the volume of the ball (or any other object) will remain constant, no matter how much it changes shape.

The use of squash and stretch proved to be the key to character animation. As animation is a medium of caricature, the movements and expressions of the cartoon characters had to be taken beyond the limits of reality to be convincing. Movements copied too literally from live action look stiff and uninteresting on the screen. To bring their characters to life, the animators had to exaggerate. Squash and stretch gave them the freedom to do so. They learned that audiences would accept extreme distortions in a character's shape as long as the volume remains unchanged.

If the animator allows the volume of an object to change, it loses all feeling of solidity and takes on an unpleasant, Silly Putty quality. According to Frank Thomas and Ollie Johnston,

To increase the sense of the animals' size, animator Woolie Reitherman kept the point of view low when he staged the battle between the Stegosaurus and the Tyrannosaurus in "Fantasia."

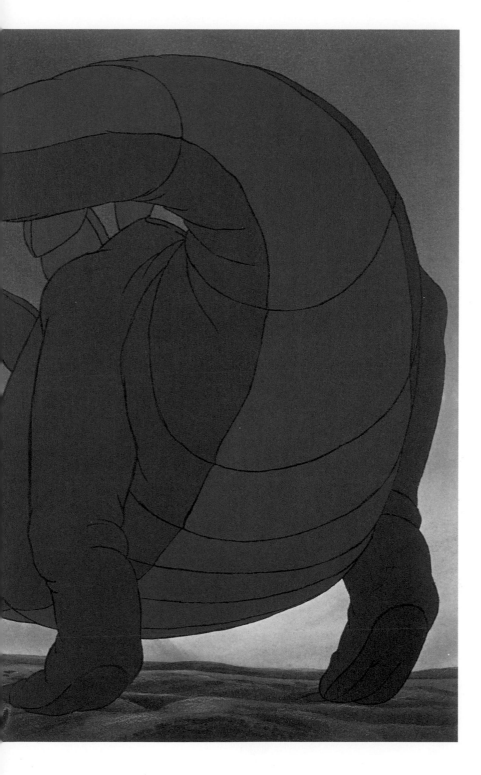

the Disney animators kept the image of a half-filled sack of flour in mind. Its volume remained fixed, although its shape was almost infinitely flexible.

The movements of living creatures result from the complex interplay of muscles, bones and connective tissues. Working with live-action reference footage, the Disney animators dissected movements, studying their components and the order in which they occur.

They learned that the elements of a movement do not all happen at the same time, and began to work with *follow-through* and *overlapping action*. Anyone who has participated in a sport is familiar with these principles. A golf swing, for example, does not end when the head of the club strikes the ball. The follow-through is essential. The point of contact with the ball must be part of an arc that continues beyond it if the stroke is to impart the proper force and direction.

That same golf swing is made up of a series of overlapping actions. First, the player focuses his attention on the ball by inclining his head and fixing his eyes on it. The swing begins at the shoulders, then continues through the arms. The wrists turn near the bottom of the arc and the weight shifts from one foot to another. The arms continue through the arc until they are positioned over the opposite shoulder; the head turns as part of the follow-through.

Follow-through is especially easy to observe—and fun to animate—on hefty characters, because the masses of fat lag slightly behind the muscles and bones at the beginning of a movement and continue beyond them at the end. Whenever Hyacinth Hippo moves in the "Dance of the Hours" sequence of "Fantasia," her enormous hips continue to shift after she stops.

The artists also applied principles used in the theater to their animation: secondary action, anticipation, staging and timing. A *secondary action* is one that supports or emphasizes the primary action and/or mood. If a character falls flat, he may wipe dirt off his face, shake his head or clench his fists as he gets up. Getting up is the primary action. Wiping, shaking and clenching are secondary actions that may indicate whether he is embarrassed, surprised or angry. The trick is to make the secondary actions support the primary movement and not detract from it.

Anticipation is used to emphasize an action by suggesting what is going to happen next. Mimes, dancers and acrobats use it extensively. Anticipatory movements often run counter to the main movement: a character may shift his weight or look to the left before moving to the right. One of the most commonly used examples of anticipation in cartoons is to have a character pause, leaning back with one foot in the air, before running off. The preliminary moment of stillness makes the run seem that much faster.

Staging in animation is quite similar to staging in the theater or in live-action films. Its purpose is to ensure that the key actions in a scene are clear and at the focus of the audience's attention. The animators often used silhouettes of their characters to see if the staging could be read from the poses alone. Woolie Reitherman explained that when he staged the fight between the Tyrannosaurus and the Stegosaurus in "Fantasia," he was careful to keep the point of view low: the audience was always looking up at the dinosaurs, so that their size and power were emphasized.

Timing is one of the most important elements in animation, yet it is also one of the most subtle and elusive. First, the basic motions of the character have to be timed. All movements have natural rhythms that must be accurately reproduced if the animation is to be convincing. One reason the characters in "Lady and the Tramp" are believable as dogs is that they walk with the proper rhythms.

Even more elusive and subjective is the timing of a character's "business," the gestures and movements he performs that help to define him as an individual and to advance the story. Here, the animator is required to act through his drawings. The Disney artists studied the principles of acting through reading, observation and lectures, and the results were impressive. Animator Tom Sito observed: "In a film like 'Pinocchio,' the gestures and the acting are so perfect that the characters cease to exist as drawings: you accept them as living individuals."

The artists also explored the possibilities offered by *straight-ahead* and *pose-to-pose* animation. Much of the earliest animation was done straight ahead: the animator began a scene by making drawing No. 1, then continued doing each drawing in order until he came to the end. This method can produce lively, natural motion, but the results are difficult to control. The character can easily miss the object he's supposed to reach for or exit in the wrong place. As Thomas and Johnston wrote: "The animator is often as surprised as anybody at the way the scene ends up."

Winsor McCay urged the audience at his 1927 testimonial to work in pose-to-pose animation, which he thought he had recently devised—not realizing the method was already widely used in the industry. With this type of animation, the animator begins by making key drawings in a motion, then fills in the gaps with "in-betweens." As the name suggests, pose-to-pose animation emphasizes the character's beginning and end positions. These strong poses make it easy to present story points. However, pose-to-pose animation rarely produces motion as natural as straight-ahead; it can easily become stiff and jerky.

"Old animation was done from pose to pose without much thought," said Huemer. "It was almost like it was a design, without any weight. Whereas Disney immediately gave his characters weight, and life and breath, and naturalness. In Disney, the animation flowed from thing to thing, and our stuff went from extreme to extreme."

The Disney animators finally worked out a compromise that Luske's "General Outline" described as: "Combination of advantages of two previous methods. Putting in extremes and then working straight ahead with the extremes as guides for the in-betweens. Elaborating or simplifying resulting drawings for caricatured action."

The artists were able to improve their animation because of another Disney innovation, the *pencil test*. The animators' rough drawings were shot on cheap black-and-white stock, then projected or shown on a Moviola and studied for errors. Corrections or changes were drawn, shot, cut into the tests and studied further.

All these techniques were used primarily by the character animators, who strove to create believable personalities on the screen. Separate crews were beginning to experiment with different sorts of motion: falling leaves, fire, lightning, water, snow, smoke, etc. *Effects animation* required artists with different powers of observation and draftsmanship. The effects animators made important contributions to the visual richness of the Disney shorts and features. In "Hell's Bells" (1928), Iwerks's stiffly moving flames resemble paper cutouts; six years later in "The Goddess of Spring," the fires of Hades burn with realistic grace.

"If an animator is sitting on the porch and people walk by, the character animator will sketch the way they walk," comments Roy E. Disney. "The effects animator will study the way their reflections move in the puddles on the sidewalk."

In addition to creating credible flames and snowstorms, the effects animators could add charming touches that complemented the character animation. A highlight of the celebration that ends "The Cookie Carnival" is the multicolored spotlight (a candle shining through translucent lollipops) that tints the characters and backgrounds as it revolves.

Disney remained at the center of all this activity, watching over every aspect of the studio's productions, moving men from one area to another, seeking to use every talent most effectively. He often rummaged through the animators' wastebaskets at night, occasionally retrieving a discarded drawing —which he would pin to the table with a note admonishing the artist not to throw away "the good stuff."

More has been written about Walt Disney than any other figure in the movies except Charlie Chaplin, yet he remains an elusive figure. His personality is an enigma to anyone forced to rely on reminiscences and published accounts. At times, Walt almost seems to have been a human Rorschach test: everyone who worked with him saw something different in him.

"You couldn't help feeling awe in the presence of genius," said Dick Huemer. "Figuratively, we could feel him coming down the hall, our hair would stand on end, the backs of our necks would cringle. . . . When he came into a room and people jumped into their seats, he bawled them out. 'Don't be afraid of me. I don't want to see you jumping into your seat like that. If you ever do it again, you'll hear from me! Don't be afraid of me. I don't mind you standing around. If you feel restless, go out and walk in the garden!' . . . And as a result, he got more work out of them because they worked out of love for what they were doing.''

"I think he was deliberately a different person to different people," comments Marc Davis. "He read something in you and behaved accordingly toward you. I'm sure he behaved differently to me than he did to other people; I think I knew a very different Walt than Art Babbitt or Frank Thomas or most of the others."

His artists raised character animation to new heights, and Disney animation became the standard for excellence in the medium. The Silly Symphonies and Mickey Mouse cartoons simply outclassed the work of the other studios. But the most beautifully animated film is only an empty exercise in technique if it fails to tell a story, and it was in this area that Walt made his greatest contributions. Disney's talents as a storyteller and editor were unequaled.

Leo Salkin, who moved to the story department after working as an assistant animator, recalled: "Of all the people I've worked under and with since, it's been very rare to find anyone who responded directly to what was there on the [story]boards as Walt did. I remember Homer Brightman—who was what in later years was called a 'great presenter'—was working on a film called 'Officer Duck.' There were twenty or so people in the room for a story meeting, including Walt. The film had a lot of broad, slapstick action. Homer went through it all, and the room was largely hysterical. You had the feeling this was a pretty funny story. When Homer finished, Walt turned to the secretary and said, 'Mary, were you laughing at Homer or at the story?' She said, 'At Homer,' and Walt launched into his criticism. He was very aware of the difference between what was being acted out and what was there on the boards—which is what would be there in the film."

By all accounts, Walt was a spellbinding storyteller. There are numerous anecdotes about how he seemed to become the various characters as he described the plot of a film. When his nephew, Roy Edward Disney, had the chicken pox as a boy, Walt came to visit and spent the better part of an hour sitting on his bed, telling him the story of Pinocchio, which the studio had just begun. When he saw the finished film, Roy found: "It was nowhere near as good as when Walt told it. I've seen it recently, and realize what a splendid piece of work it is. But there's still that funny little aftertaste of Walt's performance, and the knowledge that it could have been that much better."

All Disney's powers as an actor, storyteller, salesman and leader were called into play in the creation of one of his most ambitious projects: "Snow White and the Seven Dwarfs."

According to his daughter's biography, Walt got the idea to make an animated feature in 1935, when he and his brother

Roy went to Paris to receive a scroll and a gold medal from the League of Nations for the creation of Mickey Mouse, "an international symbol of good will." He saw a theater in Paris playing a program of six Disney shorts and decided that audiences would accept an hour or more of animation.

The idea of doing an animated feature was both a bold stroke and a logical follow-up to his unparalleled success in cartoon shorts. Short films produced only very limited revenue, and all the great live-action comics had switched to features. During the early 1930s, there had been talk of a combination animation/live-action feature of "Alice in Wonderland" with Mary Pickford in the title role or "Rip Van Winkle" with Will Rogers, or a full-length version of "Babes in Toyland."

"As a matter of fact, we were practically forced into the feature field," Disney later wrote. "We not only had to have its new story material, but also we had to have feature profits to justify our continuing expansion, and we sensed that we had gone about as far as we could in the short subject field without getting ourselves in a rut. We needed this new adventure, this 'kick in the pants,' to jar loose some new enthusiasm and inspiration."

Ken Anderson, who served as an art director on many Disney films, including "Snow White," remembers the announcement that they were going to make the film came "as a complete surprise." "One day Walt came around to a bunch of us, gave us each fifty cents and told us to have dinner and come back to the sound stage afterwards. Walt had all the lights on the stage dimmed but one. We sat on the tiered seats

The Sugar Cookie Girl in "The Cookie Carnival" (1935), who represented one of the animators' first attempts to create a convincingly feminine character. An original animation drawing by Grim Natwick.

The multiplane camera added an illusion of three-dimensionality to Disney films, beginning with "The Old Mill" (1937).

near the projection booth and he absolutely enchanted us. He told us the whole story and took on the characteristics of some of the characters. He inspired me and the others with his vision of this magnificent opus. I really think that the animators then would've climbed a mountain of wildcats to do 'Snow White.' We didn't even realize it was impossible."

"Snow White" presented enormous difficulties. The characters would have to express complex emotions and hold the audience's interest for an hour and a half, which meant the animation would have to be more subtle and sophisticated than anything done previously. The classes in drawing and acting were stepped up. In 1935, Disney put Don Graham in charge of a recruitment campaign to find 300 new artists (a year earlier, his entire staff numbered only 187). Among the qualities Disney instructed him to look for in a candidate were good draftsmanship; knowledge of caricature, action, acting, the mechanics of animation, story structure and audience values; an ability to think up and put over gags.

Many of the Silly Symphonies from the mid-1930s served as testing grounds for techniques and effects intended for "Snow White." For example, the Sugar Cookie Girl in "The Cookie Carnival" represented one of the animators' first attempts at creating a genuinely feminine character. With a few exceptions like Betty Boop, female cartoon characters had essentially been males with long eyelashes, skirts and a few dainty gestures.

Perhaps the most curious of these experiments is "The Goddess of Spring," an attempt at telling a serious story, the legend of Persephone. Although the vapid heroine is fairly well drawn, she does little but prance around her domain with some cutesy elves. Pluto, the God of the Underworld (depicted as the Devil), wraps a cloak about himself and points in pseudo-operatic gestures. Neither of the main characters communicates the emotions needed to tell the story, nor could they hold an audience's interest through a feature. The many contrasts in style (semirealistic heroine vs. stagey villain vs. cartoon attendants) are jarring. The animators obviously weren't sure what they were trying to do—yet.

Disney dazzled both audiences and his staff with another experiment, which he described as "just a poetic thing." Like "The Skeleton Dance," "The Old Mill" (1937) is a mood piece, with no gags or real characters. It depicts one night in a ruined windmill with lyrical realism. A gentle sunset gives way to an impressive thunderstorm; the birds and animals that nest in the mill shiver in the fury of the tempest. The storm passes, dawn breaks and life resumes. What made the Oscar-winning short a showstopper was the incredible illusion of depth, created with the newly perfected *multiplane camera*.

When an animated film is photographed, the cels are laid over the background on a horizontal surface under the camera; a heavy sheet of glass called a platen holds everything in place while the film is exposed. The nature of the process makes it difficult to create an appearance of three-dimensionality. The solution to the problem was the multiplane camera, developed by William Garity. (Iwerks worked on a similar idea at about the same time.) On the multiplane, layers of artwork are placed on glass sheets set several inches apart, "like a baker's pie wagon." When the results are photographed, the layers of artwork seem to recede into great depth, especially in trucking shots.

Many histories of animation have praised the multiplane camera as an epoch-making innovation, comparable to the introduction of sound or color. In fact, it had very little effect on the general development of the art, despite the impressive results it produced. Disney's multiplane camera was unwieldy (it stood more than fifteen feet high), expensive to build and difficult to operate. The lighting for the artwork and the rates of the camera movements required extensive calculations. One multiplane shot in "Pinocchio" that lasts less than a minute on screen cost an estimated $45,000. Only Disney made extensive use of the multiplane camera.

Disney wanted "Snow White" to have the look of an old European storybook, a look he found in the work of Albert Hurter and Gustave Tenggren. The Swiss-born Hurter was one of the studio's most influential designers. He had a unique drawing style and an uncanny ability to find life and personality in any shape or object. His designs were featured in many of the Silly Symphonies, and ranged from the living safety pins in "Lullaby Land" to the animated sweets in "The Cookie Carnival." A noted children's book illustrator, Tenggren contributed handsome watercolor studies. They brought the style of nineteenth-century illustrations to the screen.

As the designs for the characters evolved over a period of months, the animation began. No one artist did all the drawings of any character, but when one animator showed an ability to handle a character particularly well, he was allowed to take the lead. Most of the Wicked Queen's sequences went to Art Babbitt, who gave her an icy, regal demeanor that accented her hard-edged beauty.

After her dramatic transformation into a hag, the character was animated by Norm Ferguson. His handling of the crone was straightforward, direct and thoroughly frightening. The Witch in "Snow White" embodied the archetype so perfectly that countless animated witches have been copied from her. As several critics observed, the ultimate villain in George Lucas's "Star Wars" trilogy, the evil Emperor of the Galaxy in "The Return of the Jedi," bore a striking resemblance to the Witch in "Snow White."

The most difficult character was the heroine, who had to be appealing, believable and feminine, without being stiff, overly cute or cartoony. Ham Luske shot extensive reference footage of a young dancer, Marge Belcher—the future Marge Champion. Grim Natwick, who was chosen to animate many of Snow White's scenes because of his extensive art training,

points out that the reference footage could not be traced: the proportions of the drawn character were too different. The cartoon character was drawn only about five heads high; a normal human figure is eight heads high. Champion added: "They never copied it [the live-action footage] frame for frame, because it was not cartoon action. Still, anybody who knows me can see me in Snow White."

More than 150 girls auditioned for Snow White's voice. The role went to eighteen-year-old Adriana Caselotti. According to an often-repeated story, a Disney agent called her father, who was a singing teacher, asking for candidates. Adriana, who had been listening on the extension, said, "How about me?" She auditioned, Disney liked her voice and she got the role.

Because of his fine draftsmanship, Natwick was also assigned the animation of the Prince, the least successful character in the film. Despite reference footage of Champion's dance partner, Lewis Hightower, the Prince was not convincing, and his role in the film was eventually cut to a few short scenes. The creation of a hero who was masculine without being wooden, flexible without seeming effeminate, remained a vexing problem for the Disney artists for many years.

Probably no other characters in the history of animation have undergone such intense scrutiny at their creation as the Seven Dwarfs. In the Grimm version of the story, the personal-

A preliminary study of the Witch at her cauldron for "Snow White" shows the influence of European book illustrations.

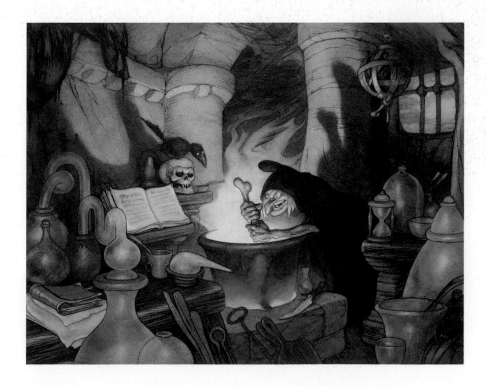

Opposite: The Wicked Queen discovers the Huntsman has brought her a pig's heart instead of Snow White's. "Snow White and the Seven Dwarfs" introduced powerful human emotions into American animated films. Above: A cel setup of Snow White sending the Dwarfs out to wash before dinner. Disney realized that to hold the audience's attention, the Dwarfs would need distinct personalities.

ities of the Dwarfs are not differentiated. Disney realized that strong, individual characters would be needed to advance the story as well as provide humor and appeal.

To create a single believable personality on the screen and imbue it with a unique style of movement is difficult enough; to create seven characters who look alike but think and act differently and who can interact presented enormous difficulties. Fred Moore, Bill Tytla, Fred Spencer and Frank Thomas, a relative newcomer, were put in charge of the Dwarfs.

Disney threw out the first six months' worth of work because he felt it was no longer good enough. The animators were developing their skills so rapidly that they superseded

their own achievements. In the "sweatbox sessions" (named for the cramped, stuffy editing room where they took place), Disney would often decide that a scene should be redrawn because it didn't meet the standard he wanted to set with "Snow White."

As the picture approached completion, Walt scrapped two entire sequences: in one, which had been completely animated, the Dwarfs ate the soup Snow White has cooked for them; in the other, which had been partially animated, they built a bed for Snow White. Disney removed these scenes, not because they were bad, but because he realized that they impeded rather than advanced the flow of the story.

All this time and animation was costing a great deal of money. The staff had grown to 600 by 1937 (and 800 more were hired by 1940). Roy was forced to borrow increasing sums from the Bank of America. In Hollywood, the film was being called "Disney's Folly." Like Oscar Wilde, Walt knew that being talked about was better than not being talked about, and did nothing to discourage the rumors. Looking back in 1941, he wrote:

> I thought we could make "Snow White" for around $250,000. At least that's what I told Roy. The figure didn't make much sense because we were spending about that much on every three Silly Symphonies or 2,500 feet of picture. Roy was very brave and manly until the costs passed a million. He wasn't used to figures of over a hundred thousand at a time. The extra cipher threw him. When costs passed the one and one-half million mark, Roy didn't even bat an eye. He couldn't; he was paralyzed. And I didn't feel very full-blooded, either. We considered changing the name of the picture from "Snow White" to "Frankenstein." I believe the final figure, including prints, exploitation, etc., was around two million. We sort of half-way explained this to everybody by charging a million of it off to research and development. You know, building toward the future. And this was true, although we hadn't exactly planned it to be that way.

"Snow White and the Seven Dwarfs" premiered on December 21, 1937, under a new releasing agreement with RKO, to glowing reviews and land office business. According to studio estimates, more people saw "Snow White" on its initial release than "Star Wars": it earned $8 million, an enormous sum in 1937–38. The characters became the subject of a merchandising campaign second only to Mickey's.

In 1939, Disney received a special Academy Award—one full-sized Oscar with seven small ones behind it—inscribed: "To Walt Disney for 'Snow White and the Seven Dwarfs,' recognized as a significant screen innovation which has charmed millions and pioneered a great new entertainment field for the motion picture cartoon."

Good as the animation is, it is the carefully plotted and superbly paced story that holds the viewer's attention. Color, lighting and sound all contribute to the drama. Snow White's terrified flight through the forest of sinister trees and the Wicked Queen's dungeon laboratory are the embodiment of every child's darkest dreams. In addition to three hit songs ("Whistle While You Work," "Someday My Prince Will Come" and "Heigh Ho"), Frank Churchill, Larry Morey, Paul J. Smith and Leigh Harline contributed an effective film score that emphasizes the changing situations and the moods of the characters.

While everyone agreed that "Snow White" was a masterpiece of animation, most critics failed to note that it was—and is—an extraordinary piece of filmmaking. Lewis Jacobs (*The Rise of the American Film*) was one of the few observers to call attention to its technical excellence: "Disney is unexcelled among directors in his exploitation of the full resources of his tools. An unlimited technical range of effects marks his structure: his camera swoops, glides, shoots, zooms, rides, bounces, and uses other movements that would be impossible in conventional studio pictures."

"Snow White" was not the first feature-length animated film, as has sometimes been claimed. That distinction belongs to Quirino Cristiani's "The Apostle" (Argentina, 1917). Lotte Reiniger had completed her silhouette feature, "The Adventures of Prince Achmed," in Germany in 1926. While it is unlikely that Disney or anyone on his staff had seen Cristiani's film, Reiniger's work had received considerable attention in Europe and the animators may have been aware of it.

But "Snow White" was the first American feature; the first feature made by a studio, rather than an independent filmmaker; the first Technicolor feature. And the success of "Disney's Folly" made it one of the most significant films in the history of animation. "Snow White" established the basic pattern for almost every subsequent American animated feature, and its influence can be seen in films made decades later.

By the time "Snow White" was released, story work and some animation had already been done on "Pinocchio" and the film that would become "Fantasia"; preproduction work on "Bambi" began in late 1938. Disney's master plan called for the release of a new feature every year on a three-year production schedule. That meant three had to be in production at any given time, plus the Silly Symphonies and Mickey Mouse shorts.

With this plan in mind, Walt and Roy bought a fifty-one-acre tract of land in Burbank for $100,000 and began building a large modern studio that was intended to be both a showplace and an animator's paradise. The staff had long outgrown the facilities on Hyperion Avenue, and Disney wanted to bring order and comfort to this sprawling disarray.

The twenty buildings set amid handsome, landscaped grounds comprised a state-of-the-art facility. The entire studio was air-conditioned, both for comfort and to prevent changes in temperature and humidity from damaging the water-based paints used on the animation cels. An underground corridor joined the Ink and Paint Building to the Camera Building, so cels could be transported without exposing them to the elements. Those buildings were also sealed against dust and lint. (Cels attract dust, and any particles that are not removed will be visible in the finished film.) A gym, steam room, sun deck, soda fountain and restaurants were provided for the animators.

This careful organization did not encourage the casual exchange of ideas and information the way the random congestion of the Hyperion studio had. "I think the line of demarcation in the era of good feeling at the Disney studio was the move from Hyperion to Burbank," said Bill Melendez. "Suddenly, everything was compartmentalized in an unartistic fashion; it was the beginning of a loss of morale." (Melendez's own studio rambles amiably among three old houses on Larchmont Avenue, near Hollywood.)

Not surprisingly, Disney was proud of his new studio, which cost nearly $4 million. The staff moved in as the various buildings were completed, beginning in August 1939 and continuing well into 1940. Meanwhile, the animators were at work on "Pinocchio," "Fantasia" and the beginnings of "Bambi."

"Snow White" was based on a brief fairy tale, and Disney had removed the epilogue, in which the evil Queen is forced to dance herself to death in red-hot iron shoes at Snow White's wedding. "Pinocchio" began as a rather rambling Italian serial. Carlo Lorenzini, who wrote the story as "Carlo Collodi," had been paid by the word and often wrote like it. His living marionette was considerably less than lovable.

Disney's Pinocchio was originally conceived as a sarcastic, rambunctious wise guy, along the lines of Charlie McCarthy. But after six months of work, Disney rejected the concept as lacking appeal and discarded all the footage. The characters were redesigned and the story restructured before the animators went back to work on the film.

Ollie Johnston recalls his experimental animation: "Pinocchio started out more like a real wooden puppet, but Walt looked at the footage and felt the character needed to be more appealing; so he became more like a real boy, with more squash and stretch in his movements. We would have animated the movements of the wooden character differently—which might have been interesting."

One of the major changes in the story was the increased importance of Jiminy Cricket, Pinocchio's conscience. (In the original story, the Talking Cricket is a very minor character, whom Pinocchio smashes with a hammer.) He gradually became the film's narrator and an effective foil for much of the action. Ward Kimball, who was in charge of the character's design, said:

> I had a lot of problems with the Cricket. Normally, an artist caricatures an animal by learning to draw it correctly—then the caricature becomes a simple problem of degree. But with an insect, you're in trouble, because insects are very ugly and unappetizing. A cricket looks like a cross between a cockroach and a grasshopper. For the first designs, I started with a real cricket, with toothed legs and antennae, but Walt didn't like it. I did twelve or fourteen versions, and gradually cut out all the insect appendages. I ended up with a little man, really, wearing spats and a tail coat that suggested folded wings; he looked like Mr. Pickwick, but with no ears, no nose and no hair. The audience accepts him as a cricket because the other characters say he is.

For the experimental animation, the artists worked with a speeded-up tape of story man Ted Sears reading the dialogue. Disney decided to use a child for the voice of Pinocchio, although cartoon children's voices were normally supplied by adult actors. The role went to twelve-year-old Dick Jones, a

Jiminy Cricket performs "Give a Little Whistle" in "Pinocchio." The background suggests the richly detailed, Old World storybook look of the film.

Stromboli locks Pinocchio in an old bird cage.
Superbly animated by Bill Tytla, Stromboli proved
to be one of the most effective Disney villains.

successful boy actor who had already appeared in almost a hundred films.

Reference footage was shot of Jones's facial expression and lip movements. He also posed in costume and makeup with other actors for the sequence in which Honest John and Gideon persuade the puppet to abandon school and become an actor. Jones's only real difficulties with the part came in the scenes in which Pinocchio searches for Geppetto under the sea: "They had a real problem trying to make me sound like I was underwater. First, they tried having me read the lines with water in my mouth, but that just came out as 'glub, glub, glub,' and I spewed water all over the place. Then they had me lie on a table and poured water into my mouth while I tried to read the dialogue—I almost drowned. They finally came up with a gadget that looked like a squirrel cage with baffles on it. They rotated it as we talked into it, and that seemed to work."

Although most of the animators express a special fondness for "Snow White," "Pinocchio" is generally considered Disney's best feature. From the complex opening shot that follows Jiminy Cricket's point of view as he jumps into the film, every frame is crowded with motion and beauty. If the animators made the Silly Symphonies as they explored a new medium, "Pinocchio" shows them at the height of their powers, reveling in their ability to create *anything*. Nothing was too difficult or too complicated for the Disney artists to draw.

"Pinocchio" is one of the few animated features in which all the characters are interesting, even the Good Guys. Geppetto, animated by Art Babbitt, shows a fumbling absentmindedness that saves him from the blandness of the Prince in "Snow White." Figaro the kitten and Cleo the goldfish provide charming support. Some older commentators complained of a lack of resolve in Pinocchio, but it is his uncertainty that makes the character so readily understandable to children growing up in the uncertain post–World War II era.

These heroes are pitted against villains that range from the suave J. Worthington Foulfellow and his inept assistant, Gideon, to the chilling Wicked Coachman, who takes the boys to Pleasure Island. But the grandest of all Disney heavies is the flamboyant puppeteer, Stromboli, superbly animated by Bill Tytla. (Fellow animator T. Hee, who was rather heavy at the time, remembered posing in gypsy costume for reference footage of Stromboli.) The figures in many of Tytla's drawings look improbably stretched and distorted, but on the screen they flow magnificently to create a character that animation historian John Canemaker described as "an overweight monster of mercurial moods, capable of wine-soaked, garlic-breathed Old World charm one second and knife-wielding, chop-you-up-for-firewood threats the next."

Few scenes in live-action film can match the terror of Lampwick's transformation into a donkey on Pleasure Island or the attack of the gargantuan Monstro. Woolie Reitherman remembered that to create the whale the animators were essentially told to "take a three-story building and move it in perspective." For sheer size and malevolent power, Monstro eclipses the stop-motion beasts that have ravaged miniature sets of Tokyo.

"Pinocchio" represented a tremendous effort by every department in the studio. This was the first feature for which the artists made extensive use of reference models. A special shop prepared a marionette of Pinocchio, a statue of Monstro (painted in oils, so that the animators could tell where highlights would appear on his skin), a five-foot whale's rib cage with articulated vertebrae and mock-ups of all the toys in Geppetto's workshop. Leigh Harline, Ned Washington and Paul J. Smith contributed a score that featured five songs, four of which became hits: "Hi Diddle Dee Dee (An Actor's Life for Me)," "I've Got No Strings," "Give a Little Whistle" and "When You Wish Upon a Star." Production costs came to a staggering $2.6 million, with prints, dubbing and promotion bringing the total to over $3 million. ("The Wizard of Oz," which was released in August 1939, cost $2.77 million.)

The film opened on February 23, 1940, to generally ecstatic reviews. (One of the few unfavorable comments came from Lorenzini's nephew, who complained that Disney had made Pinocchio seem American, rather than Italian.) Otis Ferguson wrote in *The New Republic:* "Walt Disney's 'Pinocchio' is a delight and at times will take your breath away, for the limits of the animated cartoon have been blown so wide open that some of the original wonder of pictures—wonder and terror too, as when the train roared up into the camera—is restored." Archer Winsten said: "In writing of 'Pinocchio,' you are limited only by your own power of expressing enthusiasm. To put it in the simplest possible terms, this film is fantastically delightful, absolutely perfect, and a work of pure unadulterated genius."

Although technically superior in almost every way, "Pinocchio" failed to match the box office success of "Snow White." Audiences did not find these characters as endearing as Snow White and the Dwarfs. The outbreak of World War II in Europe had a devastating effect, as foreign markets had been providing 45 percent of the studio's income. Disney products were now barred from Fascist Germany and Italy and the conquered states of Austria, Poland and Czechoslovakia. Revenues from France and England were frozen.

The financial failure of "Pinocchio," coupled with the expenses of the new studio and the rising production costs of

Walt Disney, Deems Taylor and Leopold Stokowski pose amid storyboards for "Fantasia."

"Fantasia," put Walt and Roy $4.5 million in debt. They were forced to make the first public offering of stock in Walt Disney Productions in April 1940. The issue of 155,000 shares of preferred stock and 600,000 shares of common stock quickly sold out, bringing in a much-needed $3.5 million.

In an article published early in 1941, Disney defended the film: " 'Pinocchio' is yet to return its original investment. It has been called a flop. Actually it was the second biggest box-office attraction of the year. 'Gone With the Wind' was first. 'Pinocchio' might have lacked 'Snow White's' heart appeal, but technically and artistically it was superior. It indicated that we had grown considerably as craftsmen as well as having grown big in plant and numbers, a growth that is only important in proportion to the quality it adds to our product in the long run."

History has justified Disney's faith in "Pinocchio." In its 1984 re-release, "Pinocchio" earned $26 million in the United States. But when Disney wrote that defense, he was still dealing with the box office failure of what was in many ways his most original—and controversial—work, "Fantasia."

Like many Disney projects, "Fantasia" began as a modest idea: a Silly Symphony illustrating Paul Dukas's "The Sorcerer's Apprentice." Most sources agree that Walt had conceived of "The Sorcerer's Apprentice" in late 1936 as a sort of comeback vehicle for Mickey Mouse. Mickey had become an increasingly nice guy, and had fallen in popularity behind Donald, Goofy and, in some polls, the Fleischers' "Popeye."

One night in late 1937, while dining alone at Chasen's in Beverly Hills, Disney saw Leopold Stokowski, also alone, and invited the conductor to join him. During the course of a three-hour conversation, Disney mentioned his plans for "The Sorcerer's Apprentice." Stokowski offered to waive any fee and conduct the recording of the music. The conductor also suggested that he and Disney join forces to create "a fanta-*zee*-ah," a feature that would illustrate several pieces of classical music.

As production costs on the film soared to $125,000, it became obvious—especially to Roy—that no short could ever earn back so much money. Walt began to listen to Stokowski's suggestions about doing a feature. In February 1938, plans began for a work tentatively entitled "The Concert Feature." Stokowski's contract had to be renegotiated, as the music for the film would be performed not by the studio musicians who had played "The Sorcerer's Apprentice" but by the renowned Philadelphia Orchestra. The distinguished musicologist Deems Taylor was hired to act as commentator. Disney put his engineers to work on a more powerful and realistic sound system; they eventually devised the multitrack Fantasound, a precursor of stereo.

Stokowski, Disney and the studio staff played records and studied printed scores, looking for suitable musical selections. Preliminary sketches were done for a number of pieces that Disney rejected, including "The Flight of the Bumble Bee." Animation was done to Debussy's "Clair de Lune."

Disney decided to open with Stokowski's fulsome orchestral transcription of Bach's Toccata and Fugue in D Minor. The inspiration for the visuals came from the films of Oskar Fischinger, who in 1934 had proposed to Stokowski that they make an abstract animated short set to the Bach transcription. A celebrated independent animator in Germany, Fischinger had come to America in 1935, as all abstract art was anathema to the Nazi regime.

The collaboration between Disney and Fischinger was not a felicitous one, as neither man seemed able to appreciate the other's talents. Fischinger was used to working as an independent artist, making all the decisions and doing all the artwork for his films himself. He did not adapt well to the demands and collaborative nature of studio filmmaking. Earlier assignments at Paramount and MGM had ended unhappily. Disney did not care for Fischinger's abstractions and realized they would not appeal to the film's mass audience. Fischinger left the studio after nine months; his name does not appear in the credits, probably at his own request.

Nothing had ever been done in animation that called for such subtly luminous effects and translucent textures as the selections from Tchaikovsky's popular *Nutcracker* ballet. This minutely scaled vision of an enchanted woodland opens with "The Dance of the Sugar Plum Fairy" as tiny fairies spangle leaves, a dandelion puff and a spider's web with glowing dewdrops. Textured cels with a "toothed" surface were used in "The Dance of the Reed Flutes" to retain the delicate quality of Elmer Plummer's pastel inspirational sketches. Special paints had to be developed for the veil-like fins of the seductive goldfish in "The Arabian Dance." Some images of the frost fairies in "The Waltz of the Flowers" involved such extensive use of stipple, translucent inks, dry brush and airbrush techniques that five hours were required to ink and paint each cel.

But what most people remember from the *Nutcracker* is not the special effects but the charm of Hop Low and the dancing mushrooms, animated by Art Babbitt (who also created the Russian thistles that perform the *trepak*). Only 60 seconds long, "The Chinese Dance" remains one of the most widely praised sequences in the history of animation.

A number of artists worked on Mickey Mouse in "The Sorcerer's Apprentice," notably Les Clark and Preston Blair. Fred Moore oversaw the work to ensure that Mickey retained his boyish appeal. The resulting animation is a superb pantomime that expresses a wide range of emotions. Mickey radiates cockiness as he prances about with the enchanted broom and exudes terror as he frantically searches for the counterspell. Bill Tytla animated the forbidding master magician, Yen Sid—"Disney" spelled backwards.

Dick Huemer recalled that "out of nowhere" during a story meeting for "Fantasia," "Walt asked, 'Say, is there any kind of music that would support the idea of the creation of the world, or the beginning of life on this world?' And before he was finished saying it, almost, Stokowski said, 'Why, yes! The *Sacre!*' Walt said, 'The sock?' And Stokowski said, 'Yes, *Le Sacre du Printemps* by Stravinsky—which means *The Rite of Spring*.'" Disney listened to a recording of Stravinsky's ballet of primitive Russia, and liked what he heard. The artists went to work.

A pastel preliminary sketch for the *Nutcracker* sequence of "Fantasia."

The animators and designers took considerable liberties with the history of life on earth. The narrow, triangular heads of the dinosaurs were drawn as blocky rectangles to make them easier to animate. The Tyrannosaurus and Stegosaurus that meet in the climactic battle to the "Glorification of the Victim" actually lived tens of millions of years apart. The theory that the extinction of the dinosaurs was caused by a drought has been abandoned in the face of contradictory evidence.

These caveats aside, *The Rite of Spring* is an extraordinarily vivid evocation of the prehistoric past, imbued with a feral power. Countless children have been inspired to study paleontology by "Fantasia." As Huemer concluded: "In my opinion, dinosaurs will never again be represented that well on the screen. It was really a perfect job of animation—the mood, the coloring, everything."

According to studio sources, after Stravinsky saw the film, he said perhaps that was what he had really meant when he wrote the music. He later complained bitterly about the small fee he received and the way the score had been rearranged. He damned Stokowski's performance as "execrable" and dismissed the visuals as "an unresisting imbecility."

Huemer said the idea for the "Pastoral Symphony" segment came from a short piece in a French ballet, *Cydalise et le*

Below: Hyacinth Hippo casts an amorous glance at her exhausted but adoring swain, Ben Ali Gator, in "The Dance of the Hours." Opposite top: Original drawing of Tchernobog by Bill Tytla for "Night on Bald Mountain." Opposite center: Preliminary drawing by Kay Nielsen for "Night on Bald Mountain." Opposite bottom: A preliminary pastel drawing by Nielsen for the proposed "Ride of the Valkyries" sequence for "Fantasia."

Chèvre-Pied (*Cydalise and the Faun*). But the music proved too short and lacked contrasts that could be keyed to visuals.

The early sketches for the "Pastoral" had a languid sensuality that suggested the work of the nineteenth-century Symbolist painters. Ken Anderson, who worked as an art director on the sequence, cannot remember who suggested switching to an Art Deco idiom. But Walt, who wanted a distinctive style for each section of the film, liked his first painting of a mountain at sunrise and chose that look. Anderson said he still feels the style is "not earthy enough for the music." Art Deco touches like the graceful figure of Diana lend elegance to what is otherwise a veritable orgy of cuteness, often cited as an example of Disney at his most tasteless.

Interestingly, the "Pastoral Symphony" is one of the few pieces of Disney animation that have been bowdlerized—twice. Pressure from the Hays office led Disney to put flower bras on the centaurettes, who had been designed bare-breasted. In recent releases, the two Nubian/zebra centaurettes who attend Bacchus have been edited out (except for a brief glimpse when the trio enters), as has a pickaninny centaurette who shined the others' hooves.

Ponchielli's "The Dance of the Hours" remains one of the funniest pieces of animation ever created at the Disney studio and a masterful send-up of classical ballet. Marge Champion devised the choreography for the elephants, ostriches, hippos and alligators ("The hippo rising out of the pool was greatly influenced by Vera Zorina in the 'Goldwyn Follies' . . ."). Three stars of the Ballets Russes de Monte Carlo posed for the animators working on this sequence: Irina Baronova (Mlle Upanova, the ostrich), Tatiana Riabouchinska (Hyacinth Hippo) and David Lichine (Ben Ali Gator).

The segment depicting Mussorgsky's "Night on Bald Mountain" is widely regarded as one of the few unchallenged masterpieces of the animator's art. The noted illustrator Kay Nielsen ("East of the Sun, West of the Moon") served as art director and designed the mighty form of Tchernobog, the black god of Russian legend. Bela Lugosi was hired to pose for reference footage, but Tytla, who did the key animation of the figure, was dissatisfied with the results and made sequence director Wilfred Jackson take off his shirt and go through the poses.

Tytla's extraordinary animation reflects his knowledge of anatomy and sculpture. When Tchernobog reaches skyward, the muscles in his arms and torso are described in a dramatic play of light and shadow; when he turns his hands, as flaming demons dance in his palm, there is an extraordinary three-dimensionality to the movements. The agonized, straining curves in the body of the black god as he cringes before the church bells at dawn express his impotent rage at a power greater than his own.

Because Disney was concerned that the "Bald Mountain" might be too frightening an ending for children, Schubert's

"Ave Maria" was added as a finale. Pretty lines of hooded pilgrims carry glowing candles through a forest, whose tall trees suggest a Gothic cathedral. Enormous technical problems had to be overcome to produce the illusion of misty depth, but the results hardly seem to warrant the effort. After the primal strength of "Bald Mountain," the "Ave Maria" seems pallid and saccharine, and "Fantasia" ends on a weak note.

"Fantasia" opened on November 13, 1940, at the Broadway Theater in New York—where Mickey Mouse had debuted in "Steamboat Willie" twelve years before (it was then called the Colony Theatre). Critics agreed that the film was an innovation in its marriage of sound and animated imagery; beyond that, there was no consensus. *Commonweal*'s Philip Hartung praised it as "a new artistic experience of great beauty." Music critics railed at this sacrilegious approach to the classics. Franz Hoellering called it "a promising monstrosity." In an extraordinarily vitriolic review, Dorothy Thompson of the New York *Herald* wrote: "Nazism is the abuse of power, the perverted betrayal of the best instincts, the genius of a race turned into black magical destruction, and so is 'Fantasia.' "

Disney planned to show the film only in twelve theaters that had been outfitted with banks of ninety-six speakers and Fantasound equipment (at a cost of $85,000 per theater). The plan failed. Audiences balked at paying road-show prices, especially for children. "Fantasia" had been almost as expensive to produce as "Pinocchio"—$2.28 million—and, like "Pinocchio," it lost money on its initial release.

"Fantasia" was a milestone, an animated concert that attempted to fuse music, color, sound, form, motion and illustration into a single multimedia experience—a bold departure from the stories and joke telling that animation had been used for since its inception. It contains both the best and the worst of Disney's vision of the medium.

Had "Fantasia" been as successful as "Snow White," there would have been sequels—Disney had plans to update the film regularly by adding new sequences—and the history of animation would have been very different. Instead, the Disney artists devoted most of their subsequent efforts to retelling familiar stories.

After several reissues, "Fantasia" was put into permanent selective re-release in 1969, earning about $2 million each year. Although the visuals had been preserved, the sound track deteriorated; in 1981, the executives at the Disney studio decided to rescore the film in state-of-the-art digital sound. Film conductor Irwin Kostal was chosen to conduct an orchestra of 127 Los Angeles musicians. Although Kostal had to match Stokowski's beats to keep the music synchronized with the animation, he made some changes. The Stokowski orchestration of "Night on Bald Mountain" was replaced with Mussorgsky's original; some retiming in the Beethoven disguised the excision of the black centaurettes.

Strikers from the studio picket "The Reluctant Dragon" at the Hollywood Pantages Theater in 1941. Their signs feature a caricature of Walt as "The Reluctant Disney."

When the new sound track was premiered in the spring of 1982, everyone agreed it was a technological masterpiece. But purists complained about the removal of Deems Taylor, and many listeners had qualms about the performance. Kostal was not a conductor of Stokowski's stature, nor was his pickup group the Philadelphia Orchestra. Los Angeles *Times* music critic Martin Bernheimer pointed out that the visuals had been created to match the music; the new recording reversed the process. Film historian Ronald Haver tactfully wrote: "Its new sound track makes it a completely new experience." When asked how he liked the digital sound track, Art Babbitt replied: "I think it lacks balls." (In late 1988, the studio announced plans to restore the original Stokowski sound track for the film's fiftieth-anniversary re-release.)

As quarrels among the paladins of the Round Table helped bring about the downfall of Arthur's Camelot, internal divisions and dissent contributed to the end of Disney's "golden age." The troubles in the studio crystallized around the strike of 1941, which animators still refer to as The Strike.

The union movement in the animation industry was a long and bitterly fought struggle. The organizers were opposed not only by management but often by the animators themselves, who felt they were artists—not workmen who belonged in a union. And nowhere did the effort produce deeper and more lasting divisions than at Disney.

The studio was very much Walt's personal domain. The artists shared a personal relationship with Walt that meant more to most of them than any contract: they felt Walt knew the quality of their work and rewarded them accordingly. In fact, his praise was valued over money. Conversely, Walt felt an obligation to take care of his employees, especially the animators, whom he referred to as "my boys."

The drawback to this paternalistic and benevolent regime was its utterly arbitrary nature: Walt's favor was the sole criterion for promotions, raises and bonuses.

Most of the men seem to have been content with the arrangement as long as they felt they maintained that personal relationship with Walt—which became increasingly difficult as the studio expanded. Obviously Disney could not remain close to more than a thousand employees.

Efforts had been made to organize the Disney artists during the mid-1930s by representatives from the IATSE (the International Alliance of Theatrical and Stage Employees), which was dominated by organized crime at the time. The result was the formation of the Federation, a rather inactive company union. But by 1941, an increasing number of animators at other studios had joined the Screen Cartoonists' Guild, affiliated with the AF of L Painters and Paperhangers Union. The Guild's representative was the colorful and controversial Herb Sorrell, who set out to organize the Disney studio and quickly came into conflict with Walt and Roy.

Tensions rose, exacerbated by the studio's precarious financial situation. In February, Walt made a speech in which he outlined the fiscal problems, gave a pep talk and concluded by saying the company recognized the right of the workers to unionize. In May, a number of employees were laid off, including many of the union activists, which resulted in a strike led by the Screen Cartoonists' Guild. Walt was amazed to find a picket line in front of the studio when he arrived on May 29, 1941.

About one-third of the artists joined the strike. While many of them held lower-paid jobs, Art Babbitt and Bill Tytla also went out. "People like Art and Bill had everything to lose and nothing to gain by going out on strike," said Bill Melendez, who joined the strike, although he had initially opposed it. "They weren't underpaid, but they felt honor-bound to try to do something for the lower echelons."

The division between the strikers and the artists who stayed on the job grew increasingly bitter. (Some animators still hold grudges about the strike nearly fifty years later.) A nonstriker reportedly poured a circle of gasoline around a group of picketers and threatened to drop a lighted cigarette on it. One day when Walt drove by in his open car, Art Babbitt grabbed a bullhorn and shouted: "Walt Disney, you ought to be ashamed of yourself!" Disney stopped the car, took off his coat and started to come at Babbitt, but thought better of it. The two men had never gotten along well, and they never spoke again.

Ironically, "The Reluctant Dragon" was released on June 20, 1941, shortly after the strike began. This combination live-action/animation feature showed Robert Benchley going through the Disney studio, where films were made by one big, happy family. It was also at this time that Nelson Rockefeller, the government's Coordinator of Inter-American Affairs, asked Walt to go on a filmmaking and goodwill tour of South America. Walt reluctantly agreed to go, and the strike was finally settled in his absence.

Disney grew increasingly conservative in his political views after the strike, which he damned in print as "Communistically inspired and led." He subsequently appeared before the House Committee on Un-American Activities and denounced Sorrell and layout artist Dave Hilberman.

Walt also fired Art Babbitt for his union activities, in violation of the Wagner Labor Relations Act. A series of trials through the Labor Boards ensued, which Babbitt won. Babbitt was reinstated and worked on the "Bongo" sequence of "Fun and Fancy Free," before leaving the studio for good. Despite the importance of his work, all mention of his name was omitted from studio histories for the next forty years.

Some artists who had friends on both sides quit animation rather than be caught in the middle. Walt Kelly, Virgil "VIP" Partch and Sam Cobean ultimately went on to successful careers as print cartoonists. The greatest loss to Disney—and animation—was Bill Tytla, who had tried to act as peacemaker and failed. Although Walt took him back, Tytla was unhappy in the changed atmosphere of the studio, and left in 1943. While he lived another twenty-five years, none of his later work approached the brilliance of his achievements at Disney.

"For a long time, we harbored bad feelings about the guys who went through our lines," said Melendez, "and they never forgave us for destroying the spirit of the studio. We hadn't destroyed it—the spirit of the studio went when we moved to Burbank. What I think the strike really taught the guys who went out was that there was an outside. There was Warners and MGM and Screen Gems, and they weren't bad studios; the kids that stayed at Disney never learned that. I have my own studio—which I'd never have if I stayed there."

Three of the artists who had been involved in the strike, Dave Hilberman, Zachary Schwartz and Steve Bosustow, later founded UPA (where they were joined by Babbitt, Hurtz, John Hubley et al.), the first studio to break with the Disney style.

In many ways, the many small studios that were formed after the war were the ultimate legacy of the Disney strike. But the strike also marked the end of a program of unprecedented and unmatched growth and experimentation that irrevocably transformed the medium of animation and the public perception of it.

Woolie Reitherman summarized his fellow animators' feelings when he said: "There has never been anything like the Disney studio during that era, and there never will be again."

A cel and background from "Popeye the Sailor Meets Sinbad the Sailor" (1936), the first of the Fleischers' two-reel color Popeye featurettes.

THE
STUDIO CARTOON,
1929–1941

*We didn't know where we were going, but we sure knew we were
doing something that hadn't been done before; that was true at
Disney, and it was true at our place.* —CHUCK JONES

While Disney and his artists were perfecting the art of animation, pursuing greater realism and beauty, animators, writers, designers and directors at other studios were transforming the old silent short into the Hollywood cartoon, a unique American contribution to film comedy.

Much of the inspiration for these films came from Disney, especially from his development of character animation, and the success of Mickey Mouse and the Disney films led the major studios to establish either an in-house studio or a distribution deal with an independent producer. Whenever a Disney cartoon premiered, animators from other studios rushed to the theater to study it. ("Of course we stole from Disney then," comments veteran Warners director Chuck Jones. "*Everybody* stole from Disney then.") But as the animators learned and/or borrowed, they made what they took their own. They began to push the principles the Disney artists discovered further—and in different directions.

They found that distortions and exaggerations too extreme for the lifelike Silly Symphonies could get laughs in brasher comedies with freer animation. This skill at comedy did not develop overnight. Many early-thirties cartoons simply aren't very good, although some hard-core fans delight in their rubbery charms. These meandering comic adventures, inane musicals and raucous slapstick farces reveal the uncertainty of their creators. The animators and directors were still learn-

ing how to time and stage a gag; how to pace a six-minute film; how to make a rambunctious character funny but not obnoxious. By the end of the decade, the studio cartoon had become something new and wonderful and funny.

For many years, the studio least affected by Disney's innovations was the Fleischer studio, which also became its most serious rival. The Disney artists strove to break away from the loose rubber hose animation of the silent shorts. Their emphasis on fine drawing and the careful observation of anatomy and motion pushed the medium toward greater realism. The Fleischer animators took rubber hose animation to its logical conclusion: a loose-limbed, exuberant, metamorphic style, as fluid as a blob of mercury on a glass plate.

"The Fleischer staff really did not believe that there were any principles or any specific point of view that one should adopt for any project," explains Shamus Culhane, who worked at both Disney and Fleischers during the 1930s. "Whether it was a scene or a script, it was all done ad lib, without examination to see if there was a consistent structure. They pooh-poohed these ideas when the West Coast people came to work on the features and tried to apply them to the Fleischer material."

Although the Fleischers had been making Song Car-Tunes that combined sound and animation since 1924, they did not make the transition to sound films smoothly. Their first efforts were the Screen Songs, beginning with "The Sidewalks of

New York'' (1929). The Screen Songs were essentially synch sound versions of the Song Car-Tunes, complete with Bouncing Ball. Most of the earliest ones used old standards like ''Dixie'' and ''Goodbye, My Lady Love.''

The series ran through 1939, and many of the later Screen Songs became vehicles for popular entertainers, including Rudy Vallee, Ethel Merman, the Boswell Sisters, Irene Bordoni, Louis Armstrong, Baby Rose Marie and the Mills Brothers. Most of these films are disappointingly static. Stolid live-action footage destroys whatever momentum the animated inserts build.

In June 1929, the imminent debut of the Paramount Talkartoons was announced. The series opened in October with ''Noah's Lark'' (1929), followed by ''Accordion Joe'' (1929) and ''Marriage Wows'' (1930). The animators don't seem to have been quite sure what they were doing, as these first films rely heavily on repeated cycles of drawings, and look a lot like Paul Terry's cartoons.

Ko-Ko, whose popularity waned after the debut of Mickey Mouse, was temporarily retired. A new cartoon star was sought, one that had no associations with silent shorts. The artists came up with Bimbo, an anthropomorphized dog. Like most cartoon characters of this period, he bore more than a passing resemblance to Mickey Mouse. With a casualness typical of the Fleischer films, Bimbo was sometimes drawn as a white character with a black outline (which made him look like a modified version of Ko-Ko's old companion, Fitz), sometimes as solid black. His final design was a compromise: black with a white face and stomach, which only emphasized the resemblance to Mickey.

The Fleischer animators began to hit their stride with ''Hot Dog'' (1930), in which Bimbo's reckless driving in pursuit of a pretty girl lands him in court. He wins his freedom with an upbeat vocal performance that sets the courtroom dancing.

One of their very best early films is ''Swing, You Sinners'' (1930), set to the popular song. As Bimbo walks through a graveyard, the stone wall closes over the gate, locks itself, grows a mouth and swallows the key. Gravestones elongate into ghostly shapes and accuse Bimbo of stealing chickens and shooting dice; terrified, he cringes and whines his repentance. When he takes refuge in a barn, a feed sack grows a face and stubby limbs to perform another chorus of the song. By the end of the film, everything in the frame is writhing and bouncing in time to the music.

While ''Swing, You Sinners'' was in production, several of the studio's leading artists left for the West Coast. The assistants, including Shamus Culhane, Al Eugster and Rudy Zamora, suddenly found themselves promoted to animator, under the supervision of Ted Sears and Grim Natwick.

The Fleischers' most famous character had made an unimpressive debut a few months earlier in ''Dizzie Dishes'' (1930). While Bimbo, as an inept waiter, stumbles around a night-

A publicity drawing for the Fleischer cartoons from the early 1930s features Ko-Ko, Betty Boop and Bimbo.

club, an early version of Betty Boop performs a song. In numerous interviews, Natwick has recounted how he created the character by adding a pair of pretty girl's legs to a cute little dog, and how her spit curls were inspired by the hairdo of the popular singer Helen Kane. As Natwick concedes, the original Betty was ugly, even grotesque. He continued to work on the design, turning her floppy ears into long earrings; Betty became completely human and much more attractive.

The artists developed Betty into a dumb but endearing character, capable of delivering lines like ''I guess the people who moved out don't live here anymore.'' She was the archetypical flapper, the speakeasy Girl Scout with a heart of gold—already something of an anachronism in 1930. Despite the advent of the Great Depression, the Betty Boop cartoons remained rooted in the Jazz Age.

In many ways, Betty was the first truly feminine animated character. Up to this point, cartoon females had essentially been males with long eyelashes, high-heeled shoes and a few dainty gestures. Ms. Boop had a decidedly female shape and, more importantly, a convincing feminine grace to her movements.

Betty's femininity was reflected in her considerable sex appeal. In "Is My Palm Red?" (1933), Bimbo sneaks around to peek at her silhouette as the light shines through her skirt. A frightened Betty jumps out of her clothes, revealing frilly undies, in "The Old Man of the Mountain" (1933), and she does a hula in "Betty Boop's Bamboo Isle" (1932), wearing only a lei and a grass skirt.

Although Betty became a human character, Bimbo remained a dog, which gave a curious tone to their relationship. But Betty's appeal transcends biological limits. She attracts everyone and everything, including an amorous devil in "Red Hot Mama" (1934). When she gives him the cold shoulder, hell literally freezes over.

Despite numerous trials, the slightly tattered flag of her virtue always waves at the end. A lecherous ringmaster paws her, asking, "Wanna keep your job?" in "Boop-Oop-A-Doop" (1932); when Koko rescues her, she assures him, "He couldn't take my boop-oop-a-doop away!"

Several actresses provided Betty's high-pitched giggle in the first cartoons, including Little Ann Little, Margie Heinz, Kate Wright and Bonnie Poe. Mae Questel, an accomplished mimic, took the role in 1931 for "Betty Co-Ed" and did the voice for all the cartoons through the end of the series in 1939.

The popularity of the character led to a spate of merchandise. Betty Boop dolls, soap, candy, scarfs, tea sets, tablets, flipbooks, etc., soon appeared in stores. A daily comic strip ran in 1934–35 and a Sunday panel continued through 1937. There was even a Betty Boop and Bimbo Club, although it failed to achieve the success of Disney's Mickey Mouse Club.

Betty's renown displeased Helen Kane, the singer who had unknowingly provided a model for the character. In 1934, she filed a $250,000 suit against the Fleischers and Paramount, charging that they usurped her singing style with Betty Boop, thereby limiting her earning power. The testimony in this curious trial seems to have centered on who had coined the phrase "boop-oop-a-doop."

"It just happened that she was popular with that boop-boop-ba-doop before us," Dave Fleischer recalled. "But it was a song. And anybody could use the song if he got permission, and we did that. But we called the character Betty Boop, and that was not a boop-boop-ba-doop. In the courtroom that's all you heard, we were all talking boops and boop-boop-ba-doops and boopety-boop-boops, and we'd say, 'It's not a boop, it's a boopety-boop . . .' And it was pretty funny."

The Fleischers won the case by proving that a black entertainer named Baby Esther had used "boop-oop-a-doop" before either Helen Kane or Betty Boop. But as Leslie Cabarga points out, Ms. Kane's claim that Betty was "a deliberate caricature of me" was true.

Voice actress Mae Questel and producer Max Fleischer pose with cutouts of Betty and Bimbo. Ms. Questel became the voice of Betty in 1931; fifty-seven years later, she reprised the role for the Touchstone/Amblin hit "Who Framed Roger Rabbit."

Opposite: Betty Boop in her later phase, 1936 (with Pudgy). She wears a modestly cut dress and no garter in this drawing from "More Pep."

Two of the most memorable Betty shorts are set to songs by Cab Calloway. In "Minnie the Moocher" (1932), Betty runs away from home after a fight with her parents, who insist that she eat some noxious porridge. (When a potted flower coaxes her by tasting a spoonful, it loses all its petals and withers.) She and Bimbo enter an eerie haunted cavern where a ghost-walrus, rotoscoped from Calloway, performs the title tune. The frightened pair flee, pursued by a gaggle of weird specters. One ghost tears off chunks of itself that become identical ghosts. When they reach home, Bimbo hides in the doghouse and Betty cowers in her bed. Dave Fleischer said that when Calloway saw the finished film, he "laughed so much that he fell right down on the floor of the projection room and kicked his feet in the air."

"Snow White" (1933), which uses only the barest bones of the original fairy tale, is even stranger than "Minnie the Moocher." The Magic Mirror tells the long-nosed Queen: "You're the fairest in the land"—until Betty arrives to see "my stepmama, the Queen." When the Mirror proclaims Betty the fairest and kisses her, the enraged Queen orders her beheaded. But Bimbo and Ko-Ko, the Queen's guards, haven't the heart to carry out the sentence and they contrive her escape. After rolling down a hill in a huge snowball, Betty ends up frozen in a coffinlike block of ice. The Seven Dwarfs carry her into the Mystery Cave, followed by Ko-Ko and Bimbo.

Inside the cavern, the Queen, having transformed herself into a witch, passes the Magic Mirror over Ko-Ko. He turns into a long-limbed, rubbery ghost and performs "The St. James Infirmary Blues." The metamorphoses he undergoes illustrating the words to the song are pure animation, with only the most tenuous ties to reality—despite the fact that many of the movements were rotoscoped from Calloway. The backgrounds, delicate ink-wash paintings of skeletons clutching cards, dice and whiskey bottles, emphasize the spooky atmosphere. After further improbable adventures, the Queen turns into a dragon and pursues the trio; Bimbo defeats her by yanking her tongue—which turns her completely inside out. The film ends with Betty, Ko-Ko and Bimbo dancing happily in the snow.

"Snow White" is a bizarre film, but an enormously entertaining one that provides a textbook example of the Fleischer studio's unique, utterly animated style. Every element in the frame moves—even normally inanimate things, like the ici-cles that sing a greeting to Betty. Objects grow and shed limbs as needed; shapes casually metamorphose.

This uninhibited approach to animation gives the Fleischer films a rambunctious vitality rarely found in the technically superior Silly Symphonies. Much of the charm of the Betty Boop cartoons derives from the combination of naïve drawing and absurd dialogue. When Betty comes across Bimbo, her long-lost husband, in "The Bum Bandit" (1931), she demands: "What happened to you the night you went out to get milk? Didn't you find that cow yet?" In the Disney shorts, all the visual elements are used to advance the story; in Fleischer cartoons like "Snow White," the story is reduced to a vehicle for the animated business.

Unhappily, Betty fell victim to the smarmy Production Code of the mid-1930s, said to have been adopted in response to the success of Mae West, another sexy Paramount star. A collar, sleeves and a demurely lowered hemline were added to Betty's short, strapless dress; the garter vanished from her left leg. The irresistible flapper became a respectable bachelorette/hausfrau. The lecherous admirers and goggle-eyed specters were replaced by the overly cute little dog, Pudgy, and the gadget-happy Grampy. Cabarga suggests that Grampy reflected the Fleischers' own interest in inventions and tinkering; he was certainly more interesting than most of the new co-stars.

Attempts were made at pairing Betty with various characters from newspaper strips, like Carl Anderson's Henry and Otto Soglow's Little King. None of them worked well enough to warrant a second film. By the time the series ended in 1939, nothing remained of Betty's original risqué élan. Since the early 1980s, Ms. Boop has enjoyed an enormous resurgence in popularity, but the vision of the character is derived from her earlier, frisky phase, rather than the later, domestic one.

One comic strip character who made his debut in a Betty Boop film became the star of his own cartoon series. Popeye made his first appearance on the screen in 1933, when he joined Betty for a hula in "Popeye the Sailor." With the benefit of hindsight, it's easy to see that Elzie Segar's popular comic strip "Thimble Theatre" was an obvious property for animation. It featured a memorable array of odd, appealing characters—not only Popeye and Olive Oyl, but Eugene the Jeep, the Sea Hag and Alice the Goon—whose designs offered the potential for interesting movements.

Popeye's raspy growl was initially provided by William Costello, known as "Red Pepper Sam" on the radio. But Costello quickly grew infatuated with his own success, became difficult to work with and was fired. His replacement was Jack Mercer, an in-betweener in the studio. Although initially reluctant to take the part, Mercer supplied the voice for the next thirty years, except for a few films made during the war, when Mae Questel substituted for him.

Baritone Gus Wickie did the voice of Bluto. Although

Brutus had appeared briefly in the strip in 1932, Bluto was created for the animated series. The Fleischers asked Segar to provide a villain who could serve as a rival for Olive's affection. Segar's assistant, Bud Sagendorf (who took over the strip in 1938), researched all of Popeye's tough-guy enemies from previous adventures. Segar then devised a composite heavy— Bluto, the guy audiences love to hate. Sagendorf later used the character in the newspapers, but called him Brutus.

Mae Questel supplied Olive's nasal bawl. "If you listen to that voice, you'll hear a little of ZaSu Pitts," she explains. "When Max showed me a storyboard of Olive Oyl and I looked at this scrawny creature, I could think of only one woman who would sound like that [she slips into the voice and begins wringing her hands]: Oh dearrrr . . ."

Although an occasional film might focus on Swee'pea, Poopdeck Pappy or Eugene the Jeep, the great majority of the Popeye cartoons had one basic plot: Bluto lures or abducts Olive; Popeye eats some spinach, thrashes Bluto and rescues her. But within that limited story structure, the artists and writers managed to find enough variations to keep the audience entertained. It was never clear just what the two men saw in their skinny, often capricious inamorata: their devotion to her has to be taken as a given.

One of the most popular Popeye films is "A Dream Walking" (1934). Olive awakens Popeye and Bluto when she goes sleepwalking off the flagpole outside her bedroom window. As the two fight over who is going to rescue her, she blithely strolls along a series of precariously balanced girders at a construction site. (This sequence provides an interesting contrast with a similar one of Goofy in Disney's "Clock Cleaners.") After defeating Bluto, Popeye maneuvers Olive back to her bed. When she wakes up and sees the sailor at her window, she accuses him of being a Peeping Tom and hurls the alarm clock, a vase, picture frames, etc., at him. "I saw my duty and I done it! 'cause I'm Popeye the Sailor Man," he says, sighing.

In "Morning, Noon and Nightclub" (1937), Popeye and Olive perform à la Fred Astaire and Ginger Rogers in Wimpy's cabaret. When Olive rejects Bluto's advances, he sets out to ruin their act. Popeye ultimately defeats Bluto through a very funny series of exaggerated apache dances in which all the characters get tossed around like rag dolls.

A telegram from "The Popeye Fan Club" admonishing the characters to "act more refined" interrupts the opening brawl of "It's the Natural Thing to Do" (1939); the wire concludes: "P.S. Now go on with the picture." Popeye, Olive and Bluto dress up in their best and try terribly hard to be genteel at a tea party. Their clumsy attempts at "elegant" gestures quickly degenerate into slapstick mishaps which lead to a free-for-all. Amid the chaos that ends the film, Olive delightedly proclaims that their usual rowdiness is "the natural thing to do," and she's right.

The animation in the Popeye films is more solid and less

Above: An animation drawing of Popeye and Olive Oyl from the mid-1930s. Opposite: Bluto and Popeye bluster at each other before getting down to fisticuffs, in "Popeye the Sailor Meets Sinbad the Sailor" (1936).

plastic than that in the Betty shorts, although Olive's limbs often seem as rubbery as anything in "Minnie the Moocher." (Chuck Jones remarks that anyone who made love to Olive would have a hard time getting untangled.) Quirks in the designs of the characters, such as Popeye's prognathous jaw and outsized forearms, did not lend themselves to realistic animation. The artists continued to fill the screen with motion. When Bluto/Sinbad sings his opening song in "Popeye the Sailor Meets Sinbad the Sailor" (1936), an assortment of wonderfully bizarre monsters appear from every corner of the frame to join in the chorus.

At the Disney studio, the sound track of each film was recorded first, to ensure that the animation would match the dialogue and the music perfectly. Most of the Fleischer cartoons were done "post-synch": the animators drew the mouth movements to an approximate rhythm and the voice actors would watch the film and try to match the lines to the completed animation.

"The sound effects man, all the musicians and the performers would be in the studio," says Ms. Questel. "We would rehearse for three or four days with a bouncing ball on the left-hand side of the screen, which we used to time the script. Very little was written, and the ad-libs were fantastic! The minute Betty Boop would turn her shoulder, we'd ad-lib something; same thing with Popeye and Olive. I would say it took at least a week between the rehearsals and the recording session to do each cartoon."

The obviously improvised comments lend spontaneity and

charm to many of these films. The audience has to listen carefully to catch the asides Mercer constantly mumbles under his breath. When Popeye rubs vanishing cream onto his wrists in "Popeye Meets Ali Baba and His Forty Thieves," he mutters: "There's a farewell to arms." As Olive Oyl, Ms. Questel keeps up a steady litany of "Oh, dear; oh, my; oh, mercy," etc.

The Popeye cartoons proved so successful that by 1938 some polls showed the Sailor Man had become more popular than Mickey Mouse. The Fleischers decided to break with the pattern of black-and-white shorts and put the characters in three two-reel color featurettes: "Popeye the Sailor Meets Sinbad the Sailor" (1936), "Popeye Meets Ali Baba and His Forty Thieves" (1937) and "Aladdin and His Wonderful Lamp" (1939). Like "Snow White," these films use only scattered bits of the original stories, but are highly entertaining.

In "Sinbad," the title character (Bluto with a few changes in his attire) catches sight of Popeye's ship through his spyglass and is instantly smitten with Olive. He instructs his pet Roc to sink the ship, "but bring the woman to me!" The destruction of the ship is nicely animated, and includes some effective use of the monstrous bird's shadow on the waves. Of course, Popeye manages to save himself (and Wimpy) and soon settles Bluto's hash. The rather freewheeling "Ali Baba," which spoofs desert epics, is even more fun. After eating the mandatory can of spinach, Popeye alters the famous command to "Open sez me!" and the door to the treasure cavern obeys. Both films scored big hits. "Aladdin," which uses the gimmick of Olive writing a script for herself and Popeye, is the least imaginative adventure of the trilogy.

All three films provided a showcase for a special camera setup Max designed that used miniature sets mounted on a turntable in place of drawn backgrounds. This 3-D effect had also been featured in some of the black-and-white shorts, like Popeye's "For Better or Worser" (1935) and "Housecleaning Blues" (1937) with Betty Boop.

The tridimensional camera proved to be an interesting but ultimately unsuccessful experiment. Because the miniature sets turned, the animators had trouble calculating the relative positions of objects from frame to frame. Although no figures are available, the process involved a great deal of extra work and must have been expensive to use. The system provides a striking illusion of depth in the cavern of treasure in "Ali Baba," but the discontinuity between the two-dimensional characters and the three-dimensional environment is visually jarring. Fleischer's invention was eclipsed by Disney's multiplane camera, which suggested the third dimension in animation more satisfactorily.

The Fleischers' best and most successful works were also their most original ones. Yet they came under increasing pressure to emulate Disney, which ultimately proved disastrous. In 1934, they began a series of Color Classics, obviously

modeled after the Silly Symphonies. The first installment was "Poor Cinderella," with Betty Boop in the title role. Because Disney still had exclusive use of three-strip Technicolor, the film was made in the two-strip Cinecolor process. The results are decidedly odd: Betty's normally black curls come out the color of a pumpkin pie.

Even the Technicolor Fleischer films, like the Popeye two-reelers, have a strange, rather acid palette that is less effective than the subtle interplay of grays in their other cartoons. The gritty, urban charm of the Popeye and Betty series seems better suited to black and white than to the lush pastels of the Silly Symphonies.

The Fleischer artists couldn't duplicate the Disney films. The animators lacked the training needed for the realistic drawing and subtle depiction of emotions. The writers and directors had never dealt with such carefully structured and affecting stories. (Although Dave Fleischer is listed as the director of all the shorts, Shamus Culhane has pointed out the impossibility of one man directing more than thirty-six films each year.) The antics of Betty and Popeye may be enjoyable, but they don't involve the viewer's feelings the way many of the Silly Symphonies do. In an effort to "do Disney," the men turned their backs on the qualities that gave their own work its appeal.

Attempts at being cute, like "The Little Dutch Mill" (1934), "The Song of the Birds" (1934) or "Somewhere in Dreamland" (1936), appear cloying and saccharine. The "humorous" entries in the series, like "Ants in the Plants" (1940), are painfully unfunny. Not content to leave well enough alone, the Fleischers later gave Popeye four nephews. Peepeye, Pipeye, Poopeye and Pupeye were miniature clones of their uncle who displayed even less individuality than Donald Duck's nephews, on whom they were obviously modeled.

The unexpected success of Disney's "Snow White and the Seven Dwarfs" led Paramount to pressure the Fleischers to make an animated feature. Although they had produced two long educational films during the 1920s, there is no evidence that Max and Dave had any interest in undertaking such an enormous project. They certainly hadn't prepared for it, and their staff had to be increased more than threefold (from around two hundred to seven hundred). Rather than try to rent additional office space in Manhattan, Max decided to move the studio to Florida.

According to accounts in the popular press, Max had a vacation home in Miami and liked the city. The warm climate would allow the artists to wear loose, comfortable clothes, "so their imaginations can work." Aside from the high rents in New York, the fact that Florida was offering substantial tax breaks to studios in an effort to attract film production undoubtedly counted for more than the animators' attire.

Florida also had a reputation as an anti-union state. Efforts had been made to unionize the Fleischer studio since 1935; the

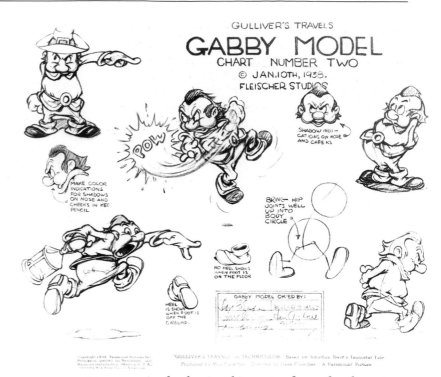

movement to organize had gained impetus from the departure of Dan Glass, a promising and well-liked in-betweener. Many of his co-workers felt that the wretched living conditions resulting from a salary of $12 a week (comparable to what other animation studios paid) had caused him to contract pulmonary tuberculosis, which proved fatal.

A strike in the spring and summer of 1937 had been fought with a bitterness equaled only by the Disney strike of 1941. When Max and Paramount tried to ignore the picketers, who chanted: "We're Popeye the union man," they organized noisy protests in theaters and succeeded in having Fleischer films banned from more than five hundred movie houses. As Max had pleaded poverty during the negotiations over salary increases, the announcement of plans to build an air-conditioned, 32,000-square-foot plant in Florida at a cost of $300,000 came as a rude surprise to the union members.

After receiving the commission from Paramount to make a feature, the Fleischers are said to have spent six months considering material. Jonathan Swift's *Gulliver's Travels* was not an inspired choice. "Snow White and the Seven Dwarfs" was based on a well-loved, brief fairy tale that offered romance, a sympathetic heroine and supporting characters with comic possibilities. *Gulliver* was a sophisticated, episodic satire that most Americans had read in English classes, if they had read it at all.

If the six-month figure is correct, "Gulliver" was produced in a little more than a year and a half (it opened on December 22, 1939). Disney had spent almost four years on "Snow White," preparing the animators, developing the characters and refining the story. More importantly, Walt and his crew had hammered out a solidly constructed story with compelling scenes that gave the animators a chance to stretch their medium.

Opposite: A model sheet of Gabby from "Gulliver's Travels" (1939). Many critics felt the broadly comic Town Crier of Lilliput stole the show from the more realistic main characters. Right: Producer Max Fleischer "at work" on "Gulliver's Travels" in 1939. In this obviously posed publicity still, Max is "drawing" with a pencil on a slick acetate cel. Below: Gulliver arises and frees himself in a cel setup from "Gulliver's Travels."

The Fleischers managed to hire back some of their former animators who had gone to work for Disney, including Grim Natwick, Shamus Culhane and Al Eugster. But Miami was far from the centers of the animation industry, Hollywood and New York. Max was forced to establish training programs in an effort to turn local art school students and graduates into painters, inkers and even assistant animators.

"I felt awful when I saw how my work in 'Gulliver' had been mangled by half-assed inking and bad in-betweening," states Culhane. "If I hadn't signed a contract, I would have left on the spot."

Dave Fleischer, who was better at thinking up gags than at creating a sustained narrative, insisted on a lighter, "more Gilbert and Sullivan" approach to the story. Swift's gigantic Brobdingnagians, civilized Houyhnhnms and brutish Yahoos were replaced with slapstick gags and cute characters.

The hostilities between Lilliput and Blefuscu over which end of a boiled egg should be cracked, Swift's mordant parody of the causes of war and the conflict between the churches, was reduced to a quarrel over the "rival" national anthems, "Faithful" and "Forever." (The resolution of singing them together as "Forever Faithful" was pathetically obvious.) A romance between Prince David, the son of King Little, and Princess Glory, the daughter of the enemy King Bombo, was added, in a bland and blatant imitation of Snow White and Prince Charming. Much of the focus of the story was shifted to Gabby, the Town Crier of Lilliput, and King Bombo's comic spies, Sneak, Snoop and Snitch.

The character of Gulliver was heavily rotoscoped, as were Prince David and Princess Glory. Cal Howard, one of the writers, served as the model for David. "I had legs like a

Prince David and Princess Glory in a tender moment from "Gulliver's Travels."

An original cel and background from "Raggedy Ann and Raggedy Andy" (1941). The film failed to generate enough interest to initiate a series, despite the popularity of Johnny Gruelle's doll characters.

chicken," he growls. "They had to put two inches of padding on my thighs." The other characters were animated in a looser style more typical of the Fleischer cartoons. The contrasts of the stolidly realistic Gulliver, the somewhat realistic lovers and the broad comic characters are never resolved in the film.

"Gulliver's Travels" has some genuinely entertaining sequences: the binding of Gulliver with a vast array of miniature cranes, hoists and carts; the upbeat dance by King Little with two of Gulliver's fingers as his partner. The funny business for Gabby and the Sneak-Snoop-Snitch trio works nicely, probably because their actions are so close to the antics of Popeye and Betty. But these high points are balanced against the seemingly endless rantings of the two kings, the vapid wooing of the ingenues, the pedestrian songs, the uneven pacing and the general lack of inspiration.

As the production neared completion, Dave Fleischer boasted in interviews that " 'Gulliver's Travels' contains no horror stuff—no evil spirits or creatures to scare the youngsters. We've profited by past screen fantasies which many parents refused to permit their children to see for fear they'd be scared to death"—a thinly veiled jab at the scarier scenes of the Wicked Witch in "Snow White" that had alarmed some parents. One of the greatest weaknesses in the "Gulliver" script is the absence of real heroes and villains and, hence, of any substantial dramatic conflict.

The film opened to mixed, but generally favorable reviews. Although it did good business in the United States, the outbreak of the war in Europe cut off that lucrative market. "Gulliver" failed to become the blockbuster Paramount had hoped for. The comparisons to "Snow White" were inevitable, and inevitably unflattering.

After the release of "Gulliver," the Fleischer brothers were faced with the problem of keeping the newly expanded staff occupied. They needed something to replace the Betty Boop series, which had ended in 1939, and the Color Classics, which finally limped to a halt the next year. During 1940–41, they created three new cartoon series, none of which proved particularly successful.

The Stone Age Cartoons were essentially collections of gags with no recurring characters. They leaned heavily on puns, as titles like "Way Back When a Night Club Was a Stick" (1940) and "Way Back When a Razzberry Was a Fruit" (1940) suggest. As various observers have pointed out, their use of "prehistoric" versions of modern appliances anticipated Hanna-Barbera's Flintstones by two decades.

The Fleischers made Gabby, the town crier from "Gulliver," the star of his own series, which lasted less than a year. Similarly, Sneak, Snoop and Snitch were given a series with Twinkletoes, King Bombo's cockeyed messenger pigeon; it also lasted less than a year. These characters had derived much of their appeal from the situations in "Gulliver": their personalities weren't strong enough to sustain an audience's interest.

A two-reel "comic" featurette based loosely (*very* loosely) on Edgar Allan Poe's poem "The Raven" (1942) did not generate much interest; nor did a featurette using Johnny Gruelle's Raggedy Ann and Raggedy Andy dolls in 1941. The latter film might have made an interesting feature if the story had been properly developed. But "Raggedy Ann and Raggedy Andy" goes by too fast for the personalities of the characters to emerge or for the story to generate much momentum.

Dave Fleischer insisted that he had been reluctant to embark on their next series:

> I didn't want to make Superman. Paramount wanted it. They called me over and asked why I didn't want to make it. I told them because it was too expensive, they wouldn't make any money back on it. The average short cost nine or ten thousand dollars, some ran up to fifteen: they varied. I couldn't figure how to make Superman look right without spending a lot of money. I told them they'd have to spend $90,000 on each one. . . . They spent the $90,000. But [the films] were great.

The Superman cartoons *were* great. Some of the best animation the studio ever produced brought the dramatically staged actions of the popular comic books to life. The character designs preserved the look Jerry Siegal and Joel Schuster had originated in Action Comics in 1938. From its premiere in September 1941, the Superman series was a hit. The films introduced the phrases "Look! Up in the sky! It's a bird! It's a plane! It's Superman!" and "Faster than a speeding bullet, more powerful than a locomotive, able to leap tall buildings in a single bound."

A poster announcing the debut of the Fleischers' "Superman" series, c. 1941.

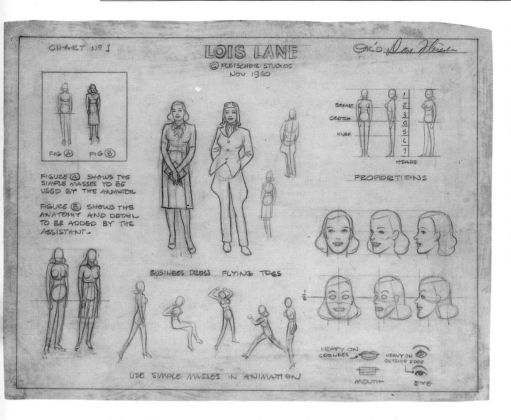

A model sheet of Lois Lane from 1940 suggests the sophisticated drawing in the Fleischers' "Superman" series.

Lois Lane emerges as a spunky newswoman, reminiscent of Rosalind Russell in "His Girl Friday." Her eagerness to get the story for *The Daily Planet* invariably lands her in perilous situations from which only Superman can extricate her. Fortunately, he's always on hand, just as Clark Kent always manages to miss all the excitement. In "The Mechanical Monsters," Lois hides inside one of the giant robots that loot a jewelry exhibit. Superman follows them back to the mad scientist's lair, where he single-handedly destroys an entire robot army. Lois is nearly caught when she stops to rescue a child from the escaped gorilla that wreaks havoc on the big top in "Terror on the Midway" (1942). Superman arrives just in time to subdue the monster primate and rescue her.

The Superman cartoons look like the lavishly budgeted films they were. The animators were able to pencil-test much of their work, a luxury that had never been permitted on the Betty Boop shorts. The figures—some rotoscoped, some drawn freehand—are carefully shaded to suggest three-dimensional forms.

The backgrounds are often elaborately rendered: "Terror on the Midway" evokes the look of circus poster art. Unusual camera angles and movements—which often forced the artists to draw the characters in exaggerated perspective—heighten the sense of drama. The stylized artwork and sophisticated use of the camera give many of the Superman shorts the brooding atmosphere of live-action *film noir*. Unlike "Gulliver's Travels," these cartoons do contain "horror stuff." Children were undoubtedly frightened by the giant ape in "Terror on the Midway," the guardian mummies that come to life in "The Mummy Strikes" (1943) and the winged men who try to dip Lois in a vat of boiling wax in "The Underground World" (1943).

While these shorts were in production, the Fleischers focused much of their attention on the creation of a second feature. Dave Fleischer said he got the idea for the film from Maeterlinck's *The Life of the Bee*. As the rights were not available, he devised an original story involving insects. The plot of the finished picture owes more to Frank Capra than Maurice Maeterlinck, yet Fleischer complained that Paramount insisted on calling it "Mr. Bug Goes to Town," to play off the success of Capra's "Mr. Deeds Goes to Town."

"Mr. Bug" opens with a long panning shot over an enormous three-dimensional model of New York City. The model received considerable attention in the press, as it had taken four months to build and included 16,000 tiny panes of glass. The results justified the effort: the opening shot is so impressive that the viewer wants to brush the credits out of the way, to get an unimpeded view.

The basic premise of animated insects trying to avoid the destruction wrought by the careless rotoscoped "human ones" is clever, but suffers from weak execution. The minute the endearingly clumsy, Jimmy Stewart-esque Hoppity ("Golly, weeds!") appears, the audience knows he'll defeat the nasty C. Bagley Beetle, marry Honey Bee and make everything turn out okay. There are also problems with the time scale, and concurrent events take place both too quickly and too slowly.

The designs of the characters are awkward mixtures of human and insect. There are strangely human feet on the ends of Mr. Beetle's skinny legs, which are stuck onto an insect abdomen. Honey has an outsized head with huge eyes and no nose, a small body with an impossibly tiny waist, no hips and skinny legs. "You can draw a bug and make it cute as hell—as cute as a bug's ear, in fact," comments Howard, "but I thought those character designs were gruesome. Hoppity has a big, bloated head stuck on a skinny body."

Hoagy Carmichael and Frank Loesser contributed an uneven batch of songs. Four bug performers in a nightclub offer a catchy, upbeat specialty number, "Katy Did, Katy Didn't." But the treacly marching song, "Boy oh boy! We've got fun, we've got freedom, we've got joy!" is far from impressive. (There's also something incongruous about a crowd of bugs singing such elaborate choral arrangements.)

Like "Gulliver," "Mr. Bug" contains some good sequences. After touching a live wire, Hoppity does a wild jitterbug rendered in colored lines on black backgrounds to produce a neon effect. Rotoscoping and freehand animation are very effectively juxtaposed when the insects rush up the girders and boards of the skyscraper that's being constructed on their home lot. But these entertaining moments are separated by long, pedestrian scenes that allow the audience's interest to wander.

The early Fleischer films had a charming innocence that easily won the viewer's affection, an innocence "Mr. Bug" lacks. There's something too obviously calculated about the comic bits involving Mr. Beetle's inept henchmen, Swat the Fly and Smack the Mosquito, just as the romantic scenes between Hoppity and Honey reveal the artists trying too hard to be touching. This self-conscious quality makes the entire picture seem effortful.

It seems unlikely that the film would have been a box office success under the best of circumstances. As it was, Paramount made little effort to promote the film, which was released three days before the bombing of Pearl Harbor. It was re-released as a second feature a few months later under the title "Hoppity Goes to Town."

The failure of "Mr. Bug" marked the end of the Miami studio. The Fleischer brothers were deeply in debt to Paramount for the studio and the features, and a bitter quarrel between Max and Dave prevented them from working together effectively. The Paramount executives fired the two brothers, changed the name to Famous Studios and put studio

manager Sam Buchwald, story man Izzy Sparber and animator Seymour Kneitel (Max's son-in-law) in charge. The studio was moved back to New York and the animators were forced to take a cut in pay. Production continued on the Popeye and Superman series, but the characters lacked their old spark.

Max went to work on training films for the Jam Handy Company of Detroit; Dave moved to the West Coast and found a job at the Columbia studio. Seven years later, Max tried to contest the legality of the takeover and sued Paramount. Matters had grown impossibly tangled, with the ongoing quarrel between the Fleischer brothers adding complications. Paramount won the case.

Despite its ignominious end, the Fleischer studio was one of the most significant in American animation. Their films represented a real alternative to Disney at a time when other animators were trying to imitate his work. As long as the Fleischer artists remained true to their vision of what the medium should be, their work displayed a strength and charm it retains to this day. When they bowed to external pressure and tried to copy Disney, they inevitably fell short. The creation of Ko-Ko, Betty Boop, Popeye and Superman represented an important contribution to American animation and popular culture, a contribution that retains its vitality long after the mistakes and feuds of Max and Dave Fleischer have been forgotten.

Below, a storyboard drawing of Swat the Fly, and, right, a cel setup of Hoppity and Honey Bee's father, Mr. Bumble, from the Fleischers' second feature, "Mr. Bug Goes to Town" (1941).

The staff of the Ub Iwerks studio posed for this group photograph during the mid-1930s. Iwerks himself is in the center.

Ub Iwerks left Walt Disney in early 1930 to start his own studio. Despite their long friendship and mutual respect, the two men apparently disagreed over how animation should be done. Iwerks wanted to continue doing all his own drawings, with assistants just adding details in the cleanups. Disney wanted him to work the way other animators did—making only the key drawings himself and letting assistants fill in the in-betweens.

Iwerks was one of the greatest animators of the rubber hose era, but his loose, weightless and appealing style of animation would have eventually clashed with the increasingly realistic look Disney was developing. It was probably inevitable that he would leave either Disney or animation. He ultimately did both. But in 1930, there was widespread speculation within the animation industry that Ub Iwerks was the "secret genius" who was really responsible for the success of Walt Disney's cartoons.

For his first series, Iwerks chose a character he had created in 1928: Flip the Frog. (His original name was Tony Frog; no one seems to know the reason for the change, although alliter-ative character names were in favor.) In the initial designs, Flip looked like a real frog, with webbed hands and feet. A bow tie and a line of buttons down his front were the sole concessions to cartoon style. Flip didn't talk in the first two shorts, "Fiddlesticks" (1930) and "Puddle Pranks" (1930), made in two-strip Technicolor; he just moved, dancing and performing sight gags to a post-synchronized sound track.

Pat Powers, who had financed the studio, was not happy with the results, and urged Iwerks to redesign the character. The webbed hands and feet were replaced with thick-fingered gloves and chunky shoes. In his new short pants and soft hat, Flip looked like an ugly little human boy with no nose and a big, oddly shaped mouth. More than one observer noted how much he looked like a certain mouse.

The next cartoons were considered more satisfactory, and Powers was able to arrange a distribution deal with MGM—that studio's first venture into animation. Iwerks hired an impressive array of animators from New York and Hollywood, including Grim Natwick, Rudy Zamora, Shamus Culhane and Al Eugster, plus music director Carl Stalling. Powers and MGM undoubtedly hoped that Flip would challenge Mickey Mouse's popularity—not an unreasonable expectation, given the talented staff.

The Flip the Frog cartoons never caught on, probably because they weren't very good. These shorts are weakest in the areas of story and structure, where Disney was strongest. Meandering plots and uniform pacing keep them from building to real climaxes. And while Iwerks devised a lot of visual business for the character, only some of it works as gags. An extremely quiet, self-effacing man, Iwerks had little flair for comedy.

Many of the Flip cartoons have good premises and amusing bits that suggest they could have been developed into better cartoons. Flip builds a robot to take over his chores in "Techno-Cracked" (1933) and the mishaps that result could (and should) be much funnier than they are. At the end of "The Bully" (1932), Flip's opponent literally knocks him out of this world: an effect produced by the clever combination of a live-action globe and an animated frog. Still, the film remains less than the sum of its parts.

"Iwerks was a brilliant animator," explains Chuck Jones, who began his animation career as a cel washer at Iwerks's studio. "He was one of the first—if not *the* first—to give his characters depth and roundness. That title sequence of Flip the Frog playing the piano is probably the first example of

Facial expressions from a model sheet of Flip the Frog. In this later version, Flip has lost all his frog-like features and resembles an unattractive little boy.

really solid animation. But he didn't have any story capacity and I don't think he knew very much about humor; he wasn't a funny man at all."

After thirty-seven films, Iwerks ended the Flip the Frog series in late 1933 and replaced it with Willie Whopper. Like Flip, Willie had to be redesigned after his first few films. He became a chubby, freckled, tousle-headed boy with a little dog as his companion. Each cartoon opens with Willie at the piano asking: "Say, did I ever tell you about this one?" An animated "whopper," a tall tale full of wildly improbable actions, makes up the bulk of each film.

In "Hell's Fire" (1934), Willie discovers the Devil presiding over an inferno inside a volcano. He watches fiends torment a caricature of a prohibitionist and takes part in a lot of furnace gags that recall "Hell's Bells," which Iwerks had animated at Disney's in 1928. Dr. A. King, the dentist, gives Willie too much gas and turns him into a human dirigible in "Stratos Fear" (1933). Willie floats away to a weird planet inhabited by odd, rather sinister scientists and their bizarre creations. The cartoons all end with Willie saying: "Now *you* tell one!"

Although most of the Willie Whopper films were shot in black and white, Iwerks had the cels and backgrounds painted in color, which produced a more interesting range of grays. But even the richest production values cannot disguise the fact that these films are built around a central character with no personality.

Natwick feels that Iwerks failed to grasp how quickly and decisively cartoons were changing during the early 1930s. The Flip the Frog and Willie Whopper films seem like holdovers from the early 1920s. Both feature passive characters who do little more than react to their environments. By 1934, audiences expected a cartoon character to have a recognizable personality. Ironically, Iwerks had helped create Mickey Mouse, the strongest of these new cartoon personalities.

If Iwerks lagged behind other studios aesthetically, he stayed far ahead of them technologically. Everyone who worked with the man describes him as a mechanical genius who was happiest tinkering in his workshop. During the 1930s he devoted more of his time to solving technical problems and less to animating, directing and running his studio. Using parts from an old Chevrolet, Iwerks devised a version of the multiplane camera that predated Disney's. Iwerks's multiplane held the layers of artwork horizontally rather than vertically and was less flexible—it didn't allow the camera to truck through a scene, the way Disney's could. But it was much

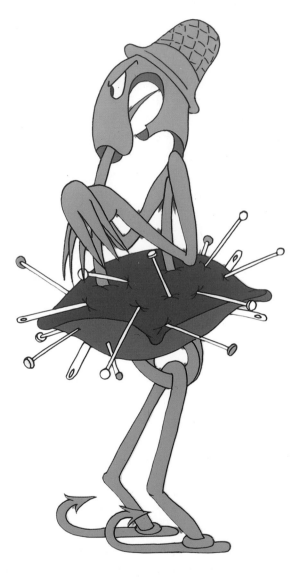

Above: An original cel of the spiny villain from Iwerks's "Balloonland" (a.k.a. "The Pincushion Man"), 1935.

smaller and had been made for a fraction of the cost. Culhane estimates he spent less than $300 on the parts.

Iwerks used the device in the Comicolor Cartoons, a series he began at the end of 1933. Made with the two-strip Cinecolor process, the Comicolor shorts were obviously modeled after the Silly Symphonies. Multiplane shots give an impressive illusion of depth in films like "The Headless Horseman" (1934) and the Willie Whopper short "The Cave Man" (1934). But the illusion of the third dimension is just elaborate icing on a bad cake; neither film is particularly entertaining.

Many of the Comicolor films could be described as near-misses: they resemble Disney cartoons that somehow went wrong. In "Jack Frost" (1934), a naughty baby bear sneaks out of bed and plays in the forest—where he gets caught by approaching winter. After a great deal of cowering and whining, he manages to get safely back to bed. The premise of the story is no weaker than many of the Silly Symphonies, and the production values are nearly as lavish. But the story is badly paced and the baby bear fails to develop as a character.

The garish colors and odd-looking characters in "Balloonland" (also known as "The Pincushion Man") (1935) have made the film a camp favorite. It's easy to imagine a Silly Symphony about an inflatable world whose inhabitants live in fear of a spiny villain. But Disney would have insisted on a more tightly focused story and more endearing designs for the balloon hero and heroine, and made an appealing fairy tale, rather than a bizarre novelty.

MGM wasn't interested in the Comicolor films, and their contract ended with the Willie Whopper series in 1934. Powers distributed the films on his own, but his Celebrity Productions could not possibly get as many bookings or earn as much in rentals as a major studio like MGM. Iwerks found himself in an economic bind, and many of his artists, including Culhane, Eugster and Natwick, quit or were fired during 1935.

In 1936, Powers withdrew his backing and Iwerks switched from independent production to subcontracting. He directed two cartoons for Warner Brothers producer Leon Schlesinger in 1937, an assignment that was widely perceived as bailout by Schlesinger. "Porky and Gabby" and "Porky's Super Service" were animated by two young Warners artists on loan to Iwerks, Chuck Jones and Bob Clampett. Neither cartoon proved outstanding. Iwerks started work on four shorts featuring "Gran' Pop," an aged chimpanzee who was the subject of very popular magazine cartoons by the British artist Lawson Wood. The films were never completed.

Iwerks then signed with Columbia to produce cartoons for their Color Rhapsodies series. His only memorable film from this period is the stylized "Merry Mannequins" (1937), in which two dummies from a department-store window display get married one night. Essentially an animated takeoff on a Fred Astaire–Ginger Rogers routine, "Merry Mannequins" features striking Art Deco designs and colors.

In 1940, Iwerks finally threw in the towel. The decision to return to the Disney studio must have been difficult, but it was also sensible. While their friendship was never fully restored, Iwerks stayed with Disney for the next thirty-one years, until his death in 1971. He concentrated on special effects, winning Oscars for his work with optical printing and traveling mattes. Although he did no further animation himself, he revolutionized the process by adapting a photocopy machine to transfer the animators' drawings directly onto the cels, thus eliminating the time and effort needed to ink them by hand. The technique was showcased in 1961 in "101 Dalmatians."

Iwerks possessed extraordinary mechanical abilities and an exceptional talent for animation. He lacked the flair for self-promotion a studio head needs, as well as the qualities of a great director and businessman. The decision to leave Disney in 1931 was a bad one. The films he made on his own show flashes of brilliance, but they don't represent the real scope of his great talent.

When J. R. Bray closed his animation studio in New York in 1927, Walter Lantz came to Hollywood, where he soon found a job writing gags for Mack Sennett at Universal. Lantz later said that he learned how to use physical comedy and milk a gag from Sennett and these live-action shorts.

When Carl Laemmle, the head of Universal and owner of the rights to Oswald, took the rabbit away from Charles Mintz and established an animation studio at Universal, he chose Walter Lantz to run it. Although Lantz remained in charge of the staff of more than a hundred, he made Bill Nolan the

Below: A poster for Walter Lantz's "Oswald the Hunter" (1931).

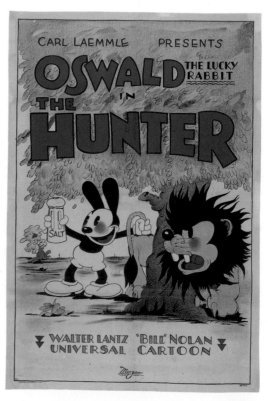

supervisor of his own unit; the two men were responsible for producing twenty-six cartoons each year.

Lantz was called in to provide an animated prologue for Universal's 1930 feature "The King of Jazz," starring Paul Whiteman. The narrator explains that Whiteman earned his title while big-game hunting. An animated caricature of the portly bandleader is seen being pursued and captured by a rubbery 1920s-style lion. Things look bad for Whiteman, until he picks up a violin and starts to play. The lion begins to dance, and soon the whole jungle is jiving. Oswald even appears, licking his thumbs alternately in a Charleston step known as pickin' cherries, to the *"Danse de Ventre."* A monkey clunks Whiteman on the head with a coconut, and the lump swells into the shape of a crown as the sequence ends.

The picture was shot in a two-strip Technicolor process that produces a pastel tan and green palette. Lantz encountered many of the same problems Disney would face in 1932, trying to find color paints that would adhere to the slick surface of the cels. Only 2½ minutes long, this sequence was the first animation in Technicolor, predating "Flowers and Trees" by two years.

"The fascinating thing about the studio was that there was no story department," says Leo Salkin, who joined the staff in 1932. "They would put a little notice up on the bulletin board saying: 'The next Oswald will take place at the North Pole. Anybody having any gags, please turn them in before such and such a date.' If you turned in gags regularly, the way Tex Avery, Cal Howard, Jack Carr and two or three others of us did, you'd be called into the gag meeting. The group would go into Walt's office and talk about whatever the subject of the cartoon was. Walt would put it into some kind of form and that was the story—no scripts, no storyboards."

Oswald is typical of the relentlessly cheerful but essentially characterless cartoon stars of the early 1930s. He has little personality aside from good-natured pluck. The gags and story situations carry the films, rather than the personality of the main character. Oswald's voice was originally provided by Mickey Rooney, who had recently appeared in a series of two-reel comedies. After Rooney's career took off, Bernice Hansen supplied the voice.

Most of the Oswald shorts are no better or worse—nor appreciably different—than other studio cartoons of the time. Like Flip the Frog and other contemporary characters, Oswald has largely been forgotten by audiences today. "Confidence" (1933), the one really famous Oswald film, is known more for its political message than its artistic merits.

All is well on Oswald's egg ranch until the night a black-robed specter labeled "Depression" rises out of a nearby swamp. The hens wander about in a daze and stop laying; the local bank has to shut down after a run. When Oswald seeks help, the doctor points to a picture of Franklin Roosevelt and announces: "There's your doctor!" Oswald flies to Washington to meet F.D.R., who performs an upbeat ditty about confidence and presents his rabbit constituent with a hypodermic needle filled with the stuff. Oswald returns home and injects his hens and neighbors with confidence. Instantly, the chickens go back to laying; the farmers put their money back in the bank; everybody sings and dances; the Depression specter perishes. "Confidence" is one of the most blatant pieces of animated propaganda ever released as entertainment by Hollywood.

In late 1935, Lantz established himself as an independent producer. Much of the impetus for the decision came from changes in management at Universal in 1935–36, including the departure of Carl Laemmle. The change in status had little effect on the daily operation of the studio. The animators still worked on the Universal lot (the staff moved to a building on Seward Street in Hollywood during the early 1940s), and Universal continued to distribute the cartoons.

This poster announcing a personal appearance by Walter Lantz at a Pasadena theater in 1936 features two versions of Oswald Rabbit.

Leo Salkin

The musicians from Walter Lantz's "The Amateur Broadcast" (1935) have the goggle-eyed look of early 1930s cartoon characters.

By this time, the Oswald series was running out of gas. There was evidently a limit to the number of stories the character could sustain. Although Oswald was ostensibly the star of many cartoons during this period, his role was sometimes reduced to a brief, irrelevant cameo. Lantz completely redesigned the character in 1936, turning him into a white Easter Bunny sort of rabbit. Although the graphic innovations helped to keep the character going, Oswald made fewer and fewer appearances on the screen. "The Egg Cracker Suite" (1943) was the character's 260th—and final—film.

Lantz began looking for a new character; he experimented with Snuffy the Skunk, Elmer the Great Dane, Doxie the Dachshund, the Canvas Back Duck family, the exceedingly cute Babyface Mouse and various one-shot films. A series of Cartune Classics modeled on the Silly Symphonies and made in a two-strip color process lasted for six installments in 1934. (Lantz didn't switch over to full-scale color production until 1939.) Beginning in 1936, three rowdy chimpanzees named Meany, Miny and Mo indulged in slapstick antics that recalled the Three Stooges. There was talk of an animated feature of "Aladdin and His Wonderful Lamp," which Lantz said he could make for the modest sum of $750,000, but no backers could be found for the project.

Although he was spending only about $8,000 on each cartoon, Lantz clearly needed a star character to sustain a series of films. The arrival of the first giant panda ever seen in the United States in 1936, followed by a group of pandas two years later, sparked a craze for panda products. In 1939, Lantz scored a hit with "Life Begins for Andy Panda," a title that played off the Mickey Rooney film "Life Begins for Andy Hardy."

Andy begins life as a chubby, cute baby, and the announcement of his birth electrifies the other animals in the forest. Dim-witted Papa Panda tells his son to keep away from the hunters, who'll put him in a newsreel. Andy decides that's exactly what he wants ("I'm gonna be in a newsweel!") and causes no end of trouble for poor dumb Dad. Andy's personality owes a lot to Fanny Brice's Baby Snooks; he was an immediate success.

Andy remained a baby for about three years in shorts that continued the pattern of the naughty child outwitting his terminally dim father. He was redesigned as an adult for "Goodbye Mr. Moth" (1942) and given gloves, shoes and pants. Papa Panda was discarded, and Andy began to develop a more passive personality, similar to Mickey Mouse's. He became a genial straight man to whom things happened, rather than a child who gleefully initiated the mischief.

While still a child, Andy, in "Knock Knock" (1940), introduced the character who would soon eclipse him: Woody Woodpecker. Lantz has often told the story of how he based Woody on a real bird. When he and his wife, Gracie, spent their honeymoon in a cabin on Sherwood Lake in California, they were repeatedly awakened before dawn by a noisy woodpecker. They thought the bird was funny until a rainstorm revealed the holes he had made in the cabin roof. Gracie suggested Walter make the bird into a cartoon character, and a star was born.

Like Disney's account of the origin of Mickey Mouse, the birth of Woody is the kind of story people love to read in newspaper features, and it's been printed all over the world. Unfortunately, it isn't true: the Lantzes weren't married until 1941.

In "Knock Knock," Woody bursts onto the screen as an obstreperous pest who bedevils Papa Panda. ("Guess who? Ah-ha-ha-HA-ha!") Andy spends most of the film sneaking around with a saltshaker, trying to sprinkle salt on the woodpecker's tail. Woody ridicules his efforts until he discovers it works: he's been captured! Two woodpeckers in white coats arrive to take Woody to the funny farm, but they turn out to be as nutty as their patient. The trio drive away amid shrieks of raucous laughter.

Audiences enjoyed Woody's brash shenanigans. The release of "Woody Woodpecker" six months later acknowledged the character's popularity and initiated his solo career. Lantz had found the cartoon star he'd been seeking.

Like the early versions of Daffy Duck and Bugs Bunny, who also made their debuts around this time, Woody represented a new kind of cartoon character. He was an aggressor who tormented his fellow creatures, not because they provoked him, but because he enjoyed it. Woody was always ready to toss off a wisecrack, peck somebody on the head or let loose his maniacal laugh. This brassy, aggressive, often violent style of humor was well suited to the equally brash mood of the early 1940s.

The initial design for Woody was quite ugly, with a long, thin beak, a small head with bulging eyes, an underslung jaw, a gap between his two teeth and thick, stubby legs. With his blue back, red crest, green tail and orange-yellow beak and legs, he was a discordant symphony of brilliant colors. Subsequent revisions in his physical appearance made Woody rounder and more appealing. His voice and signature laugh were originally created by Mel Blanc. When Warners signed Blanc to an exclusive contract a few years later, various people supplied the voice, including animator Ben Hardaway. In 1951, Gracie Lantz became Woody's permanent voice.

Lantz enjoyed a reputation as a gentle maverick. He chose animals for his characters that no one else used—a woodpecker, a panda and, later, a walrus and a penguin. He takes pride in the fact that he was the only cartoon producer who could draw his characters. Like Disney, he financed his own films, retaining ownership of them and of the characters.

Lantz also employed one of the very few women working as a full-fledged animator: LaVerne Harding. The only jobs women held in the animation industry through most of its history were noncreative ones, usually inking and painting. Many men who began as inkers or cel washers moved up to assistant, then animator and even director, but very few women did.

"LaVerne came to me with a beautiful portfolio," Lantz recalls, "so I gave her a job. She became one of my top animators and was the only woman animator in the business for years. Most producers didn't believe a woman could draw the exaggerations needed for action, that they could only

The first model sheet for Woody Woodpecker (1940) shows the character in his most raucous screwball phase.

handle birds and bees and flowers. They were wrong, of course."

During the 1930s, Walter Lantz managed to make many transitions relatively smoothly: from silent films to sound, from New York to Hollywood, from black and white to color and from studio employee to independent producer. But his best films were still ahead of him.

Animation also had its B studios, production companies whose work had less of an impact on audiences and the development of the medium. In some cases, the work itself simply wasn't good enough to command widespread attention or to exert a major influence. In others, a lack of exposure caused good-quality work to be ignored. Sometimes, a studio disbanded or an artist quit the medium before the work was recognized.

The brief and somewhat checkered existence of the Van Beuren studio provides an interesting example of a minor production house with considerable promise that was never fully realized. Almost completely forgotten by the general public, the Van Beuren films are treasured by a small group of animation devotees.

In 1921, Paul Terry joined with Amedée Van Beuren of Fables Pictures to produce his Aesop's Fables series. Van Beuren knew little about animation, and apparently founded the studio as an investment. It was backed by Keith-Albee, a company whose many theaters comprised one of the major vaudeville circuits. Keith-Albee not only provided money; it guaranteed the release of the films. With Terry at the helm, the studio ground out a short every week for most of the next decade, filling the screen with the formula antics of countless cats and mice.

Van Beuren bought out Keith-Albee in 1928, and announced he was switching from silent to sound production. (Keith-Albee—which later became part of RKO—continued to release the films.) This news led to a series of conflicts with Terry, who balked at spending the additional money sound would require. He added sound tracks to some already completed cartoons, but the results were far from satisfactory. Terry left the company early the next year and struck out on his own. Van Beuren chose John Foster to replace him. The release schedule was cut from fifty-two films a year to twenty-six, in recognition of the problems the transition to sound production would create.

At most studios, sound did more than add another dimension to cartoons; it required a completely different approach to animation, which involved extensive planning and preproduction work. Animators could no longer throw in any piece of business that came to mind while they were drawing, nor could they continue a sequence until they ran out of ideas—as had often been the case in the silent days. The gags and the story lines had to be planned before the sound track was re-

Posters from two of Van Beuren's short-lived series.
Top: "Tom and Jerry" (1933)—the pairing of a tall,
skinny character with a short, chubby one may have
been suggested by Bud Fisher's "Mutt and Jeff."
Above: "The Little King" (1934) was based on Otto
Soglow's comic strip.

corded. Once the track was completed, the animators had to
time the action to it. Only the Fleischers continued to use
"post-synch" sound tracks.

Although Van Beuren somehow managed to produce the
requisite number of films each year, it obviously required an
enormous effort, as shorts like "Making 'Em Move" (1931)
demonstrate. "I've always wanted to see how they were
made," a lady cat tells the doorkeeper of a cartoon studio.
Inside, robust chaos reigns; the lady visitor is forgotten as cartoon cats, dogs, lions and monkeys appear in gags spoofing
studio work. Later, a finished cartoon with stick-figure characters is shown to an enthusiastic audience.

The film has a loose, unstructured feel, more typical of
shorts made five years earlier. By 1931, Disney and the Fleischers were making considerably more sophisticated cartoons
like "The Ugly Duckling" and "Bimbo's Initiation." The inventiveness of the stick-figure film-within-a-film stands out in contrast to the more ordinary work that surrounds it. The coordi-
nation of the action and the sound still seems awkward and
tentative.

The animators started making films with Farmer Al Falfa,
but Terry insisted the character belonged to him and the series
came to a halt. In their search for a continuing character, the
Van Beuren artists began to work with mice that resembled
Mickey and Minnie. The basic design came from the generic
animated mice virtually every studio had used during the silent era, but the animators did more than adapt the prototype.
The borrowing was so obvious in films like "The Office Boy"
(1930) that Disney went to court and obtained an injunction
forbidding Van Beuren to continue using his character.

Any comparison of the Van Beuren and Disney mice only
emphasizes the superiority of Disney's animation. The Van
Beuren artists were still learning how to keep a character's
design consistent, and their mouse looks slightly different in
each scene; his ears change shape every time his head moves.

The Van Beuren studio was on Broadway across from the
Fleischer studio, and the two groups of animators regularly
staged paper-airplane battles. Bill Littlejohn, who started
working at Van Beuren in 1931, recalls: "Alex Lovy and I made
a paper airplane ten feet long. We pushed it out a window on
the seventeenth floor, and it flew beautifully. Then the paper
struts began to flutter, and it took a tremendous dive. Ten feet
of paper collapsed right in front of a cop! The cops finally put a
stop to the airplanes. The sanitation department complained
we left so much paper on the sidewalk, it looked as if a parade
had gone by."

Not everyone shared Littlejohn's enthusiasm. Frank Tashlin
found working at Van Beuren so unpleasant that he created
"Van Boring," a newspaper comic strip satirizing his old boss.

In 1932, George Stallings and George Rufle came to Van
Beuren, where they helped Foster develop the studio's first
original characters: Tom and Jerry, a tall guy/short guy duo

A cel and background from Van Beuren's "Parrotville Old Folks" (1935). This colorful series has been forgotten by all but the most hard-core animation fans.

who made their debut in "Wot a Nite." Probably their best-remembered film is "Piano Tooners" (1932), in which they wrestle with a recalcitrant sour note. The wriggling, tadpole-like note struggles valiantly and finally has to be flushed down an off-screen toilet.

As Van Beuren had established the studio as an investment, he was unhappy with the reactions—and revenues—these cartoons were generating. He replaced John Foster with George Stallings in 1933. That same year, Mannie Davis designed Cubby Bear, another black-and-white character in the Felix the Cat tradition. Cubby made his debut in "Opening Night," a

film created for the opening of RKO's mammoth Roxy Theater in New York. In addition to the Tom and Jerry and Cubby series, Van Beuren bought the rights to Otto Soglow's comic strip "The Little King." The choice was not an inspired one: Soglow's mild-mannered character was too passive to be an effective personality on the screen, and the films failed to generate much interest.

Still seeking a hit, Van Beuren hired Charles Correll and Freeman Gosden to provide the voices for an animated adaptation of their "Amos 'n' Andy" radio show—the most popular program in the country. Its humor didn't translate onto the screen, and the series ended after only two installments. Van Beuren replaced Stallings with Burt Gillett, the highly respected director of Disney's runaway success, "Three Little Pigs."

Gillett tried to introduce Disney's time-consuming and expensive production methods, such as pencil-testing the animators' work. He came up with three new series: Toddle Tots, Parrotville and Rainbow Parades. A cloying mixture of live-action kiddies and animated characters, the Toddle Tots had a mercifully brief run. The Parrotville shorts were animated Westerns with a cast of birds. "The parrots ran around like crazy, slipping and sliding," says Littlejohn. "There were lots of scenes where you could whip the characters around in the kind of wild action I loved to do. A lot of it worked out pretty well, much to my surprise."

The Rainbow Parade series was Gillett's answer to Disney's Silly Symphonies. Made in a two-strip process, then in Technicolor, these shorts certainly tried to live up to their name. Films like "Molly Moo-Cow and the Butterflies" (1935) are so full of color and motion that the story gets lost in the confusion. The most famous of the Rainbow Parades is "The Sunshine Makers" (1935), a tale of rival groups of elves. The "Joys" bottle sunshine as a happiness elixir and overcome their dour rivals, the "Glooms." Animator I. Klein has documented the making of this pleasant, if simpleminded, fable that has become a minor cult favorite.

By 1935, the young, talented staff of Van Beuren should have been producing more impressive films. Many of the artists would make significant contributions to animation at other studios: Pete Burness, Jack Zander, Sid Marcus, Joe Barbera, I. Klein and Shamus Culhane, as well as Littlejohn, Lovy and Gillett himself.

The poorly run studio hung on for one more year. Gillett took on two new properties: Fontane Fox's newspaper comic strip "Toonerville Folks" and a revival of Felix the Cat. "Toonerville" must have seemed like an ideal subject for cartoons: the favorite of literally millions of loyal readers, it had already inspired a series of live-action comedies and a line of toys. But Gillett's brightly colored films failed to capture the essence of Fox's satire on rural life and his loose, calligraphic style. The Van Beuren version of Felix lacked the wit and imagination of Messmer's original and, not surprisingly, failed to duplicate its success.

The ax fell in 1936 when Disney left United Artists and signed a distribution deal with RKO. The distributor of the Silly Symphonies and Mickey Mouse cartoons obviously didn't need the Parrotville, Felix or Toonerville shorts. The animators completed the films they had contracted for the 1935–36 season, and the studio quietly closed. Van Beuren died of a heart attack a year later.

At their best, the Van Beuren shorts have naïve charm, reminiscent of the early Fleischer cartoons. The rubbery characters cavort in surreal settings, unbounded by the laws of gravity and anatomy. But this camp appeal is balanced against the often crude animation, slipshod storytelling and inadequate characterization. While some animators cherish their innocent ebullience, modern audiences have consigned the Van Beuren films to oblivion—where they seem likely to remain.

When the Van Beuren studio closed, many of the animators went to work for his former manager, Paul Terry. Terry was one of the first professional animators; his experiments began soon after Blackton's and McCay's. He rose quickly in the studio hierarchies, and during the early silent days, his cartoons were considered among the best on the market. Disney once aspired to make films as good as Terry's Aesop's Fables.

Having established a successful formula, he stuck with it, and his work quickly stagnated. Terry produced innocuous, mildly amusing, loosely animated, virtually plotless cartoons during the teens, and he continued to produce them through the thirties, long after other studios had refined their draftsmanship, polished their animation and developed more sophisticated approaches to storytelling and humor. There is little appreciable difference between the Aesop's Fables of the 1920s and the Terrytoons of 1940.

Despite the length of his career and the hundreds of cartoons he produced, Terry's influence on animation was largely restricted to management and business practices, rather than aesthetics. "The Dinner Party" (1928) may have been the first synch-sound cartoon, but its impact was minimal. "Steamboat Willie" demonstrated how effective the combination of sound and animation could be.

Terry unwittingly set the pattern for the Saturday-morning kidvid industry of the 1970s and 1980s by treating animation as a commodity that could be produced cheaply, quickly and profitably. He never pretended to be concerned with art, and everyone who worked at Terrytoons remembers the dictum that apparently summed up his attitude toward animation: "Disney is the Tiffany of this business, and we're the Woolworth's."

After leaving Van Beuren in 1929, Terry joined with Frank Moser to set up a studio in the Audio Cinema building in Harlem. Joseph Coffman of Audio Cinema was the third partner. In addition to his duties as producer, Terry devoted his attention to writing stories for the cartoons.

"Terry approached creating a cartoon this way," recalls Art Babbitt, who came to Terrytoons in 1929. "He kept a file of A gags, B gags and C gags. The A gags would get a hilarious laugh, the B gags would get a friendly response and the C gags were not so successful. He would concoct a mixture of A, B and C gags, lay them out on a panorama and that would be the picture. It didn't matter what the hell the story was."

Regardless of their quality, the gags were often weakened by

Producer Paul Terry (center) with his partner
Frank Moser and composer Philip Scheib (seated)
during the early 1930s.

the way Terry used them. Many of his films seem to have been
built around two basic principles: (1) if a joke is funny once, it
should be funny a second or third time; and (2) if having one
character perform an action is funny, having two or three
characters perform the same action should be funnier. Nor
did the schedule of twenty-six films per year allow the relatively small Terry staff time to develop their staging and timing. Still, a Terrytoon somehow appeared every other week.

"Terry had a philosophy that was very cut-and-dried and
businesslike," comments Joe Barbera. "He'd say, 'You get
used to seeing a bottle of milk on the stoop every morning,
that's why I deliver a cartoon every other week.' He delivered
them, and at a price, and didn't worry."

"What we were doing was just crud," states Babbitt. "All the
characters and action were drawn in profile; nobody dared to
do anything in front view or three-quarter view, except Bill
Tytla when he first came there. I was learning a craft, but the
films never got any better. Terry didn't care—he was out for
the bucks."

Music for the films was provided by Philip Scheib. Disney
had original songs written for his cartoons; the composers and
arrangers at Warners and MGM could draw on huge studio
libraries of popular tunes. Terry refused to pay composers'
royalties, so Scheib had to piece the sound tracks together out
of material in the public domain, supplemented by his own
imitations of current hits. The Terrytoons sound tracks soon

became as repetitious and formulaic as the stories. Children
who watched them on television during the 1950s soon realized that they included only one splash, one metallic crash,
one thump, etc., and learned to recognize that very finite
repertoire.

Terry's partner, Frank Moser, spent his time at the drawing
board. Veterans of Terrytoons remember him as an extremely
fast artist, who sometimes did half the animation for a film.
Terry considered him an exceptional animator; Babbitt was
not impressed:

"Moser was a man devoid of humor. He worked very rapidly, but his work was crude and without feeling. Of course,
everybody's work was crude in those days, but he constantly
told you he was the fastest animator in the world. I undiplo-
matically told him that was like being the fastest violinist in the
world. You can play very fast, but you can't play worth a
damn!"

Moser and Terry parted under highly questionable circumstances. The Terrytoons were released by 20th Century–Fox,
who bought them from Educational Pictures. In response to
complaints about the inferior quality of the Terry films, the
president of Educational Pictures declined to renew the contract in early 1936. Terry offered to buy out Moser's share in
the studio and seek backing elsewhere on his own. The week
after Moser sold out, Terry got a new, two-year contract with
Educational that included an agreement to improve his cartoons. Moser later sued both Terry and Educational —
unsuccessfully.

About a year after Moser's departure, many of Terry's
artists, including Jack Zander, Joe Barbera, Ray Kelly and
Carl Meyer, quit en masse. Fred Quimby, who needed animators for the in-house studio he was trying to establish at MGM,
set out to round up all the talented people he could find. As
many of these younger artists had grown impatient with
Terry's restrictive practices and uninspired films, they eagerly
accepted the offer to come to California and the prestigious
MGM studio. Their exodus effectively ended any hope of
improving the quality of the Terrytoons. However, as Barbera
points out, "even though a bunch of his animators left, he kept
right on going—for years."

Except for Farmer Al Falfa, Terry eschewed recurring characters in favor of one-shot films, many of them involving what
had become standard cartoon mice and cats. He kept a library
of common movements like walks and runs, and used them in
film after film—a practice subsequently adopted by Saturday-
morning television producers. These measures did help keep
costs down: during the middle 1930s, Terry was spending only
about $7,000 per film.

In 1936, two new characters made their debuts in Farmer Al
Falfa shorts: Puddy the Pup in "The Hot Spell" and Kiko the
Kangaroo in "Farmer Al Falfa's Prize Package." Both charac-
ters were designed in the very simple style of the mid-1920s, a

look that most studios had already abandoned; neither character proved particularly successful.

Two years later, Terry made "String Bean Jack," his first
color cartoon. With its uninspired caricatures of ZaSu Pitts
and W. C. Fields, the film is more interesting as a milestone in
studio history than as an entertainment. For the next five
years, some of the Terrytoons were released in color or sepia
tone; black-and-white production was not phased out until
1943.

In 1938, Terry initiated a series of films featuring Gandy
Goose. Gandy's high-pitched voice, twittering mannerisms
and addled personality had obviously been taken from Ed
Wynn's "Perfect Fool." Initially, audiences responded well to a
character that seemed so familiar, but it soon became evident
Gandy was as lacking in personality as the other Terry players.
In an effort to bolster Gandy, one of the many cats was resusci-
tated and pressed into service as a straight man. Sourpuss's
voice and demeanor were cloned from Jimmy Durante. The
pattern was set, and the cartoons followed it monotonously.

In 1940, both Fox and Bank of America expressed interest in
an animated feature, but Terry declined. Paul Terry was
obviously satisfied producing innocuous, mildly amusing,
loosely animated, virtually plotless cartoons, as he had been
doing for the last two decades. The changes and innovations
that transformed the animated short during the 1930s and
1940s continued to pass him by.

Like Van Buren, the Charles Mintz studio has been almost
entirely forgotten by contemporary audiences. The husband of film distributor Margaret Winkler, Charles Mintz
began his career in animation with a new series based on
Herriman's "Krazy Kat" in 1925. Bill Nolan, who had already
animated one version of the character, was initially put in
charge of production. He was subsequently replaced by the
team of Ben Harrison and Manny Gould.

It's difficult to understand why Mintz chose "Krazy Kat" to
launch his studio. Although a favorite of the intelligentsia,
"Krazy Kat" never enjoyed the widespread popularity of "The
Gumps" or "Barney Google."

Mintz's animators took little more than the title of the strip
for their film series. The characters were redesigned and the
intriguing narrative was replaced with standard gags. After the
success of Mickey Mouse, Krazy was given a large, rounded
head, a falsetto voice, a similarly designed female counterpart
and a pet dog. Herriman's androgynous, moonstruck dreamer
became, in these films, just another undistinguished animated
character.

In 1928, Shamus Culhane got a job as an inker at the Mintz
studio. He judges the cartoons harshly: "The films were atro-
cious, the worst crap you can imagine. They never used the
characters. Offissa Pup rarely appeared, Ignatz Mouse was not
in love with Krazy; they never used the desert landscapes. The

Below and opposite: A poster and two animation
drawings for the Mintz "Krazy Kat" series. As
these illustrations suggest, the studio artists borrowed more heavily from Felix the Cat and Mickey
Mouse than from Herriman's comic strip.

childhood pastimes, but they gradually became more fantastic. Plots remained a major weakness of the Scrappy cartoons. The films break into segments that were obviously animated by artists working largely in isolation and adding gags at random. The story lines ramble and falter, and rarely come to any real conclusions.

At the suggestion of Oopie/Vonsey, Scrappy decides to stage a celebration for himself in "Scrappy's Birthday Party" (1933). They invite not only a standard assortment of Hollywood caricatures—Greta Garbo, Laurel and Hardy, Jimmy Durante, the Marx Brothers—but George Bernard Shaw, Mahatma Gandhi, Albert Einstein, Babe Ruth, Benito Mussolini and John D. Rockefeller as well! The animators failed to capitalize on the opportunities that bringing such a bizarre assortment of people together should have offered. The characters basically dance in (all doing the same step), cheer Scrappy, then dance back out.

"Scrappy's Birthday Party" seems innocuous enough, until the viewer remembers that in 1933 the Fleischers made "Snow White" and Disney produced "Three Little Pigs." The Mintz cartoons lack the casual surrealism of "Snow White," while the polish of "Three Little Pigs" makes the Scrappy films look like home movies. Scrappy was redesigned several times, becoming more realistic, but not more interesting. Various directors and animators continued the series through 1940.

Publicity drawings of Scrappy, Betty, Yippy and Oopie/Vonsey. The artwork for the cartoons was done with considerably less care.

staff just batted the stuff out as fast as they could for something like $750 apiece."

Like many contemporary cartoons, the Mintz Krazy Kat films display occasional flashes of imagination or humor. But overall, they remain an undistinguished body of work, largely unwatchable by modern standards.

Early in 1930, Mintz signed a distribution deal with Columbia and moved some of his staff to California, including Harrison, Gould, Allen Rose, Art Davis, Harry Love and office manager Jimmy Bronis. ("He dumped the rest of us," comments Culhane.)

Mintz hired veteran animators Sid Marcus and Dick Huemer to do a short-lived series for RKO, featuring a dog named Toby the Pup. When the series ended, Huemer, Marcus and Art Davis devised a new character. Mintz talked Columbia into distributing a second series, and Scrappy made his debut in "Yelp Wanted" (1931).

Scrappy was a little boy with a round head, big round eyes, round ears and a small, pudgy body. His limbs resembled segments of thick pipe, and his shoes looked like outsized jelly beans. Scrappy spoke in a high, rather grating whisper. He was soon joined by a diminutive, equally rounded playmate, called Oopie in some cartoons, Vonsey in others. Scrappy's terrier, Yippy, and a little girl named Betty completed the cast.

The Scrappy films were better than the Krazy Kat cartoons. The presence of so many Fleischer alumni—Huemer, Marcus, Davis, et al.—may account for some of the pleasantly rubbery animation. At first the stories involved fairly normal

Veterans of the Mintz studio describe it as a much less enjoyable place to work than Disney or Fleischers or Warner Brothers. Bells rang signaling the time for work to begin and end, and Bronis apparently kept a close watch on his employees. "They worked people like it was Siberia," says Culhane. "Nobody could loaf as much as two minutes at the water cooler." Many very talented animators worked at the Mintz studio; unfortunately, they didn't stay—a pattern reminiscent of Terrytoons.

In 1934, Mintz started the Color Rhapsodies, his answer to the Silly Symphonies. The series began with a special Scrappy, "Holidayland," which received an Academy Award nomination. Most of the subsequent entries borrowed heavily from the Disney films, but the writers at the Mintz studio failed to duplicate the tightly structured, carefully paced stories of the Silly Symphonies. The artists copied the cute, rounded look of the Disney characters, but their limits as animators prevented them from expressing credible emotions through those characters. As a result, the Color Rhapsodies seem superficial and uninvolving. By 1937, half the series had been subcontracted to Ub Iwerks.

That same year, Mintz received a second Oscar nomination, for "The Little Match Girl," the studio's best film. Based on the Hans Christian Andersen story, this lavish cartoon shows a tiny girl with red cheeks and blond curls trying to sell her matches to cruelly mocking holiday revelers. Late at night, she huddles by the warmth of a single match and dreams of a brightly colored Heaven, replete with cherubs and toys. When an icy wind shatters her dream, the hapless child collapses into the snow. An angel bears her soul away from the indifferent city to the Heaven of her vision. "The Little Match Girl" is a genuine tearjerker, and the Mintz artists never achieved this depth of feeling again.

Whatever their artistic limitations, the Color Rhapsodies were decidedly opulent. Their costs put Mintz deeply into debt to Columbia, who gradually took over the studio. Mintz continued to manage it until his death in early 1940, at forty-four.

The management of the studio changed almost annually after Mintz's death. The most significant reshuffling occurred in 1941, when Frank Tashlin became production manager. An innovator in his own right, Tashlin hired many of the young, creative artists who had been active in the Disney strike, including John Hubley, Dave Hilberman, Zachary Schwartz, Sam Cobean and Phil Klein. This influx of talent raised the quality of the Columbia cartoons almost immediately.

Chuck Jones cites Tashlin's "The Fox and the Grapes" (1941), a collection of short gags about a dim-witted fox trying to wrest a bunch of grapes from a clever crow, as a major influence on his own Road Runner–Coyote films. The source of many of the elaborately planned schemes that backfire can be seen in the earlier cartoon.

More interesting from a graphic standpoint is "Professor Small and Mr. Tall" (1942), which John Hubley and Paul Summer co-directed. Except for some mildly amusing wordplay—Mr. Tall is short and Professor Small looks like an NBA center, which produces a "Who's on first" confusion wherever they go—the cartoon is not particularly funny. But the stylized, two-dimensional look of the characters and backgrounds anticipates the work of UPA by a decade, and the film must have seemed very bold in 1942.

The Columbia renaissance lasted only about a year; Tashlin quarreled with the studio management and was replaced by Dave Fleischer. Fleischer's direct approach to humor and lack of graphic sophistication quickly brought him into conflict with his young artists. They had come to Columbia because Tashlin allowed them to experiment with modern visual styles. When the atmosphere at the studio changed, many of them left. A potential stylistic revolution in animation came to a premature end, and the Columbia films slipped back into mediocrity.

Warner Brothers and MGM, the two studios that ultimately challenged Disney's leadership and took the Hollywood cartoon in a different, funnier direction, were among the last to be established. Ironically, both were founded by two Disney veterans, Hugh Harman and Rudy Ising. Despite the importance of their contribution to anima-

Rudy Ising (left), Hugh Harman (right) and an unidentified friend in the early 1930s.

tion, Harman and Ising remain relatively unknown figures. As Mike Barrier observes: "They did not so much create characters as they created studios," and these studios were taken over by other men and given other names.

Both Harman and Ising began their careers working with Walt Disney in Kansas City during the early 1920s, along with Carmen "Max" Maxwell, Rollin "Ham" Hamilton, Norman Blackburn, Friz Freleng and Ub Iwerks. After Disney left for California, Harman, Ising and Maxwell remained in Kansas City and animated a pilot film for an Arabian Nights series. No buyer could be found, and all three artists later joined Disney in Hollywood, working on the Alice and Oswald films.

Ising and Disney parted company amicably in 1927, after Ising fell asleep while running the animation camera. He made two educational films on plastic surgery, then joined Harman, Maxwell, Hamilton and Freleng working on Oswald shorts at the Charles Mintz studio.

"While Hugh was still working for Disney, we decided we were going to start our own company," says Ising. "Sound had just come in, so we decided to use real talking. We made 'Bosko, the Talk-Ink Kid,' a test film about 400 feet long that featured mouth synchronization and dancing. Hugh designed Bosko's physical appearance, and 'Max' Maxwell was his voice."

Made during the summer of 1929, "The Talk-Ink Kid" was never released theatrically. The film opens with live-action footage of Ising at his drawing board, sketching Bosko. The character comes to life, speaks and sings in one of the first examples of lip-synch animation and performs some dance steps. The short ends as Ising returns Bosko to the inkwell.

"By the time we finished 'The Talk-Ink Kid,' we were all out of work," adds Freleng. "I had to get a job, so I accepted when Mintz asked me if I wanted to go to New York and work on Krazy Kat. While I was working there, I tried to peddle the Bosko picture."

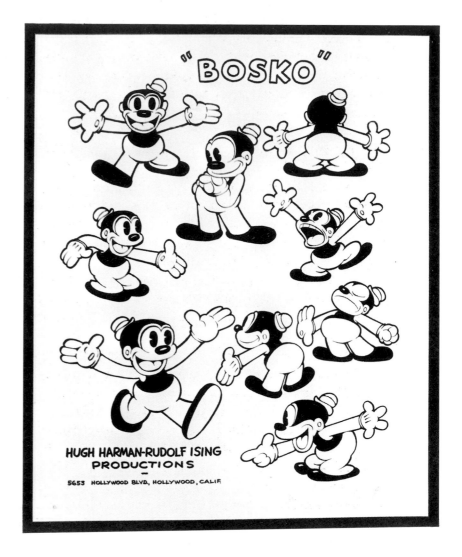

Right, top: An early model sheet of the unfailingly cheerful Bosko. Right, bottom: A promotional drawing of Bosko and Honey for "Ups 'N Downs" (1930).

Back in California, Harman and Ising finally arranged a distribution deal for their Bosko character with Leon Schlesinger, the head of Pacific Art and Title.

"Sound was still new," explains Ising, "but I would guess better than fifty percent of Leon's business was making dialogue cards for silent films. He wondered what was going to happen, and I guess he was interested in getting into something else, so he put up a few thousand dollars for the first cartoon. He had nothing to do with the production: he got the contract from Warner Brothers for the Looney Tunes series, and we had a contract from him."

"Sinkin' in the Bathtub," the first Looney Tune, was released in May 1930. Its title plays off "Singin' in the Bathtub" —the first of many song/cartoon tie-ins. The story line is minimal. After taking a bath, Bosko, an elastic black golliwog, takes his girlfriend, Honey, for a ride. During the course of the film, not only "Singin' in the Bathtub" but "Tip Toe Through the Tulips" and "I'm Forever Blowing Bubbles" are heard on the sound track. Everything is drawn in the same rubbery, bouncy style—even such normally inanimate objects as the bathtub. Like "Steamboat Willie," "Sinkin' in the Bathtub" radiates an innocent enthusiasm for the medium.

Of all the cartoon characters devised during the late 1920s and early 1930s, Bosko is probably the most relentlessly cheerful. His large, square teeth seem to remain fixed in a broad grin, no matter what he does. Beyond that inexhaustible good

cheer, he shows little personality. However, one question did arise: Felix was a cat; Oswald, a rabbit; Mickey, a mouse. What was Bosko?

"I never knew what Bosko was," replies Mel Shaw, who describes himself as "one of the original Harman-Ising boys." "Hugh designed him like Felix the Cat; if you took the same head and put pointed ears on him, Bosko would be Felix. That was very typical of the early cartoon characters—they all had pipestem legs and no anatomy."

"We never knew what he was," agrees Ising. "A lot of people who saw the films thought Bosko was a little colored boy, but we never thought of him that way. He was just a character with a Southern voice. When Rochelle Hudson did the dialogue for Honey, she used a Southern voice, too."

"She and Maxwell did wear blackface makeup," he continues, "but that was part of our recording process. We shot them in live action at the same time we recorded the dialogue, then we studied the footage on a Moviola. Each animator also had a mirror in which he studied his own mouth movements. By the time we learned how to read the voice tracks, we had made charts of lip motions."

The first Looney Tunes drew such a favorable response from audiences that Warner Brothers renewed the contract and added a second series, dubbed Merrie Melodies. (Both names obviously played off Disney's Silly Symphonies.) Harman took over the Looney Tunes, which continued to feature Bosko, while Ising developed the Merrie Melodies, one-shot cartoons that highlighted songs, rather than characters. Most of them were fairly mindless musicals and romances.

"Warner Brothers owned three music publishing companies," explains Ising, "and it was in our contract that we had to use part of a new song in every picture. Usually, the name of the picture was the name of the song."

Released in 1931, the first Merrie Melody, "Lady, Play Your Mandolin," featured a new character, usually called Foxy (Ising remembers him as Freddy Fox), who was strikingly similar to Mickey Mouse. Foxy's ears were of a slightly different shape and his tail was a thick bush, but the rest was the same. The character was dropped after three films, a decision that may have been influenced by objections from Disney. Harman and Ising also experimented with Piggy, a.k.a. Patty Pig, and Goopy Gear, a humanized dog. Neither lasted for more than two or three cartoons.

The last character created during the Harman-Ising era at Warners was Buddy, who has frequently been described as "Bosko in whiteface." An utter nonentity, Buddy appeared in numerous films over the next two years, usually accompanied by Cookie, his girlfriend, and Towser, his dog.

Although they were well received by audiences, the Buddy and Bosko cartoons of 1933 are hardly better than "Sinkin' in the Bathtub." The plots are simpleminded and the humor formulaic. The directors allow the music to dominate the

An animation drawing of Buddy and Cookie from "Buddy's Adventures" (1934).

films, regardless of the constraints it puts on the stories and the animation.

In mid-1933, Harman and Ising broke with Schlesinger and Warners. In an effort to improve his films, Harman kept requesting larger budgets; Schlesinger, who was notoriously tightfisted, kept refusing.

Having learned from Disney's experience with Oswald, Harman and Ising retained the rights to Bosko. They took the character with them when they left, and made a deal to produce cartoons for MGM about a year later. Left with the Warners contract and most of the animation staff—bolstered by a few outsiders, like Jack King and Tom Palmer—but no experienced directors and no star character, Schlesinger promoted Friz Freleng.

In 1934, Schlesinger started making the Merrie Melodies in two-strip Cinecolor, beginning with Earl Duvall's "Honeymoon Hotel" and Freleng's "Beauty and the Beast." The favorable response to these cartoons led Schlesinger to make all the Merrie Melodies in color within a year. (The Looney Tunes remained in black and white until "The Hep Cat" in 1941; Warners finally switched to full color production in 1943.)

In 1935, Freleng introduced Porky Pig, Warner Brothers' first successful character. The earliest Warners cartoon that audiences still watch for its entertainment value, rather than as a novelty, "I Haven't Got a Hat" depicts a pageant in Miss Cud's elementary school class. Kitty, a little girl cat, struggles to get through "Mary Had a Little Lamb" while miming a desperate need to go to the bathroom. The twin pups, Ham

and Ex, offer a terrific rendition of the title tune: "I'd tip my hat to you / I'd do just that / I'd tip my hat to you / But I haven't got a hat!" Porky appears as a chubby, stuttering schoolboy trying to recite "The Midnight Ride of Paul Revere."

" 'I Haven't Got a Hat' was one of the first Warners cartoons that defined the personalities of its characters," says Freleng. "There was no personality animation in the Buddy and Foxy films—they were just bland characters. We repeated Porky because he stood out. We didn't really have any star characters at the time—we were just kind of floundering."

The Warners cartoons took a major turn for the better in 1936, when Schlesinger hired three extremely talented individuals: Frederick "Tex" Avery, Carl Stalling and Frank Tashlin. Avery had been working for Walter Lantz as an animator, and already had a reputation for being unusually funny.

His first film for Warners was "The Golddiggers of '49" (1936), a title that played off the popular Busby Berkeley musicals. But instead of chorus girls, Avery gave the audience *real* golddiggers—miners. Porky was transformed into a monstrously fat adult; Kitty, the nervous reciter from "I Haven't Got a Hat," became his daughter. Her suitor—and Porky's partner—was a bold cat named Beans, the ostensible hero of the piece.

Avery later refined and sharpened many of the gags he used in "Golddiggers," like making a group of singers rush off the screen, only to return and finish the last chorus before dashing away again. But they get laughs, even in this imperfect form.

A lobby card featuring the cast of Friz Freleng's "I Haven't Got a Hat" (1935), including Porky (a.k.a. "Piggy"), Little Kitty, Oliver Owl, Beans the Cat, the twin pups, Ham and Ex and an unnamed turtle.

Unlike the vast majority of the early Warners shorts, "The Golddiggers of '49" is aggressively funny. Avery began to discard the legacy of cute characters and situations left over from the Harman-Ising musicals in favor of a wilder, faster-paced style of comedy.

When asked about the eagerness that characterized Avery's unit (and quickly spread to the rest of the animators), Chuck Jones replied: "Coming out of art school during the Depression, the idea of getting a job was surprising; the idea of getting a job doing something you liked was beyond belief. If a picture wasn't getting finished in time, everybody worked overtime. The animators might do in-betweens, or the in-betweeners might do ink and paint, and they didn't get paid for it. The enthusiasm was real. When you felt like it, you worked overtime, whether you had to or not. If you got a piece of work you really enjoyed, you would spend the extra time on it cheerfully —it never occurred to you not to."

Carl Stalling had made the transition from theater organist to film composer by writing the scores for "Steamboat Willie" and the other early Disney sound cartoons. He left Disney to join the Ub Iwerks studio in 1930 and came to Warners in 1936.

Stalling had a flair for creating light, clever tunes; he also had access to Warner Brothers' enormous library of popular songs, which included hits from their big musicals. From these two sources, Stalling fashioned sophisticated but unpretentious scores that complemented the animation without becoming intrusive. (Like most major studios at the time, Warners maintained a large professional orchestra for their films.)

Even devoted fans of the Warner cartoons seldom recognize Stalling's contribution. Anyone who can muster the willpower to turn his back to the screen during one of the films will discover that the score is far richer and more complicated than he realized. Given the fact that Stalling sometimes had as little as one week to score six minutes of film, his achievements seem doubly impressive.

Frank Tashlin made his debut as a director at Warners in 1936. A restless and versatile talent, he had worked in newspaper and magazine cartooning and live-action filmmaking as well as animation. Tashlin's greatest contribution to the Warners cartoons was his application of a more sophisticated filmmaking vocabulary.

Most shorts of the early 1930s are very straightforward cinematically: the camera stays in one place and the action unfolds in front of it. Tashlin experimented with varying camera angles and rapid cutting to punch up the humor in his pictures. "Porky's Romance" (1937) provides an outstanding example of this technique. When Petunia refuses Porky's proposal, he dejectedly walks away. Suddenly, she catches sight of the box of candy he's carrying. In a lightning flash of energy, she dashes out of her house, grabs Porky, hauls him back inside and starts eating the candy. Some of the shots in this

famous sequence last only six frames—one quarter of a second.

Tashlin also helped introduce the reflexive gag into the Warners shorts: the animated figure breaks character and reveals he knows he's in a cartoon through his words or actions. Petunia grows increasingly flustered as she attempts to read a welcoming statement at the opening of "Porky's Romance." When the off-camera announcer tries to calm her, she turns in his direction and screams: "I'M NOT EXCITED!"

The idea of reflexive gags obviously delighted Avery and his writers, including Tedd Pierce, Cal Howard and Dave Monahan; they quickly expanded and exploited the concept. The wolf chases Grandma around her cottage in "Little Red Walking Hood" (1937), until a telephone call interrupts. Granny turns to the audience and excuses herself: "It's the grocer, folks." She places her order (including a pint of gin), and the chase resumes. When Prince Charming arrives at the cottage in "Cinderella Meets Fella" (1938), he discovers a note reading: "Got tired of waiting and went to a Warner Brothers show." (He later finds her at the movie theater.)

The second famous Warners character made his debut in Avery's "Porky's Duck Hunt" (1937). In that film, Daffy Duck appeared as an aggressive wacko who bounced and "woo-hoo'd" all over the frame. The "darnfool crazy duck" even slid over the letters of "That's all, folks" on the closing title card, laughing insanely. The original Daffy was ugly, with a narrow

"That darnfool crazy duck": a rather stubby version of Daffy makes his debut in "Porky's Duck Hunt" (1937).

beak, big feet, skinny legs and a pudgy body. Like the original version of Woody Woodpecker, he represented a new, aggressive breed of cartoon character.

"Daffy was a real zany, an insane character," says Freleng. "He was tamed down later and turned into more of a greedy character, as aggressive as hell. I don't think you could say he became an adversary of Bugs Bunny really—he was kind of an aggressive pal."

In 1937, Schlesinger "loaned" animators Chuck Jones and Bob Clampett to Ub Iwerks. As Iwerks's studio was in trouble, Schlesinger farmed out two cartoons to him, "Porky and Gabby" and "Porky's Super Service." Neither film proved particularly memorable. The arrangement with Iwerks ended, and Jones and Clampett returned to the Warners lot. Joining them there was a man who would become one of the best-known contributors to the Warners films: Mel Blanc.

Blanc began his career in radio in 1927 with a program called "The Hoot Owls" on KGW in Portland, Oregon. His most famous work on the airwaves was done for the Jack Benny show, and included the voice of the train conductor who recited the litany of unheard-of towns, concluding with "Anaheim, Azusa and CUC-amonga."

The first assignment Blanc got from Schlesinger was the drunken bull in "Picador Porky" (1937). He soon began doing Porky's stutter, and supplied the voices for almost all the Warners characters. (The most important exception was Elmer Fudd, whose voice was Arthur Q. Bryan.) Blanc did more than supply funny little voices for these cartoon characters. Working with the directors, he suggested a broad range of moods and emotions that were as important in delineating the characters' personalities as the individual voices he gave them.

Bob Clampett was promoted to director in 1937, shortly after he returned from his stint with Iwerks. Unmindful of minor concerns like gravity, logic and sanity, he created wildly surreal shorts that demonstrated the power of animation to render *anything*.

The unbounded imagination of Clampett's "Porky in Wackyland" (1938) makes it an animator's delight. Porky flies past "Dark Africa" and "Darker Africa" to reach "Darkest Africa," the habitat of the Do-Do Bird, valued at $4 zillion. Wackyland turns out to be inhabited by a clutch of bizarre creatures, including a half dog/half cat that continually fights with itself, a beast shaped like a taxi horn that honks its own bulb, a ducklike being who slides along on one knee crying "Mammy" à la Jolson and a man whose three heads are caricatures of the Three Stooges (he explains that his mother had been frightened by a pawnbroker's sign).

The Do-Do Bird proves to be a wily and elusive beast, capable of lifting up the horizon line and ducking under it like a curtain. Porky finally succeeds in capturing him, only to discover that the Do-Do isn't unique after all: Wackyland is full

Bob Clampett at work at the Warners animation studio in the mid-1930s.

"Cedars of Looney Tunes"—some of the Warners artists pose for a gag photograph in 1937. Left to right, John Burton, Frank Tashlin, unidentified woman, Bugs Hardaway, Leon Schlesinger, unidentified man and woman, Ace Gamer, Tex Avery, Treg Brown and Henry Binder.

of them. The blithe insanity of "Porky in Wackyland" continues to delight and amaze audiences.

Throughout his tenure at Warners, Clampett directed some of the looniest Looney Tunes, with the wildest gags and most extreme distortions.

Chuck Jones became a director in 1938; his personal style emphasized solid draftsmanship and strong character animation. Of all the Warners directors, Jones was the most strongly influenced by the Disney films, especially by the work of Fred Moore. Many of his earlier films involve rather uninteresting characters—Sniffles the Mouse and the Two Curious Pups. In cartoons like "Sniffles and the Bookworm" (1939) and "Stage Fright" (1940), the viewer can see Jones begin to explore the more subtle brand of comedy he would develop over the next decade.

The Warner Brothers animators are often referred to as "the Boys of Termite Terrace," after the dilapidated building in which they were housed. The animation unit actually occupied three separate but equally shabby structures at various times. The months they spent in the bungalow dubbed "Termite Terrace" more or less coincided with Avery's tenure (1936–42), but the name has stuck in the popular lexicon.

Whatever the unit lacked in decor, it made up in lunacy.

Everyone who worked there has a fund of stories about the gags, pranks and practical jokes played there.

Paul Julian, who started as a background painter in late 1939, describes it as "a giant barn turned into a bachelors' quarters. The ink and paint ladies were upstairs and severely cloistered—you didn't see a woman downstairs. The place was kind of bawdy and kind of messy and kind of scroungy; a place where people threw things."

Using curtains, cardboard and odd scraps of wood, the animators divided the long rooms into little cubicles for privacy and to cut out excess light. ("It looked like a shanty-town," says animator Phil Monroe.) Empty film cans, firecrackers, pushpins and water balloons circulated freely among the cubicles. To keep each other off guard, the animators would alternate real firecrackers with carefully made dummies.

"Chuck and two or three of his animators would trade gag drawings and caricatures back and forth," adds Julian. "Sometimes by the end of the day they'd build up a stack one-half or three-quarters of an inch thick."

The pranks helped to release the tension built up by hours of precise drawing—the top men at Warners were expected to produce from 25 to 30 feet (about 20 seconds of screen time) of animation each week, considerably more than their Disney counterparts. The boisterous atmosphere helped put the artists in the mood to create the madcap gags in their cartoons and contributed to the esprit de corps vital to the synergetic process of studio animation.

The development of Bugs Bunny, Warners' most popular character, illustrates how collaborative the creative process was. In recent years, controversy has erupted over who "invented" Bugs. In fact, no one individual can claim responsibility for him: Bugs is the son of many fathers. Directors Tex Avery, Bob Clampett, Friz Freleng, Chuck Jones, Bob McKimson and Frank Tashlin; voice artist Mel Blanc; designer Charlie Thorson; writers Warren Foster, Mike Maltese and Tedd Pierce; and more than a dozen animators all contributed to his development.

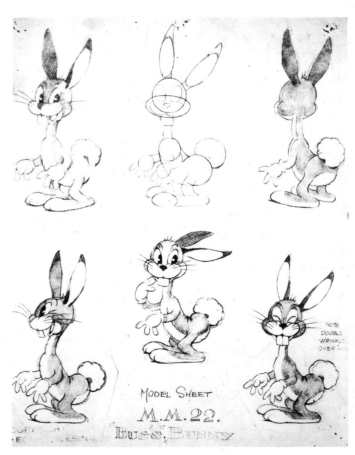

Opposite: An animation drawing of the ugly screwball rabbit in "Porky's Hare Hunt" (1938), the first prototype of Bugs Bunny. "Bugs was really just Daffy Duck in a rabbit suit in that picture," says Friz Freleng. "Hardaway thought Daffy was funny, so he decided to do the same thing with a rabbit. The character 'woo-woo'd all over the place, jumped up and landed on his head—exactly like Daffy." Above: A cel of Bugs zapping a hunter with his joy buzzer, from Ben "Bugs" Hardaway's "Hare-um Scare-um" (1939). Right: A model sheet by Charlie Thorson for "Hare-um Scare-um." The artists referred to the character as "Bug's Bunny," later dropping the apostrophe.

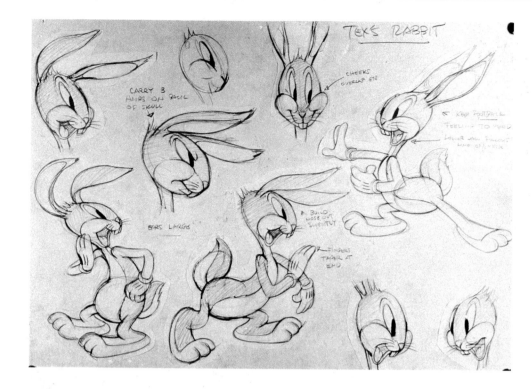

Bugs matures. Left: A model sheet for "A Wild Hare" (1940) by Robert Givens. In two years, the character has grown considerably more attractive, although he's still a bit rubbery-looking. Below: This model sheet by Jean Blanchard (c. 1947) shows a better-looking and more expressive version of Bugs. Opposite: Bugs and the unnamed black character from "All This and Rabbit Stew" (1941).

Below: "Eh, what's up, Doc?" Bugs Bunny and Elmer Fudd meet for the first time in "A Wild Hare" (1940), the film that launched Bugs's career. Bottom: A drawing of Egghead dressed as a cowboy. Tex Avery's weird, bulbous-nosed character was a partial ancestor of Elmer Fudd.

Avery established Bugs's basic personality in "A Wild Hare" (1940), in which Elmer Fudd first admonished the audience: "Be ve-wy, ve-wy quiet. I'm hunting wabbits"; and Bugs first inquired: "Eh, what's up, Doc?" Blanc describes the nasal drawl he first gave Bugs in that film as a mixture of Brooklyn and Bronx accents. Charlie Thornson, who had designed Max Hare in Disney's "The Tortoise and the Hare," came up with a more appealing rabbit, although many observers noticed his resemblance to the earlier Disney character.

Bugs's appearance was still somewhat crude and his personality had not yet coalesced into the deft, witty rabbit he ultimately became. But for the first time, he showed a spark of life, and audiences responded to it.

Over the next several years, the Warners artists continued to experiment with Bugs, gradually improving his physical appearance and refining his personality into something marvelously versatile and entertaining. These efforts added to their growing reputation for producing the funniest cartoons in the industry. Leo Salkin, who was working at Disney during the late 1930s, recalls: "Milt Schaffer and Nick George and I were working on shorts for 'Gerry' Geronimi; Milt and I were especially jealous of how funny the Warner Brothers cartoons were just before the war. We thought: 'All this personality stuff isn't really funny. It's cute and people kind of chuckle at it, but Warners cartoons get *laughs*.' "

What neither Salkin nor anyone else knew was that as the writers and directors hit their strides during the next decade, the Warners cartoons would get even funnier.

After breaking with Leon Schlesinger in 1934, Hugh Harman and Rudy Ising began looking for a new distributor. They had made the Looney Tunes and Merrie Melodies on their own, and only released them through Schlesinger and Warners. The studio was still a viable entity, as many of the animators, including Mel Shaw, Carmen Maxwell, Rollin Hamilton, Norman Blackburn and the McKimson brothers, Robert and Tom, chose to stay with them.

It took about a year to get a contract, and they eventually signed with MGM. During that year, Harman and Ising made two cartoons in the Cubby Bear series for Van Buren and did preproduction work for an animated feature based on Tchaikovsky's *Nutcracker* ballet. As the Bank of America declined to finance the film, and MGM was interested only in short cartoons, the project had to be abandoned.

In September 1934, MGM released "The Discontented Canary," the first installment in the series of two-color shorts called Happy Harmonies (yet another play off Silly Symphonies). The studio was still divided into two units: Harman used Bosko in a few cartoons, then dropped the character. Ising initially concentrated on one-shot films, including "The Chinese Nightingale" (1935).

Although the new shorts had substantially larger budgets than the Looney Tunes, most were not appreciably better.

Ising developed two series with recurring characters. The Pups, playful spotted twins who look a bit like Ham and Ex, first appeared in "Two Little Pups" in 1936. Later in 1936, Little Cheezer, a cute little mouse who ultimately served as a partial model for Jerry, made his debut.

In 1937, Shaw redesigned Bosko as a recognizable black boy: "They felt Felix the Cat-type characters didn't have enough personality," he recalls. "In a couple of meetings that I had with Hugh, I made some sketches of a real little pickaninny-type character with a big straw hat. We thought we could do more with him as a real little black boy, and get more gags out of him playing or doing chores on a farm."

Harman used this new version of a Bosko in his Jazz Frog films. These bizarre, surreal shorts feature frog caricatures of prominent black entertainers like Fats Waller, Bill Robinson, Louis Armstrong and Stepin Fetchit. When Bosko refuses to share his bag of cookies in "Bosko in Baghdad" (1939), the Fats Waller and Louis Armstrong frogs put him on a sinister chain of conveyor belts that lead to a giant bottle of castor oil. A frog musician uses a valve from his trumpet to inject himself in the arm in "Swing Wedding" (1937).

Although story remained a weak point, the Harman-Ising artists made enormous technical improvements in their films between 1934 and 1937. The animation grew smoother and more subtle, the designs more pleasing and the direction more skillful. Harman later said he began studying "the craft of films" at this time, and sought to apply the principles of Sergei Eisenstein and V. I. Pudovkin to his work.

But progress proved expensive, and the Happy Harmonies often ran over budget. In 1937, the MGM executives decided to forgo outside producers and set up an in-house animation studio. For reasons that have never been explained, they chose Fred Quimby to head the project. A former film salesman and executive, Quimby knew nothing about animation. According to all reports, he had no sense of humor, and was the most thoroughly disliked producer in the animation industry. (Cal Howard once taught his son's Cub Scout troop to shout: "Quimby is a red-faced jerk!" when they drove past the producer's office.)

In addition to hiring away as many of the Harman-Ising artists as he could, Quimby raided other studios for talent. He rounded up many of the better young animators, including Jack Zander, Joe Barbera, Bill Littlejohn and Emery Hawkins. He also lured Friz Freleng away from Leon Schlesinger with promises of more money and artistic freedom.

A cel and pan background of the later version of Honey, Bosko's girlfriend, from "The Old House"
(1936). Black characters frightened by haunted houses were a stock element in both animated and
live-action comedies during the 1930s and early 1940s.

MGM purchased the rights to "The Captain and the Kids,"
Rudolph Dirks's version of "The Katzenjammer Kids."
Freleng was not happy about this assignment. "I said: 'Oh no,
not *them!* They speak with an accent, they're the meanest little
bastards in the world, and they're humans.' I didn't think any
human characters would work."

Quimby remained adamant about the choice, and Freleng
had to proceed. Although they were released in sepia tone as
an economy measure, the Captain and the Kids shorts were
given lavish budgets. The new MGM crew did some fine work,
but the public demanded more from a cartoon than just skillful
animation. The characters remained unsympathetic, and the
series flopped—as Freleng had predicted.

Quimby brought in newspaper cartoonist Milt Gross, the
creator of "Nize Baby," "Count Screwloose of Tooloose" and
"That's My Pop!" in 1939.

"Gross couldn't deal with the Captain and the Kids, so

he came up with a storyboard using his own Count Screwloose characters," remembers Bill Littlejohn. "The guys all
said they couldn't animate them—they had no structure,
their heads couldn't be turned, their elbows were in the wrong
place."

"I got tired of hearing it," he continues, "so I stayed at the
studio till around four one morning and animated about five
seconds—which proved you could move those characters. We
made two pictures with them, 'Jitterbug Follies' and 'Wanted:
No Master,' and they were the funniest films in the studio—the
guys were rolling in their chairs. But Quimby looked at them
and said: 'These films will never be distributed—they would
violate the dignity of MGM.' " Despite Quimby's initial reaction, MGM did release the two films.

Gross was replaced by Harry Hershfield ("Abie the Agent"),
whose leadership proved even more disastrous. When Friz
Freleng's contract ended, he returned to Schlesinger and

promptly went back to making funny, innovative cartoons like "You Ought to Be in Pictures" (1940): "I had to take a cut in salary from around $375 a week to $200—Leon didn't like to hand out money," he says drily. "But I didn't argue. I just wanted to get away from MGM—that was a horrible place to be. The politics were terrible! Everybody was stabbing you in the back, and the guys from New York were pitted against the guys from California."

To resolve the worsening chaos, Quimby was finally forced to hire back the men whose studio he had taken over. Meanwhile, Harman and Ising (and their animators) had been involved in an unusual project that demonstrated just how polished their animation had become: they made a Disney cartoon—literally.

"Walt was involved with 'Snow White,' and they were worried about falling behind on their schedule of Silly Symphonies," says Ising. "So Roy called and asked if we could lend them our ink-and-paint department. In return, we asked if they could give us a cartoon."

The Disney artists had done some story work and preliminary sketches for a sort of sequel to "Water Babies" (1935). That Silly Symphony had been about little boys who lived underwater; the new film would be about little girl mermaids in a subaqueous setting. Disney agreed to subcontract "Merbabies" to Harman and Ising, with Ben Sharpsteen and Otto Englander checking their work on a weekly basis.

Released in late 1938, "Merbabies" is a plotless, undersea pageant. The animation compares favorably with Disney's, although the minimal story line doesn't require the characters to express many emotions. While pleasant and pretty, it's not a memorable cartoon.

Harman and Ising planned to do at least two more Silly Symphonies, but Disney canceled the arrangement because of objections from RKO, his distributor. (Harman later claimed Disney was plotting to take over their studio.) The two pictures they began, Harman's "Goldilocks and the Three Bears" and Ising's "The Little Goldfish," were completed for MGM.

It seems odd that Harman and Ising would agree to work for Quimby, the man who had undercut them. But as Ising points out, there were a limited number of studios that would distribute animated shorts, and neither partner seems to have aggressively pursued new markets. They returned to MGM as producer-directors and essentially picked up where they had left off.

Ising began working with the low-key, lumbering Barney Bear, who made his debut in "The Bear That Couldn't Sleep" (1939). With his short legs, sagging bottom and heavy, wrinkled brow, Barney looked like a beanbag chair come to life. His sleepy mannerisms were copied from actor Wallace Beery and Ising himself, whose tendency to fall asleep in meetings earned him the nickname "the Sleepy Bear."

The scenes of Barney snuggling amid his quilts and pillows were well animated. But the combination of a lethargic personality and rather gentle gags was hardly the sort of humor that would appeal strongly to an audience, especially in the late 1930s, when most cartoon characters were growing increasingly aggressive.

In 1939, Harman produced two of his three favorite pictures: "The Blue Danube" and "Peace on Earth." (He had made the third, "The Old Mill Pond," in 1936.) A musical fantasy set to the famous waltz, "The Blue Danube" has largely been forgotten.

"Peace on Earth" is generally considered his best film. When twin baby squirrels hear the line "Peace on the earth, good will to men" from the Christmas carol "It Came Upon a Midnight Clear," they ask their grandfather what men are. The old squirrel's narration of how humanity foolishly engineered its own extinction through war is accompanied by stark, roto-scoped footage of soldiers and weapons. After the last two soldiers have killed each other, the animals discover a Bible in the ruins of a church. They decide to live by its precepts and build their community accordingly.

"Peace on Earth" is anything but subtle in its message; however, the film's straightforward graphics retain their strength to this day. The film received numerous awards, including an Oscar nomination—the first for an MGM cartoon. Bill Hanna and Joe Barbera remade the film in Cinema-Scope in 1955 under the title "Good Will to Men."

The Harman-Ising films of the late 1930s contain some excellent animation, and they began to win awards. Ising finally wrested the Oscar from Disney's seemingly permanent possession with "The Milky Way" in 1940. But there were still problems at the studio. The division between the East and West Coast animators persisted; politicking and infighting continued, apparently encouraged by Quimby. Although they had two cartoon units in full production, MGM released only thirteen shorts in 1939; Disney managed to do that many with two features in production, while Warners made forty-four, Terry his usual twenty-six and Lantz twenty.

Under pressure from Quimby to increase production, Ising let two members of his unit, Bill Hanna and Joe Barbera, make a cartoon. Hanna had tried directing a couple of the "Captain and the Kids" films in 1938. The results were unimpressive and he returned to working as a story man. Barbera was an animator noted for his ability to create quick, vivid sketches; fifty years later, some animators still remember the vitality of his drawings.

The abilities of the two men complemented each other. When they projected a Leica reel of their sketches and layout drawings with a scratch track, it drew a good response from the animators. The finished film, "Puss Gets the Boot," was a big hit and earned an Oscar nomination. It also introduced a round-faced cat and a chubby-cheeked mouse: the duo that would soon become famous as Tom and Jerry. (In this film, Tom is called Jasper and Jerry doesn't have a name.)

The redoubtable, partially seen Mammy Two-Shoes warns Jasper that if he breaks one more object, he'll be thrown out into the cold. "Jerry" overhears her threat and seizes the chance to avenge the mistreatment he's endured. Most of the film consists of skillfully animated pantomime of the mouse threatening or attempting to smash a vase or a plate—and Jasper trying desperately to thwart him. Cat-and-mouse films had been standard cartoon fare for decades, but Hanna and Barbera cleverly reworked many of the familiar gags. Jasper finally loses the struggle and is thrown out; Jerry adds a sampler reading "Home, Sweet Home" to his mouse hole as the film ends.

"Puss Gets the Boot" proved so successful that Quimby let Hanna and Barbera make a sequel, "The Midnight Snack" (1941), essentially a reworking of the same material. The characters were given the names Tom and Jerry at this point, although no one seems to remember who christened them.

Despite the favorable response to "Puss Gets the Boot" and "The Midnight Snack," Joe Barbera says the series nearly ended with its second installment. "Quimby told us: 'Listen, fellas, let's not put all our eggs in one basket; let's not make any more of these.' Fortunately, he got a letter from an exhibitor in Texas named Besa Short asking: 'Are we going to get any more of these delightful cat-and-mouse cartoons?' Quimby

had great respect for this woman, and if her letter hadn't arrived, we would have stopped making Tom and Jerrys."

They next made "The Night Before Christmas" (1941), which earned their second Oscar nomination; the series continued for more than fifteen years. Like the Warner Brothers cartoons, the Tom and Jerry shorts would only get funnier as Hanna and Barbera honed their skills and developed the characters.

The 1930s were crucial years for American animation, when the studio cartoon evolved from a casually made time filler into a sophisticated, tightly structured, well-animated miniature comedy. The impetus initially came from Disney's development of the medium of animation at the beginning of the decade, but by the late 1930s directors, animators and writers at other studios were applying the Disney discoveries to a new style of humor.

"When I look at those cartoons today, I can see a progression very clearly," comments Friz Freleng. "In only three or four years, unbelievable changes took place. The films that were made in 1938 and 1942 are as different as night and day."

During the next fifteen years, the artists—especially the ones at Warner Brothers and MGM—would crown their achievements with an extraordinary array of brilliant cartoons that have yet to be surpassed anywhere in the world.

A cel of Barney Bear with the title character from "Unwelcome Pest" (1945).

ANIMATION GOES TO WAR, 1941–1945

He was the top man at his craft
But then his number came up
And he was gone in the draft.
He's in the army now . . .
—DON RAY AND HUGHIE PRINCE,
"Boogie Woogie Bugle Boy"

When America entered World War II, the Hollywood animators and their characters devoted themselves to the war effort as assiduously as their live-action counterparts. After paying his income tax to support the military, Donald Duck joined the Army (he wasn't officially discharged until 1984). The Seven Dwarfs explained how to drain swamps to prevent malaria.

The animated training film, pioneered by Max Fleischer during World War I, played a vital role in the education of the men and women in the various branches of the armed services. Animated shorts were often a more effective means of instruction than live-action films or illustrated lectures, because the trainees watched them more attentively.

Soon after America entered the war, many animators enlisted in the 18th Air Force Base Unit (First Motion Picture Unit), which was organized in 1942. Rudy Ising was commissioned as a major and put in charge of the animation unit, assisted by Captain Ray Fahringer and Sergeant Major Gus Ariola (the creator of the comic strip "Gordo"). Frank

Thomas, Bern Wolf, Van Kaufman and Joe Smith headed the four production groups.

Although their work has largely been ignored in histories of the medium, these artists demonstrated the enormous potential of animation as a teaching tool through their development of the training film. Based at the old Hal Roach Studio in Culver City, the FMPU (referred to as "Fum-Pooh" by the men) had a staff of between 125 and 150 officers, enlisted men and civil servants. This group included some of the most talented animators from the major studios—Disney, Warners, Fleischers and MGM.

Despite its status as a military organization, the FMPU allowed these artists more freedom in their work than the studios had. Ising placed no creative restrictions on his men, and allowed them to make films as they thought best. Like their live-action counterparts, the animators turned out enormous amounts of film. During the war years, they produced more animation than any studio in Hollywood.

"Just looking at the volume of work can be misleading," cautions Ising. "A lot of the work was really duplication, because once we made a map, certain films were very simple to do, using what we called 'scratch-off animation.' You started with a line going from this point to that point. The films were shot in reverse, and the cameraman wiped off a little bit of the line before he shot each frame."

Probably the FMPU's best-known animated film was "Posi-

Opposite: A cel setup of Bugs Bunny in uniform, probably for a bond-selling campaign. Like the top movie stars, Hollywood cartoon characters were used to boost morale and raise money for war-related causes.

The staff of the animation unit of the 18th Air Force Base Unit (First Motion Picture Unit).

tion Firing," which explained a difficult but essential principle. A gunner should not aim at an enemy plane where he sees it, but where it will be when the bullet arrives, a fraction of a second later.

"Position Firing" introduced the character Trigger Joe. Bill Hurtz, who animated on the film, describes him as "kind of based on [actor] Bill Bendix, a heavy Brooklyn type. The narrator kept goading him and sharpening his skills while Trigger Joe protested."

"Trigger Joe was a waist gunner," adds Frank Thomas. "We didn't want to put on anything that would upset the waist gunners and get them a bad rap from the other guys. We tried to make him appealing enough, but not too bright, and dedicated to what he was doing; he tried his hardest."

The film proved to be an effective teaching tool that substantially cut the training time needed to prepare gunners for their missions; it was also extremely popular. When "Position Firing" was put in the ten-cent viewing machines in the commissary at Fort Meyers, the soldiers preferred watching it to the Dinah Shore films that were also available.

"At times, we were so busy we just couldn't breathe," recalls Kaufman. "For one film I did with Bernie, we had to go back to New York and use artists from the Signal Corps, because nobody in the unit was available. At other times, we didn't have anything to do for two or even three months. But when

we worked, we sometimes worked Saturdays, Sundays, nights, everything. It really wasn't the Army in that way; we just worked as if we were a bunch of free-lance commercial artists and we had to do it."

The Air Force was the most recently established branch of the armed services, and it was generally perceived as the least tradition-bound and the most freewheeling. But there are limits to how freewheeling any military organization can be, as the animators discovered when they made "How to Fly a Lazy Eight."

A lazy eight is a basic maneuver that resembles an infinity sign—a horizontal figure eight. The pilots had to be taught to execute the maneuver slowly, because if they went through the turns too quickly, their planes would stall and spin out.

"I remembered that Mae West sang the song 'I Like a Man What Takes His Time' in 'She Done Him Wrong,' " says Bern Wolf, who served as a master sergeant in the FMPU. "So I got the idea of using a caricature of her as the central character. I suggested to the powers that be in charge of casting at the post that it would be a good idea to use her voice. They liked the idea."

When Miss West appeared at the studio for the recording session in an evening gown and jewels, accompanied by a hulking bodyguard, she was instantly surrounded by a ring of officers. After performing a slightly modified version of the song, she purred a few ad-libs, like "Well, fellas, you've got to take it easy when you go into that roll . . ." Bill Hurtz, who had been assigned the animation of her character, had to ask how she would perform certain movements.

"She turned to me, batted those great eyelashes and said: 'All right, Corporal, what's your problem?' " he remembers. "Like the young men in her films, I blushed deeply, but I managed to stammer: 'Uh . . . Miss West, how would you get up from a chaise longue?' She went over to this old, broken-down Victorian horsehair sofa and reclined upon it in the manner of the drawing we showed her. Then she floated up with—believe it or not—her pelvis leading and everything else following through and settling into place. It was an extraordinary feat, as that isn't the way anyone could get up.

"When I asked her how she would perform a gesture, she replied: 'Do something like this.' She raised her elbow to shoulder height, then brought up her hand. All her diamond bracelets went clank-clank-clank and slid down to her elbow. She turned to me and said: 'Service stripes!' "

"When we finished the picture, it was a classic on how to fly that maneuver," says Wolf ruefully. "We sent it on to General Hap Arnold, who was chief of the Air Force then. He had a theater in his home, and ran the training films every Sunday for his wife and daughter. They objected strenuously to 'How to Fly a Lazy Eight.' We got orders to emasculate it. We did—which just about wrecked it for us—and sent it out."

Most of the animated films were considerably less flamboyant. The regular narrator for the FMPU pictures was a young lieutenant from the live-action branch of the FMPU: Ronald Reagan. "He was usually the genial classroom instructor who gestured toward the blackboard with a pointer," Hurtz comments. "The diagram would go into animation, illustrating what he had said—that was the usual formula."

The artists at the FMPU collaborated on one project that was such a carefully guarded secret that only the men involved knew its true nature: preparing briefing films for the pilots who bombed Japan.

"A sound stage was sealed off and some of our background painters were ordered to appear there for a top secret project," Hurtz says. "For months they would disappear there. When we'd pump them about what was going on, they'd turn pale just at being asked about it."

"The United States government had no information on Japan—they had never flown any reconnaissance planes over to take pictures," explains Joe Smith, who was the most deeply involved of the animators. "One colonel who had been living in Japan just before Pearl Harbor had gone to all the bookstores and bought every map of Japan he could find. Those maps were absolutely unbelievable—they showed every house, every tree, every railroad track, every building. The Air Force translated them and blew them up into huge maps, from which we made tremendous sets."

Three cel setups of the FMPU's Trigger Joe, the waist gunner who made his debut in "Position Firing." Center, his hands hold the top secret Norden bombsight.

These sets were highly detailed, three-dimensional models of Japanese cities and their surroundings. Constructed as modules on ten-foot squares of plywood, they could be assembled like mosaics. The camera was "flown" over them on beams in scale to the speed that the bomber would fly over the real city—stopping periodically to highlight a target. The films were shot in Los Angeles and developed on the way to Guam on board a special plane equipped with a laboratory. The pilots studied these films before taking off on their bombing runs.

It is difficult to evaluate the work of the FMPU artists, because little—if any—of it survives. Unmindful of their aesthetic and historic value, the Air Force kept the films only as long as the equipment they depicted remained current. When the planes, gunsights, etc., they depicted were replaced, the films were discarded. Many of the films (and much of the unit's equipment) were shipped to Denver at the end of the war, where they were reportedly burned.

Below: A photograph of one of the large modular maps that were used to brief bomber pilots for their raids over Japan. Bottom: The sound stage setup for filming the maps.

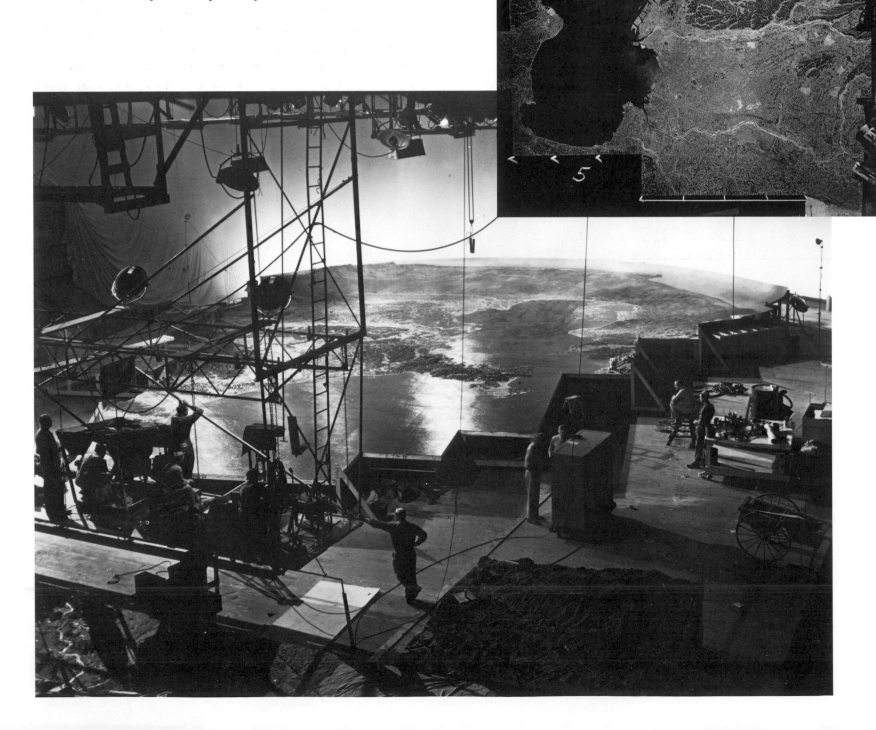

John Hubley's caricature of a distraught Master Sgt. Frank Thomas trying to elicit a response from the reticent Indian chief, Major Rudy Ising.

Herb Klynn, who later became the head of the Civil Service group attached to the FMPU, began working with the Army Signal Corps animation unit in Dayton, Ohio, in 1941. "It consisted of 150 photo retouchers—we didn't even understand how animation was done back there." He contrasts the films made by the Signal Corps and the FMPU: "In Dayton, we used to go into the projection room with what we called the 'nuts and bolts' pictures, and the minute they turned the lights out, the guys we were making them for would go to sleep. The films that were made at the FMPU were *entertaining*. The artists brought humor to them, and it was the introduction of humor that made their training films effective."

The work of the artists at the FMPU undoubtedly contributed to the war effort; it also had a profound, if delayed, effect on the history of animation. Many of the men who later worked at the UPA studio, including Jules Engel, John Hubley, Bill Hurtz, Herb Klynn and Bill Scott, struck up friendships and became aware of each other's talents during the time they spent at "Fort Roach."

By bringing these animators, designers and writers together, the U.S. Air Force inadvertently helped transform the look and content of the American animated film.

The outbreak of the war had a more immediate effect on the Disney studio. Even before America entered the conflict, the war in Europe had cut off a major portion of Disney's overseas revenues, exacerbating the studio's financial plight.

A few hours after the bombing of Pearl Harbor, Disney received a telephone call informing him that the Army was commandeering part of his studio. For the next eight months, the sound stage, the parking garages and some of the other buildings were used to billet men and store ammunition intended for the defense of the California coast. Security checks were run on the studio employees, and everyone was required to wear an identification badge—even Walt and Roy.

Disney may have foreseen America's entry into the war and the need it would create for training films. Early in 1941, he produced the studio's first educational film, "Four Methods of Flush Riveting," a straightforward documentary using limited animation of diagrams. Although intended to train riveters at Lockheed, Disney made the picture on his own initiative and at his own expense. In an article about educational films that appeared near the end of the war, Disney wrote: "More or less unconsciously, we had been preparing for this task for a long time."

When John Grierson, the organizer of the National Film Board of Canada, saw "Four Methods of Flush Riveting" in April 1941, he immediately purchased the Canadian rights. He also commissioned Disney to produce "Stop That Tank," an instructional film on a new antitank rifle, and four short trailers urging Canadian citizens to buy War Bonds. As these films had to be produced quickly and on an extremely limited budget, Disney reused characters and animation from earlier pictures.

Lord Hee Haw, one of the Nazi caricatures from the "Nipponews" reel in Norm McCabe's "Tokyo Jockio" (1943).

AIRCRAFT WARNING SERVICE

VOLUNTEER OBSERVER

Remember PEARL HARBOR

WALT DISNEY

The Three Little Pigs returned to the screen in "The Thrifty Pig," but the Big Bad Wolf sported a Nazi armband, and Practical Pig's redoubtable home was fortified with government bonds. The diamond mine sequence from "Snow White" was included in "The Seven Wise Dwarfs," along with new footage of the Dwarfs exchanging their gems for bonds. "Donald's Decision" was the Duck's first appearance in a patriotic/public service film. Many more would follow. A host of Disney characters paraded in front of the Canadian government buildings in Ottawa in "All Together." Aboard a float, Mickey Mouse conducted the musicians in reused animation from "The Band Concert."

By the time the Canadian trailers were completed in early 1942, the Disney artists were at work on a series of short films for the U.S. Navy on aircraft identification. During the next three years, they made dozens of training films on various technical subjects, most of them for the Navy.

In 1944, Lieutenant Grant Leenhouts, USNR, reported that the Navy maintained an average of 1,000 training films in production. The majority were done in live action, but a substantial portion either were animated or contained animated inserts, usually by Disney. Although nearly one-third of the staff had been drafted, production at the studio skyrocketed. Before the war, Disney's greatest annual output had amounted to 37,000 feet of film; by the end of fiscal year 1942–43, the total had risen to 204,000 feet, 95 percent of it for the military.

"In an effort to keep his organization together, Walt really made his studio into a military reserve, with military security," comments Marc Davis, who remained at Disney throughout the war. "They had the Norden bombsight there, which was apparently the top one any country had for aircraft bombing. It arrived every morning with a bunch of military guards, and they stayed with it all day long, wherever anyone worked with it. I never saw it, except as a package coming in and going out. At that time, you were not encouraged to mill around in some areas of the studio."

The hectic production schedule and minimal budgets (many of these films were made for $15,000 or less) did not permit the use of full animation. Like the work of the FMPU, most of the Disney training films involved limited animation of diagrams, charts, schematics, etc. These films went through the studio so quickly that the animators retain little memory of them.

"We'd work on the training films in between other things," says Ward Kimball, one of Disney's key animators. "I'd dash out the animation—maybe spend a week on it."

In addition to the training films, Disney artists designed logos for more than 1,400 military units and civilian organizations. Some of them featured famous Disney characters: Pluto rode a flying shell for Battery A, 244th Coast Artillery; Dumbo peered through a spyglass for the Sixth Reconnaissance Squadron. Mickey, Minnie, Goofy and Jiminy Cricket appeared on various insignia. Perhaps because of his volatile temper, Donald Duck proved to be the most popular: he was featured on nearly one-quarter of the logos.

Other designs included specially created figures, like the bulldog for the Marine Fighting Squadron 321 or the charging grasshopper for Company F, 114th Infantry. Although the logos cost about $25 apiece to create, Disney provided them free, saying he felt he owed it to the kids serving their country who had grown up on Mickey Mouse.

During the war years, Disney also produced more than two dozen educational films, most of them for the Coordinator of Inter-American Affairs. As titles like "Cleanliness Brings Health," "How Disease Travels" and "Planning for Good Eating" suggest, many of them dealt with social problems affecting Latin America. It's not clear how effective these films were as teaching tools for largely illiterate audiences. Their limited animation and avuncular, didactic tone seem rather stodgy today.

The animators actively disliked "The Winged Scourge" (1943), in which the Seven Dwarfs demonstrate preventative

Opposite: Mickey admonishes the Volunteer Observers for the Aircraft Warning Service to do their duty, in one of the hundreds of logos the Disney studio produced during the war.

Below: "Taxes to Beat the Axis!" A cel and background of the ruined Nazi war machine, from Disney's "The New Spirit" (1942).

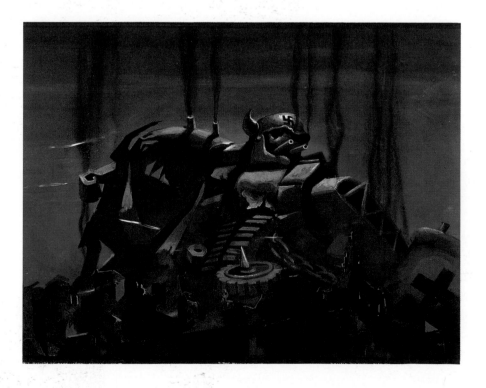

measures against the anopheles mosquito. Having spent years developing the individual personalities of the Dwarfs and making them an integral part of the story, the artists felt constrained by the format of an educational film whose nature prevented them from expressing those laboriously crafted characters.

One of the commissioned films became an object of widespread controversy and caused Disney to be accused—unjustly—of wartime profiteering. In late 1942, Walt was summoned to Washington by Henry Morgenthau, the Secretary of the Treasury. New tax laws would require 15 million people to pay federal income tax for the first time in 1943. Morgenthau wanted a film that would encourage people to pay by showing them how their tax dollars helped to fight the war. And he wanted it in the theaters in six weeks.

The Disney staff quickly put together a story in which Donald Duck learned how easy it was to complete a short tax form. When Disney presented the storyboards to Morgenthau and his staff, aides objected to the use of Donald Duck and suggested replacing him with a "Mr. Taxpayer" character. Disney angrily replied that giving them Donald Duck was the equivalent of MGM giving them Clark Gable—the studio's biggest star—and got approval to proceed with the film.

When Donald's radio asks him: "Are you a patriotic American, eager to do your part?" the Duck replies that he certainly is, even if it means doing something unglamorous that won't earn him a medal. He's surprised to learn he can help by paying income tax, but he complies, declaring: "Taxes to beat the Axis!" When he discovers he owes $13, Donald races across the country to deliver his check to the government himself.

An estimated 60 million people saw "The New Spirit" in 1,100 theaters, and the film accomplished exactly what Morgenthau wanted. A Gallup poll indicated that 37 percent of the taxpayers were more willing to pay after watching it. The cartoon received highly favorable reviews. Ashton Stevens wrote in the Chicago *Tribune* that Disney had transformed "a national bellyache into a national bellylaugh."

However, the Treasury Department had to request a special allocation from Congress to pay the $80,000 bill for the film ($40,000 in production costs, and an equal amount for 1,000 Technicolor prints). The request arrived as Republicans were looking for examples of Democratic overspending. Congressmen denounced the $80,000 expenditure as an outrageous boondoggle, and the subsequent debate unleashed a storm of unfavorable publicity. Disney received hate letters accusing him of profiteering.

These charges were completely unfounded. Disney had donated his services, and the $40,000 figure was about $7,000 below his actual production costs. In addition, the studio lost at least $40,000 more in film rentals when theater owners showed "The New Spirit" (which they got free) instead of a Disney cartoon they would have paid for.

The Academy Awards ceremony that took place in February 1942 must have consoled Walt after this brouhaha. He received the Irving Thalberg Memorial Award and won Oscars for Animated Short ("Lend a Paw") and Best Score for a Musical ("Dumbo"). Disney, Leopold Stokowski, William Garity, John Hawkins and RCA were also given special awards for "Fantasia."

Not even the combined resources of the FMPU and the Disney studio could satisfy the demand for training films. For additional material, the military turned to the Hollywood cartoon studios and to independent contractors like Mel Shaw and Hugh Harman.

Shaw left Disney during the strike in 1941 to form a partnership with Harman, who had recently quit MGM. They planned to produce a feature based on the legend of King Arthur, but soon found themselves making films for the U.S. Army.

"We were able to get some Army contracts, but we didn't have a studio," Shaw comments. "We were working out of my house in Encino, while Hugh ran around like crazy looking for a place. We finally took over Ub Iwerks's old studio in Beverly Hills. We did training films and started working on 'King Arthur.'

"Our training films were very technical," he continues. "We did one in color on gonorrhea for the U.S. Public Health Service, but it was only for physicians. We did films about aligning guns aboard ship, about artillery, about aircraft identification. Some of them were full animation, some were animation/live-action combinations. We turned out films at an unbelievable rate. We made money and were able to pay off the studio."

While they were making training films, Harman and Shaw met Orson Welles. The three men began to plan an ambitious project: a live-action/animation feature based on Antoine de Saint-Exupéry's *The Little Prince*, with Welles as the aviator.

"Orson and I got up the storyboards for the film," explains Shaw. "It was fun working with him—he had started out as an artist. We got pretty far along, and I think we had a pretty good story. But we were in full war by the time we were ready to go ahead on the film. They insisted we do more training films—they needed the footage—so we had to cut back on 'The Little

Opposite: Animation for the war effort. Above, an animation drawing (left) and a model sheet (right) of Private Snafu, created by the Warner Brothers artists for "The Army-Navy Screen Magazine." Below, a model sheet of "Hook" (left), the Navy's equivalent of Snafu, and (right) the title card from one of the character's films.

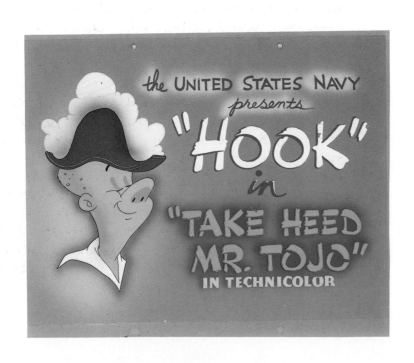

Above: As this animation drawing of Daffy confronting an avian Nazi officer in Friz Freleng's "Daffy Commando" (1943) suggests, the division between entertainment and propaganda grew tenuous during the war.

Below: A storyboard drawing (c. 1941) by Orson Welles, probably of the Geographer, for the proposed live-action/animation feature based on *The Little Prince*.

Prince.' Then Orson got involved in a tent show he was going to put on for the Army and the Navy."

Although he was working on films for the military, Shaw was soon drafted. He served in the FMPU as a live-action director and worked on a documentary about the Burma campaign. Despite later efforts by Shaw, Harman and Rudy Ising, neither "King Arthur" nor "The Little Prince" ever progressed beyond the storyboard stage.

In addition to some technical films for the Navy, the animators at Warner Brothers produced a series of mildly didactic short cartoons for "The Army-Navy Screen Magazine" starring a character named Private Snafu. (Snafu was a popular acronym for "situation *n*ormal—*a*ll *f*ouled/*f*ucked *u*p.") The series was written by Ted Geisel (Dr. Seuss) and Phil Eastman. Each film presented some sort of message or piece of advice in a humorous way.

Snafu ignores safety regulations in "Malaria Mike," and goes swimming in a jungle stream where he encounters an anopheles mosquito. Observing the soldier's bare behind, the mosquito says: "It's Snafu—I never forget a face." In "Rumors," Snafu and his buddies start spreading rumors, and soon their camp is under attack from "flying baloneys." A drunken Snafu learns that loose lips can literally sink ships in "Spies," when he blabs classified information about his ship's departure to a buxom spy equipped with a tape recorder.

Although the Pentagon had to approve the storyboards, Chuck Jones recalls that he and the other directors were given a great deal of latitude in the way they handled the material and were allowed to add comic business. As the Snafu series was intended for an audience of GIs, the gags included lots of cheesecake shots, sexual innuendo, bare posteriors and an occasional "damn" or "hell." Although considered risqué during the 1940s, these cartoons would barely qualify for a PG rating today.

Like their counterparts at Warner Brothers, the animators at Metro-Goldwyn-Mayer made training films for the Army and the Navy. In addition to nuts-and-bolts pictures, they produced a few Private Snafu cartoons and created the character of Bertie the Bomber, a little anthropomorphized airplane. When asked about the plane's human features, Avery told Joe Adamson: "You've got to put a little something in there or the boys'll go to sleep. So we attempted a little humor, as much as we could get and still stay in the same vein."

"Warner Brothers started doing the Snafus, then they got spread out to other studios," says animator Michael Lah. "Making them even helped to categorize us as an essential industry. George Gordon handled some of the training films, and when he left, I moved in and took over the Snafus. We did a couple of them.

"I remember working on one Snafu entitled 'How to Get a

Fat Jap Out of a Cave' that involved a sumo wrestler character," he adds. "It was a very funny picture, and just as we were ready to go under the camera, the Bomb was dropped. We got a call from headquarters to stop all military production. They came a week later and took all the cels, all the animation—we had to keep them separate from the other production. Owen Fitzgerald did the layouts, and I wish I could find some of those drawings, as they were very, very funny."

Walter Lantz also produced films for the military, including a series of stop-motion films for the Navy, animated by background artist Fred Brunish. Director Shamus Culhane recalls: "At least half my time was devoted to military stuff then."

Woody Woodpecker, Andy Panda and Oswald Rabbit soon began appearing on military logos. Woody's flamboyant personality made him the most popular of the studio's characters. In addition, Lantz and his artists painted murals of Woody and his cartoon friends in the mess halls of various military bases.

Like the films of the FMPU, the military films made by the various Hollywood studios were apparently destroyed at the end of the war. Of the uncounted thousands of feet of animation, only some of the Snafu shorts remain in circulation. Their casual destruction contrasts sharply with the dedication and labor of the men and women who produced them.

Walter Lantz surrounded by representatives of some of the armed forces units for which his studio prepared logos and insignia.

Donald's conscience extols the virtues of saving in "The Spirit of '43," one of Disney's war-related shorts.

THE HOME FRONT: ANIMATION, 1941–1945

Any similarity to that little %!@# Hitler is not coincidental . . .*
—Title card from "The Blitz Wolf" (1942)

While many animators worked on training films for the armed services during World War II, the Hollywood cartoon characters helped to keep military and civilian morale high as they tackled the Axis, sold bonds and dealt with wartime shortages.

The bombs that rain down on the Hitler caricature in Tex Avery's "The Blitz Wolf" (MGM, 1942) turn into War Bonds, then dissolve back into shells. When the narrator in Bob Clampett's "Coal Black and de Sebben Dwarfs" (Warners, 1942) declares: "The Wicked Queen was as rich as she was mean," the audience sees her surrounded by gold, jewels, coffee, sugar and white sidewall tires.

"Any Bonds Today?" (1941), a plotless short featuring Bugs Bunny, Porky Pig and an early version of Elmer Fudd doing "the Yam," had the widest circulation of any Warner Brothers cartoon. Andy Panda planted a Victory garden. Daffy Duck tried to dodge the draft, but parachuted behind German lines to bop a caricature of Hitler with a mallet. In "Super Rabbit" (1943), an airborne Bugs looks down and announces: "This looks like a job for a *real* super hero!" He ducks into a phone booth and emerges in uniform, to march off to "Tokyo, Berlin and Points East" singing "The Marines' Hymn" in his Flatbush twang.

During the war years, the aesthetic leadership in animation began to shift. Disney remained the master of lifelike animation and the only successful producer of feature-length films.

But the artists and directors at Warners and MGM took the lead in the field of short films, creating the wild, boldly funny cartoons that still delight audiences.

The distinction between propaganda films like "The New Spirit" and the entertainment shorts Disney produced during the war became extremely tenuous—especially in 1943, when he released "Der Fuehrer's Face," "Education for Death," "Reason and Emotion" and "Chicken Little."

The Oscar-winning "Der Fuehrer's Face" is the most famous Disney cartoon of the World War II era, and Spike Jones's recording of Oliver Wallace's theme song became a smash hit. As a disgruntled Nazi, Donald Duck saws a slice from a wooden loaf of bread and sprays the dining room with the aroma of bacon and eggs. Taking a single, hoarded coffee bean from the wall safe, he tenderly dips it into a cup of hot water. His job in a munitions factory is a wonderfully surreal nightmare of accelerating work loads, skyrocketing shells and caricatures of Hitler. Donald awakens from this dream in a bedroom decorated with American flags. As he kisses a model of the Statue of Liberty, he sighs: "Am I glad to be a citizen of the United States of America!"

Loosely based on Gregor Ziemer's book *Education for Death*, the film shows how children are indoctrinated with Nazi propaganda. After a montage that includes book burnings and stained-glass windows being shattered, the audience sees ranks of icy, goose-stepping soldiers dissolve into rows of

"Education for Death" (1943): Hitler's wooing awakens slumbering Germania, depicted as an obese Valkyrie.

tombstones. The only humor in this grim short occurs when a scrawny caricature of Hitler appears in medieval armor to awaken slumbing Germania, a monstrously fat Brünnhilde.

"Reason and Emotion" ranks as the oddest of the wartime shorts. Proper little characters representing "reason" vie with wild little figures personifying "emotion" inside the heads of a man and a woman. (The thuggish male "emotion" character is actually a caricature of animator Ward Kimball.) When "emotion" takes control, the woman goes on an eating binge; the man makes a pass at her and gets his face slapped. Ultimately, unfettered emotion causes the man to succumb to the blandishments of Nazi propaganda.

The relict entertainment value of "Reason and Emotion" comes from the exuberant actions of the volatile "emotion" figures. Ollie Johnston feels his work with the female character suggested a new approach to the animation of women.

"I don't think we'd ever had a broad cartoon girl," he says thoughtfully. "She might have established a new type of girl character we could have used in our pictures—one that could be handled broadly and still be convincing. Unfortunately, there wasn't enough of her in the picture or enough different types of situations to test the idea—she was just highly emotional and very excitable."

Disney's most ambitious wartime project was "Victory Through Air Power." In his controversial book, Major Alexander P. de Seversky argued that the use of airplanes, particularly long-range bombers, had irrevocably transformed modern warfare. He asserted its superiority over more traditional land and sea forces, and called for the creation of an air

force that would be an independent branch of the armed services. The book was an unlikely subject for a film, especially an animated one.

"Victory" opens with a tongue-in-cheek history of aviation —the only humorous segment in the film. For the remainder of the picture, the Disney artists used limited animation of diagrams, blueprints, charts and maps to illustrate various concepts and arguments. Seversky appears in several live-action scenes, expounding his philosophy and berating the "earthbound minds" that oppose it.

"Victory Through Air Power" premiered on August 13, 1943, to mixed reviews. *New York Times* critic Thomas Pryor wrote: "If 'Victory Through Air Power' is propaganda, it is at least the most encouraging and inspiring propaganda that the screen has afforded us in a long time. Mr. Disney and his staff can be proud of their accomplishment."

However, James Agee offered a strongly dissenting opinion in *The Nation:* "I only hope Major de Seversky and Walt Disney know what they are talking about, for I suspect an awful lot of people who see 'Victory Through Air Power' are going to think they do. I have the feeling I was sold something under pretty high pressure, which I don't enjoy, and I am staggered by the ease with which such self-confidence, on matters of such importance, can be blared all over a nation, without cross-questioning."

The modern viewer will probably agree. Except for the dramatic confrontation between the octopus and the eagle, "Victory Through Air Power" is long, slow and very dull. Through repetition, the pan shots of swooping airplanes and falling bombs and the many explosions lose much of their strength. The film hammers away at the audience, relentlessly expounding Seversky's gospel of the airplane.

An inspirational drawing by Marc Davis of the battle between the octopus (the Japanese Empire) and the eagle (the U.S. Air Force) for "Victory Through Air Power" (1943).

The box office failure of "Victory Through Air Power" (it lost nearly $500,000) probably helped persuade Walt to give up the idea of a feature based on Roald Dahl's stories about gremlins. Described as elves of bad luck, gremlins were blamed for the technical problems that vexed RAF pilots at the beginning of the war. No one had ever seen a gremlin, and no one knew what one was supposed to look like. After working for more than a year, the Disney artists didn't know either.

Legal questions arose over the rights to the gremlin characters, and preproduction costs climbed past $50,000. The project was abandoned shortly after the opening of "Victory Through Air Power"; all that survives are some sketches in the Disney archives.

Released at the end of October 1941, "Dumbo" can be described as the first of Disney's wartime features or the last of his prewar features. In either case, it remains one of the best animated films ever made at the Disney studio—or anywhere else.

The story of a baby elephant who is rejected because of his outsized ears, but manages to triumph over the cruelest adversity, runs the gamut of emotions and is ideally suited to the medium. Perhaps because it was made quickly and inexpensively (in only eighteen months and costing less than $1 million), the picture displays an exuberance and spontaneity matched only by the early Silly Symphonies.

Much of the key animation of the title character was done by Bill Tytla, who said his work was inspired by his infant son. Although utterly unlike the dark, muscular forces he evoked in "Fantasia," "Pinocchio" and "Victory Through Air Power,"

Tytla's work in "Dumbo" is equally powerful. The scene in which the lonely little elephant visits his imprisoned mother and is rocked to sleep in her trunk still brings tears to viewers' eyes.

Ward Kimball ranks the animation of the jaunty crows who give Dumbo confidence in the form of a "magic feather" among the best work of his career. A jazz fan and a musician, he found the crows "exactly what I had in mind for animation. I realized that if you took a bunch of crows, you had to create a personality for each one, just as Walt had always insisted that the Dwarfs had to have seven distinct personalities with clean demarcations between them. I had the little guy with the little felt hat and the big pink glasses, and Jim Crow, the leader, who wore a derby and was slightly tough, as the extremes. The rest were in-between characters."

The crows, who emerge as black characters—rather than black stereotypes—perform the catchy "When I See an Elephant Fly." Their loose-limbed movements include some impossible exaggerations: when the littlest crow rolls his eyes, the pupils circle the rims of his glasses, beyond the curve of his head. These distortions help give the crows the visual interest needed to follow one of the wildest sequences in the history of animation: "Pink Elephants on Parade."

Dumbo and Timothy, the brash circus mouse, inadvertently get drunk on a bucketful of champagne. When Timothy challenges Dumbo to blow an enormous bubble, its shimmering pink form turns into a cartoon elephant. Several minutes of the most wonderfully surreal insanity follow, as the pink pachyderms merrily grow, shrink, multiply, divide, metamorphose and change color. The fluid motion and constantly

Two "Technicolor pachyderms" share a surreal moment in the "Pink Elephants on Parade" sequence from "Dumbo" (1941).

shifting imagery demonstrate how utterly limitless the imagi-nation of Disney's artists—and the medium of animation—could be.

"When I give talks to students, invariably one of the ques-tions at the end is: 'What were you guys on when you did such things as the pink elephants?'" comments Kimball. "And they're shocked to find that we had an occasional martini at the Tam O'Shanter and that was about all. Modern students cannot accept that we did not use LSD to think that way; well, God, it was just the way we thought!"

RKO complained that at 64 minutes "Dumbo" was too short to release as a feature, but Disney refused to lengthen it. The critical and financial success of the film vindicated his deci-sion, and the $850,000 profit it earned brought welcome relief to the financially troubled studio.

Preliminary work on "Bambi" began in 1937 or 1938—the accounts vary. Disney read Felix Salten's popular novel about a young deer growing to maturity, and saw its potential as an animated film. But for the picture to be believable, the ani-mals would have to be very realistic in their designs and movements.

Photographer Maurice Day was dispatched to the Maine woods, where he shot thousands of feet of reference film, capturing everything from various animals and plants to shift-ing light on spiderwebs to the effects produced by the chang-ing seasons. Rabbits, owls, ducks, skunks and two fawns were brought to the studio for the animators to sketch.

Disney hired Rico Lebrun, a noted animal painter, to teach at the studio. As the drawing lessons progressed, Disney had four of his best young artists—Frank Thomas, Milt Kahl, Ollie Johnston and Eric Larson—begin animating. Because of his exceptional knowledge of animal anatomy, Marc Davis was assigned to work with director Dave Hand, story director Perce Pearce, story adaptor Larry Morey and the rest of the crew developing the plot and the business for the characters. To help the animators evoke the emotions of the little fawn, Davis studied a book on infant psychology and adapted the expressions on the babies' faces to a deer's anatomy.

The antlers of the majestic Prince of the Forest and the adult Bambi presented special difficulties. None of the artists could keep them in perspective and maintain their volume. The pencil tests looked rubbery and seemed to wobble. Thomas and Johnston report that the problem was solved by sculpting models of the deer's heads that were the same size as the drawings. One of the models would be held under a drawing, and the antlers traced onto it.

After six years of work, "Bambi" premiered in the summer of 1942 to generally favorable reviews. The critics who disliked the film complained that it was too cute and, ironically, too realistic. In *The New Republic*, Manny Farber wrote: "The robust irrationality of the mouse comedies has been squelched completely by the syrup that has been flowing over

Opposite: Bambi encounters his first butterfly while Thumper and his siblings watch, in "Bambi" (1942).

Below: Some of Tyrus Wong's preliminary mood sketches for "Bambi." His exquisite studies inspired the animators and helped to set the tone of the film.

the Disney way. In an attempt to ape the trumped-up realism of flesh and blood movies, he has given up fantasy, which was pretty much the magic element ... Mickey wouldn't be caught dead in this.''

Although it has had several popular reissues, ''Bambi'' failed to duplicate the success of ''Snow White.''

''Two films came out around the beginning of the war, 'Bambi' and 'Fantasia,' and for somewhat different reasons, both of them were highly unsuccessful,'' explains Roy E. Disney. '' 'Fantasia' was ahead of its time. 'Bambi' was a sweet little story about please don't kill the deer, when we were talking about killing human beings, and it just didn't sell.''

''Bambi'' contains little of the sustained fantasy of ''Dumbo'' and ''Pinocchio.'' In its place is a lyrical and idealized—but rather tame—vision of life in the forest. The style of the film varies sharply. In some scenes, realistic deer bound in per-

fectly observed arcs against delicate wash backgrounds, inspired by the drawings of designer Tyrus Wong. In other sequences, the animals do cartoon takes more typical of Warner Brothers than Disney.

The draftsmanship is uniformly excellent: The animators captured both the grace and the spindly-legged gawkiness of the young fawn. When reprimanded by his mother, Thumper behaves like a small boy caught with his hand in the cookie jar. His body language and expressions convey the perfect balance of fear and embarrassment as he struggles to remember his lessons.

The film also contains some of the most dramatic and frightening moments in any Disney feature: the forest fire, Faline's pursuit by the hunting dogs, Bambi's duel with a rival buck. The death of Bambi's mother has made generations of children—and adults—cry. One of Disney's daughters reportedly reproached him for allowing the hunters to kill the mother. When Walt protested that it happened in the book and he couldn't change it, she replied that he had changed other things in the book, and he could have changed that too.

In 1941, Disney was asked to make a goodwill tour of South America by John Hay "Jock" Whitney, who served as head of the Motion Picture Division for Nelson Rockefeller, the Coordinator of Inter-American Affairs. Officials in the CIAA office were concerned that German and Italian immigrants there might be generating pro-Axis sentiment. The Disney characters were popular in Latin America, and Whitney wanted to capitalize on that popularity. (His decision may well have been influenced by Disney's chief counsel, Gunther Lessing, who had been appointed chairman of the short subjects committee for the CIAA the year before.)

Walt was initially reluctant to accept the offer. He had never been a particularly outgoing man, and the request came at a very bad time. A third of his employees were on strike, and his debt to the Bank of America had risen to $3.4 million. Whitney added an incentive: the government would underwrite $70,000 in tour expenses and advance up to $50,000 apiece for up to five films based on the tour.

Disney left Los Angeles on August 17, 1941. Among the sixteen members of his entourage (dubbed "El Groupo") were Mrs. Disney, Norm Ferguson, Webb Smith, Bill Cottrell, Ted Sears, Lee and Mary Blair and Frank Thomas. During the next several weeks, Disney and his artists visited Brazil, Argentina, Bolivia and Chile.

Sixteen-millimeter footage of the trip was used in "South of the Border with Disney," a half-hour film released late in 1942. This travelogue has largely been forgotten, and is interesting only for the sketches it contains of José Carioca, Pedro the Mail Plane, Goofy in gaucho costume and other characters that would later appear in "Saludos Amigos."

Disney originally considered making as many as twelve shorts about South America, but decided to release them as features in packages of four. "Saludos Amigos," which opened in February 1943, was the first of the package features. The four cartoons are loosely strung together with travel footage of "a group of musicians and artists."

In "Lake Titicaca," Donald Duck plays the tourist and tries to cope with a balky, aloof llama, regally animated by Milt Kahl. "Pedro" is essentially a variation on the story of the little engine that could: a little mail plane has to take his father's place and fly over the Chilean Andes. Goofy wreaks havoc throughout the Pampas in "El Gaucho Goofy," a segment that features some outstanding straight-ahead animation by Woolie Reitherman. Donald returns for the final segment, "Aquarela do Brasil" ("Watercolor of Brazil"), and learns the samba from the jaunty parrot, José Carioca.

"Saludos Amigos" opened in South America before it did in the United States. The enthusiastic response the film received

Carmen Molina with a few of her attendant cacti in "The Three Caballeros" (1945).

in Latin America was somewhat dampened by local jealousies. People in the countries Disney hadn't visited or used as a setting for a cartoon—especially Venezuela, Cuba and Uruguay—resented their "exclusion."

"Saludos Amigos" feels more like a choppy series of shorts than a coherent feature, and the uninspired live-action sequences have become hopelessly dated. The film has never been reissued in its entirety, although the individual cartoons have been shown both in theaters and on television. Most people regard it as a prelude to the more imaginative "The Three Caballeros," which was released two years later.

Fast-paced and overflowing with energy, "Caballeros" bursts onto the screen in a welter of characters, explosions, montages, special effects and striking live-action/animation combinations. Bosley Crowther aptly described it as "a brilliant hodgepodge of Mr. Disney's illustrative art—a literal spinwheel of image, color and music which tumbles at you with explosive surprise."

The film was originally entitled "Surprise Package," as it opens with Donald receiving a box of birthday presents "from his friends in Latin America." The first gift consists of a projector, a screen and a can of film. The film-within-a-film, "Aves Rares" ("Strange Birds"), is divided into three parts.

The first segment tells the story of Pablo, a wistful little penguin, who yearns to leave the frigid Antarctic for the balmy Galápagos Islands. Pablo's saga is followed by the introduction of the Aracuan, a dizzy tropical bird that nonchalantly pops in and out of the frame. The section ends with the story of the little gauchito and his flying burro, told by "an old gaucho from Uruguay."

Donald's next present is a pop-up book on Brazil. José Carioca emerges from the pages to shrink Donald and take him on a train ride to Baía. There the two Caballeros encounter Aurora Miranda (Carmen's sister), who performs "Os Quindins de Yaya" ("The Cookies of Yaya"). Smitten with the actress's charms, Donald kisses her, producing the first of many explosive live-action/animation fantasies in gloriously garish Technicolor.

Emerging from the book, Donald and José reinflate themselves to normal size. After a series of mishaps, Donald begins to grow into a piñata. José shatters the expanding duck, and the third Caballero emerges: Panchito, a Mexican charro (cowboy) rooster. The trio perform the title song in an exuberant, madcap sequence animated by Ward Kimball.

"I really didn't know what I was going to do with that sequence," he recalls. "I sat there a week and listened to the song over and over. Then one day I said: 'Why don't I be literal? If they talk about bookends, they'll become bookends; if they mention serapes, serapes will appear.' I started to smile—I knew that was the solution, and I couldn't wait to work on it. I sat down and did thumbnails of the whole thing."

The song ends with Panchito holding the last note for an impossible twenty seconds, while Donald and José scramble for ways to silence him. Director Clyde Geronimi objected to Kimball's illogical handling of the sequence: Donald may exit to the right and come in from the top. But Disney liked the scene, and as Kimball remarks, "that was all that mattered." It appears in the film unchanged.

In the strangest sequence of all, Carmen Molina performs the Zandunga and the Jesusita in animated settings with Donald as her partner. During the latter dance, lines of rather phallic saguaro cacti serve as a chorus. The end of the sequence segues into the film's finale, replete with animated fireworks.

The intricate combinations of animation and live-action footage are extremely complex and represented the state of the art. (Airbrushed shadows give Donald a look that approximates the three-dimensional human characters.) But for all the technical polish, the result is less than the sum of its parts. As the reviewer in *The New Yorker* observed: "A somewhat physical romance between a two-foot duck and a full-sized woman, though one happens to be a cartoon and the other pleasantly rounded and certainly mortal, is one of those things that might disconcert less squeamish authorities at the Hays office. . . . It might even be said that a sequence involving the duck, the young lady and a long alley of animated cactus plants would probably be considered suggestive in a less innocent medium."

Despite decidedly mixed reviews, "The Three Caballeros" did reasonably well at the box office. Like "The Reluctant Dragon" and "Saludos Amigos," it has never been re-released theatrically, probably because so much of it seems passé to contemporary audiences. Still, this frenetic, often surreal film ended Disney's wartime efforts with an undeniable bang.

Richard Shale estimates that about 40 percent of the Warner Brothers cartoons made during the war contain material relating to the conflict or home-front situations. Their use of topical material varies from blatant propaganda shorts to odd references and spot gags.

In "Draftee Daffy" (1945), Daffy Duck is so desperate to escape the little man with his draft notice that he blows himself to hell. But he patriotically resists—and outwits—Hata Mari, the pigeon se-duck-tress/Axis spy, in "Plane Daffy" (1944).

Norm McCabe caricatured Hitler, Mussolini and Hirohito as barnyard fowl in "The Ducktators" (1942); the film opens with an apology "to all the nice ducks and geese in our audience." "Dot Bugsenheimer Bunny" dresses up as Brünnhilde and Joseph Stalin to bedevil Hermann Goering and "Der Fuehrer" in Freleng's "Herr Meets Hare" (1945). The trainload of valuables Bugs robs in "Buckaroo Bugs" (1944) carries butter, sugar, tires and gasoline. But he suddenly jumps off the caboose of another train in "The Unruly Hare" (1945) because "us civilians ain't supposed to do any unnecessary travelin' for the duration."

One of the wildest wartime shorts is Bob Clampett's "Russian Rhapsody" (1944), in which a clutch of tiny gremlins—depicted as homunculi—sing "We Are Gremlins from the Kremlin" (to the tune of "Dark Eyes") as they gleefully sabotage a German bomber headed for Moscow. Most of the gremlins are caricatures of Warners staff members, including Friz Freleng, Mel Blanc, Mike Maltese, Leon Schlesinger and Clampett himself. Clampett wanted to call the film "Gremlins from the Kremlin," but Disney had asked the other cartoon producers not to use "Gremlins" in any titles while he was working on his feature, and Schlesinger had agreed.

Regardless of the subject they tackled, the Warners animation directors were clearly hitting their stride. They began to use the knowledge of comedy and timing they had gained from their experiments during the late 1930s to construct the solid, fast-paced cartoons that built their reputations. During the war, the Warner Brothers roster included five top-flight directors—Tex Avery, Bob Clampett, Friz Freleng, Chuck Jones and Frank Tashlin.

Avery continued to develop the fast pacing, extreme takes and off-the-wall humor that became the hallmarks of his distinctive style. In "Cross Country Detours" (1940), the most famous of his travelogue spoofs, he rotoscoped a stripper for a sequence of a lizard shedding its skin. When the narrator praises a polar bear's ability to withstand frigid arctic weather, the bear interrupts with "I don't care what you say, I'm cold."

Daffy in a semi-demure moment from Clampett's "The Wise Quacking Duck" (1943). Note that the paint on the cel has begun to flake away.

A model sheet of the gremlin from Bob Clampett's "Falling Hare" (1943).

He had Porky make his own cartoon in "Porky's Preview" (1941). The clever film-within-a-film features rubbery animation of childish stick-figure characters. Porky modestly dismisses the applause his work receives from the cartoon audience: "But it wasn't hard, because, shucks, I'm an artist."

In "A Wild Hare," Avery had introduced not only Bugs Bunny but Elmer Fudd. (Elmer was essentially a more refined version of Egghead, a round-headed, bulbous-nosed, goofy character he had created in 1937.) But in the second Bugs cartoon, "Tortoise Beats Hare" (1941), he let a family of sneaky turtles outwit the wascally wabbit.

Avery inadvertently proved in "Tortoise Beats Hare" that Bugs has to be a winner. He's not funny when he loses, as Elmer and Daffy are. Among the least successful Bugs cartoons are two in which someone gets the better of him—Clampett's "Falling Hare" (1943) and Jones's "Rabbit Rampage" (1955).

Avery left Warner Brothers in early 1942. After a brief stint at Paramount, where he helped develop "Speaking of Animals," a comedy series that combined live-action footage of animals and cartoon mouths, he took over Hugh Harman's old unit at MGM. Although Avery would make his best and funniest films at Metro, his influence at Warners was widespread and profound.

"Tex was the best director I ever worked for," says Virgil Ross. "He had such terrific ideas and his stuff was so different. So far as I know, he invented the off-screen narrator, which lent itself to an entirely new range of gags. And his gags were so far-out that they were really funny."

"Tex Avery was a genius," declares Chuck Jones. "I learned from him the most important truth about animation. Animation is the art of timing, a truth applicable as well to all motion pictures. And the most brilliant masters of timing were usually comedians: Keaton, Chaplin, Laurel and Hardy, Langdon—and Fred 'Tex' Avery."

Although Bob Clampett toned down the surreal anarchy of "Porky in Wackyland" (1938) and "The Daffy Doc" (1938), his animation remained the rubberiest, his characters the zaniest and his gags the most outrageous.

In "The Henpecked Duck" (1941), Daffy accidentally makes his egg disappear while practicing magic tricks. His horrified reactions are exaggerated and extreme, but lack the Silly Putty distortions of Clampett's earlier Daffys. After being struck on the head, Daffy dreams he's the famous detective Duck Twacy in "The Great Piggy Bank Robbery" (1946). He tackles a bizarre array of villains that go beyond anything Chester Gould ever imagined, including "Juke Box Jaw," "Mouse Man," "Pickle Puss" and "Neon Noodle."

Clampett's version of Bugs Bunny was the screwiest and most emotional. When Bugs lands on a cow's skeleton in "Bugs Bunny Gets the Boid" (1942), he thinks he's seeing his own exposed bones and bursts into tears. He literally beats the drum for himself as he tries to lobby the Motion Picture Academy into giving him the Oscar for Best Actor in "What's Cookin', Doc?" (1944). When he loses to Jimmy Cagney, Bugs makes such a fuss that the members give him a bogus award.

Bugs is probably at his wackiest in two of Clampett's best-known cartoons, "A Corny Concerto" (1943) and "The Big Snooze" (1946—his last Warners short). A rumpled Elmer Fudd plays Deems Taylor and introduces "A Corny Concerto," which spoofs "Fantasia." A Daffy-esque ugly duckling tries to join a family of swans in the opening sequence, set to "The Blue Danube."

Above: Four cels of Bugs in his ballerina costume from "A Corny Concerto" (1943) capture the vitality of the animation.

Left: A lobby card for "Wabbit Twouble" (1941). During this period, Elmer Fudd was drawn as a very fat little man who looked a bit like voice actor Arthur Q. Bryant.

A lobby card for "Horton Hatches the Egg" (1942),
the first cartoon based on a Dr. Seuss story.

In the second section, Bugs outwits Porky and a hunting dog to "Tales of the Vienna Woods." When an irate squirrel fires Porky's rifle at them, the three characters clutch their hearts and collapse. Porky and the dog cautiously inspect their chests and discover they're unharmed; Bugs peeks at his, screams and melts. When the weeping duo pry the Rabbit's fingers apart, they discover he's wearing a baby-blue bra. Bugs, now clad in a matching blue tutu, screams, wraps the bra around their heads like a cowl and cavorts off in a series of balletic leaps.

Fed up with playing the fall guy, Elmer tears up his contract with Warner Brothers at the beginning of "The Big Snooze." Bugs invades Elmer's dreams, determined to get him back—to save both their careers. He ties Elmer to a railroad track and uses an adding machine to produce scores of baby bunnies that run over him like a train. He dresses Elmer in an evening gown, high heels and a wig, then dumps him at Hollywood and Vine. Pursued by zoot-suited wolves, the hapless Fudd jumps off a cliff and falls back into reality. This "howwible nightmare" convinces him to go back to work.

"Clampett clung to the 'Wild Hare' syndrome," comments Jones. "In his pictures, Bugs doesn't seem to need provocation to attack—he acts more like Woody Woodpecker. He's a thoroughly amoral lunatic—with flashes of greatness."

Clampett's reputation rests on his zany, funny shorts. But he revealed a gentler side of himself in 1942, when he made a sympathetic adaptation of the Dr. Seuss story "Horton Hatches the Egg," a film quite faithful to both the story and the illustrations. Clampett left Warners in 1946 to pursue other activities, including puppetry.

Friz Freleng was regarded as the blue-ribbon director of the studio. He did most of the color films and hadn't had to bother with the Buddy/Cookie characters. He earned that respect with top-notch films like "You Oughta Be in Pictures" (1940), "Rhapsody in Rivets" (1941) and "The Trial of Mr. Wolf" (1941).

"You Oughta Be in Pictures" is an extremely imaginative combination of live action and animation. Daffy persuades Porky to quit Warners and find work at another studio "opposite Greta Garbo" at a fabulous salary. Porky asks Leon Schlesinger (who portrays himself) to tear up his contract, and sets out to seek his fortune.

Porky's excursion into the world of live action proves disastrous. He inadvertently drives onto the set of a Western, right into the path of a cattle stampede. To escape, he has to fight his way through a Burbank traffic jam. Meanwhile, Daffy is trying to talk Leon into making him a cartoon star. (Curiously, even in the scenes they had together, Schlesinger never noticed that Daffy's lisp was patterned on his own.) Porky finally returns, gets his old job back and proceeds to beat the cookies out of Daffy.

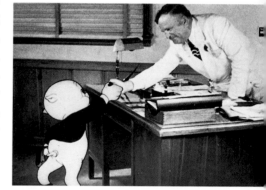

"I made 'You Oughta Be in Pictures' because I thought it was novel and I had the freedom to do it," says Freleng. "I think Schlesinger let me because showing him as the boss appealed to his ego. You'll notice Ray Katz isn't in it, nor Henry Bender. It's just Leon."

"Rhapsody in Rivets" show-cases Freleng's ability to blend images and music. A lion com-

bines the duties of construction foreman and orchestral conductor as his crew erects a skyscraper to Liszt's Hungarian Rhapsody No. 2. The film is done entirely in pantomime to the music, with the sight gags keyed to the various instrumental motifs.

Even funnier and much broader is "The Trial of Mr. Wolf," the story of Red Riding Hood told from the Wolf-Defendant's point of view. Grandma runs a fur salon and dances the conga; Red, who speaks in a Katharine Hepburn voice, kidnaps the Wolf, hoping to get his pelt. When Granny moans in fake pain, the Wolf asks what's wrong. Red replies: "It's Grandma: she

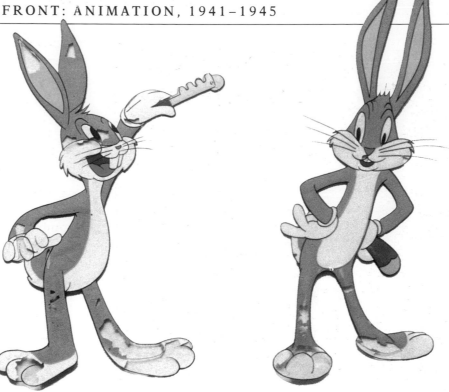

Right: Two cels from Freleng's "Jack Rabbit and the Beanstalk" (1943). At this phase in his development, Bugs had shorter limbs and was painted taupe, rather than gray.

has a terrific hangover—I mean she's terribly ill, *rally* she is." When his farfetched tale fails to convince even a jury composed of wolves, the Defendant proclaims that if he hasn't told the truth, "I hope I get run down by a streetcar!" A trolley obligingly crashes through the courthouse wall and knocks him flat.

"Friz was wonderful," states animator Phil Monroe. "He was the first director I ever worked for. He always knew his pictures were funny; they got better every year he was there, and everybody recognized it. He taught me so much about staging things in simple forms."

Chuck Jones was the most eager to experiment with new graphic styles and types of humor. In 1941, he took the diminutive native from "The Little Lion Hunter" (1939) and paired him with a mysterious Mynah Bird in "Inki and the Lion." The Mynah hops along inexorably to Mendelssohn's "Fingal's Cave Overture," blithely going over or through everything in his path. He stops for nothing, not even the ravenous lion, and never misses a beat in his syncopated hop step.

Jones insists that he never understood this bizarre, minimal film and that he was as surprised as anyone by its popularity. He used the characters in two other cartoons, "Inki and the Mynah Bird" (1943) and "Inki at the Circus" (1947), then declined to make any more.

During production of one of the Inki films, animator Ben Washam discovered Shamus Culhane's unique approach to his work: "On Monday, Shamus didn't draw a line," he recalled. "He just sat at his drawing table, ate peanuts and stared at the paper while the rest of us worked. Tuesday, Wednesday, Thursday, it was the same story. Then he came in on Friday and whipped through his scene in a couple of hours. When I asked why he hadn't done anything all week if he

could work that fast, he looked at me and said: 'You have to think about it first!'"

Another of Jones's early experiments proved to be one of his more popular films: "The Dover Boys ('At Pimento University')" (1942), a spoof of Victorian "mellerdrammers." The Dover Boys—Tom, Dick and Larry—from "dear old P.U." woo dear, rich Dora Standpipe, despite the efforts of "that coward-bully-cad-and-thief," Dan Backslide. The designs anticipate the flattened graphics the artists at UPA would use a decade later. The animation is equally stylized: Dora slides through the film as if she had casters instead of feet. "The Dover Boys" remains a very funny cartoon, and its distinctive look must have surprised audiences in 1941.

An original background of the instructions on how to remove dear, rich Dora Standpipe from the tree she's clutching in Jones's "The Dover Boys" (1942).

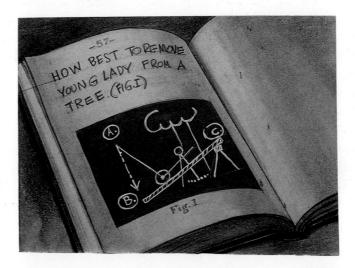

Below, Pepe LePew, introduced by Chuck Jones in 1945, in a model sheet from "Scent-i-mental Romeo" (1951); bottom, a cel setup of the character from "The Cat's Bah" (1954).

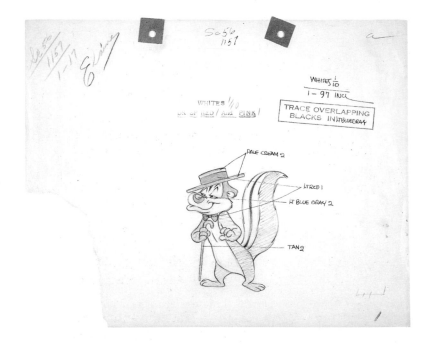

Jones introduced Pepe LePew, the amorous French skunk, in "Odor-able Kitty" (1945) and his own version of an ursine trio in "Bugs Bunny and the Three Bears" (1944). Apoplectic little Poppa Bear, big, stupid Junyer and slatternly Mama try to lure Goldilocks to their house. As they don't have any porridge —just some old carrots—Mama makes carrot soup, which brings Bugs. To avoid being captured, Bugs romances Mama —who then pursues him in various costumes, including a Veronica Lake wig and negligee. She eventually follows him down his rabbit hole, begging him to "tell me more about my eyes."

Not all Jones's experiments proved successful. Phil Monroe recalls that his work with Conrad, a cat modeled after comic actor Ben Blue, "laid some of the biggest eggs you've ever seen." Many of his wartime cartoons were good, but he would do his best work after the war.

In 1943, Frank Tashlin returned to Warners after five years at Disney and Columbia, and essentially picked up where he left off. His first cartoon was "Scrap Happy Daffy," in which Daffy defends his scrap heap against the depredations of a metal-eating Nazi goat sent by Hitler.

A caricature of Frank Sinatra as a rooster distracts Porky's hens from laying at "Flockheed Eggcraft" in "The Swooner Crooner" (1944). Porky tries to coax them back to work with Eddie Cantor, Al Jolson, Cab Calloway and Jimmy Durante caricatures, but to no avail. Finally, a Bing Crosby rooster arrives to challenge Sinatra; their vocal duel sends the hens into such raptures that they lay mountains of eggs.

Tashlin stayed in the animation unit for only about two years. His last cartoon was "Hare Remover" (1946), a Bugs Bunny–Elmer Fudd short. He moved into live action, writing and, later, directing comedies with Bob Hope, Jane Russell, Dean Martin, Jerry Lewis, Danny Kaye, Jayne Mansfield and Tony Randall. Film historians have pointed out the strong affinities between his cartoons and the more frenetic moments in his live-action features, such as "Will Success Spoil Rock Hunter."

In addition to Pepe LePew and Jones's Three Bears, three other popular Warners characters made their debuts during the war. In 1942, Tweety made his first appearance in Bob Clampett's "A Tale of Two Kitties." Clampett originally intended to make him pink, but was told that made the little bird look "too naked." He gave Tweety a coat of yellow feathers and turned him into a canary. Tweety's classic line, "I taw I taw a putty tat!" was an instant hit.

Freleng introduced Tweety's familiar nemesis, the loose-lipped putty tat Sylvester, three years later, in "Life with Feathers." Tweety and Sylvester weren't paired until 1947, when Freleng brought them together in "Tweetie Pie." That film won Freleng and Warners their first Oscar, and set the pattern for all the subsequent cartoons (although Sylvester is called Thomas in it).

In 1945, Freleng created another of his enduring characters in "Hare Trigger": Yosemite Sam. Many cartoon fans have asserted that the red-haired, hot-tempered, pint-sized Sam was a partial caricature of Freleng, which he denies.

"That story is an after-the-fact thing," Freleng explains. "I was looking for a little tiny cowboy to hold up a train; I wanted the smallest guy I could find with the biggest voice I could find. So I sketched this little guy and Hawley Pratt worked over the drawings—he was a very good designer. Sam didn't change much: he was as final in that film as he is today."

Freleng would spend the better part of the next decade working with these three characters—devising ways for Sylvester to outwit himself in his efforts to catch Tweety, and blowing Sam to smithereens. Freleng and Jones would dominate Warner Brothers animation during the postwar era, creating some of the funniest and best-known cartoons in the history of the medium.

Two animation drawings of the wolf making his prison break in Tex Avery's "Dumb-Hounded" (1943).

By 1941, MGM had a well-established reputation for producing lavish and beautifully animated cartoons. Like most of the animation created for the war effort, their training films have been forgotten. But the studio's animation department remains famous because during the 1940s the genius of Tex Avery blossomed like a manic flower and Tom the cat chased Jerry the mouse, guided by Bill Hanna and Joe Barbera. (Avery took over Hugh Harman's old unit when Harman left to become an independent producer. When Rudy Ising went into the military, his artists were absorbed into the Hanna-Barbera unit.)

Animation historian John Canemaker observed: "Warners was a practice ground for Tex Avery. When he moved in 1942 to the MGM cartoon studio, his experiments in timing, layering gags, and free expressive use of the medium came to fruition." The first film he directed there was "The Blitz Wolf," an outrageous and topical retelling of the story of the Three Little Pigs, brimming with the kind of gags Avery would use again and again—always to good effect.

When Adolf Wolf enters (in a small tank labeled "Der Fewer der Better"), he holds up a sign that says "Go on and hiss! Who cares," and gets hit with a tomato from off screen—as if someone in the audience had thrown it. Confronted with a mud puddle, Adolf lifts up the treads of the tank like a skirt (revealing lacy underpinnings) and tiptoes through the muck; then he rolls on.

The foolish Pigs, who build their houses of straw and sticks, try to reason with the Wolf: "But, Adolf, you have a treaty with us—you wouldn't go back on your word!" After he blows down their homes, a sign appears reading: "Gone With the Wind"; a second one adds: "Corny gag, isn't it?" The frightened Pigs seek refuge with "Sergeant Pork," their practical brother, and wage war on Adolf from his gun-encrusted house of bricks. When Adolf launches a barrage of shells, Pork prevents them from striking by showing them a pinup in *Esquire*. The shells screech to a halt, let out a wolf whistle and fall to the ground, spent.

"The Blitz Wolf" was nominated for an Academy Award, but lost to Disney's "Der Fuehrer's Face." The next year, Avery directed five shorts, four of them excellent: "Dumb-Hounded," "Red Hot Riding Hood," "Who Killed Who?," "What's Buzzin', Buzzard?" and "One Ham's Family."

"Dumb-Hounded" introduced the phlegmatic basset hound Droopy, one of Avery's few recurring characters. Droopy was inspired by the "Mr. Wimple" character Bill Thompson did for the "Fibber McGee and Molly" radio show. (Thompson also provided a similarly dry, nasal voice for the cartoon character.)

At first glance, the stolid, unflappable Droopy seems out of place in the madcap world of Avery's cartoons. No matter how chaotic the action becomes, Droopy remains nonplussed; if he were any more low-key, he'd be off the left end of the piano. His unshakable sangfroid provides an essential contrast to the insanity that surrounds him. When an artist wants to create the effect of a deep black, he juxtaposes it with an area of white; Droopy's calm makes the other characters' activities seem that much more frenetic.

When the Wolf (a modified version of Adolf) breaks out of prison, he finds he can't escape Droopy. No matter how fast he runs or how remote a hideout he chooses, Droopy remains hot on his heels, sometimes beating the fugitive to his destination. Driven nearly insane by frustration and anger, the Wolf returns to jail and ponders how Droopy manages to be everywhere at once. In the closing shot, the audience discovers that there are dozens of identical Droopys.

"Dumb-Hounded" also contains one of the most famous examples of what critics describe as Avery "demolishing the barrier of the screen." When the racing Wolf cuts a corner too sharply, he skids over the edge of the frame, past a simulated line of moving sprocket holes and into the blank screen that lies beyond the film. Gags like this one represent the ultimate extension of Avery's earlier reflexive jokes.

"Red Hot Riding Hood" opens with a conventional retelling of the fairy tale: a kindly Grandma, a tough-looking Wolf, a curly haired moppet in a red cloak and an unctuous narrator's voice. Suddenly, the Wolf throws down his hat and refuses to continue: he's fed up with this hackneyed treatment of the story. The other characters agree they're sick of it too. "Every cartoon studio in Hollywood has done this picture this way," sniffs Red in a Bronx accent. The narrator has to give in, and the cartoon starts over.

This time, the Wolf is a Hollywood lounge lizard and Red has become a sexy nightclub chanteuse. She does a dynamite rendition of "Daddy, I Want a Diamond Ring" (splendidly animated by Preston Blair) that sends the Wolf into paroxysms of lust. He flies into the air and stiffens in what has been described as a caricature of an erection. He whistles, howls, pounds the table and bangs his head in sheer desire.

When Red refuses to leave the club with him, he follows her to Grandma's penthouse. But that sweet old lady has been transformed into a man-hungry swinger. He finally jumps out a window to escape her clutches. Sitting in a nightclub, a

A cel of Red as the title character in Tex Avery's "Swing Shift Cinderella" (1945). Superbly animated by Preston Blair, Red starred in some of MGM's most popular wartime shorts.

somewhat battered Wolf vows to shoot himself if he ever so much as *looks* at another dame. Red makes a second entrance and knocks him for a loop again. He shoots himself, but his ghost reenacts the spasms of desire.

"Red Hot Riding Hood" raised eyebrows and brought down the house. Audiences—especially GIs—loved the film. Censors at the Hays office and/or the studio deleted some of the Wolf's takes from release prints of the film, although servicemen were allowed to see the uncut version. MGM reported that "Red Hot Riding Hood" and later "Red" films were the most popular shorts the studio ever released.

When a carrion shortage develops in "What's Buzzin', Buzzard?" two identical vultures try to devour each other in an extended joke on wartime rationing and meat shortages. (The photograph of a magnificent T-bone steak that appears in one vulture's fantasy is repeated at the end of the film—by popular request.) Avery recalled that producer Fred Quimby disliked the violent action in this cartoon and refused to acknowledge its quality, even when it was selected for preservation by the Library of Congress.

Avery tried to create a Warners-style character in 1944, and devoted three films to Screwy Squirrel: "Screwball Squirrel," "Happy-Go-Nutty" and "Big Heel-Watha." (The character also appears in "The Screwy Truant," 1945, and "Lonesome Lenny," 1946.) Screwy is even more zany and aggressive than the early versions of Daffy Duck and Woody Woodpecker. He's so abrasively loony that there's no reason for the audience to like him. He doesn't work as a fall guy, the way Daffy does, and he lacks Bugs's charm. The Screwy Squirrel films have their moments, but they don't represent Avery's best work.

"Aside from Droopy, Tex seldom bothered with a character that was really endearing, that you cared about," Jones observes. "He really can't be included in the character animation the rest of us were doing, because so much of his stuff was done through sheer graphics—moving graphics, to be sure. Tex is one of the greatest animators, greatest directors and greatest comedians that ever lived, but he went about things differently than the rest of us."

Meanwhile, in the adjacent animation unit at MGM, Bill Hanna and Joe Barbera continued to develop their Tom and Jerry series. Influenced by the swift timing in Avery's cartoons, they began to quicken the pace of their films and by the mid-1940s had achieved a level of excellence that won them Academy Awards in 1943, 1944, 1945 and 1946 for "Yankee Doodle Mouse," "Mouse Trouble," "Quiet Please" and "The Cat Concerto." (They garnered three additional Oscars in 1948, 1951 and 1952 for "The Little Orphan," "Two Mouseketeers" and "Johann Mouse"—a run exceeded only by Disney during the 1930s.)

Every animation fan has a favorite Tom and Jerry cartoon from this era which he touts as "the best." But there are so

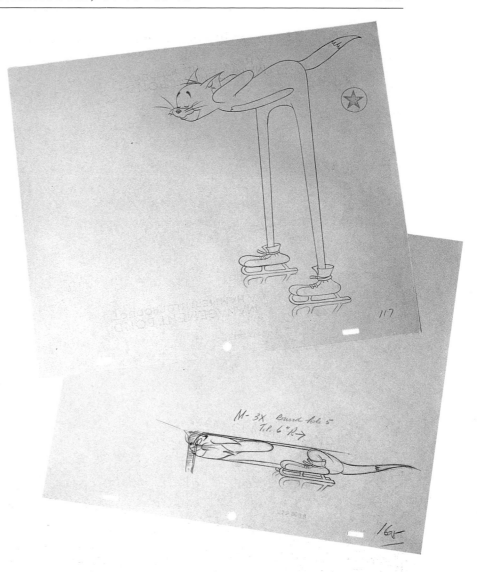

Tom ice-skates over a barstool, under a cabinet—and into an ironing board, in these animation drawings by Irv Spence from "Mice Follies" (1954). Hanna and Barbera quickly turned their cat-and-mouse team into a pair of extraordinary physical comics.

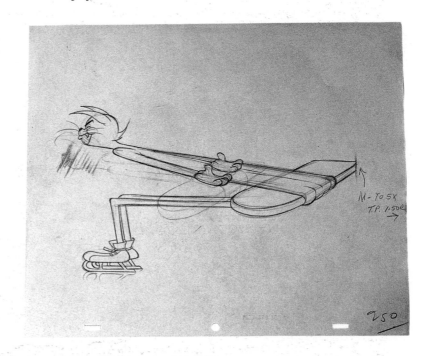

Tom and Jerry assist Gene Kelly in this publicity
still for "Anchors Aweigh" (1945).

"Joe could draw like hell—I still admire his skill," says Bill
Littlejohn. "Joe would do the storyboard and shoot the drawings for a Leica reel, which he'd project with a scratch track to
see where the picture was going—those reels were *funny*.
Then he would go on to the next picture, while Bill polished
the first one. He would do the bar sheets, hand out the animation and make sure the layouts were done."

In 1944, Hanna and Barbera worked on the live-action feature "Anchors Aweigh," when Gene Kelly got the idea of doing
a dance with Jerry the mouse.

"Kelly and Bill and Joe and I went to meetings, supposedly
to decide what to do and what could be done and what the
limitations were," recalls Lah. "But Kelly already had it all
figured out. All he would say was: 'Can you do it?' If we said we
could but that it would be a hell of a lot more expensive than if
we did it another way, he'd say: 'I don't care about that. This is
what I want. Can you do it?' We said we could do it."

And they could. The sequence had to be very carefully
planned: the camera couldn't truck in or out of a shot, because
matching the movement in perspective would present too
many difficulties. Kelly was filmed doing the dance by himself
and the animators (Lah, Irv Spence and Ken Muse) matched
the motions of the cartoon mouse to the live action. Jerry's
movements are so well blended with Kelly's that the sequence
strikes the viewer as a charming fantasy, rather than a feat of
technical legerdemain.

By the mid-1940s, Hanna and Barbera were clearly
regarded as the blue-ribbon team at MGM. Despite his initial
resistance to doing more cat-and-mouse pictures and putting
"all our eggs in one basket," producer Fred Quimby was
happy to accept the Oscars the Tom and Jerry shorts won.

"Quimby was strictly a business guy," Lah states. "If it didn't
go at the box office, he was worried—his head was at the box
office. But when the awards came out, he didn't invite the guys
to come down and get them. *He* went down and got them
himself—he must have had some image of himself as another
Disney. I can't excuse him for that."

many good shorts in the series that these judgments reflect the
individuals' tastes, rather than the quality of the films.

In the unusually topical "Yankee Doodle Mouse," Tom and
Jerry battle it out in the basement, with Jerry launching "hen
grenades" (eggs) at Tom. The conflict builds to a fever pitch
and ends with Tom being shot off on an enormous skyrocket
that explodes into a red, white and blue American flag.

Animator Thomas Sito praises "Zoot Cat" (1943) as "an
outstanding period piece." In an effort to win his girlfriend's
heart, Tom transforms himself into a "hepcat" with a snazzy
zoot suit made from an old hammock. One of the highlights of
the film is an up-tempo jitterbug by the feline couple, animated by Ken Muse. Other fans prefer the spot gags on sports
in "Bowling Alley Cat" (1942) and "Tee for Two" (1943).

Hanna and Barbera worked on the stories together with the
writers, and then Barbera would make the storyboard drawings. Hanna would time the film, prepare the exposure sheets
and work with the animators.

During the war years, Walter Lantz started using jazz sound
tracks in the Cartune series, beginning with "Scrub Me,
Mama, with a Boogie Beat" (1941). Music director Darrell
Calker knew all the big-name performers. He knew who was
in town. More importantly, he knew who was between bookings and could be coaxed into recording a cartoon sound
track. King Cole, Jack Teagarden, Meade Lux Lewis and Bob
Zurke were among the jazz greats who performed for Lantz
films.

The spirited, up-tempo scores gave these shorts a propulsive
energy that pleased audiences. The second jazz film, "The
Boogie Woogie Bugle Boy of Company B" (1941), became the
first Lantz cartoon to receive an Oscar nomination. To the
modern viewer, the visuals—a collection of spot gags about

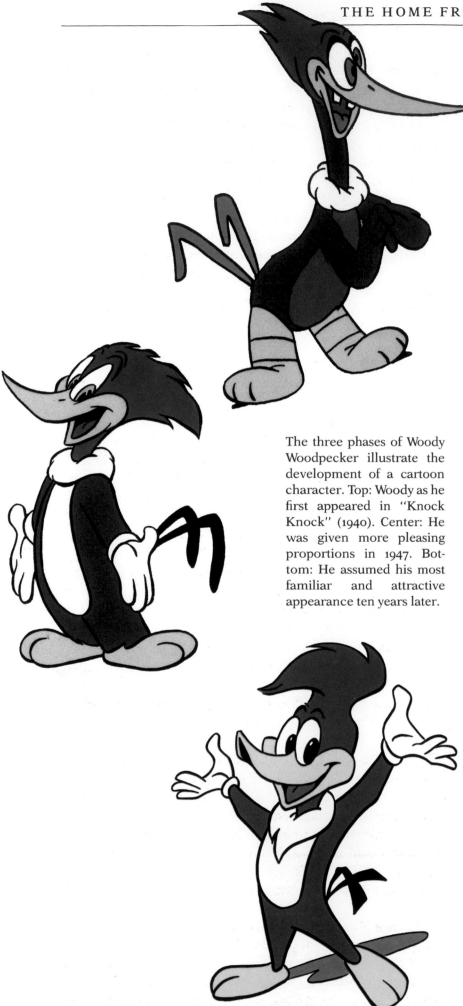

The three phases of Woody Woodpecker illustrate the development of a cartoon character. Top: Woody as he first appeared in "Knock Knock" (1940). Center: He was given more pleasing proportions in 1947. Bottom: He assumed his most familiar and attractive appearance ten years later.

thick-lipped black characters shuffling their way through the Army—seem less entertaining than the lively rendition of the title song.

The series was rechristened Swing Symphonies in 1942. Subsequent entries directed by Alex Lovy and Shamus Culhane include "Juke Box Jamboree," "Yankee Doodle Swing Shift" (1942); "Cow Cow Boogie," "The Boogie Woogie Man Will Get You If You Don't Watch Out" (1943); "Jungle Jive" and "Abou Ben Boogie" (1944). The series ended in 1945 with "The Pied Piper of Basin Street" and "The Sliphorn King of Polaroo."

Although its vaguely Middle Eastern setting of minarets and ogive arches owes more to the El Morocco club than to Baghdad, Culhane's "Abou Ben Boogie" stands out among Swing Symphonies. The centerpiece of the film is a dance to the song, performed by a harem girl in gauzy pantaloons. Her graceful movements are juxtaposed with the clumsy steps of a dopey-looking camel. The harem dancer—and the other pretty girls in the series—were not rotoscoped, but animated freehand by Pat Matthews.

Like their counterparts at Warners and MGM, the Lantz characters had to deal with wartime problems, as titles from 1942 like "Andy Panda's Victory Garden," "Pigeon Patrol" and "Radio Warden" suggest. In 1943, Andy and Woody found themselves coping with food shortages in "Meatless Tuesday" and "Ration Bored."

Culhane also directed the best-known Woody Woodpecker cartoon from the war years, "The Barber of Seville" (1944). Woody enters a barbershop, discovers the proprietor is out and takes over for him, wreaking havoc on the unfortunate customers. As he shaves a man, Woody belts out the familiar "Figaro, Figaro, Figaro" refrain of the "Largo al factotum." The Woodpecker's motions accelerate with the music to a manic pace. Culhane suggests the character's lightning speed by splitting him into two, three, four and even five images that appear on the screen simultaneously.

While working on "The Barber of Seville," layout artist Art Heinemann redesigned Woody Woodpecker's physical appearance, bringing it into line with the more sophisticated styling of the Warners and MGM characters.

The Lantz cartoons of the middle 1940s showed a marked improvement over the prewar films. But even with the jazz sound tracks and the sleeker version of Woody, these shorts failed to break new ground, as the Warner Brothers and MGM films did. Lantz wasn't interested in being an innovator. In 1942, *Boxoffice* magazine assigned the Lantz cartoons fourth place in their annual ratings of theatrical shorts.

"Our films didn't have a prayer against Warners or Disney or MGM," states Culhane. "We didn't have writers like Tedd Pierce or Mike Maltese—you could lean pretty heavily on those guys. Ben Hardaway, who was in charge of story, couldn't compete with those guys; neither could the other

story man, Milt Schaffer, although he had a better idea of structure.

"It was no secret that Walt Lantz didn't have the money the other guys did," he continues. "Even Warners probably spent half again as much per cartoon; Disney spent three or four times as much. Still, we managed to do some interesting films, considering the limitations."

Although Paul Terry's studio produced some military training films, business continued pretty much as usual for Terrytoons. Despite the added work of the government films, the production schedule remained unchanged: a Terry cartoon still appeared every other week, "like a bottle of milk."

A number of Terrytoons focused on war-related subjects. Gandy and Sourpuss turned up in the uniforms of various branches of the armed services to fight the Nazis. But their wartime shenanigans were no funnier than their peacetime activities.

In 1942, the one-shot cartoon "All Out for 'V' " received an Oscar nomination—Terry's first. He received two additional nominations during the war years for "My Boy, Johnny" in 1944 and "Gypsy Life" (a Mighty Mouse short) in 1945. Not an impressive record for a studio that stayed in business for almost forty years.

In 1942, Terry broke a long-standing rule and bought the rights to a comic strip: Ernie Bushmiller's "Nancy." The choice was not an inspired one. Nancy and Sluggo were flat, stiffly drawn characters that did not lend themselves to animation. As "Nancy" had never been funny in the newspapers, there was no reason to expect it to be funny on the screen, and it wasn't. Terry used the Bushmiller characters in two cartoons, "Doing Their Bit" and "School Daze," then abandoned them.

That same year, Terry introduced Mighty Mouse, the character that would become his biggest star. Animator I. Klein wrote that he came up with the idea of spoofing Superman with a cartoon about an incredibly strong *fly* while working in the story department at the studio. Terry, he said, "considered himself Mr. Story Department for Terrytoons, from whom all ideas originated. Other people's ideas were merely fillers. Nevertheless, he expected and demanded support from the 'backfield.' " Terry liked the idea of the parody, but changed the fly character to a mouse.

Opposite: Gandy Goose and an early version of Mighty Mouse appear ready to do their bit, in a poster for Paul Terry's "Ickle Meets Pickle" (1942).

The character who appears in "The Mouse of Tomorrow" as Super Mouse is thinner and more wiry than the later versions. The film isn't much of a satire—all the gags involve appending the adjective "super" to every product the mouse touches: super cheese, super soap, super celery, etc. The plot of the first film—a heroic flying mouse uses his super powers to save his fellow rodents from the clutches of a group of cats—set the pattern for the entire series, with only minor variations.

Although the narrator of "The Mouse of Tomorrow" concludes: "Thus ends the adventure of Super Mouse . . ." the cartoon received an unusually good response from theater audiences. Six weeks later, Terry released another Super Mouse film, "Frankenstein's Cat," and the formula was established.

In February 1944, Terry changed the character's name to Mighty Mouse for reasons that are not entirely clear. D.C. Comics, which owned the Superman character, may have objected. Former Terrytoons business manager Bill Weiss told Leonard Maltin that a disgruntled studio employee created a comic book version of Super Mouse at the same time, and Terry tired of inadvertently promoting the other character.

The change seems to have had little effect on the films. For the next several years, whenever a bunch of cats was about to capture a group of mice, Mighty Mouse was sure to appear as a hero *ex machina*. Although he was the star of the series (and its only recurring character at this point), the audience saw very little of Mighty Mouse. He arrived only at the moment of direst need and left as soon as the foe had been defeated. Even by the undemanding standards of super heroes, he had little personality.

Bill Tytla returned to Terrytoons in 1943, and his animation of the demon-cat in "The Green Line" and the dancing girl-mice in "The Sultan's Birthday" gave these Mighty Mouse shorts a rare visual strength. But Tytla disliked the conditions at Terrytoons and soon left. The Mighty Mouse cartoons then sank back into graphic anonymity.

After the departure of Max and Dave Fleischer in 1942, Paramount changed the name of the studio to Famous (later Paramount/Famous) and within a year moved the artists back to New York. The Superman and Popeye series were continued.

The last few Superman cartoons, which may have been started under the Fleischers, are among the scariest in the series. In "The Underground World" (1943), Lois and a scientist are captured by a race of winged men that turn their captives into statues by dipping them in molten wax. Superman arrives just in time to rescue Lois from being lowered into the boiling vat. Giant mummies—the guards of an ancient pharaoh—come to life and attack the visitors at an Egyptian exhibit in a museum in "The Mummy Strikes" (1943).

Superman also subdued enemy agents and prevented a gargantuan top secret bomber from being captured by the Axis in "The Japoteurs" (1942). The Japanese were the favorite target of the Famous artists, as Popeye titles like "You're a Sap, Mr. Jap" (1942) and "Scrap the Japs" (1942) indicate.

Famous ended the Superman series during the 1943–44 season and began producing Popeye in Technicolor. Not even the brightest colors could disguise the fact that these Popeye films lacked the panache of the earlier black-and-white cartoons. The series continued for more than a decade, gradually devolving into weary repetition.

At the same time, Paramount unveiled a new series starring Marge Henderson Buell's Little Lulu character. A skinny, impudent moppet with corkscrew curls, Lulu appeared in a popular series of captionless cartoons in *The Saturday Evening Post.*

The animated version of Lulu was somewhat less sophisticated and more conventionally mischievous. The rather mild humor in these cartoons was closer in tone to the shorts of the

early 1930s than to the breakneck hilarity of contemporary Warners and MGM shorts. Although successful at the time, the Lulu series has largely been forgotten. In 1948 Famous replaced Lulu with Little Audrey, an oppressively good girl, who also appeared in comic books.

In addition to the Lulu and Popeye shorts, Famous released a series of one-shots called Noveltoons. The only familiar characters in wartime Noveltoons were Raggedy Ann and Raggedy Andy, who appeared in two undistinguished shorts, "Suddenly It's Spring" (1944) and "The Enchanted Square" (1945). The rest of the Noveltoons proved equally forgettable, although Casper made his debut in "The Friendly Ghost" (1945). Two and a half years would pass before Famous got around to doing a follow-up. Casper became their most popular (and profitable) character during the postwar era.

"Our work certainly didn't stack up too well against Warners or MGM," concludes Al Eugster. "Occasionally a good job came out of Famous, but it's hard to explain why things didn't jell there overall. They had the talent; they had the animators."

The personnel at Columbia changed so frequently and so rapidly during the war years that it's hardly surprising the studio failed to produce a coherent body of work. Frank Tashlin began an aesthetic revolution there when he took over the animation department in 1942. But he left in 1943 and returned to Warners. Tashlin was followed by Dave Fleischer, who was succeeded by Hugh McCollum in 1944. Two years later, Harry Binder and Ray Katz came over from Warners to replace McCollum.

A number of impressive talents passed through Columbia during the mid-1940s on full-time or free-lance basis, including Bob Clampett, Cal Howard, Mike Maltese, Dave Monahan and Alex Lovy. But they passed through so quickly that they seem to have had little effect on the films.

The Fox and Crow remained the mainstay of the Columbia cartoons, but without Tashlin and his brilliant crew, the characters degenerated into pallid imitations of themselves. Occasionally a Fox and Crow film shows a flash of inspiration, but most of the series is just dull.

Columbia's most ambitious wartime project (and probably its most disastrous failure) was a series based on Al Capp's "Li'l Abner." The original comic strip was a highly sophisticated mixture of comedy and sociopolitical satire disguised in a backwoods setting. The animated version dropped the satirical elements and reduced "Li'l Abner" to a collection of hillbilly gags. Audiences were not amused.

Director Bob Wickersham attempted to build a series around the character of Flippy the Canary, beginning with "Catnipped" (1946), but the series ended after four films.

After so many changes in personnel and so many bad films, the management of Screen Gems (Columbia's parent studio)

Below: A cel setup of Casper as he appeared in his first film, "The Friendly Ghost" (1945). Bottom: Joe Oriolo's original concept drawing of Casper, 1942.

was happy to disband their animation unit and subcontract their cartoons to UPA in 1948. John Hubley directed the Fox and Crow short "Robin Hoodlum," and promptly won the studio its first Academy Award nomination. For the next eleven years, UPA would produce a brilliant array of award-winning, influential animated films that Columbia would distribute.

The 1940s were also the heyday of ethnic humor in American cartoons, a skeleton many animators prefer to leave in the closet. This dubious tradition stretches back to the origins of the medium, when J. Stuart Blackton ended "Humorous Phases of Funny Faces" with the "Cohen/Coon" gag in 1907.

Much of the humor in animated cartoons came from vaudeville routines and newspaper comic strips, which relied heavily on stock figures and ethnic stereotypes. The images are familiar: Jews are peddlers with hooked noses and Eastern European accents; dark, hairy Italians sing and sell fruit from carts; Latinos take siestas under sombreros; Chinese wear queues, jabber incomprehensible syllables and run laundries; lazy American blacks love watermelon and steal chickens (blacks in tropical settings are cannibals). The list goes on, and it is not a pretty one.

Blacks were the most frequent targets for ethnic jokes, and while these depictions are considered offensive today, they reflect an imagery that pervaded American popular culture through the forties (and even later in some parts of the country). Audiences accustomed to laughing at "Amos 'n' Andy" enjoyed the antics of George Pal's Jasper, MGM's Bosko (in his later incarnation as an identifiable black boy) and Walter Lantz's Li'l Eightball. At the time, most people considered this style of humor both good fun and good taste.

"There were an awful lot of live-action short subjects with black actors then," observes Mel Shaw. "The blacks were always depicted as being afraid of ghosts, doing extreme takes, etc. That we used a little black boy in our cartoons wasn't unusual. In the Jazz Frog films, we were just going through the usual rigamarole of using extreme caricatures of people that were in the limelight. Frogs have big mouths, and that was the standard caricature of a black person at the time."

Some cartoons contain caricatures of such black entertainers Cab Calloway, Fats Waller, Bill Robinson and Stepin Fetchit. Calloway's flamboyant motions, Waller's gravelly voice and pudgy shape, Robinson's elegant tap style and Fetchit's shuffling walk and nasal drawl made them natural subjects. They generally fared no worse—and no better—than their white counterparts. The cartoons of the 1930s and 1940s are filled with references to Katharine Hepburn's broad Bryn Mawr vowels; Greta Garbo's Scandinavian accent and big feet; W. C. Fields's raspy tones and rotund form; Clark Gable's large ears and full lower lip.

These caricatures of Duke Ellington and Cab Calloway, originally done for "Clean Pastures" (1937) and reused in "Have You Got Any Castles?" (1938), are good-natured spoofs, no more unflattering than images of white movie stars used in other cartoons.

The caricature of Cab Calloway that prances through Disney's "Mother Goose Goes Hollywood" (1938) is essentially a good-natured spoof. The figure burlesques Calloway's celebrated blend of conducting and jazz dancing, not his race. The Cats Waller figure in Bob Clampett's "Tin Pan Alley Cats" (Warners, 1943) is a recognizable caricature of the black performer, but the film satirizes the jazz clubs of the era and there are no racial gags.

In a few cartoons, the character's race is more or less ignored, as in Chuck Jones's Mynah Bird series. Inki could be any color (or size or sex or species) and it wouldn't affect the films. A samurai, a rabbi or a Viking could provide equally effective reactions to the understated hopping of the seemingly invincible Mynah. The character just happens to be a pigmy blackamoor.

But when the ethnicity of the characters becomes the basis for the gags and/or story line, it becomes difficult for contemporary audiences to deal with the cartoons. The humor is so divorced from current standards of taste that the films often elicit gasps of astonishment.

Nicodemus, the central character in "Sunday Go to Meetin' Time" (Warners, 1936), bangs his head when he sneaks out of church to steal chickens. After a nightmare of punishments for crimes that include stealing watermelons, he repents, and the film concludes with a fantasy of black couples doing the

Nicodemus gets dragged to church in this lobby card for "Sunday Go to Meetin' Time" (1936).

cakewalk to the title tune. An appalling collection of black stereotypes dozes amid the cotton bales, shanties and watermelon patches of Lazyville in the opening of Walter Lantz's "Scrub Me, Mama, with a Boogie Beat." A pretty, light-skinned girl arrives on the riverboat from up North and her rendition of a song about "The Boogie Woogie Washerwoman" soon has the whole town jivin'.

Van Buren's "Laundry Blues" (1930) is a loosely constructed series of gags about Chinese cats who hiss and chatter amid the teacups, fans and washtubs. There's also a gag about a mouse who comes in with a bundle labeled "Kosher" in Hebrew.

When the animators depicted Nazis and Fascists, they usually caricatured specific figures—Hitler, Goering, Goebbels, Mussolini. While they also used caricatures of Admiral Tojo, they tended to caricature the Japanese as a race, with slanting eyes, buck teeth and thick glasses, rather than satirize a specific political group. When Bugs Bunny passes out "Good Rumor" bars containing hand grenades to the Japanese soldiers in "Bugs Bunny Nips the Nips" (Warners, 1944), he calls out: "There ya go, Monkey Face," "Don't push, Slant Eyes," and so on.

It's easy to dismiss these films as examples of changing tastes, but thornier difficulties arise when ethnic imagery intrudes on otherwise good or important films.

Tex Avery turned Harriet Beecher Stowe's story topsy-turvy —and spoofed the "tall tale" tradition—in his uproarious "Uncle Tom's Cabana" (MGM, 1947). Little Eva has been transformed into Red, the dazzling nightclub chanteuse. ("Little Eva got the penthouse suite, and that ain't all she got, yowzuh!") Uncle Tom turns his urban sharecropper's shack into a nightclub to pay the mortgage Simon Legree holds on it. Legree cuts Uncle Tom in half in a sawmill, runs him over with a steamroller and shoots him from the back of an elephant; finally, Tom loses his temper and hurls the Umpire State Building (with Legree clinging to the top) into outer space. It's probably impossible to watch "Uncle Tom's Cabana" without laughing, but some people object to the designs of the main character and the little black boys and girls who hear his extravagant tale.

In the Tom and Jerry cartoons, Tom lives in terror of Mammy Two-Shoes, the gravel-voiced black maid who rules the roost with an iron broom. Her threat to throw him out on his ear if a dish gets broken or the house gets messed up gives Jerry the weapon he needs to use against his feline adversary. Jasper, the central character in a popular series of stop-motion films by George Pal, is a little black boy who lives in a rural shack. The Bill Robinson frog uses a juicy slice of watermelon to tempt Bosko to give up the cookies he's taking to his grandmother in "Bosko in Bagdad" (MGM, 1938).

In "All This and Rabbit Stew" (Warners, 1941), Bugs outwits not Elmer Fudd, but a shuffling, drawling black hunter

("Ah'm gonna ketch me a ra-a-a-bbit"), eventually winning all his clothes from him in a crap game. "Fresh Hare" (Warners, 1942) ends with an embarrassing vision of a minstrel show, with Elmer and a chorus of mounties in unflattering blackface makeup performing "Dixie" on banjos.

Attempts have been made to excise the ethnic humor from some films, with varying degrees of success. Disney's "Three Little Pigs" (1933) was partially redubbed and reanimated: the Big Bad Wolf initially disguised himself as a Jewish peddler. The change is extremely minor and doesn't damage the cartoon. But when "Mother Goose Goes Hollywood" was broadcast on "The New Mickey Mouse Club" in the late 1970s, all the black caricatures were removed, and only about half the film was shown.

The ethnic cartoons of the 1930s and 1940s remain a problem for animators, programmers and audiences. These cartoons reflect the era in which they were made, and it is not entirely fair to condemn them when they fail to meet contemporary standards. Efforts to censor these films falsify both the history of animation and American popular culture. The question is how to present these films without further insulting the minority groups that provided the butt of the jokes.

An animation drawing of the Queen, who orders Murder, Inc., to "black out So White" in Bob Clampett's uproarious "Coal Black and De Sebben Dwarfs" (1942).

Daffy Duck makes what he hopes is a dramatic entrance in this cel set-up from Chuck Jones's "Dripalong Daffy" (1951).

WABBIT TWACKS IN THE SANDS OF TIME, 1946-1960

Jones-McKimson-Freleng are in the Sennett tradition, which uses the whole sphere of man's emotion and behavior simply as a butt for humor, no matter what it leads to. The aim is purely and simply laughter.
—MANNY FARBER, *Short and Happy*

During the 1950s, the Disney artists remained the unchallenged masters of character animation and the feature-length animated film. But in short cartoons, the beautifully rendered but rather stolid antics of Mickey Mouse, Donald Duck, Chip and Dale et al. were eclipsed by the faster, wilder and funnier characters at Warners and MGM.

"We never thought we were in the same league as Disney," says Warners director Chuck Jones. "We stood in awe of the golden age of Disney shorts, which was from 1933 to 1940—then all the guys went into features. There were a few good shorts made after that, but they were mainly imitating themselves. I don't think there's any question that our best pictures came after the war. That was our golden age, although we didn't realize it. I've never heard of anyone who knew he was in a golden age."

The Warners animation studio created the only cast of characters to rival Disney's in enduring popularity: Bugs Bunny, Daffy Duck, Elmer Fudd, Tweety, Sylvester, Porky Pig, Yosemite Sam, Foghorn Leghorn, the Road Runner, Wile E. Coyote, Pepe LePew and Speedy Gonzalez. And they did it at a fraction of the cost. Even in the late 1950s, the budget for a Warners cartoon was only about $30,000; Disney had spent $37,000 on "The Goddess of Spring" in 1934.

"We didn't try to do what Disney did," explains director Friz Freleng. "We didn't have the budget or that kind of talent. Walt hired major artists just to paint scenes to influence the mood.

We couldn't afford to do that—everything we did had to be in the films. Walt spent more on storyboards than we did on films."

The animation department at Warner Brothers was divided into three units, each headed by a director: Friz Freleng, Chuck Jones and Bob McKimson. Although all three men used many of the same characters and a similar style of humor, each had a distinctive approach to the material and an individual way of handling the characters.

As Freleng was promoted to director well before the others, his personal style had already matured and underwent little change during this period. "I can see a progression when I look at my films now," he comments. "An unbelievable change took place in only three or four years: the films we made in 1938 are as different from the ones we made in 1942 as night and day. During the last fifteen years, there was little change."

Freleng's ability to put over a gag derived from his extraordinary sense of timing. Timing is the essence of comedy, and every comedian knows that a fraction of a second can make the difference between a joke receiving a big laugh, getting a polite chuckle or falling flat. Freleng honed the timing in his films down to the individual frame.

He used that sense of timing to juxtapose sequences of fast, often frantic action with moments of utter calm. When Sylvester takes the baby mouse he's adopted for a walk in "A Mouse

Divided" (1953), the audience sees him proudly push the carriage out the gate, around the corner and out of sight. Nothing in the frame moves for a long beat. Obviously *something* is about to happen, but what? Suddenly, the action erupts as Sylvester dashes back around the corner with a pack of scroungy alley cats hot on his heels. That moment of stillness makes the movements seem that much wilder—and funnier.

"High-Diving Hare" (1949) is essentially a one-gag cartoon: Yosemite Sam tries to make Bugs jump off a diving board into a tub of water, and Bugs tricks Sam into jumping off himself. But it stands out as an example of Freleng's razor-sharp timing. Again and again, Sam ascends the ladder, guns blazing, only to plummet earthward after a silent pause.

The pause is essential to the gag. It allows the audience to anticipate what's about to happen. But that moment of anticipation is exceedingly fragile: if it lasts too long, the viewers get

Left: A model sheet of the four cats in Bob Clampett's "Kitty Kornered" (1946), including an early version of Sylvester. Below: Tweety makes a cameo appearance in Jones's "No Barking" (1954).

restless and the film loses momentum; if it's too short, the payoff arrives prematurely and the director steps on his own laugh. Freleng knows exactly how long to pause—down to the twenty-fourth of a second.

At Warners, Freleng had what amounted to exclusive use of Speedy Gonzalez, Yosemite Sam and the team of Tweety and Sylvester. (Jones and McKimson treated Sylvester differently, in films without Tweety.)

Freleng occasionally paired Sylvester with other characters. The hapless cat struggles to wrest a vital can opener from a mouse in "Canned Feud" (1951). Elmer Fudd tries to sleep through Sylvester's back-fence renditions of "Moonlight Bay," "You Never Know Where You're Going 'Til You Get There!," the inevitable "Largo al factotum" and an amazing Spike Jones-esque version of "Angel in Disguise" in "Back Alley Oproar" (1948). But the combination of the sputtering, loose-lipped puddy tat and the adowable wittle bird proved to be one of Freleng's most popular and successful properties.

Tweety is basically a passive character who stands by and watches as Sylvester formulates elaborate and inevitably unsuccessful schemes to capture him. Tweety gets laughs by offering a commentary on Sylvester's mishaps. When Granny inadvertently tosses the luckless feline into a yard full of vicious bulldogs in "Ain't She Tweet" (1952), Tweety observes: "Ah, the puddy has pink skin under his fur coat."

"It wasn't easy to draw Tweety," comments animator Virgil Ross. "He was such a chubby little thing. He ran with feet that were so big on legs that were so small that you really had to sweat it out. Any character that has long limbs is easier to animate—you can twist 'em around and make them do funny things. You can't bend a little fat character like Porky or Elmer or Tweety around much. I always preferred working with Bugs, Yosemite Sam and Sylvester."

Sylvester's real nemesis in many of these cartoons is Granny, Tweety's owner. A feisty little old lady with a voice provided by Bea Benaderet (later by June Foray), Granny was always ready to belt Sylvester with her umbrella. Dressed as an Indian, Sylvester stalks Tweety (dressed as a cowboy) in "Gift Wrapped" (1952). Just as he captures his victim, he gets clobbered. The camera pulls back to reveal Granny, also dressed as an Indian: "Didn't count on Pocahontas, did you, Geronimo?"

But like Jones's Wile E. Coyote, Sylvester is ultimately his own worst enemy. The more grandiose the scheme he conceives, the more certain it is to backfire.

"Tweety never did a damned thing but say: 'I taught I taw a puddy tat,' " states Freleng. "Sylvester destroyed himself, the way the Coyote destroyed himself. He was a character that fell on his face all the time, who planned to defeat himself."

Sylvester may have defeated himself, but Freleng triumphed with him. He won a third Oscar in 1957 for "Birds Anonymous," a hilarious cartoon that spoofs both Alcoholics Anony-

mous and the stylized graphics of the UPA cartoons. Sam, an orange tabby, persuades Sylvester to join "B.A." and swear off eating birds. Assaulted by images of birds on the radio and television, Sylvester writhes in torment. Finally he breaks down and bursts into tears: "After all, I am a pussycat!"

"Mel Blanc put a certain personality into those voices," adds Freleng. "His acting in 'Birds Anonymous' was really great, especially when Sylvester says: 'After all, I am a pussycat!' Without Mel, it wouldn't have been the same, and I don't think I would have used it. But the track was so good, the character couldn't fail."

Freleng also pitted Sylvester against the hyperkinetic Speedy Gonzalez, "the fastest mouse in all Mexico." Speedy made his first appearance in Robert McKimson's "Cat-Tails for Two" (1953). Freleng took over the character in 1955, and promptly won an Oscar for "Speedy Gonzalez."

Like the black characters of the 1940s, Speedy has fallen victim to changing social attitudes toward ethnic stereotypes. The timing and the gags in Freleng's "Speedy" cartoons remain as good as they ever were. But contemporary audiences are uncomfortable with a Latino character who exclaims "Holy frijoles!"

Far more durable are the films that matched Bugs Bunny against the fiery Yosemite Sam. "I always thought Yosemite Sam was the perfect adversary for Bugs," says Freleng. "I didn't think Elmer Fudd was much competition—he was such a weak little character. I don't know why they thought Bugs was so clever when he outwitted a guy with the brain of a chicken. I thought Yosemite Sam was perfect: he was so aggressive that you had to be pretty sharp to outwit him."

Freleng clearly enjoyed working with Yosemite Sam, casting him as a pirate, a cowboy, an Arab, a knight, a Roman legionnaire and a Confederate soldier who doesn't realize the War is over. "I put him in a different costume in almost every picture," remarks Freleng. "And he was really a cowboy. But everybody seems to remember him as a pirate."

Although he is a lot louder, Sam isn't really that much sharper than Elmer. In "Bugs Bunny Rides Again" (1948), the pint-sized cowboy shoots at Bugs's feet, yelling: "Dance, Rabbit!" Bugs obligingly goes into an elaborate buck-and-wing, then calls out: "Take it, Sam!" Sam repeats the combination perfectly, but concludes with a "Shuffle Off to Buffalo" down a mine shaft.

Sam derides Bugs as a "long-eared galoot," "an idjit" and "a flea-bitten varmint," while proclaiming himself "the roughest, toughest," "the rootin'-tootin'est," "the riffiest raff to ever riff a raff," etc.—always at top volume. But his bluster is no match for Bugs's wiles. In fact, his mercurial temper and apoplectic tantrums make him the perfect foil for Freleng's cocky, self-assured version of Bugs.

When Bugs overhears Yosemite Sam deciding to woo Granny for the $10 zillion she's inherited in "Hare Trimmed"

Yosemite Sam in two of his many guises: top, as a Roman soldier inspecting a malfunctioning catapult in "Roman Legion Hare" (1955); above, as a sheik in a drawing for the lobby card for "Sahara Hare" (1955).

(1953), he announces: "Looks like this Boy Scout's gonna do his good deed for the day!" and sets out to thwart him. Jones or McKimson might have used some of the gags that follow in this very funny cartoon, but they wouldn't have made Bugs intervene in an affair that didn't really affect him.

Freleng's "Sahara Hare" (1955) opens with a gag Jones often uses. Bugs tunnels into the scene and emerges from his rabbit hole to discover he's in the wrong place—the Sahara Desert, rather than Miami Beach. Jones's Bugs would recognize his mistake immediately. He'd consult a map and declare: "I knew I shoulda taken that left turn at Albuquerque!" Freleng plays with the situation longer: Bugs runs across miles of sand, puzzled that the beach is so wide ("Must be a low tide . . ."), and mistakes a small oasis for the Atlantic Ocean. McKimson's Bugs would never mock "Riff Raff Sam" the way Freleng's does, calling out: "Yoo-hoo, Mr. A-rab!" (Naturally that taunt has the desired effect: Sam attacks and gets blown to smithereens.)

"If, say, the cannon fired in Sam's face, Friz usually didn't show anything happening to the character," explains Ross. "It would be covered up or Sam would go off camera, there'd be an awful crash and you'd see little sparkles and his face would be all cinders. The audience could imagine the awful crash, but they didn't actually see it. If you had to animate it, you couldn't animate all that they'd imagine. The gag got a better laugh that way."

In addition to his cartoons with the popular characters, Freleng continued to blend animated action and music in cartoons like "The Three Little Bops" (1957), a jazzed-up version of "Three Little Pigs" narrated by Stan Freberg, and "Pizzicato Pussycat" (1955), in which a nearsighted, piano-playing mouse and a cat with a cool sense of rhythm form a jazz combo.

Probably Freleng's best-known musical cartoon from this era is "Show Biz Bugs" (1957), in which he handles the Bugs-Daffy rivalry more evenhandedly than Jones does in his "Rabbit Fire" films. Jones makes Daffy an inept, greedy survivalist who becomes the victim of his own delusions of grandeur. Freleng's Daffy is vain: he refuses to tip the cabdriver,

Right: Bugs demonstrates how he escaped from a gang of dogs, in five animation drawings by Virgil Ross from "A Hare Grows in Manhattan" (1947). The center drawing shows how the artists could distort a character to create an illusion of motion: as the drawing would only be on the screen for 1/24th of a second, viewers' eyes wouldn't register it as a separate image.

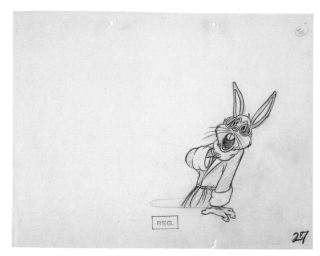

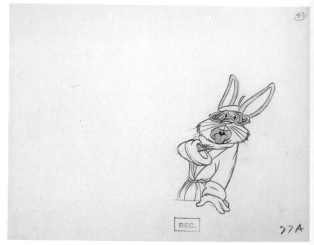

announcing: "It's enough that you've had a star of my magnitude in your hack!"—and often inept: his trained-pigeon act is a bust, and his efforts to sabotage Bugs's vaudeville routines backfire painfully. But this Daffy is also an excellent tap dancer, and the audience can understand his desire to have his talent recognized.

Freleng and the other directors were allowed to do just about whatever they wanted in their films. Leon Schlesinger, who technically remained the producer through 1944, paid little attention as long as the cartoons did well at the box office.

" 'Poppa' always smelled of Parma Violet and he dressed like a vaudeville hoofer who had suddenly come into money," comments Julian. "He had no aesthetic sense, he didn't know boo about anything but the money his cartoons made."

" 'Smokey' Garner, who was the projectionist, shot our pencil tests," Jones continues. "He also had to develop the film, because Leon was too tight to send it out. For a long time, Leon wouldn't let us hire anybody to cut the film into a test reel, so Friz and I both learned how to splice."

In 1944, Schlesinger sold the studio to Warner Brothers and retired. His replacement was Edward Selzer, a studio executive who knew even less about animation and who managed to make himself even less popular with the artists. Schlesinger had generally been regarded as an annoying nonentity; Selzer was seen as an adversary. Chuck Jones cites the time Selzer burst into a hilarious gag session and demanded to know "what the hell all this goddamned laughter has to do with making animated cartoons."

The animators managed to make brilliant films despite Selzer's interference. And one of his curious pronouncements inadvertently inspired an excellent cartoon: "Mike Maltese and I were working one day when Eddy appeared in the doorway, and he was mad," explains Jones. "He said: 'I don't want any pictures about bullfights; there's nothing funny about bullfights.' Then he turned and walked out. I looked at Mike; he looked at me, then looked at his fingernails and said: 'I never knew there was anything funny about bullfights, but

Daffy, Bugs and Elmer in "Rabbit Fire" (1951). Elmer is befuddled; Daffy is angry; Bugs remains cool and confident.

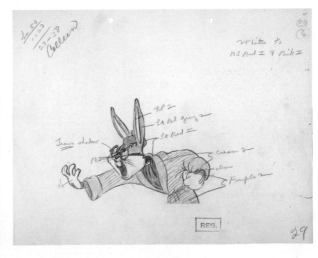

Eddy's never been right before . . .' " The result was "Bully for Bugs" (1953), in which Bugs makes hamburger out of a bad-tempered *toro*. ("What a gulli-bull! What a nin-cow-poop!")

Jones continued to experiment with new characters, new styles of humor, new graphic looks. Writer Mike Maltese recalled that Jones would accept stories he wouldn't have even shown to the other directors. Not all of these experiments succeeded, but the ones that did include some of the best cartoons in the Warners canon—"One Froggy Evening" (1955), "Duck Dodgers in the 24½th Century" (1953), "Duck Amuck" (1953), "A Bear for Punishment" (1951) and "What's Opera, Doc?" (1957).

A sprightly parable of greed, "One Froggy Evening" may be Jones's most acclaimed film. A worker demolishing an old building discovers a metal box hidden in the cornerstone. Inside is a frog (unnamed in the film, but Jones refers to him as Michigan J.) who does the cakewalk and sings dynamite renditions of such turn-of-the-century favorites as "I'm Just Wild about Harry," "Hello, My Baby" and a Jones-Maltese pastiche, "The Michigan Rag." The man tries in vain to exploit the frog's talent but discovers that Michigan J. will sing only for him. Bankrupt and defeated, he finally dumps the frog into the cornerstone of a new building. Another man exhumes him a hundred years later and the cycle begins again.

"One Froggy Evening" also serves as an example of the disciplines Jones set for himself. The cartoon is carefully planned so that the audience hears no dialogue, just sound effects, the score and the frog's singing voice. Everything else is done in mime: a sequence in a skeptical talent agent's office takes place behind glass.

He put even sterner restrictions on "High Note" (1960), a minimal cartoon that prefigures his Oscar-winning adaptation

of "The Dot and the Line," eschewing both voices and recognizable characters. The film plays off the graphics of a piece of sheet music: the notes become characters that resemble ants, a quarter rest turns into a Scotty, etc. Jones planned to make the film entirely in black and white, but added areas of color at the insistence of Selzer, who felt that as he was paying for Technicolor, he should see color on the screen.

Jones also liked to put familiar characters into unusual situations and graphic environments. Daffy tries to sell Jack Warner a script in "The Scarlet Pumpernickel," and uses the Warners characters as repertory players: Porky appears as a Claude Rains-esque nobleman; Sylvester, a rival cavalier; Mama Bear, a lady's maid; Henery Hawk, a page. In "Duck Dodgers in the 24½th Century," Daffy stumbles through a bizarre, futuristic world created by Maurice Noble.

Noble's clean, elegant designs complemented the rapid cutting that gives Jones's work its crisp, sharp edge. As the two men made it a rule never to repeat a layout or a background exactly, Noble often had to devise up to one hundred backgrounds for a single film—three or four times as many as the other directors used.

The most striking of the Jones-Maltese-Noble experiments is "What's Opera, Doc?," a highly stylized spoof of Wagner. When Elmer appears as Siegfried singing "Kill the Wabbit!" to "The Ride of the Valkyries," Bugs disguises himself as Brünnhilde in helmet, braids, corselet and false eyelashes. His entrance on an overstuffed white horse to the strains of "The Pilgrims' Chorus" from *Tannhäuser* dazzles Elmer.

The Teutonic twosome performs a balletic pas de deux in a setting that satirizes the "Dance of the Hours" sequence of "Fantasia." (Jones and his artists had studied the movements of Tatiana Riabouchinska and David Lichine when they were

"Hello, My Baby!" The talented frog (later christened "Michigan J.") does the cakewalk in "One Froggy Evening" (1955).

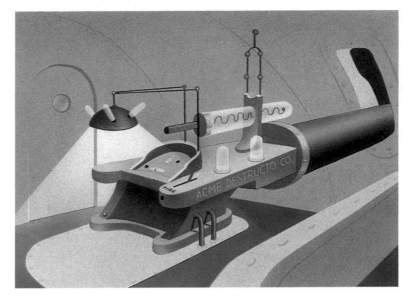

Above: Left, Maurice Noble's layout drawing of Daffy's spaceship in "Duck Dodgers in the 24½ Century" (1953); right, Phil De Guard's background painting of the same scene.

at Warners making ballet films.) Visually, the cartoon is a tour de force of angular settings, gargantuan shadows, rapid cuts, odd colors and dramatic camera angles.

The elaborate production values of "What's Opera, Doc?" contrast sharply with the stark look of "Duck Amuck." Daffy is tormented by a fiendish off-screen animator who toys with the setting, the sound track and even the hapless duck's physical appearance. In his efforts to cope with his unseen foe, Daffy punches himself after being split in two, gets blown up and has his parachute turn into an anvil. At the end of the film, Daffy demands to see the perpetrator of this abuse. The camera moves back to reveal Bugs at the drawing board, grinning: "Ain't I a stinker?"

"Duck Amuck" has been widely discussed by critics, who see it as an existential parable, open to interpretation on many levels. Richard Thompson called it "Daffy's Book of Job." As Jones observes: "Daffy can live and struggle on an empty screen, without setting and without sound, just as well as with a lot of arbitrary props. He remains Daffy Duck." To make a character come alive on a blank screen is an impressive achievement that demonstrates just how far the Warners artists had come in the twenty years that separate "Duck Amuck" from "Buddy's Beer Garden."

Daffy fares only slightly better in his on-screen confrontations with Bugs. Jones's version of Bugs is the suavest and subtlest. Jones uses a flicker of an eyebrow to set up a gag and let the audience know something's about to happen.

"Bugs started out in a sort of a Harpo Marx mode, then moved through Groucho Marx," he explains. "He became a very sophisticated character—a combination of Rex Harrison playing Professor Higgins (who normally would prefer to stay in and mind his own business, although still a very intellectual bird), D'Artagnan (because of the things he was able to do) and

Daffy confronts a dismayed Marvin Martian on Planet X in "Duck Dodgers."

Dorothy Parker (because of the quips). If you blend those elements together, you have a pretty good idea of what Bugs was all about.''

The preference for staying at home and minding his own business is essential to Jones's conception of the character. His Bugs never initiates a conflict the way Woody Woodpecker does, but once he enters the fray, he insists on total victory.

In ''Long Haired Hare'' (1949), Bugs is perfectly content to lounge outside his rabbit hole and sing ''What Do They Do on a Rainy Night in Rio?'' But when operatic tenor Giovanni Jones smashes his banjo and beats him up, Bugs declares: ''Of course you know this means war!'' What follows may or may not be justice, but it's definitely swift and terrible. Disguising himself as Leopold Stokowski, Bugs wrecks both the singer's recital and the Hollywood Bowl.

Jones's ''Rabbit Fire''–''Rabbit Seasoning''–''Duck Rabbit Duck'' trilogy (1951–53) delineates his versions of the personalities of Elmer, Daffy and Bugs. Elmer is the perfect patsy. He believes whatever he's told—that it's rabbit season, duck season or mongoose season, that there's a severe penalty for shooting a ''fwicasseeing wabbit'' without a ''fwicasseeing wabbit license.''

Daffy is clever enough to have some sense of the situation, but too vain to realize that he can't control it. He lets himself get carried away by his own words, and gets his beak shot off again and again. Bugs knows he's smarter than the other two. He remains in control by keeping his cool. He sizes up his opponents and creates opportunities for them to stumble over their own weaknesses—which they obligingly do.

An extremely articulate man, Jones uses dialogue much more extensively than Freleng or McKimson. In the ''Rabbit Fire'' films, Bugs turns into something of a flimflam man, hoodwinking the rubes with his patter. Jones also made Daffy a highly verbal character—one who commits the fatal error of flattering himself, then believing his own spiel.

Conversely, the popular Road Runner cartoons, which use no dialogue at all—just an occasional subtitle, sign or label. Jones introduced the characters of the Road Runner and Wile E. Coyote in ''Fast and Furry-ous'' (1949). Audiences enjoyed the antics of the scrawny Coyote and his swift nemesis, and the series continued for more than a decade, forming a vast fugue on the theme of The Chase.

Jones likes to quote Santayana's definition of a fanatic— ''one who redoubles his effort after he loses sight of his goal'' —to describe Wile E.'s monomaniacal pursuit of the Road Runner. In the first few cartoons, the Road Runner played a more active role, taking a mischievous delight in adding to the Coyote's woes. But he soon lost even those few character traits and became a speeding cipher whose only contribution to the films was an occasional ''beep-beep.'' (A sound Paul Julian invented one day when he was trying to get through a crowded hallway.)

Below, Noble's initial gouache sketch for a set spoofing the ''Dance of the Hours'' sequence of ''Fantasia''; bottom, the finished background, painted by De Guard, for ''What's Opera, Doc?'' (1957).

Color models for Elmer (as Siegfried) and Bugs (in and out of disguise) from "What's Opera, Doc?"

As all the Road Runner shorts share a single plot, the fun comes from the baroque schemes the Coyote hatches, and the ways they misfire. In "Lickety Splat" (1961), he launches a flock of dynamite sticks on wings that not only explode his gas balloon but plague him for the rest of the cartoon. The catapult in "To Beep or Not to Beep" (1964) manages to drop the boulder on him regardless of where he stands. When he hides under the catapult, it collapses on top of him.

Like Freleng, Jones honed the action in his films down to a fraction of a second: "I found that if the Coyote fell off a cliff, it would take eighteen frames for him to disappear, then fourteen frames later he would hit. It seemed to me that thirteen frames didn't work in terms of humor, and neither did fifteen frames; fourteen frames got a laugh."

Most of the Coyote's props in these films come from the Acme Company, a running gag Jones kept going for years. Acme provides the Earthquake Pills in "Hopalong Casualty" (1961) that have no effect on road runners but seem geared to a coyote's body chemistry. Acme also supplies the endless quan-

tities of giant rubber bands, dynamite, jet-propelled roller skates, birdseed and anvils, as well as the Batman suit in "Gee Whiz-z-z" (1956) that enables Wile E. to fly—right into the face of a cliff.

"The substance of all the Road Runner–Coyote pictures is not how to catch a road runner; it's how many ways you *can't* catch a road runner," explains Jones. "The relationship between the Coyote and the Acme Company is very much like a squirrel's to a tree. The Coyote supports the Acme Company by buying or at least using the things they manufacture, and the Acme Company survives by supplying them to him."

With a red nose and a slightly darker pelt, Wile E. became Ralph Wolf: Jones pitted him against Sam the Sheepdog in a series that began in 1953 with "Don't Give Up the Sheep." Ralph devises elaborate schemes to steal sheep and gets his lights punched out by Sam—but only from nine to five. When the five o'clock whistle blows, the two characters stop whatever mayhem they're committing, fill out their time cards and walk home together.

Wile E. Coyote performs with his typical aplomb, in these cels from the mid-1950s. Director Chuck Jones has often remarked that his films are "not about how many ways you can catch a Road Runner, they're about how many ways you *can't* catch a Road Runner."

Daffy prepares to challenge Friar Tuck (Porky Pig) to a duel with quarterstaves, in this cel setup from Jones's "Robin Hood Daffy" (1958).

Jones transformed Porky Pig into a fussy old bachelor who remains blithely unaware that Sylvester is saving him from murderous mice and even aliens in "Scaredy Cat" (1948), "Claws for Alarm" (1954) and "Jumpin' Jupiter" (1955). But his final version of Porky was a subtle, distinctly tongue-in-cheek foil to Daffy's vanity—the "eager young space cadet" in "Duck Dodgers," the "typical Western sidekick" in "Dripalong Daffy" (1951) and, best of all, the convulsed Friar Tuck in "Robin Hood Daffy" (1958). ("How jolly can you get?")

In addition, Jones continued to work with Pepe LePew; Hubie and Bertie, two rowdy mice who disrupt the peaceful life of Claude Cat; and Marc Anthony, a bulldog with a heart of gold. His Three Bears series climaxed in 1951 with "A Bear for Punishment." In this uproarious send-up of Father's Day celebrations, Junyer makes life sheer hell for poor Papa, dumping breakfast in bed all over him, filling his pipe with gunpowder and shaving him with a dull razor. The high point of the film is Mama Bear's high-kicking tap dance, performed with the frowsy élan of Edith Bunker auditioning for the Ziegfeld Follies. Jones praises Ken Harris's extraordinary work on that sequence as "one of the finest pieces of animation ever done anywhere."

The three Warners directors were expected to turn out ten six-minute cartoons each year—one every five weeks, with two weeks' vacation. (The length had gradually been whittled down from seven or even eight minutes by pressure from exhibitors to keep their programs exactly two hours long and by the producers' efforts to limit costs.)

Animator Ben Washam recalled that Jones used to juggle the time cards for his unit. As the Road Runner cartoons were relatively simple to produce, the artists might need only three weeks to get one out. The extra two weeks could be devoted to a more complicated film, like "What's Opera, Doc?" But as far as the bookkeepers (and Selzer) knew, each cartoon took five weeks.

One hour of animation a year seems like an easy schedule thirty-odd years later, when the Saturday-morning houses often turn out more than that in a week. But the Warners artists knew their counterparts at MGM and Disney had bigger budgets and lighter work loads: Bill Hanna and Joe Barbera, who worked as a team directing the Tom and Jerry cartoons, usually made about eight shorts per year.

And at Warner Brothers, each cartoon had to be pretimed to exactly 540 feet, or six minutes. The budgets made virtually no allowance for editing the films beyond removing any mistakes the cameraman made during shooting. The MGM and Disney directors could watch their cartoons, then tinker with them to perfect the timing; at Warners, they had to plan everything in advance.

Each director at Warner Brothers had his own designer, background artist and team of animators. During this period, Freleng had animators Virgil Ross, Gerry Chiniquy, Ken Champin and Manuel Perez; Jones had Ken Harris, Ben

Washam, Phil Monroe, Lloyd Vaughn, Robert "Bobe" Cannon and Abe Levitow; McKimson had Rod Scribner, J. C. "Bill" Melendez, Charles McKimson, Phil DeLara and John Carey.

Warren Foster wrote most of the stories for Freleng, Mike Maltese for Jones and Tedd Pierce for McKimson. All the writers and directors joined in the regular "jam sessions" or "gag sessions," where everyone offered ideas for cartoons that were in preproduction. Only suggestions were allowed at these freewheeling meetings: the word "no" was not permitted.

All three directors worked with Carl Stalling, who remained music director until 1958, when he retired and was replaced by Milt Franklyn, his former arranger. Mel Blanc continued to supply almost all the voices, and Treg Brown, the sound effects.

A model sheet for Chuck Jones's version of the Three Bears explains the designs of the characters and suggests their relationships.

Robert Porter McKimson, Sr., has received less critical attention than the other major Warners cartoon directors. Jones and Freleng have been honored by the British Film Institute and the Academy of Motion Picture Arts and Sciences, and retrospectives of their work have been held at film festivals all over the world. Avery, Clampett and Tashlin have been the subjects of numerous articles; Harman and Ising have devoted fans.

McKimson remains the forgotten man. Only Art Davis, who worked as a director at Warners right after the war, receives less attention. But Davis's tenure was brief and his work had little influence; McKimson spent nearly forty years at the studio.

One reason for this neglect is that McKimson, like Ub Iwerks, was rather quiet. Everyone who worked with him remembers McKimson as a pleasant, genial, smiling man; they agree that he was an excellent draftsman and a fine animator.

"I felt McKimson was the easiest and best director to work for," says background artist Richard Thomas. "He was just a completely beautiful man, so nice to everyone. He was not aggressive; he was not the type to go out and meet the public, the way that Chuck and Friz did. He more or less stayed in the background and let his pictures do the talking."

McKimson died in 1976, before animation became the object of much serious critical study in America. Most of the honors Jones and Freleng (and other important animators) have received were bestowed after the mid-1970s. Had he lived longer (and given more interviews), McKimson would probably have received more widespread recognition.

But for all his talent as a draftsman and an animator, McKimson was the least imaginative of the Warners directors. When he was good, he could be very good, and his best films still bring down the house. But the body of his work includes a much higher percentage of duds than Jones's or Freleng's. Many of his shorts seem to represent cartoon business as

usual, and the viewer looks in vain for Jones's innovative spirit or Freleng's flawless timing.

Bob McKimson came to Warners in 1930—when it was still Harman-Ising—after a two-year stint at Disney. Ten years of intensive study of anatomy, combined with Don Graham's lectures at Chouinard, had sharpened his natural ability as a draftsman, and he soon became a full-fledged animator.

McKimson was promoted to director in 1946, when Frank Tashlin left the studio for the second time. His first film was "Daffy Doodles," in which Officer Porky tries to apprehend a mad graffiti artist—a rather manic version of Daffy. He scored his first hit later that year with "Walky Talky Hawky."

Jones had introduced the diminutive Henery Hawk four years earlier in "The Squawkin' Hawk." McKimson paired him with a wonderful new character, a Southern blowhard rooster named Foghorn Leghorn, obviously inspired by Senator Claghorn from Bighorn, Kenny Delmar's character on the Fred Allen radio show.

Foghorn Leghorn proved to be one of McKimson's most popular and entertaining creations. Much of his appeal came from his endless bluster, which Blanc delivered with gusto: "This kid's about as sharp as a bowling ball." "You're built too low to the ground, boy. The fast ones go right over your head." And after one particularly devastating explosion: "Fortunately, ah keep my feathers numbered for just such an emergency."

The ingenuous Henery's search for a chicken (without knowing what one looks like) makes him a convenient pawn in the ongoing feud between Leghorn and an unnamed barnyard dog. Each convinces the gullible little hawk that the other is a chicken, and an especially toothsome one at that. Somehow, Henery manages to come out on top and drag Leghorn —and the dog in some films—home to the pot.

McKimson often dispensed with Henery, and set Miss Prissy, a skinny spinster of a hen, on Foghorn's trail. With a little help from the dog, she builds an elaborate Rube Goldberg device to knock him on the head with a bowling ball in "Lovelorn Leghorn" (1951), then drags him home, caveman fashion. She even manages to get him to the altar in "Of Rice and Hen" (1953).

Prissy also appears as "Widow Hen" in "Little Boy Boo" (1954), one of the funniest films in the series. Realizing that his own ramshackle dwelling will never keep him warm during the impending winter, Leghorn courts the wealthy widow. ("Ah need your love to keep me warm.") She agrees to marry him if he can prove he'll be a good father to her son, a bespectacled, intellectual runt. Using elaborate mathematical calculations, the runt manages to trounce Foggy in every game they play. Beaten in both body and spirit, Leghorn returns the child and announces the courtship is over: "Madame, ah don't need your love. Ah've got, ah say, ah've got my bandages to keep me warm!"

McKimson favored a hammy, nineteenth-century style of acting for his characters, with the gestures and expressions duplicating the content of the lines. If someone says "He's nuts," the character will rotate an index finger by the side of his head. Thomas recalls: "Bob had some classic poses that he used—Bugs used them, Foghorn Leghorn used them—like getting down on one knee. (He strikes a thinking pose with his elbow resting on one knee.) They were very typical of McKimson's directing." This overstated style of delivery—which worked splendidly for Foghorn Leghorn—contrasted sharply with the more understated techniques of Freleng and, especially, Jones.

That florid delivery is also well suited to the melodramatic pronouncements of Sylvester's son, Junior, whom McKimson introduced in "Pop 'Im Pop" (1950). Sylvester boasts of his prowess as a mouser to Junior, then runs into Hippety Hopper, the baby kangaroo McKimson had created two years earlier in "Hop, Look and Listen." When Sylvester mistakes the kangaroo for a giant mouse, he gets scared, then beaten up. Humiliated, Junior proclaims that he'll have to go around with his head in a paper bag, that people will point and say: "There goes the kid whose father was beaten by a mouse!" "Oh, the shame of it!"

McKimson's dislike of underplaying is particularly evident in his handling of Bugs Bunny, whom he described as "a pixie character, the kind of character that did everything that people would love to do, but don't dare." His Bugs is the goofiest and the least sophisticated. McKimson sometimes put him in silly situations that Freleng or Jones would never have used. In "Gorilla My Dreams" (1948), Bugs has to dress up as a baby

Below: A publicity drawing of Henery Hawk, Foghorn Leghorn and the unnamed dog, from the mid-fifties. Right: The dog smugly sets a plan in motion in Bob McKimson's "Leghorn Swoggled" (1951).

to placate a lonely mother gorilla—and annoy her husband. He falls for the electric rabbit lure at a dog track in "The Grey Hounded Hare" (1949), without realizing that she's mechanical.

In 1950, McKimson used Bugs and Elmer to narrate Bugs's rise from small-time vaudevillian to motion picture star in "What's Up, Doc?" (a cartoon Peter Bogdanovich later included in his Barbra Streisand–Ryan O'Neal comedy of the same name). But McKimson's Bugs is at his best when confronted with even more stupid foes, like the outsized gorilla in "Hurdy Gurdy Hare" (1950) ("Obviously a barbell boy") or the Ozark bumpkins in "Hillbilly Hare" (1950).

His funniest opponent is the Tasmanian Devil, a voracious whirlwind of teeth, claws, bloodshot eyes and growls, who debuted in "Devil May Hare" (1954). According to McKimson, Selzer insisted on discontinuing the Tasmanian Devil (he thought the character was "too obnoxious"), until Jack Warner announced he had received "boxes and boxes of letters" about him, so McKimson continued with the Tasmanian Devil.

During the later 1950s, McKimson embarked on a series of spoofs of television programs. Bugs and Daffy wander from studio to studio in "People Are Bunny" (1959), and Daffy appears as an English detective in "China Jones" (1959). Jack Benny supplied his own voice (and made a cameo appearance) in "The Mouse That Jack Built" (1959), reportedly asking for a print of the film instead of a salary.

A cel setup of one of the twin bumpkins (Curt and Pumpkinhead Martin) in McKimson's "Hillbilly Hare" (1950).

A color chart of Bugs and the Tasmanian Devil for "Bill of Hare" (1962).

The best of these cartoons is "The Honey Mousers" (1956), with Daws Butler and June Foray providing the voices of Ralph, Morton and Alice—caricatures of Jackie Gleason, Art Carney and Audrey Meadows as mice. In an attempt to sneak food past a cat, Morton disguises Ralph in a tin can; Alice interrupts, remarking: "Now don't tell me there's a market for canned slob!" Gleason threatened to block the film's release, but was so pleased with the print McKimson sent him that he withdrew his objections.

McKimson subsequently made two more cartoons with the characters: "Cheese It, the Cat" (1957) and "Mice Follies" (1960). The weak point in all three films (and in most of the other TV parodies) is that he sticks too close to his models and fails to exploit the opportunities animation affords. The Honey Mousers cartoons and "The Mouse That Jack Built" are little more than live-action skits done in mouse masks.

In 1953—the height of the 3-D craze—Jack Warner commissioned Chuck Jones to make a 3-D cartoon to show with features like "House of Wax." "Lumberjack Rabbit" proved

The results are utterly hilarious, and include some of the funniest cartoons ever made.

"King-Sized Canary" (1947) is probably Avery's best-known film. When a low-life alley cat sneaks into a house in search of something to eat, the mouse he finds inside a can of cat food tells him: "You can't eat me—I've seen this picture before, and before it's over, I save your life!"

The family canary turns out to be too scrawny to bother with, so the cat pours Jumbo Gro plant food down the bird's gullet. The canary quickly swells to the size of a gorilla and attacks him. To save himself, the cat drinks some Jumbo Gro and expands to the dimensions of a mastodon. Other characters start drinking the plant food. The canary finds an ally in a bulldog as big as a good-sized dinosaur. The mouse—now taller than a six-story building—scares away the dog and the bird, only to be pursued by the even more gigantic cat.

The last half of the cartoon is essentially a duel between the cat and the mouse to see who can drink the most Jumbo Gro. Finally the mouse announces they're going to have to end the picture because "we just ran out of the stuff." The camera pulls back to reveal the gargantuan cat and mouse standing precariously on the earth, like two elephants on a circus ball.

"King-Sized Canary" has been a favorite of critics in the United States and France. One wonders what Avery's reaction would have been to comments like Ronnie Scheib's: "The enormous distended bodies of the characters, with their tiny heads and hands and giant swollen bellies, give a peculiar edge to the inexorable Hegelian duality of postwar realpolitik

that the 3-D process is not suited to drawn animation. The film resembles a pop-up book, with the flat characters moving on four distinct levels. The only truly three-dimensional effect occurs in the titles, when the Warners shield seems to fly out into the audience.

"Lumberjack Rabbit" was a disappointment technically and artistically—even in 2-D, it's not one of Jones's better films. Warner thought the entire film industry was about to switch to 3-D. ("Believing that the next generation would be born with one red retina and one green one," comments Jones drily.) As cartoon production in 3-D was ineffective and expensive, he closed the animation unit.

The 3-D fad died as quickly as it had boomed, and four months later, Warner reopened the animation department. Jones, Freleng and McKimson went back to work.

During the postwar era at MGM, Tex Avery somehow managed to make films that were even funnier than his wartime efforts. The pacing grew faster, the action more frantic, the takes more extreme, the puns more shameless.

A model sheet of the characters in Tex Avery's classic "King Size Canary" (1947)—*before* they begin drinking "Jumbo Gro."

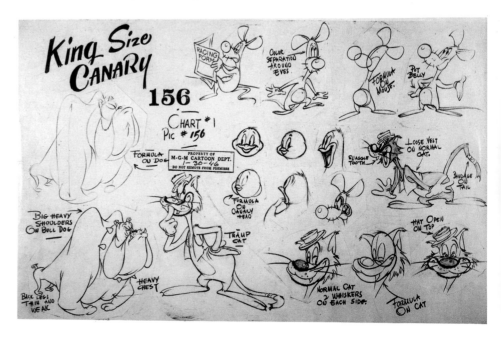

that destroys the initial class solidarity between suburbia-excluded lower-class cat and mouse . . ."

"We found out early that if you did something with a character, either animal or human or whatnot, that couldn't possibly be rigged up in live action, why then, you've got a guaranteed laugh," Avery told Joe Adamson. "If a human can do it, a lot of times it isn't funny in animation. Or even if it is funny, a human could do it funnier. . . . But if you can take a fellow and have him get hit on the head and then he cracks up like a piece of china, then you know you've got a laugh!"

He used equally extreme gags in "Bad Luck Blackie," which Chuck Jones calls "one of the most perfect cartoons ever made."

A nasty bulldog mercilessly torments a little white kitten until a rescuer appears in the guise of a black cat, who crosses the dog's path to the strains of "Coming Through the Rye." Instantly a flowerpot falls on the bulldog's head. The cat hands the kitten a tin whistle and tells him to use it if he ever needs help again. Each time the bulldog bothers him, the kitten toots the whistle and the cat appears—in unlikely places and poses—and an increasingly heavy object clunks the dog on the head.

After a long series of disasters, the bulldog gets the whistle and accidentally swallows it. He hiccups, the whistle sounds, and a bathtub immediately falls out of the sky—followed in rapid succession by an airplane, a bus, a steamroller and an ocean liner! The terrified bully gallops away, as the cat and the snickering kitten triumphantly shake hands.

"I found out the eye can register an action in five frames of film," Avery explained. "Say we had an anvil falling, we would bring it in perhaps four or five frames before the hit, that's all you need. Djuuuu . . . Bam! It's there and you don't know where in the hell it came from. It makes the gag that much funnier. If you saw this thing coming down, and you panned down with it and it hits—uh-uh."

Avery continued to make cartoons with the Wolf and Red, the nightclub chanteuse. "Swing Shift Cinderella" (1945) opens with a typical Tex Avery gag. The Wolf chases little Red Riding Hood, until she sees the titles and announces they're in

Screwy Squirrel discovers there was more than four horseshoes hidden in his boxing glove in "Lonesome Lenny" (1946).

the wrong picture. She leaves and the Wolf decides to look in on Cinderella—who turns out to be Red. Avery brought Red, the Wolf and Droopy together in "The Shooting of Dan McGoo" (1945), a send-up of the old Robert W. Service chestnut that Patrick Brion praises as "an absolute masterpiece."

"Little Rural Riding Hood" (1949) is a variation on the story of the city mouse and the country mouse. When the Country Wolf comes for a visit, the suave, Ronald Colman-esque City Wolf is appalled by his rowdy, libidinous reaction to Red's performance of "Oh! Johnny, Oh! Johnny." But when the City Wolf gets a look at the hillbilly Red Riding Hood who's been unsuccessfully chasing his cousin, the roles are suddenly reversed, as he goes into typical Avery spasms of desire.

"Quimby didn't like the Red character because I could only animate about fifteen feet of her a week, and we were supposed to do twenty-five feet," says Preston Blair. "So for 'Little Rural Riding Hood,' Grant Simmons took the previous Red films and rotoscoped her scenes. Her dance in that cartoon is a composite of bits and pieces of the animation I had done for the earlier films."

During this period, Avery also experimented with the possibilities offered by a big, dumb, overly affectionate character, apparently based on Lenny in John Steinbeck's *Of Mice and Men*. He began with the last Screwy Squirrel short, "Lonesome Lenny" (1946), in which a rich old lady buys Screwy as a companion for the title character, a loutish dog.

He continued the theme with two vagabond bears, George and Junior, in "Henpecked Hoboes" (1946), "Hound Hunters" (1947) and "Red Hot Rangers" (1947). The best-known entry in this series is "Half-Pint Pygmy" (1948). George and Junior comb Africa, hoping to earn a $10,000 reward by capturing the world's smallest pygmy. They think they've done it when they finally catch a little fellow, literally knee-high to a grasshopper, but he informs them: "You've never seen my Uncle Louie . . ."

The George and Junior shorts were only moderately successful and failed to generate much interest. Droopy, who appeared in more than a dozen cartoons between 1945 and 1955, remained Avery's only recurring character.

"The problem was, we'd go through the jokes at the story meetings and we'd laugh like hell," explains animator Michael Lah. "We'd get into a laughing jag where nothing could miss. When we put it on film, people who hadn't been in the meetings didn't laugh. The jokes were there, but they didn't get the laughs we expected. After we had a couple of pictures bomb out, we realized that we had been laughing at each other and at Tex, who could be funny as hell.

"After that, Tex began to feel like he was burning out and becoming inadequate—he was putting everything together and it wasn't funny," Lah continues. "I told him: 'I think you've been working too hard and worrying too damn much about it. Let's make some more Droopys.' He couldn't get enthusiastic about them until I laid them out, then he got excited. The spark was still there, but it was hard to keep it up.''

Droopy and the Wolf appear as rival toreadors at the Chili Bowl in ''Señor Droopy'' (1949). Droopy ultimately defeats both the Wolf and the bull, to end up in the lap of actress Lina Romay in a sequence that combines animation with live-action footage. The master of Droopy and Spike the bulldog leaves everything to Droopy in ''Wags to Riches'' (1949). Spike is so surprised by the news that his jaw drops through the table, breaking a hole in it. As Droopy goes to sleep counting sheep in ''Drag-a-long Droopy'' (1953), the audience sees his sheep go to sleep counting Droopys.

No one worked harder on his cartoons or worried more about them than Avery. He constantly tinkered with the timing during production, usually tightening scenes by taking out drawings and trimming frames from the pencil tests and even the work print.

Joe Adamson recalls watching ''Uncle Tom's Cabana'' (1947) with Avery during the early 1970s. ''When Little Eva went into the up-tempo refrain of 'Carry Me Back to Old Virginny,' Tex said: 'I should have had her rip her skirt off.' He was still trying to improve the cartoon twenty-five years later.''

For all the brash hilarity of his films, Avery was a quiet man who disliked making public appearances. Compliments embarrassed him. He never realized how important and influential his work was.

Overwork and exhaustion led Avery to take a leave of absence from MGM in 1950. Quimby replaced him with Disney veteran Dick Lundy, who received the unenviable assign-

Droopy and Wolf trade shots in a cel setup from ''Drag-a-long Droopy'' (1953).

A model sheet of the unfortunate dogcatcher from Avery's "Three Little Pups" (1953).

ment of reviving the Barney Bear character yet again. The results were reasonably successful, but pale when contrasted with Avery's work. Because MGM kept a sizable backlog of cartoons, the studio was able to issue Tex Avery shorts during the hiatus; some of Lundy's films weren't released until 1954, three years after he left.

Avery's films from the 1950s show no slackening of talent or energy. In "Magical Maestro" (1951), Misto, a ragged magician, is badly treated by the operatic tenor, Poochini (Spike the bulldog). As Poochini begins to sing "Largo al factotum," Misto transforms him into a cowboy singing "Clementine," a child with a balloon, a gibbering Chinaman, Carmen Miranda (belting out "Mama yo quiero") and a Polynesian doing "The Hawaiian War Chant," assisted by two energetic rabbits.

One of Avery's wildest gags is the introduction of an animated hair in the projection gate, which vibrates in the middle of the frame until the irritated Poochini reaches over and yanks it out. The hair has been known to drive projectionists crazy, as they assume it's real and try to remove it.

Avery's love of verbal/visual puns climaxed in "Symphony in Slang" (1951), a collection of wincingly terrible wordplays. When the main character says, "Suddenly, I felt a tug at my elbow," a harbor boat appears next to him in the bar. He hits bad times and everything looks black, "but I carried on." The audience sees him lugging the word "on." Quimby disliked the storyboard for this film, and didn't want to make it. Avery got it into production by telling him that nothing else was

ready: it was a choice of making "Symphony in Slang" or closing the unit.

Avery gave Droopy two brothers for "The Three Little Pups" (1953), the funniest of all "Three Little Pigs" spoofs. The trio takes on a dim-witted Wolf/dogcatcher, who talks in a mouth-full-of-mush Southern drawl, provided by Daws Butler. When the Wolf gets the seat of his pants chomped by a bulldog, he hangs them up—dog and all—and dons a new pair. A few scenes later, he walks by, sees the bulldog still hanging from the pants and says: "You can let go now, boy, the joke's over."

Avery hoped to make "The Three Little Pups" into a series, but problems at the studio intervened. He left MGM in 1954, when the cartoon unit was beginning to feel the crunch of rising production costs and reduced revenues. Two of his top animators, Michael Lah and Preston Blair, were promoted to director.

"Quimby erred; in trying to create a new Hanna-Barbera team, he put Preston Blair and myself together to revive the Barney Bear series," says Lah. "Without telling Quimby, we divided the work in half: you take the first story that comes along, I'll take the second. The 'team' lasted about four pictures."

Lah also directed Droopy cartoons, earning an Oscar nomination for "One Droopy Knight" (1957). But the results just weren't the same: Lah was talented, but he wasn't Avery. And the diminutive, understated Droopy looked lost on the vast CinemaScope screen, especially in the sparse, UPA-influenced environments of the later films. The last entry in the series, "Droopy Leprechaun," was released in 1958.

Avery's work at MGM during the postwar era has been acclaimed for its brilliance, originality, hilarity and significance. But that acclaim has come long after the fact. From 1943 through 1955, Avery never won an Academy Award, and he received only a single nomination—for "Little Johnny Jet" in 1953. Avery and his unit were very much the junior partner to MGM's gold-star team of Bill Hanna and Joe Barbera.

His influence on that team becomes obvious when the Tom and Jerry shorts made before and after his arrival are compared. In the later films, the pacing grows faster, the timing sharper and the takes wilder. Hanna and Barbera kept the general level of quality high, and usually produced at least one brilliant film each year.

"Bill and Joe were trying to outdo Tex," says Lah. "I'll never forget the time Bill and Joe ran one picture for Quimby. He said: 'That's moving so fast, I can't understand it. It's too fast for me, and if it's too fast for me, it's too fast for the general public.' I understood the film; everybody in the business would have understood it—they were up on it. But a slower-thinking guy like Quimby gave you the average person's opinion. So Bill and Joe had to catch themselves, as they were going a little too damned fast. But they were knocking out some great pictures, and a lot of it had to do with the pacing, which changed after Tex got there."

Bill Hanna (left) and Joe Barbera with producer Fred Quimby in their offices at MGM in 1948.

The Oscar-winning "The Cat Concerto" (1947) stands out as the most elegant film in the series. Tom, resplendent in white tie and tails, performs Liszt's Hungarian Rhapsody No. 2, disturbing Jerry, who's asleep inside the piano. During the elaborate runs, Jerry gets bounced the length of the keyboard by the moving hammers, to his enormous chagrin. He starts popping out from under keys and heckling Tom, who bats and slaps at him without missing a note of the piece.

Tom's movements were modeled after the Russian virtuoso Vladimir de Pachmann, and music director Scott Bradley posed for the animators, to ensure that his fingerings and wrist motions were correct. "The Cat Concerto" is both a funny cartoon and an impressive example of character animation: Tom's polished style of motion contrasts strikingly with Jerry's sprightly movements.

Scott Bradley contributed much more than his services as a model to the MGM cartoons, especially the Tom and Jerry series. His sophisticated, modernistic scores strongly support the pantomime action. Lou Raderman, the concertmaster of the MGM orchestra, jokingly complained: "Scott writes the most blank-blank-blank difficult fiddle music in Hollywood."

If "Cat Concerto" and "Johann Mouse" stand out as the most artistic of the Hanna-Barbera shorts, "Mouse Cleaning" (1949) must rank as the quintessential Tom and Jerry cartoon. Animator Mark Kausler describes the film as "my candidate for best cartoon of the series; [it] is not only a great showcase for the animators, but integrates story and gags beautifully."

"Mouse Cleaning" is essentially a faster, funnier remake of "Puss Gets the Boot" (1940), the first Tom and Jerry short. Mammy Two-Shoes informs Tom that the house is spotless and it had better still be that way when she returns from shopping, or he's out on his ear. Jerry overhears her and naturally sets out to wreck the place. The fun comes from the way he makes Tom an unwitting accomplice. He tricks the cat into heaving a tomato at him, which splatters all over a wall. Tom frantically tries to clean it up, but Jerry adds blue ink to the bucket of soap and water. When Tom sees the mess he's inadvertently made, he registers a perfect Tex Avery take: four sets of eyeballs pop out of his head, and his jaw crashes to the floor with a clang. As a grand finale, Jerry diverts a coal chute into the living room, and a flood of coal sweeps Tom and the returning Mammy Two-Shoes out the door and into the yard. Mammy initially mistakes the sooty cat for a black man, but soon realizes her error—the cartoon ends as she beans Tom with a chunk of coal.

Hanna and Barbera used pose reels (filmed preliminary drawings timed to a rough sound track) to help perfect the pacing of cartoons like "Mouse Cleaning." Michael Lah, who did pose reels for both Avery and Hanna-Barbera, thinks the practice was instituted by Fred Quimby as a way of keeping tabs on what Avery was doing, "because storyboards from Tex were scribblers."

Above: Tom, Jerry and Spike the Bulldog in an unusually civil moment from "The Truce Hurts" (1948). Left: Tom does two different "takes" in these animation drawings by Irv Spence from "Mouse Cleaning" (1948).

Opposite: Top left and bottom, two publicity stills of Tom and Jerry from the early 1950s; top right, Jerry's balletic frolicking fails to amuse Tom, in this cel setup from "Johann Mouse" (1953).

The Tom and Jerry shorts reflect the larger budgets the MGM artists enjoyed—the Warners directors were never permitted the luxury of a pose reel. By the mid-1950s, the cost of a Tom and Jerry film had risen to $40,000—a substantial sum at the time. "Heavenly Puss" (1949), for example, looks almost as lavish as a Disney cartoon, and has noticeably richer production values than the Warners films.

Tom dreams that he's been barred from Heaven because of his cruelty to Jerry. He has a terrifying vision of the devil as a bulldog, standing by a boiling cauldron and laughing demonically—"Let me have him! Send him down!" St. Peter sends Tom back to earth for one hour. If he can get Jerry to sign a Certificate of Forgiveness, he'll be admitted to Heaven. Most of the film is devoted to Tom's frantic efforts to get that vital signature. When Tom awakens from his nightmare, he's so relieved to find himself safe and sound that he kisses the thoroughly astonished Jerry.

Unlike the Warners directors, who made extensive use of dialogue and voice characterizations, Hanna and Barbera relied almost exclusively on mime in their cartoons. "Occasionally we'd develop a plot that required a paragraph of dialogue to set up," says Hanna. "But we usually used silent characters, which meant you had to think gags and you had to think pantomime and you had to think action."

Having established a successful formula in the early 1940s, Hanna and Barbera stuck with it. While they sometimes put the characters in unusual settings, virtually all the Tom and Jerry shorts feature the same basic conflict or chase between a cat and a mouse, which provides a framework for the gags.

"I think the reason the series was so popular was the slapstick comedy and the hard gags and the little guy triumphing over the aggressor," adds Hanna. "We always used to say: 'The harder they hit, the harder they laugh.' I enjoyed doing the Tom and Jerry cartoons, and if we had never done anything else, I would have been—and still would be—perfectly satisfied."

In "The Milky Waif" (1946), Hanna-Barbera introduced Jerry's cousin, Nibbles (sometimes called Tuffy), an even smaller mouse with a babyish voice. Nibbles appeared in several cartoons over the next decade, including "Two Little Indians" (1953), "Touché, Pussy Cat" (1954) and the Oscar-winning "The Two Mouseketeers" (1952). The latter film is set in seventeenth-century France, with all three characters dressed in musketeer's tunics. Tom fails to protect a royal banquet from the depredations of Jerry and Tuffy, and he's hauled off to the guillotine at the end of this rather unsettling short.

Nibbles never really caught on, perhaps because the presence of a speaking character violated the order of the pantomime world of Tom and Jerry. Mammy Two-Shoes could talk, but as a human being, she remained outside that world. A quacky-voiced little duck who debuted in "Southbound Duck-ling" failed to generate much interest, although he later appeared on "Yogi Bear" as Yakky Doodle.

Hanna and Barbera also experimented with Spike and Tyke, a father-son bulldog team they introduced as Tom and Jerry's neighbors in "Love That Pup" (1949). Spike and Tyke proved to be somewhat less than memorable, although their relationship prefigured Auggie Doggy and Doggy Daddy on "Quick Draw McGraw." With "Give and Tyke" (1956), they became the stars of a brief but forgettable series.

During the early 1950s, Hanna and Barbera also worked on live-action/animation sequences for two MGM features. Tom, Jerry and an octopus caricature of co-star Fernando Lamas frolic under the sea with Esther Williams in "Dangerous When Wet" (1953). Gene Kelly asked them to create the animated serpent that dances with him in the "Sinbad the Sailor" sequence of "Invitation to the Dance" (1956).

" 'Invitation to the Dance' was a real challenge," says Lah. "Everything else we had animated with live action had arms and legs to work with, whereas with the serpent, we had to invent things. Kelly did the serpent dance with Carol Haney, and she did a beautiful job. We studied the footage of her, then invented similar actions and poses for the serpent."

Although "Invitation to the Dance" proved less successful commercially than "Anchors Aweigh," most critics singled out "Sinbad the Sailor" for special praise.

Despite their critical success—and seven Academy Awards—Hanna and Barbera began to feel the increasing financial pressure as the 1950s progressed. During the 1940s, their cartoons often ran eight minutes; at Quimby's insistence, they were pared to a maximum of seven minutes, with six preferred. They also began to turn out occasional "cheaters," like "Smitten Kitten" (1952)—cartoons that reuse footage from previous films under the guise of some sort of reminiscence.

In 1954, MGM released "Pet Peeve," the first CinemaScope Tom and Jerry cartoon; by 1956, all the MGM cartoons were released in CinemaScope, which added to their cost. The switch to the wide-screen format created problems for the animators similar to the ones the magic lantern artists had faced in the 1830s: their drawings were so greatly magnified that any flaw in a line or looseness in the animation was readily apparent on the screen. The animators met the challenge by drawing tighter in-betweens and streamlining the characters' appearances. The ink and paint artists began using thicker, heavier outlines.

"I don't think we ever did true CinemaScope," says Hanna. "But we did change the layout system and cut things down on the top and bottom—which made a kind of bastard Cinema-Scope. It was a little more difficult to plan—your drawings were smaller and they didn't animate quite as well—at least I didn't think so. I don't think the effect was as good on the screen. You were taking something smaller and blowing it up larger, so anything that was off was magnified."

George Pal, Walt Disney, Walter Lantz and Stephen Bosustow share a laugh, in a photograph from the early 1950s.

When Fred Quimby retired in 1955, Hanna and Barbera were promoted to producers. In 1955–56 they made what turned out to be their last batch of Tom and Jerry cartoons. Some of them, like "Muscle Beach Tom," are quite good. Others are strikingly unfunny: the plot of "Blue Cat Blues" centers on the characters' plan to commit double suicide. The flattened graphics of the UPA cartoons were beginning to influence the MGM artists, but this angular style proved difficult to reconcile with the rounded designs of Tom and Jerry.

"Blue Cat Blues" turned out to be almost prophetic. In 1957 MGM closed its animation unit.

"We got a phone call and were told to discontinue production and lay off the entire animation staff," says Barbera. "Twenty years of work suddenly ended with a single phone call!"

"We would have kept making Tom and Jerrys, except for the fact that MGM got in big trouble," he continues. "The decision to stop came from Arthur Loew, Sr., who looked at the books and saw that a reissue of a cartoon could make up to 90 percent of what a new one would earn. MGM was apparently out of money, so he decided to close the best damned studio there was—which was actually making money—and just put out reissues to get in as much cash as they could."

The Tom and Jerry shorts—and the other Hollywood cartoons—were the inadvertent victims of a 1949 U.S. Supreme Court decision that forced the film studios to sell off the theaters they owned and discontinue the practice of block booking. Under block booking, if a theater owner wanted to show a studio's hit film, he also had to take a second feature, a cartoon and, often, a newsreel. A percentage of the rental fee for the entire package was used to finance the studio animation department.

Film programs had changed by the middle 1950s. The extravaganzas that had run for an entire afternoon during the 1930s were replaced by double features. Theater owners refused to pay more than a minimal rental fee for a short. It became increasingly obvious that cartoons could not earn back their production costs *on their initial release,* and one by one, the studios stopped producing cartoons. MGM was among the first to close.

No one seemed to realize that a cartoon could be re-released over a period of years—and earn a substantial profit. The continuing popularity of the classic Warners, MGM, Fleischer and Disney cartoons on television and, subsequently, on videocassette has proved just how long-lived good animation is. Unfortunately, studio executives during the 1950s were too shortsighted to recognize that fact, and the Hollywood cartoon was needlessly sacrificed.

The first animated films to fall victim to the combination of rising production costs and shrinking revenues were the George Pal Puppetoons, released by Paramount. Born in Cegléd, Hungary, in 1908, George Pal became a cartoonist when he was unable to find work as an architect. He began making animated commercials, and his first stop-motion film was an advertisement for French cigarettes. Pal did not invent puppet animation, as has sometimes been claimed, but he did devise the *replacement system* of stop motion: instead of adjusting the face or limb of a model between exposures, he exchanged the face or limb for one that was slightly different.

Pal moved to Berlin, then to Paris, where he produced his first "Puppetoon," "The Ship of the Ether" (c. 1938), done entirely in glass. He established a studio at Eindhoven in Holland, where he made films and commercials for various companies, including Philips Radio and Horlick's Malted Milk. Shortly before the Nazi invasion in 1939, Pal and his family left Holland for the United States.

In New York, Barney Balaban, the head of Paramount, saw one of the Puppetoons and struck a deal with Pal. "Western Daze," the first entry in what was originally called the Madcap Models series, debuted in January 1941. A spoof of cowboy movies that features tenderfoot Jim Dandy; Prunella, a lovely milkmaid; and two bad guys, Grabit and Hide, "Western Daze" received highly favorable reviews. That same year, Pal earned the first of five Academy Award nominations for another puppet film, "Rhythm in the Ranks." (Pal never won the Oscar for Animated Short, but was presented with a special Academy Award for his innovative work in 1943.)

Jasper, a little black boy who was led into mischief by

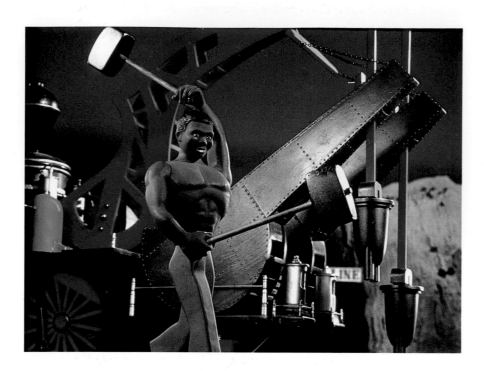

Two stills from "John Henry and Inky Poo" (1946)
reveal Pal's use of dramatic lighting and staging.

Professor Scarecrow and Black Crow, made his debut in 1942. Jasper proved to be Pal's most popular creation, appearing in more than a dozen and a half shorts, including the Oscar-nominated "Jasper and the Beanstalk" (1945). Although far milder than many American cartoons from the 1940s, the Jasper shorts did feature the standard references to watermelon and other stereotypical black images. In 1947, *Ebony* magazine reported:

> While Pal says, "Little Jasper is the Huckleberry Finn of American folklore in my opinion," his Puppetoons have been criticized by Negro and white newspapers, organizations and notables as perpetuating the myth of Negro shiftlessness, fear and childishness. . . . As a European not raised on race prejudice, he takes America for what he finds in it. To him there is nothing abusive about a Negro boy who likes to eat watermelon or gets scared when he walks past a haunted house. But to American Negroes attempting to drown the Uncle Tom myth that Negroes are childish, eating nothing but molasses and watermelons, and are afraid of their own shadow, Jasper is objectionable.

The same issue of *Ebony* praised Pal's use of black characters in "John Henry and Inky Poo" (1946), an adaptation of the folk tale about the steel-drivin' man who defeats a steam-powered machine. "It is the first film that deals with Negro

folklore that has a Negro as its hero. Miracle of miracles, it is that rarest of Hollywood products that has no Negro stereotypes, but rather treats the Negro with dignity, imagination, poetry and love."

Pal also made a number of one-shot cartoons, including film versions of Ted Geisel's Dr. Seuss stories, "The 500 Hats of Bartholomew Cubbins" (1943) and "To Think That I Saw It on Mulberry Street" (1944). He satirized the Nazi troops as the Screwball Army, a goose-stepping assemblage of mechanical parts, in "Tulips Shall Grow" (1943). After witnessing the destruction of their country, a little Dutch boy and girl pray for rain in the ruins of a church. Their prayers are answered: the water rusts the robot invaders and enables the tulips to blossom once more.

Probably Pal's most endearing Puppetoon is "Tubby the Tuba" (1947), the story of an eager little horn who wants his song to be heard. The film features charming animation of the title character and some impressive scenes of the instruments in the orchestra performing Tubby's theme. André Kostelanetz provided lush scores for "Tubby" and the other Puppetoons. At one point, Pal announced he was considering a puppet version of an opera—perhaps an adaptation of Verdi's *Otello* for the Jasper character.

Pal abandoned his shorts "because costs went up 164 percent in five years, while our grosses went down, if anything." In an interview in 1974, he explained: "After making so many Puppetoons, I wanted to get out of the short business, because I began to see the handwriting on the wall that the short business was going to go out of business. I tried to get into the regular feature-making business, and I thought I would start with something of what I know best—special effects— because the cartoons, especially the Puppetoons, were nothing but special effects: you try to make things in miniature that you normally do on a big scale."

Pal used both puppetry and stop-motion techniques to create the performing squirrel in his first feature, "The Great Rupert" (1949). But it was the success of "Destination Moon" (1950) that established him as a successful producer/director of science fiction and fantasy films. He subsequently won Academy Awards for the special effects in "War of the Worlds," "Tom Thumb," "The Time Machine," "The Wonderful World of the Brothers Grimm" and "The Seven Faces of Dr. Lao."

In the United States, animation has usually been synonymous with *drawn* animation; the popular Puppetoons were a rare example of stop-motion entertainment films. By all accounts, Pal was a kind and gentle man, and his work reflects these qualities. With their little dowel noses and wide, painted eyes, his puppets have the ingenuous charm of the best folk art. Although the racial imagery of the Jasper series seems dated, many of the other Puppetoons retain their charm, and deserve the continuing attention of a larger audience.

Tubby shares his problems with a wise frog in "Tubby the Tuba" (1947).

Walter Lantz's most popular character, Woody Woodpecker, became the center of national attention in late 1947, when two musicians, George Tibbles and Ramey Idriss, wrote "The Woody Woodpecker Song," featuring his raucous laugh. Radio star Kay Kyser's recording of it was an enormous hit in 1948. Other artists "covered" the song, until nearly two million records were sold. Lantz began to use the tune as Woody's theme song.

References to the song—and Woody—turned up on the radio, in comic strips and political cartoons, on billboards and in newspaper "color" stories. The ubiquitous song sparked a brief craze for Woody Woodpecker fan clubs, special Woody Woodpecker matinees, a Woody Woodpecker haircut.

One person not amused by the Woodpecker fad was Mel Blanc, who had created Woody's signature laugh in "Knock Knock" eight years earlier. Blanc made his own recording of "The Woody Woodpecker Song," which proved almost as popular as Kyser's, but he felt—probably correctly—that the song owed its enormous success (and profits) to his laugh. Blanc filed suit against Lantz, seeking $520,000 in estimated lost fame and income. In a widely debated decision that affected broadcast copyright practices, Blanc lost the suit. His lawyers were preparing to appeal when Lantz settled out of court.

Pianist Andy Panda encounters an unusual musical problem, in "The Poet and the Peasant" (1946).

After experimenting with various voice artists for Woody (and even using him as a pantomime character), Lantz unknowingly chose his wife for the job in 1951. She had slipped an anonymous recording into a stack of audition discs. "Her diction was so good," says Lantz, explaining his decision. "She had been an actress on stage and in radio."

Beginning with "Termites from Mars" (1952) when she delivered the single line "Termites!" Gracie Stafford Lantz spoke all Woody's dialogue and provided his brassy "ah-ha-ha-HA-ha!" until the series ended in 1972. (The laugh sounds slightly lower when she does it in person, as her voice was speeded up on the sound tracks.) She declined screen credit, as she felt it might disillusion Woody's fans if they knew his voice was supplied by a woman, and the producer's wife at that.

Woody annoyed and escaped a variety of foes during the later 1940s and 1950s. Buzz Buzzard, an all-purpose criminal, appeared for the first time in "Drooler's Delight" (1949). Gabby Gator, who kept trying to make a meal out of Woody, arrived in 1961 in "Southern Fried Hospitality." Daws Butler provided his Georgia cracker accent.

Woody regularly torments Wally Walrus, a dumpy character who talks like a Swedish-dialect comedian. Many of their cartoons revolve around food: Wally has it, Woody wants it and connives to steal it. Woody produces so much noise and smoke that Wally never gets any rest in "Smoked Hams" (also known as "Sleep Happy") (1951). In one memorable scene

animated by Grim Natwick (who declared: "I loved that crazy woodpecker"), Woody turns the unfortunate Walrus's brass bed into a steam calliope.

Donald Duck had Daisy and Huey, Dewey and Louie; Mickey Mouse had Minnie and Ferdy and Morty. Woody was given a rather forgettable girlfriend, Winnie Woodpecker. In 1956, Splinter and Knothead, a niece and a nephew voiced by June Foray, made their debut on the screen in "Get Lost." The pair had already appeared in the Woody Woodpecker comic books published by Dell.

Even after the craze of the late 1940s died down, Woody Woodpecker remained the most popular of the Lantz characters. George Pal used a short animated sequence of Woody to explain how a rocket engine works in "Destination Moon." In 1957, "The Woody Woodpecker Show" debuted on ABC; each program featured three theatrical shorts and a five-minute look at how cartoons were made. Lantz hosted the how-to segments after Woody introduced him: "Here's my boss, Walter Lantz."

Lantz continued to produce Andy Panda shorts and one-shot cartoons. He also tried to develop new series, like the Maw and Paw cartoons, which borrowed heavily from the popular Ma and Pa Kettle films. In 1953, director Alex Lovy introduced a morose little penguin in "Chilly Willy." The character was not a success and remained more or less forgotten until Tex Avery arrived from MGM in 1954.

Rather than work with Woody Woodpecker, who already had a well-established personality and style of humor, Avery took the rather nondescript Chilly Willy and made him genuinely funny in "I'm Cold." Most of the laughs come from the goofy dog who guards the cache of furs Willy tries to rob, rather than from the penguin himself.

Even better is "The Legend of Rockabye Point" (1955), written by Mike Maltese, and arguably the funniest cartoon Walter Lantz ever produced. Chilly Willy and a dopey polar bear both try to filch part of a shipload of bluefin tuna, only to discover the fish are guarded by a vicious bulldog. When the dog opens his mouth, his jaws curl back onto themselves, revealing an array of fangs like a set of matched cutlery. Typical Avery mayhem follows. The bear elbows Willy aside, Willy wakes the slumbering dog, the dog bites the bear, who desperately sings "Rockabye Baby" to lull the dog back to sleep. The bear ends up marooned atop an iceberg with the bulldog, whom he must continue to rock and serenade. The Old Salt who opens and closes the cartoon tells the audience the pair can still be heard twenty years later.

In "Crazy Mixed-up Pup" (1954), a suburban husband gets hit by a car while walking his dog; the ambulance attendants mistakenly give the man and the dog each other's transfusions. The man starts to bark, bite and scratch at fleas, while the dog acts like a human. Daws Butler provides both voices and deftly switches characterizations.

Woody appears to doubt the flimflam man's pitch, in this cel setup from an unidentified short from the late 1940s.

Mighty Mouse clobbers a marauding wolf in this typical cel setup from the late forties/early fifties.

"Crazy Mixed-up Pup" and "The Legend of Rockabye Point" earned the first Oscar nominations for Best Cartoon Short Lantz had received since 1946. Perhaps in recognition of that fact, Lantz offered to make Avery an independent producer— a singular proposition that he declined. In a later interview, Lantz said:

> The reason Tex didn't work out too well for me was that he insisted on doing one-shot deals, instead of developing a particular character and staying with him for several cartoons. That has no commercial value. Comic books are not interested in featuring a one-shot character. And you wouldn't get any of the licensee business that I have for my cartoon characters. The only way you can have by-products is by creating a famous character, and Tex never did that. He did make some of the funniest pictures that have ever been made, and I admire his work very much. . . . If Tex had stayed with me, I think he would have been one of the top producers in the business, and would have become a very famous person.

Avery told Adamson that in the contract Lantz offered, "I was getting my percentage off the bottom instead of the top. By the time all the charges went in, why, my goodness, there was nothing left." He directed one more cartoon, "Sh-h-h-h" (1955), then moved to the Cascade studio and started making television commercials. Other directors at the Lantz studio began using his exaggerated takes and faster pacing, but never as well.

While other studios were beginning to cut back or eliminate their cartoon shorts, Lantz continued making films, and making them on strict budgets. During the 1950s, his cartoons cost around $25,000 apiece, or roughly one-third of what Disney was spending.

He took advantage of the layoffs at MGM, Disney and Warners to hire veteran artists and writers, including Jack Hannah, Mike Maltese, Homer Brightman, Grant Simmons and Ray Patterson, but these men remained better known for their work at other studios. The Lantz films of the postwar era are an uneven lot, ranging from entertaining works like Andy Panda's "Playful Pelican" (1948) and "Poet and Peasant" (1946) to some uninspired duds.

More importantly, these films broke no new ground. While the artists at MGM and Warners were developing a bold, new style of humor and the designers and directors at UPA were revolutionizing the look of American animation, Lantz and his staff continued to make cartoons similar to the ones they had made before. The changes they included were learned from UPA, Warners or MGM, rather than from their own experiments.

The Paramount/Famous films of the 1950s exhibit the same weakness as their efforts from the 1940s. Despite the presence of talented animators like Bill Tytla, Al Eugster, Dave Tendlar and Myron Waldman, the Famous staff failed to develop into a real creative unit. Their films lack a recognizable style, and are generally known only for an utter dearth of humor.

"I think the problem lay in the attitude of the management," says animator Lee Mishkin, who worked as in-betweener at Famous in 1949–50. "The bosses would go to screenings with a list of all the gags in a film on a clipboard. They'd put a check after each gag that got a laugh and use it in the next picture. If a gag got a laugh in three pictures in a row, it became a standard and they'd use it in every picture after that. They had a real nuts-and-bolts approach to making films." As the Famous output includes some of the most formulaic cartoons ever released, Mishkin is exaggerating only slightly—if at all.

The only character left at Famous from the Fleischer era was Popeye, but little remained of the feisty sailor who had once rivaled Mickey Mouse in popularity. Although Jack Mercer and Mae Questel continued to provide the voices for Popeye and Olive, the later shorts lack the spontaneity and free-flowing zaniness of the 1930s films. Popeye was tamed and domesticated, and all the fun went out of the cartoons. The series finally ground to a halt in 1957, when Paramount sold the entire library of Popeye films to television.

After attempting to revive the old Screen Songs, Famous introduced several new cartoon series, featuring characters that could only be described as one-note. The grotesquely outsized duckling Baby Huey made his debut in "One Quack Mind" (1951). He invariably either gets in his mother's way or is rejected by a group of little birds whom he later saves from a fox.

Buzzy the Crow, whose gravelly voice sounds like Eddie Anderson's Rochester character, outwits various animals who must literally eat crow to cure whatever ails them. In "No If's, Ands or Butts" (1954), the only way for a cat to quit smoking is to "eat a salad with fresh crow meat"—a premise as unfunny as it is unappetizing.

Maurice Horn neatly summarized Famous's Herman and Katnip cartoons, which began in 1950 with "Mice Meeting You," as "scaled-down versions of Tom and Jerry, minus the wit, the pace and the inventiveness." The never-ending battle between Herman and Katnip embodied all the clichés of the inane cat-and-mouse cartoon: bricks, flowerpots and sticks of dynamite flew like autumn leaves. Many animators point to these films as the most senselessly violent cartoons ever animated.

Famous's most popular character was Casper the Friendly Ghost. After an unimpressive debut in "The Friendly Ghost" (1945), the character was revived in "There's Good Boos

Model sheets of the Famous Studio's characters Katnip (below) and Baby Huey (bottom) from the mid-1950s.

Tonight'' (1948) and ''A-haunting We Will Go'' (1949). Sam Buchwald, the president of Famous, decided to expand the Ghost cartoons into a series in 1950. Virtually all these films have the same story line: Casper tries to make friends with some animals or people, who scream ''A g-g-ghost!'' and run off. The lonely little ghost finally manages to befriend some child or young animal who ultimately enables Casper to prove he's okay. ''With the Casper series, you never knew what picture you were working on,'' observes Mishkin, ''because they were all exactly the same.''

Unlike other theatrical shorts, the Famous Studio cartoons were aimed exclusively at children. In 1949, Casper and the other Famous characters were licensed to appear in Jubilee comic books. The next year another comic-book publisher, St. John, took over the contract. Many of the Famous artists and writers worked on both the films and the St. John comics, developing a cast of characters that included Casper, Nightmare the Ghost Horse, Spooky, the Ghostly Trio and Wendy, the Poor Little Witch Girl.

The Harvey Company replaced St. John in 1953 and four years later bought the rights to all the Famous characters and their old cartoons from Paramount (except the Popeyes, which had already been sold). The films were retitled Harveytoons and given a new logo featuring a large jack-in-the-box. Casper, Spooky, Baby Huey, Herman, Katnip, Little Audrey et al. continued to appear both on television and in comic books, with each medium bolstering the other.

In 1956, Famous Studios was reorganized as Paramount Cartoon Studios. The staff was reduced, initiating a further decline in quality. Around the end of the decade, Paramount began distributing films from outside producers. William Snyder's ''Munro,'' based on a pointed satire of the U.S. military by Jules Feiffer, won the Oscar for Best Animated Short in 1960—the first and only nomination Paramount ever received. The studio subsequently bought a series of cartoons about a character named Nudnik that Gene Deitch, the director of ''Munro,'' had produced in Czechoslovakia.

In the early 1960s, Paramount switched to television production, grinding out literally hundreds of films featuring various comic strip characters, including Popeye, Beetle Bailey, Snuffy Smith and yet another version of Krazy Kat. Their resources were obviously inadequate for this staggering volume of work, and most of it had to be subcontracted to various

''Here I come to save the day!'' An original cel and background of Paul Terry's ''Mighty Mouse,'' in his classic pose, from the late 1940s.

Heckle and Jeckle once again find themselves in trouble: an original background from "Merry Chase" (1950).

studios and independent artists in New York and California. The resulting cartoons have rightfully been consigned to oblivion.

Not surprisingly, a Paul Terry cartoon continued to appear in the theaters every other week, "like a bottle of milk." Nor is it surprising that the Terrytoons of the late 1940s and early 1950s are virtually indistinguishable from the Terrytoons of the 1930s and early 1940s. The same capable if uninspired directors—Conrad "Connie" Rasinski, Mannie Davis and Eddie Donnelly—continued to work with many of the same animators on the same types of stories involving some of the same characters.

Like many contemporary animated television programs, the Terrytoons were made quickly, cheaply and profitably. Fox distributed them all over the world, and even insisted that

Terry supplement his annual output of twenty-six cartoons by re-releasing a certain number of older films each year.

During the later 1940s, the Terry crew also began to incorporate elements from their musical spoofs of Victorian "mellerdrammers" into the Mighty Mouse shorts. Mighty Mouse was given a sweetheart, the blandly virtuous Pearl Pureheart, and a regular nemesis, Oil Can Harry, an evil feline in a silk hat and spats. The plot seldom varied. When Pearl Pureheart spurns Oil Can Harry's advances, he kidnaps her and/or threatens her with some dire peril. Mighty Mouse arrives in the nick of time, bugling: "Here I come to save the day!" in a hammy baritone. While the narrator solemnly intones: "What a mouse, what a mouse," Mighty Mouse trounces Oil Can Harry without receiving so much as a scratch.

Mighty Mouse never developed into much of a character because the audience only saw him when he was engaged in some sort of derring-do. Traditionally, figures like Superman, Batman and Spiderman lead a dual existence. In addition to their heroic roles, they have everyday lives that allow them to express their personalities and deal with more mundane problems, including romance. The need to guard the absolute secrecy of their "super" identities—even from their sweethearts—generates the tension in many story situations.

But if Mighty Mouse had an everyday life, no one ever saw it. Once he had rescued Pearl Pureheart or defeated the gang of cats, he flew away amid cheers of gratitude. As a result, he remained a one-dimensional hero, albeit a popular one—both in theaters and on television.

After the phenomenal success of MGM's Tom and Jerry series, every studio had to have its own cat-and-mouse team. Terry introduced another mouse, Little Roquefort, and Percy, a slow-witted cat, in "Cat Happy" (1950). For the next five years, Percy pursued Roquefort and Roquefort tormented Percy in a series of cartoons that blur into an indistinguishable succession of formula skirmishes and chases.

In 1946, Heckle and Jeckle made their screen debut in "The Talking Magpies." Terry had apparently been considering the idea of twin characters for some time, and the two birds were identical in both design and animation. Neither the audience nor the animators could tell Heckle from Jeckle. Only their voices were different: one (and it was never clear which one) spoke in a low-pitched Bronx accent, the other in rather fluty British tones.

Heckle and Jeckle represented Terry's version of the brasher, more aggressive cartoon characters that appeared during the 1940s. The two Magpies were more mischievous—and more entertaining—than any of the other Terry characters. Although still vastly inferior to the work of Warners or MGM, the Heckle and Jeckle shorts of the late 1940s have a rambunctious energy that sets them apart from other Terrytoons. Paul Terry correctly assessed them as the best films his studio ever made.

Like Woody Woodpecker, Heckle and Jeckle are aggressors. They need no real provocation to wreak havoc wherever they go—an ocean liner ("Stowaways," 1949), a pastoral retreat ("McDougal's Rest Farm," 1947) or even a prison ("Out Again, In Again," 1948). "The Power of Thought" (1949) is probably the high point of the series. The two Magpies realize that because they're in a cartoon, all they have to do is think of something for it to occur. They use their newly discovered powers to bedevil a bulldog/policeman, until he realizes how the process works and slaps them in the pokey "by doing a little thinking of my own."

The quality of the Heckle and Jeckle cartoons declined during the early 1950s, as the Terry crew fell into their all-too-familiar pattern of using and reusing the same situations and pieces of business. The pressure of producing a cartoon every other week may not have allowed the writers and animators the time they needed to develop and refine their ideas. Heckle and Jeckle may have been too limited as characters to sustain a series of films over several years. Whatever the reason, the later Magpie films lack the qualities that made the earlier ones the best postwar Terrytoons.

In 1955, Paul Terry abruptly sold all his assets to CBS for $3.5 million. He apparently didn't even bother to inform his staff of these plans. Studio veterans with decades of service, who had expected to receive a share of the business and its profits eventually, were dumbfounded.

Although $3.5 million was a considerable sum in the mid-1950s, this settlement constituted one of the few bad financial decisions Terry ever made. Television broadcasts of his films and sales of license products based on his characters (a sideline he had never really bothered to exploit) earned millions for CBS. Nevertheless, Terry spent his sixteen remaining years in well-heeled retirement, and was honored with other animation pioneers at Expo '67 in Montreal.

To head the studio, CBS selected Gene Deitch, who brought in talented young artists and writers like Ernest Pintoff and Jules Feiffer. Despite the resentment of the older animators, Deitch began producing new cartoons for television and theatrical release that borrowed heavily from the work of the UPA studio.

For all their graphic sophistication, the new theatrical Terrytoons were as limited in animation as—and no funnier than—the adventures of Mighty Mouse and Heckle and Jeckle had been. For the Terrytoons studio, the new regime represented more of a change in focus than an improvement.

The postwar years were a glorious time for American animation, a time when studio writers, directors and animators created many of the funniest and most imaginative cartoons ever made. But by the late 1950s, it was clear that an era was drawing to a close.

Dinky Duck nestles in the bosom of his adopted family, in a publicity cel from the Paul Terry studio.

"Listen well, all of you!": Maleficent prepares to give her curse. Marc Davis, who did the key animation of the character, explains that she was designed like a "giant vampire bat" to create a feeling of menace.

DISNEY:
THE SILVER AGE,
1946–1960

Television and the changes it has brought about in the motion picture industry has provided an exciting new stimulus to our creative efforts. We are now able to work closer to the entertainment appetite of the public—much closer than when most of our production was animation and had to be planned in anticipation of the public's moods and market conditions well into the future. This change of pace has been very good for us, I believe, and our whole organization has gained in versatility and efficiency because of it.

—WALT DISNEY

The postwar era was a time of change at the Disney studio; the production of cartoon shorts was gradually phased out, and the focus of Walt's attention slowly shifted from animation to live-action filmmaking, television production and amusement parks. Roy Disney compared the studio at the end of the war to a bear emerging from hibernation: "We were skinny and gaunt and we had no fat on our bones. Those were lost years for us."

The image is not entirely apt. Walt and Roy did face the considerable tasks of phasing out war production, rebuilding their prewar staff and returning to pure entertainment. But the government policy of budgeting military films at a profit, combined with the revenue from the wartime entertainment films, had substantially reduced the deficit created by the box office losses of "Pinocchio," "Fantasia" and "Bambi." In 1945, the studio reported a net profit of over $50,000. As Richard Shale observes: "The end of the war found the Disney studio in the best financial shape it had been in since the 1930s."

This solvency proved short-lived. Disney began production and preproduction work on several films, and within a year had run up a debt of $4.3 million with the Bank of America. To help keep the studio afloat, he made films for various corporations, including Westinghouse, Texaco, General Motors, Firestone and Dow Chemical in 1945 and 1946. Disappointed by the limited returns of educational and industrial films, Disney abruptly ceased their production. With the exception of "How to Catch a Cold" in 1951, he made no other sponsored films until 1964.

The studio's precarious financial situation precluded making a feature-length cartoon. An animated feature represented a big gamble, and it would take three or four years to get one into the theaters. Disney's creditors wouldn't wait that long.

Instead, Walt decided to make the first of the "package features," "Make Mine Music." The format was similar to "Fantasia"—a series of illustrated musical interludes. But the classical score and innovative visuals of "Fantasia" had been aggressively "highbrow" in tone. "Make Mine Music" involved popular performers—Benny Goodman, Dinah Shore, Nelson Eddy, the Andrews Sisters, Jerry Colonna—and broader, cartoon-style animation. The resulting film, which has been called "the poor man's 'Fantasia,'" is a decidedly mixed bag that contains both genuinely charming moments and some of Disney's most egregious lapses in taste.

The high point of the film is unquestionably "The Whale Who Wanted to Sing at the Met," an *opéra-pathétique.* Nelson Eddy provides the voice(s) for Willie, the title character, who can sing not only bass, baritone and tenor but solos, ducts, trios and even the entire sextet from *Lucia*—by himself.

The artists play the whale's enormous bulk against the dainty gestures of his flippers—and his diminutive audience. (When Willie bursts into tears as Pagliacci, he floods the orchestra pit.) The animation and music blend neatly in this gentle fantasy, and Willie's death at the harpoon of Tetti Tatti has reduced many viewers to tears.

According to Diane Disney Miller, Prokofiev once showed her father the unpublished score of *Peter and the Wolf,* saying: "I've composed this with the hope that someday you will make a cartoon using my music." But the object of Prokofiev's musical tale was to make children use their imaginations to visualize Peter's adventures. The segment in "Make Mine Music" usurps that role. The animation is delightful, but the narration is both too literal and too cute for its own good.

"I really enjoyed *Peter and the Wolf,*" recalls Ollie Johnston. "Eric Larson and I worked very closely together on it, and hoped there wouldn't be any narration. We were heartbroken when Walt looked at it and said: 'I think we ought to get somebody to narrate it—how about Sterling Holloway?'"

Although Johnston feels the sequence "worked out real well," his initial impression was correct: *Peter and the Wolf* would be stronger without the narration. "Without You" ("A Ballad in Blue") is also too literal—a tree turns into a Gothic arch at the words "I pray"—and too self-consciously artsy.

Critics were unanimous in condemning the "Ballade Ballet" set to Dinah Shore's rendition of "Two Silhouettes" as the absolute nadir of Disney's taste. Rotoscoped footage of ballet stars Tatiana Riabouchinska and David Lichine is combined with hearts, cupids and sparkles in an orgy of kitsch that resembles a cinematic version of a dime-store valentine.

"Make Mine Music" is a pleasant diversion, but the viewer looks in vain for dramatic strength and emotional power. The film also lacks the energy and inspiration that had characterized prewar Disney animation. "Make Mine Music" was obviously crafted by talented, well-trained professionals, but the excitement is missing; much of the film feels like the animators were marking time.

Similar problems affected the other two package features, "Fun and Fancy Free" (1947) and "Melody Time" (1948). "Fun and Fancy Free" consists of two segments: "Bongo," based on an original story by Sinclair Lewis, and "The Legend of Happy Valley," a variation on "Jack and the Beanstalk," with Mickey Mouse, Donald Duck and Goofy dividing the role of Jack.

"Bongo," the tale of a performing bear who escapes from the circus to find happiness in the forest, would have made a good six-minute short. The film stretches it to about twenty minutes—far more than it can sustain. The ending is a foregone conclusion: Bongo will defeat the brutish Lumpjaw and win Lulubelle's affection. It's just a question of how long it will take to reach that conclusion. The one surprise in the story is the number in which Bongo learns that a slap from another bear is a sign of affection, not rejection.

"Happy Valley" represented Disney's last attempt to revive Mickey's popularity in a feature. Although he's given some entertaining business, like slicing bread so thinly that it's transparent, Mickey never breaks out of the role of pleasant

straight man. Donald, Goofy and Willie the Giant (a comic character, very different from the giant Mickey fought in "The Brave Little Tailor") get the laughs and steal the show.

The cartoon sequences are bracketed with live-action/animation combinations (done via techniques Disney had perfected in "Song of the South," 1946), in which Luana Patten, Edgar Bergen, Charlie McCarthy and Mortimer Snerd interact with Jiminy Cricket and Willie the Giant.

"Melody Time" is almost entirely animation, and many critics consider it the best of the package films. Roy Rogers and the Sons of the Pioneers sing "Blue Shadows on the Trail" to Bobby Driscoll and Luana Patten to introduce the very funny sequence about Pecos Bill. The wildly exaggerated adventures of Bill, his horse, Widowmaker, and his cowgirl ladylove, Slue Foot Sue (who ultimately bounces to the moon on the bustle of her wedding gown), offered material that was better suited to animation than the rather maudlin account of Johnny Appleseed.

"'Johnny Appleseed' just seemed very bland," says Johnston. "It was hard to get your teeth into that and find what there was about this guy that made him interesting to the audience. 'Pecos Bill' was a funnier picture with more imagination and more chance for characters."

Set to Joyce Kilmer's hackneyed poem, "Trees" is the film's one bow to a deliberately "artistic" style. In another regrettable lapse of taste, a tree slowly turns into a silhouetted cross at the end of the sequence. "Once Upon a Wintertime," a stylized evocation of Victorian greeting cards, plays the courtship of two comical rabbits against the wooing of a human couple.

"Blame It on the Samba" feels like a reprise of "The Three Caballeros": the aracuan mixes up a "samba cocktail" to cure the blues that afflict Donald and José Carioca. (They are not only mournful, but powder blue in the opening shots.) Ethel Smith appears within the bowl of an enormous goblet, and the resulting mixture of live-action footage, dancing cartoon characters and animated background elements looks far more surreal than "Bumble Boogie," an attempt to repeat the success of the "After You've Gone" sequence in "Make Mine Music."

There's nothing really wrong with any of the package features. Many of the segments were successfully released as shorts and/or television programs. But the films lack unity, and they rarely involve the audience's emotions on any but the most superficial level. The stories and the interactions of the characters seem less interesting than the diverse graphic styles, like the Christmas-card look of "Once Upon a Wintertime."

While the package features were in production, Disney embarked on another experiment, combining live action and animation to present Joel Chandler Harris's Uncle Remus stories. Walt had always been interested in becoming a live-action director; animator Marc Davis describes "Song of the South" as "a way to get into live action, and have his cartoon too." The film required a much more convincing marriage of elements than any of Disney's previous efforts, and matching the brilliant palette of the Technicolor images presented additional challenges.

"Song of the South," which opened in the fall of 1946, remains an impressive piece of technical legerdemain. As Uncle Remus, James Baskett seems to walk down cartoon paths into a world where he interacts casually and naturally with the animated characters. When he begins to tell the Chandler stories (including the Tar Baby, the Briar Patch and the Laughing Place), Br'er Fox, Br'er Bear and the wily Br'er Rabbit appear on the screen and take over for him.

Unhappily, the live-action sequences that frame the cartoon segments are far less enjoyable. The story of the friendship between Uncle Remus, the shrewd ex-slave, and Johnny, the lonely little rich boy, seems weak, despite fine performances by Baskett (who won a special Oscar for his portrayal) and the child actors Bobby Driscoll and Luana Patten. The film is about 70 percent live action and 30 percent animation, which, Bosley Crowther noted with withering accuracy, is "the ratio of its mediocrity to its charm."

Critics complained about Uncle Remus's passivity and the

Willie the Whale imagines himself performing "I Pagliacci" at the Met, in "Make Mine Music" (1946).

idyllic depiction of plantation life, with the field hands singing as they march off to work in neatly pressed clothes. Both the NAACP and the National Urban League voiced objections to the film; and its re-release, ten years later, stirred further controversy. After being withdrawn from circulation during the late 1960s, "Song of the South" was reissued in the 1970s and 1980s, to favorable box office response.

Many of the complaints about the live-action story were justified, but they caused the excellence of the animated segments to be overlooked. The interactions of Br'er Fox, Br'er Rabbit and Br'er Bear were more subtly delineated than anything the animators had done since before the war.

Although "Song of the South" did good business, it had been expensive to produce—$2,125,000. The $226,000 profit the film earned was undoubtedly welcome, but failed to make much of a dent in the studio's debts. For his last production of the 1940s, Walt turned to material that had gone into development (and even animation) almost a decade earlier.

" 'Wind in the Willows' had started out as a feature before the war," explains Frank Thomas. "It was the brightest, liveliest and funniest forty-eight-minute Leica reel that anyone had put together. At forty-eight minutes, it was just a jewel. A lot of the sequences had lots of life and sparkle, and it was going good, then all of a sudden, it sort of died. The full animation was killing the lively spirit of the   thing. I, for one, was completely perplexed.   Walt really

"Don't throw me in that briar patch," Br'er Rabbit pleads to Br'er Fox. "Song of the South" (1946) featured the most vivid animated characters the Disney artists had created since "Bambi," four years earlier.

pinpointed the trouble. There was no overriding theme that you got caught up in—yet there was in the book.

"The story built to a climax, gag-wise," he continues. "Here's this guy who's always trying something new, and when you've finally got him to give the thing up, here he comes in an airplane! I commented one time that 'Wind in the Willows' was the only story we had with a natural ending, and John Hubley said 'Yeah,' and did a sketch of these film cans covered with spiderwebs and dust lying on a shelf."

Hubley's cartoon turned out to be prophetic: "Wind in the Willows" was shelved until the late 1940s, when Disney decided to revive it. He instructed his artists to cut the film to a half hour, and paired it with a featurette based on Washington Irving's "The Legend of Sleepy Hollow." Disney had several properties in development at the time, and no one seems to know why he chose to link these two stories. "The Adventures of Ichabod and Mr. Toad" emerged as something of a compromise between a traditional feature and a package film.

Narrated by Basil Rathbone, the "Mr. Toad" segment is enjoyable in its own way, although little remains of Kenneth Grahame's gentle, insouciant story.

"The Legend of Sleepy Hollow" receives a much more straightforward treatment. Although he's used primarily as a foil for the gawky Ichabod Crane, Brom Bones is a far more credible male character than the Princes in "Snow White" and "Cinderella." His burly form and lantern-jawed face com-

Brom Bones warns Ichabod Crane about the Headless Horseman in "The Adventures of Ichabod and Mr. Toad" (1949). Masculine without seeming wooden, Bones was a more believable male character than most of the Disney princes.

municate a greater range of moods and emotions than either of the stiff, blankly handsome heroes.

The chase by the Headless Horseman is the high point of the sequence (and the entire feature). Animators Woolie Reitherman and John Sibley balance the terror of the phantom rider against some very funny business, such as Ichabod and his horse scrambling over each other in an effort to escape.

While both sections of the film have been shown on television many times, "The Adventures of Ichabod and Mr. Toad" performed indifferently at the box office. Disney needed a hit of the magnitude of "Snow White." His debt to the Bank of America continued to grow, forcing him to introduce economy measures at the studio.

The situation was growing desperate. Every film Walt had made since the war had done badly; he seemed to have lost both the large, general audience that provided the studio's bread and butter and the intellectuals who had taken him up during the 1930s. Once again, Disney decided to stake everything on a full-length animated film. The question was: which one? Preproduction work on "Cinderella," "Lady and the Tramp," "Alice in Wonderland" and "Peter Pan" had been going on for years. Walt favored "Alice," Roy preferred "Cinderella." Roy's taste prevailed after what seems to have been an unusually bitter argument between the brothers.

It proved a wise choice. Like "Snow White," "Cinderella" is a familiar, well-loved fairy tale that focuses on what Thomas describes as "a pretty young girl in trouble." Also, both stories are brief, which allowed the artists to develop business for the characters to demonstrate their personalities and entertain the audience.

Story man Bill Peet explains that the heroine holds the story together, while most of the action occurs around her. Among those actions were a subplot about the King's desire for grandchildren and another involving the struggle of Cinderella's friends, the mice and the little birds, against the spoiled cat, Lucifer.

"Cinderella" was the first animated feature that was shot entirely in live action before the animation began. The actors who provided the voices performed the scenes before a camera. Photostats the size of animation paper were made of the frames of film for the animators' reference.

"Walt decided: 'We've got to do something here we can do for a price; we've got to know what we're doing all the way through, so that we don't have to make a lot of changes,'" explains Ollie Johnston.

As the animators studied the live-action frames, they discovered that the movements of the human form were even more complicated and subtle than they had imagined. But tracing live action produces dull, lifeless animation; the poses and expressions must be exaggerated and caricatured to work effectively on the screen. The live-action footage could be a useful reference—or an annoying hindrance.

"I think the live action is very helpful," says Marc Davis. "You can do things the hard way, which is to animate out of your head to create a first rough; the live action gives you that first rough. It also establishes a unity to the use of the character, as one person generally does not do all of a character's scenes. But if you depend on it too heavily, you end up with something like Ralph Bakshi's films: you trace and you get big fat things on the screen, and that doesn't work."

"Shooting the film in live action made sure everything worked," cautions Frank Thomas, "but you felt as an animator that your feet were nailed to the floor. Anytime you'd think of another way of staging a scene, they'd say: 'We can't get the camera up there.' Well, you could get the animation camera up there! So you had to go with what worked well in live action."

"Cinderella" proved to be the hit Disney had been seeking. The film grossed more than $4 million on its initial release, which helped to reduce the studio's debt to $1.7 million.

Cinderella is a more mature character than Snow White, but the animators gave her the same gentle virtues. The scenes of her awakening to the call of the birds, and her rendition of "Sing, Sweet Nightingale" as she scrubs the floors, accompanied by the tiny images of herself reflected in the soap bubbles, help to establish her as a kind, sympathetic figure.

The mice supply comic relief as they dodge the indolent, spiteful Lucifer, and fashion a gown for Cinderella out of the Stepsisters' discarded scraps. But the sequence of Gus and Jaq struggling to get the enormously heavy key up the stairs to Cinderella after the Stepmother has locked her in the tower builds real dramatic tension. The Stepsisters' destruction of her new dress is the most heartrending scene in a Disney film since Dumbo visited his imprisoned mother.

"Cinderella" is a handsome, well-crafted film, with genuinely charming and moving moments. But it lacks the imagination and innovation of the prewar Disney features. Except for the scene of the King and the Grand Duke bouncing preposterously high on the outsized royal bed, the scenes with the human characters seem earthbound—the effect of the live-action reference footage.

The only real magic in "Cinderella"—literally and figuratively—occurs when the Fairy Godmother appears, cradling the weeping heroine's head in her lap. In her absentminded way, she turns the pumpkin into a coach and the mice into horses with a flurry of sparkles that became known as "Disney dust"—a sequence that was a personal favorite of Walt's.

Once Cinderella puts on the glass slipper, her Stepsisters simply disappear. In Perrault's original story, they fall at her feet and beg forgiveness—which she freely gives; in the Grimm version, birds peck out their eyes at her wedding. It was uncharacteristic of Disney to leave a story point unresolved.

Bolstered by his first unqualified success since "Snow White," Disney turned his attention to "Alice in Wonderland," a project that presented an entirely different set of problems.

"Snow White" and "Cinderella" were based on fairy tales that existed in many versions; no one cared if the artists changed the wording of a speech or added someone to the cast. *Alice in Wonderland* was an acknowledged masterpiece of English literature, and its many admirers would object to the slightest tampering with the story or Sir John Tenniel's celebrated illustrations.

Although Disney had contemplated a film of *Alice* for almost twenty years, the animators who worked on the cartoon complain that Walt didn't know what he wanted. The vision that had guided the creation of "Snow White" down to the smallest detail was missing. Frank Thomas describes the difficulties he had animating the Queen of Hearts: "First, I made her sort of grumpy and growly; Walt looked at it and said: 'You've lost the humor in the thing.' So I went and did some silly, bouncy stuff, and he said: 'Now you've lost your menace.' Everything was negative. So I said: 'There's nothing for her to do to convey any of this stuff. Give me some business and I'll give you a character.' He said: 'Naw, give me a character and I'll give you some business.'"

The resulting film is a cold, episodic mishmash of elements from *Wonderland* and *Through the Looking Glass*, with some purely Disney inventions thrown in. Of all the studio's features, "Alice" remains the most uneven.

The Fairy Godmother prepares to give Cinderella her ball gown as a truly magical moment in animation history begins.

Parts of the film are brilliant. Ward Kimball brought a rambunctious energy to the Mad Tea Party, with Ed Wynn and Jerry Colonna giving delightfully zany performances as the Mad Hatter and the March Hare. The letters and pictures the Caterpillar produces with the colored smoke from his hookah provide an effective visual counterpoint to his dialogue. The understated insanity of the Cheshire Cat makes him both the craziest and the most appealing character in the film. The Croquet Game features some impressive animation of the Queen's card attendants, and the Caucus Race has a pleasant zest.

But the attempt to illustrate bits of the first verse of "Jabberwocky" bears no relation to what Carroll intended; Tweedledum and Tweedledee don't do much of anything, despite all their bouncing. "The Walrus and the Carpenter" has been rewritten (and not improved). The trial sequence lacks the topsy-turvy logic of its model, and no mention is made of the Gryphon, the Mock Turtle or the Duchess. Carroll would have been horrified by the preachy song Alice sings about giving herself Very Good Advice (but very seldom taking it).

The reviews of "Alice" were overwhelmingly negative. The premiere was held in London, and the British critics decried the liberties Disney had taken with the story. The public didn't like the film any better. "Alice" lost an estimated $1 million. Frank Thomas remembers production supervisor Ben Sharpsteen's reaction to the film's disastrous showing: "We shouldn't feel bad, fellas; it's just something Walt had to get out of his system."

At the same time Disney was making his "Alice," Lou Bunin was at work on another adaptation of the story. A puppet animator best known for his stop-motion prologue to MGM's "Ziegfeld Follies," Bunin made his film in Paris. J. Arthur Rank underwrote most of the production costs, which amounted to over $1 million. Disney took Bunin to court in an effort to block the rival film, but lost the case.

The March Hare and the Mad Hatter attempt to silence the Dormouse, in one of the more successful sequences in Disney's "Alice in Wonderland."

Actress Carol Marsh and the White Rabbit in Lou Bunin's live-action/puppet-animation film of "Alice in Wonderland" (1951).

Bunin also claims that Disney pressured Technicolor into denying him their services. Forced to work in the inferior Ansco color process, he had to deal with numerous technical problems and was unable to do the matte shots he had planned.

Although possible, it is difficult to credit this account. Walt Disney didn't have that kind of clout during the late 1940s. He had made only a few features, most of them had done poorly at the box office and he was deeply in debt. Also, Ansco was an accepted process at the time, and its use would not have precluded matte work.

Bunin's "Alice" opened within a few days of Disney's to even worse reviews and poorer business. After being shown a few times on television, the film disappeared from circulation.

The growing importance of several new interests may have kept Walt Disney from devoting his attention to "Alice" as fully as he had to the earlier animated features.

Not long after the war, Disney had sent the husband and wife photography team of Alfred and Elma Milotte to Alaska, with the idea of making some sort of travelogue or documentary. After a visit to Alaska in 1947, Walt began to study the Milottes' film with greater interest, especially the footage of seals on the Pribilof Islands.

In 1949, Disney released "Seal Island," the first installment in the True-Life Adventure series. "Seal Island" proved very

successful, winning the Oscar for Two-Reel Documentary. "Beaver Valley" (1950), "Nature's Half Acre" (1951) and "Water Birds" (1952) also won Oscars, and in 1953 Disney released his first feature-length nature film, "The Living Desert."

Like many other war-ravaged countries, Britain had suspended payments to U.S. film studios. Disney found himself with several million dollars in frozen assets that could only be spent in England. Rather than move his animators to London —or train a new group of artists there—he decided to begin live-action production.

"Treasure Island," based on Robert Louis Stevenson's novel, premiered in 1950. The film was not terribly well received by the critics or the public; neither were "The Story of Robin Hood" (1952), "The Sword and the Rose" (1953) and "Rob Roy, the Highland Rogue" (1954). It was the enormous success of the American-made features "20,000 Leagues Under the Sea" (1954) and "Davy Crockett, King of the Wild Frontier" (1955) that established Disney as a live-action filmmaker.

According to Bob Thomas's official biography, Walt began planning an amusement park, tentatively called "Mickey Mouse Park," around 1948. However, Rudy Ising recalled that as early as 1920 he and Walt "used to go out to an electric park; it was one of the best amusement parks in Kansas City then. One time Walt said to me: 'One of these days I'm going to build an amusement park—and it's going to be clean!' "

In his efforts to finance Disneyland, Walt turned to the new medium of television, another interest that would take him

Ward Kimball and Walt Disney aboard Kimball's full-size locomotive, c. 1951. Disney, Kimball and animator Ollie Johnston were all railroading enthusiasts.

away from animation. Ironically, his first television program was "One Hour in Wonderland" (1950), a Christmas special promoting the upcoming "Alice" feature. Kathryn Beaumont, who provided the voice of Alice, served as hostess.

The excavation for Disneyland began in Anaheim in August 1954, and on October 17 the "Disneyland" television show premiered on ABC. The park opened on July 17, 1955, and on October 3 "The Mickey Mouse Club" debuted, also on ABC.

All these projects meant that the studio was no longer "hanging on one picture," and they ultimately made Walt Disney very rich. But their increasing importance also meant that he devoted less of his time and attention to the animated films.

"What puzzled me on 'Peter Pan' was that Walt had had it for eleven years and had dragged it out time and again," says Frank Thomas. "He never seemed to have a hold on that picture, the way he did with 'Snow White' and 'Pinocchio' and 'Cinderella.' I never quite knew why. It had everything you needed: funny characters, and the human characters weren't *that* human (at least they didn't look like they were going to be), and all kinds of good material—everybody liked it. He said: 'Fellas, we've got a hold of something here—we've gotta be careful how we handle this,' and he seemed sort of unsure."

Bill Peet complains that Walt let too many story men pre-

A cel setup of Peter, Wendy, John and Michael flying over London, one of the high points of "Peter Pan."

pare too many sequences. "They had boards going on forever, and it got cumbersome. When we finally got around to it, a comparative few of us did the final version. Without ninety-five cooks stirring the broth, we got the personalities of the characters into a form where everybody understood what we were doing."

Sir James Barrie's play *Peter Pan* had been a holiday standard for children since its premiere in 1904. The Disney artists broke with what had become the traditional stage conventions. For the first time, the role of the title character was voiced by an actor, rather than portrayed by an actress (Bobby Driscoll in his last role in a Disney film). They discarded the famous scene in which Peter asks the members of the audience to clap their hands, to confirm that they *do* believe in fairies, as a theatrical effect, rather than a cinematic one.

Disney also decided to depict Tinker Bell as a recognizable female character, rather than a beam of light, a decision that received widespread criticism. Disney's characterization is actually in keeping with Barrie's descriptions of Tinker Bell as very feminine, if somewhat temperamental and even vulgar.

Many animation histories assert that the artists used Marilyn Monroe as a model when they designed Tinker Bell—an idea Marc Davis, who animated many of her scenes, dismisses. "She would have made a marvelous model. It'd be great if you could draw Marilyn Monroe, but she was not a consideration."

Ward Kimball's caricature of himself and his fellow studio artists performing as "The Firehouse Five Plus Two" during the early 1950s. Recordings by this jazz group remain popular, more than 35 years later.

Once again, live-action footage was shot of the actors and actresses. Kathryn Beaumont, who had been photographed as Alice, performed Wendy's scenes and Margaret Kerry posed as Tinker Bell.

In Barrie's descriptions, Captain James Hook maintained "something of the grand seigneur" in his demeanor: "He even ripped you up with an air." The Disney artists kept the pirate chief's volatile temper, but they broadened his gestures and attitudes, transforming him into the first (and one of the best) of the studio's comic villains. The blustering animation of Hook is complemented by Hans Conried's bombastic vocal performance. The whining Mr. Smee of the book became his flighty, befuddled sidekick.

In addition to Peter Pan, Hook must contend with his other nemesis, the ravenous crocodile who was never seen in the stage productions. The animators turned him into an outsized comic character with a pudgy body and pop eyes who moved jauntily to the catchy refrain of "Never Smile at a Crocodile." The crocodile's efforts to devour the Captain include some of the best slapstick in any Disney feature.

Although he stressed the dreamlike nature of "Peter Pan," Disney lost (or discarded) the wistful yearning for the fleeting innocence of childhood that had characterized the original story, replacing it with a robust Yankee energy. Peter is a mischievous all-American boy, rather than the conceited British popinjay Barrie had envisioned. This upbeat approach proved more successful with "Peter Pan" than it had with "Alice in Wonderland," as many aspects of the original Neverland suggest a rowdy vitality that Carroll's more proper fantasy world lacks.

In the *New York Times*, Bosley Crowther complained that "Mr. Disney has completely eliminated from his film the spirit of guileless credulity in fairy magic that prevails in the play." But despite his reservations, he concluded: "However, that's not to say it isn't a wholly amusing and engaging piece of work within the defined limitations of the aforementioned 'Disney style.' The Disney inventions are as skillful and clever as they have ever been—perhaps even more so, in some cases, as in the encounter of Captain Hook with the Crocodile."

Like "Cinderella," "Peter Pan" offered no real innovations, but proved to be a highly successful and widely loved film.

Disney had begun planning a film about a proper cocker spaniel in 1937. While he was developing the idea, he read "Happy Dan, the Whistling Dog," a story by Ward Greene. According to Bob Thomas, Walt suggested: "Your dog and my dog have got to get together." In 1943, Greene produced another story, "Happy Dan, the Whistling Dog, and Miss Patsy, the Beautiful Spaniel." Like so many other projects, the film was shelved, but later revived. Walt insisted on changing the title to "Lady and the Tramp," despite objections from both Greene and RKO.

Perhaps Disney was still smarting from the critical rebukes he received about changing *Alice* and *Peter Pan* when he issued a publicity release explaining the reasons for choosing an original property for his next feature: "We were free to develop the story as we saw fit, which is not the case when you work on a classic. Then you must adhere rigidly to the sequences conceived by the author, which are familiar to your audience. Here, as the characters came to life and the scenes took shape, we were able to alter, embellish, eliminate and change to improve the material."

Like many Disney films, "Lady and the Tramp" seems superficial at first glance, but actually touches deeply felt emotions. Lady, the coddled pet of Jim Dear and Darling, experiences something akin to sibling rivalry when their baby arrives. She gradually falls in love with Tramp, the debonair mongrel from the wrong side of the tracks who manages both to rescue her and to get her in considerable trouble. He redeems himself by rescuing the baby from a marauding rat in a dramatically staged fight during a thunderstorm.

Set in a small New England town at the turn of the century, "Lady and the Tramp" has a realistic but slightly softened look that suggests a gentle nostalgia. The camera is kept low in many sequences, to suggest a world seen from a dog's perspective. Claude Coates and Bruce Bushman crafted one-inch scale models of several settings, to help the artists keep track of where things were in the traditional, cluttered interiors.

Like "Bambi," "Lady and the Tramp" called for believable animal characters. If the audience didn't accept the dogs as dogs, the story would simply fall apart. The Disney artists went back to studying animal anatomy.

"As work began on this picture," Eric Larson wrote in 1977, "a very thorough study of the anatomy, mannerisms, personalities and action of dogs was made by animators and story men. This, with the application of human thought processes and behavior, contributed greatly to the character development of the dogs and, in turn, to the picture's appeal. . . . We *must know* the real thing before we can caricature it."

The results are impressive. The artists captured the nuances of canine movement, accurately depicting the extension of a stretch, the rhythm of a walk, the precarious balance of a two-legged stance. In some sequences, the animators seem to have done their job almost too well, and the results are little more than drawn live action.

One of the most entertaining sequences in the film is the spoof of prison movies that takes place when Lady gets thrown into the dog pound. The setting and the dialogue play off films like "The Big House," including a line about Nutsy "taking the long walk." In the pound, Lady meets Peg, the faded star of the Dog and Pony Follies. Jazz singer Peggy Lee, who co-wrote the songs in the film, supplies Peg's voice for "He's a Tramp," a number that details the racy life of Lady's beau. Eric Larson's vivid animation blends with the vocal performance to create a delightful portrait of a shady lady—a canine Diamond Lil who's hit the skids, but still remembers when she played the Palace.

The film suffers from an inconsistent treatment of the characters. Most of the dogs and Lady's owners, Jim Dear and Darling, are drawn realistically; Tony and Joe, the Italian restaurateurs, and Aunt Sara and her spiteful cats, Si and Am, are animated in a broader, cartoon style. The artists seem to have been unable to decide whether to tell the story from a dog's point of view or approach it as a human vision of a canine world.

"You had to ask Walt to come into meetings on 'Lady and the Tramp,'" explains Ollie Johnston. "Earlier, particularly before the war, he was always rummaging around in every room, looking to see what people had done, getting either a lift or a disappointment. He had a lot of things going at the time of 'Lady and the Tramp,' and there were only so many he could handle, even with his fine mind. And I think he had really spent himself on what he wanted to do in animation, although he was still interested in it."

"Lady and the Tramp" was the first Disney feature shot in CinemaScope, which increased the cost of the film by nearly one-third, to $4 million. In *Films in Review*, Ward Kimball wrote: ". . . in CinemaScope, *cartoon characters* move, not the backgrounds. Because there is more space, the characters can move about without getting outside the visual angle. They can also move about more in relation to each other. In Cinema-Scope cartoons, the characters no longer perform in one spot against a moving background, *but are moved through the scenes.*"

Other animators disliked the wide-screen format and the additional space their drawings had to fill. (The increased dimensions also complicated the creation of "Sleeping Beauty.") The reviewer in *The New Yorker* complained that CinemaScope gave the dogs "the dimensions of hippos."

The film received favorable reviews, although some critics complained about excessive sentimentality. Walt's publicity for the film on the "Disneyland" television program probably had more effect than the reviews. Scamp, Lady and Tramp's puppy, who's briefly seen in the final minutes of the film, became the subject of a series of comic books and a newspaper comic strip.

"Lady and the Tramp" was also the first animated feature to be distributed by Disney's Buena Vista Company. RKO had handled both the Disney shorts and features since "Snow White," but the studio had been in decline since 1948, when Howard Hughes purchased it. Walt and Roy were not happy with the treatment they'd been receiving from RKO, especially when the sales force balked at trying to sell the feature-length documentary "The Living Desert" to theater owners.

Roy's response was to organize his own sales company, named after the street in front of the studio. After the enormous success of "The Living Desert" (which earned $4 million, against $300,000 in production costs), Buena Vista distributed all the Disney films.

"Lady and the Tramp" proved that a full-length cartoon based on an original story could be a box office success. But Disney turned to another familiar fairy tale for what would prove to be his most artistically ambitious animated feature since "Fantasia": "Sleeping Beauty."

Preproduction work on the film had begun in 1950, but the project was postponed and started again in 1954. Eric Larson, who directed about two-thirds of "Sleeping Beauty," remembers that Disney told the artists not to hurry and to make what they did beautiful: he wanted "a moving illustration." It took four and a half years—longer than any animated feature until "The Black Cauldron" (1985)—and one million finished drawings, but they gave him what he asked for.

Unlike the earlier Disney features, which had been drawn in a style derived from nineteenth-century storybook illustrations, "Sleeping Beauty" was designed to evoke the stylized imagery of fifteenth-century French illuminated manuscripts. The man most responsible for this formalized beauty was Eyvind Earle, who did the key color and design work.

"I worked in the style I had been painting in since I was ten," he states. "I was strongly influenced by Dürer, Bruegel, van Eyck, the *Très Riches Heures de Jean, Duc de Berry* and other French manuscripts and tapestries: the entire spectrum of the art of that period. The backgrounds are rendered in perfect focus, unlike the ones in previous animated films—or photographs. I chose to emulate the style of van Eyck, in which a highlight in the foreground and a tree ten miles in the background are rendered with the same crispness."

This striking style is apparent from the opening of the sumptuous procession that serves as a prologue to the film, with its rippling blue banners, its knights on caparisoned horses, its jewel-like colors and flattened perspective. "Sleeping Beauty" offers an unparalleled vision of medieval life as a splendid pageant.

But the film lacks a story that can support these opulent visuals, a problem the animators attribute to a dearth of input from Walt and the coldness of the angular style. "The biggest problem we faced within that rigid drawing style," says Thomas, "was trying to maintain the warmth of character we had developed in previous pictures."

"He's a tramp, but I love him . . ." Animator Eric Larson sneaked into a burlesque show when he was animating Peg in "Lady and the Tramp," but he found singer Peggy Lee a more inspiring model.

Overleaf: Tony and Joe serenade the title characters from "Lady and the Tramp" with "La Bella Notte."

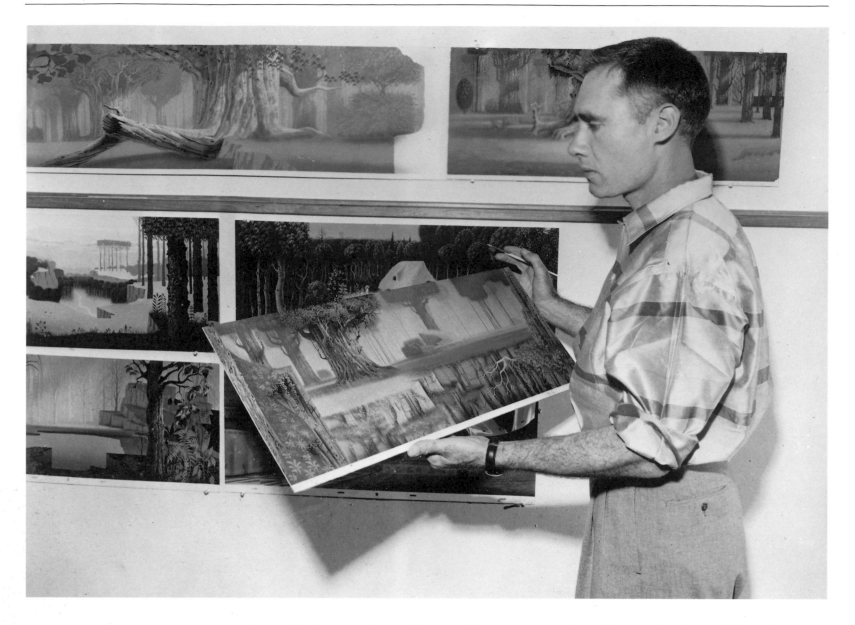

Eyvind Earle at work on "Sleeping Beauty" during the mid-1950s. The look of fifteenth-century French illuminated manuscripts inspired his designs for the film.

Disney's story crew kept very little of Perrault's fairy tale: this Beauty sleeps only a single night, not a hundred years. The story of the ageless princess slumbering in a vine-shrouded castle was replaced with a mixture of "Snow White" and a Hollywood boy-meets-girl story.

Princess Aurora may well be the loveliest of the Disney heroines, but she remains a rather distant character, without the dainty charm of Snow White or the unassuming warmth of Cinderella. Most of the animation of Prince Philip was done by Milt Kahl, who made him a much more dynamic figure than the Princes in "Snow White" and "Cinderella." Both human characters seem too close to the live-action reference footage to be very interesting in animation. Although rendered with consummate skill, their waltz in the forest seems dull.

The animation of the Good Fairies by Frank Thomas and

Ollie Johnston suggests the movements of dear, if slightly befuddled, spinster aunts. Flora, Fauna and Merryweather provide most of the comedy in the film, with their bumbling attempts to bake a cake and their duel with magic wands over the color of Aurora's gown. But all three characters are so unfailingly nice that the artists never have the chance to explore their personalities in any depth. Nothing they do suggests the complex emotions Grumpy must confront as he learns to accept, then love, Snow White.

Maleficent, one of the most frightening of all Disney villains, dominates the film. Although she bears little resemblance to the wizened old fairy in Perrault's tale, she epitomizes the evil sorceress of fantasy literature. Her face is beautiful, but cold and reptilian. Tiny, snakelike pupils stare out from beneath her heavy eyelids and arching brows. Her black robes undulate in serpentine folds, and lightning crackles from her staff when she is angered.

The Disney artists gave "Sleeping Beauty" the most dramatic climax of any animated feature—perhaps to compensate for the flatness of the rest of the story. Aided by the Good Fairies, Prince Philip escapes from Maleficent's dungeon and gallops across the countryside to the slumbering Princess Aurora.

As Philip reaches the causeway leading to King Stefan's castle, Maleficent hurls herself across the sky as a glittering pinwheel of fire, landing before him in a burst of flame. She shouts a wrathful invocation in her commanding voice, and the chartreuse fires that surround her explode into a mighty column of flame, higher than the turrets of the castle. The black form of the sorceress, darkly silhouetted against the fire, twists and elongates. The shadow waxes and solidifies, as if evil itself were coalescing within that inferno, and becomes an enormous dragon with a terrible horned head and glowing yellow eyes.

Unlike the stop-motion creatures in monster movies, this

Princess Aurora from "Sleeping Beauty" with actress Mary Costa (left), who provided her voice, and Helene Stanley, who performed her movements in the live-action reference footage.

The climactic battle between Prince Philip and the dragon. Animator Eric Cleworth modeled the movements of the dragon's head and neck after a rattlesnake striking.

dragon seems real. Its battle with Prince Philip has a remarkable, almost primal power, rarely equaled in animation—or live action.

The dragon's motions have a ponderous, reptilian grace that suggests powerful muscles moving a bulky body over the rocky terrain. The long neck and narrow head dart with a serpentine fluidity as the monster snaps at Prince Philip or tries to blast him with its fiery breath—movements that animator Eric Cleworth modeled after a rattlesnake striking.

Animator Woolie Reitherman, who directed the sequence, summed up its power: "It's something you can't just draw, and that's the beauty of animation. It can only be done in animation . . . you start to get the feeling of a force of nature out of it—it's a little bit like sex."

Like "Fantasia," to which the animators compare it, "Sleeping Beauty" was not a financial success initially. Released in 1959 in 70mm with six-channel stereophonic sound, the film earned back its $6 million production cost, but the additional expenses for promotion and distribution put the film—and the studio—more than $1 million in the red. A relatively unpublicized re-release in 1970 failed to generate much interest.

Rather than the small children and families who traditionally attend Disney cartoons, it was the students and young adults of the fantasy audience who made the 1979 and 1986 reissues successful. Although not strictly the stuff of contemporary sword-and-sorcery adventures, "Sleeping Beauty" offers a cinematic vision of a heroic world unlikely to be equaled.

"Sleeping Beauty" proved to be the glorious finale of the grand Disney style that had been developing since preliminary work began on "Snow White." The studio's next animated feature would be considerably more modest in its aims and style.

"Even if you had the money to make 'Sleeping Beauty' today, where would you find the talent?" asked Larson in a 1979 interview. "The staff was at the peak of its powers then, and their animation was about as perfect as you could get. Since 1934, we had been drawn into a world of work, study and perfection because of Walt; animators today just don't have that experience. There was nothing like it before, and there never will be again."

Although Disney's reputation had initially been built on his cartoon shorts, the success of "Snow White" reduced them to secondary importance. During the postwar era, Walt continued to approve each short film, but his interests lay elsewhere.

"We were geared to make features," says Ward Kimball. "The features made money; on the shorts, the profit margin was very small. Walt asked for little added touches no other studio would have taken the time to do, and we did take the time to provide the little niceties people expected in a Disney cartoon. The shorts were something to keep the animation and story departments afloat between features; if Walt was having a problem with a new feature, you'd mark time by picking up work on a short."

The postwar Disney cartoons were the most lavish shorts of their era. The polished animation, handsomely rendered backgrounds and careful attention to details prove that Walt still spent more money on them than any other producer would or could. But the Disney shorts no longer set the style for the animation industry, as they had before the war. Lacking the razor-sharp timing and brash humor of the Warners and MGM cartoons, they look a bit old-fashioned and tame. The mild deeds of Mickey, Goofy, Pluto and even Donald don't seem as funny as the madcap antics of Bugs Bunny, Daffy Duck, Wile E. Coyote and Tom and Jerry.

In "Duck Pimples" (1945), Donald gets involved with the characters from a murder mystery, including a siren who looks suspiciously like Tex Avery's "Red." The situation produces some funny bits of business, and director Jack Kinney is obviously trying to capture the freewheeling zaniness of the Warners and MGM films. But he doesn't know how to use their wildly exaggerated takes and split-second timing, and the results are only mildly amusing. "Duck Pimples" is one of the first Disney cartoons that clearly emulate another studio's style—something that would have been unthinkable ten years earlier.

Although Mickey Mouse remained the universally recognized symbol of the Disney studio, in 1949 Irving Wallace reported in *Collier's* that Mickey ranked "a step behind Donald Duck and Bugs Bunny in popularity among people under thirty, and second to Donald Duck among persons over thirty."

Disney explained that "Mickey's decline was due to his heroic nature. He grew into such a legend that we couldn't gag around with him. He acquired as many taboos as a Western hero—no smoking, no drinking, no violence."

The artists had always regarded Mickey as a sort of alter ego for Walt, and when Disney grew older, he lost some of his youthful exuberance. Because he was too busy to spend the necessary time in recording sessions, and because years of heavy smoking had roughened his voice, Walt stopped doing Mickey. Sound effects man Jim Macdonald began providing the character's voice during production of the "Mickey and the Beanstalk" section of "Fun and Fancy Free."

"Nobody but Walt could do the Mouse," says Ollie Johnston. "He was the only guy who felt how to handle Mickey. After 'The Sorcerer's Apprentice,' there really wasn't a good Mickey. Then they started drawing him in a different way, with different proportions. But the drawing wasn't the problem; it was that they just didn't have the right things for him to do."

Between 1941 and 1965, Disney made 106 Donald Duck cartoons and 49 Goofys, but only 14 shorts starring Mickey Mouse. And in those few films, Mickey often served as a foil for Pluto. In "Mickey and the Seal" (1948), he's cast as a mild-mannered suburban bachelor. When he feeds the animals at the zoo, a baby seal crawls into his picnic basket and gets loose in his house. Pluto's outraged reactions to the little invader provide the laughs; Mickey just gives a bemused chuckle.

The audience that grew up during the late 1940s and early 1950s knew Mickey as the genial host of "The Mickey Mouse Club" ("Everybody neat 'n' pretty?"), rather than the rowdy scamp who tried to steal a kiss from Minnie in "Plane Crazy."

Donald Duck's wartime popularity carried over into the next decade. Jack Hannah directed so many of these cartoons that he got "damned tired of that duck's voice." When America moved to the suburbs, Donald went along, usually in the role of Daisy's suitor and/or the guardian of Huey, Dewey and Louie.

Like Minnie Mouse, Daisy Duck never really developed a personality of her own. Her actions and attitudes give Donald something to react to; beyond that, she remains a cipher. Her voice was always a problem: Clarence Nash originally provided it, but he made her sound too much like Donald. During the 1940s, the studio tried using the normal voices of various soft-spoken women from the ink and paint department, which made her sound too different.

Daisy's one big moment occurs in "Donald's Dilemma" (1947), after a falling flowerpot has transformed the Duck into a Bing Crosby-esque crooner. Faced with a choice between regaining her beau or "the world having his beautiful golden voice," Daisy screams "Me! Me! Me!" in an uncharacteristically vivid display of greed and jealousy.

Donald becomes a boob father in the dubious tradition of television sitcoms when he has to deal with the rather generic Huey, Dewey and Louie. The Duck is usually his own worst enemy in these films. Huey, Dewey and Louie win a new car for him in "Lucky Number" (1951), but Donald wrecks it before they can give it to him. When they take the money from their piggy bank to buy a box of cigars as a birthday present in "Donald's Happy Birthday" (1949), he accuses them of smoking, and wastes his present making them sick.

In the postwar Warners cartoons, the audience sympathizes with Bugs Bunny, because he never bothers anyone until he's been attacked. It's difficult to know whom to root for in many of the Donald Duck cartoons from this period. The temper tantrums that were so funny when a young rascal threw them in "The Band Concert" seem inappropriate for someone who is supposed to be an adult and a parent. No wonder Daisy tries to stop them in "Cured Duck" (1949).

But Donald is also portrayed as the victim of arbitrary

Donald Duck greets Humphrey in a rare peaceful moment from "Beezy Bear" (1955).

mistreatment—unlike Wile E. Coyote, who always engineers his own defeat. In "Don's Fountain of Youth" (1953) his nephews are obnoxious brats who scream when he tries to take away their comic books and show them the Florida scenery. Huey, Dewey and Louie have no reason to spoil his date with Daisy in "Mr. Duck Steps Out" (1940), nor do Chip and Dale in "Crazy Over Daisy" (1950). As a result, the audience's sympathy goes to Donald, and his abuse by the other characters seems unwarranted and unfunny.

The films that pit Donald against some external foe are usually more fun. In "Tea for Two Hundred" (1948), Donald sets out on a picnic, and ends up waging an unsuccessful war against a whole tribe of invading ants. He plays the tourist in "Grand Canyon Scope" (1954), annoying everyone with his incessant flash photography, including an ancient puma.

One of Hannah's most successful adversaries for Donald was a honeybee named Spike. The source of their conflict varies from film to film. Donald attempts to rob the hive in "Honey Harvester" (1949) and "Bee on Guard" (1951); Spike mistakenly tries to visit the flowers on Donald's new wallpaper in "Inferior Decorator" (1948). The results, however, are always the same: Spike diving, stinger first, at Donald's plump, exposed rear.

Hannah pushed the gags further—and got funnier results—

in the. cartoons that involve Donald, a prissy park ranger, J. Audubon Woodlore, and a no-account bear named Humphrey. (A bear similar to Humphrey hid from gun-happy hunters in Donald's cabin in the 1953 short "Rugged Bear"; his name and conniving personality were added later.)

In "Grin and Bear It" (1954), Humphrey must balance his greed for Donald's picnic against the fear of being made into a rug if he's caught stealing. He tries to burgle Donald's honey farm in "Beezy Bear" (1955), but has to hide his actions from Donald, Woodlore and the angry bees. The animators give

Humphrey wildly distorted takes and play his bulky, pear-shaped body against the frantic movements of his limbs, with hilarious results. The Donald-Humphrey-Woodlore cartoons show that the Disney artists could have competed with Warners and MGM if they had tried—or been allowed to try.

During the later 1950s, Disney began to feature Donald in educational and didactic films, like "How to Have an Accident in the Home" (1956) and "Donald Duck in Mathmagic Land" (1959). "The Litterbug" (1961) marked his last appearance in a theatrical short until 1983.

Goofy portrayed both team captains as well as the referee in "Hockey Homicide" (1945), one of the funniest cartoons in the How To series on sports.

Donald also appeared in other media throughout the 1940s and 1950s. His comic strip, begun by Al Taliaferro in 1936, remained popular, and in 1942 story man Carl Barks drew "Pirate Gold," the first Donald Duck comic book. Barks turned Donald into a comic adventurer, sending him everywhere from Yucatan to the Himalayas to Atlantis. (Among Barks's inventions was the fabulously wealthy Scrooge McDuck, who later became an animated character.) In addition, Donald was regularly seen on television, beginning with the fourth episode of "Disneyland," titled "The Donald Duck Story."

Goofy was probably the only Disney character who became more popular after the war than he had been before it. Dick Huemer directed the first cartoon to focus on him, "Goofy and Wilbur," in 1939. But it was the success of the "How to Ride a Horse" segment of "The Reluctant Dragon" (1941) that established the Goof as a cartoon star and set the pattern for the popular and funny How To series, directed by Jack Kinney.

The format remained the same in all these shorts. The polished narrator (story sketch man John McLeish, a.k.a. John Ployardt) delivers a straightforward lecture on a particular sport, while Goofy tries to illustrate each point in mime. Naturally, things go spectacularly wrong, and the contrast between McLeish's unshakably calm voice and the escalating mayhem on the screen make the How To films some of the funniest Disney cartoons of the postwar era. Kinney had Goofy try a variety of sports, including baseball, swimming, sailing, basketball, fishing, golf, tennis and skiing, with equally disastrous—and funny—results.

"Hockey Homicide" (1945) is probably the best entry in the series. This fast-paced cartoon lampoons not only the game of hockey but its overly enthusiastic fans and announcers. The titanic final brawl features quick shots of exciting images from other Disney films, climaxing with Monstro the Whale from "Pinocchio." "Hockey Homicide" also includes several studio "in" jokes. The dueling star players are "Icebox" Bertino and "Fearless" Ferguson (animators Al Bertino and Norman Ferguson), and the referee's name is "Clean-Game" Kinney.

Making Goofy a silent character (except for an occasional laugh, scream or "Garsh") also eliminated a potential problem. Pinto Colvig, who provided the character's voice, had left the studio in 1939; Goofy's few lines could be dubbed from old films or done by someone else.

During the course of the How To series, the genial dimwit Art Babbitt had described in 1934 was transformed into a less dreamy, more enthusiastic character. The new Goofy was as eager as he was maladroit, ready to try anything and blithely unaware of his lack of ability. Many of his more flamboyant mishaps were animated by two artists noted for their handling of dynamic action, John Sibley and Woolie Reitherman. Reitherman described his work in these cartoons as having "vitality and an 'I don't give a damn, try it' quality."

"Plunk": the ancestry of modern stringed instruments is explained in the stylized short "Toot, Whistle, Plunk, and Boom" (1953).

During the 1950s, Goofy grew less gangly and more attractive; his buckteeth and floppy ears were downplayed. His slouching, loose-jointed walk became a brisk, erect trot. The Goof metamorphosed into an easygoing, suburban Everyman in a series of domestic sitcoms with titles like "Fathers Are People" (1951), "Two Weeks Vacation" (1952) and "Father's Day Off" (1953). He portrays both the sane, courteous Mr. Walker and the snarling, irrational Mr. Wheeler in Kinney's "Motor Mania" (1950), a pointed satire on American driving habits.

"Goofy became our resident *Homo sapiens*—with a dog face—our man who represented the common humanoid," says Ward Kimball. "It was Goofy against the world."

In addition to the shorts with the familiar characters, the Disney artists made a number of one-shot cartoons during the 1940s and 1950s, including experiments with CinemaScope and 3-D.

Writer Bill Peet demonstrated the talent that would later make him a popular children's author in "Susie, the Little Blue Coupe" (1952), the tale of one small car's career, from shiny new status symbol to dilapidated clunker to the beloved jalopy of a teenage boy. Ham Luske's "Ben and Me" (1953) tells the story of Benjamin Franklin from the point of view of Amos, the little mouse who gives the Colonial writer-inventor all of his ideas.

Probably the best known of these one-shot films is the Oscar-winning "Toot, Whistle, Plunk, and Boom" (1953), a history of Western musical instruments. Co-directed by Charles Nichols and Ward Kimball, this educational short traces each family of instruments back to its prehistoric origins. It was originally planned for the educational market, but Disney decided to reshoot it in CinemaScope and release it theatrically.

Animation historians often point to "Toot, Whistle, Plunk, and Boom" as an example of Disney borrowing the UPA style—a charge Kimball denies: "Nobody had a patent on that look," he says. "We all subscribed to *Graphis* magazine. I was accused of imitating UPA by some of the other artists while Walt was in Europe, but the owl and the birds in the schoolroom are fully animated—exactly as we would have animated anything else. Only the figures on the charts were done in a limited style, to differentiate them from the 'real' birds. The overall effect is that the film was done in limited animation, which is not true."

"Toot, Whistle, Plunk, and Boom" is an entertaining and informative cartoon, but there doesn't seem to have been any artistic reason to make it in CinemaScope. (Kimball recalls that Disney reshot the film in the new format at Darryl Zanuck's request.) Nothing in the film really plays off the larger frame, and it's every bit as enjoyable in the standard format.

Except for a few bits of abstract animation in the equally stylized "Melody" (1953), the Disney artists didn't use 3-D any more effectively than their counterparts at the other studios. "Flowers and Trees" (1932) and "The Old Mill" (1937) were breakthrough films that showcased technical innovations; in "Melody" and "Toot, Whistle" the new techniques are little more than gimmicks.

The influence of the UPA cartoons can clearly be seen in "Pigs Is Pigs" (1954), the story of two overly fecund guinea pigs who swamp a railroad station with their progeny. The rhyming narration, flattened graphics, angular characters and limited animation are more reminiscent of "Gerald McBoing-Boing" than "The Band Concert." The pacing of the film and the timing of its rather mild gags also echo the work of the UPA directors.

By the middle 1950s, Disney was spending up to $100,000 on each cartoon. The shrinking market for short films made it impossible to recoup those costs, and the production of shorts was phased out in 1955–56. The studio continued to release one or two special short films a year from 1957 through 1962, most of them twenty-minute "featurettes," like "Paul Bunyan" (1958), "The Truth about Mother Goose" (1957) and "Goliath II" (1960).

However, the classic Disney cartoons remained in the public view. Walt recycled many of them on various "Disneyland" shows and on "The Mickey Mouse Club." A new generation of viewers—the sons and daughters of the original Disney audience—beheld the wonders of "The Cookie Carnival," "Three Little Pigs," "The Old Mill" and "Brave Little Tailor" after Annette, Bobby or Darleen gave the invocation: "Meeska, Mooska, Mouseketeer; Mouse Cartoon Time now is here!"

As the genial host of "The Mickey Mouse Club," Mickey introduced the members of the baby-boom generation to the wonders of the classic Disney shorts.

UPA AND THE GRAPHIC REVOLUTION, 1943-1959

The best way to identify United Productions of America is to say: "They're the people who made 'Gerald McBoing-Boing.'" And the best way to identify the quality of their product is to say that every time you see one of their animated cartoons you are likely to recapture the sensation you had when you first saw "Steamboat Willie," the early Silly Symphonies, "The Band Concert"—the feeling that something new and wonderful has happened, something almost too good to be true. —GILBERT SELDES

Although it flourished for only a brief time, United Productions of America, better known as UPA, profoundly altered the course of animation. Only the Walt Disney studio has had a more far-reaching influence. Disney brought order and an elevated standard of draftsmanship to the sloppy, anarchic cartoons of the 1920s. The UPA artists challenged the realistic look of the Disney films, and infused social comment and avant-garde graphics into their work.

The origins of UPA lay in the Disney strike of 1941. Many of the strikers were young men with extensive art training and a strong interest in current trends in the graphic arts. Their sophisticated artistic views were supported by strong, liberal political beliefs and a conviction that the arts, including the art of animation, could be used as a tool for social reform.

These young men chafed at the restrictions of Disney animation—the traditional, almost Academic style of drawing; the animal characters; the emphasis on humor; the familiar stories. They wanted to expand the medium, to explore con-

temporary graphic styles and different kinds of storytelling. Among the active members of this group were Zachary Schwartz, Dave Hilberman, Leo Salkin, John Hubley, Bill Melendez, Stephen Bosustow and Bill Hurtz.

After the strike several of these artists, including Schwartz, Hilberman and Hubley, were hired by Frank Tashlin, who had recently been put in charge of the animation unit at Columbia. For about a year, they worked with Tashlin, making funny cartoons like "The Fox and the Grapes" (1941) and the graphically bold "Professor Small and Mr. Tall" (1942). But when Tashlin ran afoul of the Columbia management and left the studio, the more imaginative animators also left.

Many of the artists who later joined UPA served in the First Motion Picture Unit: John Hubley, Bill Hurtz, Willis Pyle, Herb Klynn, Van Kaufman, Phil Monroe, Jules Engel and Bill Scott. The FMPU gave them the opportunity to experiment with the design and content of animated films—experiments they would continue to develop and explore at UPA.

Steve Bosustow went to work at Hughes Aircraft, making explanatory drawings to help workers who couldn't read blueprints; he also taught classes in three-dimensional sketching to engineers and tool designers at the California Institute of Technology (Cal Tech).

In 1943 Bosustow joined Zack Schwartz and Dave Hilberman (who were renting studio space in the Otto K. Oleson building in Hollywood) to form the Industrial Film and Poster

Opposite: Gerald McBoing-Boing and Mr. Magoo as Tiny Tim and Ebenezer Scrooge in "Mr. Magoo's Christmas Carol" (1962). This entertaining adaptation of Dickens's holiday classic proved to be the characters' last hurrah.

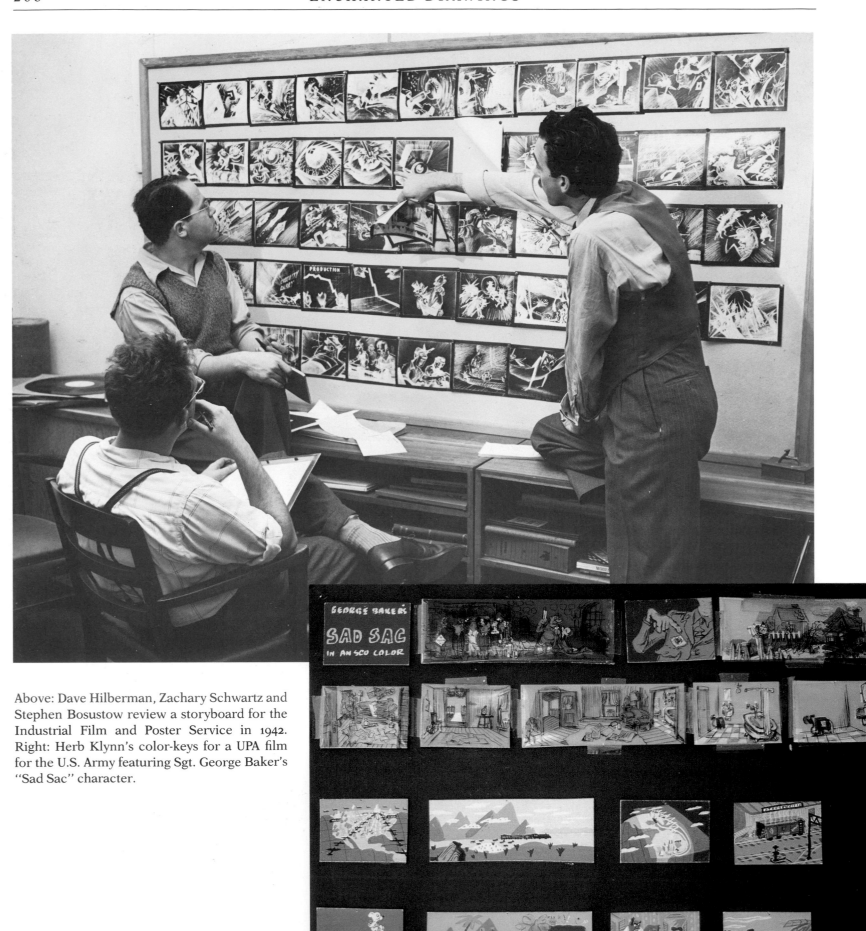

Above: Dave Hilberman, Zachary Schwartz and Stephen Bosustow review a storyboard for the Industrial Film and Poster Service in 1942. Right: Herb Klynn's color-keys for a UPA film for the U.S. Army featuring Sgt. George Baker's "Sad Sac" character.

Service. Their first project, a welding-safety filmstrip, "Sparks and Chips Get the Blitz," proved successful, and soon Industrial Film and Poster was producing films, film strips and graphic materials for defense contractors and the Army and Navy. The volume of work grew too large for the three partners to handle alone, and studio animators, including many of the artists at the FMPU, began helping on a free-lance basis.

"After working at the FMPU all day, I would stop at my apartment and grab a sandwich, then go to work at Industrial Film and Poster at seven. Sometimes I'd stay till two in the morning," recalls Herb Klynn, who later became production manager at UPA. "The creative freedom we had there no longer exists."

The fledgling studio received its first big break in 1944: a contract from the United Auto Workers to produce a film supporting Franklin Roosevelt's campaign for a fourth term, "Hell-Bent for Election."

"Hell-Bent for Election" had a budget of only $9,000—hardly adequate for several minutes of animation. Most of the work was done at night by free-lancers for minimal wages. Chuck Jones, who directed the film—after putting in a full day at Warner Brothers—received $125 for his services. Earl Robinson wrote the songs for the film, and E. Y. "Yip" Harburg supplied the lyrics.

"Hell-Bent for Election" features caricatures of the two candidates as trains: Franklin Roosevelt is a streamlined superchief, the Win the War Special; Thomas Dewey, the Defeatist Limited, is a ramshackle, coal-burning locomotive that belches black smoke. An evil Southern senator tries to trick Joe Worker into literally falling asleep at the switch and not voting—which would enable the Defeatist Limited to win. But Joe awakens just in time. The Limited gets derailed as the F.D.R. Special sails to victory. At the conclusion, the audience is invited to sing along with a Roosevelt campaign song.

The film remains bright, stylish and persuasive. It's impossible to assess what effect—if any—the film had on the election. (No other presidential candidate has bothered to exploit the potential of animation to sway opinions.) But "Hell-Bent for Election" did attract a great deal of attention to the Industrial Film and Poster Service.

Many of the FMPU artists who had been moonlighting at Industrial Film and Poster came to work there when the war ended and the unit was disbanded.

The next major project the studio undertook was the "Flight Safety" series for the U.S. Navy. The first installment became the studio's second well-known film: "Flat Hatting" (1945) warned against the dangers of hot-dogging stunts, like buzzing

Three stills from "Hell-bent for Election" (1944), with caricatures of presidential candidates Franklin Roosevelt and Thomas Dewey as the Win the War Special and the Defeatist Limited (top). The Dewey caricature does a "take" (center) before crashing (bottom).

civilian areas. John Hubley directed the film (and the series), assisted by Bill Hurtz; Paul Julian did the backgrounds and Phil Eastman much of the story work.

In late 1945, the rapidly expanding Industrial Film and Poster Service was reorganized as United Productions of America. Actually, the studio was anything but united. Increasing tensions had developed among the three partners. A few months later, Schwartz and Hilberman offered to sell their shares in the company to Bosustow, who quickly raised the $9,000 they requested and bought them out.

Animators and film historians have debated Bosustow's methods and motives for this acquisition for more than forty years. In an interview with John Canemaker in 1979, Dave Hilberman explained his reasons for leaving UPA and cleared up many unanswered questions.

During the war, the Soviet Union had sent a commission under Michael Kolatozoff of the Leningrad studio to Hollywood to learn American filmmaking techniques. Kolatozoff became friends with Hilberman (who had spent six months in the U.S.S.R. in 1932, working and studying at the Leningrad State Theater) and invited him to come to Russia to help establish animation studios in each of the ten Soviet republics and two more in Moscow.

"Well, that was a helluva challenge," said Hilberman. "I kept it very quiet, but I did talk to Zack, because we were very close friends. I said: 'I want to do this thing. If I pull out of UPA, would you want to buy my share?' He said: 'No, but if you're not going to be there, then I don't want to be there, because

Herb Klynn at work on a cut-paper film at the UPA studio during the late 1940s.

I've got my family's money invested in this. It's a shaky thing, so I'd want to sell out too.' So we decided to sell."

With the benefit of hindsight, Hilberman lambasted the decision to sell their shares of the studio to Bosustow as "an idiotic thing to do." His plan to work in the Soviet Union was destroyed by the postwar political changes and purges in the Soviet Union. He and Schwartz moved to New York and joined with William Pomerance to form Tempo Productions, a commercial studio; Schwartz later left Tempo to pursue a successful career in advertising.

Stephen Bosustow now held the controlling interest in UPA. As the studio rose to prominence, articles in many magazines and newspapers focused on him, often comparing him to Walt Disney. The popular journals implied that Bosustow was personally responsible for the artistic innovations of UPA, much as they had once credited Disney with the creations of his entire studio. The consensus among the artists is that Bosustow lacked Disney's all-encompassing vision and consummate story sense. He apparently had little involvement in the nuts-and-bolts decisions that went into the making of the individual films.

Because his aesthetic contributions were limited, some animators make the mistake of dismissing Bosustow's role at UPA. He made the studio a place where creativity flourished. The artists enjoyed an unprecedented freedom in their work, in marked contrast to the administration of Eddie Selzer at Warner Brothers or Fred Quimby at MGM.

"If it were not for Steve's persistence and determination to make UPA go, it never would have held together," says Ade Woolery, who began working at the studio before it was officially organized as Industrial Film and Poster. "There were plenty of opportunities for the doors to close and everybody to go his way, but Steve would have no part of it. He'd go out and scrounge, and come up with either a few dollars or a job."

Shortly after Bosustow took control of UPA, the studio produced another short film for the UAW that received favorable notices in the press: "The Brotherhood of Man." The Auto Workers commissioned the film when their recruiting campaign in the South encountered an unexpected obstacle: white and black workers balked at joining the same locals.

The reasons for making "The Brotherhood of Man" may have been prosaic, but director Robert "Bobe" Cannon took advantage of the opportunities the project offered for innovation. Based on *The Races of Man*, a pamphlet by Gene Weltfish and Ruth Benedict, the film systematically demolishes the fallacies that underlie racial prejudice. A little green man, who represents the bigot hidden within the genial central character, voices the old stereotypes about race affecting intelligence, blood, lifestyle, etc. He slinks away during the closing scenes of people of various ethnicities working and playing together.

The central message—"An equal start in life . . . an equal

chance for a job! Then we can all go forward together"—seems considerably less revolutionary today than it did in 1946. But "The Brotherhood of Man" is an effective piece of filmmaking that presents a message skillfully. Archer Winsten praised "Brotherhood" (and "Flat Hatting") as "wonderful" in the New York *Post:* "Not since the first Disney cartoons established new standards of humor, art and animation for the movie cartooning industry has anything as startling as these pictures and their makers come along."

Two years later, Bosustow signed a contract with Columbia to produce cartoons for them for theatrical release. The management at Columbia was unhappy with the quality of their cartoons, and with good reason. The head of their Screen Gems studio had been changed seven times in the last eight years, but the films had not improved—except during Frank Tashlin's brief tenure. For the UPA artists, theatrical shorts represented a more prestigious, stable and lucrative market than the sponsored films and commercials they had been producing.

On the strength of the Columbia release, UPA began building a modern showcase of a studio in Burbank—not far from Disney. They moved from temporary quarters on Highland Avenue to the new studio in late 1949.

The contract with Columbia had one major drawback: they wanted the new cartoons to feature the studio's only remaining characters—the Fox and Crow Tashlin had introduced in 1941. The UPA artists didn't want to work with any animal characters, let alone a pair that had degenerated into shopworn clichés during the intervening years.

John Hubley, now vice president of creative affairs at UPA, directed three Fox and Crow shorts: "Robin Hoodlum" (1948), "The Magic Fluke" (1949) and "Punchy De Leon" (1950). He

Producer Steve Bosustow accepts UPA's first Oscar (for "Gerald McBoing-Boing") from Phyllis Kirk in 1951.

A cel and background of the Everyman character in Bobe Cannon's "The Brotherhood of Man" (1946).

Above: A typical chase sequence from Columbia's Fox and Crow series (1939). John Hubley revivified the characters in "Robin Hoodlum" (1948) and (below) "The Magic Fluke" (1949), and received Oscar nominations for both films.

managed to revivify the threadbare duo, and the first two films received Oscar nominations.

"Hub sort of went back to the sure, Disney concept of space," says Bill Hurtz, who assisted him on the films. "He wanted to get some spatial animation. He was sick to death of a little character with legs on a separate cel trotting back and forth across the screen. He wanted characters to move in space and go up spiral staircases, so he bludgeoned 'Robin Hoodlum' through."

Despite the success of the new Fox and Crow shorts, Hubley, Bosustow and the rest of the UPA staff chafed at their restrictions. They had joined the studio to get away from the funny animals and slapstick gags that constituted the standard fare of Hollywood cartoons. They wanted to make films with human characters and a different style of humor.

In 1949, they initiated the Jolly Frolics series with "Ragtime Bear," the first theatrical cartoon made in the UPA style. The story centered on a nearsighted little green curmudgeon who mistook a grizzly bear for his nephew in a raccoon coat. The little man—unnamed in the cartoon, but subsequently christened Quincy Magoo—became UPA's most popular character.

Mr. Magoo, his nephew, Waldo, and the title character of "Ragtime Bear" (1949). This cel, laid over an original background, was used for a color test at the studio.

This popularity has led various artists to vie for the title of "Magoo's father," with each claimant offering his own version of the character's origins. John Hubley, who directed three of the first seven Mr. Magoo cartoons, including "Ragtime Bear," said he had patterned the old geezer after a stubborn Midwestern uncle he disliked. (The animators credit Hubley as the principal creator of Magoo.) In 1958, Jim Backus, who supplied Magoo's raspy voice, told Richard Nason of the *New York Times:* "I don't think I'm revealing anything irreverent when I state that I embodied something of my father in the characterization. . . . Dad was a wonderful guy and a very successful manufacturer of machinery. But you couldn't tell him a thing that he didn't want to think existed. That's the way Magoo is."

In addition, articles in various publications recounted the story of Magoo's unexpected rise to stardom. He supposedly began as a minor, throwaway character who had to be continued to satisfy public demand. The Boston *Herald,* December 13, 1959: "Curiously, Mr. Magoo wasn't born a star. In fact, he wasn't even intended to carry on. He was simply an incidental character tossed in for a few laughs in a picture about a grizzly bear addicted to music. But the force of his personality stole 'Ragtime Bear,' as the 1949 cartoon was called."

Entertaining as these stories are, Bosustow dismissed them all as fabrications by the studio's publicists. (A look at "Rag-time Bear" confirms this statement: Magoo is clearly not "an incidental character.") Mr. Magoo, he said, was really created in response to demands by Columbia for a series to replace the Fox and Crow.

When he returned from New York, Bosustow called in writer Millard "Butch" Kaufman from MGM. (Bosustow had given Kaufman one of his first jobs, working on the Navy "Flight Safety" series.) Kaufman wrote "Ragtime Bear" for Bosustow, and Magoo was born.

One important ancestor of Magoo was W. C. Fields. "It's a Gift" was John Hubley's favorite film, and Magoo's bulbous nose, intransigent attitude and muttered asides clearly show the influence of that redoubtable comedian. Pete Burness, who directed most of the Magoo cartoons, later acknowledged the influence: "We got W. C. Fields pictures and ran them and studied them just to see what they would suggest. We wanted to see if there were dimensions that we were missing that we could put into Magoo. . . . He was similar to Fields in that neither one of them had patience with weakness or inequities as they saw them. Of course, Fields was basically a con man. Magoo was terribly civic-minded. . . . We studied the Fields pictures in terms of the way Magoo walks through a situation, which in many cases was the same way Fields would move through a situation."

Like any other studio cartoon character, Mr. Magoo was the

product of a communal effort by the writers, directors, designers, animators, voice actor et al. Each person contributed something to the character, and no single artist created him.

"Ragtime Bear" was much closer to what the UPA staff wanted to do than "Robin Hoodlum" or "The Magic Fluke." Although critics and audiences liked the film, it had really been designed to please the artists themselves. The success of Mr. Magoo enabled them to make the films they wanted, while Steve Bosustow assumed the unenviable task of trying to persuade the Columbia executives and sales representatives to accept these highly individual shorts in place of the more conventional cartoons they expected.

During 1950–51, the artists at UPA turned their attention to a variety of projects that bore little resemblance to the cartoons being produced at other studios. Hubley, who never wanted to repeat anything, turned Mr. Magoo over to animator Pete Burness after the second cartoon, "Spellbound Hound" (1950). (Hubley directed one more Magoo short, "Fuddy Duddy Buddy," in 1951.) Burness made four Magoo films during this period, including the Oscar-nominated "Trouble Indemnity" (1950) and the outstanding "Grizzly Golfer" (1951). He continued working with the character through 1958.

Critics praised the fantasy sequence done in the style of children's drawings in Art Babbitt's "The Family Circus" (1951), but "Giddyap" (1950), the story of a broken-down iceman's horse who had been a vaudeville star, was closer to a conventional cartoon. Babbitt studied footage of Fred Astaire in "Flying Down to Rio" before animating the horse's elaborate tap dance. David Raksin, who composed the jazzy score, named this sequence "Hoofloose and Fancy Free."

The iceman's horse—before he reveals his skill as a tap dancer—in Art Babbitt's "Giddyap" (1950).

In 1951, Bobe Cannon won UPA's first Oscar for one of the most famous and very best films the studio produced: "Gerald McBoing-Boing." The story of Gerald McCloy—who "didn't talk words . . . he went boing-boing instead!"—began as a poem written by Ted "Dr. Seuss" Geisel and recorded by Hal Peary ("The Great Gildersleeve"). Geisel and Bosustow were good friends, and they agreed to try making an animated cartoon based on the poem.

Working with designer Bill Hurtz, Cannon created unique graphic devices that helped to set "Gerald" apart: "We worked out this crazy linear pattern that plays all the way through the film, almost on a continuous line," says Hurtz. "Where the character ends up in one scene is where he picks up in the next. Also, the props were all silent characters. You couldn't tell what the rooms in that house were like, so the animation carved out the space. That was a strong thing that Bobe was really excited by."

"Gerald McBoing-Boing" played an impressive 30,000 theater dates, showing simultaneously in three first-run houses in New York City. *Life* magazine ran a two-page spread of art from the film, and critics praised "Gerald" ecstatically: "Audiences are simply bearing out the basic conviction of the UPA people, that cartoons need not be all cuteness or all violence. That cartoons can be artistic and intelligent and still be popular. Like 'Gerald McBoing-Boing' " (Arthur Knight, *Theatre Arts*). "Little Gerald's talents are too specialized for many other stories, but in its own way, his 'Boing!' may prove as resounding as the first peep out of Mickey Mouse" (*Time*).

The extraordinary success of "Gerald," coupled with the popularity of Mr. Magoo and the critical acclaim the other UPA films were receiving, made it clear that Bobe Cannon and John Hubley had emerged as the creative leaders of the studio.

John "Hub" Hubley ranks among the key figures in the history of animation. A restless, relentlessly creative artist, Hubley constantly strove to expand the medium, experimenting with design, color, texture, sound and story. His co-workers unanimously acclaim him as a genius, and regret their failure to save even his doodle pads and gag drawings.

"Hub could draw like nobody else—very expressive drawings that would capture the essence of almost anything, in a

Opposite: Eight cel setups tell the story of "Gerald McBoing-Boing." Top row: His parents discover that he doesn't talk—"he goes 'boing-boing' instead," a diagnosis the physician confirms. Second row: His sound effects startle his father. Third row: His inability to speak makes it difficult to find friends at school and causes his father to cut himself while shaving. Bottom row: Rejected by his father, Gerald flees into the night, but he finds work as a radio sound effects artist.

John Hubley, c. 1952. One of the guiding forces of UPA (and, later, of independent animation), Hubley sought to expand the medium of animation, in both content and graphics.

soul to a design, not through the copying but through the transformation of reality"—reflects Hubley's influence.

In 1952, Hubley also directed "Rooty-Toot-Toot," a honky-tonk courtroom retelling of the story of Frankie and Johnny, which remains one of the most widely praised UPA cartoons. The graphics of the film are so sophisticated that critic Robert Benayoun compares the stylized face of Nellie Bligh to the head of a Modigliani odalisque.

In New York, Bill Scott had seen a musical comedy in which Valerie Bettis danced the trial of Frankie. He pitched the concept to Hubley, who "took the idea, enlarged upon it, made it his own: [he] set the style of it, decided to do it as a combination ballet and animated film."

"Rooty-Toot-Toot" was the only UPA film to be censored. When Nellie Bligh gives her occupation as singer, Frankie furiously declares: "That's a lie! she's no singer, she's a . . ." Columbia objected to the phrase "she's a . . ." and had it excised from the sound track—the first of many controversies in which John Hubley would become embroiled.

It would be difficult to imagine two more dissimilar personalities—or two more divergent approaches to animation —than John Hubley's and Robert "Bobe" Cannon's. For all his brilliance, Hubley could be a difficult man: he commanded a sharp wit and was a devastating caricaturist. Cannon was quiet, very sensitive and subdued. Everyone at the studio seems to have loved him, albeit a bit impatiently.

style that was completely the opposite of what was done at Disney and the rest of the industry," says Bill Melendez. "I always felt it was Hub that started us in the direction of caricaturing humans, rather than animals—which includes almost everything that's animated now. On top of that, he had a great mind for story. If Hubley had any kind of weakness, it was his impatience. He'd start a project, then pretty soon he'd be off on another one. He found it difficult to complete one from beginning to end."

Working with designer Paul Julian, Hubley created seven short pieces of animation to link the scenes in "The Four Poster" (1952), Stanley Kramer's live-action feature tracing the course of a marriage over thirty-five years. The deceptively simple animated sequences serve as transitions to indicate the passage of time and/or changes in the characters and the world. The death of the couple's son in World War I is reduced to a bleak tableau of bayonets, helmets and rain.

This dramatic and imaginative use of the medium impressed the Yugoslavian artists and designers who founded the animation unit of Zagreb Film in 1954. Their "Collective Statement"—which describes animation as "a protest against the static condition" and asserts: "To animate: to give life and

Artwork from one of John Hubley's animated inserts for the live-action feature "The Four Poster" (1952).

Above: "And to the tiger in the zoo, Madeline just said 'pooh-pooh.'" A cel setup from Bobe Cannon's adaptation of Ludwig Bemelmans's children's book (1952). Right: Bobe Cannon at work at UPA in 1956. A quiet, gentle man, Cannon directed some of the studio's most charming films.

"I believe two major things pretty much ruled what Bobe would do," said Bill Scott. "First, he loved ballet, was crazy about ballet. He considered animated movement a form of ballet. I don't necessarily mean classical ballet, but certainly as far as choreographed motion. Second was that Bobe could not stand conflict. He hated and despised conflict. He did not like loud things. He did not like argument. I remember that one of the toughest times we had in doing the adaptation of the Gerald McBoing-Boing story was getting in a scene where a kid's parents reject him—this is what drives him out of the house. And Bobe simply could not deal with that."

In "Gerald McBoing-Boing" and "Madeline" (1952), Cannon introduced a plastic style of motion. In both films, the movements of the characters seem to flow across the screen, effortlessly carrying the viewer's eye in a graceful path—a marked contrast to Hubley's more staccato cutting in "Rooty-Toot-Toot." Cannon achieved this fluid motion through a rather unconventional process.

"Bobe loved show tunes, and he would have a record on while he was animating," explains writer Leo Salkin. "What he'd animate would have nothing to do with what was on the record, except the rhythm was one he wanted to get in the animation. Although it sounds ludicrous, he'd just kind of respond to the music and he would get animation that was choreographic. After seeing 'Madeline' several times, I began to see how subtly Bobe kept everything fluid from beginning to end, without a cut. He kept the characters on the screen and dissolved the backgrounds in and out. The movements of the characters seemed to be uninterrupted—they flowed from scene to scene, as though it were choreography. I thought it

A cel setup from "Fudget's Budget" (1954), Cannon's spoof of household money management.

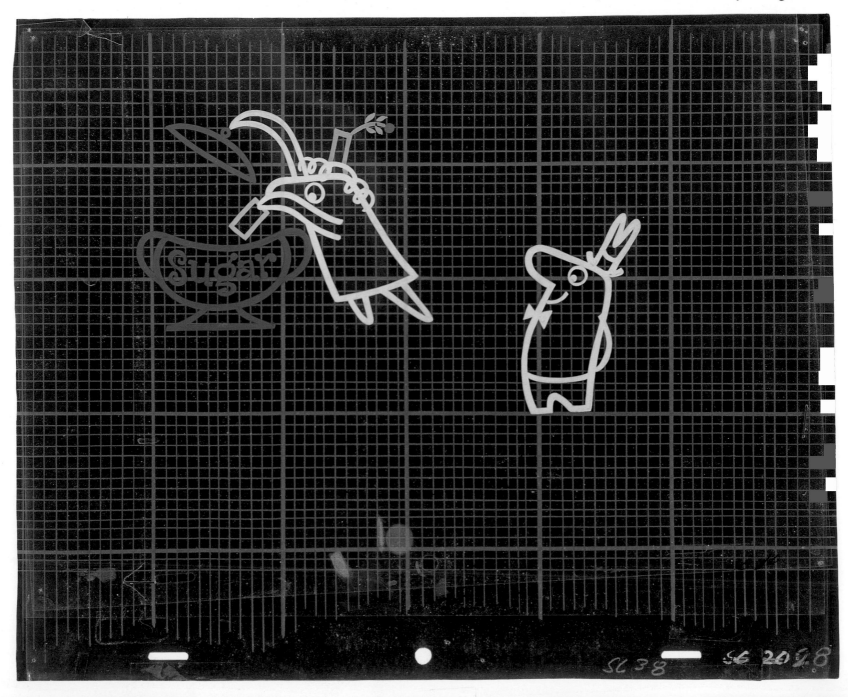

was one of the most unique talents I'd ever witnessed in animation.''

His preference for innocent, whimsical fantasies often led Cannon to make films about children, including ''Gerald McBoing-Boing'' and ''Madeline.'' ''Christopher Crumpet'' (1953) is the story of a little boy who transforms himself into a chicken when he doesn't get his own way. ''The Oompahs'' (1952) uses the theme of classical music vs. jazz to portray tensions within a family of instruments. In ''Willie the Kid'' (1952), Cannon turns a game of ''cowboy'' into a spoof of westerns.

Cannon's best films are genuinely charming. ''Gerald McBoing-Boing'' continues to delight audiences with its gentle insouciance. ''Madeline'' is a lovely adaptation of Ludwig Bemelmans's popular children's book. ''The Oompahs'' remains an effective metaphor for the conflict between parental aspirations and a child's career ambitions.

But the aversion to conflict sometimes becomes a weakness. When Christopher Crumpet refuses to demonstrate his metamorphic abilities before a witness, his father whines and begs and pleads, but never loses his temper. The audience tires of the intractable child and begins to root for the parent.

''There was a conflict of approach between Hubley and Bobe, and this conflict of temperament kept turning up in everything the studio did,'' says Paul Julian. ''It was quite obvious that Hub was a stronger director, in terms of coming out with films that had some validity or some real comment. Bobe and T. Hee were agreeable components of a very agreeable pattern, doing small, quiet things with an original turn of mind. But there was never any bite to them—it was as if Bobe didn't have any front teeth. Hubley made a point of working comment in, whatever he was doing. Even with the Magoos, Hubley had some kind of side point.''

The experimental films of Hubley and Cannon won awards and were justly acclaimed for their artistry. They tended to overshadow the work of the third important UPA director, Pete Burness. While Hubley and Cannon explored the aesthetic potential of the animated film, Burness directed the Mr. Magoo series, which provided the studio's bread and butter. The Magoo films represented the UPA version of a standard Hollywood cartoon short. They may have lacked the graphic innovations of ''Rooty-Toot-Toot'' or ''Madeline,'' but they pleased theater audiences—and the Columbia management, who might otherwise have dropped the UPA release.

In the early films, Magoo is a dynamic but crotchety old geezer whose galloping myopia causes him to live in a world of his own—without ever realizing it. He's funny, not because he's blind as a bat, but because he's too stubborn to acknowledge the mistakes his nearsightedness produces. The world errs, not Quincy Magoo.

''Magoo was very spiky when Art Babbitt animated him,''

comments Bill Hurtz. ''He was all flinty edges and mean looks and outthrust jaw. His head was much smaller than the baby-doll head he got later, and he walked with this purposeful, aggressive stride.''

But as the series progressed, Burness softened Magoo. The character lost his sharp edges and became a dear, dim old uncle who puttered about a confused never-never land. The early Magoo walked through a plate-glass window and snarled: ''Confound it, they wrap everything in cellophane these days!'' The later Magoo was far less dynamic and purposeful. In the Oscar-winning ''When Magoo Flew'' (1955), he mistakes an airplane for a movie theater and goes for a stroll on one wing, muttering that the air conditioning is set too high.

Magoo always had a genial, self-satisfied side. He jerks the handle of a pump in ''Grizzly Golfer,'' mistaking it for the host's hand. Hearing no reply to his greeting, Magoo strolls away, chuckling delightedly: ''Oh, these New Englanders. They're taciturn, they're tight!'' But an almost senile geniality gradually replaced stubbornness as his dominant trait.

Bill Scott felt the turning point came in Hubley's ''Fuddy Duddy Buddy'' (1951), when they allowed him to realize he's mistaken a walrus for his tennis partner. Magoo instantly recovers his aplomb: ''I don't care [if he is a walrus]—I like him! I *like* him!'' But this admission of weakness—''an old man tricked by his failing eyes''—ultimately led to an emphasis on the more kindly but less amusing side of his nature.

Hubley complained that the series lost the situation comedy and character conflict of the first cartoons, and degenerated into formula gags about nearsightedness. Burness subsequently doubted the wisdom of transforming Magoo.

By the time the series ended in 1959, the character had run his course. There was nothing left for him to mistake for something else. Like the later, gentler version of Mickey Mouse, the nice Magoo lacked the forceful personality that sustained more rambunctious cartoon characters over years and even decades.

Hubley, Cannon and Burness were three of the principal exponents of what was acclaimed as ''the UPA style.'' Although the UPA films were as immediately recognizable as the Silly Symphonies of the 1930s, the artists never used a monolithic style. The dark, brooding backgrounds Paul Julian painted for Ted Parmalee's ''The Tell-Tale Heart'' (1953) evoke the work of Dali, de Chirico and Eugène Berman. They have little in common with the bright watercolor look designer Art Heinemann created in ''Madeline.'' The linear figures in ''Christopher Crumpet'' don't look like the cutouts of musical instruments in ''The Oompahs''—which bear no resemblance to the boldly stylized characters of ''Rooty-Toot-Toot.''

''No two UPA pictures were ever done in the same style,'' states Herb Klynn. ''And that includes the Mr. Magoo series, the Gerald McBoing-Boings and the Jolly Frolics. Every time we did something, it became a creative experiment and an innovative search. That's what made the studio what it was, and that's why it wasn't just a rebellion against Disney and the limitations of sweet characters."

Despite their graphic diversity, almost all of the studio's films share three characteristic elements: unconventional stories, often with modern settings, contemporary graphics and a more stylized approach to the animation itself.

Scott said that the two things a writer at UPA had to avoid at all costs were what the artists termed "Disney cute" and "Warner Brothers humor." Many of the men had felt frustrated during their years at the Disney studio, and Walt seemed to be repeating himself, retelling classic fairy tales like "Cinderella." The former Warners artists had less of an ax to grind. With the exception of Bobe Cannon—who hated the slapstick animation he had done for Chuck Jones—they had enjoyed their work. Still, there was a general belief at UPA that the brash cartoons of Warners and MGM had been taken about as far as they could.

The gentle fantasy of "Gerald McBoing-Boing" and the wry satire of "Rooty-Toot-Toot" represent an alternate vision of the cartoon that is very different from the fast-paced hilarity of "Rabbit Seasoning" and "A Mouse Divided" or domestic sitcoms like "Mickey and the Seal" and "Fathers Are People."

At Walt's behest, the Disney artists adapted the style of nineteenth-century European storybook illustration to animation during the 1930s. They drew rounded, three-dimensional forms that derived from a traditional, Academic draftsmanship rooted in the work of the Renaissance painters. Many of the UPA artists were fine draftsmen, but they wanted to be advanced and avant-garde. Their heroes were Matisse, Cézanne, Dufy, Klee, Modigliani and Picasso, rather than the Renaissance masters. They liked the new jazz styles, and sought to infuse their work with the same spontaneity. They also admired the sophisticated cartoonists of *The New Yorker:* Robert Osborn, Saul Steinberg, Sam Cobean, James Thurber.

At Disney, they said, the animator was king. The characters were designed to move easily in three dimensions and to look good from as many angles as possible. At UPA, design took precedence over animation. It was important for the characters to look good by the standards of contemporary graphics. The animators had to devise ways of moving them that harmonized with those designs.

Obviously, an angular, two-dimensional cartoon figure couldn't move like a rounded Disney character—realistic movement in three dimensions would clash with its design. To accommodate the new, flatter style, the artists often had to rethink their approach to animation. They avoided moving the characters in depth, restricting the action to the picture plane. They timed motions as carefully as before, but used fewer in-betweens and emphasized strong poses. Melendez

describes the result as "animation with no unnecessary drawings."

Although the style was dubbed "limited animation," the UPA films should not be lumped together with the static television programs of the 1970s. All the characters in "Rooty-Toot-Toot"—Frankie, Johnny, Nellie Bligh, the attorneys—have individual ways of moving. But their movements are exaggerated and unnatural: the animation is as stylized as the designs.

Nor was the motion always limited in UPA shorts. In "Grizzly Golfer," Art Babbitt used "at least twice as many drawings as there would normally be" to animate a bear trying to catch a dandelion puff in slow motion. The sequence is wonderfully fluid and balletic, but no effort is made to reproduce the movements of a real bear.

Limited animation in a UPA film was a stylistic choice, not the result of an effort to cut costs. Their films had budgets comparable to the fully animated cartoons produced at Warners.

"During the early 1950s, we received $30,000 per film from Columbia," says UPA veteran Ade Woolery. "Our effort was to make them for $27,500, then take the difference of $2,500 and put it in the bank. Well, we always ended up spending about $3,000 extra, so we had to go to Columbia for another $2,500 or $5,000 to keep us in business. I think we had 25 percent of each picture, and we would have to sell a portion of our percentage back as collateral for the loan—which was never repaid. Therefore, when it came time to divide the properties years later, UPA had very little interest left in them."

The mannered approach of the UPA artists to animation was not entirely new. Chuck Jones had experimented with stylized motion in "The Dover Boys" a decade earlier. Dick Huemer maintained that the "Baby Weems" segment of "The Reluctant Dragon" was the first example of limited animation. John Hubley's work at Columbia, especially "Professor Small and Mr. Tall," had anticipated much of the UPA style. Many of the FMPU films featured stylized graphics and limited motion.

But the UPA experiments with limited animation were the first to receive widespread critical attention. By 1952, their cartoons were being praised in art journals that had rarely even acknowledged the existence of animation—let alone discussed it as a valid medium of expression. Although the studio subsequently received numerous awards and honors, 1952 probably represented the artistic zenith of UPA. Dragon's teeth had been sown during the founding of the studio, and the warriors were about to arise.

The fight to unionize the animation studios had not ended with the Disney strike of 1941. The battles over how the entertainment industry would be unionized—and by whom—continued during the postwar years. The strife was exacerbated by the notorious hearings of the House Committee on Un-American Activities. The screen cartoonists constituted only a tiny fraction of the film industry, in both numbers and dollars, but they had ties to the major studios and were inevitably drawn into the conflict.

In 1947, Walt Disney appeared before HUAC as a "friendly witness." He described the strike of 1941 as "a Communist group trying to take over my artists and they did take them over," and complained of Communists "hiding behind this labor setup . . . so that if you try to get rid of them they make a labor case out of it." He also denounced layout man Dave Hilberman, one of the founders of UPA:

> I feel there is one artist in my plant, that came in there, he came in about 1938, and he sort of stayed in the background, he wasn't too active, but he was the real brains of this, and I believe he is a Communist. His name is David Hilberman . . . I looked into his record and I found that, number 1, he has no religion and, number 2, that he had spent considerable time at the Moscow Art Theatre studying art direction, or something.

"We were all on the list of sympathizers or otherwise from the Disney strike on," comments Bill Hurtz. "We were all busy in labor activities, making labor films."

The situation was further complicated by the struggle between the Screen Cartoonists' Guild and the IATSE (International Alliance of Theatrical and Stage Employees), a very powerful combination of unions that had strong ties to organized crime at that time. The liberal artists at UPA strongly disapproved of the IATSE because of its corruption and its growing involvement in Red-baiting activities. They preferred the independent Screen Cartoonists' Guild.

Technically, UPA was an independent producer, but Columbia financed their cartoons and controlled their release. The consensus among the artists is that Columbia pressured Bosustow into breaking with the Screen Cartoonists' Guild, negotiating with the IATSE and purging UPA of "Communists."

Bill Hurtz remembers: "Columbia sent us a list of people who had to go or they'd yank the release. Face-saving devices were arranged for people to leave. People volunteered to leave, rather than sink the studio—because it was that bald: either these guys left or the studio went under. Those of us who were labeled 'com-symps' stayed."

Few—if any—of the UPA artists had any Communist sympathies, but most of them were liberals and/or union activists. During the HUAC hearings, many of them felt vulnerable because they might have belonged to "undesirable" liberal organizations in the past or attended meetings at which Communists might have spoken. These artists were faced with three distasteful choices: to leave the studio and try to find work elsewhere, to appear as a "friendly witness" before the committee or to pay bribes.

"In those bad old days, you would be approached by a representative or a friend of a representative from the committee, who would assure you that for *x* amount of dollars,

Director Pete Burness with the Oscar for "Magoo's Puddle Jumper" in 1957.

they could see that your file was at the bottom of the pile," stated Scott. "In other words, if the hearings lasted long enough, you would be called up, but the chances were that you wouldn't be called up publicly, because your dossier kept slipping to the bottom of the stack. The going price, I believe, at that time was four to five thousand dollars, though it may have been more as far as, maybe, a head of a studio was concerned. At any rate, that was the current wisdom, the conventional wisdom and the underground chatter. That's what happened at—and to—UPA."

Whether anyone at UPA actually made these payoffs is uncertain: no one admits to it. A story circulates among the artists about $50,000 that somehow disappeared from the studio's "petty cash" and was paid in bribes. But no one has any proof that this mysterious sum ever existed, and it may be just a story.

Zachary Schwartz chose to testify before HUAC—and earned the continuing dislike of many of his fellow artists. Despite the condemnations, Hilberman never had to appear. Many of the finest talents left UPA, including John Hubley, Phil Eastman and Bill Scott, and found work elsewhere in the industry. Scott joined John Sutherland, who produced industrial films. Hubley started his own studio, Storyboard Films, and quickly became a very successful producer of animated TV commercials.

But the stigma of being "named" before HUAC created very real problems for people involved in animation, as it did for other entertainment industry professionals. Faith Hubley (John's widow) recalled that despite the success of Storyboard, John had to use a "front man" to deal with the advertising agencies. Some animators believe Hubley's politics were the source of many of the problems that surrounded his ill-fated effort to make an animated feature based on the musical *Finian's Rainbow*.

Hilberman said that he and his partners sold their Tempo studio because of increasing pressure from CounterAttack, "one of those vulture organizations that fed off the Un-American Activities hearings to produce blacklists for a fee and keep the agencies apprised of who had been named and what the connection was."

The loss of these men—especially Hubley—was a serious blow to the studio. Perhaps as significant was the inevitable loss of the esprit de corps that had characterized UPA. Since its inception, the artists had been bound together by mutual respect, affection and a common vision of what the animated film could be. As one animator stated: "They believed in UPA like a religion." The suspicion and distrust produced by the HUAC hearings irrevocably damaged that camaraderie. Some

of the animators refuse to discuss their experiences years, and even decades, after the fact.

The changes in UPA were not immediately apparent. In 1953 the studio released "Christopher Crumpet" and two other important films: Bill Hurtz's "The Unicorn in the Garden" and Ted Parmalee's "The Tell-Tale Heart." "Unicorn" is a charming, literal adaptation of one of James Thurber's "Fables for Our Time"; *Time* magazine praised the film as "just about the best seven minutes now showing on any screen." Hurtz chose the story "because it dealt with human beings—the others are just animals," and set out to preserve Thurber's lumpy, ingenuous drawing style.

"I literally studied every drawing he ever did," Hurtz explains. "I got the idea for the arm extending to close the Venetian blinds from Thurber; the legs in the run came out of a Thurber run. Whenever this repressed soul broke loose, part of his body extended, which seemed to be what Thurber had in his cartoons. Using color bothered me at first, but I thought if he ever got around to it, he'd probably do it this way—as long as it was strongly linear."

In contrast to Hurtz's literal approach to "The Unicorn in the Garden," "The Tell-Tale Heart" is a very loose retelling of Edgar Allan Poe's chilling account of murder and madness. Bill Scott, who adapted the story, delighted in pointing out that not one sentence in the narration is entirely Poe's —it just sounds like Poe (an illusion heightened by James Mason's haunting performance). Very little animation appears on the screen. Camera movements over static artwork suggest motion, rather than depict it. Otis Guernsey, Jr., wrote that the film "looks like a cross between Salvador Dali and woodcut illustrations for a horror story, and it is thoroughly fascinating." Originally designed for 3-D, "The Tell-Tale Heart" was released only in conventional format.

In retrospect, it's clear that by the mid-1950s, the most imaginative era at UPA had passed—but that was not apparent at the time. The studio expanded and continued to win awards and critical praise. An office in New York at Fifty-third Street and Fifth Avenue handled additional commercial work. (By 1955, commercials accounted for $1 million of the studio's total gross of $2.25 million.)

In 1956, Steve Bosustow and UPA vice president and treasurer Ernest Scanlon toured Europe to widespread acclaim. Bosustow later sent Herb Klynn and Leo Salkin to London to open a third branch of the studio. Salkin served as head of UPA/London, a venture that failed due to poor planning, stiff competition from British and European studios and an enormous overhead.

A cel of "Abdul Azziz Magoo" and the Wizier from "A Thousand and One Arabian Nights" (1959).

In 1955, the Museum of Modern Art staged "UPA: Form in the Animated Cartoon," a retrospective of the studio's films, accompanied by an exhibit of drawings, photographs, sketches, cels and other artwork. That same year, a giant balloon of Gerald McBoing-Boing appeared in Macy's Thanksgiving Day parade. All three of the nominees for the Oscar for Animated Short in 1956 were UPA films: "Gerald McBoing-Boing on the Planet Moo," "The Jaywalker" and "Magoo's Puddle Jumper," which won. Not even Disney had achieved that distinction.

In 1955–56, the UPA artists undertook their most ambitious effort, "The Gerald McBoing-Boing Show," for CBS. Until then, the studio had been producing eight to ten seven-minute theatrical shorts each year; CBS wanted thirteen half-hour programs. To meet the demand for increased production, producer Bobe Cannon hired a number of bright young artists

and designers, many of whom later achieved prominence in the field—Ernest Pintoff, Fred Crippen, Jimmy Murikami, Duane Crowther, Gene Deitch, John Urie.

"Bobe hired all these young guys—a marvelous group of people—but there were probably no writers or story men among them," explains Salkin. "They weren't people from the animation field. They were generally designers or people that had some kind of artistic ability."

Cannon was always open to new ideas in animation, and he allowed these young artists to make short experimental films. But previews revealed that these films had little appeal for the average viewer. Cannon called in Bill Scott to punch up the humor.

Despite the production problems, inadequate budgets and horrendous deadlines, "The Gerald McBoing-Boing Show" premiered on December 16, 1956. The program was entirely

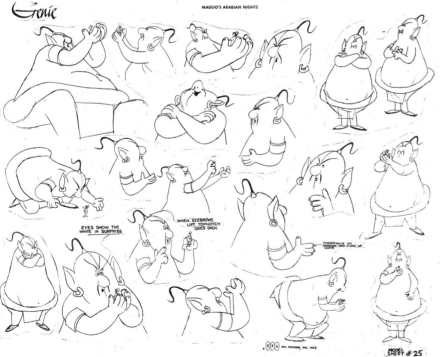

Two model sheets from "A Thousand and One Arabian Nights."

animated, with McBoing-Boing serving as host and Bill Goodwin providing off-camera narration. In addition to old UPA theatrical shorts, the show featured a number of regular segments. "Dusty of the Circus" centered on a boy who could talk to animals. The Twirlinger Twins, two rotund little girls, studied music and dance with more energy than polish. "Legends of America and the World," "Meet the Artist" and "Meet the Inventor" were didactic sequences. "Mr. Charmeley Meets a Lady" taught basic etiquette. Unlike most cartoon shows, which had rigid formats, "Gerald McBoing-Boing" was flexible: a one-minute film might follow a six-minute short.

Critics had nothing but praise for the show: "All too rarely do we see on television a work of such poetic imagery, wit, charm and entertainment" (*Radio-TV Life*). In the Los Angeles *Times*, Cecil Smith wrote: "The set of geniuses who make up UPA have the remarkable facility to tickle the funny bone of a philosopher as easily as they delight a 2-year-old."

Audiences did not share the critics' enthusiasm, and "The Gerald McBoing-Boing Show" ended its run on March 24, 1957, four months after it began. While much of it was highly imaginative, and some of the segments were entrancing, the program was too tame, too didactic and, at times, too sophisticated to appeal to children. As George Woolery wrote: "A token of good taste, fresh in concept as well as execution, the parts were better than the whole."

Although UPA dominated the Academy Awards in 1956, eight of the ten cartoons the studio released that year were Mr. Magoo shorts—as were all nine of their releases in 1957. The days of "Madeline" and "Rooty-Toot-Toot" had clearly passed. In 1958, Lew Keller introduced two new characters, a little girl named Hattie and a musician called Ham Hamilton, in "Trees and Jamaica Daddy." The film earned UPA its last Oscar nomination, and all the remaining shorts starred either Magoo or the Ham and Hattie team.

After the demise of the "McBoing-Boing Show," the artistic and financial decline of UPA accelerated. The London venture had proved disastrous, and in 1958 the New York studio closed due to rising overhead and the increasingly intense competition in commercial production. Ironically, many of the rival studios were run by UPA veterans, including Tempo, Storyboard, and Ade Woolery's Playhouse Pictures.

In August 1959, Herb Klynn and Buddy Getzler, two of UPA's key officers, left to found Format Films, taking many talented people with them, including Jules Engel, Leo Salkin, Vera McKinney, Allan Zaslov and Roy Morita. By this time, Bill Scott, Bill Hurtz, Lew Keller, Ted Parmalee and Pete Burness had moved to Jay Ward Productions, where they collaborated on the wonderful "Rocky and His Friends."

Almost since its inception, there had been talk of UPA making an animated feature. Various properties had been discussed in newspaper articles—Ben Jonson's *Volpone, Don Quixote*, James Thurber's *The White Deer*, Helen of Troy, the

A preliminary watercolor drawing by John Hubley of Frankie and her lawyer Jonathan Bailey (Honest John, the crook) for "Rooty-Toot-Toot" (1952).

operettas of Gilbert and Sullivan. Despite the announcements of imminent production, none of the films materialized.

Klynn explains that most of these announcements were issued by the studio publicists for the benefit of the trade papers. *The White Deer* was the only project that progressed as far as the storyboard stage, although Aldous Huxley did preliminary work on a script for a version of *Don Quixote* starring Mr. Magoo. When UPA finally did produce a feature, it broke little new ground artistically.

"When I got back from London in 1957, Steve had promoted money from somewhere to do a feature," says Leo Salkin. "When we were talking, various things came up, and one of them was the *Arabian Nights*. Steve was saying: 'Well, we could do all these stories,' and I said: 'Look, you've got to take one story—take the Aladdin story, which is the most fun—that's enough to carry the feature, then you can do all the embroidering and building around it.' "

In December 1959, "A Thousand and One Arabian Nights" premiered. Ostensibly a retelling of the story of Aladdin and his magic lamp, much of the action centered on Aladdin's exceedingly nearsighted uncle, one Abdul Azziz Magoo. *Newsweek* complained that "his myopic blunders seem to have lost some of their imagination" and noted: "In the first minute of the movie, Magoo remonstrates with a flock of birds which he thinks are schoolboys, puts the coffeepot on the fishbowl instead of the stove, mistakes a camel for his nephew, and pats a stool thinking it is his cat (which is named Bowzir because to Magoo it is a dog)."

"Arabian Nights" isn't really bad; it's just bland and unexciting. Many observers had hoped for a boldly innovative film that would transform the animated feature the way the early work of UPA had altered the cartoon short, but nothing in "Arabian Nights" approaches that level of imagination. *Newsweek* summarized the feature as "Middling Magoo."

It was not a box office success, and it proved to be the last hurrah of the moribund studio. After the departure of the Format group, only Steve Bosustow remained from the original team. He sold UPA to producer Henry Saperstein three months later. The great experiment in animation ended, fifteen years after it began.

Under Bosustow, UPA produced 43 seven-minute Magoo shorts between 1949 and 1959, 2 of them Academy Award winners. Under Saperstein, UPA produced 155 five-minute Magoo films between 1960 and 1962—all of them abysmal—plus 130 five-minute cartoons for "The Dick Tracy Show." A little of the old Magoo could be detected in "Mr. Magoo's Christmas Carol" (1962), an hour-long special directed by Abe Levitow for NBC. As Ebenezer Scrooge, he recaptured some of his original curmudgeonly personality. Levitow also directed "Gay Purr-ee" (1962), a forgettable feature about cats with the voices of Robert Goulet, Judy Garland and Hermione Gingold.

In 1964, "The Famous Adventures of Mr. Magoo" debuted on NBC. He portrayed various literary figures, including Cyrano de Bergerac, Puck from *A Midsummer Night's Dream*, Friar Tuck from *Robin Hood*, Don Quixote and Rip Van Winkle. None of the roles really suited Magoo, and the program was mercifully short-lived. UPA and DePatie-Freleng joined forces to produce the painfully unfunny Saturday-morning show "What's New, Mister Magoo?" (1977). They paired Magoo with an equally blind dog named McBarker—which halved, rather than doubled, the fun. It was an ignominious end for a character who used to mistake fire hydrants for dogs and strike them with his cane, crying "Down! Down, I say!"

The influence of the UPA films was widespread and diverse. During the 1950s, the studio dominated American animation artistically, as Disney had during the 1930s. The MGM and Warners cartoons began to reflect the UPA aesthetic. Droopy went from being a pudgy, rounded character to a flat, angular one. Bugs Bunny and Wile E. Coyote acquired harder edges and began cavorting in more stylized, two-dimensional settings.

The UPA look became so familiar that Friz Freleng could spoof their dramatic shots of windows and shadows in "Birds Anonymous" (1957). Even Disney began to employ a flatter look and more stylized animation in films like "Toot, Whistle, Plunk, and Boom" (1953), "Pigs Is Pigs" (1954), "The Truth about Mother Goose" (1957) and "Paul Bunyan" (1958).

UPA exerted the strongest influence on Terrytoons, which had been the least progressive of the major studios. After Paul Terry's retirement, UPA veteran Gene Deitch introduced several highly graphic characters, including John Doormat, Gaston Le Crayon and a blue elephant named Sydney. These creatures remain outstanding examples of hip mid-1950s design, but they aren't very entertaining. In "Sick, Sick Sydney" (1958), the title character moans about being "terribly insecure" in a heavy-handed attempt to provide sophisticated humor, but the results are neither sophisticated nor humorous.

In 1957, UPA alumnus Ernest Pintoff created "Flebus," another "adult" fable of neuroses: the Steinberg-esque title character runs to a psychiatrist when he discovers someone doesn't like him. The extremely limited animation and whiny sound track may have seemed amusing in 1957, but modern audiences are more likely to side with Rudolph, the man who resolutely dislikes Flebus. The next year, Al Kouzel and designer R. O. Blechman animated Blechman's book *The Juggler of Our Lady*, based on the medieval legend. The fragile drawings combine with Boris Karloff's understated narration to give this minimal film a charm the other 1950s Terrytoons lack. Most of these films prove just how much the stories and direction contributed to the UPA cartoons: something more than advanced graphics was needed.

An important factor in the aesthetic hegemony of UPA was the highly favorable coverage the studio received in the press. No animation studio had garnered such favorable reviews since Disney during the 1930s. Many of these articles suggested, either implicitly or explicitly, that the UPA approach to animation was somehow right and all other cartoons were wrong.

Critics acclaimed the UPA films as art, while they ignored or dismissed the slapstick cartoons that had delighted audiences

Director Jack Kinney, music director Morris Stoloff, composer George Dunning and producer Steve Bosustow during production of "Arabian Nights."

for two decades. The most frequent target of these artistic contrasts was Walt Disney. Despite the continuing popularity of his films, Disney's critical reputation fell to an all-time low during the early 1950s. Sometimes the writers seem more interested in whacking Disney than in praising UPA. In an article in *Theatre Arts* (significantly titled "Up From Disney"), Arthur Knight wrote:

> The most obvious thing about "Gerald," and to many, the most endearing, is that it is so completely unlike anything ever turned out by Disney and his horde of imitators. Missing are the cute animals, the rabbits, the chipmunks, the kittens, mice and puppies. Missing too are the detailed backgrounds, the trees that look like trees, the water that flows like water. In this little film, all the characters are true cartoon caricatures, animated two-dimensional figures moving through settings that make no attempt to conceal the fact that they are drawings.

The UPA approach to animation was not superior to Disney's, any more than a Picasso drawing is superior to a Rembrandt portrait. They represent two different but equally valid aesthetic visions, and each deserves to be judged on its own merits.

Despite their enormous influence, most of the UPA films have proved far less durable than the contemporary Warner Brothers and Disney cartoons. "The Bugs Bunny Show" continues to earn high ratings after more than twenty-five years on the air. "The Gerald McBoing-Boing Show" lasted only a single season. The best UPA shorts still delight audiences when they are screened. "Rooty-Toot-Toot," "Gerald McBoing-Boing," "Madeline," "The Unicorn in the Garden" and "Grizzly Golfer" are excellent cartoons by any standard. But UPA programs are rarely seen at revival houses and film festivals, which regularly feature Warners, MGM and Disney animation.

Some of the films have not aged gracefully. The graphic style that made "Willie the Kid" and "Christopher Crumpet" bold artistic statements thirty years ago now looks decidedly passé. Many UPA films rely heavily on narration—a device that has fallen out of favor and contributes to the dated tone.

Once UPA established the concept of limited animation, the idea was taken up by the infant television industry and run into the ground. What began as an artistic experiment became a way of getting more footage from fewer drawings (and, therefore, at a lower cost), even if it meant shortchanging the viewer. Reflecting on the abuse of limited animation by the TV studios, Bill Scott once remarked: "UPA may have a lot to answer for on Judgment Day."

Probably the most enduring contribution of UPA to the art of animation (as opposed to the industry) was the idea that artists at one studio could employ disparate styles and use the animated film as a vehicle for personal expression. Their efforts to meld motion and contemporary design led other animators to experiment with new and different graphic styles.

This philosophy was adopted by the artists at Zagreb Film, which became *the* international center of creativity in the medium after UPA declined during the later 1950s. The National Film Board of Canada (which replaced Zagreb as the artistic focus of world animation a decade later) maintains a similar aesthetic freedom, partially modeled after the UPA-Zagreb paradigm, partially developed independently. The graphic diversity of contemporary world animation can be seen as the ultimate legacy of UPA.

"If God were merciful, UPA would have survived," concludes Leo Salkin. "It really was one of the most delightful places I ever worked. The people were excited about what they did, at least most of the time, and the really good people, the talented people, were given as close to total freedom—within economic boundaries—as is possible to give anyone in making films."

A cel setup of the musician characters from Lew Keller's "Trees and Jamaica Daddy" (1958).

Linus and Lucy in a cel setup from "It's the Great Pumpkin, Charlie Brown" (1966), one of the best "Peanuts" television specials.

ON THE SMALL SCREEN: THE TELEVISION YEARS

TV is such a monster. It swallows up all this animation so fast that nobody seems to care whether it's good or bad. These kids' shows are badly done technically; it seems as though nobody really looks at them but the kids. . . . The networks don't look at the show, they just look at the ratings. If the ratings are good, to heck with the show. They don't care whether it's just a bouncing ball. —FRIZ FRELENG

Television was originally a minor outlet for the flourishing animation industry of the postwar era, but as the theatrical studios closed during the late 1950s and early 1960s, it grew in importance until it dominated the medium.

Today, critics regularly deplore the sorry state of television animation, and animators bitterly condemn the programs that are now the mainstay of the industry. In a *Variety* interview, John Hubley explained why he refused to work on Saturday-morning programs: "It's assembly-line stuff which can have no feeling, no personal attention. As a filmmaker and artist, I'm not interested."

Television production transformed animation as profoundly as the advent of sound or color. It began unobtrusively in 1949, when a diminutive rabbit dressed as a knight galloped across the screen to a mock-heroic fanfare.

"Crusader Rabbit" was the first cartoon series produced for television and the first series done in limited animation. Created by Jay Ward and Alexander Anderson, Jr., the program was financed by distributor and executive producer Jerry Fairbanks for NBC.

The first of many, many comic-adventure television series about a mismatched duo, "Crusader Rabbit" debuted on local NBC stations in the fall of 1949. A small, quick-witted bunny, Crusader was the brains of the pair; his big, dumb sidekick, Rags (short for Ragland T.) the Tiger, provided the brawn.

From their home, a hollow tree in Galahad Glen, they solved mysteries and aided anyone in distress.

When the Sultan of Rinsewater began bleaching the stripes off tigers to make India ink, Crusader and Rags rode to the rescue. Their regular nemesis, Dudley Nightshade, found a way to extract the "happiness vitamin" from orange juice, making "pure gloom juice." He plotted to become a movie star by using his discovery to poison the smiles of all the Hollywood cowboys—only to be thwarted by Crusader and Rags. Among the other unlikely characters the partners encountered were Minnie the Merbunny, Achilles the Heel and the Brimstone Brothers, Bigot and Blackheart.

The clever scripts often featured sophisticated humor in an ingenuous guise. When Crusader and Rags told a dragon with two bickering heads (named Arson and Sterno) that it was helping the bad guys, the heads acknowledged the fact, but added: "A job's a job, and think of the residuals we'll get."

The stories were divided into four-minute episodes with cliffhanger endings; narrator Roy Whaley usually concluded each installment with an ominous phrase—"Uh-oh, this looks like the end for our heroes . . ." One or two were shown each day on various children's programs. The names of the adventures and the individual episodes were shameless puns, like "West We Forget" and "A Midsummer Night's Scream"—a practice Ward continued in his later shows.

The animation was more limited than anything produced at

Top: A presentation cel of Crusader Rabbit as he appeared in the opening of his show. Above: A production cel of Crusader and Rags in Robin Hood costumes.

UPA. Ward said: "We wanted to get the effect of an animated comic strip," and the visuals were little more than black-and-white storyboard drawings linked by simple pans and walk cycles. All of the humor and most of the action came from the scripts, ably read by Lucille Bliss (Crusader) and Vern Louden (Rags). "Crusader Rabbit" proved very popular and was soon outdrawing "Howdy Doody" and "Hopalong Cassidy" in some markets.

Production ended in 1951, after a complicated lawsuit over the ownership of the series. Shull Bonsall, who ultimately acquired the rights, produced a second version of "Crusader Rabbit" in color with Creston Studios in 1957–58; Wolper TV Series did a third in 1965–69. The real heirs to Crusader's legacy were Ward and Anderson. They retained the rights to other characters they had created, including Bullwinkle the Moose and Dudley Do-Right of the Royal Canadian Mounties, who had been designed for a program tentatively called "Frostbite Falls Follies"—which ultimately became "Rocky and His Friends."

Another early television series was "Winky Dink and You," which premiered on CBS in 1953, with Jack Barry as the host. A little boy dressed in a jester's costume, Winky Dink had a tiny body, a huge head with enormous eyes and a shock of blond hair that resembled a five-pointed star. With his faithful dog, Woofer, Winky Dink went on rather tame cartoon adventures.

At key moments in the story, children were asked to help Winky Dink solve a problem. The viewer put a special sheet of plastic over the television screen to connect a series of dots, to draw in some missing component with "magic" crayons (a bridge over a river, a door to a tunnel) or to receive a secret message—the first example of interactive children's programming. Millions of "Winky Dink Kits" containing a sheet of plastic film, a box of crayons and an eraser cloth were sold through the mail at fifty cents apiece, although many children discovered that waxed paper and ordinary crayons worked nearly as well.

During the early 1950s, children's television essentially became a dumping ground for old theatrical shorts. While a certain number of films could be recycled each year in various foreign and domestic markets, outlets for black-and-white cartoons all but disappeared after the advent of color. Older films from working studios, like Warners' "Buddy" and "Bosko" series, and cartoons from defunct studios like Van Buren and Ub Iwerks, gathered dust on the shelves until networks, syndicators and independent producers bought them and began showing them, again and again, on television.

The sale of these old films led to the emergence of a sort of generic kiddy show on local stations. A live host, usually in some sort of costume (clown, cowboy, rabbit, etc.), introduced the cartoons with his brand of patter. During their earliest years, the children of the baby-boom era watched the same rubbery-limbed golliwogs their parents had seen in theaters two decades earlier. Most of the topical references in the old cartoons were incomprehensible to them, and much of the racial imagery seemed odd to students who attended the increasing number of integrated schools. An article in *Television Age* in 1962 summarized animated children's programming c. 1952–56: "Little was offered to the local stations besides antique theatrical cartoons or short subjects. Much of this material was dated beyond use, much of it was offensive by today's standards of taste and much of it was of poor print quality; still, in 1953, one industry survey showed 20–25 stations regularly running cartoons shows—the majority of which were getting high ratings."

CBS acquired the entire Terrytoons library in 1955. "The Mighty Mouse Playhouse" debuted on CBS in December of that year, followed by "The Heckle and Jeckle Show" in 1956.

Walt Disney showed old short cartoons and sections of features on the "Disneyland" (1954) and "Mickey Mouse Club" (1955) programs on ABC. Although both shows were primarily live action, Disney had new animation done for them, including an elaborate title sequence for the hour-long version of "The Mickey Mouse Club." Disney's TV animation was more lavish than the theatrical cartoons other studios were producing during the 1950s.

"The Woody Woodpecker Show" (1957) brought the Walter Lantz shorts to television. Lantz appeared on the program, explaining how various aspects of animation were done in short live-action sequences.

The debut of "The Bugs Bunny Show" on ABC in 1960 made Tuesday a special night for millions of children. Bugs and Daffy did an upbeat song-and-dance routine in the newly animated titles, and various Warner Brothers characters appeared as "guest hosts." The many excellent Warners shorts made "Bugs Bunny" the best of the recycled cartoon shows. (And the most durable: more than twenty-five years after their TV debut, programs of Warners films continue to earn good ratings.)

The late 1950s have been called the "golden age" of television animation, and little produced after the mid-1960s has matched the imagination, humor or charm of the programs done between 1956 and 1962. "The Gerald McBoing-Boing Show" was the most artistic of several rather experimental animated series done for children. Although highly praised by critics, this gentle experiment failed to attract large audiences and UPA produced only a single season's worth of episodes.

In 1957, Gene Deitch began producing "Tom Terrific" at Terrytoons for "Captain Kangaroo" on CBS. Tom Terrific was a miniature superhero who could transform himself into virtually anything. (No matter what he became, he retained his

© Marvel Screen Enterprises, Inc.

Winky Dink, the star of the first interactive children's program. Mae Questel provided his voice (and all the others for the show).

Left: The cast of "Gumby" celebrates the title character's birthday, in one of the new adventures created for syndication. Bottom: Art Clokey's little clay boy as he appeared in 1955.

funnel hat as a kind of visual signature.) With the lethargic and rather timorous Mighty Manfred, the Wonder Dog, Tom fought a variety of villains. His main adversary was the nasty Crabby Appleton, described as "rotten to the core." Like "Crusader Rabbit," "Tom Terrific" was a miniserial: one five-minute chapter was broadcast each day, with five episodes making a complete story.

The animation in "Tom Terrific" was minimal, and the character designs were as simple and stylized as Deitch's other creations. But unlike Sydney the Elephant and Clinton Clobber, Tom had charm. The unpretentious and often imaginative use of the medium for his various metamorphoses proved far more entertaining than the theatrical Terrytoons of the mid-1950s.

"Gumby" developed from "Gumbasia," an experimental clay animation film Art Clokey made in 1953. Clokey showed his film to producer Sam Engel, who felt the clay technique could be applied to children's entertainment. He had Clokey make a pilot featuring a character—rather than the abstract, geometric forms of "Gumbasia." Clokey recalls: "I set out to create a shape and size that were functionally practical from the film-animating standpoint. Animating clay for hours under hot lights created a problem: I found it necessary to have a shape and size that were easily reproduced, so that a fresh figure could be substituted as the old one

became dirty and completely misshapen through excessive manipulation."

Clokey chose a seven-inch figure, cut from a half-inch-thick slab of forest-green clay and stiffened with wire. The distinctive, uneven shape of Gumby's head was inspired by the outsized cowlick in an old photograph of Clokey's father; his name came from "gumbo," a slang term for the thick mud of his creator's native Michigan.

Five-minute Gumby episodes began appearing on "Howdy Doody" in 1955, and two years later the character was given his own show on NBC, with Bob Nicholson and Pinky Lee as hosts. The stories played Gumby's kind personality against the more skeptical nature of his clay horse, Pokey. As the duo explored strange places and had various adventures, the cast was expanded to include Gumby's parents, Gumbo and Gumba; Prickle, a small dinosaur; a clay girl named Goo and a pair of rivals, the Blockheads.

The stop-motion animation in "Gumby" was far less polished than that in George Pal's Puppetoons or contemporary commercials with "Speedy Alka-Seltzer," but children enjoyed the unusual technique. Clokey used real toys as props in many of the stories, and the novelty of seeing familiar playthings in a fantasy setting added to the program's appeal. During the 1980s, Gumby became the object of an extensive merchandising campaign.

Top: Sketches by an unknown animator show Bullwinkle the Moose in various moods and poses. Center: A presentation cel of Rocky and Bullwinkle from "Rocky and His Friends." Bottom: The archfiends Boris Badenov and Natasha Fatale.

Paradoxically, the best-loved cartoon program of the era failed to achieve high Nielsen ratings: Jay Ward's "Rocky and His Friends," which debuted November 19, 1959, on ABC. "Rocky" never featured great animation—or even good animation—but that didn't prevent it from being a great show.

The adventures of Rocky, the plucky flying squirrel, and his terminally dim partner, Bullwinkle the Moose, were a zany, freewheeling spoof of old movie serials. The episodic structure and the pairing of a small, bright character with a big, dumb one in a comedy-adventure format obviously owed a great deal to "Crusader Rabbit." But "Rocky" took the premise further—the plots were more outlandish, the satire more pointed and the puns more shameless.

The witty, topical scripts were written by Chris Hayward, Chris Jenkins, Lloyd Turner, George Atkins and Allan Burns, who now rank among the most successful writers of live-action television comedies. Bill Scott, who served as co-producer, head writer and the voice of Bullwinkle, explained the multilayered nature of the scripts:

> The stories were always slam-bang, moving ahead very, very quickly, and lots of things were happening. That was one level that a four-year-old could watch. . . . Then there was the second level, the standard jokes. You know, people getting blown up and falling out of windows and doing crazy things; Rocky zipping through the air, Bullwinkle crashing through walls . . . that kind of *animated* humor. The third level really was the fun level to write—that was the satire, parody, verbal jokes, puns.

Rocky and Bullwinkle (as Porthos and Aramoose) had to come to the aid of Athos, the last, aging musketeer, at the castle of Chateau Briand, when François Villain usurped the throne of Applesauce-Lorraine. Bullwinkle tried to break into the movies as Crag Antler, a spoof of Marlon Brando, who studied acting under "The System." When Captain Peter "Wrong-Way" Peachfuzz told Bullwinkle he worked for the government, the moose replied: "Hmmm, you must be that mess in Washington I keep hearing about."

Not everyone was amused by these shenanigans. Moonmen Gidney and Cloide came to Earth in search of the fabulous Kurwood Derby, a hat that made whoever wore it brilliant. Durward Kirby's lawyer sent a cease-and-desist letter to Ward—who offered to pay all the legal fees if Kirby would promise to sue. Ward avoided network interference by working so close to deadline that prints of the show arrived at ABC just hours before the broadcast.

Ward lost one confrontation: "The Great Boxtop Caper." The sponsor, General Mills, didn't think Boris Badenov's scheme to wreck the nation's economy by counterfeiting box tops was at all funny. The story had to be concluded in less than a week.

General Mills not only sponsored the show; they owned it. Under a curious arrangement, Ward had creative control over the program, but the cereal company retained ownership.

When company executives discovered they could save almost $500,000 a year by having the animation done outside the United States, a studio was hastily assembled in Mexico City with Gerry Ray at the helm. The five directors—Pete Burness, Gerard Baldwin, Lew Keller, Jim Hiltz and Bill Hurtz, all veterans of Disney and/or UPA—stayed in Los Angeles and tried to direct long-distance.

The resulting animation was extremely limited—about four drawings per second—and quality control was minimal. Keller recalls: "Once Bullwinkle came walking into a scene in mid-air: his feet were the equivalent of four feet off the ground. But those problems didn't seem to bother the audience."

The characters in "Rocky" are always aware they're in a cartoon, and a sloppy one at that. When Papa Bear starts to go upstairs to investigate Goldilocks's presence in a "Fractured Fairy Tale" of "The Three Bears," his puzzled wife remarks: "I thought this was a one-story house." In an episode of the serial, Boris argues with the narrator and tears up the script, confusing everyone.

The nutty dialogue was brought to life by what amounted to a small repertory company of respected voice artists: June Foray, Paul Frees, Bill Scott and Daws Butler, supplemented by Hans Conried, Charles Ruggles and Edward Everett Horton. The first four actors often doubled up on parts, and many "Fractured Fairy Tales" with multiple characters are really dialogues as Butler and Ms. Foray constantly change voices. William Conrad served as the beleaguered narrator of the Rocky and Bullwinkle adventures.

The men behind the madness: Bill Scott (left) and Jay Ward (right) make a publicity appearance with an unidentified television host in the San Francisco Bay Area during the early 1960s.

Each day, Rocky and Bullwinkle thwarted the nefarious schemes of Boris Badenov and Natasha Fatale in two three-and-a-half-minute cliffhanger episodes. The remainder of the show consisted of "Fractured Fairy Tales," irreverent send-ups of classic stories; "Peabody's Improbable History," in which a canine super-genius traveled through time with his boy, Sherman, via the Way-Back Machine; and "Aesop and Son," which appended new, punning morals to old fables. Bullwinkle tried to answer questions as "Mr. Know-It-All" and read poetry on "Bullwinkle's Corner."

But "Rocky and His Friends" was not a big hit, despite a series of baroque publicity stunts, including the "Statehood for Moosylvania" campaign. ABC canceled the show in September 1961.

"It was never No. 1, and if it were to return today by some strange miracle, it still wouldn't be No. 1," said Scott in a 1985 interview. "But it was a show with an intensely loyal audience. . . . It was a show that affected people, especially bright kids growing up. I'm fond of saying that we corrupted an entire generation."

"Rocky and His Friends" moved to NBC (1961–64) as "The Bullwinkle Show," hosted by a moose puppet (voiced and manipulated by Scott). When he told the audience to hide the knobs of the TV set ("That way we'll be sure to be with you next week"), some 20,000 children complied. NBC officials hit the ceiling, and the next week the puppet told them to put the knobs back on with glue ("And be sure it sticks"). "The Bullwinkle Show" also introduced the thick-witted but virtuous Dudley Do-Right of the Royal Canadian Mounties, who later became the star of his own program.

"Rocky and Bullwinkle" proved that a talented staff *can* make entertaining cartoons despite the short deadlines and minimal budgets that too often characterize TV production. Unhappily, few animators followed this example, and the show remains a rare, bright light in the sorry history of television animation.

I n February 1949, Warner Brothers veteran Bob Clampett introduced a fifteen-minute puppet show, "Time for Beany," on KTLA in Los Angeles. Daws Butler and Stan Freberg manipulated the puppets on the air and provided the voices for Beany Boy and Cecil, the Sea Sick Sea Serpent. A popular program with both audiences and critics, "Time for Beany" ran through 1955 and won three Emmys.

A decade later, Elliot Hyman, the president of Associated Arts Productions (AAP) (a releasing organization that later merged with United Artists), asked Clampett to develop a new cartoon series for television. Working with his wife, Sody, Clampett produced a pilot film, "Beany and Cecil Meet Billy the Squid" in 1959. He agreed to make an animated series based on "Time for Beany" that UA would distribute theatrically outside the United States.

Mattel Toys took over the sponsorship of the series in 1960, and in 1962 the characters made their debut on ABC in "Matty's Funday Funnies with Beany and Cecil." The name was shortened to "Beany and Cecil" a year later, and the show ran through 1967.

Chubby, good-natured, blond Beany (whose name came from his propeller cap) and the goofy, affectionate Cecil were joined aboard the sailboat *Leakin' Lena* by Beany's uncle, Captain Huffenpuff, and Crowy, the lookout. Dishonest John, whose "nya-ah-ah" laugh was adopted by children all over the country, supplied an especially entertaining brand of comic villainy. While Beany, the Captain and D.J. were regular cartoon characters, Cecil seemed to remain a puppet. The audience never saw his tail—just a length of green body that suggested the sleeve of the original. In a 1978 interview, Clampett said: "I always felt that not seeing Cecil's tail was very much like not seeing the face of a veiled Arabian maiden. It is much more intriguing before you pull the veil aside and actually see what she looks like."

"Beany and Cecil" was done in limited animation, which precluded using the wildly surreal visuals that had character-

The regular cast of "Time for Beany": above, the nefarious Dishonest John; below, Captain Huffenpuff, Cecil and Beany.

ized Clampett's work at Warners. Instead, the program's humor came from clever scripts that contained some of the most excruciating puns in cartoon history.

Harecules Hare (Ben Hare's Heir) goes "nuclear fishin' under the spreading chemis-tree," while his athletic father exercises and drinks "Rabbit Punch." Beany, Cecil and the Captain search for the singing "Dinasor" on the tropical "No Bikini Atoll." In "Davy Cricket," Dishonest John operates Citrus Pictures ("If it's a Citrus picture, it's a lemon") out of a phone booth. When he discovers (in *Variety*) that "Pie-N-Ear Pictures" is offering $100,000 to sign Davy, he remarks: "Gad! How low can you get? I've made B pictures before, but never cricket pictures."

Many baby-boomers rank "Beany and Cecil" second only to "Rocky and His Friends" in their affection.

The last of the experimental cartoon programs of the early 1960s was "The Alvin Show" (CBS, 1961), adapted from singer-songwriter Ross Bagdasarian's novelty single, "The Chipmunk Song." Bagdasarian supplied the falsetto voices for the chipmunk trio, as well as the long-suffering David Seville.

On the program, Seville remained the put-upon manager-guardian of the Chipmunk brothers: pudgy, giggling Simon, tall, scholarly Theodore and little, mischievous Alvin. Most of the stories centered on their singing career—rehearsals, recording sessions, concerts, tours. Alvin invariably got himself and his brothers into trouble, provoking Seville's familiar crescendo: "Alvin? ALVIN! ALLL-VINN!!!" Each episode also featured a sing-along to a well-known song like "Yankee Doodle Dandy" or "How Much Is That Doggy in the Window?"

In a secondary series, the addlepated scientist Clyde Crashcup invented things that already existed—like the wheel. Whatever he drew would instantly appear, but things never quite worked out as they were supposed to, and Crashcup had to be rescued by his practical, silent assistant, Leonardo.

"The Alvin Show" was the first cartoon series based on a pop-music group (albeit an imaginary one). The premise was soon expanded to include real singers—which led to such undistinguished offerings as "The Beatles" (ABC, 1965), "The Jackson 5ive" (ABC, 1971) and "The Osmonds" (ABC, 1972).

The future of television animation (and children's programming) lay not with the individual creations of Ward or Clampett, but with a modest and likable comedy/adventure series that debuted to little fanfare on NBC in late 1957: "The Ruff and Reddy Show."

When MGM closed their cartoon unit in 1957, Oscar-winning producer-directors Bill Hanna and Joe Barbera pooled their resources, and with some additional backing from director George Sidney, formed the Hanna-Barbera studio. Their proposal to make six-minute television cartoons for $3,000 apiece (or less than one-tenth of what a Tom and Jerry of the same length cost) was, in Barbera's words, "turned down by the entire television industry."

The management at Screen Gems had been considering entering the television animation market. When problems developed with a proposed series, they signed Hanna and Barbera to produce the first episodes of "Ruff and Reddy" for $2,700 apiece.

Left: Ruff the Bulldog and Reddy the Cat, the stars of the first television series from the Hanna-Barbera studio, "The Ruff and Reddy Show." Opposite: "That oh-so-merry, chuckleberry, Huckleberry Hound." The genial blue dog scored a big hit for Hanna-Barbera in 1958.

"People said to us: 'How can you do those cartoons? Don't you want to do them the old way?' We told them: 'We've only got $2,700,' " says Barbera. "We had to use all the know-how we had to set those things up and move them, using a system we had devised twenty years earlier."

Barbera's "system" was the use of pose reels, carefully timed compilations of story sketches, layout drawings and animation extremes. Animator Mike Lah recalls:

Bill and Joe's pose reels were funny, but when it came to the finished pictures, we saw a change. On the pose reel, a drawing would read—it would be there and you could see it. But when you added the animation, the timing was so fast you couldn't see that drawing anymore—it wasn't there long enough. So there was a problem of the pose reels being funnier than the films because there were too many drawings in there.

When we analyzed the pictures to see how we lost a certain amount of funniness, we would say: "It might be fun just to add a few little leg walks and head moves, and we'd have limited animation, like 'Crusader Rabbit.' " And "Crusader Rabbit" was a hell of a big hit in the TV market then.

Although more skillfully designed and animated, "Ruff and Reddy" clearly owed a great deal to "Crusader Rabbit." The little cat, Reddy, was the clever partner; Ruff, the bulldog, was the amiable, not-too-bright one. Reddy's voice was supplied by Daws Butler; Ruff's by Don Messick. The actors worked well together, and created a believable rapport between their char-

acters. They subsequently did the voices for many Hanna-Barbera duos, including Yogi Bear and Boo Boo, Pixie and Dixie, Augie Doggie and Doggy Daddy.

Like Crusader and Rags, Ruff and Reddy foiled criminals, solved mysteries and helped anyone in distress. Among the characters they encountered were the Mastermind of the metal planet of Muni-Mula ("aluminum," spelled backwards); Killer and Diller, the Terrible Twins from Texas; Scarey Harry Safari and the Chickasaurus, a birdlike dinosaur that called "Greek-greek."

"I think the stories we did then were cute little stories," says Hanna. "And the idea that we were able to turn out a cartoon for $3,000—as compared to $35,000—made us feel good. And we were overjoyed by the fact that the films were our own."

Screen Gems used the six-minute episodes of the "Ruff and Reddy" adventures to open and close a package show that included a live host with puppets and old Columbia theatrical cartoons. "Ruff and Reddy" enjoyed a moderate success, but the live-action/animation format reduced the new characters to a secondary role. Hanna and Barbera realized that to succeed in television animation, they would have to make programs that were entirely their own.

"The Huckleberry Hound Show" debuted in syndication in 1958. The title character and host was an amiable, bright blue dog. An incurable optimist, Huck blithely stumbled into all sorts of odd situations and met a variety of curious characters, including the last survivors of the feuding Pennsyltucky Huckleberry and Dingleberry families. Huck's genial, easygoing nature softened the slapstick humor; somehow, he always managed to come out on top, singing "Clementine" in his off-key Southern drawl.

Huckleberry Hound sounded a lot like the dim-witted dog-catcher/wolf in Tex Avery's "Three Little Pups." Daws Butler, who supplied both voices, explains their differences (slipping in and out of character as he does): "The attitude is a little different, and the writing tells you how to do it. The wolf is completely dumb: 'Ah wanna tell yew, tha's a well-built dawghouse.' Huck was laconic; he was soft-spoken, like Jay Ward, and made a statement when he had to. Huck was sincere: 'Ah can't imagine him evuh tellin' a falsehood.' He does his job, not realizing that it isn't the greatest job in the world and he doesn't get any fringe benefits."

"The Huckleberry Hound Show" also featured the antics of Pixie and Dixie, two mice who bedeviled a cat named Mr. Jinx ("I hate meeces to pieces!"). The duo bore more than a passing resemblance to Jerry and Tuffy, but a comparison of their films illustrates the difference between full and limited animation. When Jerry ran from point A to point B, every step in his run was accurately depicted. When Pixie and Dixie made a quick exit, they would hang in midair for a split second with their legs moving in circles—then they were jerked off screen in a fast pan.

Huckleberry Hound was soon upstaged by a secondary character on the program: Yogi Bear. A loafer and a conniver, he lived in "Jellystone National Park" with his small, gentle sidekick, Boo Boo. Yogi frequently proclaimed he was "smarter than the average bear," and applied all his devious intelligence to swiping food from campers' "picanic baskets"—despite Ranger Smith's efforts to impose discipline. Yogi became the star of his own program in 1961.

"The Yogi Bear Show" was the second Hanna-Barbera series broadcast during the dinner hour, and an even bigger success than "Huckleberry Hound." Warners veterans Mike Maltese and Warren Foster wrote many of the first stories, and Yogi quickly became one of the most popular cartoon characters created for television.

In addition to Yakky Doodle, a rather self-consciously cute little duck, "The Yogi Bear Show" introduced the hammy mountain lion, Snagglepuss. Children immediately adopted his favorite line, "Exit, stage left" (usually delivered as he dashed away to avoid trouble). If, as some commentators have observed, Yogi sounded a lot like Art Carney's Ed Norton character, Snagglepuss sounded even more like Bert Lahr's Cowardly Lion.

Many early Hanna-Barbera characters were similarly modeled after live actors: Doggie Daddy was Jimmy Durante; Hokey Wolf, Phil Silvers; Fibber Fox, Paul Lynde; etc. Although the practice lacked imagination, audiences accepted it as an easy-to-watch formula.

Huck and Yogi were all but eclipsed by what proved to be Hanna-Barbera's biggest success of the 1960s: "The Flintstones." Barbera spent two months trying to find a sponsor for the program before the networks would consider it.

Finding a sponsor proved to be only the first problem. Hanna recalls: "Joe and I wrote the first 'Flintstones' episode, and we were stuck to go beyond that because of the pressure of doing one a week. For the next sixteen weeks, Warren Foster wrote a half-hour 'Flintstones' script each week and storyboarded it. If it hadn't been for him, we never would have been able to deliver the show. I don't think anyone had done that amount of work before, and I doubt that anyone has equaled it since."

The first—and still the most successful—program animated for prime time, "The Flintstones" premiered on ABC in 1960. It scored an immediate hit, and watching the show quickly became a Friday-night ritual.

A publicity cel of the cast of "The Yogi Bear Show" (1961): Yakky Doodle, Snagglepuss, Boo Boo and Yogi.

Fred and Wilma, the "modern Stone Age family" from Hanna-Barbera's prime-time hit "The Flint-stones" (1960).

As the title song stated, the Flintstones were "the modern Stone Age family." The town of Bedrock, 10,000 B.C., was portrayed as a 1960s suburb, and the program resembled a domestic sitcom with a prehistoric setting. Much of the humor came from sight gags about Paleolithic versions of everyday conveniences. A baby mastodon became a vacuum cleaner, sucking up dirt with his trunk; the phonograph consisted of a bird who touched his long beak to the grooves in a revolving stone record.

As more than one observer has noted, "The Flintstones" was basically Jackie Gleason's "The Honeymooners" in caveman costume. Like Ralph Kramden, big, loudmouthed Fred Flintstone was always getting involved in some get-rich-quick scheme, and always getting the worst of it. No matter how often their plans backfired, little Barney Rubble continued to look up to Fred, the way Ed Norton looked up to Ralph. Like Ralph and Norton, Fred and Barney went bowling (with stone pins and bowling balls) and belonged to a lodge, the Royal Order of Water Buffaloes. However, their rather long-suffering wives, Wilma and Betty, were less acidulous than Alice and Trixie.

During the 1962–63 season, Wilma became pregnant—another cartoon first. After the birth of Pebbles Flintstone in February 1963, the Rubbles adopted an unnaturally strong baby boy named Bamm Bamm. The focus of the stories shifted to parental worries and conflicts.

Bill Hanna (left) and Joe Barbera confer with some of their stars, in this publicity photo from the early 1960s.

The popularity of the show enabled Hanna-Barbera to license the production of nearly 3,000 Flintstones products. A Pebbles doll by Ideal earned almost $20 million in 1963. General Mills introduced a Pebbles sugar cereal, and Chocks offered chewable Flintstones vitamins for children. The characters were also adapted to both a newspaper comic strip and comic books.

During its final season, the program began to falter, as the writers resorted to gimmicks like caricatures of show business celebrities: Ann-Margrock (Ann-Margret), Stoney Curtis (Tony Curtis) and attorney Perry Masonry (Raymond Burr). Shortly after ABC dropped "The Flintstones" from its prime-time lineup, NBC repeated the series on Saturday mornings.

A fourth Hanna-Barbera program, "Quick Draw McGraw," debuted in syndication in 1959. A spoof of Westerns, "Quick Draw" borrowed heavily from Red Skelton's Clem Kadiddlehopper and Sheriff Deadeye characters. The best-remembered character from the show is Snuffles, the dog who went into spasms of ecstasy over dog biscuits.

"Top Cat" (ABC, 1961), a feline version of Phil Silvers's "You'll Never Get Rich," did better on Saturday morning than it did in prime time—as did "The Jetsons" (ABC, 1962), a

futuristic sitcom that borrowed from "The Flintstones" and various live-action comedies, notably "Hazel."

The blissfully automated world of "The Jetsons" epitomized the "Futurelux" fantasies of the early 1960s. A renewed interest in the style led to a "Jetsons" revival during the 1980s that involved an extensive merchandising campaign and the creation of new episodes for first-run syndication.

Hanna-Barbera's last prime-time series, "The Adventures of Jonny Quest," ran for a year on ABC before moving to Saturday morning. The son of the eminent scientist Dr. Benton Quest, Jonny traveled the world with his father and a team that included jet pilot "Race" Bannion, Hadji, an East Indian boy, and a bulldog puppy named Bandit. Together they fought monsters and villains in exotic locales. This durable action/science-fiction program eventually ran on all three networks.

Hanna-Barbera's "The Jetsons," which premiered in 1962, enjoyed a resurgence in popularity twenty-five years later.

"Frankenstein Jr. and the Impossibles," "The Lone Ranger," "Mighty Heroes," "The New Adventures of Superman" and "Space Ghost and Dino Boy" on CBS and "Cool McCool," "Space Kidettes" and "The Super Six" on NBC. None of these programs could be described as memorable.

Because so many hours of airtime must be filled each week, television consumes programs with incredible speed. For the 1980–81 season, the Filmation Studio alone produced seventy-six half-hour shows—the equivalent of twenty-five features. While these programs were not intended to be masterpieces of the animator's art, the sheer volume of work is staggering. Even at the height of production, Disney or Warners only did between two and four hours of theatrical animation a year.

Animation became a cheap way of filling large blocks of time, instead of an entertainment or an art form. In the never-ending search for quantity, quality was gradually compromised out of existence. FCC chairman Newton Minow once described television as "a vast wasteland"; Saturday-morning television became more of a vast landfill.

The artists at UPA had developed limited animation as an aesthetic response to the problems of moving flattened, graphically sophisticated figures. The Saturday-morning producers used limited animation to cut costs: the budgets for these early programs were minimal. Lou Scheimer, the president of the Filmation Studio, recalls that in 1966 "The New Adventures of Superman" cost only $36,000 per half hour (or about what Walt Disney spent on a seven-minute short thirty years earlier). The budgets stayed low. For the 1986–87 season, one half-hour episode of a kidvid series cost between $230,000 and $300,000—approximately half the price of a prime-time animated special and far less than a live-action show.

Many Saturday-morning programs were basically retreads of old live-action shows, like "The Addams Family" (NBC, 1973), "Jeannie" (CBS, 1973), "The New Adventures of Gilligan" (ABC, 1974), "Fonz and the Happy Days Gang" (ABC, 1980). Others, like "Hey, It's the King" (part of "CB Bears"; NBC, 1977) and "The Oddball Couple" (ABC, 1975), substituted animal characters for humans but kept the premise of their live models. These shows ignored the creative potential of animation and offered only a pallid reflection of live action.

As limited animation grew more limited and less animated, it also proved less durable. The well-animated characters of the theatrical shorts (and the not-so-well-animated but imaginative characters in the early TV shows) continued to delight audiences years and even decades after their films were released. The forgettable characters that populated Saturday mornings displayed all the individuality of Dixie cups—and proved equally disposable. Few remained on the air for more than a single season.

Even more damning was the failure of the studios to establish any sort of artistic identities. During the 1940s and 1950s, audiences could easily tell if a cartoon was from Warners or

The stars of Hanna-Barbera's "The Adventures of Jonny Quest" (1964): Jonny, Bandit, Hadji and "Race" Bannion.

The year 1966 was a turning point in television animation. For the first time, all three networks offered an entire lineup of new children's cartoon shows on Saturday morning. Although these programs were not appreciably different in quality or content from many of the networks' previous offerings, the focus on an audience composed exclusively of children was significant.

Theatrical cartoons had been made for large, general audiences. The early animated TV programs, particularly the ones shown during prime time, were intended to entertain both children and adults. But the growth of the Saturday-morning industry during the 1960s led Americans to equate animation with limited, child-oriented programs—a shibboleth that still dogs the art in the United States.

The 1966 season included "King Kong," "Magilla Gorilla" and "The Peter Potamus Show" on ABC, "The Beagles,"

Disney or MGM: each studio had an immediately recognizable style of design and animation. During the 1960s and 1970s, Saturday-morning cartoons were generally regarded as a vast, anonymous heap of film. Critics and historians rarely bother to differentiate among the products of the four dominant studios: Hanna-Barbera, DePatie-Freleng, Filmation and Ruby-Spears.

During the first few seasons of Saturday-morning programming, it consisted mostly of action/adventure series that centered on superheroes (Aquaman, the Fantastic Four, Batman) or mortals that somehow got involved in supernatural conflicts (the kids on "Shazzan!" who met a sixty-foot genie or the crew of the miniaturized submarine on "Fantastic Voyage").

In answer to the growing criticism of the allegedly violent content of the superhero programs, Filmation introduced "The Archie Show" on CBS in 1968. Based on the popular comic book series created by Bob Montana, "Archie" depicted teenaged characters in situations that were closer to everyday life. The program got an unexpected boost in 1969, when Betty, Veronica, Archie, Reggie and Jughead formed a rock band, "The Archies," and their bubble-gum single, "Sugar, Sugar," became a number one hit.

"The Archie Show" proved phenomenally successful. Although the format changed, it ran for a decade as "Archie's Funhouse" (1970), "Everything's Archie" (1973), "The U.S. of Archie" (1974), etc. Its popularity engendered a spate of comedy/variety series ("Cattanooga Cats," "Skatebirds") and shows about rock groups ("The Hardy Boys," "Butch Cassidy and the Sun Dance Kids," "Josie and the Pussycats").

"Archie" also gave rise to a highly successful spinoff, "Sabrina, the Teenage Witch," a sort of juvenile version of the popular live-action comedy "Bewitched." The young sorceress first appeared on "The Archie Show" in 1969, but became the star of her own series in 1970. A Sabrina comic book followed in 1971.

Hanna-Barbera scored a big hit in 1969 with the comedy/adventure series "Scooby-Doo, Where Are You?" The title character was a cowardly Great Dane, the mascot of four teenage sleuths. Freddy, Velma, Daphne and Shaggy solved mysteries that always seemed to involve haunted houses and chase scenes with the villains disguised as ghosts. Scooby-Doo shivered, cowered and, finally, turned tail and ran.

Scooby was never a "real" dog, like Bandit on "Jonny Quest." The animators used human facial expressions and body language to depict his craven reactions to frightening situations. Don Messick gave Scooby a voice that was a mixture of barking sounds and garbled words. Similarly anthropomorphized dogs became a feature of many subsequent Hanna-Barbera shows.

In 1969, DePatie-Freleng brought their successful Pink Panther theatrical cartoons to Saturday mornings. Friz Freleng had created the suave, rose-colored cat for the title sequence

Based on Bob Montana's comic book series, Filmation's "The Archie Show" proved to be one of the most durable kidvid shows of the 1970s.

of Blake Edwards's comedy "The Pink Panther" in 1964. Both the film and the character proved so popular that DePatie-Freleng began producing theatrical shorts for United Artists. Their first effort, "The Pink Phink" (1964), won an Academy Award.

In addition to the cool, silent Panther, the NBC show featured "Texas Toads," a redubbed version of the theatrical series Tijuana Toads; "The Inspector," a caricature of Peter Sellers's Inspector Clouseau character; Misterjaws, a near-sighted shark, and his sidekick, Catfish; Crazylegs Crane; the Aardvark and the Ant. While the Pink Panther films couldn't compare with the brilliant cartoons Freleng had directed at Warners, they used movement more skillfully than the made-for-TV series and provided a bright spot on Saturday mornings during the early 1970s.

Jay Ward's last cartoon show, "George of the Jungle" (ABC, 1967), featured even more puns, satire and mischief than "Rocky and His Friends." The title character was an incredibly stupid Tarzan figure in the best Elmo Lincoln tradition. George mistook his elephant, Shep, for a dog ("great big gray peanut-loving bow-wow"); and referred to his wife, Ursula, as "that funny fellow who never need to shave." Ape, the Oxford-educated gorilla, tried in vain to unscramble George's perceptions of the world.

These cartoons spoofed every cliché of the "Tarzan" genre. George wrecked the plans of white hunters and would-be developers; he learned the news of the jungle from the cries of the Tooki-Tooki Bird and wrestled Leon the lion for fun. When network officials complained about the depiction of the black natives in "nearby Umbwebwe Village," Ward had them redrawn as Caucasians. (The chief of Umbwebwe and his

Part of the cast of Jay Ward's "George of the Jungle": Ursula, George, the Tooki-Tooki Bird and Shep.

witch doctor were caricatures of Ward and co-producer Bill Scott.)

Best of all were the adventures of Superchicken. One glass of "Super Sauce" and the mild-mannered Henry Cabot Henhouse III was transformed into an inept, swashbuckling hero in a cape, plumed hat and mask. Assisted by Fred, his faithful, dumb lion/butler, Superchicken battled archfiends like the evil wizard Merlin Brando, who lived on the Isle of Lucy. When Appian Way stole the state of Rhode Island, Superchicken flew to the rescue in the Supercoop. (That villain turned out to be the descendant of a fine old Rhode Island family—"the Ways of Providence.") When things went wrong —as they invariably did—Superchicken would tell Fred: "You knew the job was dangerous when you took it!"

"George of the Jungle" had a more polished look than "Rocky" or the unsuccessful "Hoppity Hooper" (ABC, 1964), because it was animated in the United States on a larger budget. Despite an intensely loyal audience, only sixteen episodes of "George" were made. The program went off ABC in 1970, but has remained popular in syndication ever since.

Two years later, Filmation introduced their most highly acclaimed show, "Fat Albert and the Cosby Kids" (CBS). Based on comedian Bill Cosby's monologues about his childhood, "Fat Albert" centered on a group of poor black kids who hung out in a junkyard—Russel, Old Weird Harold, Rudy the Rich Kid, Dumb Donald, Mushmouth et al.

Created in conjunction with Cosby and a panel of educators from UCLA, the program dealt with many problems and frustrations children face in daily life: show-offs, bullies, liars and learning to accept different types of people. Cosby supplied several voices (including the title character's rumbling signature line, "Hey, hey, hey!") and served as the live-action host of the series. His low-key chats underscored the morals presented in the cartoons.

Two previous shows had centered on black characters— "The Harlem Globetrotters" (CBS, 1970) and "The Jackson 5ive" (ABC, 1971), but "Fat Albert" was praised by parents and teachers for its positive depiction of minorities and pro-social values. The program earned impressive ratings and ran on ABC through 1981.

The quality of Saturday-morning programming gradually declined during the 1970s. Animators (including many of the artists who created it) and critics damned it as "Sat-schlock," "illustrated radio" and "creative bookkeeping with moving arms and legs."

The general consensus among animators is that the medium hit rock bottom sometime during the late 1970s. As the decline was gradual, it is difficult to pinpoint one program or year as the absolute nadir, but every animator has a personal candidate for the title. At animation programs and seminars, at least one parent would demand to know why the

Above: Fat Albert confronts Rudy the Rich Kid, in the popular Filmation series based on Bill Cosby's monologues about his childhood. Left: Fat Albert's hero, the inept "Brown Hornet."

cartoons his child watched weren't as good as the ones he had seen thirty years earlier. The lugubrious truth was that Saturday-morning programming was bad because there was no reason for it to be good.

Corporate acquisitions of the studios suggest just how much the networks were spending—and how profitable Saturday-morning animation had become. In December 1966, Taft Entertainment bought Hanna-Barbera for $12 million, then bought Ruby-Spears in 1981 for $1.6 million. TelePrompTer acquired Filmation for $3 million in 1969, and was in turn acquired by Westinghouse–Group W in 1981 for $659 million. ("We accounted for about $659 of that," laughs Scheimer.)

The networks imposed deadlines on the kidvid studios that caused more problems than the limited budgets. Those deadlines were tightened during the 1970s, creating a pattern that has continued through the 1980s. In March—or even April—the networks sign the contracts for the next season's programs. The first episodes are due in September. Dozens of hours of animation have to be written, recorded, drawn, shot and edited in six months or less. Disney spent four years working on "Snow White," which was only 83 minutes long.

To meet these demands, the studios have devised a frantic, disbalanced work schedule. The months of January, February and March are devoted to optioning properties, developing ideas and negotiating contracts. Once the contracts are signed, production begins at a breakneck pace. Initially, the studios hired every available animator in Southern California and paid vast amounts of overtime; as the shows were delivered in the fall, most of the artists were laid off until the next year—when the cycle began again.

As the amount of production needed to fill the Saturday-morning time slots grew, most studios switched to "runaway" or "overflow" production. Much of the ink-and-paint work—and even the animation itself—was subcontracted and done cheaply by artists in other countries: Japan, Taiwan, Korea, Australia, Spain. The writing, design, direction and recording were done in America. Of the Saturday-morning houses, only Filmation kept all of their production in the United States.

Overseas production proved attractive financially but disastrous aesthetically. The foreign animators, who were often minimally trained, had no real contact with the directors. The resulting animation was rarely more than adequate and often terrible. During the 1980s, foreign studios like TMS (Tokyo Movie Shinsha) began to enter the U.S. market and bid against their former sponsors.

Efforts by the Screen Cartoonists' Guild to stem the flow of runaway production were largely unsuccessful. A strike in 1979 led to an imperfect but promising contract that offered some protection to American animators. Unfortunately, these gains were erased by a calamitous and poorly planned strike in 1982.

In addition to the lost job opportunities, runaway production made it difficult, if not impossible, for young artists to gain a thorough understanding of animation. The men who drew the classic studio cartoons learned their craft by working on full animation eight hours a day, five days a week. The young animators lacked the knowledge and understanding that could only come from hours at the drawing board. They couldn't do limited animation as well as their predecessors—let alone full, character animation.

During the late 1960s and early 1970s, the content of the Saturday-morning shows was greatly altered by the rise of pressure groups like the Boston-based Action for Children's Television (ACT), who objected to the allegedly violent content of the programs and who sought to promulgate "pro-social values." Their widely publicized campaigns yielded

Calvin offers a critique of contemporary kidvid, in Bill Watterson's comic strip "Calvin and Hobbes."

CALVIN AND HOBBES By Bill Watterson

some indisputably beneficial results. Children's programming began to include minority and female characters who took an active part in solving problems. While ethnic humor had gradually been phased out of cartoons during the 1950s, the stereotypical shorts of the 1940s were still being broadcast in some markets. More positive images were long overdue.

The campaign to eliminate "violence" in cartoons had more dubious consequences. While watching violent entertainment *can* lead to aggressive behavior in children, it is by no means certain that watching violence necessarily *does* lead to such behavior. What, if any, long-term effects watching violence has and how children perceive fantasy, animation and animated violence have yet to be established. Nor is it clear what constitutes "violence"—as opposed to legitimate dramatic conflict or slapstick humor.

"I was particularly disturbed by the Donald Duck and his nephews cartoons which promote spanking as the appropriate and only way to discipline children," wrote Thomas Radecki, M.D., of the National Coalition on Television Violence, in a newsletter decrying alleged violence on the Disney Channel in 1984. "Three Donald Duck cartoons put down non-violent attempts to deal with problem children and offered no alternative type of discipline other than corporal punishment."

In a 1983 interview, Radecki excoriated Filmation's syndicated series "He-Man and the Masters of the Universe" without having seen a single episode of the program:

> The "He-Man" series is a blatant attempt to sell violence to children through the peddling of violent action toys. The fact that there's no blood or gore doesn't mean that there's no violence—the way to sell violence is to clean it up. Cleaning up violence only makes it seem more wholesome. The brutal barbarian is still held up as model. It's incompatible with the survival of a democratic society. This violence is opposed to the Judeo-Christian ethic on which our society is based.

This hyperbolic denunciation recalls the notorious book *Seduction of the Innocent,* in which Frederic Wertham, M.D., damned the supposedly violent and/or sexual content of comic books as a major cause of juvenile delinquency. Its publication resulted in a large-scale "cleanup" of the comics industry during the mid-1950s, but failed to stem the incidence of delinquency.

Faced with these pressures, the networks adopted "standards and procedures" codes that often seemed to equate violence with action. Crashes, explosions and falls had to take place off camera. Animated characters were forbidden to strike each other, perform any "imitatable" action or do anything that might be construed as "suggesting violence." These strictures were even extended to commercials.

"We recently had a spot where you would see a kitchen knife breaking the smooth surface of a newly opened jar of peanut butter—an exciting moment for a kid," Bill Scott recalled in 1983. "We had to change the knife to a butter spreader because somebody at the network thought the kitchen knife entering the peanut butter implied violence."

In an effort to excise all suggestion of violence, ABC began bowdlerizing the classic Warner Brothers cartoons on "The Bugs Bunny Show." Collisions, falls and explosions were suddenly classified as pernicious and were excised. The fact that these explosions, pratfalls and pie-in-the-face gags had entertained audiences for decades was ignored. (As Chuck Jones observes: "Anybody in this country under forty-five was raised on these cartoons.") Nor was the aesthetic excellence of the shorts taken into consideration. The films were casually and clumsily censored. Only the artists who made them and a few hard-core animation fans objected.

Like classic fairy tales, cartoons had traditionally shown small, apparently helpless characters using their wits to overcome bigger, more powerful characters. Psychologists—notably Bruno Bettelheim—argue that these stories reassure children about their ability to deal with problems. The push to emphasize cooperation and getting along together resulted in a spate of animated programs that stressed collective action over individual initiative. (This theme was also used in many of the features based on license product characters during the 1980s.)

If one character tried to do something by himself, he usually failed and/or caused trouble for everyone. Only when the group acted together could they resolve a crisis or overcome a foe: Collective action became the only effective means of solving a problem. Dissenting opinions were rarely heard, and "pro-social" requirements grew increasingly stringent during the 1970s. The standards seem to have been relaxed somewhat during the 1980s, although the emphasis on group action remains.

The title character from Filmation's "He-Man and the Masters of the Universe": a threat to a democratic society?

©1988 Hanna-Barbera Productions, Inc.
and Sepp International, S.A.
Smurfs®

Three kidvid hits from the 1980s based on previously existing material. Left: Hanna-Barbera's "The Smurfs" was adapted from a popular Belgian comic strip. Below: Publicity art for Disney's "The New Adventures of Winnie the Pooh." Bottom: DIC's "The Real Ghostbusters" was inspired by Ivan Reitman's hit comedy.

During the 1980s, Saturday-morning cartoons improved a little. In 1981, Hanna-Barbera introduced "The Smurfs" on NBC, an adaptation of Pierre (Peyo) Culliford's popular Belgian comic strip, "Les Schtroumpfs" (Flemish for "whatcha-macallit"). Happy little blue men ("three apples high") who dwell in an enchanted forest, Smurfs are troubled only by the evil wizard, Gargamel, and his cat, Azreal. The Schtroumpfs were originally identical, but Hanna-Barbera made minor alterations in the designs and added a female, Smurfette. "The Smurfs" was a big hit, and regularly drew a Nielsen audience share of 39 to 44.

Some of the most prominent figures in fantasy entertainment entered the Saturday-morning cartoon market, with mixed results. "Muppet Babies" (CBS, 1984) featured infant versions of Jim Henson's popular creations. Although the program did well in the ratings, critics correctly observed that the attempt to adapt puppetry to animation negated both art forms. "Ewoks" and "Droids" (ABC, 1985) used characters taken from George Lucas's "Star Wars" films.

Many animators were aghast when Disney agreed to produce two shows animated in Japan for the 1985–86 season, "The Wuzzles" (CBS) and "The Gummi Bears" (NBC). Both programs were considerably more lavish than the average Saturday-morning show, and "Gummi Bears" was nicely animated and often charming. The trend toward better animation continued in 1986 with "Galaxy High School" (CBS) and the elaborate special effects on "The Real Ghostbusters" (ABC).

Above: Animator David Daniels demonstrates his Strata-Cut technique; in the close-up, he slices the clay block with a machete. Below: One of Columbus's ships at sea, from an episode of "Pee-wee's Playhouse."

However, it would be premature to hail the mid-1980s as the advent of a renaissance in Saturday-morning animation. Many of the same problems remained. The writing failed to match the visuals on the better-animated programs: the mean-spirited scripts for "Galaxy High School" all seemed to focus on publicly humiliating Doyle, the Earth boy. Despite the popularity of their live-action models, "The Real Ghostbusters," "Teen Wolf" (CBS, 1986), "ALF" (NBC, 1987), "Ewoks" and "Droids" proved to be very ordinary Saturday-morning fare.

"Kissyfur" (NBC, 1986), "Little Clowns of Happytown" (ABC, 1987), "The Adventures of Raggedy Ann and Andy" (CBS, 1988), "Superman" (CBS, 1988) and "Pound Puppies" (ABC, 1986) were just dull. And in 1985, CBS premiered "Hulk Hogan's Rock and Wrestling," an abominable mixture of bad animation, ethnic stereotypes and caricatures of professional wrestlers that was enough to make viewers long for a return of "Partridge Family: 2200 A.D." or "Valley of the Dinosaurs."

While it is easy to blame the producers and the networks, part of the responsibility for the state of Saturday-morning cartoons must be borne by parents who allow their children to watch programs they consider inferior, violent, inane, etc. As long as a show earns good ratings, the network will continue to broadcast and renew it. Parents who feel their children are being shortchanged by kidvid programs can make those feelings known. On Saturday mornings—as on prime time—the "off" button provides an absolute veto power.

Even before Saturday-morning cartoons came to dominate television animation, specials—especially the ones shown during prime time—were considered more prestigious. As the theatrical studios closed, many of the industry's top directors, designers and animators began to work on specials, attracted by the bigger budgets and longer production schedules.

The better specials, like "A Charlie Brown Christmas," "How the Grinch Stole Christmas," "A Doonesbury Special," "A Christmas Carol" or "An Adventure in Color," comprised some of the high points in the history of television animation. Some of the holiday-themed specials became perennial entertainments that earned good ratings year after year. Others proved more ephemeral than TV series: they were shown once, then consigned to oblivion—until the 1980s, when many of them were reissued on cassette.

Not all specials were wonderful. Many were hastily cranked out by foreign or domestic studios for Christmas or Easter family viewing. Their stories invariably seemed to center on some little animal who helped "save" the holiday from a villain's shoddy plot.

The first special animated for television was a fifteen-minute version of Igor Stravinsky's ballet *Petroushka*, which appeared as a segment of "The Music Hour" on NBC in 1956. Directed

Director John Wilson and composer Igor Stravinsky with artwork from the 1956 special based on the ballet *Petroushka*.

by John Wilson, a veteran of Disney and UPA, the film featured animation by Phil Monroe, Bill Littlejohn and Dave Hanan.

"NBC decided they would do *Petroushka* if I could get Stravinsky to conduct it," says Wilson. "I heard he was living on Sunset Drive, so I went up there and knocked on the door. His wife, Vera, answered, and I said: 'I'm here to see the Maestro. I want to do an animated film with him.' She said: 'I don't think you have much chance—he hates animation.' But I was lucky. She introduced me to Robert Craft, and he thought it was a good idea."

At Wilson's request, Stravinsky rearranged the score for the program, cutting it from forty minutes to fifteen. He also agreed to serve as conductor, but insisted on using the Los Angeles Philharmonic, rather than a studio orchestra. NBC approved the request, and the recording took place on the sound stage of the Goldwyn studio—the most lavish sound track ever created for an animated television program.

While the cartoon version of the ballet failed to capture the opulent vision of a Russian Shrovetide fair that dazzled Parisians in 1911, it remained faithful to the story of the ingenuous puppet whose spirit transcends death. "Petroushka" won sev-

eral international awards and was the first animated film screened at the prestigious Venice Film Festival.

The first four installments of the Bell Science series remain among the best-remembered specials of the 1950s. The destruction of Hiroshima and the accelerating nuclear arms race had produced a highly unfavorable image of scientists in America at a time when the country faced a critical shortage of them. Working through their advertising agency, N. W. Ayers, the directors of the Bell Telephone System decided to underwrite a series of hour-long programs that would simultaneously interest young people in science and improve the public image of scientists.

Academy Award–winner Frank Capra was chosen to direct the series. For the first program, "Our Mr. Sun," he decided on a multimedia approach that would combine still photographs, live-action footage and animation. Frank Baxter, an instructor at USC noted for his entertaining and informative lectures on Shakespeare, became the narrator. The contract for the animation went to the UPA studio.

"Our Mr. Sun" received excellent reviews. Bell offered free prints of it (and the subsequent entries in the series) to school systems around the country.

Shortly after completing "Our Mr. Sun," Bill Hurtz left UPA to head the Los Angeles branch of Shamus Culhane Productions, where he directed the animation for the next three specials. Probably the most successful entry in the series, "Hemo the Magnificent" (1956) dealt with human anatomy and biology. "The Strange Case of the Cosmic Rays" (1957) featured puppets by Bil Baird, and "The Unchained Goddess" (1958) focused on meteorology.

Despite the critical and artistic success of the series, Capra retired after "The Unchained Goddess"; the subsequent programs were made at Warner Brothers. The Bell Science series remained a standard of elementary and junior high school classes for years. Their deft blending of animation and live action, science and fantasy, influenced the scholastic careers of untold numbers of children.

A turning point in the history of the TV special came in 1965 when Lee Mendelson and Bill Melendez produced "A Charlie Brown Christmas" for CBS, the first half-hour animated special. Although the characters from Charles Schulz's comic strip "Peanuts" had appeared in a series of Ford Falcon commercials in 1957, they had never been animated for entertainment before.

At first glance, Schulz's simple graphic style seemed too minimal to offer much potential for animation. But Melendez followed the UPA tradition of allowing the design to dictate the style of motion and simplified the characters' movements. In a further break with tradition, real children were chosen to supply the characters' voices—rather than adult actors imitating children, a technique John and Faith Hubley had pioneered in their commercials and personal films.

A cel setup from "A Charlie Brown Christmas" (1965), the first "Peanuts" special.

Grammy-winning composer Vince Guaraldi contributed a crisp jazz score that emphasized the timeless quality of the story.

The result was a modest and charming program that pleased critics and audiences alike. "A Charlie Brown Christmas" won both an Emmy and a Peabody Award; CBS rebroadcasts it every holiday season.

Melendez estimates he and Mendelson initially lost about $20,000 on the show, which was budgeted at $96,000—a substantial sum at the time. But the success of "A Charlie Brown Christmas" led to the production of more than two dozen "Peanuts" specials, which won four more Emmys and an additional Peabody over the next twenty years. Schulz, Mendelson and Melendez also used the characters in four feature films and a Saturday-morning series.

The second special, "It's the Great Pumpkin, Charlie Brown" (1966), probably ranks as the best. In an imaginative and very funny fantasy sequence, Snoopy appears as the World War I Flying Ace, piloting his doghouse/Sopwith Camel through enemy fire. Melendez supplies the beagle's laughs, cries and howls.

The phenomenal popularity of the comic strip contributed to the enormous success of the "Peanuts" specials, and vice versa. The series seemed to run out of steam in the late 1970s, as the stories began to violate rules Schulz had set for the strip—like allowing the audience to see Heather, "the little red-haired girl," in "It's Your First Kiss, Charlie Brown" (1977).

In 1966, Chuck Jones directed the Peabody Award–winning "How the Grinch Stole Christmas." Jones and his skillful crew (which included several artists from his unit at Warners) managed to preserve Ted (Dr. Seuss) Geisel's popular children's story, while expanding it for animation. Boris Karloff served as both the narrator and the voice of the curmudgeonly Grinch, "whose heart was two sizes too small." Audiences never seemed to tire of "How the Grinch Stole Christmas"; like "A Charlie Brown Christmas," it was rebroadcast each holiday season.

The success of "The Grinch" led to a spate of programs based on Dr. Seuss books. Jones earned a second Peabody Award for "Horton Hears a Who" (1970), and served as co-producer on "The Cat in the Hat" (1971). Directed by Warners veteran Hawley Pratt, "The Cat in the Hat" features a rousing production number in which the Cat (voiced by Allan Sherman) gives his name in various languages: "Cat in a Hat / In French, Chatte-Chapeau / In Spanish, I'm El Gato in a Sombrero," and concluding: "I'm a Gwunka in a Bunkagwunk in Eskimo."

But as the quality of the specials began to decline during the 1970s, Geisel grew disenchanted with animation and finally ceased to authorize production.

Most of the better specials continued to focus on holiday

themes. Richard Williams won an Oscar in 1973 for his handsome adaptation of "A Christmas Carol." To evoke the look of Dickensian London, Williams chose designs based on nineteenth-century steelcuts—a style he had begun to explore in the animated title sequences for Tony Richardson's "The Charge of the Light Brigade" (1968).

In regular animation, it would be virtually impossible to keep the crosshatched shading in registration. Williams avoided the problem by using "soft cuts"—quick dissolves from one drawing to the next. The result was a moody and dramatic film that refreshed Dickens's holiday chestnut.

The Oscar-winning husband-and-wife team of John and Faith Hubley offered a different vision of an animated special in 1976 with "Everybody Rides the Carousel," a study of human growth and development, based on the work of psychologist Erik Erikson.

The last collaboration of the Hubleys was "A Doonesbury Special" (1977), based on Garry Trudeau's Pulitzer Prize–winning comic strip: John died, unexpectedly, during the storyboard stage. The program offered both a satire of and a wistful elegy to the idealism and social activism of the 1960s. Character animation had essentially disappeared from television by 1977, and to see characters walk in ways that demonstrated their personalities was a rare treat: B.D. swaggered, Zonker pranced to his different drummer (or rhythm section) and Michael plodded stolidly along. The film earned both an Oscar nomination and a Special Jury Prize at the Cannes Film Festival.

The Grinch plays pool with a Who family Christmas tree ornament, in Chuck Jones's award-winning "How the Grinch Stole Christmas" (1966).

Top: Zonker confronts B.D. on the playing field, in "A Doonesbury Special" (1977). Above: A preliminary sketch by Pulitzer Prize–winning cartoonist Garry Trudeau indicates the relative sizes of the characters.

NBC broadcast "Doonesbury" on Thanksgiving weekend, back to back with a more typical example of 1970s television animation: Rankin-Bass's unlovely adaptation of J. R. R. Tolkien's *The Hobbit*. Drawn in Japan, this leaden film failed to capture the magic and poetry of Tolkien's Middle Earth. Rankin-Bass produced even less impressive shows based on *The Return of the King* (1980), the third volume of the *Lord of the Rings* trilogy, and *The Wind in the Willows* (1983).

Chuck Jones used the old Warners characters in programs like "A Connecticut Rabbit in King Arthur's Court" (1978), but full, character animation proved too expensive for a television special: Bugs Bunny became a pale reflection of his former, brash self—like an old vaudevillian doing a star turn at a benefit. The films Jones made with other characters, like the Grinch or Rudyard Kipling's Rikki-Tikki-Tavi (1974), proved more satisfying.

Warners began splicing together pieces of old cartoons to make "new" specials like "How Bugs Bunny Won the West" (1978). These visually jarring and painfully unfunny hodge-podges casually mixed scenes from films made in different years by different directors. The timing and pacing that made the original cartoons so enjoyable were destroyed. However, the formula proved successful financially, and was expanded into a series of cut-and-paste theatrical features.

Specials that reflected an original vision—like R. O. Blech-man's highly personal interpretation of Stravinsky's "The Sol-dier's Tale" (1984)—became increasingly rare during the late 1970s and the 1980s. Animators complained that the networks insisted on "presold" properties, which almost invariably meant a special had to involve a line of toys, comic strip characters or both. These characters could be made interest-ing and entertaining, as Eric Goldberg demonstrated in "Ziggy's Gift" (1982). Based on Tom Wilson's one-panel strip, this Emmy-winning special proved that a new generation of talented young animators could do top-quality work, if given a chance.

Aside from these exceptions, specials settled into a formu-laic rut; the characters sometimes seemed to sleepwalk through the gags. Kidvid characters like the Smurfs joined Garfield and Charlie Brown on prime-time programs during the 1980s, and it became increasingly difficult to distinguish the once exciting realm of network specials from Saturday-morning TV.

The title character quails at the sight of a can of icky dog food in Brad Bird's hilarious "Family Dog" (1987).

The first animation of Charles Schulz's "Peanuts" characters was done for a series of commercials for the Ford Falcon.

Since the earliest days of television, much of the best animation has been done not for series or specials but for commercials. Some of the most talented artists in the history of the medium have consistently used the boldest graphics, the most fluid animation, the newest technology and the most sophisticated direction to create excellent miniature films, often as brief as 15 seconds. Many commercials were more entertaining than the programs they interrupted.

"Advertisers realize their audience is not captive," explains Bob Kurtz of Kurtz and Friends, one of the top commercial studios in America. "So we're more apt to use animation in exciting ways to grab their attention. Therefore, we have more freedom to be inventive."

Although animation accounts for only a small fraction of the commercials on network television—about 5 percent during the 1980s—a disproportionately high number of the best spots have been animated. Of the sixty-nine entries in Lincoln Diamant's "Classic Commercials 1948–58," thirty-four are animated or animation/live-action combinations. Popular characters introduced in animated spots include Tony the Tiger (Kellogg's Sugar Frosted Flakes), the Ford Dog, Bert & Harry (Piels beer), the Ajax Elves, the Trix Rabbit, Sugar Pops Pete, Bucky Beaver (Ipana toothpaste), Speedy Alka-Seltzer, the

Hamm's Bear, Marky Maypo, Cap'n Crunch, Toucan Sam (Kellogg's Fruit Loops), Poppin' Fresh (the Pillsbury Dough Boy) and Punchie (Hawaiian Punch).

Animators agree that the late 1940s and early 1950s—the early years of broadcasting—were the "golden age" of commercials, when advertising agencies gave the artists almost complete freedom to create what they chose. Among the top commercial studios then were UPA, Storyboard Productions, Shamus Culhane Productions, Playhouse Pictures and Quartet Films.

The varied styles and shorter deadlines of commercial production offered a welcome change to animators accustomed to spending months and even years drawing the same animal characters: "What made working in commercials fun then was the quick turnover of ideas," says Bill Melendez, who went on to direct over 1,000 commercials. "After working on shorts and animated features, that speed was refreshing. It was stimulating to be animating contemporary designs and caricatures of human beings, instead of old-fashioned concepts of animals."

In 1956, John Hubley began to explore the possibilities of using real children's voices, instead of those of adult actors, in a series of ads for Maypo cereal—his four-year-old son, Mark, first cried "I want my Maypo!" The Hubleys later used their children's voices on the sound tracks of their award-winning personal films, including "Moonbird" (1959), "The Windy Day" (1967) and "Cockaboody" (1973).

A commercial for Snowdrift shortening by Quartet spawned another catchphrase of the mid-1950s, "John! Marsha!" The commercial was a 60-second soap opera in miniature: John and Marsha's foundering marriage was saved when her baking improved, thanks to Snowdrift. The dialogue consisted of little more than the words "John," "Marsha" and "Snowdrift." Stan Freberg made a popular comedy record about John and Marsha, and when the Tasmanian Devil met Bugs Bunny disguised as a she-devil in "Bedevilled Rabbit" (1957), they greeted each other as "John" and "Marsha."

Production costs during the 1950s remained modest. In 1956, a fully animated 60-second spot from one of the top studios cost only about $12,000; a 30-second spot, about $8,000—approximately one-fourth of the cost in the mid-1980s. But as the price of network airtime rose, sponsors began to demand more efficient advertising. The average commercial shrank from 60 seconds to 30 (and was later cut to 20, then 15, and even 10 seconds).

Under pressure from their clients, the advertising agencies started exerting greater control over commercial production. Instead of coming to the animation studios with a rough idea, they began to write, design and storyboard the commercials themselves.

Culhane complained that by the mid-1950s "it became a rarity to be allowed to create a spot from the basic sales points

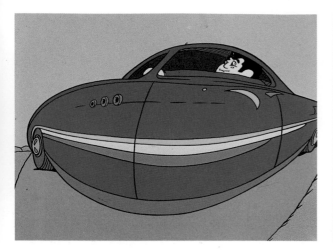 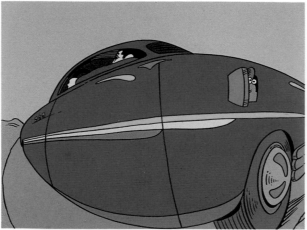 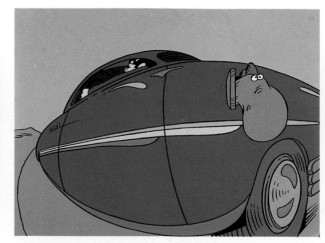

Below: The Ford Dog, one of the popular characters from 1950s commercials. Bottom: A cel of Jay Ward's befuddled Cap'n Crunch.

as we had been doing. It took all the fun out of the work, because that is really the most creative aspect of spot production." But a measure of freedom persisted through the early 1960s.

"There was a period when Kellogg's had a Hanna-Barbera character on every cereal box, and I was doing all the commercials," recalls Daws Butler. "I talked to the guys at the agency and said: 'You're just giving me sell lines and expecting me to be funny, and you can't. There has to be a story.' So I wrote one, it was animated, and from then on, they started to watch the shows and study their potential. The commercials became 30-second plays."

During the 1960s, the artists at the Jay Ward studio began producing commercials that were almost as zany as their programs—and better animated. Bullwinkle even hawked General Mills cereals for a brief time ("I'm just a moose with Cheerios to sell"). But most of Ward's commercials were done for Quaker Oats, including the "rivalry" they created between the sugar cereals Quisp and Quake.

Ward's longest-running ad campaign involved Cap'n Crunch, the befuddled skipper of the good ship *The Guppy*. With a crew of children and a canine mascot named Seadog, the doughty Cap'n stumbled through various 30-second misadventures, including a series of confrontations with the pirate Jean LaFoote. The campaign lasted well into the 1980s and proved to be the last animation done by the Ward studio.

The trend toward more sharply focused commercials continued through the 1970s and into the 1980s. Demographics, the practice of aiming a sales pitch at a specifically targeted sector of the audience, became a buzzword in advertising. As agencies exerted increasingly tight control over commercials, there seemed to be less and less room for originality. American animators began to look enviously at the greater freedom their British counterparts enjoyed.

A new group of commercial studios came to the fore during the 1970s: Duck Soup, Spungbuggy, Film Fair, Kurtz and

Above: Six frames from a Chevron "dinosaur" commercial by Kurtz and Friends highlight the use of metamorphic animation.

Friends in Los Angeles; Zander's Animation Parlor, Ink Tank, Perpetual Motion, KMPC, Ovation and Kim & Gilford in New York. In addition, every large city could boast at least one studio that handled local accounts. Despite the agency restrictions, some animators managed to produce truly original commercials that provided some of the brightest moments on television.

R. O. Blechman's depiction of a man arguing with his stomach in an Alka-Seltzer commercial ("You never liked my mother," the man says accusingly) was one of the cleverest spots of the early 1970s. In 1975, Bob Kurtz introduced what was intended to be the world's stupidest-looking cat (actually a self-caricature of Kurtz) in a hilarious trio of ads for Kitty Salmon cat food.

Two years later, Kurtz produced his best-known works: a series of ads for Chevron, in which a clutch of unlikely blue dinosaurs transform into a glob of petroleum. As the narrator gives tips on energy conservation, the camera seems to move in three dimensions around the turning, metamorphosing beasts, an effect achieved by shifting the perspective slightly in each drawing. Audiences remembered the dinosaur spots so clearly that a survey revealed many people believed they were still running a year after the campaign ended.

Up through the 1970s, most American commercials involved drawn animation. Ads using stop-motion animation, like Lou Bunin's puppet spots for Brylcream characters, or the commercials with Speedy Alka-Seltzer and Poppin' Fresh, the Pillsbury Dough Boy, were rare exceptions. Will Vinton's line of funky little raisins that danced to "I Heard It Through the Grapevine" (1986) was the first commercial in clay animation to attract widespread attention.

During the 1970s and 1980s, the new medium of computer animation had its greatest impact in the area of commercials, program logos and station identifications. Independent artists like John Whitney, Sr., had already begun to explore the artistic potential of computer-generated visuals, but commer-

The world's stupidest-looking cat: "Underwater Kitty."

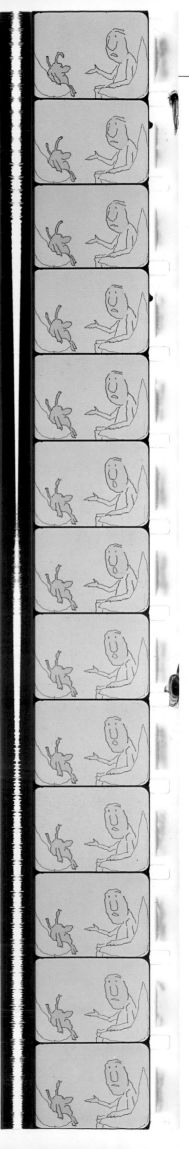

cials provided a bridge between the avant-garde and main-stream filmmaking.

The popularity of science-fiction films, from "2001: A Space Odyssey" to the "Star Wars" trilogy—and the need to excite an increasingly jaded TV audience—produced a demand for flashy, high-tech visuals. Computer-animation houses like Abel Image Research, Omnibus, Digital Productions, Cranston-Csuri, Pacific Data Images and Digital Effects supplied them: gleaming chrome-and-neon insignia zooming in and out of infinity; streaks of light exploding across starry skies; shining objects moving through complicated, three-dimensional patterns.

Bob Abel of Abel Image Research (originally Robert Abel and Associates) was one of the first to use the new technology, beginning with a series of futuristic, color-streaked logos for ABC-TV in 1971. Two years later, he and his friends Con Pederson and Tom Holland built the first digitally controlled camera stand out of $600 worth of surplus electronics equipment. The computerized camera stand allowed the artists to "paint with light"—to produce glowing, brilliantly colored images on film. They began to explore the possibilities of using a computer to create the imagery.

Abel achieved widespread prominence in 1974 with his multimedia 7-Up commercial, "Bubbles," an extravaganza of show girls, soda bottles and colored lights. Three years later, he produced a spot for Levi's, in which an actor appears to be walking the company's familiar logo on a leash.

The high cost of computer animation restricted its use to commercials and logos. By the mid-1980s, a 30-second commercial in full, drawn animation ran between $30,000 and $40,000. An advertiser might pay $100,000 to $150,000—or more—for 30 seconds of top-quality computer animation. A spot combining computer graphics with live action and/or drawn animation could run from $250,000 to $500,000 (and up) for 30 seconds. The prices remained high despite advances in both hardware and software. As the tools grew more sophisticated, artists strove to produce more complicated images.

"Whatever you're doing this week is the state of the art," says Abel. "That's how fast the medium is changing—it's constantly being redefined."

The growing use of computer-generated visuals helped to keep commercials one of the most vital areas of animation during the 1980s. As the American economy began to rebound

"You never liked my mother!" A man confronts his stomach, in R. O. Blechman's classic Alka-Seltzer commercial.

from the recession of the late 1970s, advertisers grew a little less conservative and began to allow the artists more creative freedom.

But for all their talent, commercial animators remained trapped in a strange demimonde. Their films were seen on television by vast audiences, but commercials don't include credits, and their names remained virtually unknown. "Promotional films" often proved to be the most exciting category at animation festivals, but commercials weren't perceived as being on the same aesthetic plane as personal films or features.

Television production saved the American animation industry during the late 1950s and early 1960s. Without the Saturday-morning factories, the medium might have ceased to exist in the United States outside of the Disney studio and a few small enclaves—commercial houses, schools, independent producers. But the cost was enormous. Animation had always been a popular art form that entertained audiences of all ages. It was quickly reduced to a cheap medium, suitable only for mindless kidvid. The salvation of animation by television recalls the Vietnam era phrase: "It became necessary to destroy the village in order to save it."

Computer-generated robots dance in a Hawaiian Punch commercial by Abel Image Research. This lavish spot was never televised.

During the late 1980s and early 1990s, the television cartoon industry underwent a series of shifts, some for the better, some for the worse. Many of these shifts reflected changes in the television industry, corporate finance or government regulation.

The Filmation studio, one of the main Saturday morning houses, fell victim to the corporate wheeling and dealing that typified the 1980s. On February 3, 1989, Westinghouse Electric's Group W Productions abruptly closed the studio and fired almost all of its 229 employees—one day before a federal law went into effect that would have required giving the workers a sixty-day written notice. Rumors about a possible sale had circulated for months, but the closing occurred as furloughed artists were being rehired for two new series, "Bugzburg" and "Bravo." Producer Tom Tataranowicz recalled, "The announcement just dropped out of the blue that Friday morning: 'Put down your pencils and get out.'"

The $30 million deal was negotiated by the London financier Michael W. Stevens for a European investor group backed by L'Oreal, the French cosmetics conglomerate. The purchasers wanted the studio's library of fifty television series and five features, which could be dubbed and sold to European television outlets.

Filmation had faced mounting financial problems for three years, due to the fragmentation of the syndication market, a downturn in the toy industry that eliminated underwriting product-based programs, increased competition and rising costs. Their position was exacerbated by the failure of the theatrical feature "Pinocchio and the Emperor of the Night" (1987). The $10 million film earned only $2.7 million at the box office.

Two years later, in October 1991, Ted Turner's TBS bought "the program library and production commitments" of Hanna-Barbera for a reported $320 million, outbidding MCA

"Bobby's World:" The title character finds himself amid the ruins of Tokyo as a monstrous version of his Aunt Ruth ravages the city. Comedian Howie Mandell, who created the characters, provided the voices of Bobby and his patient father.

and Hallmark Cards. The hundreds of hours of Hanna-Barbera television shows and features, added to the Warner Brothers and MGM theatrical shorts he had acquired with the 1986 purchase of the MGM/UA film library, gave Turner the necessary material for the Cartoon Channel he launched in 1993.

Unlike Filmation, Hanna-Barbera continued production, although the studio no longer dominated the medium, as it had a decade earlier. A new group of studios had come to fore during the 1980s—DIC, Nelvana, Klasky-Csupo, Film Roman, Universal—that helped to supply the burgeoning market for animated programming.

Some cable networks attempted to establish an identity with off-beat shows—e.g. "Rugrats" and "Ren and Stimpy" on Nickelodeon. Rock videos and MTV's "Liquid Television" pushed the envelope even further, with programs that included "Stick Figure Theatre" and Peter Chung's Japanese-influenced "Aeon Flux." These projects attracted artists who ordinarily wouldn't have worked in television and appealed to a young, hip audience, but they accounted for only a small percentage of television production. The tight schedules, low budgets and heavy restrictions on network programming seemed to stifle originality, and much of the network and syndication animation from the new studios proved as undistinguished as that of their predecessors.

The Saturday morning industry was further shaken in 1991 by NBC's decision to replace cartoons with live action programming, two hours of which would be aimed at children in the nine-to-sixteen age range. The effect of the pullout was mitigated by an expansion of the Fox Children's Network. Fox had entered the kidvid market with an imaginative slate of shows in 1990, and passed NBC in the ratings within a year.

These shifts made relatively little difference in the nature of Saturday morning animation; many of the "new" programs each season seemed to be little more than retreads of earlier shows.

There were bright spots. Comedian Howie Mandel provided the voice for a suburban father and his four-year-old son on "Bobby's World" (Fox, 1990). Much of the action in this charming fantasy—which owed a good part of its inspiration to Bill Watterson's "Calvin and Hobbes"—took place in Bobby's overly fertile imagination. When his father announced the impending visit of Aunt Ruth, Bobby saw himself in a 1950s Japanese monster movie, as a terrible, cheek-pinching Aunt terrorized a city. In "Taz-mania" (Fox, 1991), the ravening beast of the Warner cartoons was transformed into a none-too-bright adolescent. His underplayed father ("go off and play in the montage sequence, son") tended to steal the show.

Ralph Bakshi managed to breathe some life into the old Terrytoons character in "Mighty Mouse" (ABC, 1988), but the show became embroiled in controversy when the Reverend Donald Wildmon of the Mississippi-based American Family Association claimed that the title character sniffed cocaine in one episode. Bakshi insisted that Mighty Mouse had merely smelled some dried flowers and threatened to "do a cartoon about the right wing."

The most lavish series of the era was "The Little Mermaid" (CBS, 1992), an adaptation of the 1989 hit feature. The program attracted considerable attention because it was a rare example of a show centered on a female character—and the first time a Disney feature had been turned into a TV show. "I don't think there's been a tradition of *not* adapting the features to television," said Disney television animation president Gary Krisel. "The opportunity didn't present itself before now because of limits of the animation and other factors."

Although opulent by television standards, with several of the original vocal cast members repeating their roles, no one would have mistaken the program for the feature. Noting that the television programs were "a very touchy issue at the studio," feature animators complained privately that "the TV people should come up with new ideas that work within the limits of television animation."

The era also had its share of duds. "The Karate Kid" (NBC, 1989) and "Super Dave" (Fox, 1992) featured Asians who talked in fortune cookie phrases. Protests over Super Dave's sidekick, Fuji, led to the redesign of the character. "Wild West C.O.W.-Boys of Moo Mesa" (ABC, 1992) starred a posse of grotesque creatures who were half human and half steer.

"The California Raisins" (CBS, 1989) turned the three-dimensional figures from Will Vinton's commercials into drawn characters. To avoid making the animators draw all their wrinkles, the Raisins were redesigned with smoother bodies, which made them look more like the California Eggplants. The plots, involving the Raisins' career as a musical group, recalled the old "Alvin" show.

At the same time, new programming revived the moribund syndication market. The runaway success of Disney's "DuckTales" (1987) led the studio to expand its presence in the weekday afternoon time slot in 1989 by adding "Chip 'n Dale Rescue Rangers" and moving "The Gummi Bears" from Saturday morning to weekday afternoons to form a two-hour bloc, "The Disney Afternoon." "Tail Spin" (1990), "Darkwing Duck" (1990), "Goof Troop" (1992) and "Bonkers!" (1993) followed.

Some observers noted that Darkwing Duck bore a striking resemblance to Daffy Duck in Chuck Jones's "The Scarlet Pumpernickel"; that Bonkers D. Bobcat was essentially a clone of Roger Rabbit; that the television versions of Goofy in "Goof Troop" and Baloo and King Louie in "Tail Spin" were decidedly inferior to their theatrical predecessors. But the "Disney Afternoon" proved enormously popular with kids, and characters from the shows appeared on merchandise and at the Disney parks. In January 1994 the studio announced plans for three additional programs: "Disney's Aladdin,"

The laid-back, Ozzie Nelson-esque father watches as the kids raise typical havoc in a scene from "Taz-Mania."

based on the record-breaking feature (with Scott Weinger and Linda Larkin repeating their roles as Aladdin and Jasmine, and with Dan Castellaneta as the Genie), slated for September 1994, to be followed by "Gargoyles" in December 1994, and "The Shnookums Meat Funny Cartoon Show" in January 1995.

The success of the Disney series led to an increase in original weekday afternoon programming. Steven Spielberg and Warner Brothers joined forces for "Tiny Toon Adventures" (1990), starring what were essentially juvenile versions of the classic Warner characters: Buster and Babs Bunny, Hamton, Plucky Duck, Elmyra, Montana Max and Dizzy Devil. The show scored a big hit, and was followed in 1993 by "Steven Spielberg Presents Animaniacs." Two Warner Brothers of some indeterminate species, Yakko and Wakko, and their Warner Sister, Dot, who escaped from the studio animation department in 1930, returned sixty-odd years later to bedevil modern life.

Neither program had much in common with the classic Warner shorts, but children delighted in the mixture of frenetic action and showbiz insider jokes. ("We have pay-for-play contracts" the Animaniacs sang in their theme song.) Warner scored another hit with an animated version of "Batman" (1992), although the dark, Art Deco-influenced backgrounds tended to eclipse the stiff animation and pedestrian storytelling. "Batman" looked better in stills than it did on the screen.

"Shelley Duvall's Bedtime Stories" (Showtime, 1992) featured celebrities reading the narration to animated adaptations of contemporary children's books. Affirming and instructive without sinking into preachiness, "Stories" provided children and parents with a welcome respite from formula adventures and product-driven shows.

The growth of the cable/syndication market and the arrival of the Fox network caused an unprecedented demand for animation. For the first time in many years, producers found themselves bidding against each other for the services of a small pool of professional artists. "The animation business is busier now than I can remember," said Phil Roman, president of the Film Roman Studio, in late 1993, "and I've been in it over thirty-eight years."

But the growth of these markets also meant that more broadcasters were fighting for a limited pool of advertising revenue while production costs were rising. Part of this rise was due to the falling value of the U.S. dollar; between 1986 and 1988, the dollar lost 40 percent of its value against the Japanese yen. Although Japanese animators were regarded as the most highly skilled of the overseas artists, it had become too expensive to make television cartoons in Japan by the end of the decade. Production was shifted to studios in Taiwan, Korea, Thailand, Malaysia, the Philippines and Eastern Europe.

The most popular animated program of the era was not a kidvid show, but Fox's phenomenal success, "The Simpsons." It was the first prime time cartoon series in more than fifteen years, and the first animated hit since the heyday of "The Flintstones."

The bug-eyed family with the matching overbites was developed for vignettes on "The Tracey Ullman Show" in 1987 by James L. Brooks, Matt Groening and Sam Simon from an idea of Groening's. These sixty- to ninety-second interludes were animated almost single-handedly by David Silverman and Wes Archer. As development on the series progressed, the staff was expanded and much of the animation sent to Korea. A half-hour Christmas special in 1989 launched "The Simpsons" on Fox, and the regular Sunday evening show premiered in January 1990.

"Fox originally wanted a single special, but Jim Brooks and I said, 'No, give us a series or forget it,'" said Groening. "I knew it would take a little while—not a long time, but a little while—for an audience to catch on to the program."

A bittersweet, often outrageous look at contemporary family life, "The Simpsons" boasted some of the most sophisticated writing for animation since "Rocky and Bullwinkle." Many of the scripts parodied feature films: Maggie escaped from a repressive day-care center to the theme from "The Great Escape"; a crooked developer's pitch to build a monorail in Springfield turned a town meeting into a spoof of the "Trouble" number from "The Music Man." "Whatever makes the writing staff laugh, we put in the show," Simon explained. "That's why it's very smart and very vulgar."

A talented vocal cast brought the irreverent lines to life, with Dan Castellaneta as the loutish Homer; Julie Kavner as the well-intentioned Marge; Yeardley Smith as the all-too-precocious Lisa and Nancy Cartwright as Bart, the delinquent-in-training. Their performances were supplemented by guest voices, including Elizabeth Taylor, Michelle Pfeiffer, Ringo Starr, George Harrison, Aerosmith and the Red Hot Chili Peppers.

Although the program relied heavily on verbal humor, animating the lumpy cast posed special challenges: "Matt's characters don't follow the normal construction of the Disney or Warner characters, which are based on circles and ovals," said Silverman, who became a producer/director on the series. "Wes and I try to get the animators to think of them as puppets with cylindrical bodies, tubular limbs and wedge-shaped feet. It's harder to draw a character that's designed in a two-dimensional style than one that's intended for animation from the outset." With typical irreverence, Groening described the animation process as "a roomful of people who draw better than I do trying to draw like I do."

The program garnered rave reviews. In the *Los Angeles Times*, Howard Rosenberg wrote, " 'The Simpsons' is a guer-

Homer cheers caricatures of the Ramones. Series creator Matt Groening describes "The Simpsons" as "A family whose members love each other and drive each other crazy—which we can all identify with."

rilla attack on mainstream TV, meshing smart writing and directing with unique voices and animation to transform a conventional sitcom formula into a commentary on American values. Beyond all that, however, it's just flat-out funny." In August, Fox shifted the series to Thursday nights, where it challenged—and ultimately defeated—ratings champion Bill Cosby.

A flood of "Simpsons" merchandise, including dolls, T-shirts, posters, balls, air fresheners and cups earned an estimated $750 million in 1990, which put them just behind the Teen-Age Mutant Ninja Turtles and New Kids on the Block. The top-selling Bart T-shirt provoked a brouhaha in the spring of 1990, when some educators complained that the motto "Underachiever and proud of it" was inappropriate for schoolwear.

"The Simpsons" became so popular that during the 1992 presidential election, George Bush declared in a campaign speech, "The nation needs to be closer to the Waltons than the Simpsons." The creators replied by beginning one show with the Simpsons watching Bush's speech on TV and Bart remarking, "Hey, we're just like the Waltons. We're praying for the end of the Depression, too."

"The Simpsons" proved that a good animated program could compete successfully in prime time. It received Emmies for Outstanding Animated Program for 1989–90 and 1990–91, although Groening, Simon and Brooks argued it should be allowed to compete against live-action sitcoms in the Outstanding Comedy category. The cast members won an Emmy for Outstanding Voice Over Performance for 1991–92, and Castellaneta was singled out for his work for 1992–93. The show received numerous other citations, including the Television Critics' Award for Outstanding Achievement in Comedy 1989–90, a Stevie (British Satellite Television Award) for Most Popular Cartoon/Animated Series in 1993 and the People's Choice Award for Favorite Television Program 1990–91.

Spurred by the success of "The Simpsons," two of the Big Three networks introduced prime time cartoon shows in 1992. Neither of them matched its take-no-prisoners irreverence, and both of them flopped. "Capitol Critters" (ABC), a collaboration between Hanna-Barbera and "Hill Street Blues" creator Steven Bochco, involved the mice and bugs who supposedly inhabited the walls of the White House; "Fish Police" (CBS) was a spoof of film noir detective stories set underwater. Both shows opened to generally good reviews and low ratings.

But the biggest disappointment was the long-awaited and often-delayed "Family Dog" (CBS, 1993), which failed to recapture the anarchic glee of the 1987 "Amazing Stories" episode. In the *Los Angeles Times*, Howard Rosenberg asked "How does something as putrid as 'Family Dog' get made? and

after it is made—profits be damned—how does it get on the air?" In the *Washington Post*, Tom Shales observed, "Bart Simpson's anti-social shenanigans have a wry edge and a witty context; Homer Simpson's foibles and failings are recognizably human. But on 'Family Dog,' both family and dog are just crude and off-putting." Lambasted by critics and ignored by viewers, "Dog" quickly sank into oblivion.

In January 1994, "The Critic," created by Al Jean and Mike Reiss, two former executive producers on "The Simpsons," debuted on ABC. The title character was Jay Sherman, a bald, paunchy television film reviewer in the Siskel–Ebert mold. The first episode contained some nicely snide send-ups of Hollywood, including Arnold Schwarzenegger as an undercover cop posing as a Hasidic rabbi ("Hava Nagila, baby!") and a clever spoof of the ballroom scene from "Beauty and the Beast." But the rest of the show lacked the imagination of the parody sequences, and Sherman was a bit too much like Homer Simpson, down to the animation of his finger waves. Given the potential targets the excesses of contemporary Hollywood offered, "The Critic" seemed decidedly tame and sanitized.

Nickelodeon's outré "Ren and Stimpy" attracted more viewers, more critical attention and, ultimately, more controversy than any of the network series. The adventures of a scrawny, asthmatic-sounding Chihuahua (Ren) and a fat, doltish cat (Stimpy), the show featured distorted takes and gross jokes involving hairballs, mucous, flatulence, etc. "Of course we want to disgust people, but that's not all we do," said series creator John Kricfalusi. "We go for both the highest common denominator and the lowest. What we avoid is the middle."

The appeal to both ends of the taste spectrum proved successful: "Ren and Stimpy" quickly became the object of both a cult following and a merchandising campaign.

A contretemps arose in September 1992, when Nickelodeon announced it was firing Kricfalusi. The producer-director complained about the demands of working with the cable network and expressed a desire to stretch the boundaries of television cartoons. Representatives for Nickelodeon said the episodes they had contracted were both overdue and over budget (the series cost a relatively lavish $400,000 per episode, while Saturday morning shows averaged about $250,000 per episode).

Nickelodeon also complained that some of the shows were too offensive to air. The network shelved two programs involving a new character named George Liquor and changed the name of the season premiere episode from "Stimpy's First Fart" to "Son of Stimpy." Kricfalusi's former partner, Bob Camp, took over the series for Nickelodeon.

"Ren and Stimpy" were soon replaced at the center of controversy by an animated duo who suggested the evolutionary process had somehow slipped into reverse. In *Rolling Stone*,

Charles M. Young described them as "two thunderously stupid and excruciatingly ugly pubescent males who live somewhere in the Southwest, do rotten stuff all the time. They are cruel to animals. They vandalize their neighbors. They torture their teachers. Their libidos rage unchecked, except by the uniform unwillingness of the female sex to associate with them. And they are the biggest phenomenon on MTV since the heyday of Michael Jackson."

Beavis and Butt-Head made their debut in "Frog Baseball," a short by Mike Judge, a self-taught animator who also provided the characters' voices and nasal laughs. A week after the short appeared in a festival of "Sick and Twisted Animation" in 1992, Colossal Pictures bought the short for MTV's "Liquid Television." The series went into full production in November of that year.

"Ren and Stimpy" was often tasteless and vulgar, but the designs and movements were rooted in traditional cartoon styles. "Beavis and Butt-Head" looked like doodles from the notebook of an obnoxious junior high school student. The immediate popularity of the program, despite (or because of) its Know-Nothing stance, willful cruelty and unremitting ugliness horrified watchdog groups, especially when the characters were seen as representatives of a generation of alienated American teenagers. In a *Newsweek* cover story, John Leland wrote, "But they are not just any losers, they are specifically *our* losers, totems of an age of decline and nonachievement."

The controversy over "Beavis and Butt-Head" made headlines in October 1993, when the program was blamed for inspiring a five-year-old Ohio boy to set fire to his bed; the resulting blaze killed his two-year-old sister. Critics of the show also cited it as the cause of other fires and incidents of cruelty to animals. MTV representatives denied any link between the program and the behavior, but the network shifted "Beavis and Butt-Head" from 7 P.M. to 10:30 P.M. and deleted references

"A Wish for Wings That Work" (1991) brought the characters from Berke Breathed's Pulitzer Prize-winning comic strip "Bloom County" to the screen. Michael Bell was the voice of Opus, the neurotic penguin; John Byner provided Bill the Cat's snorts, grunts and belches.

to fire, which they characterized as a decision "to bend over backwards as responsible programmers."

The latest entry in the outrageousness sweepstakes, Klasky-Csupo's "Duckman," depicting a "politically uncorrect" avian detective, debuted in March 1994 on the USA network.

The furor over "Beavis and Butt-Head" arose as increasing numbers of Americans were expressing concern over the violent content of television in general, and of children's programming in particular. U.S. Attorney General Janet Reno and Senator Paul Simon led a push for Congressional action to reduce TV violence. A spokesman for Simon cited the "Beavis and Butt-Head" controversy as "a timely example" of the links the senator and others saw between television mayhem and violent actions. Advice columnist Ann Landers declared "It (TV violence) had to get worse before it got better, and that's what has happened. The antics of Beavis and Butt-head (sic) turned the tide."

The increasingly acrimonious debate over media violence only exacerbated the confusion within the animation industry over the enforcement of the Children's Television Act. Passed by Congress in October 1990, the act was designed to restore some of the restrictions that were eliminated in the 1984 deregulation of the broadcast industry. It limited the number of commercial minutes during children's shows to 10.5 per hour on weekends and 12 per hour on weekdays; ordered the FCC to conclude an inquiry into the "inherent commercialism" of toy-based programs and required stations to air programs that serve "the educational and informational needs of children."

Although George Bush "strongly opposed" the advertising limits as a possible violation of the First Amendment rights of broadcasters, he allowed the act to become law without signing it. The Clinton administration indicated it supported the goals of act, and that the FCC would scrutinize children's programming when stations applied for license renewals.

The restrictions on commercial time received relatively little attention within the cartoon industry. The mandated FCC investigation into toy-based programming continued a debate that had been going on since 1982, when the first "Strawberry Shortcake" special unleashed a flood of shows built around toys and license product characters.

The vagueness of the "educational and informational needs" provision recalled the requirement for stations to serve "the public interest, convenience and necessity" in the Communications Act of 1934, which established licensing procedures. Either clause could obviously be interpreted freely when FCC officials evaluated a renewal application.

But it was equally obvious that some stations had blatantly dodged the intent of the act. Applicants had claimed "The Jetsons" "instructs children about life in the year 2000," and the battles "against an evil that has the capabilities of mass destruction of society" on "GI Joe" demonstrated "social consciousness and responsibility."

"There haven't been many educational programs because they haven't been competitive," commented DIC president Andy Heyward. "If you can't compete with 'Batman,' you'll be shunted into a bad time slot. The stations will say they've fulfilled the requirement but no one will be watching."

The "educational needs" clause led to a flurry of "FCC-friendly" production. The mildly didactic "Cro" debuted on Fox in 1992; DIC based "Where On Earth Is Carmen San Diego?" (Fox, 1994) on the popular educational computer game and live action show. But no one knew exactly what stations would have to air in order to fulfill the educational mandate.

"I think it's too early to tell where this is going to go," said Jeff Segal, president of the Universal Cartoon Studio. "Nobody has defined the parameters of what exactly we're trying to do, other than to hurl around catch-phrases and to make often self-serving speeches. There's a lot of pontificating and theorizing going on by people who are detached from the mechanism of producing entertainment and/or programming it and/or evaluating it from the point of view of the audience."

The issue of violence and its depiction in children's programming remained at the heart of the controversy. Animation professionals objected to having their work singled out. Network cartoons, they noted, had been minutely regulated by network standards and practices offices for years, although children could easily find more extreme violence in news programs, "reality" shows and movies.

"In a special we did with Linda Ellerbee, 'Are You What You Watch?,' the kids told us that they know the difference between real violence and television violence," adds Herb Scannell, senior vice president for programming at Nickelodeon. "Specifically, they talked about cartoon violence; they know that when the Road Runner blows up the Coyote, it's make-believe. What came out of the discussions about real violence versus fiction was the blurring of the line on shows like 'Cops' that bring home real violence under the guise of entertainment."

The people involved in the debate—inside and outside of the industry—had already staked out positions and showed little inclination to modify them. Segal summed up opinion within the animation industry when he stated: "We are not a babysitter, we are an entertainment medium: we make no pretense about that. We're artists and production people, doing the best we can. Nobody wants to do something that's going to induce violence or behavior that's potentially damaging or self-destructive. But if everything that's perceived to be violence were suddenly removed from television, I doubt that anything in society would change. Parents have a responsibility to monitor the viewing habits of their children: I don't think that responsibility should rest with the programmers. If parents object to something their children are watching, they should turn it off."

THE CAPTAINS AND THE KINGS DEPART, 1960–1994

What's the greatest piece of animation of all time? It hasn't been done yet. Everything we've done up till now hasn't even begun to scratch the surface of what animation can do. —ART BABBITT

The years between 1960 and 1994 were a confused and confusing time in American animation when both the imminent demise and an incipient renaissance of the art were announced with dismaying frequency.

The closing of the Hollywood studios, the elimination of short films from movie theaters and the retirement or death of prominent animation figures suggested that the future of the medium was in jeopardy. Conversely, new outlets for animated films (including video games, cable television and video cassettes), the advent of computer-generated imagery and the emergence of a new generation of talented artists seemed to portend an era of renewed creativity.

Theatrical shorts had been the mainstay of the animation industry since the silent era. Their loss was devastating and none of the new outlets replaced them. Some of the young animators proved to be at least as talented as their predecessors, but the limited market for their abilities forced many to work on kidvid programs, find jobs in other countries or abandon animation for advertising, illustration, cartooning or live-action filmmaking.

America lost the aesthetic leadership of the medium—first to Zagreb Film in Yugoslavia, then to the National Film Board of Canada—just as an increasing number of people were finally beginning to recognize it as an art form. The nostalgia craze of the late 1960s and 1970s helped to stimulate this appreciation. As people studied films and collected bric-a-brac from the 1930s, they rediscovered the ingenuous charms of the early Disney and Fleischer shorts. Many underground comix artists adapted the bizarre, goggle-eyed look of old print and screen cartoons for their funky new creations.

Three films helped spur a growing awareness of the potential of animation: "Yellow Submarine" (Great Britain, 1968), "Fantasia" and "Fritz the Cat" (1972). The hip young crowd that made all three features hits was very different from the traditional family audience usually associated with the full-length Disney cartoons.

During the 1960s, the graphic revolution John Hubley and the UPA artists had tried to promote in American animation ground to a halt. All the characters on Saturday-morning TV looked as if they had been cookie-cut from the same, flat mold; the Disney artists seemed content to use minor variations on familiar rounded forms. This drab background made Heinz Edelmann's flamboyant designs for "Yellow Submarine" seem even more original and visually imaginative.

Edelmann and director George Dunning mixed styles and media to create an eclectic, brightly colored mishmash: some scenes included drawn animation, cutouts, rotoscoping, still photographs and processed live action. The designs reflected a blithe disregard for reality––some of the Blue Meanies have seven fingers on one hand and six on the other. The characters' movements were as strange as their anatomy: no attempt was made to reproduce the accurately observed motions of Disney animation.

The minimal plot of "Yellow Submarine" did little more than link the elaborate production numbers illustrating various Beatles songs, which suggest proto-typical rock videos. In this rather simple-minded morality tale, the Blue Meanies and their minions—Apple Bonkers, Snapping Turtle Turks, the Dreadful Flying Glove et al.—attack the peaceful inhabitants of Pepperland. Young/Old Fred goes for help in a yellow submarine. He reaches Liverpool, meets the Beatles and takes them back to Pepperland, where they defeat the Blue Meanies with music.

"Yellow Submarine" is long (88 minutes) and uneven. Parts of it, like the sequences set to "Eleanor Rigby," "Nowhere Man" and "Lucy in the Sky with Diamonds," are brilliant and remain unmatched for sheer visual imagination. As the film ages, the flimsiness of the story becomes increasingly evident, but plot has rarely been the long suit of movie musicals.

"Yellow Submarine" exposed American audiences to a genuinely new vision of what animation could be, and it was one of the big hits of the 1968–69 holiday season. Its main rival as an animated "head trip" film was Disney's 1940 classic "Fantasia," and the psychedelic poster for its 1969 re-release emphasized this image. Young viewers responded to Disney's great audiovisual experiment much more enthusiastically than audiences had during its initial release thirty years earlier. Walt Disney's faith in "Fantasia" was finally vindicated, but for reasons he might not have approved.

"Yellow Submarine" revealed the untapped visual potential of animation. "Fritz the Cat" showed American audiences that the medium could be used to tell contemporary stories with more adult content than mindless kidvid shows and the traditional fairy tales.

The underground comix had already had a considerable impact on graphic arts in America when producer Steve Krantz and writer-director Ralph Bakshi adapted three of Robert Crumb's popular stories to the screen. In both versions, Fritz was a mordant caricature of a superficial college student who paid lip service to the counterculture but whose only real interest was getting laid.

"Yellow Submarine": above, the logo from the ground-breaking animated feature; below, a cel of the Beatles disguised as the musicians in the original Sgt. Pepper's Lonely Hearts Club Band.

Big Bertha introduces Fritz to the pleasures of
marijuana, in Ralph Bakshi's "Fritz the Cat" (1972).

In the film, Fritz leaves NYU for Harlem, to try to become
"cool" like the blacks he admires—caricatured as crows.
Excited by marijuana and a sexual encounter with Big Bertha,
an enormous crow/black woman, he makes a rabble-rousing
speech that touches off a small riot. He flees New York for San
Francisco, where he gets involved with a Weatherman-like
gang of radicals who attempt to blow up a power station. The
explosion lands Fritz in the hospital, where he continues his
efforts to seduce anything and everything in a skirt.

"Fritz the Cat" is a gritty, sometimes funny, often angry work
that surprised and shocked viewers. American audiences,
accustomed to innocent flirtations and slapstick comedy in
cartoons, weren't prepared for its animated sex, bloody violence and outrageous racial imagery. (Despite its scandalous
reputation, "Fritz" was not the first "adult" cartoon made in
America, but earlier efforts, like the 1928 short "Buried Treasure"—usually referred to as "Everready Hardon"—were little more than animated dirty jokes.)

One person who was not pleased by the film was Robert
Crumb. He drew a final Fritz story, and turned the character
into a decadent Hollywood star exploited by "Ralphy" and
"Stevie"—caricatures of Bakshi and Krantz. A disgusted
former girlfriend murders Fritz with an ice pick: "another
casualty of the 'Sixties . . ."

"If Robert had come on staff and done the film, I think he
would have liked it better," says Bakshi. "But he wasn't asked
to, nor would he have. It's very hard to please the writer of a
particular book: I don't know that many directors please
writers a hundred percent. His criticism was very severe at the
time, but I'm not ashamed about it. I was out to make personal
films, and I wasn't doing Robert Crumb's 'Fritz the Cat' at that
point. I was doing Ralph Bakshi's 'Fritz the Cat.' "

Whether they loved or hated it, "Fritz" was a film people
talked about—and went to see. It earned more than $25
million on its initial release, against production costs of only
$850,000 (a shoestring budget, even in 1972).

Unfortunately, the success of "Yellow Submarine" and
"Fritz the Cat" came too late to save the remaining
Hollywood cartoon studios. During the late 1960s, they
stopped production, and most of the artists either retired or
went to work for the Saturday-morning houses.

After Paul Terry sold Terrytoons to CBS in 1955, Gene Deitch became creative director of the studio and initiated several new cartoon series that borrowed heavily from the work of UPA. After three years of graphically sophisticated but unfunny characters, Deitch was fired by Terrytoons' business manager and executive producer, Bill Weiss.

Weiss promptly dropped all Deitch's characters and revived the old Terry standbys, Mighty Mouse and Heckle and Jeckle. The budgets on these new shorts were so minimal and the animation so limited that they made the Terrytoons of the early 1950s look lavish.

Weiss also encouraged the writers and directors to create new characters, ostensibly for theatrical shorts, but with an eye to television production. Bob Kuwahara's Japanese mouse, Hashimoto (1959), Eli Bauer's Colonial hero, Hector Heathcote (1960), and Larz Bourne's Southern sheriff, Deputy Dawg (1960), all proved more successful on TV than in theaters.

"In New York, every theatrical short was really a pilot for television," explains Bakshi. "That was disastrous. It was limited animation, the characters were for kids on Saturday mornings—and we all know the Bugs Bunnys were for adults and kids. The producers were using the theatrical marketplace to make goddamned pilots with all the restrictions that television imposed."

One of the last important animators to work his way up through the old studio system, Bakshi started at Terrytoons as a cel polisher in 1956. He switched to animation and became one of the studio's top directors during the early 1960s. Even within the limited Terry formula, his emphasis on strong poses gave his work an undeniable energy.

In 1966, Bakshi was appointed creative director. He continued to direct many of the studio's theatrical shorts, most of them featuring James Hound, a comic canine spy in the 007 mold. His television show, "The Mighty Heroes," spoofed popular cartoon superheroes with Strongman, Ropeman, Cuckooman, Tornadoman and Diaperman. Bakshi wanted to capture the look of the artwork he admired in *Mad* magazine, but the budget precluded elaborate production values.

Bakshi left Terrytoons for Paramount/Famous in 1967, and the Terry shorts lost what little punch they had had. Weiss finally closed the New Rochelle studio in 1968, but CBS continues to distribute Terrytoons, to both television and the international theatrical market. Except for the early days of the silents, the studio never led the art or the industry, but their films ultimately proved far more profitable than many better cartoons.

After a spate of television production during the early 1960s, Famous shifted its primary focus back to theatrical shorts, grinding out repetitive and uninspired cartoons with Swifty and Shorty (a fast-talking con man and his sidekick) and various one-shots.

In 1964, Seymour Kneitel, the last survivor of the management team that had replaced Max Fleischer, died, and Howard Post, a former in-betweener and story man, became head of the studio. Post had to produce cartoons on budgets that were low even by television standards: $12,000 to $17,000 per film. The animation was so limited (and so much of it was reused) that some of the artists cranked out close to 100 feet per week, or twice what the Terry animators did. In addition to continuing the Swifty and Shorty series, Post introduced Honey Halfwitch, a determinedly cute but distinctly unfunny sorceress's apprentice, in 1965.

Post did not get on well with the Paramount executives, and after about a year he was replaced by Shamus Culhane. Dismissing the recent Famous cartoons as "a piss-poor pile of crap," Culhane tried to obtain backing from Paramount to upgrade the studio's theatrical shorts and expand into commercials, television specials and industrial films.

He directed the studio's best cartoon in at least a decade, "My Daddy, the Astronaut" (1967), in which an airman takes his son to an amusement park and promptly gets sick on the wilder rides. Told in a child's voice, with artwork based on children's drawings, the short owes a great deal to John and Faith Hubley's "Moonbird" (1959) and "The Windy Day" (1967), but it represented a distinct improvement over the Honey Halfwitch series. "My Daddy, the Astronaut" was accepted by the prestigious animation festival at Annecy, France—a first for a Paramount/Famous cartoon.

In addition to the theatrical shorts, Culhane agreed to make thirty-nine 5-minute segments of "The Mighty Thor" for producer Steve Krantz's syndicated "Marvel Superheroes" program. He added a number of new young artists to the staff, but their inexperience led to major errors that cost the studio $10,000, virtually eliminating any profit on the series.

In 1967, the Gulf + Western conglomerate bought Paramount. After checking the financial records of the animation studio, their auditors decided to end production. Culhane resigned and was replaced by Ralph Bakshi, who soon discovered he had been hired to close the studio in three months. (Famous studio manager Burt Hanft later introduced Bakshi to Krantz, who provided the backing for "Fritz the Cat" and "Heavy Traffic.") Even within the animation community, the demise of the Paramount/Famous studio generated little excitement or regret.

The gradual breakup of the brilliant crew of the postwar era led to a decline in the quality of the Warner Brothers cartoons during the 1960s. Music director Carl Stalling retired in 1958, and was replaced by his arranger, Milt Franklyn. Franklyn died four years later, and was succeeded by William Lava, who lacked the facile touch of his predecessors—and the old Warners orchestra. Arthur Q. Bryant, the voice of Elmer Fudd, died in 1959, and not even Mel Blanc could replace him. A more serious loss was the defection of writers Mike Maltese and Warren Foster, who left the studio to write television cartoons for Hanna-Barbera.

Initially, the decline was gradual. Chuck Jones made some of the best Road Runner–Coyote shorts during the early 1960s, including "Lickety Splat" (1961) and "To Beep or Not to Beep" (1963). "Rabbit's Feat" (1960) features his zaniest version of Bugs—who upsets Wile E. Coyote with non sequiturs like "Daddy! You're home from Peru—and we thought you'd been

The Pink Panther—Friz Freleng's suave, silent comic, originally created for the title sequence of a Blake Edwards comedy.

run over by an elevator!" Jones also continued his graphic experiments in unusual films like "High Note" (1960), "I Was a Teen-Age Thumb" (1962) and "Now Here This" (1962). He left the studio in 1963.

Many of Friz Freleng's later cartoons focused on Sylvester and Speedy Gonzalez—the poor, dim-witted *Gato* never quit trying to capture "the Fastest Mouse in All Mexico." Freleng handcuffed Sylvester to a dog from the city pound in "D'Fightin' Ones" (1961), a very funny satire of "The Defiant Ones." He also continued to pit the hapless cat against Tweety. A caricature of Alfred Hitchcock introduces them (and gets beaned with a brick) in "The Last Hungry Cat" (1961), a mystery spoof.

Warners closed their animation unit in 1964 and rented the space to the newly established DePatie-Freleng studio—a partnership between producer Dave DePatie (whose father was a vice president at Warner Brothers) and veteran director Friz Freleng.

"Mr. Warner leased it to us for a very small amount of money, because he wanted to give us a start," says Freleng. "I think we rented the whole facility, the building and the projection machines, desks and paper, everything we needed, for five hundred dollars a month."

One of DePatie-Freleng's first projects was the title sequence for Blake Edwards's "The Pink Panther" (1964), which led to a successful series of theatrical shorts featuring the suave, silent feline. As United Artists released the Pink Panther shorts, Jack Warner objected to their production on the Warners lot. DePatie-Freleng moved to new offices in the San Fernando Valley.

Warner Brothers decided to reactivate their cartoon series later in 1964, but to farm out the production. Between 1964 and 1967, DePatie-Freleng made thirty-eight cartoons with some of the old characters, which Warners released under their imprimatur.

These films lack the humor of the real Warners cartoons. The limited animation reveals how cheaply they were made, and the stories miscast many of the characters. Daffy Duck became the central character of the series, as a foil for Speedy Gonzalez—alone ("Assault and Peppered," 1965; "Snow Excuse," 1966) or in dubious alliance with Sylvester ("It's So Nice to Have a Mouse Around the House," 1965).

In 1967, Warners stopped releasing the DePatie-Freleng shorts and reopened their animation studio under Alex Lovy. In addition to continuing the Daffy Duck–Speedy Gonzalez series, Lovy added three new characters: Cool Cat, "the hep-talking tiger," and Merlin the Magic Mouse, a W. C. Fields caricature, and his sidekick, Second Banana. Robert McKimson replaced Lovy in 1968 and introduced Bunny and Claude, a pair of carrot-stealing rabbit outlaws. Neither director made any noteworthy cartoons during these last years, and Warners stopped cartoon production again in 1969. McKimson's Cool

Cat film "Injun Trouble" was to be the last Warner Brothers theatrical short for nearly two decades.

During the seventies and eighties, the Warners characters appeared in TV commercials and in bits of new animation that linked the segments of the cut-and-paste features. The studio began to expand production in 1984, and in 1987 released "The Duxorcist," their first theatrical short since "Injun Trouble." Written and directed by Greg Ford and Terry Lennon, "The Duxorcist" and "The Night of the Living Duck" (1988) were scheduled to be incorporated into another feature, "Daffy Duck's Quackbusters."

In early 1989, plans were announced for a syndicated television series involving juvenile versions of some of the Warners characters. Tentatively entitled "Tiny Tunes," the Warners/Amblin co-production was scheduled to debut during the fall of 1990.

MGM closed their Oscar-winning animation studio in 1957, then decided to revive the Tom and Jerry series four years later. Gene Deitch was signed to make new films with the old characters in Czechoslovakia, which MGM released in the United States. These uninspired shorts were obviously made with little money and less preparation, but they showed that cartoons could still be commercially viable. The audience response to "The Tom and Jerry Festival of Fun" (1962), a collection of the old Hanna-Barbera shorts, demonstrated the continuing popularity of the cat-and-mouse team.

After leaving Warner Brothers, Chuck Jones had formed Tower 12 Productions with Les Goldman. In 1963, MGM contracted with them to produce a series of fully animated new Tom and Jerry cartoons, budgeted at an impressive $42,000

Chuck Jones's version of Tom the Cat from the mid-1960s featured more prominent eyes and eyebrows.

apiece. (MGM later took over Tower 12, changing the name to MGM Animation/Visual Arts.) Jones reunited many of the artists from his old Warners crew, including writer Mike Maltese, designer Maurice Noble and animators Ben Washam, Richard Thompson, Tom Ray and Abe Levitow.

Tom and Jerry were redesigned with larger eyes and more prominent eyebrows. Jones abandoned Hanna and Barbera's violent slapstick-chase formula, and emphasized more subtle expressions and gestures. Despite the talented crew, the resulting cartoons were generally unimpressive. One notable exception was "The Cat Above, the Mouse Below" (1964), in which Jerry tries to sleep in an upstairs apartment while Tom, as an operatic tenor, rehearses in the ground-floor concert hall.

In 1965, Jones won an Oscar for "The Dot and the Line," a charming and unconventional cartoon that captured the best qualities of Norton Juster's book, subtitled *Romance in Lower Mathematics*. The disciplined, purposeful straight line defeats a boorish, ragged squiggle to win the heart of the flighty magenta dot. The character animation is minimal—the dot remains a perfect circle, with no squash and stretch—but this handsome film remains an outstanding example of design in motion.

As Jones became increasingly involved in television specials and other projects, Levitow, Ray and Washam took over directing the Tom and Jerry series. The MGM revival quietly ended in 1967. Two years later, the studio distributed Jones's feature "The Phantom Toll Booth," based on another book by Juster.

The Walter Lantz cartoons underwent a minor renaissance during the early 1960s. Beginning in 1962, director Sid Marcus, animator Art Davis and writer Cal Howard infused comic energy into films like "Half-Baked Alaska" (1965) and "Three Little Woodpeckers" (1965), a personal favorite of Lantz's.

In addition to the Woody Woodpecker and Chilly Willy shorts, Lantz released films about the Beary Family, a series director Paul Smith began in 1962. The Beary shorts were essentially "The Life of Riley" in fur coats: a dim-witted father, a patient wife and their even dimmer-witted son, Junior. The series ran for ten years.

After the departure of Marcus in 1966, Smith directed all the Lantz cartoons. Rising production costs, limited rental fees, stricter limits on Woody's "violent" antics and a general lack of inspiration made these theatrical films virtually indistinguishable from contemporary television animation.

By 1972, Lantz estimated it was taking ten years for his cartoons to show a profit. He gave a farewell luncheon for his staff—some of whom had been with the studio for forty years —and ended production. Universal continues to release a package of twelve old Lantz cartoons to various markets each year and maintains a Woody Woodpecker display in their studio tour. The recipient of an Academy Award for Special Achievement in 1979, Lantz remains active, supervising the licensing of his characters, painting and making personal appearances for various worthy causes.

The closing of the Lantz studio marked the end of an era. There would be no more theatrical short cartoons. But that era ended with a whimper, rather than a bang. By the late 1960s, closing the theatrical studios amounted to little more than a formality: they had long ceased to occupy the forefront of the medium, and their best work was a decade or more in the past. It was an ignominious ending for organizations that had brought so much laughter to so many viewers for so many years.

When the stylized opulence of "Sleeping Beauty" failed to attract audiences in 1959, Walt Disney turned to a more modest, contemporary story for his next feature: Dodie Smith's juvenile novel *The 101 Dalmatians*.

Pongo and his wife, Perdita, must rescue their stolen puppies when their human "pets" prove unable to solve the dognapping. Their 13 offspring—and 86 other pups—are being kept at Hell Hall, where Cruella DeVil plans to have them skinned and made into fur coats. After a harrowing journey, Pongo and Perdita take all 99 puppies home. Roger and his wife, Anita, decide to adopt the lot and start "a Dalmation plantation."

Bill Peet wrote the screenplay (a first for a Disney animated feature) and made Pongo the narrator. He explained that he

Cruella DeVil upbraids the Bad'uns, Horace and Jasper, in Disney's "101 Dalmatians."

made Roger, Pongo's owner, a songwriter because "That would give us the chance for songs without having to haul 'em in, like the old MGM musicals."

"Only Disney would do a picture with 101 spotted dogs," remarks Chuck Jones. "We would have had trouble doing a picture with *one* spotted dog." His comment reflects a real problem. In live action, a spotted dog is no harder to film than a solid-colored one. But in animation, the artists have to draw each spot, and keep it in the exact same position on the character in thousands of drawings. According to a studio press release, there are 6,469,952 spots in the film—a figure that may be accurate—and each one had to be drawn and painted by hand.

The film is dominated by one of the scariest and funniest of all the Disney villains, Cruella DeVil ("If she doesn't scare you, no evil thing will"). Unlike the Wicked Queen or Maleficent, Cruella is neither icy nor beautiful, but flamboyant and grotesque, with a sharp-cornered face that resembles a skull.

"I had several partial models in mind when I drew Cruella," says Marc Davis, who animated the character, "including Tallulah Bankhead and one woman I knew who was just a monster. She was tall and thin and talked constantly—you never knew what she was saying, but you couldn't get a word in edgewise. What I really wanted to do was make the character move like someone you wouldn't like."

A critical and popular success, "101 Dalmatians" became the first animated feature to gross over $10 million on its initial release. (The film has since grossed well over $200 million worldwide. Its 1985 release alone earned $32.1 million.)

"Dalmatians" also provided a showcase for the new technique of xerography, which was to have a widespread effect on the animation industry. Ub Iwerks modified a photocopy machine to reproduce the animators' drawings directly onto cels, instead of having human artisans trace them with fine brushes. The xerographic process produced a rougher, more friable line than the elegant, calligraphic one of the hand inkers. Many animators preferred the new technique, because the lines they had actually drawn appeared on the screen, rather than an inker's approximations.

While "Dalmatians" was still in postproduction, Davis, Ken Anderson and several other artists did preliminary sketches for what they thought would be Disney's next feature, an adaptation of *Chanticleer,* Edmond Rostand's play about a rooster who believes his crowing makes the sun rise.

"I think some of the best drawings I ever did at the studio were for 'Chanticleer,' " says Davis. "But the business people were on Walt's back to discontinue making the animated features. Their attitude was: 'It takes too damned long to do these features and they cost too much. We think you shouldn't do any more.' We finally had a meeting about 'Chanticleer,' and they came in like a bunch of pallbearers. Somebody said:

'You can't make a personality out of a chicken,' and they walked out.

"Walt was about ready to dump animation," he continues. "Then he had second thoughts. He felt the guys knew how to make these films and that he owed it to them to continue. I don't know what kind of fight he had with the business people, but it was almost the end of the features. I would say everything after 'Dalmatians' was done with a minimum of Walt's supervision."

The next Disney feature was not "Chanticleer" but "The Sword in the Stone" (1963), about the young King Arthur. Woolie Reitherman received sole directorial credit on the film—a "first" that suggests Walt's lack of involvement with the project.

The story was based not on T. H. White's *The Once and Future King* but on a juvenile novel by the same author. Bill Peet compressed White's rambling narrative, removing secondary characters and focusing on a few episodes in Wart's education by Merlin.

The high point of the film is the Wizard's Duel, in which Merlin and the Mad Madame Mim do battle by turning into various animals. The animators had to try to maintain a character's personality as he or she became a cat, a mouse, a rabbit, a crab, a rattlesnake, a rhinoceros, a billy goat and a comic dragon. Superbly timed and animated, this sequence stands out as an example of the fun that only animation can provide.

"The Sword in the Stone" earned a respectable $4.5 million on its initial release, and the reviews were generally favorable. In the *New York Times,* Howard Thompson wrote: "The humor sparkles with real, knowing sophistication—meaning for all ages—and some of the characters on the landscape of Old England are Disney pips . . ." But the film is generally regarded as a minor work in the Disney canon. For all its good humor and polished animation, it trivializes the Arthurian legends.

For years, Bill Peet had urged Disney to make a film based on Rudyard Kipling's *The Jungle Books.* Disney finally obtained the rights from the Kipling estate, and Peet began preliminary story work.

Although they respected each other's talents, Disney and Peet were strong-willed men, and their relationship had always been a stormy one. When they fought over a preliminary recording for the voice of Bagheera, the black panther, Peet left the studio and became a successful children's author. He had his name removed from the credits and never saw the film. Larry Clemmons was put in charge of the story, with a crew that included Ralph Wright, Ken Anderson and Vance Gerry.

They took little more than the names and species of the characters from Kipling. Baloo, "the big, serious, old brown

Baloo and King Louie bring down the house (and most of a ruined temple) with their jitterbug in "The Jungle Book."

bear" who taught Mowgli the Law of the Jungle, was transformed into "that shiftless, two-bit jungle bum." The ancient and subtle rock python, Kaa, became a sibilant comic villain. Hathi, the elephant (whom even Bagheera describes as "the master of the jungle"), was turned into a bumbling caricature of a British Army officer. *Time* commented: " 'The Jungle Book' is based on Kipling in the same way that a fox hunt is based on foxes."

For the first time, famous voice actors dictated the design of the characters to a large extent. Phil Harris's loose-jointed gait offered a model for Baloo's walk. Sebastian Cabot's voice suggested proper, schoolmaster attitudes for Bagheera. Shere Khan, the arrogant tiger, resembled George Sanders.

As many critics have observed, the story takes a back seat to these strong characters, and the film is little more than a series of vignettes that showcase their personalities. Taken on its own terms, "The Jungle Book" is a delightful, upbeat comedy. Terry Gilkyson received an Oscar nomination for Baloo's big number, "The Bare Necessities."

Only four of the "Nine Old Men"—Milt Kahl, Ollie Johnston, John Lounsbery and Frank Thomas—worked as directing animators on the film. (Woolie Reitherman, another member of the group, directed.) Their work displays a maturity and a degree of polish that have rarely been equaled. Every movement of Kahl's proud Shere Khan suggests deadly power barely held in check. Thomas and Johnston made the friendship between Mowgli and Baloo seem immediate and credible. Lounsbery's animation of the hilarious jitterbug duet

between Baloo and King Louie, the orangutan, ranks as the funniest scene in the film—and one of the funniest in a Disney cartoon.

"The Jungle Book" was released in the fall of 1967, thirty years after "Snow White and the Seven Dwarfs." Although critics complained about the liberties that had been taken with Kipling and the characters based on well-known actors, their reviews were generally favorable, and "The Jungle Book" earned $13 million on its initial release, a record for a full-length Disney cartoon that stood for a decade.

One factor that may have affected the success of "The Jungle Book" was its lugubrious distinction as the last animated feature that Walt Disney personally supervised. He died on December 15, 1966, at St. Joseph's Hospital in Burbank—across the street from his studio.

Walt Disney's death deprived animation of its most prominent spokesman and father figure. In the years since "Steamboat Willie," the Disney name had become synonymous with animation. And Walt, in his role of genial television host, seemed to personify the medium. The persistent rumor that his body had been frozen and would be revived at some future date reveals how reluctant audiences were to accept his passing. (In fact, he was cremated.) Obituaries and tributes all over the world proclaimed that an era had come to an end.

His death left a gap in the animation industry as well as at his studio. But for all his importance in the history of the medium, animation had occupied a very small part of Walt's interest during his last years. The focus of his attention—and the studio's production—had shifted to other areas. Live-action films, television, licensing and the theme parks had supplanted cartoons. The management team Walt had assembled, headed by his brother Roy, allowed the animators to continue making features, with Woolie Reitherman assuming the duties of producer.

Walt had already given his approval to begin preliminary work on "The Aristocats" (1970), but it seems unlikely that he would have allowed the film to proceed with such a vague, disjointed story. The setting is Paris, 1910. When the unscrupulous butler of a wealthy woman learns that he is the beneficiary of her will after her cats, he drugs them and dumps them in the countryside. Duchess, an elegant white shorthair (voice by Eva Gabor), and her three kittens are helpless in the wild.

They're rescued by the happy-go-lucky Thomas O'Malley Cat (voice by Phil Harris), who takes them back to Paris, where they meet his jazz-playing alley-cat friends. Duchess's wealthy owner adopts the whole crowd after they defeat the butler in a broad slapstick sequence. The plot clearly owes a lot to "Lady and the Tramp," but it lacks consistency and focus. The animation is competent by Disney standards, but hardly innovative.

"Aristocats" told an original story badly. The studio's next feature, "Robin Hood" (1973), tried to tell one of the most famous stories in the English language, and failed. For the first time, the Disney artists adopted the dubious Saturday-morning practice of turning human characters into animals for no discernible reason. But producer-director Woolie Reitherman defended the idea: "This business of using animals instead of humans is a whole new way of looking at a classic tale. The reason, we feel, is basic, as audiences exercise a greater [amount] of imagination with animals than with humans."

Celebrities were again cast as the voices, and many of the character designs suggested caricatures more strongly than ever. Brian Bedford supplied the voice of Robin Hood (a fox); Pat Buttram, the Sheriff of Nottingham (wolf); Peter Ustinov, King John (lion); and Terry-Thomas, Sir Hiss, the King's counselor (snake).

Phil Harris gave his third happy-go-lucky performance, as Little John—a bear dismayingly similar to Baloo. A further indication of the lack of originality that pervades the film is the scene of Maid Marian dancing on the green. Instead of devising new animation, the artists copied the drawings of Snow White dancing with the Dwarfs, making changes dictated by the differences in the characters' anatomies.

Like "Aristocats," "Robin Hood" contains some entertaining sequences. Both films did well at the box office, and their success enabled the Disney artists to continue production at a time when animation seemed in danger of extinction in America. But after the brilliant visuals of "Yellow Submarine" and

the revolutionary content of "Fritz the Cat" and "Heavy Traffic," these films look uninspired and pedestrian.

The Disney cartoons had become an established part of American culture. No one seemed to remember that "Snow White," "Pinocchio" and "Fantasia" had once been considered innovative and even daring. Instead of taking risks—as Walt had—and recapturing the initiative in animation, the studio appeared to be offering a diluted version of Disney that emphasized only the tamer, safer, less dynamic elements.

During the production of "Robin Hood," Disney finally began to recruit new animators. For more than two decades, the studio had been relying on a small corps of experienced artists. The Disney staff was generally acknowledged as the best in the world, and there was little impetus to search for new talent. (Disney was not the only studio that failed to recruit young animators; very few artists entered the field between the mid-1950s and the mid-1970s.)

Even the death of Walt failed to shake the comfortable assumption that this skilled team would continue working indefinitely. But as members of the group began to retire and die, it became necessary to find and train new artists to replace them.

Disney hired twenty-five new artists between 1970 and 1977, including Gary Goldman, John Pomeroy, Glen Keane and Don Bluth. "The Rescuers" (1977) represented the first real collaboration between the two groups of animators.

Based on Marjorie Sharp's Miss Bianca stories, the film sent two mice, dainty Bianca and timorous Bernard, to the rescue of Penny, an orphan girl. Madame Medusa, the flamboyant,

Three of Disney's top young animators—Mark Henn, Rob Minkoff and Glen Keane—during production of "The Great Mouse Detective."

grasping villainess, is making the child search a small cave for the Devil's Eye, a fabulous diamond from a pirate's hoard. With a little assistance from the animals of neighboring Devil's Bayou, Penny and the mice defeat Medusa and escape with the diamond.

Although famous actors supplied the voices, the characters were not caricatures, and the animation seemed to blend with the voices exceptionally well. Eva Gabor and Bob Newhart underplayed Bianca and Bernard, which helped to give them more depth than the standard cartoon good guys. Bernard appears hesitant and uncertain, but not dull; Bianca is chic and self-assured, yet vulnerable. Geraldine Page gave a wonderfully overstated performance as Madame Medusa, and Milt Kahl devised extravagant, theatrical gestures to match her vocal histrionics.

The blend of new and experienced talent produced delightful results. The animation had the polish of the older Disney features. When Bianca enters the Rescue Aid Society meeting, her dainty walk immediately establishes her character. But the young artists brought an enthusiasm to the film that provided a welcome contrast to the business-as-usual tone of the two previous features.

"The Rescuers" proved to be an enormous success, earning $16.3 million domestically and outdrawing "Star Wars" in Germany and France. Charles Champlin's review in the Los Angeles *Times* summed up critical opinion of the film: " 'The Rescuers' is the best feature-length animated film from Disney in a decade or more—the funniest, the most inventive, the least self-conscious, the most coherent and fast-moving from start to finish and, probably most important of all, it is also the most touching in that unique way fantasy has of carrying the vibrations of real life and real feelings."

The success of "The Rescuers" seemed to ensure the future of Disney animation. Additional artists were hired and plans were announced for an ambitious production schedule that included "The Fox and the Hound" and "The Black Cauldron." Articles began to appear about the "Nine Young Men" who were emerging as important talents, with Don Bluth as their leader.

Bluth had been an assistant animator on "Sleeping Beauty" for two years during the mid-1950s. He left the studio to pursue other interests, then returned in 1971. After working on "The Rescuers," he served as director of animation on "Pete's Dragon" (1977), a dull but technically polished animation/live-action combination. He also produced and directed the saccharine Christmas featurette "The Small One" (1978).

In September 1979, Bluth resigned from Disney; Goldman and Pomeroy went with him to found their own studio. Fourteen other animators and assistants—a substantial portion of the new Disney artists—also left to join the nascent studio. The split reflected the divisions within the animation department, and the parting was not without recrimination on both

One of Glen Keane's powerful charcoal sketches for the bear fight in "The Fox and the Hound."

sides. Bluth compared the situation to the gentlemanly rivalry that might exist between two baseball teams. In fact, it was more personal and more bitter.

The Disney studio moved the release date of "The Fox and the Hound" back a year, and stepped up the recruitment and training program. Some extremely talented young artists came to the studio during the next few years, many of them from the California Institute of the Arts (CalArts). Eric Larson, the last of the "Nine Old Men" to retire, continued to supervise their training.

If "The Rescuers" represented a collaboration between the older and younger Disney artists, "The Fox and the Hound" was the first feature to showcase the rapidly developing talents of the newer animators. Studio veterans like Woolie Reitherman, Art Stevens, Mel Shaw, Frank Thomas and Ollie Johnston contributed to the film, teaching as they worked. But the roster of directing and character animators was dominated by new artists who were developing into some of the best animators of their generation, including Glen Keane, Hendel Butoy, Daryl Von Citters, John Musker, Jerry Rees, Phil Nibbelink, Randy Cartwright, Ed Gombert and Ron Clements.

Unfortunately, the rather self-conscious story of Copper and Tod, a puppy and a fox kit who begin as friends but are later forced to become enemies, didn't offer the animators much of a vehicle. Instead of heightening the dramatic situations in the story, the eight writers seem to shy away from them and pull their punches. Chief, the older dog who teaches Copper to hunt, is hit by a train while chasing Tod. Caught between conflicting loyalties, Copper swears revenge. But Chief isn't dead. He turns up a few scenes later, with one hind leg in a cast, and a potentially moving story point is thrown away.

"The Fox and the Hound" contains one electrifying sequence: a fight that pits Tod and Copper against an enraged grizzly bear, animated by Keane. He planned to animate the fight in charcoal and photocopy his drawings onto cels, but encroaching deadlines precluded the use of this novel medium. Even rendered in pencil, the scene contains some of the most powerful animation the studio had produced since Prince Philip battled the dragon in "Sleeping Beauty."

Critics were unanimous in their praise of the animation itself, but agreed that "The Fox and the Hound" was not very exciting as a film. Many of the animators felt frustrated by its cinematic limitations.

"Mickey's Christmas Carol" (1983) presented the special challenge of animating the classic Disney characters. Mickey Mouse was cast as Bob Cratchit in this retelling of Dickens's venerable war-horse. Scrooge McDuck made his screen debut as Ebenezer Scrooge, with Donald Duck as his nephew Fred. Goofy played Marley's Ghost, and Jiminy Cricket, Willie the Giant and Black Pete were the Ghosts of Christmas Past, Present and Future.

Like "The Fox and the Hound," "Mickey's Christmas Carol" was more of a showcase for fine animation than a fine animated film. Although the familiar characters gave the story a curious poignancy, Dickens's morality tale had been greatly

A gwythaint, the pterodactyl-like messenger of the evil Horned King, snatches Hewen, the oracular pig, from Taran, in "The Black Cauldron."

watered down. Scrooge didn't consign the poor to the workhouse or the grave, nor was he forced to confront the specters of Ignorance and Want. And no audience could believe that Goofy really cheated widows and swindled orphans.

After fighting off a highly publicized takeover bid by financier Saul P. Steinberg in June 1984, the Disney family's management of the company ended when Walt's son-in-law, Ron Miller, resigned under fire in September. The new management team was composed of men from live-action backgrounds: chairman of the board and chief executive officer of the company Michael Eisner had been president of Paramount Pictures Corp.; president and chief operating officer Frank Wells was vice president of Warner Brothers.

The new leadership immediately launched a program of live-action production. Rumors that the animation department might be eliminated were fueled by the decision to move the artists off the lot and convert the animation building into offices. Those fears were allayed when Roy Edward Disney (Roy Oliver's son and Walt's nephew) took charge of the department and set up new headquarters in Glendale.

Willie the Giant made a comic Ghost of Christmas Present in "Mickey's Christmas Carol" (1983).

Although most of his experience was in live-action filmmaking (he had been an editor, writer, cameraman, director and producer at the studio, working on many of the nature films), Roy grew up with an intimate knowledge of animation. "I like to say my first exposure to animation came when my mother inked and painted cels of Mickey Mouse while she was pregnant with me," he says, grinning.

"The Black Cauldron," the first animated feature released under the new regime, made its belated debut in July 1985, after twelve years of production and preproduction work. Numerous delays—and the decision to shoot the film in 70mm (the first animated feature in that format since "Sleeping Beauty")—had raised its cost to a record $25 million.

"The Black Cauldron" was based on Lloyd Alexander's *Chronicles of Prydain*, a series of five juvenile novels inspired by Welsh legends. The Disney artists had to condense the long, complex tale into a coherent story that could be told in 80 minutes. In addition to the tangled story line, the main characters were all humans, which are far more difficult to animate than the animals and cartoon figures of "The Fox and the Hound" and "Mickey's Christmas Carol."

"The Black Cauldron" contained some genuinely impressive moments. The attack of the gwythaints, the pterodactyl-like messengers of the evil Horned King, displayed an almost feral strength and demonstrated the power of animation to render pure fantasy. The apostrophe the Horned King delivered to the heaped-up skeletons that would become his army of deathless ghoul-warriors suggested just how frightening a villain he could have been—if he hadn't been burdened with the sniggering little familiar, Creeper.

If the quality of the story had equaled the animation, "The Black Cauldron" would have helped reassert Disney's position in the field of fantasy that George Lucas and Steven Spielberg now dominated. The film recalled Bill Peet's complaint about the troubles too many writers engender. Nine received story credit, plus seven for "additional story contributions" and two more for "additional dialogue," and the story lacked an overall vision.

"The Black Cauldron" was the first Disney animated feature to receive a PG rating, although "Snow White," "Pinocchio," "Fantasia" and "Bambi" all contain material that is more frightening. The film drew mixed reviews and earned about

Tito (voice by Cheech Marin) instructs Georgette (Bette Midler) in the intricacies of salsa dancing, in Disney's record-breaking "Oliver & Company."

$25 million domestically—hardly a flop, but not the blockbuster the studio and the animation industry had hoped for.

" 'The Black Cauldron' is a remarkable film in terms of the art in it," affirms Roy Disney. "It validated animation as an art at this point in the company's development. We're very proud of it. We have said that this is a valid art and that we're going forward with it."

The young animators at the studio found a project better suited to their talents in "The Great Mouse Detective" (1986), based on Eve Titus's popular children's books about Basil of Baker Street, a Sherlock Holmesian mouse. With the assistance of the mouse/physician Dr. David Q. Dawson, Basil defeats a scheme by the insidious Professor Ratigan to kidnap Queen Moustoria on the eve of her Diamond Jubilee and usurp the throne.

Instead of trying to disguise Basil's obvious literary ancestry, the filmmakers flaunted it, simultaneously invoking and spoofing Holmes. Much of the film displayed the sort of energy the Silly Symphonies had during the early 1930s, the energy of young artists celebrating their abilities. The few weak moments—a production number for a barroom singer and the scenes with Queen Moustoria—occurred when the animators seemed to be holding back, rather than strutting their stuff.

The climactic confrontation between Basil and Ratigan was set inside the mechanism of Big Ben. Computer graphics were used to produce an ominous, complex environment of interlocking gears. The computer generated frame-by-frame images of the moving gears, which were photocopied onto cels and painted. Animator Phil Nibbelink worked with computer specialist Ted Gielow to create the scene.

"I've always enjoyed doing chase scenes, and I like point-of-view shots," Nibbelink explains. "You could never achieve them in standard animation because it's limited to flat artwork—all you can do is truck in or out, or pan left and right. When you create the entire environment in the computer, as we did for that sequence, you can spin around and turn corners and move in directions that are very dramatic."

Glen Keane designed most of the characters in the film and did the key animation of Ratigan. The final battle between Ratigan and Basil on the hands of Big Ben displays the same strength as the bear fight in "The Fox and the Hound": Ratigan sheds his comic sophistication and becomes a towering embodiment of menace.

Despite a last-minute change in title from "Basil of Baker Street" to "The Great Mouse Detective," the film did good business ($25.3 million) and received excellent reviews. The critics agreed that new artists had proved they could do animation comparable to classic Disney features.

Jeffrey Katzenberg, chairman of Walt Disney Pictures, announced he intended to keep the animation division busy: "From the outset, both Michael [Eisner] and I felt that the one area of the company that needed the most encouragement and had the greatest potential was Disney animation. They'd been releasing a new feature every three or four years. We discovered that if it's properly managed and staffed and equipped, the operation is capable of supporting twice that level of production—a new feature every eighteen months to two years—without compromising the quality of Disney animation."

Walt Disney had planned a similar production schedule during the late 1930s, but the outbreak of World War II and the initial box office losses of "Pinocchio" and "Fantasia" derailed his plans. Peter Schneider, Disney vice president of feature animation, continued to recruit and train animators for a program geared to meet Katzenberg's ambitious plan.

"Oliver & Company," a new feature loosely based on "Oliver Twist," premiered in November 1988, not quite two years after "The Great Mouse Detective." The contemporary tone and broader, more cartoon-style animation of this upbeat comedy put it in the tradition of "The Jungle Book," rather than "Pinocchio."

Oliver was transformed into a homeless kitten and Fagin's gang into a pack of stray dogs, led by (the Artful) Dodger, a super-cool mongrel (voice by pop singer Billy Joel). The best characters in the film were Tito, a frenetic Chihuahua (Cheech Marin), and Georgette (Bette Midler), a snobbish champion poodle. When Georgette performed "Perfect Isn't Easy," a paean to her own charms, she was joined by a chorus of adoring birds who performed an aerial Busby Berkeley—a nicely irreverent send-up of the little birds who attended Cinderella and Snow White.

"Oliver" opened on the same day as Don Bluth's "The Land Before Time," to mixed but generally favorable reviews and good business. (Richard Corliss of *Time* called it "the snazziest Disney cartoon since Walt died in 1966.") The film earned more than $12 million in its first two weeks. With its rock songs and hip characters, "Oliver" appealed to older children and young adults, while "Land Before Time" seemed to be aimed at four-to-eight-year-olds. Although it opened more slowly, "Oliver" won the face-off, earning more than $53 million domestically—a record for an animated film in its initial release.

By the time "Oliver" premiered, "The Little Mermaid," a film based on the Hans Christian Andersen story and scheduled for release in late 1989, was in full production. Previewed footage from "Little Mermaid" suggested that it had the potential to become the showcase the young animators had been seeking for their talents. In addition, preproduction work had already begun on "The Rescuers Down Under," a sequel to the studio's 1977 hit, "Beauty and the Beast," and a third film, with an "Arabian Nights" setting.

"My gut feeling is that people have been trying to figure out what Walt would have done and to hold on to his tradition," says Schneider. "I think Walt would have been the first person to say he had no tradition, other than excellence in storytelling and always pushing the frontiers of animation one step further. The challenge we have today is to find that excellence and to keep pushing the frontiers of animation as an art form—as opposed to looking back and trying to figure out how Walt would have done it."

Disney also announced plans to open a second animation unit at the Disney/MGM Studios in Orlando, Florida, in spring 1989. The facility would offer the first tour of a working animation studio. The artists would make featurettes, half-hour films starring the classic Disney characters—Mickey, Donald, Goofy et al.

The most innovative, imaginative and successful animated film of 1988 was a co-production of Disney's Touchstone division and Steven Spielberg's Amblin Entertainment: "Who Framed Roger Rabbit." Based on Gary Wolf's novel *Who Censored Roger Rabbit?*, the comedy-mystery set a new stan-

Eddie Valiant (Bob Hoskins) confronts a frantic 'Toon, in the Touchstone/Amblin smash hit "Who Framed Roger Rabbit."

dard for blending live action and animation: For the first time, live actors and cartoon characters seemed to share the same, three-dimensional space.

Yet when director Robert Zemeckis and animation director Richard Williams met for the first time to discuss collaborating, they agreed that mixing media wouldn't work. Williams disliked combination films, because "the cartoon cancels out the live action and the live action cancels out the cartoon, and you can't believe in either one."

The two men discovered that what they really disliked were the traditional rules governing live action/animation combinations: Don't move the live-action camera, and keep the physical interaction between the live actors and the cartoon characters to a minimum because it makes too much work for the animators.

"I told Bob I was convinced every single rule about the use of animation and live action was baloney, and that if we made the film, I'd throw them all out and let him move the camera," says Williams. "We agreed that the key to making the combination effective would be interaction. We thought the cartoon characters should always be affecting their environment or getting tangled up with the live actors."

The animation was done by an international crew in London, with a second unit in Los Angeles. The production was shrouded in secrecy, and rumors circulated about staggering technical problems and runaway costs. (Disney refuses to release an exact figure, but the film probably cost about $45 million.) There were also rumors that the animation was being done on a sophisticated computer system.

In fact, all the animation was done by hand, using the same basic technique as for "Anchors Aweigh" and "Mary Poppins." Each frame of live action was printed as a large photostat, which the animators used to match their drawings to the actors' movements. The drawings were traced and painted onto cels, photographed and combined with the live action using optical printers.

To make the characters appear three-dimensional, crews at Industrial Light and Magic shot at least three cel layers of shadows and highlights for each character in every frame. The cels were shot underexposed and out of focus to simulate the soft-edged look of real shadows.

The decision not to lock down the camera complicated the animators' work, as they had to adjust the size and position of the characters in every frame to match the camera moves. These moves caused the most serious problems when the cartoon characters stood still: They seemed to slide on the backgrounds as the point of view shifted.

"When a character walks or runs, his feet only come in contact with the ground for a few frames," explains supervising animator Andreas Deja. "But when the character is standing there and the camera is moving up and down and in little circles, it's just about impossible to lock him onto the ground—his feet seem to slip."

The artists also had to capture the style of animation in 1947 (the year in which the film was set) and to match the work of various studios. Disney licensed a number of other characters, and for the first time, Mickey Mouse, Donald Duck and Dumbo appeared in a film with Bugs Bunny, Daffy Duck, Tweety, Woody Woodpecker, Droopy and Betty Boop.

"Who Framed Roger Rabbit" was the most popular film of 1988, grossing more than $150 million domestically and earning equal sums overseas. Roger Rabbit, Jessica, Baby Herman and Benny the Cab became the subjects of a major merchandising campaign. In addition to favorable reviews, the film provoked a spate of articles about animation in the popular press. Disney announced plans to star Roger in "Maroon Cartoons" that would screen with the studio's features.

" 'Roger Rabbit' was one of the most difficult, time-consuming and challenging projects ever to come across our desks," concludes Katzenberg. "But I think it has been a pioneering filmmaking effort for this company, one that defines the type of venture Walt Disney himself was famous for. We like to think that this film is at the center of the grandest tradition we inherited from him."

The success of "Snow White" and the subsequent Disney features had established full-length cartoons as the most prestigious and potentially lucrative area of animation. When the market for theatrical shorts disappeared, studios switched to feature or television production—or closed. Between 1937 and 1965, thirty feature-length animated films were produced in the United States for theatrical release, twenty-two of them by Disney. Between 1967 and 1977, twenty-one features were released, but only three were from the Disney studio. (The number of films continued to rise during the next decade, most of them animated overseas and/or vehicles for license product characters.)

Ralph Bakshi emerged as the most successful director of animated features of the 1970s. "Fritz the Cat" (1972) sparked unprecedented critical discussions of the potential of animation, and attracted widespread attention to the medium. One year later, he released "Heavy Traffic," which many consider his best film. "Heavy Traffic" was a study of a young cartoonist coming of age in the gritty, raucous squalor of New York City. Virginal twenty-two-year-old Michael, with his mixed Italian-Jewish ancestry, was obviously a fictionalized self-portrait of the filmmaker.

Michael moved through a gaudy, low-life world inhabited by hookers, blacks, mafiosi, hustlers and punks. Bakshi mixed animation with live action, paintings and photographs to heighten the grimy realism of his vision. Much of the imagery was dark, harsh, angry and even ugly—its violence, sexual

Two scenes from Ralph Bakshi's semi-autobiographical "Heavy Traffic" show Michael's black girlfriend and his fractious parents.

content and graphic language earned the film an X rating.

In "Heavy Traffic," Bakshi made the collaborative medium of the animated feature reflect a strong personal vision, rather than a generalized studio style. His work suggested that animated features could be as immediately and intensely personal as the live-action films of the *auteur* directors.

"Since my days at Terrytoons, I had been asking: 'Why do we always pick up an animated character from the story department and try to do our best on it? Why don't we just do something that we really feel?' " says Bakshi. "My background was in Brooklyn—my Jewishness, my family life, my father coming from Russia. All these things had to be somehow represented on film."

Made for only $950,000, "Heavy Traffic" did well at the box office. Bakshi became the first man since Walt Disney to have two successful animated features back to back. He parted company with producer Steve Krantz and opened his own studio. Bakshi explains: "I opened up Bakshi Productions to do a picture called 'Harlem Nights,' which I'd sold to Paramount. I was working with Al Ruddy, the producer of 'The Godfather.' The name 'Harlem Nights' was eventually changed to 'Coonskin'—a title which is indefensible and, I would say, changed my life."

A very dark, very angry updating of "Uncle Remus" that mixed animation and live action, "Coonskin" was shown as a work-in-progress at the Museum of Modern Art in the fall of 1974. Representatives from CORE (Congress of Racial Equality) objected to the depictions of blacks and disrupted the program. As the controversy over "Coonskin" grew, Paramount declined to release it. (Bryanston, a small independent company, distributed the film when it was completed in 1975.)

After a very short run, "Coonskin" disappeared. (In late 1987 the film was released on videocassette as "Streetfight," with the disclaimer "Warning: This film offends everybody.") But the brouhaha it generated led Warner Brothers to drop their plans to finance and distribute Bakshi's next film, "Hey Good Lookin'," which was already in production. It went on the shelf—where it remained until a reworked version appeared briefly in 1983.

His first PG film, "Wizards," was released by Fox in 1977. This post-apocalyptic sword-and-sorcery fantasy depicted the battle the dark wizard, Blackwolf, and his neo-Nazi thugs waged against the virtuous Avatar and his troop of elves. According to Bakshi, the title of the film was shortened from "War Wizards" to accommodate George Lucas, as Fox was also about to release "Star Wars." "Wizards" opened strongly, and retains a strong cult following. But many Bakshi fans were disappointed to find that "Wizards" lacked the grit and personal vision of his earlier works.

Bakshi's most ambitious film was an adaptation of *The Lord of the Rings*, produced by Saul Zaentz ("One Flew Over the Cuckoo's Nest"). At various times, Walt Disney, Stanley

Kubrick and John Boorman had considered filming J. R. R. Tolkien's vast saga—and abandoned the idea. The 1,500-page trilogy was a narrative work, rather than a visual one, and attempts to streamline its complexities for the screen weakened the epic qualities that attracted readers.

Writers Chris Conkling and Peter S. Beagle tried to condense the first half of the story into two hours and fifteen minutes, which meant the film ended literally in the middle of the story, right after the Battle of Helm's Deep. (Viewers were enjoined to wait for the ending in Part II.) Only a dedicated Tolkien fan could possibly decipher the muddled fragments of the story line, but few would care to.

Instead of conventional animation, Bakshi chose a technique he had used on "Wizards": he shot the film in live action, then had his artists use (and, in the opinion of many animators, overuse and abuse) the rotoscope to copy the figures frame by frame.

As the Disney animators had learned forty-odd years earlier, simply tracing live action produces stilted, uninteresting motions. The problems with the awkward movements of the rotoscoped characters were aggravated by the decision to combine them with drawn animation and a process involving frames of high-contrast live-action footage that were transferred onto cels, painted and rephotographed.

Although the critics were unanimous in their condemnation of the incomprehensible story line and unsatisfying mixture of techniques, "The Lord of the Rings" earned back its $8 million production costs several times over. Despite its commercial success, there was no attempt to film the second part.

Instead, Bakshi turned to another personal film. "American Pop" was intended as an overview of twentieth-century American popular culture, seen through four generations of a family of musicians. All the characters were rotoscoped, and some critics asked why he didn't just make the film in live action.

Two years later, Bakshi completed "Fire and Ice," a rotoscoped sword-and-sorcery epic designed by Frank Frazetta, so bad it was unintentionally funny. During production, Bakshi announced he was retiring from animation.

He returned to New York and spent the next two and a half years painting. In 1986, he reopened his Los Angeles studio but focused on television production, including the rock video of the Rolling Stones' "Harlem Shuffle" and the sprightly remake of "Mighty Mouse" for CBS, rather than theatrical features.

It may be too early to evaluate Ralph Bakshi's contribution to American animation. Only Walt Disney made more animated features, and Bakshi enriched the medium in different ways. He attracted public attention to animation at a time when almost no one else seemed to be doing interesting work. "Fritz the Cat" and "Heavy Traffic" opened new areas of story content and offered an alternative vision of what an animated feature could say and be.

Many animators feel that he turned his back on the medium when he began using the rotoscope in "Wizards," and that his later films are essentially live-action works. "Dirty Duck" (a.k.a. "Cheap," 1977), "Heavy Metal" (1981) and "Rock and Rule" (1983) borrowed heavily from Bakshi, but during the 1980s, too many directors have turned out inane, homoge-

A cel setup of the tarnished fantasy world of Ralph Bakshi's "Wizards" (1977).

Director Bill Melendez at work in his Los Angeles studio.

nized "children's entertainment" instead of exploiting the potential suggested by "Heavy Traffic" and making films that reflect a strong, personal point of view.

With five full-length cartoons to his credit, Bill Melendez ranks behind Bakshi and Disney's Woolie Reitherman as a prolific director of American animated features.

Working with producer Lee Mendelson and cartoonist Charles Schulz, Melendez had already directed several "Peanuts" specials for television when their first feature, "A Boy Named Charlie Brown," premiered at Christmas 1969. Not surprisingly, the film resembled an expanded version of one of the "Peanuts" shows: the graphics, voices, limited animation and style of direction were all similar.

Budgeted at a modest $1.1 million, "A Boy Named Charlie Brown" earned a tidy profit. Its success, coupled with the growing popularity of the "Peanuts" characters, guaranteed a sequel. "Snoopy, Come Home" (1972) is a much more entertaining film, and remains the best of the "Peanuts" features.

The last two "Peanuts" features, "Race for Your Life, Charlie Brown" (1977) and "Bon Voyage, Charlie Brown (And Don't Come Back)" (1980), were considerably less enjoyable. The artists seemed to be losing their sense of the characters. "Race for Your Life" centered on a rafting contest at summer camp that pitted the regular characters against a group of badly designed bullies and their nasty cat. The formula competition

was far less imaginative than Schulz's handling of similar material in the strip.

"Bon Voyage" sent Charlie Brown, Linus, Snoopy, Woodstock, Marcie and Peppermint Patty to France, where Snoopy's bad driving got them in accidents and Marcie yelled insults at the other motorists. The film introduced on-screen adult characters—which violated the purely children's world Schulz had always maintained.

Through the London branch of his studio, Melendez also directed the short-lived "Dick Deadeye, or Duty Done" (1975), a hodgepodge of rewritten fragments of Gilbert and Sullivan operettas, with designs by illustrator Ronald Searle.

Hanna-Barbera also made periodic efforts to enter the theatrical features market, beginning with two limited animation vehicles for their most popular television characters: "Hey There, It's Yogi Bear" (1964) and "A Man Called Flintstone" (1967). The animation in subsequent television-inspired features grew so static that "Hey There, It's Yogi Bear" looked downright lavish when it was re-released in 1986.

A musical based on E. B. White's popular children's book *Charlotte's Web* (1972) encountered some of the same problems as Disney's "Alice in Wonderland": audiences resisted what they perceived as tampering with a beloved story. While more fully animated than the Hanna-Barbera television programs, the movements in "Charlotte's Web" were still limited, and the animators had problems keeping the relative sizes of the characters consistent.

Hanna-Barbera waited ten years before releasing their next animated feature, "Heidi's Song," a musical based on Johanna Spyri's novel. During production, Joe Barbera announced that "Heidi" would be the first in a series of original, fully animated films.

"This picture has provided a college, if you will, for full animation, and an opportunity for the guys to get back into what it's really all about," he told John Canemaker in 1981. "We take as many new animators as we can bear—the ones that have the enthusiasm and are really interested in what we're calling a 'renaissance.' But even more important, we are just interested in making great animated films and updating them into the 1980s."

Barbera added that preproduction work was already underway on two additional features: "Rock Odyssey" ("a marvelous treatment of music from the 1950s, 1960s and 1970s; a rock *Fantasia,* if you want to call it that") and "Nessie, Come Home," an "environmental" story involving the Loch Ness monster.

"Heidi's Song" proved to be considerably less than a return to full, character animation. The artists simply couldn't move the figures convincingly in three dimensions. The film, which also suffered from bad direction and syrupy songs, earned an unimpressive $5.2 million theatrically. "Rock Odyssey" has yet to be released, and the plans for feature production were temporarily shelved, until a feature-length cartoon starring "The Jetsons" was announced for Christmas of 1989.

In the fall of 1987, "Hanna-Barbera's Superstars 10," a series of ten 2-hour films starring Yogi Bear, Scooby-Doo, Top Cat, Huckleberry Hound and the Jetsons, debuted in syndication. "The Jetsons Meet the Flintstones" was the highest-rated animated program for November 1987—an impressive accomplishment for a syndicated show.

The previous year, Hanna-Barbera released the first episode of "The Greatest Adventure," a series of half-hour videocassettes based on Biblical stories. The series proved successful, and won numerous awards from religious organizations. Two years later, the studio introduced "Hanna-Barbera's Personal Favorites," 90-minute cassettes of the partners' favorite episodes from the more than fifteen hundred hours of programming they had produced together.

The remaining animated features of the 1970s were either one-shots or European films. John Wilson's "Shinbone Alley" (1970), an adaptation of the George Kleinsinger–Joe Darion musical based on Don Marquis's "archy and mehitabel" stories, featured the voices of Carol Channing and Eddie Bracken, but failed to attract much attention.

When Ralph Bakshi declined to direct the sequel to "Fritz," producer Steve Krantz hired Robert Taylor to replace him. The resulting film, "The Nine Lives of Fritz the Cat" (1974), was an aesthetic disaster.

Richard Williams's lavish Anglo-American production, "Raggedy Ann and Raggedy Andy—A Musical Adventure" (1977), featured work by great old animators (Art Babbitt, Grim Natwick, Emery Hawkins, Tissa David) and promising young artists (Dan Haskett, Michael Sporn, Eric Goldberg). But its opulent visuals sank beneath the burden of a simpleminded script, leaden pacing and Joe Raposo's many forgettable songs.

It took more than a year to find a distributor for San Rio's "Metamorphoses" (Japan/U.S., 1978), despite a sound track that featured songs by the Rolling Stones and the Pointer Sisters. This excruciating compilation of Greek myths was withdrawn, reworked and re-released in 1980 as "Winds of Change." The additional labor failed to improve it, and the film disappeared with merciful swiftness.

Martin Rosen's adaptation of Richard Adams's *Watership Down* (Great Britain, 1978) boasted an excellent script and strong performances by a vocal cast that included John Hurt, Ralph Richardson, Denholm Elliott and Zero Mostel. Balanced against these strengths were the unimpressive animation and the uninspired designs, which made it difficult to tell the various rabbit characters apart.

Controversy surrounded the production of "Watership Down." John Hubley was hired to direct the film, but left over differences with writer-producer Martin Rosen. Rosen assumed the duties of director, and a year's work had to be scrapped. However, the introduction, which explained the rabbit mythology with stylized figures reminiscent of Inuit or Oceanic art, retained Hubley's distinctive stamp.

Probably the most popular European animated feature of the 1970s was "Allegro Non Troppo" (Italy, 1977), Bruno Bozzetto's spoof of "Fantasia." The film contained some fine animation, particularly the sequence set to Ravel's "Bolero," in which a succession of wonderfully improbable animals evolved from the gunk in the bottom of a Coke bottle. "Allegro Non Troppo" remains a popular attraction at revival theaters.

An unprecedented number of animated features were released during the early 1980s, but almost all of them did poorly at the box office. "1001 Rabbit Tales" (1982) and "Twice Upon a Time," "Daffy Duck's Movie: Fantastic Island" and "Fire and Ice" (all 1983) received only limited theatrical distribution and had *combined* earnings of less than $2 million. (Cable television and cassette sales later put some of these films in the black.)

Martin Rosen's adaptation of Richard Adams's *The Plague Dogs* (Great Britain, 1983) and Nelvana's "Rock and Rule" (a.k.a. "Ring of Power," Canada, 1982) failed to obtain U.S. distribution and were shown only in film festivals and special screenings. The sophomoric "Heavy Metal" (Canada/U.S., 1981) and Don Bluth's "The Secret of NIMH" (1982) did reasonably well.

The poor showing of these features triggered discussions within the film industry about the problems of marketing and distributing an animated feature. The concern was justified. Animation was tagged as box office poison. The fact that in 1982 re-releases of "Robin Hood," "Peter Pan" and "Cinderella" earned $55 million was ascribed to the mystical power of "the Disney name."

The medium had become so stereotyped as a children's entertainment that it became difficult to "place" an animated feature before a large audience. Even a good film like Will Vinton's "The Adventures of Mark Twain" (1985) had trouble finding viewers.

Hyperion's "The Brave Little Toaster" (1987), a bright, appealing film based on Thomas Disch's story about a group of household appliances, never received theatrical distribution, but aired on the Disney Channel. Filmation's "Bravestarr: The Legend" (1988), made in conjunction with a syndicated series based on a line of toys, was shown only at weekend matinees.

However, many films did badly because they were terrible. "Rabbit Tales" and "Fantastic Island" tried to make coherent stories out of bits and pieces of old Warner Brothers shorts. The widely touted "Lumage" animation in "Twice Upon a

A series of frames from Hyperion's "The Brave Little Toaster." Bottom: The title character tries to comfort the frightened blanket as the appliances seek shelter from a storm.

Time" turned out to be a minor variation on the silhouette technique Lotte Reiniger devised in 1919. "The Secret of the Sword" (1985) and "Here Come the Littles" (1985) were just re-cut television programs.

The most successful and widely publicized challenger to the Disney studio's supremacy in animated features was Don Bluth. Animators Gary Goldman and John Pomeroy had worked with Bluth on the film that later became "Banjo, the Woodpile Cat" (1980), in a studio they set up in Bluth's garage. After leaving Disney in 1979, they organized the studio on a cooperative basis with the other disaffected artists.

Their first projects were "Banjo," a 24-minute short subsequently purchased by ABC-TV, and a 2-minute animated sequence for the live-action disco musical "Xanadu." Originally planned as a Christmas story, "Banjo" told the story of a mischievous farm kitten who runs away to the city. Lost and lonely, he's befriended by a jazz-playing alley cat named Crazylegs (voice by Scatman Crothers), who eventually helps him get home to his family. The film owed more than a little to Disney's "The Aristocats."

In 1980, Bluth formed "an exclusive association" with Aurora Productions, which helped secure the $7 million budget (plus an additional $4.5 million for prints and advertising) for his first feature, "The Secret of NIMH."

Based on the book *Mrs. Frisby and the Rats of NIMH*, by Robert O'Brien, "The Secret of NIMH" (1982) was an impressive debut that suggested that these artists would be capable of exceptional work with additional time and training. The film contained some excellent animation, particularly of Jeremy, the klutzy crow (voice by Dom DeLuise). But "NIMH" suffered from poor storytelling, fussy character designs and a tendency toward visual overkill. The artists put in so many sparkles, shadows, reflections and wisps of smoke that it became difficult to follow the main action in some scenes.

"The Secret of NIMH" was a film that looked backward, rather than forward. Bluth is an outspoken admirer of the Disney films of the 1930s, and much of "NIMH's" visual style was copied from "Snow White" and "Pinocchio." Accounts in the popular press portrayed Bluth and the new Disney artists as vying to assume Walt's mantle. But Walt's best works had been bold, experimental films, rather than attempts to recreate something out of the past.

"NIMH" earned $13 million theatrically: a respectable showing, but hardly a smash hit. During the next two years, "East of the Sun and West of the Moon," "The Little Blue Whale" and "Beauty and the Beast" were mentioned as the studio's next feature.

In July 1983, a consortium including the Don Bluth studio (animation), Advanced Microcomputer Systems (programming) and Cinematronics (manufacture/distribution) launched "Dragon's Lair," the first laser-disc video game.

mation industry. Every studio either had a deal to make a video game or was negotiating one. There was talk of animated home video games and of the opportunities the new technology offered the medium.

The Bluth studio produced 14 minutes of animation for its second video game, "Space Ace" (1984), which proved popular but failed to duplicate the runaway success of "Dragon's Lair." Later that year, Cinematronics encountered financial difficulties, then the bottom dropped out of the arcade game market. Although the animation had been completed for "Dragon's Lair II: Time Warp," the game was never released. The laser-disc video game boom ended as quickly as it began.

Bluth's second feature, "An American Tail" (1986), exhibited many of the same strengths and weaknesses as "The Secret of NIMH." Bluth and writers David Kirchner, Judy Freudberg and Tony Geiss attempted to transfer the experiences of the nineteenth-century immigrants who came to America seeking freedom from religious persecution to a world of mice. A raid by "cossack cats" spurs little Fievel Mousekewitz and his family to leave Russia for America, "where there are no cats."

Cats chasing mice were an inappropriate metaphor for religious persecution. Oppression is not a conflict between predator and prey, but the willful cruelty the members of a single species inflict on each other in the name of a spurious ideology. Roger Ebert noted that the film "tells a specifically Jewish experience but does not attempt to inform its young viewers that the characters are Jewish, or that the house burning was a result of anti-Semitism." Vincent Canby described "An American Tail" as "the first such children's film to open with a pogrom and to end with an entire species being forcibly relocated."

Above: Special effects added to the sense of danger in the "Space Ace" video game. Right: Dirk the Daring is attacked by a pair of monsters, one of the many animated perils in "Dragon's Lair."

Bluth produced 22 minutes of full animation for the game at a cost of $1.3 million.

Because the information on a laser disc can be randomly accessed, each time the player made a decision or defeated a foe in the game he jumped to a new situation that resulted from his previous action. A player might make 200 decisions to guide the hero, Dirk the Daring, through 38 situations and rescue Princess Daphne. (One game would take about six minutes if the player made all the right decisions.)

"Dragon's Lair" proved exceedingly popular, grossing more than $32 million in eight months. A line of merchandise was issued featuring Dirk and Daphne, and the Marvel studio produced a Saturday-morning kidvid show based on "Dragon's Lair."

Laser-disc games briefly became the buzzword of the ani-

Below: Henri the Pigeon meets Fievel Mousekewitz, in Don Bluth's popular feature "An American
Tail." Right: Bluth with the cast of "Space Ace."

"An American Tail" looked even more lavish than "NIMH," with more effects and details; the rounded designs were again modeled after the work of the Disney artists. The animation was full and fluid, but it often seemed at odds with the characterizations. Nehemiah Persoff gave Fievel's papa a thick accent, but the character didn't move with the body language of an old Russian Jew.

Like "NIMH," "An American Tail" suffered from poor direction and ineffective storytelling. Suspenseful situations were created, then abandoned before they paid off. The sentimental aspects of the story were overblown and treacly.

Produced and released under the aegis of Steven Spielberg's Amblin Productions, "An American Tail" was heavily promoted and merchandised in a campaign that more than counteracted its very mixed reviews. It set a box office record for an animated feature, earning more than $45 million. Cassette sales of the film topped 1.3 million units.

In 1984, Bluth met Morris Sullivan, the former CEO of a major corporate financial consulting firm, then in semiretirement. Sullivan felt the animators' financial problems were due to poor business and legal advice and decided to help them. He reached an accord with the Irish Industrial Authority to shift production to Dublin, where the ink and paint work for "American Tail" had been done.

The move made excellent fiscal sense: Wages were lower in Ireland and the Irish government offered substantial tax benefits to filmmakers. The Sullivan-Bluth Studios Ireland was established in a modern, 42,000-square-foot building on the banks of the River Liffey. "The Land Before Time" (1988), Bluth's third feature, was made entirely in Dublin.

Produced by Sullivan-Bluth for Steven Spielberg and George Lucas, "Land Before Time" told an original story about dinosaurs. After a Tyrannosaurus kills his mother, Littlefoot, a baby Brontosaurus, sets out to find the secure haven of "The Great Valley." Along the way, he befriends children of other reptile groups—a Triceratops, an Anatosaurus, a Pterodactyl and a Stegosaurus.

The story borrowed heavily from "Bambi," but indulged in a heavy-handed sentimentality that Disney wisely eschewed. Not only did the mother dinosaur die on screen, but her image appeared in the clouds to guide Littlefoot after her death ("Some things you see with your eyes. Other things you see with your heart"). Although the members of the various reptile groups learned they could get along and even help each other on the journey, the characters failed to mature the way Bambi did.

"Land Before Time" was heavily promoted and opened the same weekend as Disney's "Oliver & Company"—the first time two animated features had been released head to head. "Land Before Time" grossed over $7 million during the opening weekend—a record for an animated feature—and nearly twice what "Oliver" earned. ("Land" was booked into nearly half again as many theaters—1,410 vs. 952.) The film went on to gross an impressive $46 million domestically.

Critical opinion on the film was divided. Janet Maslin praised the "enchanting behavior of these little beings," in the New York Times, adding, "In circumstances like these, 'cute' cannot be thought of as a term of opprobrium." In the Los Angeles Times, Sheila Benson decried the "ootsie-cutesiness" that reduced the mighty dinosaurs to "little more than adorable bath toys."

In February 1988, Sullivan-Bluth signed a $70 million joint venture financing agreement with Goldcrest, a subsidiary of Brent Walker Group Plc. (a large U.K. corporation) to produce three animated features over the next three years. When "Land Before Time" opened, work had already begun on the first of these features, "All Dogs Go to Heaven." Burt Reynolds, Loni Anderson and Dom DeLuise provided character voices, and the film was scheduled for release in 1989. A second feature, with the working title "Rock-A-Doodle," was slated for 1990. In addition, plans were announced for the studio to expand into television and live-action production.

Despite the success of his films—and the media attention they have received—it is not clear what Don Bluth's ultimate contribution to animation will be. His very real talents as an

Littlefoot, the central character of Bluth's "The Land Before Time," with some of the other dinosaurs.

animator and his love for the medium must be balanced against his limits as a director: He is not an effective story-teller, and his attempts to recapture the magic of the great Disney features lack the innovative spirit that distinguishes those films. And it seems ironic that his studio, which has been presented as the savior of classic American animation, would attempt to fulfill that role from Dublin.

The publicity surrounding the brief craze for laser-disc games drew attention from another trend that would have an even greater impact on the animation industry: the rise of license product characters.

Animation has been associated with merchandising since the days of Felix the Cat, but the cartoons always came first. The popularity of Felix, Mickey Mouse, Donald Duck, Woody Woodpecker et al. created a market for products featuring their likenesses. During the early 1980s, creators discovered that animated films could provide an effective way to present their merchandise: New characters were created *in vacuo* by corporate designers and the rights to reproduce them were sold to various manufacturers.

One of the first characters to benefit from this marketing strategy was Strawberry Shortcake, a tiny girl in an outsized mop cap. When she and three related figures were launched in 1980 by a consortium of American Greetings Corp. and General Mills, they appeared on products from five companies. By 1983, the line had grown to 20 characters, who appeared on more than 1,200 items from 68 companies and accounted for hundreds of millions of dollars in retail sales. Three syndicated television specials had helped to make little girls aware of all the Strawberry Shortcake characters.

This highly successful campaign led to the formation of Those Characters from Cleveland, a licensing subsidiary of American Greetings and MAD, the Marketing and Design service of the toy group at General Mills. They subsequently created Herself the Elf and the Care Bears.

The Care Bears, a clutch of teddy bears with various insignia on their stomachs, proved to be one of the most successful of all license characters, racking up more than $200 million in retail sales in 1984. The Care Bear Cousins, a group of ten new animals, were introduced in "The Care Bears Movie" (1985). Animated in Canada by the Nelvana studio for only $4 million, the movie was a cheaper way of announcing the new line of products than a major advertising campaign.

The film itself was little more than a gargantuan commercial disguised as a story about "sharing feelings." Barefaced commercialism underlay the threadbare plot. The animation ranked a cut above Saturday-morning kidvid, but no higher. The various bears didn't embody the qualities they were supposed to represent, the way the Dwarfs did in "Snow White."

Released at a time when virtually no other films for children were in the theaters, "The Care Bears Movie" earned $23 million—besides stimulating untold millions of dollars in additional sales of Care Bears merchandise. The sequel, "Care Bears II: A New Generation" (1986), introduced another new product line (the Care Bear Cubs) and earned an additional $8.1 million. That fall, a half-hour Saturday-morning series, "The Care Bears Family," debuted on ABC.

The success of the Care Bears films led other toy manufacturers to enter the theatrical market. During 1985–86, animated features appeared "starring" My Little Pony, Transformers, Gobots, Rainbow Brite and the American Rabbit. All of these films were made cheaply and quickly overseas. (DIC reportedly produced "Rainbow Brite and the Star Stealer" in three months—a record for an animated feature.) Poorly written and badly animated, their sole purpose was to promote the merchandise.

License product characters and animation based on merchandise had an even greater impact on the television industry. A vast market for new animated programs opened in 1981 when Mattel asked Lou Scheimer, the president of the Filmation studio, to create a series based on its forthcoming line of sword-and-sorcery figures. When Westinghouse acquired Filmation later that year, Scheimer suggested developing the Mattel property for the company's distribution arm, Group W.

The film received mixed reviews but earned an impressive $46 million at the box office.

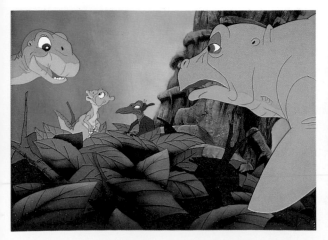

Above: Some of the action-figure toys from Mattel's "He-Man and the Masters of the Universe" line. Opposite top: The villainous Skeletor on his throne. The success of Filmation's "He-Man and the Masters of the Universe" created a lucrative market for animation in first-run syndication.

"He-Man and the Masters of the Universe" debuted in syndication in 1983 to an unexpectedly high rating: a 6 share in households and a 16 to 18 share of children in the two-to-eleven age group. Its only competition consisted of reruns of old cartoons, many of them originally made for Saturday morning.

"The year we went on the air, our ratings were phenomenal," says Scheimer. "Advertisers loved it, because with no significant children's programming off-network, they had been relegated to the Saturday-morning ghetto. It became apparent that this was a much better market for us, both financially and creatively."

The success of "He-Man" led to a spate of made-for-syndication programs, most of them financed by toy companies, including "Bigfoot," "Centurions," "G.I. Joe," "Gobots," "J.E.M.," "M.A.S.K.," "Sectaurs," "She-Ra, Prin-

cess of Power," "Thundercats," "Transformers" and "Voltron."

The stakes were high: a toy manufacturer might invest between $12 and $14 million in developing a series, and commit an equal sum to advertising on the client stations. But the potential profits were even higher: by 1985, more than $500 million worth of He-Man toys had been sold, plus an additional $500 million of related merchandise.

Like the toys they promoted, most of the syndicated programs were "sex-specific." Series that featured action figures and robots, like "G.I. Joe," "Thundercats" and "Transformers," were aimed at boys. Shows that centered on dolls or cute characters like "J.E.M.," "My Little Pony" and "Rose Petal Place," were directed at girls.

"The overcommercialization of children's television is worse than that of adult television," charged Peggy Charren, president of Action for Children's Television (ACT) in 1983. "A

show composed of commercials is insidiously horrible, although that's not to say license products are inherently ghastly—I played with a Shirley Temple doll as a child.

" 'The Masters of the Universe' [which was about to debut] is another example of programmers, writers and producers looking to toys for ideas because of their licensing potential," she continued. "When the concept of a program is to sell, it limits its creativity. It's a shame that the people who make their living telling stories no longer care about telling stories."

Dennis Marks, creative director at the Marvel studio, replied: "Wasn't the Disney show a huge promotion for Disneyland? And how is animating G.I. Joe different from a guest on Johnny Carson plugging a book or a movie? Don't networks plug shows with 'guest stars' on other shows? You can't condemn one aspect of it without condemning the entire system. TV is one big promotion."

Many animation producers felt syndication offered distinct advantages over Saturday-morning production. Although the budgets per episode were comparable, the deadlines were spread out over a longer period of time. The networks ordered only thirteen episodes of a show per season, while syndicated series were produced in packages of sixty-five half-hour episodes. Because the stations bought completed programs, the studios didn't have to submit their work to the scrutiny of the network broadcast standards departments. For years, animators had chafed at their strictures.

Despite rumors that syndicated programming had usurped so much of the audience that the networks were planning to cut back their kidvid lineups, the Big Three continued to dominate the market. In 1986, their combined audience still accounted for 85 percent of the available viewers or 13.3

million children. The syndicated programs were broadcast on Sunday mornings and weekday afternoons.

"The competition is really for the total amount of advertising dollars scheduled to be spent on programs that appeal to children," says Martin Weinberg, senior vice president of animation operations at Taft Entertainment (then the parent company of Hanna-Barbera and Ruby-Spears). "The impact on the networks is not so much a reduction in audience as it is a competition for advertising dollars."

The boom in syndicated programming quickly glutted a finite market. By the fall of 1986, there were twenty-six first-run series on the air. Taft Entertainment alone made five different series and two miniseries, totaling more than three hundred half hours.

This plethora of material caused a rapid drop in ratings. In mid-November 1986, "G.I. Joe," the most popular first-run series, had a Nielsen rating of 3.6 (3.1 million households)—hardly a smash hit, even by the more modest standards of syndication (and a failure for a network show). Only 2½ points separated "G.I. Joe" from "Gobots," the 18th-ranked children's show. At 1.4, "Gobots" had dropped 50 percent from its 2.8 rating the previous November. The ratings for "He-Man" and "She-Ra" also fell nearly 50 percent in the same time period. These statistics suggest just how fragmented the off-network audience had become.

By late 1986, the consensus within the animation industry was that first-run syndication would remain an important market, but on a reduced scale. Off-network broadcasting simply couldn't support twenty-six packages of sixty-five half-hour episodes each year, even with substantial underwriting from the toy industry. (Nor could the toy companies, many of which experienced financial difficulties during the later 1980s, continue to subsidize this amount of production.)

Disney entered the syndication market in September 1987, with "Ducktales," a cartoon series loosely based on the stories Carl Barks created for the Disney comic books during the forties and fifties. For the first time, a foreign studio (TMS, or Tokyo Movie Shinsha) animated classic Disney characters (Donald Duck and his nephews) in the limited style of Saturday morning TV. (TMS had done similar animation for "The Wuzzles" and "Gummi Bears," Disney's first Saturday morning programs, but these shows dealt with new characters in new settings.)

Although purists complained that "Ducktales" reduced the Disney characters and Barks's extravagantly farfetched stories to homogenized cartoon comedy-adventures, the series scored a big hit. It received higher ratings than any other animated series in syndication, and outdrew many live-action shows. Within two weeks of its premiere, Disney announced plans for a second syndicated series, "Chip 'n' Dale: Rescue Rangers," scheduled for the fall of 1989 in conjunction with thirty new installments of "Ducktales."

The genius of Oskar Fischinger—scenes from three of his most significant American films: top, "Motion Painting #1" (1947); center, "Allegretto" (1936); bottom, "An Optical Poem" (1937).

Some animators rejected the kidvid programs and license character films that constituted the bulk of American animation as aesthetically and morally bankrupt. The dichotomy between animation as an art form and animation as an assembly-line product became increasingly evident as independent animators began to dominate film awards—including the Oscars—and the general public gradually learned of their work.

Independent animation remains the least documented area of a critically neglected art. Filmmaking has generally been regarded as a popular entertainment. Artists who tried to use it as a vehicle for personal expression had to content themselves with small audiences composed of other artists, students and avant-garde patrons until well into the 1960s.

It's easy to decry the lack of interest in personal and/or experimental animated films as an example of the overly conservative or even philistine taste of the American public. The abstract films of such artists as Oskar Fischinger and John Whitney display unique beauties and a bracing purity: they deserve exposure to wider audiences. And the work of many experimental animators has influenced mainstream filmmaking, albeit indirectly.

"Whatever work the avant-garde does invariably finds its way into the vocabulary of mainstream film," explains Douglas Edwards, Exhibitions and Special Programs Coordinator for the Academy of Motion Picture Arts and Sciences. "Avant-garde inventions are often picked up first by the people who do TV commercials. They're always on the lookout for new techniques and effects to use to hype a product. From commercials, the techniques are adopted by narrative filmmakers. So the avant-garde functions as a sort of laboratory for mainstream filmmakers, whether they're willing to admit it or not."

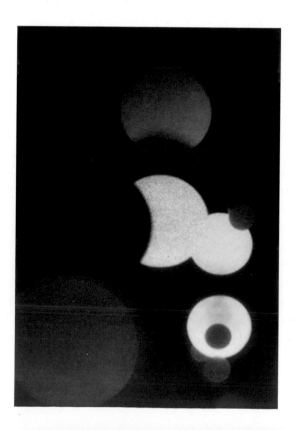

While some experimental animation is brilliant, imaginative and beautiful, even serious students of the medium find other films challenging, if not difficult to watch. Filmmaker-critic Robert Russett describes Tony Conrad's "Flicker" (1965), which consists of patterns of alternating clear and black frames, as "a classic among modern experimental films. In this abstract work, Conrad created a new filmic condition by modulating the fundamental energy source of the cinema, projected light." But screening "Flicker" is like sitting in a room with an erratically timed strobe light, and it is unwatchable by the average viewer's standards.

Winsor McCay had envisioned animated visuals replacing the static imagery of the traditional graphic arts. The first European independent animation was done around 1921—the time of McCay's last films—but more than a decade passed before artists in America started to pursue his vision of animation as a personal art form.

Independent animation began in the United States during the middle 1930s, with the first films of Mary Ellen Bute. The movement gained strength during the late 1930s and early 1940s through the experiments of John and James Whitney, Oskar Fischinger, Douglass Crockwell, Dwinell Grant, Francis Lee and, later, Jordan Belson.

Although the distinctions sometimes blur, most independent animators can be grouped into four categories. One is composed of the pure abstractionists: artists who explore the aesthetic potential of form, motion and color without recourse to recognizable imagery or conventional narrative structures. The work of Oskar Fischinger, Jordan Belson and John and James Whitney falls within this classification.

A second group use animation techniques, but their interests and influence have stronger affinities with the more avant-garde aspects of live-action filmmaking. Among these artists are Robert Breer and Zbigniew Rybczynski.

The third category comprises the technical innovators: artists who devise or adapt new tools for producing images frame by frame. In recent years, many of these animators have begun working in computer graphics. Included in this category would be John Whitney, Lillian Schwartz and Larry Cuba.

Artists in the fourth group use more conventional animation techniques in unconventional ways that reflect a personal vision. Their subject matter ranges from childhood reminiscences to sociopolitical statements to abstract imagery. They work in a variety of media, including standard cel techniques. Not surprisingly, these artists have had the most significant and widespread influence on mainstream studio animation.

A few of these animators have attained widespread recognition in America: Will Vinton, Michael Sporn, Frank and Carolyn Mouris and John and Faith Hubley. Some have moved to other countries to find the opportunities and recognition their work merits: Carolyn Leaf has made her best films at the National Film Board of Canada. Others, like Dennis Pies, George Griffin and Sara Petty, are well respected within the international animation community for their achievements, but remain little known within the United States.

These divisions, of course, are not absolutes; the work of many artists defies neat classifications. Oskar Fischinger was one of the pioneers of abstract animation, but he was also a technical innovator who devised a method for synthetically creating sound on film. John Whitney ranks as one of the pioneers of both American abstract film and computer animation, but he has also worked on title sequences for major Hollywood releases. Lillian Schwartz and Ed Emshwiller are respected for their work in both live-action film and computer animation.

With three Academy Awards ("Moonbird," 1959; "The Hole," 1963; "Tijuana Brass Double Feature," 1966), four more nominations ("Windy Day," 1967; "Of Men and Demons," 1969; "Voyage to Next," 1975; "A Doonesbury Special," 1978) and countless prizes from film festivals all over the world, Faith Elliott Hubley and the late John Hubley rank as the most celebrated independent animators in America.

John Hubley was already one of the most respected talents in American animation when he and Faith Elliott, a script supervisor and film/sound editor, met in the early 1950s during the production of the UPA sex education film "Of Human Growth." They worked together on the ill-fated cartoon ver-

Two of the collages from Frank and Carolyn Mouris's Oscar-winning "Frank Film."

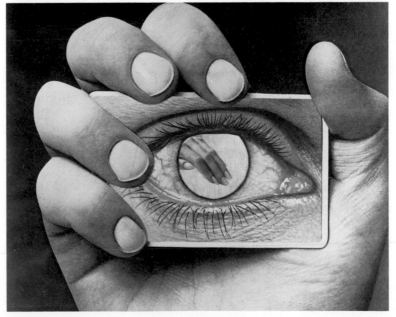

sion of *Finian's Rainbow* and were married in 1955. The Hubleys included "to make one noncommercial film a year" among their wedding vows.

In 1956, they released their first major work, "The Adventures of an *," commissioned by the Guggenheim Museum. In "Adventures," the Hubleys strove to make animation even more graphically stylized than the UPA films. Some of the characters were reduced to semi-abstract constructs of lines, drawn in wax on paper and splashed with watercolors "to produce a resisted texture."

Imaginative use of sound, color, texture, multiple exposures and abstract and semi-abstract imagery became hallmarks of the Hubley films. They were also the first animators to feature the music of important jazz artists, including Ella Fitzgerald, Dizzy Gillespie, Quincy Jones, Benny Carter, Oscar Peterson and Lionel Hampton.

John and Faith recorded the voices of their children at play, edited the tapes and used the results as the sound track for "Moonbird." Arguably their best film, "Moonbird" follows the efforts of two little boys to capture the shy and elusive title creature. The Hubleys also used their children's voices in "Windy Day" and "Cockaboody" (1973). The innovative result —a giggling, wandering story line—delighted some observers, who saw it as a profound treatment of childhood; others rejected it as self-conscious and precious. In either case, the critics treated the films as important works that merited serious consideration, rather than dismissing them as cartoons.

The unusual and imaginative films of the Hubleys contrasted sharply with the formulaic work that was being ground out for Saturday-morning TV by the major studios, and they helped to stimulate the use of innovative graphic styles and unusual music tracks in both personal and commercial animated films. The Hubleys did more to make people aware that animation was a legitimate art form than any American studio since Disney during the 1930s.

Since John's unexpected death in 1977 (during the production of "A Doonesbury Special"), Faith has maintained the studio, teaching, painting and making films of her own, including "Whither Weather" (1977), "Sky Dance" (1979), "Enter Life" (1981), "Starlore" (1982), "Hello" (1984), and "Yes, We Can" (1988). In 1985, she completed "The Cosmic Eye," a combination of old and new Hubley animation that represented the first feature-length work produced by an independent American animator.

During the late 1970s and early 1980s, independent animation began to attract larger, more general audiences. Dennis Pies ("Aura Corona," 1974; "Luma Nocturna," 1974; and "Sonoma," 1977) offered a mystic, reflective vision of nature that seemed both micro- and macrocosmic. Frank and Carolyn Mouris dazzled audiences with the Oscar-winning

Below: John and Faith Hubley at the Movieola during the early 1960s. Opposite: A scene from their television special "Everybody Rides the Carousel" (1976), an adaptation of Erik Erikson's concept of the eight stages of the human life cycle.

"Frank Film" (1973), an almost overwhelming collage of images cut from magazines that functioned as both an autobiography and a satire on a consumer society. In "Furies" (1977), Sara Petty used charcoal and pastels to transform the movements of her pet cats into Cubist abstractions.

The weird, alienated world of Sally Cruikshank's "Quasi at the Quackadero" (1978) delighted hip young viewers. Mike Jittlov's remarkable stop-motion work in "The Wizard of Speed and Time" (1980) made him a popular guest at science-fiction conventions. George Griffin explored the nature of animation in self-reflexive works like "Viewmaster" (1976), "Lineage" (1979) and "Flying Fur" (1981).

The most successful of the new, young artists was Will Vinton, who demonstrated the artistic potential of stop-motion clay animation. He and Bob Gardiner shared an Academy Award in 1974 for their technical tour de force, "Closed Mondays," then went their separate ways.

Vinton established a studio in Portland, Oregon, where he and his animators refined and expanded "Claymation." Their techniques range from realistic, three-dimensional sculpture to moving streaks of clay on Plexiglas to produce an effect that resembles an oil painting in motion.

In addition to numerous festival prizes, Vinton has earned four subsequent Oscar nominations—one for the special effects of the Gnome King in Disney's "Return to Oz" (1985) and three for animated shorts: "Rip van Winkle" (1978), "The Creation" (1981) and "The Great Cognito" (1982). He received Emmys in 1987 for "A Claymation Christmas Celebration"

An example of the complex imagery in Paul Glabicki's "Object Conversation."

(Outstanding Animated Program) and the "Come Back, Little Shiksa" episode of "Moonlighting" (Outstanding Special visual Effects).

"The Adventures of Mark Twain by Huck Finn" (1985) was the first feature done in clay animation. Vinton's most mature work to date, "Mark Twain" was free of the two problems that had weakened several of his earlier films: inadequate scripts and a tendency to overanimate. A chilling sequence adapted from Twain's "The Mysterious Stranger" reminded audiences how eerie good animation can be—a fact the simpleminded ghost shows on Saturday mornings had obscured.

But his most famous creations are the funky dancing raisins he animated for the California Raisin Board, which garnered three Clio awards and launched an extensive merchandising campaign. In the 1988 CBS special "Meet the Raisins," Vinton and his artists sought to establish the raisins as four distinct characters (Red, A.C., Beebop and Stretch), whom they planned to develop for future projects.

Vinton's films and commercials proved that clay animation —which had traditionally been regarded as a crude medium, suitable for children—could be as flexible and expressive as drawn animation.

"Claymation is a performance sculpted with the fingers," says Vinton. "The animator sits in front of the camera and *performs* this blob of clay, much the way an actor acts, trying to communicate the character's thoughts and feelings."

Since he opened his own studio in 1980, Michael Sporn seems to have almost single-handedly revived the moribund New York animation industry, which had been reduced to a few independent artists and commercial houses.

He began by making educational children's films, but his

Opposite: Will Vinton on the set of the "Meet the Raisins" television special (1988). Below: The California Raisins—Red, Stretch, A.C. and Beebop.

work for designer Tony Walton, including the animation of the cartoon character in the Broadway musical "Woman of the Year" and the titles for the films "Deathtrap" and "Prince of the City," attracted the attention of larger audiences. Sporn received an Oscar nomination in 1985 for "Dr. De Soto," an adaptation of William Steig's children's book about a shrewd mouse-dentist who outwits a conniving fox.

He followed "Dr. De Soto" with two other films based on Steig books, "The Magic Bone" and "Abel's Island"; the latter film aired on PBS in February 1989, as part of the series "Long Ago and Far Away." "Lyle, Lyle, Crocodile," a special adapted from Bernard Waber's children's book "The House on East 88th Street," aired on HBO in the fall of 1987, followed by "Santabear's High Flying Adventures" on CBS, a charming holiday show that featured the voices of John Malkovich, Kelly McGillis and jazz musician Bobby McFerrin.

Independent artists like Vinton, the Hubleys, Pies, Mouris, Griffin, Petty et al. brought originality and beauty to American animation at a time when the work of the major studios looked dismayingly uninspired. Since the Hubleys won an Oscar for "Moonbird" in 1959—the first independent animators to be nominated—small studios, independents and foreign studios (especially the National Film Board of Canada) have dominated the nominations for animated short film. The last short from a major studio to win the Academy Award was Disney's "It's Tough to Be a Bird" in 1969.

Independent animators still face enormous problems financing and distributing their work. As there is no U.S. equivalent of the Canadian Film Board or the government-subsidized studios of Eastern Europe, American filmmakers must finance their own work, which means raising thousands of dollars. The artists must teach, seek grants or corporate sponsors, work in studios or find jobs outside their art.

The market for short films remains extremely limited, and very few films earn back their production costs, let alone show a profit. Rental fees are minimal—if a distributor can be found. And while cable television offers filmmakers wide exposure, they pay as little as $125 per minute for multiple showings. Despite these difficulties, some American artists continue to devote their time, money and talent to a personal vision of what an animated film can be—and the art of animation is richer for their devotion.

The most publicized innovation in frame-by-frame filmmaking during the 1970s and 1980s was the advent of computer animation in commercial motion pictures. Computer graphics were hailed as a panacea that would cure the problems besetting the animation industry. Fantastic announcements appeared in the popular press, proclaiming that computers would soon take all the "drudgery" out of animation and produce simulations so lifelike that dead actors could be "resurrected" to appear in new films.

While these inflated claims have not been realized, computer graphics have had a profound effect on American life. But their greatest impact has been in business graphics and industrial design and manufacture. Animation accounted for barely 1 percent of the nearly $7.5 billion spent on computer graphics in 1986, and only a portion of that was applied to entertainment. The limitations of what is still a very new

An elegant mouse learns self-reliance in "Abel's Island," Michael Sporn's adaptation of a children's book by William Steig.

technology, cost and the inability of animators and computer specialists to communicate effectively have all restricted the use of computer imagery in the animation industry.

The computer represents an innovation in graphics tools, one that requires specialized skills and a new vocabulary. Some artists and animators still question its validity. They balk at terms like "raster," "fractal," "algorithm" and "frame buffer," and joke about computer specialists turning nouns like "interface" into verbs. Conversely, many of the technicians who create computer-generated images—and who delight in its recondite jargon—have little artistic training. Their work too often juxtaposes enormous technical sophistication with an aesthetic void.

Underlying all the elaborate visuals is the ability of the computer to assign values for color (a proportion of red, blue and green) and brightness for each point or pixel on a video monitor. The high-resolution monitors used for commercial computer graphics may have 2,000 or more lines running in each direction for a total of four million pixels (a standard television screen has 525 horizontal and vertical lines). Images of staggering complexity can be built out of these pixels, and millions of calculations may be required to generate a single frame of film. Sophisticated software programs instruct the computer to alter each image in a sequence to simulate movement or changes in lighting. The images are recorded onto film or videotape from the monitor, one frame at a time, to produce animation.

"The more interesting the picture, the longer it takes the computer to generate," comments James Blinn, whose work includes the simulated Voyager flybys for NASA. "You can slow down the fastest computer by giving it more to do. If you get a faster computer, your taste gets more elaborate, so it always takes about the same amount of time to make a picture. It takes between five and ten minutes to generate one frame of the films I make. That's the limit of my patience with that vision."

The first computer-generated images were created during the early 1950s at the Bell Laboratories and various universities, notably MIT, as scientists began using cathode-ray tubes to display the information in computer memory banks. (Some experimental animators, including Mary Ellen Bute, Norman McLaren and Hy Hirsch, made films using oscilloscope patterns at about the same time.) During the late 1950s, the U.S. Army's SAGE air defense system used a primitive example of interactive computer graphics to indicate potential targets. Ivan Sutherland wrote "Sketchpad" at MIT in 1962. This Ph.D. thesis created the first truly interactive graphics, enabling an artist to draw simple geometric forms.

Working independently, John Whitney began using war-surplus analog computing devices for his film experiments in 1957–58. These efforts were summarized in the film "Catalogue" (1961), and enabled John to help with the complex photography of still artwork for "Lapis" (1963–66), a film his brother James had been struggling to finish.

Two landmark computer films were completed in 1967. Abstract patterns of colored dots performed complicated motions in John Whitney's "Permutations," made under a research grant from IBM. At Ohio State University, Charles Csuri made "Hummingbird," which showed a two-dimensional drawing of a hummingbird breaking into linear fragments. Peter Foldes expanded the technique of moving pieces of lines to alter drawings and suggest motion in his ugly, Oscar-nominated short "Hunger" (Canada, 1974).

Above: Computer animator James Blinn. Right: The planet Saturn and the Voyager space probe in a simulated flyby that Blinn created for NASA.

Whitney remains one of the acknowledged leaders of the independent computer artist-animators. No human animator could possibly draw the intricate patterns of colored dots that form his exquisite film "Arabesque" (1975). Whitney has sought to distance himself from the animation community in recent years, as he continues his search for a graphic language comparable to musical notation, but his work continues to influence other artists.

Complex mathematical relationships underlie the abstract patterns in Larry Cuba's films "3/78" (1978), "Two Space" (1979) and "Calculated Movements" (1985). The austere elegance of his work imbues it with a cool, remote beauty.

Ed Emshwiller, who began working with abstract animation in 1959, uses a computer to create his personal films. "Sunstone" (1979) is a shimmering, sensual collage of silvery pointillist faces and landscapes.

Lillian Schwartz often begins her films with recognizable images and uses the computer to explore permutations of their basic forms. In "Olympiad" (1971), she transforms Muybridge's sequential photographs of a runner into aggregates of hexagons while exploring the nature of their motion. Photographs of the artist's family metamorphose into increasingly abstract shapes and groupings of color in "Pictures from a Gallery" (1976).

But these computer animators, and their colleagues—Stan VanDerBeek, Ken Knowlton, Charles Csuri et al.—face the same problems as other independent filmmakers: money (although Emshwiller has experimented with a $50 Bally computer, computer animation can be extremely expensive) and distribution. It is difficult to find an audience for a personal computer film outside of occasional festivals and the annual screenings at the SIGGRAPH (Special Interest Group for Computer Graphics) conference.

The flashier, commercial applications of computer animation have commanded a much larger audience than the experimental works. Larry Cuba has received more attention for the special effects he did in George Lucas's "Star Wars" (the plans for the Death Star that were read from R2D2's memory) than for his personal films.

The most sophisticated computer graphics remain very expensive, and their use has largely been restricted to television commercials, network logos and brief special-effects sequences in major feature films. "The Genesis Effect" in "Star Trek II: The Wrath of Khan" (1982), the swirling atmosphere of the planet Jupiter in "2010" (1984), and the stained-glass knight in "Young Sherlock Holmes" (1985) rank among the best-known examples.

"I think computer graphics will enter the film industry through the back door of special effects," says Charles Gibson, vice president of the Rhythm & Hues studio. "The mechanical aspects of integrating live action and animation are much simpler because computers understand perspective, lighting

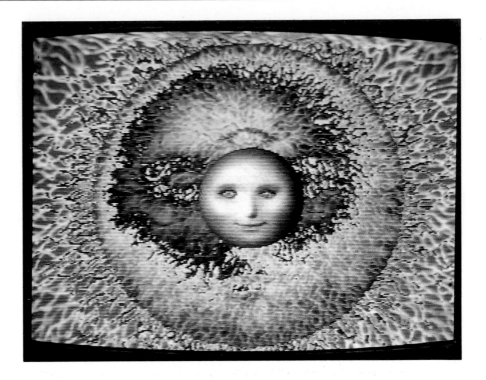

Above: An image from Ed Emshwiller's "Sunstone." Below: Lillian Schwartz lecturing in front of an illustration from "Beyond Picasso."

Computer-generated special effects: a knight comes to life out of a stained-glass window in "Young Sherlock Holmes."

and other elements. You can add, say, a photorealistic soda can to a live-action scene and it will cast shadows and share the lighting without airbrushed highlights or rotoscoped shadows."

Disney's "Tron" (1982) made extensive use of computer graphics and contained some dazzling sequences. The vaguely unnatural bias of computer-generated imagery gave the world within the computer an effectively surreal appearance. Surfaces suggested airbrushed metal or plastic, but retained a subtle difference. The race of the Light Cycles and the flight of the Solar Sailer simply didn't look like anything that had ever appeared on a movie screen.

Unfortunately, all this visual flash couldn't disguise the fact that "Tron" was a bad movie with a weak script. Despite enormous advance publicity, the film failed to attract viewers, and its poor showing at the box office probably kept it from winning the Oscar for special effects it deserved.

Similar problems beset Lorimar's "The Last Starfighter" (1984), which included the first spaceship battles done entirely with computer graphics. The state-of-the-art effects provided the only excitement in what was otherwise an undistinguished B science-fiction movie.

In the summer of 1987, a major shakeup left the computer graphics industry in a state of flux. The Canadian studio Omnibus Productions bought out two of its major rivals, Digital Productions and Abel Image Research. The Digital-Omnibus-Abel conglomerate (irreverently dubbed "D.O.A." by some artists) promptly went belly-up, followed almost

immediately by another important studio, Ohio-based Cranston-Csuri.

Artists from the defunct companies regrouped to form new studios, notably Metrolight and Rhythm & Hues in Los Angeles, but no real aesthetic or technical leader has emerged. Metrolight, Rhythm & Hues and Pacific Data Images, or PDI (one of the few producers of high-end broadcast graphics to survive the wave of failures), seem locked in a three-way race to lead the broadcast market.

Artists and executives at all three studios agree that broadcast graphics are shifting away from technical marvels and toward a greater emphasis on design and animation.

"In many ways, it's a very different industry than it was even two years ago," says Carl Rosendahl, president of PDI. "It used to be that it was a big feat if you could just render an image—now, that's assumed. Just the fact that you can make pictures with a computer isn't enough anymore: Design has become crucial to capturing the viewer's attention."

Currently, one group of computer animators believes the medium needs a major hit to make the public aware of its enormous (and still largely untapped) potential. A second group argues that computer graphics have been the subject of too many inflated reports promising marvels no extant graphics system can produce. Instead of calling attention to itself, they feel, the medium should simply be added to the repertory of filmmaking techniques.

"The visionaries out there have been our worst enemies," concludes James Kristoff, president of Metrolight Studios. "I really think there's been too much attention paid to where the [computer graphics] industry is going and not enough to where we are. When you consider how short a time we've

The enraged Ratigan pursues Basil through a labyrinth of computer-generated gears at the climax of Disney's "The Great Mouse Detective."

Mick Jagger flirts with the computer-animated title character in the rock video of "Hard Woman."

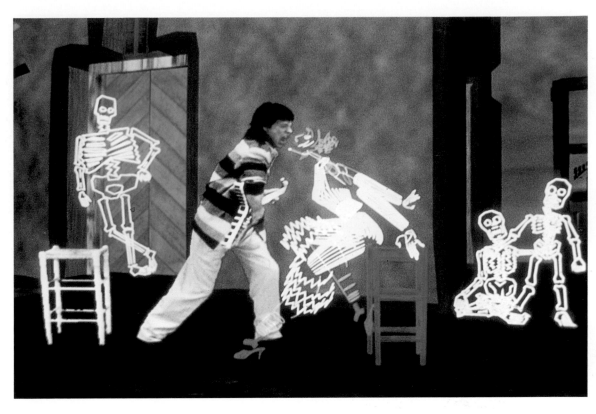

been working in this medium, we're really in a pretty good situation. We should recognize that and revel in it."

Despite its importance in the production of glitzy TV commercials, computer graphics has had a limited effect on conventional animation, especially character animation.

Many animators doubt that computers will be able to generate effective, two-dimensional character animation until they can experience emotions. (Whether computers can economically produce the stiffer, more mechanical movements of the characters on kidvid shows remains the subject of experimentation.)

However, computers are being used to complement drawn animation in potentially significant ways. Computer coloring systems are already coming into use in the industry. The computer scans the animators' drawings and records them on videotape. At interactive workstations, crews color the images on the tape, instead of inking and painting cels. Variations in the program can produce effects that simulate textured and airbrushed effects. As the new coloring systems are more efficient, they may soon replace the old ink and paint departments for television production.

Experiments combining hand-animated characters and computer-animated backgrounds have produced impressive results that reveal the different strengths of each medium. One of the first attempts was a short test film based on Maurice Sendak's "Where the Wild Things Are," made at Disney by Glen Keane and John Lasseter in 1982.

Lasseter constructed a model of Max's bedroom and the adjoining hall in the computer's memory. After the artists calculated the rates of movement for Max and his dog, the computer produced simple models, showing where the characters would be in each frame. Keane animated the characters, using the computer printouts as guides. When his drawings were entered into the computer and colored, the characters were placed in the computer-generated environment.

In the resulting footage, the camera seemed to follow Max as he chased the hapless dog around the bedroom and through the hall, jumped over the banister and pursued his pet down the stairs. Keane's animation captured the personalities of the characters, and made them seem alive. The computer made it possible to use the complex tracking shot, which would be virtually impossible to do in conventional animation, as it would be too difficult to draw everything in perspective. This experiment helped lead to the use of a computer-generated environment for the climax of "The Great Mouse Detective."

"Oliver & Company" (1988) contained 11 minutes of computer animation, including an elaborate car chase over the Brooklyn Bridge and through the tunnels of the New York subway system. The drawback to the computer-generated imagery was its hard-edged regularity: Even in a cartoon, it was difficult for an audience to accept a fleet of New York taxicabs without a single dent.

The most effective attempts to animate recognizable characters with computers have similarly exploited the special strengths of the medium, instead of trying to duplicate drawn animation.

No one would mistake James Blinn's caricatures of physicists Hendrik Lorentz and Albert Einstein in "The Mechanical Universe" (1983–87) for Disney animation. The designs are simple; the characters' movements, schematic. But the figures form part of a moving, three-dimensional graph that explains some aspects of the theory of relativity with extraordinary clarity.

It would be tedious and difficult to create these visuals or the program's many moving equations and formulas with drawn animation, and the computer does it more effectively. Blinn's awareness of standard animation techniques and knowledge of computer graphics enable him to create these deft and often amusing illustrations in motion.

Artists trained in traditional animation have been involved in the most successful attempts to produce computer-generated character animation. Their knowledge allows them to analyze an organic movement and caricature it to produce an image that suggests a personality on the screen.

The striking rock video to Mick Jagger's "Hard Woman" (1985) by Digital Productions featured vivid computer-animated figures that resembled moving neon sculptures. In one dramatic sequence, a live-action Jagger threw his guitar into the air. As it turned into a neon image, the fret board became a staircase the female character ascended.

"Computers can reproduce and, in some cases, be made to create all kinds of movement," says Bill Kroyer, a former Disney artist who did the key animation on "Hard Woman." "But movement is not, in my opinion, animation. I think of animation as a performing art. A computer can create action but not acting—a good computer animator must first be a good animator who understands and employs the principles of acting, staging, timing, etc. The computer simply becomes another tool."

A schematic of the "Hard Woman" character by Bill Kroyer illustrates one of the problems of animating in three dimensions. Although the character appears to touch the cup in both versions, her hand is in a separate plane in the lower image.

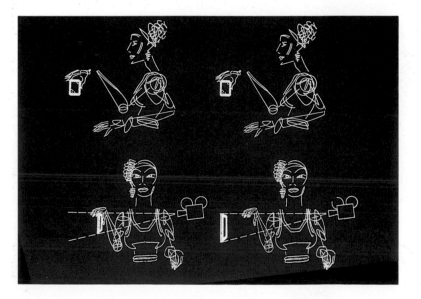

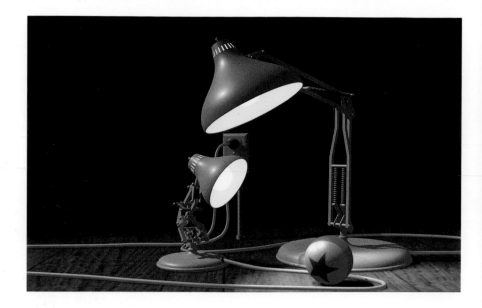

The father-and-son table lamps from John Lasseter's charming short "Luxo, Jr." (1986).

Working with computer graphics experts Alvy Ray Smith and Bill Reeves, John Lasseter designed and animated the characters in "The Adventures of Andre and Wally B" (1984) at Lucasfilm. Less than two minutes long, this short film depicted the efforts of Andre, a goggle-eyed little man, to outwit the mischievous bee, Wally. Lasseter used traditional cartoon timing and "takes" to help bring the characters to life: when Wally takes off after Andre, his feet leave four frames after his body.

While technically impressive, "Andre and Wally B" looked like an odd puppet film. The characters moved smoothly, but they had a curious rubbery appearance and looked out of place in Smith's astonishingly detailed forest setting.

The next year, a group of young artists in Montreal produced "Tony De Peltrie," a short film about a faded cabaret pianist recalling his former celebrity. Again, the film was technically impressive. Tony moved like a well-animated robot, and the final scene of the figure blowing away in a cloud of tiny fragments was a haunting visual that could only be done in computer graphics. But "Tony" suffered from bad designs—the character was very ugly—and the filmmakers relied on the sound track, rather than the motion, to carry the story.

In 1986, George Lucas decided that computer graphics were "just too time-consuming and expensive" and eliminated that division of his film company. Alvy Smith and Edwin Catmull, two of the acknowledged leaders in the field, spun off Pixar (named for a special graphics computer they devised) from Lucasfilm. Steven Jobs, the co-founder and former chairman of Apple Computers, bought controlling interest in the new company.

That same year, Pixar released "Luxo, Jr." by John Lasseter

Right: A scene from Lasseter's "The Adventures of Andre and Wally B" (1984). Below: The nightclub singer's nostalgic fantasy in "Tony De Peltrie" (1985).

Above: Snacky, a computer-animated character created by the artists at Pacific Data Images for a Japanese advertising campaign. Below: The title character flees the monstrous baby in the Oscar-winning "Tin Toy" (1988), by John Lasseter and William Reeves.

and Bill Reeves. This 90-second short used a game of ball between two realistic desk lamps to depict the affectionate relationship between a patient father and his rambunctious son. Like the best drawn animation, the film delineated the characters and their relationship through pure motion. Its one real weakness was its length: at 90 seconds, "Luxo" felt more like an exercise than a complete film. It received an Academy Award nomination, but lost to a more conventional Belgian film, "A Greek Tragedy."

"Luxo, Jr." was hailed as the "Steamboat Willie" of computer graphics, the film that represented a breakthrough into a new realm of animation. Lasseter followed "Luxo" with two longer works, "Red's Dream" (1987) and "Tin Toy" (1988). Both films represented technical advances, but lacked the charm of "Luxo," despite some impressive animation.

The organic characters (the clown in "Dream" and the monstrous baby in "Tin Toy") were not as believable as the mechanical ones, and they seemed out of place in the special world the computer generated. The robotic characters in experimental works from other studios—the automatons in Pacific Data Images' "Opera Industriel" or the hopping metronome Rhythm & Hues adopted as a logo—were more convincing in their appearance and movements than the attempts to reproduce organic surfaces and motions.

"We hope that character animation will be the next frontier," says Gibson. "The computer can give you the flexibility of cel animation, but with a three-dimensional look that is different from stop-motion models or clay animation. There's an amazing potential in computer graphics that people are just beginning to understand. It seems they're finally getting less hung up about rendering and more interested in the motion itself."

The computer graphics industry bears more than a passing resemblance to the conventional animation industry during the teens and twenties, with a small group of trained artists moving back and forth among studios that constantly open, close, merge and separate. Computers have become so ubiquitous in American life that people tend to forget just how new the technology is. Many years will probably elapse before the situation in the graphics community stabilizes.

It has become increasingly obvious that computer graphics will not be the savior of the animation industry—although the combination of the two media in "The Great Mouse Detective" and "Oliver" suggests exciting possibilities. Rather, computer animation represents another tool in the filmmaker's repertory, like live action, stop-motion photography and drawn animation.

Computer graphics will probably continue to develop more rapidly than other areas of animation. It remains to be seen whether the artists can develop their experiments in character animation to tell stories that showcase the unique qualities of the medium, the way the Disney artists developed drawn animation.

Like Truman Capote's Holly Golightly, audiences for animation in America didn't realize what they had until they had thrown it away. The recognition of animation as a legitimate art form did not become widespread in the United States until the late 1960s and early 1970s—after the major studios had closed and many of the key artists had retired or died. But that recognition—however belated—has grown throughout the 1970s and 1980s, despite the preponderance of television production.

More books on animation were published between 1970 and 1989 than in all the years since the medium was invented. John Canemaker, Mike Barrier, Jay Cocks, Richard Schickel and Leonard Maltin have begun to establish a body of serious writing about animation that is distinct from standard film criticism.

Cels and drawings from animated films, which were once sold for a few dollars as curiosities or discarded (some Disney artists tell stories about playing slip-and-slide on piles of "Fantasia" cels after photography had been completed), have become highly prized collectibles.

Many animators were surprised when cels from "Pinocchio" sold for $425 at Sotheby's Los Angeles in 1981. The value

Kermit the Frog with Waldo C. Graphic, the computer-generated Muppet, on "The Jim Henson Hour" (1989).

of animation art rose during the early 1980s, but the sale of the John Basmajian collection at Christie's East in 1984 inaugurated an era of skyrocketing prices. A cel from "Brave Little Tailor" (1938) sold for $19,000, while one from "Pinocchio" brought $18,000.

Within four years, prices had increased sevenfold. An unidentified Canadian buyer paid a record-breaking $135,000 for a black-and-white cel and background from "Orphan's Benefit" (1934) at Christie's in November 1988. Another cel and background from the same film sold for $110,000; a background of the menacing trees from "Snow White," $34,000 and a pencil drawing of Mickey Mouse being lowered into a cannibal pot from "Trader Mickey" (1932), $11,000.

These prices amazed the artists, who remembered throwing away similar material, but they fit the late-eighties pattern of unprecedented sums being paid for art and collectibles.

"Many big buyers collect this material not because they consider animation an art form, but because the Disney films mean something to them," says Joshua Arfer, animation art specialist at Christie's East. "They can't own Judy Garland in the ruby slippers, but they can have a real piece of a Disney film. A second group wants something to decorate their kid's room—they just want something cute. The third group knows that prices are rising and some of the biggest names in Hollywood are serious collectors."

In 1976, the Library of Congress presented "Building a Better Mouse," an exhibit of Disney animation art. The Whitney Museum of American Art devoted an entire floor to a

Disney exhibition/screening in 1981. The Museum of Modern Art in New York honored the fiftieth anniversary of Warner Brothers cartoons with a similar exhibition/screening in 1985–86, and the Los Angeles County Museum of Art has held major animation retrospectives annually since 1984.

As the audience for animated films has grown, so has the number of animators. More schools are offering animation classes and programs. While the best young animators have come from a few major schools—CalArts, UCLA, USC, NYU, Sheridan College in Canada—children as young as kindergartners are being taught simple animation techniques. These programs are producing a new generation of artists and audiences with a more profound understanding and appreciation of the medium.

Although certain problems persist—the lack of funding for independent artists; the preponderance of license character films and Saturday-morning kidvid; the stereotype of animation as a children's medium; runaway production—the future of animation in America looks more promising during the late 1980s than it has during the previous thirty years.

The success of "An American Tail" and "The Great Mouse Detective," "The Land Before Time," "Oliver & Company" and, especially, "Who Framed Roger Rabbit" has excited audiences about the medium and helped to overcome the negative image created by the box office failures of the early eighties. The rising cost of live-action production made animation a bargain during the later eighties. A good animated feature could be made for $8 million to $12 million (considerably less

in some cases— "Brave Little Toaster" cost only $2.3 million); the average budget of a live-action feature from a major studio hovered around $16 million.

But the greatest hope for the future of the medium is the growing number of viewers and artists who are excited about animation, who want to see and make films that will equal or exceed the best work of the past: "What Disney really did was introduce big-time cinema into animation," says Brad Bird, the director of "Family Dog." "When 'Snow White' came out, it was at the forefront of *cinema*, not just at the forefront of animation. If you look at the best scenes in 'Snow White' and compare them with the best filmmaking in 1937, it's up there. There's a whole consciousness that's been lost in animation— that when you're given a film, you're given a whole package of tools—the same tools that Chaplin and Welles and Kubrick and the other great filmmakers use. If you use every single one of them in concert, it *nails* you! Completely—the way the old Disney films, especially the Big Five ['Snow White,' 'Pinocchio,' 'Dumbo,' 'Fantasia' and 'Bambi'] do!"

Winsor McCay and Walt Disney saw their achievements in animation as preliminaries to greater works yet to be created. Both men recognized that the only limits to the medium are the artist's imagination and his ability to realize his visions. With the renewal of interest in animation and the advent of new technologies, the question is no longer whether animation will survive in America, but what forms it will take. The potential of animation remains largely unexplored more than eighty years after the experiments of J. Stuart Blackton.

A rough animation drawing by Glen Keane vividly captures Beast's indignation at Belle's refusal to dine with him in Disney's "Beauty and the Beast."

Like Carlotta, the aging in vamp in Stephen Sondheim's "Follies," the animated feature has experienced "Good times and bum times," but during the early 1990s, it underwent both simultaneously. For the Disney artists, it was an era of critical and box office triumphs, as the studio came to dominate the medium more absolutely than it had during the 1930s.

"The Little Mermaid" (1989) introduced an era of smash hits. Walt Disney had considered animating Hans Christian Andersen's wistful fable during the 1930s, when Kay Nielsen prepared a series of preliminary studies that reflected the poignance of the heroine's ill-fated quest for love. Fifty years later, co-writers/co-directors John Musker and Ron Clements transformed the tale into an upbeat, contemporary romance. Ariel (Jodi Benson) became a teenaged princess, hungry to experience something beyond life at the court of her father, King Triton (Kenneth Mars). She was especially curious about the forbidden world of humans above the surface.

Defying her father's bellowing wrath, Ariel sought the love of the mortal Prince Eric (Christopher Michael Barnes). To become human and pursue him, she bought the assistance of Ursula, the Sea Witch. Unlike the original story, all ended happily, with Ursula's schemes foiled and Triton blessing the marriage of Ariel and Eric.

Ariel represented a new breed of cartoon heroine: Independent, self-assured and capable of defying her imposing father. Eric seemed livelier than the stiffer, more realistic princes in past Disney fairy tales. Ruben Aquino's vivid animation of Ursula matched Pat Carrol's extravagant vocal performance. Resembling a cross between the transvestite actor Divine and an octopus, Ursula simpered and camped and pouted. No one doubted her admission, "They weren't kidding when they called me, well, a witch."

But the film was nearly stolen by King Triton's court composer and confidante, Horatio Thelonius Ignatius Crustaceous Sebastian. Musker and Clements knew the story would require a character who could talk to Ariel both underwater and on land. They had originally planned to use a turtle, but he was transformed into a hermit crab during storyboarding. A key turn in his development came when lyricist co-producer Howard Ashman suggested making him a *Jamaican* crab.

The combination of Sam E. Wright's mellifluous voice and Duncan Marjoribanks' animation proved irresistible to audiences. Sebastian epitomized affronted dignity as he tried to reconcile his duty to enforce King Triton's orders with his desire to indulge Ariel's whims. "He has a big ego for such a small body, and he's always in trouble because of his size," commented Marjoribanks. "His sense of dignity is at odds with his fear of being crushed."

"Mermaid" was also the first animated film with music and lyrics by Alan Mencken and Howard Ashman ("Little Shop of Horrors"). Their ability to blend appealing melodies and imaginative lyrics established the animated feature as the last bastion of the American musical. In the *New York Times*, Janet Maslin wrote of the ballad "Part of Your World," "Any Broadway musical would be lucky to include a single number this good. 'The Little Mermaid' has half a dozen of them." The Ashman–Mencken songs were not only catchy, they advanced the plot and helped define the characters. "Part of Your World" showed Ariel's impatience and desire to explore the human realm, as "Poor Unfortunate Souls" revealed the villainy lurking beneath Ursula's veneer of concern.

Sebastian tried to persuade Ariel to give up her unnatural interest in humans in the show-stopping production number, "Under the Sea," which Richard Corliss praised in *Time*: "As Sebastian limns the aquatic virtues, a Noah's aquarium of sea creatures animates a joyous Busby Berkeley palette. If ever a cartoon earned a standing ovation in mid-film, this would be it."

"Mermaid" garnered a record-breaking $84 million at the domestic box office and won Academy Awards for Best Original Score and Best Song ("Under the Sea"). It was the first animated feature to receive an Oscar since "Dumbo" in 1942. Energized by their success, the Disney artists were eager to prove that "Mermaid" was not a fluke.

The next Disney feature, "The Rescuers Down Under" (1990), represented a even greater break with tradition. It was the first animated sequel in the studio's history and the first feature since "Victory Through Airpower" (1943) that was not a musical. Bernard (Bob Newhart) and Miss Bianca (Eva Gabor), the mice from the Rescue Aid Society in the 1977 hit "The Rescuers," returned to aid Cody (Adam Ryen), an Australian boy who was kidnapped while trying to protect Marahute, a giant golden eagle, from the villainous poacher Percival McLeach (George C. Scott).

Directed by Hendel Butoy and Mike Gabriel, the film displayed non-Disney influences, including the animated sci-fi epics of Hayao Miyazaki. Although the animators did an effective job of recreating the characters from the earlier feature, "Down Under" suffered from a weak story and uninteresting characters. Ollie Johnston and Frank Thomas, two of Disney's "Nine Old Men," observed, "Not enough had been done in the story to make the boy an appealing character or a sympathetic victim, and McLeach was not quite convincing as an interesting, spellbinding member of the cast . . . he lacked that touch of charisma that would hold an audience."

The high points of the film were the flight sequences, when Marahute spread her vast wings and carried Cody above banks of clouds, over precipitous waterfalls and into the starry Australian night. These magical scenes captured every child's fantasy of having an animal as a special friend—and reasserted the power of animation to bring extravagant fantasies to the screen as effectively as the live-action adventures of George Lucas and Steven Spielberg.

ESPECIALLY MM...   ...LITTLE ARIEL

OH!   Y   E   S   S

YEH   YE   S – S   A   B   YOO

TI   FUL   VOI   CE   IF

ONLY   SHE'D   SHOW   UP   FOR RE   HEARSAL   W

ONCE   IN A   WHILE

ROW EYES

© The Walt Disney Company.

Duncan Marjoribanks' lively sketches of Sebastian from "The Little Mermaid" illustrate how an animator coordinates a character's expressions and dialogue. The artists often use one color to rough out a preliminary sketch, then do the finished drawing in a second color.

The giant eagle Marahute carries Cody across the surface of a river and over a waterfall in a magical scene from ''The Rescuers Down Under.''

''Down Under'' was the first Disney feature to be done without cels. The animators' drawings were scanned into a computer system, colored by people using a digital paint system, then digitally composited with the hand-rendered backgrounds and overlays, which had also been scanned. The resulting frames were recorded onto film. The technique had been used experimentally on a few scenes in ''Little Mermaid.''

''Rescuers'' was released with the featurette, ''The Prince and the Pauper,'' with Mickey Mouse in the double title role and Donald Duck, Goofy, Pluto, Horace Horsecollar and Black Pete in supporting parts. Some of the sequences recalled Mickey's old appeal, but at twenty-two minutes, ''The Prince and the Pauper'' ended before either character had time to explore his new identity and learn he was better off being who he was. The de facto double bill performed adequately at the box office.

''Beauty and the Beast'' (1991) repeated and expanded the musical fairy tale format of ''The Little Mermaid.'' The film had originally been envisioned as a straightforward retelling of the story, set in eighteenth-century France; the award-winning British commercial animators, Richard and Jill Purdom, were slated to direct. But when early work on the film proved less entertaining than expected, it was turned into a musical, with Gary Trousdale and Kirk Wise directing.

Walt Disney had also considered animating ''Beauty and the Beast,'' but his artists had been unable to find a way to infuse action into the claustrophobic tale of two characters who eat dinner together every night. The musical format enabled the artists to alter and embellish the story freely. The passive Beauty became the intelligent, restless Belle (Paige O'Hara); her merchant father, the befuddled inventor, Maurice (Rex Everhart); Beast (Robby Benson) was given a troupe of enchanted objects as servants. Ashman and Mencken contributed six songs, including the show-stopping ''Be Our Guest,'' which producer Don Hahn described as ''Busby Berkeley, Esther Williams and Maurice Chevalier colliding in the kitchen.''

''We were absolutely aware that comparisons to 'Little Mermaid' would be inevitable, because we were working in the same realm: A Disney fairy tale with a strong female lead,'' said Wise. ''We didn't want Belle's characterization to go in the same direction as Ariel's. Ariel was definitely the All-American teenager, while we pictured Belle as a little bit older, a little bit wiser and a little more sophisticated.''

Belle was even more independent than Ariel; she wanted

more from life than her provincial village offered, but she wanted more than a husband. And she knew she didn't want her self-appointed suitor, the braggart Gaston (Richard White), around in any capacity. The design for Belle had the same overly large eyes and thin arms as Ariel. Although she lacked the carefully observed anatomy that helped to make Cinderella and Briar Rose so appealing, Belle posed many of the same problems for the artists.

Supervising animator James Baxter noted that a beautiful character "can become very ugly very quickly—all it takes is a few misplaced lines." Trousdale added, "You can get away with more, animating an imaginary character like Ariel. Nobody really knows how a mermaid swims; they've got a little bit of an idea, but there are liberties you can take. Everybody knows how a pretty girl looks and walks."

The artists agreed that the film would basically be Beast's story. Inspired by the animals he had sketched in the London and Los Angeles zoos, supervising animator Glen Keane said "I wanted Beast to be comfortable on all fours, which was a big statement. This guy is not just a man with a beast's head on; he is actually, physically, bone structure-wise, an animal."

Beast was a character of almost operatic passion, given to towering rages that dissipated like thunderstorms, leaving him crushed by profound melancholy. Yet he appeared touchingly shy when he tried to please Belle by feeding a tiny bird from his monstrous paw. Few animated characters have expressed such a complex range of emotions: Beast made choices, wrestled with his feelings and sacrificed his own happiness by freeing Belle to return to her ailing father.

Keane described animating the latter sequence as "frustrating." "I wanted to animate the incredible turmoil that was going on inside the character, and there was no action. The only way you can express those intense emotions is by subtly tilting an eyebrow or changing the shape of the corners of the mouth. It's very delicate work—completely the opposite of what you're feeling inside."

Physical beauty has traditionally been equated with virtue in animated films; in nearly every fairy tale, the hero and heroine fall in love at first sight. The idea of a girl learning to love a gentle heart hidden beneath a baleful exterior represented a major break with the past—as did the notion that the heroine's suitor could be both handsome and villainous. Gaston stole almost every scene he was in with his swaggering arrogance, but he remained unlovable.

The drama of the romance between Belle and Beast was played against the comedy provided by Beast's principal servants. Cogsworth (David Ogden Stiers), the prissy clock, oozed self-importance as he fussed about his duties as major-domo, while the suave Lumiere (Jerry Orbach) moved with the assured grace of a man (or candlestick) of the world. Although little more than a disembodied head, Mrs. Potts (Angela Lansbury), the teapot/housekeeper, provided a maternal presence with her impish son, Chip (Bradley Michael Pierce). Like Gus and Jaq in "Cinderella," this endearing quartet allowed the filmmakers to comment on the action without giving the main characters pointed speeches.

The use of the computer paint system enabled the artists to create a detailed fantasy world that echoed the opulent look of the films of the 1930s and 1940s. The delicate patches of pink on Belle's cheeks recalled similar ones that appeared on Snow White, which the women in the ink and paint department had applied to the individual cels by hand. This labor-intensive process would have been prohibitively expensive in the 1990s, but the computer paint program could easily produce a *blend*, similar to an airbrushed effect. The computer system also combined layers of artwork to simulate complex camera mechanics, notably in the opening multiplane shots, trucking through the forest to Beast's castle.

However, the real showcase for new techniques was the sequence of Beast and Belle waltzing to the title song. Because the directors wanted to set this key moment apart emotionally, they deliberately chose a visual style distinct from the hand-painted backgrounds in the rest of the film. Using customized software, CGI (computer generated imagery) artists and engineers built the ballroom in which the hand-drawn characters appeared. Creating the three-dimensional ballroom enabled the directors to employ sophisticated cinematography that rivaled the best live-action films. The swooping pan through a glittering chandelier elicited admiring gasps from audiences, as the lengthy tracking shot did in Martin Scorsese's "Good-Fellas."

The studio mounted an aggressive marketing campaign that included screening the film as a work-in-progress at the New York Film Festival and preparing an arrangement of the title song for MTV and pop radio. "Beauty and the Beast" opened to rave reviews. Critics called it the most satisfying Disney feature since "101 Dalmatians," thirty years earlier. The romantic tone of the film made it a popular "date movie," contributing to an unprecedented domestic gross of $141 million.

It also became the first animated feature to receive an Academy Award nomination for best picture (it received five other nominations: sound, original score and three for best song—"Beauty and the Beast," "Be Our Guest," and "Belle"). *Los Angeles Times* film critic Kenneth Turan warned, "If you were to ask the Academy members which of the five nominees they liked best, 'Beauty and the Beast' would win hands down; but that doesn't mean they'll give it the Oscar." "Beast" lost to "Silence of the Lambs," but won for original score and song ("Beauty and the Beast"), as well as Golden Globe Awards for song, original score and best musical or comedy film.

The success of "Beauty and the Beast" was marred only by the death of Howard Ashman from AIDS in March 1991. The final credit for the film read: "To our friend, Howard, who gave a mermaid her voice and a beast his soul, we will be

Belle and Beast in a magical moment from "Beauty and the Beast." The artists deliberately rendered the rococo ballroom in a different style from the other backgrounds to highlight the emotional significance of the scene.

The Genie performs a snazzy jazz dance accompanied by his own hands in the show-stopping "Friend Like Me" number from "Aladdin."

forever grateful. Howard Ashman: 1950–1991."

Ashman's influence was still apparent in the studio's next feature, "Aladdin." He had suggested doing the tale as a jazz-influenced spoof of Hollywood costume epics, and had completed the lyrics for several songs before his death. Although it continued the musical romance tradition of "Little Mermaid" and "Beauty and the Beast," "Aladdin" was markedly different in tone, design and animation.

"We need to provide our animators with artistic challenges, not just in terms of the stories and the kinds of characters in those stories, but in the design, the look and the style of the films," said Jeffrey Katzenberg, chairman of The Walt Disney Studios. " 'Little Mermaid' and 'Beauty and the Beast' were attempts to recapture the fairy tale style of the most classic Disney animated movies—'Snow White' and 'Pinocchio.' From the very outset, our goal on 'Aladdin' was to go as far afield of that style as possible, and let the artists stretch a different set of muscles in terms of color palette, painting style, character design, etc."

Like "Snow White," "Mermaid" and "Beast" harked back to the detailed style of the great nineteenth- and early-twentieth-century European storybook illustrators. For "Aladdin," the Disney artists were inspired by the elegantly minimal caricatures of Al Hirschfeld.

"I look on Hirschfeld's work as a pinnacle of boiling a subject down to its essence, so that you get a clear, defined statement of a personality," said supervising animator Eric Goldberg. "There's also an organic quality in the way one line

will flow into another—it may go down the back of a neck, down the spine, across the behind and down the leg—all in one single line that is very, very elegant. I wanted the Genie to have that kind of graphic elegance."

"Hirschfeld's work teaches you fluidity, appeal and simplicity," agrees supervising animator Andreas Deja. "We now refer to some of our earlier efforts as 'chiseled realism': On Gaston's face, we established so many planes for his cheekbones and chin to achieve it. This assignment taught us to be simple and direct, then your statement will be clearer and easier to follow on the screen."

The simplified, more two-dimensional look of the characters in "Aladdin" dictated a less realistic style of animation. The artists used broader, cartoon-y motions that were influenced by old Warner Brothers and MGM shorts and some of the wilder moments in earlier Disney films, especially the "Pink Elephants on Parade" sequence from "Dumbo" and the title number from "Three Caballeros."

For the story to work, the Genie's mercurial personality had to be easy to read on the screen, even when he appeared as a dragon or a caricature of Arnold Schwarzenegger. Goldberg and his crew stressed clear, Hirschfeld-ian poses that told the audience exactly what the Genie was thinking or doing. Once he struck a pose, the artists used small motions of his hands and head and changes in his expression to keep the character alive.

Clear attitudes were also stressed in the animation of the other characters. The artists studied Tom Cruise's performance in "Top Gun" to suggest ways in which the brash, street-smart Aladdin (Scott Weinger) would move. The character's bold stances and theatrical gestures were both copied and satirized by Abu, his mischievous pet monkey. The artists had to rely on poses and body language for the magic carpet, as the character had neither head nor hands. The evil Jafar (Jonathan Freeman) exuded a slimy elegance that his sepulchral form emphasized; the appealing Jasmine (Linda Larkin) was more consistently animated than the previous Disney heroines.

But the film was dominated by the irrepressible, shape-shifting Genie, who metamorphosed into more than sixty identities, including caricatures of William F. Buckley, Groucho Marx, Ethel Merman, Jack Nicholson and Peter Lorre. The visuals kept pace with Robin Williams' frenetic vocal changes, producing a gleeful graphic insanity that embodied the essence of Williams' performance.

Critics noted the gap in quality between Ashman's lyrics and the songs that had subsequently been written by Tim Rice. Ashman's two production numbers for the Genie, "Friend Like Me" and "Prince Ali" were the real show stoppers in the film, despite the build-up for Rice's ballad, "A Whole New World." Some observers felt "Aladdin" lacked the heart of "Beauty and the Beast."

There were complaints from Arab-American groups over Ashman's opening song: "Oh, I come from a land from a far-away place/Where the caravan camels roam/Where they cut off your ear if they don't like your face/It's barbaric, but hey, it's home." Their protests caused Disney to re-dub the verse when the film was released on videocassette to "Where it's flat and immense/And the heat is intense."

But these complaints had little effect on audiences: "Aladdin" broke all previous box office records for an animated film, earning $215 million domestically and an additional $220 million overseas. It received five Oscar nominations (sound, sound effects editing, original score and song—"Friend Like Me," "A Whole New World"), and won for score and song ("A Whole New World").

Its unparalleled success confirmed Disney feature animation president Peter Schneider's assertion, "We don't want to make features for a 'cartoon ghetto.' We want them to be accepted as part of mainstream filmmaking, and I feel we've made big strides in that direction. The best picture Oscar nomination for 'Beauty and the Beast' honored the art of filmmaking as well as the art of animation."

The Disney artists followed the freewheeling hijinks of "Aladdin" with "The Lion King" (June, 1994), a dramatic coming-of-age story that required realistic animation of African animals. Simba (Jonathan Taylor Thomas/Matthew Broderick), the title character, was the only child of Mufasa (James Earl Jones) and Sarabi (Madge Sinclair), the king and queen of the "Pride Lands," a Serengeti-esque plain. Simba's evil uncle, Scar (Jeremy Irons), plotted the deaths of both Simba

and Mufasa to obtain the throne for himself. Although the story focused on Simba's learning to accept his responsibility to reclaim his throne, secondary characters provided comic relief, as they had in "Beauty and the Beast."

Elton John and Tim Rice wrote five songs, including "The Circle of Life" for the opening of the film. In this majestic sequence, the infant Simba was presented to the animals of the realm, who knelt before their future ruler. The elaborate cinematography incorporated shifts from the microscopic to the macroscopic, as the focus in a single shot moved from a line of leaf cutter ants on a foreground branch to a herd of prancing zebras.

The filmic sophistication matched the increasingly subtle character animation. For Rafiki (Robert Guillaume), the shaman-baboon, James Baxter juxtaposed a comic appearance with a wise demeanor. A combination of a Zen master and a Western wise fool, Rafiki taught Simba by mocking him. In their movements, Simba and Mufasa revealed the artists' understanding of the interplay of powerful muscles and bones; this strength was less pronounced in Scar, whose movements bespoke a treacherous guile.

In one of the film's climactic moments, Scar killed Mufasa, and nearly killed Simba, by trapping them in a gorge amid thousands of stampeding wildebeests. Using Ruben Aquino's drawn animation of a single wildebeest as a reference, a crew of five animators and engineers created a three-dimensional model and a library of behaviors. Custom software enabled the artists to direct the motions of the wildebeests over the fictional terrain of the gorge. This combination of drawn and computer animation allowed the directors to heighten the drama of the situation by showing the audience the stampede from various angles, including the terrified Simba's point of view. No film in the history of animation had ever presented so many characters in motion.

"The heightened realism of the ballroom sequence in 'Beauty and the Beast' set it apart from the rest of the film. The visually dramatic environment intensified the characters' emotions," says CGI supervisor Scott Johnston. "'The Lion King' presented us with a different problem: Unlike the visual transitions in and out of the ballroom, it was important for us to integrate the wildebeests with the hand drawn characters and the African Pride Lands environment. The 'beests had to behave naturally, but it couldn't look too realistic—they had to look like real *cartoon* wildebeests."

Slated to follow "The Lion King" was "Pocahontas" (summer, 1995), the story of the Algonquin princess who risked her life to save Captain John Smith from execution, with Eric Goldberg and Mike Gabriel directing. Other features in preproduction included "The Hunchback of Notre Dame," based on the Victor Hugo novel, "Aida," "Hercules" and new sequences for "Fantasia."

The recent Disney features were made by two crews, one in

Jack Skellington attempts to find the meaning of Christmas in "Tim Burton's The Nightmare Before Christmas." Historically, stop-motion animation has been more popular in Eastern Europe than in the United States.

Glendale, California, the other in Orlando, Florida. After "Lion King," the Florida crew was set to begin work on their own feature, "Fa Mulan," based on a Chinese fable about a warrior-princess. Additional animation for the various Disney films would be done at a recently purchased satellite studio in France.

During the summer of 1990, Disney released "Ducktales: The Movie: Treasure of the Lost Lamp," a feature based on the television series that had been animated in France. The film looked like a TV show that had been blown up and Spielbergized to fill a bigger screen. Although superior to such TV-based fare as "He-Man: The Secret of the Sword," "Lamp" was markedly inferior in concept and animation to the real Disney films. A second French-made film, "The Goofy Movie," starring the characters from the weekday afternoon series, "Goof Troop," was slated for holiday release, 1994.

In addition, Disney began to move beyond drawn animation into other media. Their first venture was "Tim Burton's Nightmare Before Christmas" (1993), a rare example of a stop-motion feature. Burton had created the original story in 1982, as a half-hour special in the tradition of "How the Grinch Stole Christmas."

Burton had been hired as an animator by Disney in 1979, but his often bizarre imagination put him at odds with the conservative management of the studio, and he left to direct live-action films. His success enabled him to strike a deal with Disney's Touchstone division, and the film was animated in San Francisco. Director Henry Selick, a fellow Disney alumnus, had done award-winning stop-motion work for MTV, commercials and personal films.

The delightfully macabre story of Jack Skellington, the spirit in charge of Halloween who tires of his job and tries to take over Christmas, "Nightmare" represented a quantum leap for the medium. No other stop-motion feature had incorporated such sophisticated character animation and contemporary cinematography. When Jack set himself afire during a triumphal parade or posed in silhouette on an oddly coiled hillside before the full moon, audiences were seeing something genuinely new.

As the puppets have to be adjusted in almost microscopic increments between frames, stop-motion animators can't begin with a rough approximation of a movement and refine it, as animators who draw can. Each series of adjustments represents a unique performance, which has made it difficult to give characters the personal styles of movement that define their drawn counterparts. But Jack walked with a self-assured strut, while Sally teetered uncertainly on her high heels, and the trio of Lock, Shock and Barrel took short, choppy steps that underscored their pudgy shapes.

The technical difficulties have also tended to make stop-motion movies uninteresting as films: The artists avoid pans and trucks to concentrate on moving the characters. No previous film could boast shots comparable to the gracefully rotating image of Jack lying in the arms of the tombstone angel. In its own way, "Nightmare" was as cinematically innovative as "Who Framed Roger Rabbit" and "Beauty and the Beast."

Critics praised the film for its extraordinary visual imagination: Kenneth Turan described it as "so profligate with exotic images that it overflows with a demented kind of genius." But reviewers also complained that the film suffered from a weak story, and criticized Danny Elfman's songs as repetitive and derivative.

The film grossed more than $50 million, enough to encourage Disney to continue in the medium. Selick is slated to direct a second feature based on Roald Dahl's ''James and the Giant Peach.'' Disney is also collaborating with PIXAR's John Lasseter, who directed the Oscar-winning short ''Tin Toy,'' to develop the first feature done in computer generated imagery, tentatively entitled ''Toy Story.''

''For the past seven or eight years, our job was to reclaim the franchise and rebuild the base we had in the 1930s, 1940s and 1950s—a strong studio with creative artists doing classic stories,'' concluded Schneider. ''But we also wanted to broaden that mandate and push the envelope of the animated feature. There are other forms of animation besides drawing, which I think are valid and interesting. Over the next five years, you're going to see us venturing into other types of animation with artists who will complement and diversify our palette. I think their work is going to be as exciting and successful as the Beauty and Beasts and the Aladdins, but it's going to look different and tell different kinds of stories.''

With the major exception of Disney, the much-heralded renaissance in feature animation largely proved a bust. Between 1986 and 1990, animated features earned over $400 million domestically, a figure that sparked a welter of production. In 1990, more features were in production than at any other time in the history of the medium. By the end of 1993, most of those films had come and gone, leaving a record that ranged from disappointing to disastrous.

In 1992, Disney's ''Aladdin'' earned $215 million, while ''Fern Gully: The Last Rain Forest'' grossed $24.6 million; ''Rock-A-Doodle,'' $11.6 million; ''Bebe's Kids,'' $7.5 million; ''Little Nemo: Adventures In Slumberland,'' $1.4 million; ''Freddie as F.R.0.7,'' $1.1 million; and the live action/animation combination, ''Cool World,'' $14.1 million. The pattern repeated in 1993: ''We're Back! A Dinosaur's Story,'' $8.6 million; ''Once Upon a Forest,'' $6.1 million; ''Batman: Mask of the Phantasm,'' $5 million; ''Tom and Jerry: The Movie,'' $2.7 million.

In 1990, David Kirschner, then chairman of Hanna-Barbera, expressed concern that the boom in animated features could be imperiled by ''studios saying 'yes' to films that need more work in the development stages before they're ready to show to the public.''

''That's exactly what happened,'' he sighed four years later. ''It was evident in the way many of the features looked and were received. Of course, no one has a marketing system like Disney's, which is very important. But their product was so superior to any of the other films that came out in the last two years: Disney seems to understand how to deliver both comedy and pathos better than almost anyone else.''

Once acclaimed as Disney's most promising—or threatening—rival, Don Bluth suffered a series of financial and artistic reversals. ''All Dogs Go To Heaven'' (1989), his first solo effort since ''The Secret of NIMH'' was soundly drubbed by critics. Peter Rainer placed it ''in the comfy, fun-for-the-entire-family category. Except, as is so often the case, it's not really a whole lot of fun for anyone.''

The muddled story involved the efforts of Charlie (Burt Reynolds), a ne'er-do-well German shepherd, to regain control of the New Orleans casino he co-owned with the villainous pitbull, Carface (Vic Taylor). Charlie and his sidekick, Itchy (Dom De Luise) got involved with an orphan, Annemarie, who could talk to animals (why she could and Charlie and Itchy couldn't was never explained), enabling her canine chums to bet successfully on horse races, kangaroo boxing matches, etc. Annemarie wanted to be adopted, and when she finally realized that Charlie was exploiting her talents to hedge his bets, she announced in an inadvertently hilarious climax, ''You're a bad dog!''

Audiences apparently agreed with the critics: ''All Dogs'' earned only $23.4 million; not a flop, but hardly a success—particularly when contrasted with the performance of Disney's ''The Little Mermaid,'' which was released at the same time.

In March of 1991, Goldcrest, the British company that had agreed to finance Bluth's work in 1988, petitioned for the liquidation of Sullivan Bluth in the Irish court system over a $298,000 loan. The petition was abruptly dropped one month later; the terms of the settlement were never made public. Early in 1992, Bluth received a much-needed $50 million from Pearl Equity Investment NV, a consortium of European investors.

His next feature, ''Rock-A-Doodle,'' opened in April 1992 to equally bad reviews and even lower attendance. The film combined elements of ''Chanticleer,'' ''The Wizard of Oz,'' fairy tales and old Elvis Presley movies in a story that was virtually impossible to follow. Chanticleer (Glen Campbell), Rostand's rooster who believed his crowing made the sun rise, became an Elvis-esque entertainer. Edmond (Toby Scott Granger), a boy whose family's farm is threatened by a flood, decides the Chanticleer in his story book is the only one who can save the day—although the Grand Duke, an evil owl (Christopher Plummer), proved the rooster had no power over the sun in the opening minutes of the film. After being turned into a kitten by the Grand Duke (for no apparent reason other than to give the animators a cute little animal to draw) Edmond goes in search of his hero. All eventually ends happily after a great many complications and forgettable songs.

Bluth once again faced bankruptcy in August 1992, when Don Bluth Entertainment had to suspend operations and lay off almost 500 employees in Ireland and America. He finally obtained additional funding from a Hong Kong consortium and struck a deal with Warner Brothers to distribute three films upon completion in 1994: ''Thumbelina,'' ''A Troll in Central Park'' and ''The Pebble and the Penguin.''

Based on the fairy tale about a tiny girl born from a flower,

"Hans Christian Andersen's Thumbelina" (March, 1994) had the potential to be an excellent film, which made its many problems all the more disappointing. The meandering storyline broke into poorly related episodes, which Barry Manilow's treacly songs failed to bridge. Thumbelina (Jodi Benson) was a very passive heroine, who had no interests, aside from falling in love. Other characters initiated the action while she pined for Cornelius (Gary Imhoff), the fairy prince. A trio of little bugs freed Cornelius from the clutches of an evil toad and his beetle henchman, rather than Thumbelina.

The film was executed in three disparate visual styles that never melded. Thumbelina, her mother and Cornelius were drawn semirealistically; the often grotesque supporting characters seemed to have been copied from the Fleischer's "Mr. Bug Goes to Town"; the highly realistic computer animation, including a traveling shot through medieval Paris, provided a jarring discontinuity.

Previewed footage of "Troll," with the ubiquitous Dom De Luise as the voice of Stanley, a misunderstood troll with a green thumb, revealed even graver story problems and designs that were marred by excessive cuteness.

Bluth suffered a further loss when John Pomeroy, a talented animator and one of his original partners, left the studio and returned to Disney in 1993. At this point in his career, Don Bluth's place in the history of American animation seems increasingly uncertain. His recent work has neither fulfilled the promise of "NIMH" nor repeated the financial success of "American Tail" and "Land Before Time."

Unlike the Bluth studio, Steven Spielberg's London-based Amblimation Studios enjoyed financial security, a guaranteed release and promotion by Universal Pictures, and Spielberg's knowledge of filmmaking. Yet the studio failed to establish an artistic identity or even much of a presence in the marketplace. Spielberg's "Tiny Toons" and "Animaniacs" TV series proved more successful critically and financially than either of the studio's features.

"An American Tail: Fievel Goes West" (1991) continued the adventures of the immigrant Mousekewitz family. Disillusioned with the poverty and crime of New York c. 1887, they decide to look for a new promised land in the West. The unscrupulous Cat R. Waul (John Cleese, essentially reprising his British sheriff from "Silverado") lures the urban mice to a desolate town where he plans to devour them. Fievel (Philip Glasser) and his vegetarian cat friend, Tiger (Dom De Luise),

Thumbelina and Prince Cornelius plight their troth amid clouds of fairy dust in "Hans Christian Andersen's Thumbelina." The film failed to attract much attention at the box office, despite its often handsome look.

Sheriff Wylie Burp rewards Fievel Mousekewitz with a deputy's badge at the end of "An American Tail:
Fievel Goes West."

defeat the plot with the aid of the broken-down canine mar-shal Wylie Burp (James Stewart, clearly enjoying kind of a self-parodying "Destry Hobbles Again").

Once the mice decided to head West, the story devolved into a string of loosely related episodes. Directors Phil Nibbelink and Simon Wells kept everything moving at a breakneck pace in an effort to infuse some energy into what little plot there was, but the result was wearing, rather than exhilarating. "Fievel Goes West" played to indifferent reviews and business.

Even more disappointing was the heavily promoted "We're Back! A Dinosaur's Story" (1993). Hudson Talbot's popular book about a group of dinosaurs who visit New York after having had their IQ's raised could have made a good half-hour television special. In an effort to fill an hour and 12 minutes of screen time, writer John Patrick Shanley padded the story with weak subplots, including a not-quite romance between two adolescent humans and an ineffectual confrontation be-tween good and evil scientists from the future.

The film's four directors, Dick Zondag, Ralph Zondag, Phil Nibbelink and Simon Wells, failed to establish real personali-ties for the dinosaurs, which robbed their misadventures of any interest. Even the sequence of the prehistoric animals rais-ing havoc among the giant balloons of Macy's Thanksgiving Day Parade failed to generate much excitement or humor. "We're Back" flopped at the box office.

Universal Pictures/Amblin Entertainment announced plans for a holiday, 1995, release of "Balto," an adventure story cen-tering on the lead sled dog who carried diphtheria serum to Nome, Alaska, in 1925 (an epic journey recreated annually in the Iditarod race), with Bob Hoskins providing the voice of the title character and Simon Wells directing. There have also been periodic announcements that the studio would animate Andrew Lloyd Webber's musical "Cats," but no date has been announced. Given the money and talent at its disposal, it's difficult to understand why the Amblimation films remain so undistinguished.

After the success of the Amblin/Disney hit, "Who Framed Roger Rabbit," animation director Richard Williams was finally able to obtain financing from Warner Brothers to complete "The Thief and the Cobbler." Williams had already worked on this personal feature for twenty-three years by 1988. During lulls in commercial production, his artists would switch to scenes from "Thief." He coaxed some the greatest animators in the history of the medium out of retirement to work on it— Grim Natwick, Art Babbitt, Ken Harris, Emery Hawkins.

A lavish tale with an Arabian Nights setting, "Thief" depicted the efforts of a wily kleptomaniac to steal the golden orbs that protected an enchanted city from harm. The film included sequences of staggering complexity, although some of the effects that had been laboriously drawn by hand during the late 1960s could easily be done with computers twenty years later.

In May 1992 the Completion Bond Co. of Century City shut down production. It was estimated that Williams had spent $20 million, but only finished seventy of an expected eighty minutes. Williams went into seclusion, and Completion Bond sought to finish the truncated epic.

Fred Calvert, whose work included the forgettable television series "Emergency + 4" and "I Am the Greatest: The Adventures of Muhammad Ali," recut the film, replaced most of the sound track and added new animation. Previewed footage from "The Thief" suggested that the film was probably unreleasable: The story was a muddle that suffered from comparisons to Disney's savvy "Aladdin"; the visuals a mishmash of full and limited animation. Although completed in September 1993, "The Thief and the Cobbler" remained in limbo in early 1994. It was a regrettable ending to a daring, if impractical, vision of what an animated feature could encompass.

Ralph Bakshi's return to feature animation after nearly a decade also proved a major disappointment. "Cool World" (1992) was a combination of animation and live action that used neither medium effectively. Comic book artist Jack Deebs (Gabriel Byrne) found himself yanked out of live action reality into an animated world based on his drawings.

The cartoon realm, inhabited by *doodles*—an obvious attempt to duplicate the Toons in "Roger Rabbit"—had a gritty,

Rex the tyrannosaurus, Woog the triceratops, Elsa the pterodactyl and Dweeb the hadrosaurus catch their breath in a New York alley in the 1993 feature, "We're Back! A Dinosaur's Story."

The wise old badger, Cornelius (Michael Crawford) sings to his niece, Michelle (Elizabeth Moss), who
has been poisoned by a toxic chemical spill in "Once Upon A Forest."

distorted look that recalled Bakshi's earlier work. But the backgrounds and all the characters zipping around the frame to distract the viewer's eye couldn't disguise the sloppiness of the live action/animation combinations. The Fleischers had blended media more effectively seventy years earlier.

The virtually incomprehensible plot involved the efforts of Holli Would (Kim Basinger) to become a *noid* (human)—something a doodle could achieve only by breaking the law and having sexual relations with a human. The advertising campaign for the film was built around the suggestive slogan, "Holli Would if she could . . . *and she will*." The failure to deliver the promised titillation might help explain the film's disastrous performance at the box office. Widely disparaged as one of the great bombs of 1992, "Cool World" appeared on numerous end-of-the-year "Ten Worst" lists.

Hanna-Barbera returned to the feature market in 1990, with "The Jetsons," a stolid recreation of the 1962 TV series. The image of a family in which Dad goes to work, Mom goes shopping and a teenager's only problem is to find a boyfriend seemed hopelessly passé, as did the idyllic, early sixties vision of an automated future.

The studio's next theatrical feature was the more ambitious "Once Upon a Forest" (1993). The story of three small animals searching for the herbs that can save a friend who has been poisoned in an industrial accident, "Forest" pushed an ecological message. But the combination of environmental preaching and cutsey characters felt tired and formulaic. The animation was considerably more polished than "The Jetsons," although still inferior to the work of Disney, Amblin or Bluth.

"Once Upon A Forest" was part of then-chairman David Kirschner's effort to upgrade the studio's output. But Kirschner left Hanna-Barbera in 1993 to start his own production company, where his first feature, "The Pagemaster," a blend of live-action, drawn animation and CGI starring Macaulay Culkin and Christopher Lloyd, was scheduled for Christmas, 1994. The musical satire, "Cats Don't Dance," was slated to follow in 1996. When Kirschner departed, Hanna-Barbera once again abandoned theatrical features.

The tiny fairy Crysta (Samantha Mathis) attempts to communicate with the addled Batty Koda (Robin Williams) in "FernGully: The Last Rain Forest."

Another Saturday morning producer, Phil Roman, made his feature directorial debut with "Tom and Jerry: The Movie" (1993), an ill-conceived attempt to revive the popular cat-and-mouse duo from the MGM shorts. Bill Hanna and Joe Barbera had never tried to get more than seven minutes out of their characters when they had some of the best animators in the business working for them. Like the Warner Brothers characters, Tom and Jerry simply didn't have deep enough personalities to sustain a story and hold an audience's attention for more than hour.

Instead of continuing their slapstick feuds, Dennis Marks's screenplay turned them into grudging allies who had inadvertently been abandoned by their owners. The mismatched duo was drawn into a threadbare story about a little girl looking for her missing explorer/gazillionaire father. After fifty-three years as pantomime characters, Tom and Jerry spoke (Richard Kind and Dana Hill, respectively) and sang some cat-and-doggerel songs. The vastly more entertaining MGM cartoons, which were readily available on video cassette and laser disc,

only underscored how pedestrian this version of Tom and Jerry looked.

The most successful non-Disney feature was "FernGully . . . The Last Rain Forest," a "modern myth" set in Australia. Zak, a human logger-in-training, and Crysta, an insect-sized fairy charged with defending the forest, share an ill-starred romance after Crysta shrinks Zak to her dimensions. The loggers have inadvertently released Hexxus, a malevolent spirit bent on destroying the forest, but by joining forces, Zak, Crysta and her fairy tribe manage to defeat him.

The ecological message was weakened by writer Jim Cox's failure to connect the threat to the environment to real life. The animation itself was about on par with a good television special, although the lush backgrounds and CGI effects suggested director Bill Kroyer was aiming higher. In the *New York Times*, Janet Maslin described the film as "an uncertain blend of sanctimonious principles and Saturday-morning cartoon esthetics." Others complained about the inane "Valley Girl" dialogue, especially Zak's description of Crysta as a "bodacious babe." Despite these weaknesses, "FernGully" played to larger audiences than its more expensive competitors.

Although cassettes of "The Brave Little Toaster" (1987) sold well, the subsequent features from Hyperion Pictures failed to connect with audiences. "Rover Dangerfield," starring a caricature of comedian Rodney Dangerfield as a Las Vegas showgirl's pet basset hound, never received theatrical distribution. Dangerfield conceived the idea in the mid 1980s and spent more than $1 million of his own money on preproduction work that convinced Warner Brothers to fund the project. Warner gave "Rover" a very brief run in a few markets in the summer of 1991, then released it on video.

"Bebe's Kids" (1992) was based on a nightclub routine by comic Robin Harris: A man who asks an attractive woman for a date ends up shepherding her son and her friend's three bratty kids around an amusement park. It was the first animated feature to center on African-American characters.

Production designer Fred Cline and art director Doug Walker created a two-dimensional, UPA-influenced look that was well-suited to film's limited animation. Although it contained some genuinely funny moments, Reginald Hudlin's script remained an overextended stand-up routine that couldn't support seventy-two minutes of animation. The title trio were so unceasingly and gratuitously loathsome that viewers quickly wearied of them. "Bebe's Kids" was released with the short "The Itsy Bitsy Spider," which Hyperion subsequently developed into a series for the USA Network.

Two foreign animated features received general releases during 1993: "Little Nemo: Adventures in Slumberland," a long-delayed Japanese film based loosely on Winsor McCay's comic strip, and "Freddie as F.R.0.7.," an egregious British spoof of James Bond movies. Both films died quickly and deservedly at the box office.

"It sounds really arrogant, but the fact is, feature animation hasn' t made a comeback, *Disney* animation has made a comeback," said a Disney animator who spoke to the *Los Angeles Times* on the condition of anonymity. "Animation—even bad animation—is a lot of work, and if you do that much work, you want people to see it, but the reality of the situation is that people won't go to see it unless it's a Disney film."

Although numerous media pieces heralded the early 1990s as a new "Golden Age" that rivaled the 1930s at Disney or the postwar era at Warner Brothers and MGM, the fact remained that success in the feature market has been restricted to a single studio. And the work of any one studio—regardless of the talent of the artists working there—is insufficient to fuel a genuine renaissance.

Even during the 1940s and 50s, when Disney enjoyed a virtual monopoly on animated features in America, other studios, notably MGM, Warner Brothers and UPA, were producing quality shorts that offered audiences alternate visions of what an animated film could be. Animators, like other artists, thrive on competition that broadens their ideas and challenges their assumptions. When a single studio or a single artist dominates a field too completely, there is a danger of stagnation.

The artist who spoke on the condition of anonymity summed up the prevailing feeling within the animation industry when he said, "It would be nice to see another studio score a big hit at the box office, especially with a breakthrough film in style or subject. It might convince the people here to do films with even more varied styles and subjects than they're doing currently."

By the early 1990s, more than eighty percent of American homes had at least one videocassette player, and a good animated feature could generate more revenue through video sales and licensing than through box office returns. Disney once again led the market. After experimenting with high-priced cassettes of their classics during the mid 1980s ("Pinocchio" sold for $79.95 when it was initially released), the studio switched to a lower price/higher volume strategy that proved wildly successful: The top five best-selling cassettes of all time were animated Disney features.

"Beauty and the Beast" became the best-selling video in history with over 20 million units—only to have its record broken by "Aladdin" with over 21 million units. Disney earned an estimated $200 million profit on U.S. sales of the "Beauty" cassette, and in 1992, revenue from Disney's Buena Vista Home Video division passed the $1 billion mark.

The modestly successful "FernGully" sold over three million cassettes; "All Dogs Go to Heaven," four million. "Happily Ever After," Filmation's misbegotten attempt to continue the story of Snow White, and other films that died in theaters, found new life in video stores. In addition, anthologies of classic theatrical shorts and compilations of network and syndicated kidvid shows were released on video and laser disc.

A large part of this video market was geared to Baby Boomer parents who had grown up on the Disney features. In the *Wall Street Journal*, Richard Turner explained, "Among the cheaply made videos aimed at kids, the Disney brand was like a Good Housekeeping seal of approval . . . Kids would watch these things ten, twenty and thirty times, making it worthwhile to buy them. Disney was a baby-sitter with good references." Or, as one animator bluntly put it, "Having the Disney videos is like having a 'pause' button on your kids. You slip a tape into the VCR, and it's quiet for an hour."

Video sales also fed the growing market for cartoon character merchandise. Although animation had been linked to license products since the days of Felix the Cat, cartoon characters were more popular than ever on clothing (especially jackets and T-shirts), toys, school supplies and bric-a-brac.

Disney and Warner Brothers opened chains of stores devoted to character merchandise.

In addition to cassette sales of over 10 million units, "The Little Mermaid" was adapted to a Saturday morning TV show and a series of compact discs, which kept the character fresh in people's minds and insured an ongoing market for related merchandise. Ariel became the second-most licensed figure in the Disney stable; only Mickey Mouse appeared on more products.

The growing perception of animation as both an art form and a source of collectibles led to increasing sales of cels, drawings and related artwork—at the very time cels were being replaced by digital ink-and-paint systems. The high end of the animation art market became the preserve of a handful of wealthy buyers during the late 1980s. In 1989, Canadian collector Herbert Black paid a record $286,000 for a black-and-white cel and background set-up from the 1934 Mickey Mouse-Donald Duck short "Orphan's Benefit." But the top of the market collapsed when Black quit buying and sold his collection at Sotheby's in 1992. The record-breaking "Orphan's Benefit" set-up brought only $88,000—considerably less than its pre-sale estimate of $100,000–$150,000. A second set-up from the same film that Black had bought for $181,000, fetched $60,500.

Sales of art from the old Disney features and special auctions of artwork from "Who Framed Roger Rabbit," "The Little Mermaid," "Beauty and the Beast" and "Aladdin" proved there were large numbers of buyers for animation art in the $10,000–$90,000 range. An even larger group bought works priced between $500 and $5,000. To appeal to these consumers, studios began issuing limited edition cels—hand-painted or serigraph reproductions of images from popular films. Sold individually or in sets, these cels (which had no archival significance) found buyers in the burgeoning collectibles market.

Although the potential profits from video and licensing helped to fuel the high level of production, merchandise tie-ins did not guarantee success. Marked-down character merchandise from failed animated films and TV programs filled the discount stores and swap meets during the late 1980s and early 1990s.

"Animation remains attractive despite the failures we saw in 1992–93," concluded Kirschner. "The kind of business 'Aladdin' did says to studio heads there is a market here if we can tap into it and deliver the right emotions. But I don't think you can just casually enter the feature animation business. It requires a long-term commitment to the talent and growing that talent in the right direction. If you hire artists for a single project, by the time you get to know them and how they work, they're off to another studio and another film. You want to keep continuity with talented people."

Joan Gratz used streaks of clay on underlit plexiglass for "Mona Lisa Descending a Staircase," her Oscar-winning survey of twentieth-century Western art.

Conditions for independent animators remained largely static. The increasingly popular programs of short animated films and some of the new channels (especially MTV and "Liquid Television"), provided outlets for their work. But only a few artists were able to earn a living from their personal films; the majority still had to rely on grants, teaching and commercial work.

An occasional film attracted media attention. In 1988, director Stephen Johnson and producer Prudence Fenton worked with forty-two animators from around the world to illustrate the thirty articles in the Universal Declaration of Human Rights issued by the United Nations. The 19-minute film was shown between acts on the Amnesty International "Human Rights Now" tour that included Bruce Springsteen, Peter Gabriel, Tracy Chapman and Sting.

Working with a single assistant, Bill Plympton spent two years making the 30,000 drawings in his feature "The Tune" (1992). But his scribbly drawing style and extremely limited animation proved better suited to the 10-second gag spots ("Plymptoons") he did for MTV.

Will Vinton announced plans for two clay animated features: "The Frog Prince," based on the Grimm fairy tale, scheduled for summer, 1996, and an adaptation of L. Frank Baum's "The Life and Adventures of Santa Claus" for 1997. Although Joan Gratz, an artist at Vinton's studio, won the Oscar in 1993 for "Mona Lisa Descending a Staircase," a survey of twentieth-century art rendered in streaks of clay on glass, the leadership of the clay animation field had shifted to London.

Aardman Animations' five-part "Lip Synch" series (1989) for

"I'd like to live in a hot country with good weather." The jaguar in the Oscar-winning short "Creature Comforts" set a new standard for the character animation of clay figures. Director Nick Park won a second Oscar in 1994 for "The Wrong Trousers."

Channel Four Television set new standards for character animation in clay. The Oscar-winning "Creature Comforts," in which an improbable array of animals complained about conditions in a London zoo, delighted audiences on both sides of the Atlantic. "Next!" a tour-de-force of both animation and choreography, featured a caricature of Shakespeare synopsizing twenty-nine of his plays in 5½ minutes.

The American-born twins Timothy and Stephen Quay were also at work in England, producing commercials and their compelling, if nightmarish, personal stop-motion shorts. In contrast to the spotless environments in traditional stop-motion films, "The Epic of Gilgamesh" (1985) and "The Street of Crocodiles" (1986) depicted scabrous worlds of peeling walls, rusting metal and gritty hallways, inhabited by an eerie array of half-mechanical, half-organic creatures. The chilling visions of the Quays were influenced by Eastern European artists and filmmakers, particularly the Czech surrealist, Jan Svankmayer.

Computer animation—also referred to as computer graphics (CG) or computer-generated imagery (CGI)-continued to evolve rapidly during the late 1980s and early 1990s. The animators and technical directors who worked in this specialized field often had to explain to reporters and audiences that the computers didn't "do it all." A computer is only a sophisticated tool that requires an artist's guidance to create anything. As one animator noted dryly, "People will attribute computer animation to a computer and ignore the role of the animator, but they would never attribute a book to the author's word-processor."

The rapid development of computer animation, which in some ways paralleled the growth of drawn animation at the Disney studio during the 1930s, was due in part to advances in computer technology. Although the most visible fraction of the imagery created on computers was used for entertainment or the arts, the vast majority of these images were produced for industrial design and manufacturing, architecture and medi-

Morphing techniques transformed a Caucasian man into an Asian woman in the music video of Michael Jackson's hit, "Black or White."

cal, scientific and mathematical research. But computer animation accounted for some of the most striking visuals in films during the late 1980s and early 1990s.

George Lucas's fantasy, "Willow" (1988), in which a sorceress turned into a series of animals, showcased a process called "morphing" (from metamorphosing). Doug Smythe devised the software to help the model makers create the distorted animals needed for the scene. Morphing enables an artist to transform one image into another by having the computer devise a series of intermediary steps.

"Our program uses a grid of control points to tell the computer where certain features are located on the object you are interested in transforming," Smythe explains. "So you put a horizontal line of dots, say, along the top of the head, and vertical lines along the edges of the body. You put other lines of dots along the top and sides of the second shape. With that information, the computer can calculate a series of interpolations between the two."

Although special effects artists had used traditional techniques for transformation scenes in earlier fantasy films, morphing allowed for smoother, more convincing metamorphoses.

The seawater pseudopod (irreverently dubbed the "water weenie") that represented the aliens' attempt to communicate with Mary Elizabeth Mastrantonio in "The Abyss" (1989) was one of the first effects that would have been impossible to create with traditional methods.

The pseudopod also provided a starting point for the dazzling effects involving the "poly-alloy" liquid metal assassin, the T-1000, in James Cameron's "Terminator II: Judgment Day" (1991). Audiences had never seen a character flow through the barred entrance to a prison or rise out of a tessellated linoleum floor, or seen hundreds of metallic fragments melt and flow together to form a metallic robot. It had never been possible to create these effects.

"I think you could have gotten some of these shots on the screen for less money with traditional methods, but they

The brachiosaurus and other animals in "Jurassic Park" represented not only a breakthrough in computer animation, but the culmination of more than seventy-five years of efforts to produce realistic dinosaurs on the screen.

wouldn't have looked as good," said ILM senior visual effects supervisor Dennis Muren. "So the director has a choice: Does he want something in the film that's going to look artificial and break the progress of the story for the audience, or does he want something that looks real? We can now do stuff that couldn' t be done before, and I don't think you can put a price on that."

Impressive as the computer effects were in "T2," they were eclipsed by "Jurassic Park." Creating the dinosaurs for Steven Spielberg's sci-fi blockbuster involved every technique in the special effects artists' repertory, from state-of-the-art computer imagery to traditional stop-motion to actors in animal suits. Animating a single *Gallimimus* realistically would have been a challenging assignment for a stop-motion animator; computer animation allowed the filmmakers to deploy a small herd of the animals. It also enabled them to include the added realism of the *Tyrannosaurus* smashing his way through a tree limb as the jeep he was pursuing drove under it. Other computer animators are quick to praise the work done at ILM for "Jurassic Park" as "the best dinosaurs ever to appear on the screen," but they also note that the project involved a large staff and a multimillion dollar budget.

"In the near future, I think a lot of the other arrows in the filmmaker's quiver are going to continue to be important," says Jay Riddle, computer graphics supervisor at ILM. "Building a model you can touch has a lot of advantages, and a human can sculpt very high levels of detail that you just can't get right now with a computer."

Although the flashy effects in "T2" and "Jurassic Park" received widespread media attention, crews have been using computer techniques to manipulate other visuals so subtly that audiences don't even realize the images have been altered. Pacific Data Images president Karl Rosendahl calls them "invisible effects—if you can't tell we touched the film, we did a really good job. The majority of the work that's being done on the film side right now involves that kind of image manipulation, as opposed to image generation or character animation."

"The situation is no different than it has been for traditional effects," agrees John Hughes, president of Rhythm & Hues. "In any of the big effects movies that were out last year, with the

The computer-animated ''Polar Express'' commercial for Coca-Cola proved so popular, additional ads featuring the polar bear characters were created for airing during the 1994 Winter Olympics.

exception of 'Jurassic Park' and 'Nightmare Before Christmas,' the effects *are* invisible; nobody knows that those are effects shots. Computer-animated effects are just a filmmaking tool: you're trying to tell a story, not call attention to the effects.''

Changes can be made so seamlessly that sometimes even an expert can't tell from a print if the film has been altered. One animator irreverently suggested transposing old footage of the cast onto the faces of the crew in ''Star Trek IV'' to make them look younger. While such extensive alteration of human faces wouldn't be effective at this stage in the technology, the Orwellian possibility of creating ersatz ''news'' footage or fraudulent ''evidence'' for a trial now exists. For ''The Babe'' (1992), PDI artists turned one tier of 1,000 extras into an overflowing stadium of fans; in ''Line of Fire'' (1993), Clint Eastwood and the actor playing the president were added to newsreel footage of

Air Force One. Some judges already refuse to admit photographic evidence.

The glitzy effects in blockbuster science fiction films eventually filtered down to television, but usually not to programs. ''In television, there's a lot of interest in doing computer-animated characters integrated in with live action, but I don't believe the economics work yet,'' says Rosendahl. ''In episode television, you don't get twelve weeks to do your animation; what people really want is a quick turnaround on a budget that television people are used to paying for a sitcom, and that is very, very difficult to do with computer-animated characters today—but that will certainly change.''

To date, computer animation has had its greatest effect in the area of commercials. As the audience for the Big Three networks continues to shrink and ''channel surfing'' becomes increasingly popular, advertisers are searching for visuals that will capture an audience's attention—and hold it through repeated viewings. Some of the most sophisticated computer animation techniques used in feature films over the last few years now appear in commercials.

"At a time when advertising is in a sharp decline, when people are spending less on production and producing less than they have in a long time, they're spending more on computer animation and effects," continues Rosendahl. "If you're not going to spend as much on advertising, you'd better make sure that you're going to create something that the viewers are going to watch, that they're going to pay attention to, that they're going to want to see over and over again; and that's something that computer animation and traditional animation do really well."

"It used to be a very difficult sell for us in the commercial world, trying to get people to do things digitally; now, it's never an issue," adds Hughes. "It's become the preferred way of doing a lot of animation and a lot of visual effects."

Some of the most striking work has involved combinations of digital effects and drawn animation to produce visuals that would be impossible to achieve through either medium alone. McLeach's sinister Bushwhacker vehicle in "The Rescuers Down Under"; the critically praised ballroom sequence in "Beauty and the Beast"; Aladdin's ride on the flying carpet through the Cave of Wonders and the Wildebeest stampede in "Lion King" rank among the most successful examples of this marriage of techniques.

The recent Disney features once again led the pack, but the use of computer animation for vehicles, roller coaster ride effects and background elements became increasingly common during the early 1990s. Warner Brothers' "Batman: The Mask of the Phantasm" opened with digital animation of the Art Deco skyscrapers of a darkly elegant metropolis; "Rover Dangerfield" began with an accelerating traveling shot through the desert to the lights of Las Vegas.

When the disparate types of animation were combined with taste and imagination, the results were doubly striking. In "Beauty and the Beast," the glittering marble ballroom heightened the emotional power of the hand drawn characters to produce a genuinely magical moment: That Belle and Beast could fall in love became believable. However, when the techniques are mixed carelessly, the discontinuity can be jarring. Nothing in either "Rover" or "Batman" matched the visual imagination of the opening scenes.

Although computer animation was widely seen in commercials, network logos, rock videos and amusement park simulator rides, outside of specialized conventions and occasional programs of shorts, computer films were rarely seen in theaters. The equipment, software and users' time were simply too costly to use for entertainment films that had little chance of receiving distribution.

"There's no market for computer 'art' films, and to do anything at the level of film quality is expensive and tough to justify from the standpoint of profit and loss," says Rosendahl. "So you have justify it as a portfolio item, either as an individual or as a company to help open doors for you. That's how we justify it: Internally, it helps us to develop our skills to push our R&D, to push our storytelling and design skills. Externally, it helps open some doors and sell people on what the technology can do."

Budget limitations and the lack of an outlet for the work have frustrated some of the efforts to do more effective character animation using computers. In recent years, there have been no breakthrough films like "Luxo, Jr." that alerted audiences and artists to heretofore unknown possibilities. Instead, the improvements have come incrementally—one commercial may show more subtle changes in a character's expressions; another, a more effective body movement. The art of computer personality animation continues to advance, but in small steps, rather than giant leaps.

"I think the development will continue to be incremental from now on," says Hughes thoughtfully. "Any kind of advancement in the quality of animation is going to be due to the individuals who are doing it. The technology itself is becoming irrelevant; the actual computers being used or the software being used doesn't matter any more. It's the quality of the individual animator. If we want to see improvements in the quality of the animation done on computers, we have to look to better animators."

In addition to "really high quality character animation," Muren notes, "I don't think CGI is really good at creating natural phenomena that move. We can't do oceans . . . I mean, we can sort of do them and we can fudge them by mixing media, but it's not quite there yet. Somewhere down the line, I know all that stuff is going to be done with the turn of a switch."

However, computer animation is still in its infancy. CGI animators have made enormous strides in the last decade, but the brightest moments of the medium still lie in the future.

"I think we have a lot to offer in terms of fluidity of motion and the quality of the image," concludes Hughes. "Somebody with a pencil and paper has an edge in capturing emotion: I think it's still easier to capture emotion with a line on paper than it is with a character in the computer. The faster computers are actually a very good force for animation. The thing about animation is, you have to repeat it: Nobody animates well the first time. You do it, and you do it again, and you do it again. It's the art of refinement, and the faster the computers are, the more repetitions you can do in a given amount of time. That's where fine animation comes from—being able to look at the test, study it and then improve it."

For a medium that had repeatedly been pronounced moribund, if not dead, from the mid 1950s through the early 1980s, animation appeared quite vital in the late 1980s and early 1990s. No longer restricted to mindless kidvid, it was increasingly accepted in America as a legitimate art form. The continuing boom in production was heralded as a new "Golden Age," although the title may have been awarded prematurely. As long as animated features and television programs continued to draw large audiences and show large profits, a high level of production was assured.

The question shifted from whether animation would survive to what forms it would take. Aesthetically, it makes little sense to have dozens, let alone the promised hundreds, of television channels if they all broadcast reruns of old shows—or new productions that look like old shows. In the theatrical arena, artists continue to search for a new "Yellow Submarine," a successful feature that will push the stylistic envelope even farther than "Aladdin" and make audiences aware of the possibilities of new graphic styles.

Ninety years after the experiments of J. Stuart Blackton, the artistic potential of animation has actually expanded as generations of talented and well-trained artists explore their visions using traditional techniques and new technologies. This promising situation confirms Walt Disney's statement that the reason he enjoyed working in animation was, "the knowledge that there's always something new and exciting just around the corner—and the uncertainty of everything else."

Young Simba finds himself trapped amid thousands of stampeding wildebeests in "The Lion King." The artists combined drawn and computer-generated animation to create a spectacular sequence that would have been impossible to achieve using either medium alone. Increasingly sophisticated blends of techniques offer new visual possibilities in animated features.

BIBLIOGRAPHY

BOOKS

Adams, Richard. *The Watership Down Film Picture Book*. New York: Macmillan, 1978.

Adamson, Joe. *Tex Avery: King of Cartoons*. New York: Popular Library, 1975.

————. *The Walter Lantz Story*. New York: Putnam's, 1985.

Agee, James. *Agee on Film*. New York: Grosset & Dunlap, 1969.

Alber. *Les Théâtres d'ombres chinoises*. Paris: E. Mazo, 1896.

Bain, David, and Bruce Harris. *Mickey Mouse: Fifty Happy Years*. New York: Harmony, 1977.

Barnes, John. *Catalogue of the Collection, Part 2: Optical Projection*. Saint Ives, Cornwall: Barnes Museum of Cinematography, 1970.

Barnouw, Erik. *The Magician and the Cinema*. New York: Oxford University Press, 1981.

Barrie, James M. *Peter Pan*. Bungay, Suffolk: Puffin, 1972.

Benayoun, Robert. *Le Dessin animé après Walt Disney*. Lausanne: J. J. Pauvert, 1961.

Bendazzi, Giannalberto. *Le Film d'animation*, Vol. 1. Grenoble: La Pensée Sauvage/Jica, 1985.

Blackbeard, Bill, and Martin Williams, eds. *The Smithsonian Collection of Newspaper Comics*. Washington, D.C./New York: Smithsonian/Abrams, 1977.

Blackham, Olive. *Shadow Puppets*. London: Barrie and Rockcliff, 1960.

Blitz, Marcia. *Donald Duck*. New York: Harmony, 1979.

Bordat, Denis, and Francis Boucrot. *Les Théâtres d'ombres: Histoire et techniques*. Paris: L'Arche, 1926.

Brewster, David. *Letters on Natural Magic*. London: John Murray, 1832.

Brion, Patrick. *Tex Avery*. Paris: Chène, 1984.

————. *Tom et Jerry*. Paris: Chène, 1987.

Cabarga, Leslie. *The Fleischer Story*. New York: Nostalgia, 1976.

Canemaker, John. *The Animated Raggedy Ann and Andy*. Indianapolis/New York: Bobbs-Merrill, 1977.

————. *Winsor McCay: His Life and Art*. New York: Abbeville Press, 1987.

Carroll, Lewis. *The Annotated Alice: "Alice's Adventures in Wonderland" and "Through the Looking-Glass."* Cleveland: World, 1967.

————. *Alice's Adventures in Wonderland*. With David Hall's previously unpublished illustrations for Walt Disney Productions. Devon, Eng.: Methuen, 1986.

Ceram, C. W. *Archeology of the Cinema*. New York: Harcourt, Brace & World, 1965.

Chasins, Abram. *Leopold Stokowski: A Profile*. New York: Hawthorn, 1979.

Couperie, Pierre, and Maurice Horn. *A History of the Comic Strip*. New York: Crown, 1968.

Crafton, Donald. *Before Mickey: The Animated Film 1898–1928*. Cambridge, Mass.: MIT Press, 1982.

Cripps, Thomas. *Slow Fade to Black: The Negro in American Film, 1900–1942*. New York: Oxford, 1977.

Crumb, Robert. *The Complete Fritz the Cat*. New York: Belier Press, 1978.

Culhane, John. *Walt Disney's "Fantasia."* New York: Abrams, 1983.

Culhane, Shamus. *Talking Animals and Other People*. New York: St. Martin's Press, 1986.

Curtis, David. *Experimental Cinema: A Fifty-Year Evolution*. New York: Dell, 1971.

Daniel, Oliver. *Stokowski: A Counterpoint of View*. New York: Dodd, Mead, 1982.

Davis, Jim. *Here Comes Garfield*. New York: Ballantine, 1982.

Diamant, Lincoln. *Television's Classic Commercials*. New York: Hastings House, 1971.

Dircks, Henry. *The Ghost!* London: E. and F. N. Spon, 1863.

Donnay, Maurice. *Autour du Chat Noir*. Paris: Bernard Grasset, 1926.

Evans, Henry. *The Old and the New Magic*. Chicago: The Open Court, 1906.

Feiffer, Jules. *Passionella and Other Stories*. New York: McGraw-Hill, 1959.

Feild, Robert. *The Art of Walt Disney*. New York: Macmillan, 1942.

Ferguson, Otis. *The Film Criticism of Otis Ferguson*. Philadelphia: Temple University Press, 1971.

Fielding, Raymond, ed. *A Technological History of Motion Pictures and Television*. Berkeley: University of California Press, 1967.

Finch, Christopher. *The Art of Walt Disney*. New York: Abrams, 1973.

Fischer, Stuart. *Kids' TV: The First 25 Years*. New York: Facts on File, 1983.

Fox, David, and Michael Waite. *Computer Animation Primer*. New York: McGraw-Hill, 1984.

Friedwall, Will, and Jerry Beck. *The Warner Brothers Cartoons*. Metuchen, N.J.: Scarecrow Press, 1981.

Gernsheim, Helmut, and Alison Gernsheim. *L. J. M. Daguerre*. Cleveland: World, 1956.

Gifford, Dennis. *The Great Cartoon Stars: A Who's Who!* London: Jupiter Books, 1979.

Goodman, Cynthia. *Digital Visions: Computers and Art.* New York: Abrams, 1987.

Gould, Stephen Jay. *The Panda's Thumb: More Reflections on Natural History.* New York: W. W. Norton, 1980.

Grahame, Kenneth. *The Wind in the Willows.* New York: Scribners, 1933.

Grant, John. *Encyclopedia of Walt Disney's Animated Characters.* New York: Harper & Row, 1987.

Greenberg, Donald, Aaron Marcus, Allan Schmidt, and Vernon Gorter. *The Computer Image: Applications of Computer Graphics.* Reading, Mass.: Addison-Wesley, 1982.

Griffin, George. *Frames: A Selection of Drawings and Statements by Independent American Animators.* Montpelier, Vt.: Capital City, 1978.

Haas, Robert. *Muybridge: Man in Motion.* Berkeley: University of California Press, 1976.

———. *Eadweard Muybridge: The Stanford Years, 1872–1882.* Palo Alto: Stanford University, 1972.

Halas, John. *Masters of Animation.* Topsfield, Mass.: Salem House, 1987.

Hall, Avery, and John Korty. *Twice Upon a Time.* New York: Simon & Schuster, 1982.

Hall, Jim. *Mighty Minutes.* New York: Harmony, 1984.

Hand, David. *Memoirs.* Cambria, Calif.: Lighthouse Litho, 1986.

Harris, Joel Chandler. *Uncle Remus: His Songs and Sayings.* New York: Viking Penguin, 1982.

Heide, Robert, and John Gilman. *Cartoon Collectibles: 50 Years of Dime-Store Memorabilia.* New York: Doubleday, 1983.

Hendricks, Gordon. *Eadweard Muybridge: The Father of the Motion Picture.* New York: Grossman, 1975.

Herdeg, Walter. *Film & TV Graphics.* Zurich: Graphis Press, 1967.

———. *Film & TV Graphics, 2.* Zurich: Graphis Press, 1976.

Hoffer, Thomas. *Animation: A Reference Guide.* Westport, Conn.: Greenwood, 1981.

Holliss, Richard, and Brian Sibley. *The Disney Studio Story.* New York: Crown, 1988.

———. *Walt Disney's Snow White and the Seven Dwarfs and The Making of the Classic Film.* New York: Simon & Schuster, 1987.

Holman, L. Bruce. *Puppet Animation in the Cinema: History and Technique.* Cranbury. N.J.: A. S. Barnes, 1975.

Hopkins, Albert. *Magic: Stage Illusions and Scientific Diversions.* London: Sampson Low, Marston & Co., 1897.

Horn, Maurice, ed. *The World Encyclopedia of Cartoons.* New York: Chelsea House, 1980.

———. *The World Encyclopedia of Comics.* New York: Avon, 1977.

Hutchins, Robert. *Zuckerkandl!* New York: Grove Press, 1968.

Huxley, Aldous. *Essays New and Old.* New York: H. M. Wilson, 1932.

Jankel, Annabel, and Rocky Morton. *Creative Computer Graphics.* New York: Cambridge University Press, 1984.

Kerlow, Isaac, and Judson Rosebush. *Computer Graphics for Designers and Artists.* New York: Van Nostrand Reinhold, 1986.

Kipling, Rudyard. *The Jungle Books.* New York: Airmont, 1966.

Leavitt, Ruth, ed. *Artist and Computer.* New York: Harmony, 1976.

Le Grice, Malcolm. *Abstract Film and Beyond.* Cambridge, Mass.: MIT Press, 1981.

Lenburg, Jeff. *The Encyclopedia of Animated Cartoon Series.* Westport, Conn.: Arlington House, 1981.

———. *The Great Cartoon Directors.* Jefferson, N.C.: McFarland, 1983.

Lewell, John. *Computer Graphics: A Survey of Current Techniques and Applications.* Van Nostrand Reinhold, 1985.

Lorenzini, Carlo. *The Adventures of Pinocchio.* New York: Macmillan, 1951.

McArdell, Roy, ed. *George Herriman's "Krazy Kat."* New York: Grosset & Dunlap, 1977.

McCay, Winsor. *Dreams of the Rarebit Fiend.* New York: Dover, 1973.

———. *Little Nemo.* New York: Nostalgia Press, 1972.

———. *Little Nemo, 1905–1906.* New York: Nostalgia Press, 1976.

———. *Little Nemo in the Palace of Ice and Further Adventures.* New York: Dover, 1976.

McDonnell, Patrick, Karen O'Connell, and Georgia de Havenon. *Krazy Kat: The Comic Art of George Herriman.* New York: Abrams, 1986.

Macek, Carl. *The Art of Heavy Metal, the Movie: Animation for the Eighties.* New York: New York Zoetrope, 1981.

Maltin, Leonard. *The Disney Films.* New York: Crown, 1984.

———. *Of Mice and Magic: A History of American Animated Cartoons.* New York: McGraw-Hill, 1980.

Melody, William. *Children's TV: The Economics of Exploitation.* New Haven: Yale University Press, 1973.

Mendelson, Lee. *Happy Birthday, Charlie Brown.* New York: Random House, 1979.

Merritt, Douglas. *Television Graphics: From Pencil to Pixel.* New York: Van Nostrand Reinhold, 1987.

Miller, Diane Disney. *The Story of Walt Disney.* New York: Dell, 1959.

Morris, Norman. *Television's Child.* Boston: Little, Brown, 1971.

Munsey, Cecil. *Disneyana: Walt Disney Collectibles.* New York: Hawthorne, 1974.

Neuville, Lemercier de. *Ombres chinoises.* Paris: O. Bornemann, 1911.

———. *Les Pupazzi noirs.* Paris: Charles Mendel, n.d.

O'Brien, Flora. *Walt Disney's Donald Duck: 50 Years of Happy Frustration.* Tucson, Ariz.: HP Books, 1984.

———. *Walt Disney's Goofy: The Good Sport.* Tucson, Ariz.: HP Books, 1985.

Osborn, Robert. *Osborn on Osborn.* New York: Ticknor & Fields, 1982.

Peary, Gerald, and Danny Peary, eds. *The American Animated Cartoon.* New York: Dutton, 1980.

Perrault, Charles. *Contes.* Paris: Garnier Frères, 1967.

Prueitt, Melvin. *Art and the Computer.* New York: McGraw-Hill, 1984.

Quigley, Martin, Jr. *Magic Shadows: The Story of the Origins of Motion Pictures.* Washington, D.C.: Georgetown University Press, 1948.

Rivlin, Robert. *The Algorithmic Image.* Redmond, Wash.: Microsoft Press, 1986.

Russett, Robert, and Cecile Starr. *Experimental Animation: An Illustrated Anthology.* New York: Van Nostrand Reinhold, 1976.

Sagendorf, Bud. *Popeye: The First Fifty Years.* New York: Workman, 1979.

Salten, Felix. *Bambi.* New York: Noble and Noble, 1929.

Schickel, Richard. *The Disney Version.* New York: Simon & Schuster, 1968.

Schneider, Stephen. *That's All, Folks: The Art of the Warner Brothers Animation.* New York: Henry Holt, 1988.

Schulz, Charles. *A Boy Named Charlie Brown.* New York: Holt, Rinehart & Winston, 1969.

———. *A Charlie Brown Christmas.* Cleveland: World, 1965.

———. *Race for Your Life, Charlie Brown.* New York: Holt, Rinehart & Winston, 1978.

———. *The "Snoopy, Come Home" Movie Book.* New York: Holt, Rinehart & Winston, 1972.

———. *You've Had It, Charlie Brown.* New York: Holt, Rinehart & Winston, 1969.

Searle, Ronald, *Dick Deadeye.* New York: Harcourt Brace Jovanovich, 1975.

Seldes, Gilbert. *The 7 Lively Arts.* New York: Sagamore, 1957.

Seversky, Alexander de, *Victory Through Air Power.* New York: Simon & Schuster, 1942.

Shales, Richard, *Donald Duck Joins Up: The Walt Disney Studio During World War II.* Ann Arbor, Mich.: UMI Research Press, 1982.

Shull, Michael, and David Wilt. *Doing Their Bit: Wartime American Animated Short Films, 1939–1945*. Jefferson, N.C.: McFarland, 1987.

Sitney, P. *Visionary Film: The American Avant-Garde*. New York: Oxford University Press, 1974.

Slide, Anthony. *The Big V: A History of the Vitagraph Company*. Metuchen, N.J.: Scarecrow Press, 1976.

Smith, Albert E. *Two Reels and a Crank*. Garden City, N.Y.: Doubleday, 1952.

Smith, Thomas. *Industrial Light and Magic: The Art of Special Effects*. New York: Ballantine, 1986.

Solomon, Charles, and Ron Stark. *The Complete Kodak Animation Book*. Rochester, N.Y.: Eastman Kodak, 1983.

Stalberg, Roberta. *China's Puppets*. San Francisco: China Books, 1984.

Stephenson, Ralph. *The Animated Film*. New York: Barnes, 1973.

Stravinsky, Igor, and Robert Craft. *Expositions and Developments*. New York: Doubleday, 1962.

Taylor, Deems. *Walt Disney's "Fantasia."* New York: Simon and Schuster, 1940.

Thomas, Bob. *The Art of Animation*. New York: Golden Press, 1958.

———. *Walt Disney: An American Original*. New York: Simon and Schuster, 1976.

Thomas, Frank, and Ollie Johnston. *Disney Animation: The Illusion of Life*. New York: Abbeville Press, 1981.

Tolkien, J. R. R. *The Hobbit: An Illustrated Edition*. New York: Abrams, 1977.

———. *The Lord of the Rings: The Fotonovel*. Los Angeles: Fotonovel Publications, 1979.

Trudeau, Garry. *John & Faith Hubley's "A Doonesbury Special": A Director's Notebook*. Kansas City: Sheed, Andrews & McMeel, 1977.

Waters, Edward. *Victor Herbert: A Life in Music*. New York: Macmillan, 1955.

Weinstock, Neal. *Computer Animation*. Reading, Mass.: Addison-Wesley, 1986.

Wertham, Frederic. *Seduction of the Innocent*. New York: Rinehart, 1954.

Whanslaw, H. W. *Shadow Play*. Redhill, Surrey, Eng.: Wells Gardner, Darton, 1950.

White, T. H. *The Sword in the Stone*. New York: Putnam's, 1939.

Whitney, John. *Digital Harmony: On the Complementarity of Music and Visual Art*. Peterborough, N.H.: McGraw-Hill, 1980.

Wilk, Max. *Yellow Submarine*. New York: New American Library, 1968.

Woolery, George. *Children's Television: The First Thirty-Five Years, 1946–1981*. Animated Cartoon Series, Part 1. Metuchen, N.J.: Scarecrow Press, 1983.

Youngblood, Gene. *Expanded Cinema*. New York: Dutton, 1970.

Ziemer, Gregor. *Education for Death: The Making of a Nazi*. New York: Oxford University Press, 1941.

ARTICLES

Adamson, Joe. "Lumage Animation for Twice Upon a Time." *American Cinematographer*, May 1983.

———. "Well, for Heaven's Sake! Grown Men!" *Film Comment*, January/February 1975.

Allan, Robin. "Alice in Disneyland." *Sight and Sound*, Spring 1985.

Alpert, Hollis. "Seven-Minute Epics." *Woman's Day*, September 1953.

———. "The Manic World of Ralph Bakshi." *S/R World*, March 9, 1974.

Ansen, David. "Hobbits and Rabbits." *Newsweek*, November 20, 1978.

Arnold, Gary. "Life After Disney: Animator Don Bluth and The Road to 'NIMH.'" *Washington Post*, July 18, 1982.

Babbitt, Art. "Character Analysis of the Goof—June 1934," *Sight and Sound*, Spring 1974.

———. "Letters." *Millimeter*, April 1976.

Abstract, Cubist shapes undergo continual transformations in Sara Petty's "Preludes in Magical Times."

Barrier, Mike. "Ralph Bakshi: The Animated Cartoon Grows Up." *Print*, March/April.

———. "The Careers of Hugh Harman and Rudolf Ising." *Millimeter*, February 1976.

———. "John and Faith Hubley: Traditional Animation Transformed." *Millimeter*, February 1977.

Bates, James. "Cartoon Firm Deals Way to Top." *Los Angeles Times*, March 8, 1988, Valley edition, Business section.

———. "Cartoon Writers Hope to Ink Union Contract." *Los Angeles Times*, October 11, 1988, Valley edition, Business section.

Beck, Jerry, "Behind *Roger Rabbit*." *Animation*, Summer 1988.

———. "Tattertown: Ralph Bakshi's New Direction." *Animation*, Fall 1988.

Beck, Jerry, and Harvey Deneroff. "Some Lace Has to Be Woven by Hand: A Conversation with Don Bluth." *Animation*, Fall 1988.

Beke, Gyorgy. "Ralph Bakshi: MOMA Will Never Be the Same." *Millimeter*, April 1975.

Benson, Sheila. "The Animated Wonders of 'Roger Rabbit': Feverishly Inventive Mix of Actors, Cartoon Characters." *Los Angeles Times*, June 27, 1988, Calendar section.

———. "Dogs, Dinosaurs from Disney, Bluth: 'The Land Before Time.'" *Los Angeles Times*, November 18, 1988, Calendar section.

———. "'Fire and Ice' Is a Marriage of Genres." *Los Angeles Times*, August 26, 1983, Calendar section.

———. "'Twice Upon a Time' Trips Over Script." *Los Angeles Times*, August 5, 1983, Calendar section.

———. "A Wide Canvas in 'American Pop.'" *Los Angeles Times*, February 13, 1981, Calendar section.

Bernheimer, Martin. "'Fantasia' Rescored: Soundlift for Stokowski." *Los Angeles Times*, March 14, 1982, Calendar section.

Bertino, Tom. "Hugh Harman and Rudolf Ising at Warner Brothers." In *The American Animated Cartoon*, Gerald Perry and Danny Perry, eds. New York: Dutton, 1980.

Boone, Andrew R. "When Mickey Mouse Speaks." *Scientific American*, March 1933.

Boston Sunday Herald. "Magoo, Now in '1001 Nights' Not Intended to Be Star." December 13, 1959.

Bower, Anthony. "Snow White and the 1,200 Dwarfs." *The Nation*, May 10, 1941.

Brady, Thomas. "Donald Doesn't Duck the Issue." *New York Times*, June 21, 1942.

Bragdon, Claude. "Mickey Mouse and What He Means." *Scribners*, July 1934.

Broadcasting/Telecasting. " 'Unarty' Modern Art: That's UPA's Formula for TV Commercial Success." October 17, 1955.

Brooks, Geraldine. "*Drawing Away:* In Children's Cartoons, Taft Broadcasting Co. Routs the Competition." *The Wall Street Journal*, September 28, 1983.

Brown, Alan M. "Show Business Is in Her Blood." *Los Angeles Times*, January 10, 1982, Calendar section.

Brown, John Mason. "Mr. Disney's Caballeros." *Saturday Review*, February 24, 1945.

———. "Recessional." *Saturday Review*, June 3, 1950.

Burton, Thomas. "Walt Disney's 'Pinocchio.' " *Saturday Review*, February 17, 1940.

Canby, Vincent. "The Screen: 'An American Tail.' " *New York Times*, November 21, 1986.

———. "Toons and Bushers Fly High." *New York Times*, July 3, 1988.

Canemaker, John. "The Birth of Animation: Reminiscing with John A. Fitzsimmons, Assistant to Winsor McCay." *Millimeter*, April 1975.

———. "The Business of $uccessful Animated Features." *Millimeter*, February 1978.

———. "The *Fantasia* That Never Was." *Print*, January/February 1988.

———. "Grim Natwick." *Film Comment*, January/February 1975.

———. "Hanna-Barbera: Will 'Heidi's Song' Be Its 'Snow White'?" *Millimeter*, February 1981.

———. "Otto Messmer and Felix the Cat." *Millimeter*, September 1976.

———. "Pioneers of American Animation: J. Stuart Blackton, Winsor McCay, J. R. Bray, Otto Messmer, Disney." *Variety*, January 7, 1976.

———. "Puppet Master." *Print*, September/October 1987.

———. "Redefining Animation." *Print*, March/April 1979.

———. "Three Films by Dennis Pies." *Film News*, Summer 1978.

———. "Vlad Tytla: Animation's Michelangelo." *Cinefantastique*, Fall 1976.

———. "Winsor McCay." *Film Comment*, January/February 1975.

Care, Ross. "Cinesymphony: Music and Animation at the Disney Studio, 1928–1942." *Sight and Sound*, Winter 1976–77.

Carroll, Kathleen. "This Mouse Has a Few Problems." New York *Daily News*, November 21, 1986.

Champlin, Charles. "Animation Moves 'Heavy Traffic.' " *Los Angeles Times*, August 9, 1973, Calendar section.

———. "Animator Bakshi Is Back at the Drawing Board." *Los Angeles Times*, July 17, 1986, Calendar section.

———. "His Yogi Bear Voice Leaves Lasting Impression." *Los Angeles Times*, May 24, 1988, Calendar section.

———. "Magna Cartoon, Signed Bakshi." *Los Angeles Times*, February 9, 1975, Calendar section.

———. "Putting New Life in the Animator's Art." *Los Angeles Times*, September 19, 1980, Calendar section.

———. "Wringing with Tolkien's Tale." *Los Angeles Times*, November 15, 1978, Calendar section.

Champlin, Chuck, Jr. "Animator Army Advances on the Tolkien Trilogy." *Los Angeles Times*, August 24, 1978, Calendar section.

Christon, Lawrence. "Tales of Jay Ward and the Bullwinkle Gang." *Los Angeles Times*, November 13, 1988, Calendar section.

Churchill, Douglas. "Walt Disney's 'Philosophy.' " *New York Times Magazine*, March 6, 1938.

Chute, David. " 'Toon Noir." *Film Comment*, August 1988.

Cieply, Michael and Charles Solomon. "Disney 'Rabbit' Hops into the Spotlight." *Los Angeles Times*, April 13, 1988, Calendar section.

Corliss, Richard. "The New Generation Comes of Age: 'The Fox and the Hound.' " *Time*, July 20, 1981.

Cocks, Jay. "Communication Received: 'Charlotte's Web.' " *Time*, March 5, 1973.

———. "Pussyfooting: The Nine Lives of Fritz the Cat." *Time*, August 12, 1974.

———. "Robin Hood." *Time*, December 3, 1973.

———. "The World Jones Made." *Time*, December 17, 1973.

Colker, David. "Disney and the Coat of Many Puppies; Or, How Nine Old Men Created Lasting Magic with Pen and Ink." *Los Angeles Herald Examiner*, December 20, 1985.

Cooper, Arthur. "Color It Black." *Newsweek*, August 18, 1975.

———. "Dear Spider: Charlotte's Web." *Newsweek*, March 12, 1973.

Crook, David. "Animator Leads with a 'Space Ace.' " *Los Angeles Times*, February 21, 1984, Calendar section.

Crowther, Bosley. "Disney's 'Peter Pan' Bows: Full-Length Color Cartoon, an Adaptation of Barrie Play, Is Feature at the Roxy." *New York Times*, February 12, 1953.

———. " 'Sleeping Beauty.' " *New York Times*, February 18, 1959.

———. " 'Saludos Amigos,' a Musical Fantasy Based on the South American Tour Made by Walt Disney, Arrives at the Globe." *New York Times*, February 13, 1943.

———. " 'Three Caballeros,' a Disney Picture, with Actors and Animated Characters, in Debut at Globe Theatre." *New York Times*, February 5, 1945.

Daily Variety. "The Boing-Boing Show." December 17, 1956.

Dalton, Susan. "Bugs and Daffy Go to War." In *The American Animated Cartoon*, Gerald Peary and Danny Peary, eds. New York: Dutton, 1980.

Dance Magazine. "Ballet-Oop!: A Happy Little UPA Satire." January 1955.

Daugherty, Frank. "Mickey Mouse Comes of Age." *The Christian Science Monitor Weekly Magazine*, February 2, 1938.

Delehanty, Thornton. "The Disney Studio at War." *Theatre Arts*, January 1943.

De Mille, William. "Mickey versus Popeye." In *The American Animated Cartoon*. Gerald Peary and Danny Peary, eds. New York: Dutton, 1980.

Disney, Roy. "Unforgettable Walt Disney." *Reader's Digest*, February 1969.

Disney, Walt. "Growing Pains." *Journal of the Society of Motion Picture Engineers*, January 1941.

———. "How I Cartooned 'Alice': Its Logical Nonsense Needed a Logical Sequence." *Films in Review*, May 1951.

———. "Humour: My Sixth Sense." *Films and Filming*, February 1961.

———. "Mickey as Professor." *Public Opinion Quarterly*, Summer 1945.

———. "The Testimony of Walter E. Disney Before the House Committee on Un-American Activities." In *The American Animated Cartoon*, Gerald Peary and Danny Peary, eds. New York: Dutton, 1980.

Dreyfus, John. "Transformers and Cabbage Patch Dolls Tops Santa's List." *Los Angeles Times*, November 22, 1985, View section.

Ebert, Roger. "A Tragic 'Tail'—Of Mice and Mensch." *New York Post*, November 21, 1986.

Ebony. "John Henry: New Movie Tells of Legendary Hero with Puppets and Poetry." January 1947.

Eisenberg, Adam. "Romancing the Rabbit." *Cinefex*, Summer 1988.

Eller, Claudia. "Uni 'Tail' Breaks B.O. Record for Highest-Grossing Ani Film." *The Hollywood Reporter*, March 12, 1987.

Elmer-DeWitt, Philip. "The Love of Two Desk Lamps: Steven Jobs' Newest Venture Produces Extraordinary Graphics." *Time*, September 1, 1986.

Emmons, Steve. "*Experts Defend Them:* Sick Jokes—Coping with Horror." *Los Angeles Times*, May 30, 1986.

Ferguson, Otto. "Walt Disney's Grimm Reality." *The New Republic*, January 26, 1938.

———. "It's a Disney." *The New Republic*, March 4, 1940.

Financial Times (London). "Broken Promises." December 14, 1959.

Fitzsimmons, John. "Winsor McCay." *Cartoonist Profiles*, March/April 1984.

Fleming, Charles. "Before Roger Rabbit There Was Obsession." *Los Angeles Herald Examiner*, June 24, 1988.

Ford, Greg. "Warner Brothers." *Film Comment*, January/February 1975.

Ford, Greg, and Richard Thompson. "Chuck Jones." *Film Comment*, January/February 1975.

Ford, John. "An Interview with John and Faith Hubley." In *The American Animated Cartoon*, Gerald Peary and Danny Peary, eds. New York: Dutton, 1980.

Gansberg, Alan. "Hanna-Barbera: 30 Years of Drawing Power." *The Hollywood Reporter*, December 11, 1988.

Garrity, William. "The Production of Animated Cartoons." *Journal of the Society of Motion Picture Engineers*, April 1933.

Garrity, William, and J. L. Ledeen. "The New Walt Disney Studio." *Journal of the Society of Motion Picture Engineers*, January 1941.

Garrity, William, and W. C. McFadden. "The Multiplane Camera for Animation Photography." *Journal of the Society of Motion Picture Engineers*, August 1938.

Gelman, Morrie. "Blue Skies Clouding Over in Syndicated Kidvid Biz." *Daily Variety*, March 18, 1987.

———. "Networks Keep Door Open for Saturday Ayem Sked." *Daily Variety*, October 23, 1986.

Gilliatt, Penelope. "An Attack of the Drabs." *The New Yorker*, August 20, 1973.

———. "Eight Lives to Go." *The New Yorker*, May 6, 1972.

———. "High Bravado from the Lower Depths." *The New Yorker*, August 25, 1975.

Greco, Mike. "Bakshi's American Dream." *Film Comment*, January/February 1978.

Guernsey, Otis, Jr. "Peter Pan." *New York Herald Tribune*, February 12, 1953.

———. "The Movie Cartoon Is Coming of Age." *New York Herald Tribune*, November 29, 1953.

Haithman, Diane. "How Image Makers Shape Kids' TV." *Los Angeles Times*, September 3, 1987, Calendar section.

Harmetz, Aljean. "Disney Incubating New Artists." *New York Times*, July 27, 1978.

———. "How a 'Rabbit' Was Framed." *New York Times*, June 19, 1988.

Hartung, Philip. "Once in a Lifetime" (review of "Fantasia"). *The Commonweal*, November 29, 1940.

Hatch, Robert. "Coonskin." *The Nation*, September 20, 1975.

———. "Yellow Submarine." *The Nation*, December 9, 1968.

Haver, Ronald. "Rescoring 'Fantasia.'" *Connoisseur*, July 1982.

Hearn, Michael. "The Animated Art of Winsor McCay." *American Artist*, May 1975.

Hibbin, Nina. "Not Good Enough." *Daily Worker* (London), December 12, 1959.

Hift, Fred. " 'McBoing' to 'Rooty Toot Toot.' " *New York Times*, March 16, 1952.

Hirschfeld, Al. "An Artist Contests Mr. Disney." *New York Times Magazine*, January 30, 1938.

Hoellering, Franz. Review of "Fantasia." *The Nation*, November 23, 1940.

Hoffer, Tom. "From Comic Strips to Animation: Some Perspective on Winsor McCay." *Journal of the University Film Association*, Spring 1976.

Horovitz, Bruce. " 'Claymation' Reshapes Prime Time, Video After Dancing Raisins." *Los Angeles Times*, November 10, 1987, Business section.

Horowitz, Joy. "An Auction of Mickey Mouse Merchandise." *Los Angeles Times*, July 3, 1981, View section.

Hubley, John. "Beyond Pigs and Bunnies: The New Animator's Art." *The American Scholar*, Spring 1975.

Hughes, Elinor. " '1001 Arabian Nights.' " *Boston Globe*, December 18, 1959.

Hughes, Robert. "An X Cartoon: Fritz the Cat." *Time*, May 22, 1972.

Hunt, Dennis. " 'American Pop's' Pop Defends His Child." *Los Angeles Times*, March 4, 1981, Calendar section.

Irwin, Michael. "Walter Lantz." *Films in Review*, April 1971.

Jones, Charles Martin. "Diary of a Mad Cel Washer." *Take One*, August 4, 1978.

———. "Farewell to a Genius of Funny." *Los Angeles Times*, August 31, 1980, Calendar section.

———. "Friz Freleng, and How I Grew." *Millimeter*, November 1976.

———. "The Roadrunner and Other Characters." *Cinema Journal*, Spring 1969.

Jacques-Louis. "Mister Magoo: Son 1er Grand Role." *Paris-Jour*, May 26, 1960.

Kael, Pauline. "A Boy Named Charlie Brown." *The New Yorker*, January 17, 1970.

———. "Metamorphosis of the Beatles." *The New Yorker*, November 30, 1968.

Karp, Walter. "Where the Do-Gooders Went Wrong." *Channels*, March 1984.

Kauffmann, Stanley. "Beatles and Other Creatures." *The New Republic*, November 9, 1968.

———. "Coonskin." *The New Republic*, September 13, 1975.

———. "Fritz the Cat." *The New Republic*, May 20, 1972.

Kaufman, J. B. *Three Little Pigs—Big Little Picture.* *American Cinematographer*, November 1988.

Kausler, Mark. "Tom and Jerry." *Film Comment*, January/February 1975.

Kerbel, Michael. "Frank's Films." *Film Comment*, September/October 1975.

Kernan, Michael. "The Bird's-Eye View: The Lantzes, the Laugh and Woody Woodpecker." *Washington Post*, December 16, 1981.

Kiesling, Barrett. "They Paint a Million Cats." *Films and Filming*, November 1956.

Kilday, Gregg. "The Animated Ghettoland of Ralph Bakshi." *Los Angeles Times*, August 23, 1973, Calendar section.

———. "Bakshi Describes 'Rings' Breakthrough." *Los Angeles Times*, November 6, 1978, Calendar section.

"The Simpsons": cartoonist Matt Groening's skewed vision of American family life was created for "The Tracy Ullman Show" but later expanded to a half-hour series.

Klein, Andy. "Who Sketched Roger Rabbit." *Los Angeles Herald Examiner*, June 24, 1988.

Klein, I. "On Mighty Mouse." In *The American Animated Cartoon*, Gerald Peary and Danny Peary, eds. New York: Dutton, 1980.

———. "The Van Buren Studio." *Film Comment*, January/February 1975.

Knight, Arthur. "A Boy Named Charlie Brown." *Saturday Review*, January 17, 1970.

———. "Odds and Ends and Middles." *Saturday Review*, May 20, 1972.

———. "Two Subs Have I." *Saturday Review*, November 16, 1968.

———. "Up from Disney." *Theatre Arts*, August 1951.

———. "UPA, Magoo and McBoing-Boing." *Art Digest*, February 1, 1952.

Kracauer, Siegfried. "Dumbo." *The Nation*, November 8, 1941.

Langer, Mark. "Max and Dave Fleischer." *Film Comment*, January/February 1975.

Leenhouts, Grant. "Story Development and Control in Training Films." *Journal of the Society of Motion Picture Engineers*, May 1945.

Le Grice, Malcolm. "Computer Film as Film Art." In *Computer Animation*, John Halas, ed. New York: Hastings House, 1974.

Louchheim, Aline. "Cartoons as Art: UPA Films Absorb an Important Function." *New York Times*, August 23, 1953.

McCay, Winsor. "How I Originated Motion Picture Cartoons." *Cartoons and Movie Magazine*, April 1927.

McGee, Rex. "All That Jazz . . . Swing . . . Pop . . . and Rock." *American Film*, July/August 1980.

Maddocks, Melvin. "Magoo in Old Baghdad: '1001 Arabian Nights' Animated at the Orpheum." *The Christian Science Monitor*, December 18, 1959.

Mahler, Richard. "Syndicators Predict Effect on Saturday, Late-Nite." *Electronic Media*, October 20, 1986.

Mann, Arthur. "Mickey Mouse's Financial Career." *Harper's*, May 1934.

Mannes, Marya. "Channels: The Animated Sell." *The Reporter*, October 7, 1954.

Maslin, Janet. "Future Schlock." *Newsweek*, May 9, 1977.

———. "Dinosaurs in Search of a Leafy Eden." *New York Times*, November 12, 1988.

Masters, Kim. "Can Spielberg Pull 'Roger Rabbit' Out of a Hat?" New York *Daily News*, November 15, 1987.

Mathews, Jack. "Maker of Frisky 'Fritz the Cat' Retires from Adult Animation." *USA Today*, January 25, 1983.

Mauceri, Jack. " 'No Conflict' Seen for UPA in CBS–Terry Deal." *Film Daily*, January 11, 1956.

Mehren, Elizabeth. "Disney Art Brings Out the Buyers." *Los Angeles Times*, December 10, 1984, Calendar section.

Moffitt, Jack. "Disney's 'Lady and Tramp' Charming Cartoon Fantasy." *The Hollywood Reporter*, April 19, 1955.

Moon, Barbara. "The Silly, Splendid World of Stephen Bosustow." *Maclean's*, December 7, 1957.

Motion Picture Herald. "Science Film Now a Staple, Pal Believes." November 10, 1951.

Moritz, William. "Abstract Film and Color Music." In *The Spiritual in Art: Abstract Painting, 1890–1985*, Maurice Tuchman et al., eds. New York: Abbeville Press, 1986.

———. "The Films of Oskar Fischinger." *Film Culture*, Nos. 58–60, 1974.

———. "Fischinger at Disney (Or, Oskar in the Mousetrap)." *Millimeter*, February 1977.

———. "You Can't Get Then from Now." *Journal*, Summer 1981.

Mosher, John. "The Music Goes Round and Round." *The New Yorker*, November 23, 1940.

Nardone, Mark. "Robert McKimson Interviewed." In *The American Ani-*

Dennis Pies imbued abstract shapes with an organic style of motion in his evocative film "Skyheart."

mated Cartoon, Gerald Peary and Danny Peary, eds. New York: Dutton, 1980.

Nason, Richard. "The 'Voice' of 'Magoo.' " *New York Times*, March 30, 1958.

Nater, Carl. "Walt Disney Studio—a War Plant." *Journal of the Society of Motion Picture Engineers*, March 1944.

New York Herald Tribune. " 'Mr. Bug Goes to Town'—Loew's State." February 20, 1942.

———. "2 Million See Macy's Gay Parade." November 25, 1955.

New York Times. "The Ascendency of Mr. Donald Duck." June 23, 1940.

———. "Disney Family." January 11, 1942.

———. "The Globe Presents 'Victory Through Air Power,' a Disney Illustration of Major De Seversky's Book." July 19, 1943.

———. "The Inkwell Man." February 22, 1920.

———. " 'Mr. Bug Goes to Town' Opens at Loew's State." February 20, 1942.

Newsweek. "Bright-Toned Fantasy: '1001 Arabian Nights.' " December 21, 1959.

———. "Mickey Mouse in Symphony: Disney and Stokowski Combine Talents in Film 'Fantasia.' " November 25, 1940.

———. "Gulliver in Technicolor: 214-Year-Old Classic Converted into Diverting Film Cartoon." January 1, 1940.

Nichols, Luther. "A Star Is Drawn—Meet Gerald McBoing-Boing." *San Francisco Chronicle*, January 21, 1951.

Orna, Bernard. "Magoo Has a Sennett Touch." *Films and Filming*, February 1956.

Orth, Maureen. "Bombshell in Disneyland." *Newsweek*, August 27, 1973.

Paegel, Tom. "George Pal, Sci-Fi Movie Pioneer, Dies." *Los Angeles Times*, May 3, 1980.

Peary, Danny. "Reminiscing with Walter Lantz." In *The American Animated Cartoon*, Gerald Peary and Danny Peary, eds. New York: Dutton, 1980.

Phillips, McCandlish. "Without Lisping Pigs: UPA Cartoons Penetrate TV's

Cultural Barrier with Esthetic Appeal." *New York Times*, March 17, 1957.

Polt, Harriet. "The Death of Mickey Mouse." *Film Comment*, Summer 1964.

Powell, Dilys. "The Indomitable Mr. Magoo." *Sunday Times* (London), December 13, 1959.

Radio-TV Life. "The Boing-Boing Show." January 19, 1957.

———. "The Life Story of Gerald McBoing-Boing." February 9, 1957.

Radio-TV Report. "UPA Animated TV Commercials Often 'Best Part of the Show.'" February 28, 1955.

Reese, Michael. "The Making of Roger Rabbit." *Newsweek*, June 27, 1988.

Reynolds, Mike. "Drawing on the Bible for the 'Greatest Adventure.'" *The Hollywood Reporter*, December 11, 1987.

Rider, David. "Just Good Friends." *Films and Filming*, July 1963.

Rieder, Howard. "Memories of Mr. Magoo." In *The American Animated Cartoon*, Gerald Peary and Danny Peary, eds. New York: Dutton, 1980.

Rifkin, Sherman. "The Pratfall Is Out." *Westward*, October 1952.

Robins, Sam. "Disney Again Tries Trailblazing." *New York Times Magazine*, November 3, 1940.

Rosenbaum, Jonathan. "Tex Avery." *Film Comment*, January/February 1975.

———. "Walt Disney." *Film Comment*, January/February 1975.

Ruark, Robert. "A Potent Tool." *New York World-Telegram*, May 21, 1946.

Scheib, Ronnie. "Tex Arcana: The Cartoons of Tex Avery." In *The American Animated Cartoon*, Gerald Peary and Danny Peary, eds. New York: Dutton, 1980.

Schickel, Richard. "Bunny Business: Watership Down." *Time*, November 13, 1978.

———. "The Great Era of Walt Disney." *Time*, July 20, 1981.

———. "Uncle Remus '75: Coonskin." *Time*, September 8, 1975.

Schreger, Charles. "An Animated Flip Through Pop History." *Los Angeles Times*, June 16, 1979, Calendar section.

———. "'Cat': 1st by Disney Defectors." *Los Angeles Times*, December 3, 1979, Calendar section.

Segal, Lewis. "'archy and mehitabel': Consider the Possibilities." *Entertainment World*, October 31, 1969.

Seldes, Gilbert. "No Art, Mr. Disney?" *Esquire*, September 1937.

———. "Delight in Seven Minutes." *Saturday Review*, May 31, 1952.

Sendak, Maurice. "'Pinocchio': At 38, He's Still a Hero." *Los Angeles Times*, December 17, 1978, Calendar section.

Shales, Tom. "Commentary." *Los Angeles Times*, December 21, 1986, TV Times section.

Slafer, Eugene. "A Conversation with Bill Hanna." In *The American Animated Cartoon*, Gerald Peary and Danny Peary, eds. New York: Dutton, 1980.

Smith, Cecil. "Look, No Humans in Boing Show Making TV Bow Today." *Los Angeles Times*, December 16, 1956.

Solomon, Charles. "Commercial Animation, Part III: Maintaining Cost-effective Production." *Millimeter*, November 1980.

———. "Commercials: Bob Kurtz—Off the Wall and on Target." *Animation*, December 1987.

———. "Disney Today." *Sightlines*, Winter 1985–86.

———. "Fun with Animation: In Great Britain, Commercials Are Different." *Emmy*, September/October 1985.

———. "John Lasseter: Drawing Emotions from a Computer." *The Hollywood Reporter*, February 25, 1988.

———. "Out of the Inkwell: Animators Draw on New Media." *The Hollywood Reporter*, Fifty-eighth Anniversary Edition, 1988.

———. "The Secrets of Tron." *Rolling Stone*, August 19, 1982.

———. "'Sleeping Beauty': A Disney Masterpiece Is Reawakened." *Rolling Stone*, October 4, 1979.

———. "Top Draw." *Film Comment*, August 1988.

———. "Top Spots: Commercials Are the Best Animation on TV today." *Emmy*, September/October 1983.

———. "Will the Real Walt Disney Please Stand Up?" *Film Comment*, July/August 1982.

———. "The Winning World of Commercial Animation." *The Hollywood Reporter*, January 22, 1987.

Spielman, Bob. "'Boing-Boing' Stanza Sophisticated Humor." *Billboard*, December 29, 1956.

Stewart, Jon. "Fritz the Cat." *Ramparts*, March 1972.

Strauss, Theodore. "Donald Duck's Disney." *New York Times*, February 7, 1943.

Sullivan, Catherine. "UPA Pictures, Inc.: The Modern Look in Animated Cartoons." *American Artists*, November 1955.

Taylor, Frank. "Pal of the Puppets." *Collier's*, January 16, 1943.

Television Age. "UPA: Creativity Basic." December 1, 1958.

———. "Promotion in Motion." March 21, 1960.

Thomas, Kevin. "Weak Characters Mar 'Good Lookin.'" *Los Angeles Times*, January 28, 1983, Calendar section.

Thompson, Dorothy. "Minority Report." *New York Herald Tribune*, November 25, 1940.

Thompson, Richard. "Duck Amuck." *Film Comment*, January/February, 1975.

Time. "Cartoons: Put a Panther in Your Tank." October 1, 1965.

———. "The Conquering Zero." January 5, 1970.

———. "Disney's Cinesymphony." November 18, 1940.

———. "Father Goose." December 27, 1954.

———. "Gulliver's Travels." January 1, 1940.

———. "Jasper and the Watermelons." March 9, 1942.

———. "Light Touch." December 31, 1956.

———. "New Magic in Animation." December 27, 1968.

———. "Popeye Boycott." September 20, 1937.

———. "Teacher Disney." August 17, 1942.

———. "The Unicorn in the Garden." October 26, 1953.

Stravinsky, Igor. "Stravinsky Replies to Walt Disney." *Saturday Review*, March 12, 1960.

TV-Radio Life. "The Life Story of Gerald McBoing-Boing." February 2, 1957.

U.S. News & World Report. "You Ain't Seen Nothin' Yet, Roger Rabbit." July 25, 1988.

Variety. "Market Realities Switch UPA to New Format and Characters." April 24, 1958.

Wallace, Irving. "Mickey Mouse, and How He Grew." *Collier's*, April 9, 1949.

Wanger, Walter. "Mickey Icarus." *Saturday Review*, September 4, 1943.

Warga, Wayne. "Schulz, Charlie Brown Finally Make It to the Movies." *Los Angeles Times*, March 29, 1970, Calendar section.

———. "The Sun Never Sets on Hanna-Barbera." *Los Angeles Times*, September 24, 1972, Calendar section.

Warren, Steve. "Pal on Pal." *Inside Cinema*, 1974.

Weinraub, Bernard. "How an Animator Broke the Rules (and Ground) in 'Roger Rabbit.'" *New York Times*, August 1, 1988.

Wharton, David. "Ralph Bakshi Works Still Getting People Animated." *Los Angeles Times*, July 27, 1988, Calendar section.

Wilson, Dick. "'Tom and Jerry' Evolves into Cartoon Empire." *Variety*, July 7, 1977.

Winge, John. "Cartoons and Modern Music." *Sight and Sound*, Autumn 1948.

Winsten, Archer. "Disney's 'Peter Pan' at Roxy." *New York Post*, February 12, 1953.

———. "New Cartooning Technique Blazes Path of Humor." *New York Post*, April 26, 1946.

Wright, Milton. "Inventors Who Have Achieved Commercial Success." *Scientific American*, April 1927.

Zimmerman, Paul. "Beatles in Pepperland." *Newsweek*, November 25, 1968.

SPECIAL PUBLICATIONS

Adamson, Joe. "Dave Fleischer: Oral History"; "Friz Freleng: Oral History"; "Dick Huemer: Oral History." AFI-UCLA Oral History Project, 1969.

Bailey, Chris. "Animating Characters by Computer." In "Conference Proceedings, National Computer Graphics Association '88," *Tutorials*, Vol. 2.

Balzer, Richard. *Optical Amusements: Magic Lanterns and Other Transforming Images: A Catalog of Popular Entertainments.* Watertown, Mass.: privately printed, 1987.

Barrier, Mike. *Building a Better Mouse: Fifty Years of Animation.* Washington, D.C.: Library of Congress, 1978.

———. "Silly Stuff: An Interview with Hugh Harman." *Graffiti*, Spring 1984.

Beaudet, Louise, and Raymond Borde. *Charles R. Bowers, ou Le Mariage du slapstick et de l'animation.* Montreal: Cinémathèque québécoise, 1980.

Canemaker, John. "A Day with J. R. Bray." Yearbok of ASIFA/Hollywood, 1975.

———. Interview with J. R. Bray, Bridgeport, Conn., March 25, 1974. Unpublished transcript.

———. Interview with David Hilberman, Santa Cruz, Calif., June 16, 1979. Unpublished transcript.

———. "Winsor McCay's Little Nemo and How a Mosquito Operates— Beginnings of 'Personality, Animation.' " In *The Art of the Animated Image: An Anthology,* Charles Solomon, ed. American Film Institute, 1987.

Crafton, Donald. "J. Stuart Blackton's Animated Films." In *The Art of the Animated Image: An Anthology,* Charles Solomon, ed. American Film Institute, 1987.

Culhane, Shamus. "Dave Fleischer: Pseudo-director." *Animafilm,* Summer 1985.

Deneroff, Harvey. "Dan Glass: A Cautionary Tale of the Golden Age of Animation." *Graffiti,* December 1984.

———. "Screen Cartoonists on Strike." *Graffiti,* October 1982.

Etcheverry, Paul. Interview with William Scott, Los Angeles, Calif., November 2, 1982. Unpublished transcript.

Friedwald, Will. "Hugh Harman (1903–1982)." *Graffiti,* Spring 1984.

Johnston, Ollie. "Fred Moore, 1910–1952." 12th Annual Annie Awards Program, 1983. ASIFA/Hollywood.

———. "Hamilton S. Luske." 13th Annual Annie Awards Program, 1984. ASIFA/Hollywood.

Korkis, Jim. "The Bob Clampett Interview." *Mindrot,* November 1, 1978.

Kroyer, Bill. "Character Animation By Computer." In "Conference Proceedings, National Computer Graphics Association '88," *Tutorials,* Vol. 2.

Martin, André. "Barre l'introuvable"/"In Search of Raoul Barre." In program of the 1976 Ottawa International Animated Film Festival.

Museum of Modern Art (New York). Press Release No. 57, for release Wednesday, June 22, 1955.

Scott, Allen. "Solidarity Forever? The Pursuit of Bread in the Age of Runaway Production." *Graffiti,* October 1984.

Scott, Bill. "FMPU Reunion Attracts a Bunch." *Graffiti,* October 1980.

Smith, David. "New Dimensions—Beginnings of the Disney Multiplane Camera." In *The Art of the Animated Image: An Anthology,* Charles Solomon, ed. American Film Institute, 1987.

Solomon, Charles. "Cal Howard." 9th Annual Annie Awards Program, 1980. ASIFA/Hollywood.

———. "Pure Animation." *Graffiti,* October 1984.

———. "A Salute To U.P.A." Notes for a program at the Academy of Motion Picture Arts and Sciences, January 23, 1984.

———. "Vladimir William ('Bill') Tytla (1904–1968)." 10th Annual Annie Awards Program, 1981. ASIFA/Hollywood.

Thomas, Frank. "Wilfred E. Jackson." 12th Annual Annie Awards Program, 1983. ASIFA/Hollywood.

Whitney Museum of American Art (New York). "Disney Animation and Animators." Bulletin accompanying exhibition, June 24–September 6, 1981.

WALT DISNEY PUBLICATIONS

Ave Maria: An Interpretation Inspired by Walt Disney's "Fantasia." Lyrics by Rachel Field. New York: Random House, 1940.

Dance of the Hours from Walt Disney's "Fantasia." New York: Harper & Brothers, 1940.

The Illustrated Disney Song Book. New York: Random House, 1979.

Magic Moments. Milan: Arnoldo Mondadori Editions, 1973.

Mickey Is Sixty! Special commemorative magazine published by Time Inc., 1988.

The Nutcracker Suite from Walt Disney's "Fantasia." Boston: Little, Brown, 1940.

Snow White and the Seven Dwarfs. New York: Grosset & Dunlap, 1938.

Snow White and the Seven Dwarfs. New York: Viking, 1979.

Stories from Walt Disney's "Fantasia." New York: Random House, 1940.

Treasures of Disney Animation Art. Preface by Robert Abrams; introduction by John Canemaker. New York: Abbeville Press, 1982.

Treasury of Children's Classics. New York: Abrams, 1978.

Treasury of Stories from Silly Symphonies. New York: Abrams, 1981.

Walt Disney Presents "Fantasia." Film program, 1940.

For the Oscar-winning documentary "You Don't Have to Die," John Canemaker animated the illustrations that Adam and Tim Gaes did for their brother Jason's book about undergoing cancer treatments.

ADDITIONAL BIBLIOGRAPHY

Ansen, David, with Lynda Wright, Jeanne Gordon, and Abigail Kuflik. "Just the Way Walt Made 'Em: Disney's 'Beauty and the Beast' Is an Instant Classic." *Newsweek*, November 18, 1991.

Bates, James. "Filmation Shuts Plant, Beats Closing Law Deadline by 1 Day." *Los Angeles Times*, February 8, 1989.

_____. "'Tooned Out: Sale of Woodland Hills' Filmation to French Group Leaves Former Workers in Suspended Animation." *Los Angeles Times*, February 14, 1989, Valley edition.

Benesch, Connie. "Big-Screen Boom." *Hollywood Reporter*, January 25, 1994.

Bernstein, Sharon. "NBC's Saturday Morning Makeover." *Los Angeles Times*, December 7, 1991.

Braxton, Greg. "Protest Sends 'Super Dave' Back to the Drawing Board." *Los Angeles Times*, November 10, 1992.

Brennan, Steve. "Reeling Bluth Animation Lays Off 480 in Dublin, LA." *Hollywood Reporter*, August 24, 1992.

Cawley, John. *The Animated Films of Don Bluth*. New York: Image Publishing, 1991.

Cerone, Daniel. "'Ren & Stimpy' and Its Creator: A Parting of Ways." *Los Angeles Times*, September 28, 1992.

_____. "Toontown Terrors." *Los Angeles Times*, August 9, 1992.

Corliss, Richard. "Aladdin's Magic: The Funny, Fabulous Feature from Disney Heralds a New Golden Age of Animation." *Time*, November 9, 1992.

_____. "Festive Film Fare for Thanksgiving." *Time*, November 20, 1989.

Fox, David J. "Disney Will Alter Song in 'Aladdin.'" *Los Angeles Times*, July 10, 1993.

Frook, John Evan. "Kricfalusi: Final 'Ren' is Gift to Nickelodeon." *Daily Variety*, January 13, 1993.

Galbraith, Jane. "It's Burton's 'Nightmare,' but He Called Shots." *Los Angeles Times*, November 18, 1993.

Gritten, David. "Ralph Makes a Man Out of Mighty Mouse." *Los Angeles Herald Examiner*, April 29, 1988.

Grove, Martin A. "Hollywood Report: Handicapping the Race for Picture Oscar." *Hollywood Reporter*, February 27, 1992.

Hall, Jane. "'Beavis' Move Not Enough, Its Critics Say." *Los Angeles Times*, October 20, 1993.

Holden, Stephen. "Elvis Really Is Still Alive, Only He's a Rooster Now." *New York Times*, April 3, 1992.

Johnston, Ollie, and Frank Thomas. *The Disney Villain*. New York: Hyperion, 1993.

Kasem, Casey, and Jay Goldsworthy. "No Magic in 'Aladdin's' Offensive Lyrics." *Los Angeles Times*, May 17, 1993.

Kaufman, Debra. "Be Afraid, Be Very Afraid." *Animation*, Winter 1994.

Kleinfield, N. R. "Cashing in on a Hot New Brand Name." *New York Times*, April 29, 1990.

Kronke, David. "Just Boys or Civilization Destroyers?" *Los Angeles Times*, September 12, 1993.

Landers, Ann. "Too Much Crime? Blame the TV Set." *Los Angeles Times*, December 22, 1993.

Leland, John. "Battle for Your Brain." *Newsweek*, October 11, 1993.

McDougal, Dennis, and Daniel Cerone. "Ullman Has a Cow Over 'Simpsons.'" *Los Angeles Times*, April 19, 1991.

McGilligan, Pat, and Mark Rowland. "Year of the Low-Costs." *Los Angeles Times*, January 10, 1993.

Margulies, Lee. "Child's Death Prompts MTV to Retool 'Beavis.'" *Los Angeles Times*, October 14, 1993.

Maslin, Janet. "Andersen's 'Mermaid,' by Way of Disney." *New York Times*, November 15, 1989.

_____. "Animated Tale Has Serious Message." *New York Times*, April 10, 1992.

_____. "Critic's Notebook: The Inner Workings of the Animator's Magic." *New York Times*, September 30, 1991.

_____. "Disney's 'Beauty and the Beast' Updated in Form and Content." *New York Times*, November 13, 1991.

_____. "Disney Finds Magic in Aladdin's Lamp." *New York Times*, November 11, 1992.

_____. "Target: Boomers and Their Babies." *New York Times*, November 24, 1991.

Masters, Kim. "The Mermaid and the Mandrill." *Premiere*, November, 1991.

Parisi, Paula. "Drawing Power." *Hollywood Reporter*, January 26, 1993.

_____. "Looking Forward . . . and Back." *Hollywood Reporter*, January 26, 1993.

Rainer, Peter. "Bluth's 'All Dogs Go to Heaven' Is Bland Family Fare." *Los Angeles Times*, November 18, 1989.

_____. "'Cool World' Flirts With the Erotic." *Los Angeles Times*, July 11, 1992.

Rhodes, Joe. "Disney Dreams of Genie." *Los Angeles Times*, November 8, 1992.

Rohter, Larry. "Hollywood, Seeking Profits, Revives the Animated Film." *New York Times*, May 16, 1991.

Rosenberg, Howard. "Bart and Family Try to Make the Grade . . ." *Los Angeles Times*, October 11, 1990.

_____. "It's No 'Simpsons,' but Toon in." *Los Angeles Times*, January 26, 1994.

_____. "Smart, Vulgar, Subversive, Quirky, Hilarious—and a Hit." *Los Angeles Times*, February 23, 1990.

Sanoff, Alvin P., and John Lee. "Horizons: You Ain't Seen Nothin' Yet, Roger Rabbit." *U.S. News & World Report*, July 25, 1988.

Schickel, Richard. "Furry Fun: The Rescuers Down Under." *Time*, November 19, 1990.

Schmidt, Katherine A. "Mighty Mouse Flying High? Preacher Accuses Cartoon Character of Sniffing Cocaine." *Los Angeles Herald Examiner*, June 10, 1988.

Shaheen, Jack G. "Arab Caricatures Deface Disney's 'Aladdin.'" *Los Angeles Times*, December 21, 1992.

Sharkey, Betsy. "When You Wish Upon a Star." *New York Times*, November 8, 1992.

Shay, Don, and Jody Duncan. *The Making of Jurassic Park: An Adventure 65 Million Years in the Making*. New York: Ballantine Books, 1993.

Sheehan, Henry. "Computer Comes to the Rescuers: Disney's Modest Mix of Animation and Digital Images Hints at the Medium's Future." *Los Angeles Reader*, November 16, 1990.

Simpson, Blaise. "The Concept: Jack-o'-Santa." *Los Angeles Times*, October 10, 1993.

Solomon, Charles. "Bart vs. Bill: 'The Simpsons' Faces a Tough Draw Against Cosby." *Los Angeles Times*, August 22, 1990.

_____. "Building a Magical 'Beast.'" *Los Angeles Times*, November 10, 1991.

_____. "Disney's 'Beauty' Revives Classic Flair in Story, Style." *Los Angeles Times*, January 5, 1992.

———. "How They Did That." *Los Angeles Times*, November 16, 1991.

———. "It's Tough to Stay Afloat in the Film-Cartoon Business." *Los Angeles Times*, January 4, 1994.

———. "The Saga of a Calypso Crab." *Disney Channel Magazine*, May/June, 1991.

———. "Q/A With Matt Groening: 'Simpsons' Back 'as Crude and Crass as Ever.' " *Los Angeles Times*, September 30, 1993.

———. "Which Way Animation?" *Hollywood Reporter*, January 25, 1994.

———, and Robert W. Welkos. "Bond Firm Takes Over 'Thief.' " *Los Angeles Times*, May 20, 1992.

Sragow, Michael. "Free Spirits." *New Yorker*, November 30, 1992.

Turan, Kenneth. "The 1,001 Delights of 'Aladdin.' " *Los Angeles Times*, November 11, 1992.

———. "A 'Beast' With Heart: Animated Disney Feature Is Most Satisfying in Years." *Los Angeles Times*, November 15, 1991.

———. "Burton Dreams Up a Delightful 'Nightmare.' " *Los Angeles Times*, October 15, 1993.

Turner, Richard. "Tape Transfer: Disney Leads Shift From Rentals to Sales in Videocassettes." *Wall Street Journal*, December 24, 1992.

Waters, Harry F. "Family Feuds." *Newsweek*, April 23, 1990.

Wilmington, Michael. " 'Little Mermaid' Makes Big Splash." *Los Angeles Times*, November 15, 1989.

Young, Charles M. "The Voice of a New Generation: MTV's Beavis and Butt-Head on What's Cool and What Sucks." *Rolling Stone*, August 19, 1993.

INDEX

Note: Page numbers in *italics* refer to illustrations.

All illustrations not otherwise credited are from the collection of the author.

Page 2: Collection of Mike and Jeanne Glad. 4: UCLA Research Library, Special Collections. 5: (top) Collection of Richard Balzer. (lower right) Photo by Greg Clarke; shadow puppets courtesy of the Los Angeles County Museum of Science and Industry, "Cinemagic" exhibit. 6: State Historical Society of Wisconsin. Courtesy of the Academy of Motion Picture Arts and Sciences; © Copyright Academy of Motion Picture Arts and Sciences. 7: Courtesy of the Academy of Motion Picture Arts and Sciences. © Copyright Academy of Motion Picture Arts and Sciences. 8: Collection of Richard Balzer. 9: (left) Collection of Richard Balzer. (right) Courtesy of La Cinémathèque Québécoise. 10: (left) Collection of Richard Balzer. (right) Courtesy of the Academy of Motion Picture Arts and Sciences. © Copyright Academy of Motion Picture Arts and Sciences. 11: Courtesy of Stanford University Libraries, Department of Special Collections and University Archives. 12: (left) Collection of Richard Balzer. (right) Collection of Mike and Jeanne Glad. 13: (left) Courtesy of Anthony Slide. (right) Courtesy of Piggyback Productions. 14: Collection of John Canemaker. 15: Collection of John Canemaker. 17: Collection of Mike and Jeanne Glad. 18: Collection of John Canemaker. 19: Collection of D. J. Halver. 20: Collection of Mike and Jeanne Glad. © Felix, King Features and Felix the Cat Productions. 22: Courtesy of La Cinémathèque Québécoise. 23: Courtesy of Piggyback Productions. 24: (top) Courtesy of Piggyback Productions. (bottom) From the Walter Lantz Collection. Reprinted with permission. 25: Courtesy of the American Museum of the Moving Image. 26: (top) From the Walter Lantz Collection. Reprinted with permission. (bottom) Courtesy of Piggyback Productions. 27: Collection of Mike and Jeanne Glad. © 1927 Universal Pictures Corporation. 28: Courtesy of Piggyback Productions. 29: Collection of Nick and Tee Bosustow. 30: Courtesy of the Louis B. Mayer Library of the American Film Institute. 31: Courtesy of Piggyback Productions. 33: From the Walter Lantz Collection. Reprinted with permission. 35: Collection of John Canemaker. © 1989 King Features Syndicate, Inc. 36: Courtesy of La Cinémathèque Québécoise. 37: The Walt Disney Company. © The Walt Disney Company. 38: (lower left) The Walt Disney Company. © The Walt Disney Company. 39: The Bob Clampett Collection. 40: (left) The Walt Disney Company. © The Walt Disney Company. (right) Courtesy of Piggyback Productions. 41: The Walt Disney Company. © The Walt Disney Company. 42: Courtesy of Christie's East, Animation Art Department. © The Walt Disney Company. 44, 45, 48 (left), 53, 54–5, 57, 58, 63, 64–5, 66, 68, 69 (bottom). The Walt Disney Company. © The Walt Disney Company. 46: Collection of Ward Kimball. 47: Collection of Mike and Jeanne Glad. © The Walt Disney Company. 48 (lower right): Collection of Mike and Jeanne Glad.

© The Walt Disney Company. 49: Courtesy of Art Babbitt. 50: (left) Collection of Ward Kimball. (right) Courtesy of Mel Shaw. 51: Collection of Ward Kimball. 59: Collection of Marc Davis. © The Walt Disney Company. 60: Courtesy of Christie's East, Animation Art Department. © The Walt Disney Company. 61: Collection of Mike and Jeanne Glad. © The Walt Disney Company. 67: Collection of John Canemaker. © The Walt Disney Company. 69 (top and center): Collection of Mike and Jeanne Glad. © The Walt Disney Company. 70: Courtesy of Leo Salkin. 72: Courtesy of Mae Questel. © 1989 King Features Syndicate, Inc. 74: Courtesy of Mae Questel. © King Features Syndicate, Inc./Fleischer Studios, Inc. 75: Courtesy of Mae Questel. 76: Collection of Mike and Jeanne Glad. © King Features Syndicate, Inc./Fleischer Studios, Inc. 78: Collection of Mike and Jeanne Glad. © 1989 King Features Syndicate, Inc. 79: Collection of Mike and Jeanne Glad. © 1989 King Features Syndicate, Inc. 80: Museum of Modern Art Film Archives. © Fleischer Studios, Inc. 81: (upper right) Bison Archives. (bottom) Collection of Mike and Jeanne Glad. © Fleischer Studios, Inc. 82: (lower left) Courtesy of Christie's East Animation Art Department. (upper right) Collection of Mike and Jeanne Glad. 83: Private collection. Superman is a trademark and copyright of DC Comics Inc. © 1941. 84: Collection of Mike and Jeanne Glad. 85 (right): Collection of Mike and Jeanne Glad. 86: (upper left) Courtesy of Nick and Tee Bosustow. (bottom) Courtesy of Gerry Muller. © Celebrity Productions. 87: Collection of Mike and Jeanne Glad. © Celebrity Productions. 88: Collection of Mike and Jeanne Glad. © 1931 Universal Pictures Corporation. 89: (left) Courtesy of Leo Salkin. © 1933 Universal Pictures Corporation. (lower right) From the Walter Lantz Collection. Reprinted with permission. 90: Collection of Mike and Jeanne Glad. © 1935 Universal Pictures Corporation. 91: Courtesy of Walter Lantz Productions, Inc. © 1940 Walter Lantz Productions, Inc. 92: Collection of Mike and Jeanne Glad. 93: Collection of Mike and Jeanne Glad. 95: Bison Archives. 96: Collection of Mike and Jeanne Glad. 97: (upper left) Collection of Mike and Jeanne Glad. (lower right) Museum of Modern Art Film Archives. 98: The Bob Clampett Collection. 99: Collection of Steve Schneider. Bosko and Honey ™ and © Warner Bros., Inc., 1930. Artwork © Steve Schneider. 100: Collection of Steve Schneider. Buddy and Cookie ™ and © Warner Bros., Inc., 1934. Artwork © Steve Schneider. 101: Private collection. All characters ™ and © Warner Bros., Inc., 1935. 102: Daffy Duck and Porky Pig ™ and © Warner Bros., Inc., 1937. 103: Courtesy of The Bob Clampett Collection. 104: (upper left) Collection of Steve Schneider. Artwork © Steve Schneider. (lower right) Collection of Steve Schneider. Bugs Bunny ™ and © Warner Bros., Inc., 1938. Artwork © Steve

Schneider. 105: Collection of Steve Schneider. Bugs Bunny ™ and © Warner Bros., Inc., 1939. Artwork © Steve Schneider. 106: (left) Collection of Steve Schneider. Bugs Bunny ™ and © Warner Bros., Inc., 1940. Artwork © Steve Schneider. (right) Bugs Bunny ™ and © Warner Bros., Inc., 1947. Artwork © Steve Schneider. 107: (upper left) Collection of Mike and Jeanne Glad. Bugs Bunny ™ and © Warner Bros., Inc., 1941. (right top) Bugs Bunny and Elmer Fudd ™ and © Warner Bros., Inc., 1938. (right bottom) Courtesy of Virgil Ross. Egghead ™ and © Warner Bros., Inc., 1938. 108–9: Collection of Mike and Jeanne Glad. 111: Collection of Mike and Jeanne Glad. 112: Collection of Mike and Jeanne Glad. Bugs Bunny ™ and © Warner Bros., Inc. 114: Courtesy of Joe Smith. 115: Collection of Mike and Jeanne Glad. 116: Courtesy of Joe Smith. 117: (left) Courtesy of Frank Thomas. (right) Collection of Steve Schneider. Lord Hee Haw ™ and © Warner Bros., Inc., 1943. Artwork © Steve Schneider. 118: The Walt Disney Company. © The Walt Disney Company. 119: Collection of Mike and Jeanne Glad. © The Walt Disney Company. 121: (upper left) Collection of Steve Schneider. Private Snafu, Hook ™ and © Warner Bros., Inc. Artwork © Steve Schneider. (upper right and bottom) Collection of Mike and Jeanne Glad. Private Snafu, Hook ™ and © Warner Bros., Inc. 122: (upper left) Collection of Mike and Jeanne Glad. Daffy Duck ™ and © Warner Bros., Inc., 1943. (lower left) Courtesy of Mel Shaw. 123: From the Walter Lantz Collection. Reprinted with permission. 124: The Walt Disney Company. © The Walt Disney Company. 126: (left) The Walt Disney Company. © The Walt Disney Company. (right) Collection of Mike and Jeanne Glad. © The Walt Disney Company. 127: The Walt Disney Company. © The Walt Disney Company. 128: Courtesy of Tyrus Wong. © The Walt Disney Company. 129: Courtesy of Christie's East, Animation Art Department. © The Walt Disney Company. 130: The Walt Disney Company. © The Walt Disney Company. 132: (left) Collection of Steve Schneider. Character ™ and © Warner Bros., Inc., 1943. Artwork © Steve Schneider. (right) Daffy Duck ™ and © Warner Bros., Inc., 1943. 133: (left) Private collection. Bugs Bunny, Elmer Fudd ™ and © Warner Bros., Inc., 1941. (right) Collection of Eric Goldberg. Bugs Bunny ™ and © Warner Bros., Inc., 1943. 134: (upper left) Private collection. Character ™ and © Warner Bros., Inc., 1942. (right) Daffy Duck, Porky Pig ™ and © Warner Bros., Inc., 1941. 135: (upper right) Bugs Bunny ™ and © Warner Bros., Inc., 1943. (lower right) Courtesy of Chuck Jones. © Warner Bros., Inc., 1942. 136: (above) Collection of Steve Schneider. Pepe LePew ™ and © Warner Bros., Inc., 1951. (below) Collection of Mike and Jeanne Glad. Pepe LePew ™ and © Warner Bros., Inc., 1954. 137: Private collection. © 1989 Turner Entertainment

Company. All rights reserved. 138: Collection of Mike and Jeanne Glad. © 1989 Turner Entertainment Company. All rights reserved. 139: Private collection. © 1989 Turner Entertainment Company. All rights reserved. 140: © 1989 Turner Entertainment Company. All rights reserved. 141: (top) © 1940 Walter Lantz Productions, Inc. (center) © 1947 Walter Lantz Productions, Inc. (bottom) © 1957 Walter Lantz Productions, Inc. 142: Collection of Mike and Jeanne Glad. © Viacom. 144: Collection of Mike and Jeanne Glad. © Harvey Publications, Inc., 1989. 145: Collection of Steve Schneider. © Warner Bros., Inc., 1937. Artwork © Steve Schneider. 146: Private collection. © Warner Bros., Inc., 1936. 147: Collection of Steve Schneider. Character ™ and © Warner Bros., Inc., 1942. Artwork © Steve Schneider. 148: Collection of Steve Schneider. Daffy Duck ™ and © Warner Bros., Inc., 1951. Artwork © Steve Schneider. 150: (left) Collection of Steve Schneider. Characters ™ and © Warner Bros., Inc., 1946. Artwork © Steve Schneider. (right) Collection of Mike and Jeanne Glad. Tweety ™ and © Warner Bros., Inc., 1954. 152: (left, top) Collection of Steve Schneider. Yosemite Sam ™ and © Warner Bros., Inc., 1955. Artwork © Steve Schneider. (left, below) Courtesy of Chuck Jones. Yosemite Sam, Bugs Bunny ™ and © Warner Bros., Inc., 1955. 152–3 (bottom): Collection of Steve Schneider. Bugs Bunny ™ and © Warner Bros., Inc., 1947. Artwork © Steve Schneider. 153 (right): Daffy Duck, Bugs Bunny, Elmer Fudd ™ and © Warner Bros., Inc., 1951. 154: Private collection. Character ™ and © Warner Bros., Inc., 1955. 155: (top) Courtesy of Chuck Jones. © Warner Bros., Inc., 1953. (bottom) Marvin Martian, Daffy Duck ™ and © Warner Bros., Inc., 1953. 156: Courtesy of Chuck Jones. © Warner Bros., Inc., 1957. 157: Collection of Steve Schneider. Elmer Fudd, Bugs Bunny ™ and © Warner Bros., Inc., 1957. 158: Collection of Mike and Jeanne Glad. Wile E. Coyote ™ and © Warner Bros., Inc. 159: Collection of Mike and Jeanne Glad. Daffy Duck ™ and © Warner Bros., Inc., 1958. 160: Collection of Steve Schneider. Characters ™ and © Warner Bros., Inc. Artwork © Steve Schneider. 161: (left) Collection of Steve Schneider. Dog, Foghorn Leghorn, Henery Hawk ™ and © Warner Bros., Inc. Artwork © Steve Schneider. (right) Collection of Steve Schneider. Character ™ and © Warner Bros., Inc., 1951. Artwork © Steve Schneider. 162 (lower left): Collection of Steve Schneider. Bugs Bunny, Tasmanian Devil ™ and © Warner Bros., Inc., 1962. Artwork © Steve Schneider. 162–3 (top): Collection of Steve Schneider. Character ™ and © Warner Bros., Inc., 1950. Artwork © Steve Schneider. 163 (lower right): Collection of Steve Schneider. © 1989 Turner Entertainment Company. All rights reserved. Artwork © Steve Schneider. 164: Private collection. © 1989 Turner Entertainment Company. All rights reserved. 165: Collec-